The Literature of Journalism

The Literature of Journalism

AN ANNOTATED BIBLIOGRAPHY

Warren C. Price

UNIVERSITY OF MINNESOTA PRESS, Minneapolis

To L and K and B and P

THE FOUR WHO WAITED

Foreword

Relatively few efforts have been made in journalistic research toward compiling general and descriptive bibliographies of the press as a whole. Through the years journalists have been prolific writers on all conceivable subjects. Commentators about journalism as a profession or craft, from both within and without the field, have likewise been numerous. The selection of more than 3,000 titles provided herein indicates no lack of literature on the press and its modern-day allies (advertising, public relations, radio and television, to name a few). But up to the present time journalists have done little in the way of assembling data on what books are readily available or of judging the quality of the literature.

Whenever extensive bibliographical studies of journalistic areas have been made, the scholars preparing them have tended to restrict themselves to specific subject matter, chronological periods, or geographical regions. Examples of such specialized bibliographies are the excellent *History and Bibliography of American Newspapers (1690–1820)*, by Clarence S. Brigham (No. 2926); *Propaganda, Communication, and Public Opinion*, by Smith, Lasswell, and Casey (No. 2986); and *International News and the Press*, by Ralph O. Nafziger (No. 2954). A good case could be made that these are the best journalistic bibliographies ever published.

On the general literature of journalism only two book-length bibliographies are of any quality or importance.

Journalism: A Bibliography (No. 2927), by Carl L. Cannon of the New York Public Library, has been for 35 years the most thorough work. Based on the journalism holdings of the New York Public Library as of 1924, Cannon's book is unsurpassed for its cumulative listings up to that year. Yet the subsequent years have seen hundreds of volumes added to journalistic literature. Further, Cannon's work is unselective and only partially annotated and carries only an author index. Many county

vii

histories of newspapers that relate only to local situations take up disproportionate space. Many of the hundreds of pamphlets which he lists are of doubtful value. Also, when Cannon prepared his bibliography the allied fields that have so enlarged the scope of journalism had not yet developed. Today journalism has become a branch of mass communications (with whatever interpretation one wishes to put on the broader term); and for journalism in this broad context Cannon's bibliography may not be as helpful as those of Smith, Lasswell, and Casey.

The Journalist's Bookshelf (No. 2946), by Roland E. Wolseley of Syracuse University, has been the other helpful general bibliography of the present day. Professor Wolseley's book has appeared in six editions, 1939 through 1955. It presently includes about 1,300 entries, all books, with extensive annotations in most cases; many of the annotations are quite highly impressionistic.

In many respects I have expanded upon Wolseley, and this book is more parallel to his than to Cannon's. But whereas Wolseley, like Cannon, holds to journalism in its standard newspaper-magazine meaning, I have sought to go somewhat further. Sections VIII through XII of this book provide selected entries relating to journalistic periodicals, management of the press, public opinion (including some contemporary books in communication research), radio and television, and foreign press and international communications agencies. In addition, the section on bibliographies and directories (XIII) goes well beyond journalism in its limited meaning. On the other hand, two of Professor Wolseley's classifications, journalistic fiction and high school journalism, are omitted here on the premise that they do not particularly apply to the needs of the more advanced reader or researcher. The Wolseley bibliography will provide nearly 200 titles in these two fields.

The task of trying to prepare a book of this kind for subject matter as wide in scope as journalism is not without peril. Certainly, not every volume that touches on one of the subject categories can be included, and, in the mass of titles to be considered, significant ones may be overlooked. But, with due regard for the dangers involved, the boundaries of this study have been deliberately kept extremely loose. Any work was considered that was about journalism, or by a writer whose career was wholly journalistic or at least journalistic in connection with the writing of a particular book. Likewise, I included a number of general history books if it appeared that their content carried important journalistic overtones.

One firm control was that the book be in the English language, and this was followed rigidly. As a result many valuable foreign-language works on journalism were kept out. A bibliography of these would make today a considerable addition to what is contained in this book. I have also avoided going deeply into books on printing and book publishing, although these fields frequently skirt the edges of journalism.

Except in a few instances only published books have been included. To have opened the bibliography to more than a small number of especially significant articles, pamphlets, and theses would have made the project unwieldy and the organization — a difficult task in itself — much more complicated.

The base of the book is frankly historical and biographical, with more than two-fifths of all the titles in these two categories. The largest individual category contains biographies and autobiographies of journalists (most of them newspapermen) and books about men with close journalistic connections. This is the area in which the literature is concentrated and is most readily accessible in libraries. Journalism has always been intensely personal, and only in recent years has there been enough other journalistic production to reduce slightly the great margin that biography always has held.

Other large categories consist of general journalistic and individual newspaper history, appraisals of the press, and legal aspects of the press. As in the case of the biographies, these are heavily concerned with the newspaper.

Books on the business side of the press (contained in Section IX on Management) seem to be somewhat less substantial in their content than those of a historical, biographical, analytical, or literary nature, although this interpretation may have been influenced by my own editorial-side training. However, considering the size of the whole bibliography, the books that concern individual histories of newspapers are surprisingly limited. In the bibliography, including some promotional histories of a rather shallow sort, there are only 171 newspaper histories (Nos. 91–261), and these include histories of the regional and specialized press. Books like Meyer Berger's *The Story of the New York Times* (No. 104) or the London *Times'* own four-volume *History of the London Times, 1785–1948* (No. 204) are distinctive not only because they are excellent but because there are so few newspaper histories like them.

In my selected listing of works in the allied areas of communication and of works on general subjects that carry useful journalistic information, I have made no effort to be comprehensive. The entries are those that would be expected in a collection of representative titles. The volumes relating to the newspaper press, on the other hand, should be extensive enough to serve most reference needs.

Several hundred titles relate to books on journalism in Great Britain and the British Commonwealth. Well over 100 additional volumes, including the entire section on the Foreign Press, concern journalism in other areas of the world. A large number of these, because of their ready access, are biographies and selected publications of the United Nations Educational, Scientific, and Cultural Organization (UNESCO). This total, of course, does not make much of a dent in non-United States writing in journalism. But except for Nafziger's, there has been no previous annotated bibliography of British, European, and Asiatic journalism on an extended scale.

Another extensive inclusion is Section III, more than 550 titles under the heading Narratives of Journalists at Work and Anthologies of Journalistic Writing. The bulk of this section represents work *by journalists*, principally reporters, as distinguished from work *about journalism*. Most of this reporting concerns foreign and war correspondence, with another subcategory being political reporting. Other divisions cover general news and features, editorial writing, photography and cartooning, columns and criticism, and sports.

Some questions with regard to Section III naturally will arise. Is the literature of journalism limited to that which relates to the men and women who engage in the profession and to that which concerns appraisals of news and the newspaper, the legal status of the press, management problems, and journalistic phases of radio and television? Or does the literature include also writing by any practitioner of the art, whatever his subject matter may be? It is quite clear that many of the books in Section III are nonjournalistic in content. Nevertheless, the authors in most cases were engaged in the practice of journalism at the time they wrote, and their work certainly was not open to question as reporting or commentary.

Therefore, I have decided to regard these books as fit candidates for entry in the bibliography. The listing of them had to be extremely selective, for to include a limitless total of books on everything any reporter wrote about would be absurd, as well as impossible. But I felt a representative list would be useful. So far as I know, most of the previous journalistic bibliographies have been restricted to works about journalism as a topic and have not included many works by journalists that were undertaken as part of regular assignments. These latter books, incidentally, have in many instances been of the highest quality. Critics of the press have too often been inclined to forget the journalistic sources of reportorial narratives that have won their approbation as works on specific subjects.

Another question will arise: Is a book accessible? This bibliography was compiled at one of the largest university libraries in the Pacific Northwest, with the additional aid of more than 400 volumes through interlibrary loans and of many references to Library of Congress author-and-subject cards. Among university libraries, the one in which I worked, however, is far from the most extensive. Nevertheless, it has 75 to 80 per cent of all the books that are listed here. It is reasonable to believe that a majority of all the titles given can be found in most moderately sized university libraries and in many of the larger public libraries. Interlibrary loan service, further, should make it possible for anyone who wishes to consult a given volume to do so.

Although for the most part this bibliography is based on titles issued only through 1957, a careful selection of 1958 publications has been included. The beginning date is open; but since journalistic literature is, in relation to general literature, distinctly contemporary, the majority of the titles are of the 20th century. I made some effort to be as complete as possible in books since 1924, in order to fill the gap since Cannon's book appeared. Although 19th-century works are well represented, their subject matter is centralized heavily in the standard "old-line" categories of history and biography, early reportorial narratives, and some analysis of the press. As for the 18th century or earlier, only a scattered number of titles are to be found.

The bibliography includes more than 200 bibliographies and directories. I would not attempt to estimate how many titles in press literature can be obtained by referring to the items carried in these volumes. The number seems to me, after I have worked with 3,000, to be tremendous. In any case, I hope that the books listed in the first 12 sections of this work, plus those that can be obtained by reference to the volumes listed in Section XIII, will be helpful to any student who wishes to pursue more particularized research.

Certainly, many books that should be in this bibliography are not listed, and I welcome information on them. Also, with the thousands of minute facts involved, errors may well have crept in. I am wholly responsible for these, and for any errors in classification, and I should be glad to hear about them.

Many friends and colleagues have assisted me in gathering titles for this bibliography. I am grateful to all of them — for their knowledge, for their patience, and for their confidence that something would come out of all the searching.

Those who bore the brunt of my requests for help were individual members of the staff of the University of Oregon Library, all of whom went far beyond professional duties to help in running down particular problems.

Eugene Barnes, acquisitions librarian, located books long out of print, and many of these books later were obtained for the library.

Miss Elizabeth Findly and Mrs. Leila Beatty, both of the Reference Department, filled out hundreds of interlibrary loan applications, and these borrowed books came to me from libraries throughout the United States and Canada. And Miss Clarice Krieg, head catalog librarian, always was ready to push a specific book through to the Circulation Department — sometimes on less than 24 hours' notice.

Miss Dorothy Randall of Circulation continually was looking for journalism books about which I might not have heard, and Miss Edith Colignon and Bruce Morris of Reference helped in checking confusing entries. It seemed to me sometimes that librarian Carl Hintz might actually have advised his staff to meet all my requests, however much they impinged on library time.

Dean Charles T. Duncan of the University of Oregon School of Journalism helped in providing departmental financial assistance for checking titles against Library of Congress cards; and he understood, too, the fine line of balance that must be kept in meeting the problem of managing time, when research is competing with classroom teaching demands.

Professor Edwin Emery of the University of Minnesota School of Journalism gave me considerable encouragement and sound advice in suggesting annotations sufficiently detailed and analytical to be meaningful. Professor Ralph D. Casey, emeritus director of the University of Minnesota School of Journalism, made — at the very start of the project early in 1954 — one of the most valuable of all the suggestions I received: that in order to be of most value nearly all the titles should have some annotation. This therefore became more than a listing of books.

Professor Frank L. Mott of the University of Missouri School of Journalism encouraged me to go into extensive detail on personal narratives of foreign and war correspondents. This part of the work, at it turned out, became the most enjoyable in which I engaged.

One who probably did not know at all about the project at the start, but from whose seminar in southern history I first got in 1953 the idea of an extended journalistic bibliography, is Professor Alice Felt Tyler of the University of Minnesota.

Among the staff of the University of Minnesota Press I met new friends, and to the editors of the press I owe much for valuable suggestions that helped to stave off numerous inconsistencies in organization.

My wife, Lillian Shidell Price, took it all patiently and assumed added chores of her own that I should have shared — and did not. At the close, night after night, she helped to read proof and to check the index.

It is only honest, perhaps, to deny what is commonly attributed to those who engage in bibliographical research, namely, that it must be a hobby. The truth is that, as a newspaperman, I had never had more than

FOREWORD

a passing interest in bibliography before 1953, except for utilitarian purposes. The book began merely as a single paper on pre-Civil War journalism in Mrs. Tyler's course. That led down strange avenues which went far afield, and to which there seemed no ending. As it happened, one book in the bibliography actually turned up with the title *Open Every Door.*

WARREN C. PRICE

Eugene, Oregon
May 1959

Contents

III. NARRATIVES OF JOURNALISTS AT WORK AND ANTHOLOGIES OF JOURNALISTIC WRITING, *page 216*

IV. APPRAISALS OF THE PRESS, ETHICS OF THE PRESS, AND LAW OF THE PRESS, *page 281*

V. TECHNIQUES OF JOURNALISM, INCLUDING TEXTBOOKS
(items 2154–2302), *page 316*

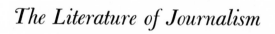

The Literature of Journalism

NOTE ON ORGANIZATION

SUBJECT MATTER *is the controlling factor in presenting the 13 major categories of this bibliography. General works — mostly journalistic history and histories of individual newspapers — have been placed first. These are followed by the extensive biographical section and then by the personal narratives of journalists. Bibliographies, check lists, catalogues, and indexes, because of their specialized nature, have been put at the close. The user of the book should consult the table of contents for the specific organization of the various sections.*

Insofar as possible, I have tried to follow the Library of Congress system of making entries: author, title, place of publication, publisher, date of publication, and pages. Frequently the particular edition is noted, as are series titles, the titles of earlier or British editions, the number of illustrations, and other pertinent information.

In the great majority of cases I have seen the book and have made the entry directly from it; in every case I have checked to verify inclusions through a Library of Congress card or through the British National Bibliography. *The number of titles in this bibliography that are not also in the Library of Congress is negligible.*

I have sought to include in the annotations only the material that is necessary to indicate the content and value of the books. For some entries, however, annotations are fairly extensive — especially in the case of long works that include among diverse subjects important information on journalism. Wherever possible, I have tried to point out the major journalistic references. In many instances I could list only high points, and I recognize that some misjudgments have probably been made. This is particularly true in the case of books that lacked both index and table of contents. It should be noted too that the volumes listed in the first section (History) contain a wealth of general information that cannot be abstracted except in the broadest manner. The user of this bibliography will have to go to these books themselves in most cases, although I have done as much as possible in the annotations to get at specific content that is relevant to journalism.

The annotations are, I hope, reasonably objective and fair. I sought consciously to avoid injecting my own literary efforts into the notes. In a few instances of particularly valuable and fascinating books, however, there are subjective comments.

No book is listed more than once. Since many volumes can be classified in several ways, the user will find it profitable to refer to the index if he does not find a book in the category in which he first expected it. For example, a volume on Dexter Fellows, a circus press agent, is included in the biographical section. One seeking this book could find the entry number under four headings in the index: Dexter Fellows; Biographies, promoters and propagandists; Public relations; and Ringling Brothers. See the Note on Index, p. 434, for further information on the organization of the index.

History

A. General Histories of Journalism in the United States and Canada

1. Bartow, Edith Merwin. *News and These United States.* New York: Funk and Wagnalls Co., 1952. viii + 292pp.

   A popular treatment of the history of journalism through the history of news stories. Artistic nameplates of various newspapers illustrate the text.

2. Bleyer, Willard G. *Main Currents in the History of American Journalism.* Boston: Houghton Mifflin Co., 1927. x + 464pp.

   An excellent over-all account of the press; for many years the leading work of general scholarship. Since 1941 it has been superseded by Mott (no. 18 below) and more recently by Emery and Smith (7). There is an excellent introductory chapter on English backgrounds.

3. *Cambridge History of American Literature.* New York: G. P. Putnam's Sons; Cambridge, England: Cambridge University Press, 1917–1921. 4 vols. (Edited by William P. Trent, John Erskine, Stuart P. Sherman, and Carl Van Doren.)

   Contains numerous articles on literary phases of the press. See particularly "Franklin," I:90–110; "Colonial Newspapers and Magazines," I:111–123; "Transcendentalism," I:326–348; "Magazines, Annuals, and Gift Books, 1783–1850," II:160–175; "Newspapers, 1775–1860," II:176–195; "Mark Twain," III:1–20; "Minor Humorists" (including comic journalism), III:21–30; "Later Magazines," III:299–318; "Newspapers since 1860," III:309–316; and "Book Publishers and Publishing," IV:533–553. The articles include a bibliography for each topic.

4. Commager, Henry Steele. *The American Mind.* New Haven: Yale University Press, 1950. ix + 476pp.

   A general intellectual history of America from the mid-1880s to 1950. One excellent chapter on the press, "Transition Years in Literature and Journalism," covers the vast changes that took place in the 1890s.

5. Dill, William Adelbert. *Growth of Newspapers in the United States.* Lawrence: University of Kansas Department of Journalism, 1928. 80pp.

6. Eggleston, Wilfrid. "Literature: The Press," in *The Culture of Contemporary Canada*, pp. 81–95. Ithaca, N.Y.: Cornell University Press, 1957. (Edited by Julian Park.)

   A useful capsule survey of Canadian journalism issued as part of a general work on the country's literature and art, scholarship, philosophy, education, and science. Eggleston is director of the Department of Journalism, Carleton University, Ottawa, and in World War II was director of censorship for Canada.

7. Emery, Edwin, and Henry Ladd Smith. *The Press and America.* New York: Prentice-Hall, 1954. xiv + 794pp.

   The latest general history; includes the recent history of radio and television, magazines, and other communication agencies. Going beyond their predecessors, the authors have sought to place the story of the press in perspective as part of America's political, economic, and social scene. The suggested readings in extensive chapter bibliographies go far beyond specialized books on journalism. There are particularly sound analyses of the Colonial period and the continental European background and of modern-day newspapers.

8. Eriksson, Erik McKinley. *Official Newspaper Organs and the Presidential Elections of 1828, 1832, and 1836.* Nashville, Tenn., 1927. 247pp.

   Reprints articles from the *Tennessee Historical Magazine*, vols. VIII–IX. Originally a Ph.D. thesis at the State University of Iowa.

9. Ford, Edwin H., and Edwin Emery, eds. *Highlights in the History of the American Press: A Book of Readings.* Minneapolis: University of Minnesota Press, 1954. xi + 398pp.

   Twenty-seven well-chosen articles discuss the major conditions that have affected the press and the men who have shaped the American newspaper. The articles are grouped by historical period from English antecedents to modern times, with introductory essays by the editors outlining the main trends of each period.

10. Greene, Laurence. *America Goes to Press: Headlines of the Past, the History of the United States as Reported in the Newspapers of the Days from the Boston Tea Party to the World War.* Indianapolis: Bobbs-Merrill Co., 1936; Garden City, N.Y.: Garden City Publishing Co., 1938. 372pp.

    Reprints material from newspapers beginning with a selection from Benjamin Harris's *Publick Occurrences* and carrying down to the sinking of the Titanic and Sarajevo.

11. Harlow, Alvin F. *Old Wires and New Waves: The History of the Telegraph, Telephone, and Wireless.* New York: D. Appleton-Century Co., 1936. xiv + 548pp.

    A general history of telecommunications, with half of the book devoted to the period up to the Civil War. There is a separate chapter on the rise of the Associated Press. Numerous newspapers and their connections with the telegraph are mentioned. The bibliography includes leading books on telegraphy and some periodical articles.

HISTORY

12. Hudson, Frederic. *Journalism in the United States from 1690 to 1872*. New York: Harper and Brothers, 1873. 789pp.

First of the general histories, except for Thomas's *History of Printing* (see no. 284 below). Hudson, managing editor for James Gordon Bennett, Sr., includes many detailed personal recollections, but he is long-winded and inaccurate.

13. Jones, Robert W. *Journalism in the United States*. New York: E. P. Dutton and Co., 1947. xvi + 728pp.

Least satisfactory of the general histories; lacks sound organization and is poorly written. The bibliography offers only a list of the commonest titles.

14. Lee, Alfred McClung. *The Daily Newspaper in America: The Evolution of a Social Instrument*. New York: The Macmillan Co., 1937. xiv + 797pp.

A thorough general study from the sociological and economic points of view. The text is solidly buttressed by statistical data on the newspaper industry from 1710 to 1936. The organization is wholly topical: physical plant, labor, ownership and management, chains and associations, advertising, weekly and Sunday issues, societal adjustment to the press, press associations, feature syndicates, and problems of the editorial staff.

15. Lee, James Melvin. *History of American Journalism*. Boston: Houghton Mifflin Co., 1917; revised, 1923. xiv + 462pp.

The first history after Hudson's; now superseded by more substantial studies. One useful inclusion is Lee's state-by-state treatment of early journalistic developments and first newspapers. The volume has frequent errors, however, and is difficult to read.

16. McNaught, Carlton. *Canada Gets the News*. Toronto: Ryerson Press, 1940. ix + 271pp.

McNaught tells how the news is gathered and presented for Canadian consumption. The volume is thoroughly done, but now dated. The history of the Canadian Press and its news networks takes up more than a fourth of the book. There is an introductory chapter on the daily newspapers of Canada.

17. Mathews, Joseph J. *Reporting the Wars*. Minneapolis: University of Minnesota Press, 1957. x + 322pp.

Mathews traces the evolution of war news from the mid-18th to the mid-20th century. He covers in some detail the inseparable association between war news and censorship and propaganda. There is excellent treatment of specific wars, the profession of war correspondence, and the literature of war correspondence. The notes and index are extensive.

18. Mott, Frank Luther. *American Journalism: A History of Newspapers in the United States through 260 Years, 1690–1950*. New York: The Macmillan Co., 1941; revised, 1950. xiv + 835pp.

An outstanding general history, valuable both as a textbook and as an encyclopedic reference work. Highly readable. Each of ten major topical groupings has a highly selective, briefly annotated bibliography.

19. Nelson, William. *Notes toward a History of the American Newspaper*. New York: Charles F. Heartman, 1918. 644pp.

A partial history only; covers the newspapers of 30 states and territories, alphabetically arranged from Alabama through New Hampshire. The book was intended to be the first of two volumes, but the second was not completed.

20. North, S. N. D. *History and Present Condition of the Newspaper and Periodical Press of the United States, with a Catalogue of the Publications of the Census Year.* Washington, D.C.: Government Printing Office, 1884. vi + 446pp. (Published as part of House of Representatives Miscellaneous Document No. 42, Part 8, 47th Congress, 2nd Session.)

By a special agent for the U.S. Census of 1880, this history of newspapers from 1639 to 1880 includes extensive statistical tables and a catalogue of all periodicals published in 1880. It represents the first concentrated effort (except for the works of Thomas and Hudson) to bring American journalistic history into focus, but North did not discuss the character, power, or influence of the press; nor did he weigh the personal service of individual editors. The book's value lies in its factual matter, which goes down to the county level.

21. Park, Robert E. "The Natural History of the Newspaper," in Park, Ernest W. Burgess, and Roderick D. McKenzie. *The City*, pp. 80–98. Chicago: University of Chicago Press, 1925.

One of a series of ten pieces by three sociologists seeking to describe human nature and social life under modern city conditions. Park emphasizes the newspaper circulation struggle, the growth of metropolitan journalism, and the rise of an "independent news press" and a "yellow press." The article has long been used as one of the principal social science studies into newspaper background.

22. Parrington, Vernon. *Main Currents in American Thought.* New York: Harcourt, Brace and Co., 1927. 3 vols.

A masterpiece in American literary study, much of it of great journalistic value, by a distinguished professor of English at the University of Washington. Vol. 1 carries the story to 1800, vol. 2 to 1860, and vol. 3 (published posthumously in fragmentary form) to the contemporary period. There are penetrating analyses of Benjamin Franklin, John Dickinson, Samuel Adams, Philip Freneau, H. H. Brackenridge, William Cullen Bryant, Horace Greeley, William Lloyd Garrison, and Margaret Fuller.

23. Payne, George Henry. *History of Journalism in the United States.* New York and London: D. Appleton and Co., 1920. xx + 453pp.

The best of the pre-Bleyer general histories. Payne's work is helpful for the detail given on journalism's early years; more than half of the book considers periods preceding the establishment of the New York *Herald.* The Zenger case, the American Revolution, and the Alien and Sedition acts are well handled.

24. Pollard, James E. *The Presidents and the Press.* New York: The Macmillan Co., 1947. xiii + 866pp.

A careful study of the relations between newspapers and the executive branch of the government from Washington through Truman, with emphasis on the "strong-willed" presidents beginning with Jackson. Notes to sources are thorough.

25. Salmon, Lucy Maynard. *The Newspaper and the Historian.* New York: Oxford University Press, 1923. xliii + 566pp.

One of the truly scholarly historical studies. Miss Salmon, of Vassar, prepared this book in an effort to discover the advantages and limitations of periodical press publications as historical source material. She considers news developments from Roman days; newspapers as "personalities"; guarantees to the press; the press and allied public activities; news-gathering and distribution; reporters and correspondents and reportorial techniques; the position of editors, critics, and advertisers, and authenticity and authoritativeness in the press.

26. Stewart, Kenneth, and John Tebbel. *Makers of Modern Journalism.* New York: Prentice-Hall, 1952. x + 514pp.

A survey paying particular attention to personalities. In a sense this is a textbook based upon biography. One of the best features is the inclusion of sketches of contemporary living journalists (1930–1950) on whom little biographical material is yet available.

B. Special-Period Histories of Journalism in the United States

27. Andrews, J. Cutler. *The North Reports the Civil War.* Pittsburgh: University of Pittsburgh Press, 1955. x + 813pp.

The most ambitious of the histories of Civil War newspaper coverage, with a thorough documentation of sources. Much of the material was obtained from reporters' own letters, diaries, and dispatches. Andrews established the identity of many reporters for the first time and offered new light on the relation between the press and leading military figures; a listing of several hundred northern reporters and their newspapers is included.

28. Bertier de Sauvigny, Guillaume de. "The American Press and the Fall of Napoleon in 1814," in American Philosophical Society *Proceedings*, vol. 98, no. 5 (Oct. 15, 1954), pp. 337–375.

29. Brantley, Rabun Lee. *Georgia Journalism of the Civil War Period.* Nashville, Tenn.: George Peabody College for Teachers, 1929. xvi + 134pp.

Originally a Ph.D. thesis at George Peabody College.

30. Brigham, Clarence S. *Journals and Journeymen: A Contribution to the History of Early American Newspapers.* Philadelphia: University of Pennsylvania Press, 1950. xiv + 114pp.

Useful, brief sketches. Brigham discusses early newspaper names, circulation and subscription problems, the time lag in news coverage, early news rooms, Colonial newspaper collections, and illustrations.

31. Churchill, Allen. *Park Row: A Vivid Re-Creation of Turn of the Century Newspaper Days.* New York and Toronto: Rinehart and Co., 1958. 344pp.

A romanticized history of New York journalism, 1883–1931, focusing upon Joseph Pulitzer and the New York *World.* The book is eminently readable if not always historically solid. There is considerable detail on yellow journalism, the Spanish-American War, David Graham Phillips, Stephen Crane, Richard Harding Davis, and the decline of Park Row in the modern day.

32. Cook, Elizabeth Christine. *Literary Influences in Colonial Newspapers, 1704–1750.* New York: Columbia University Press, 1912. xi + 297pp. (Columbia Studies in English and Comparative Literature.)

Analyzes typical literary efforts in the influential weekly Colonial press. Articles discussed come from the *New England Courant,* the *New England Weekly Journal,* Bradford's *American Mercury,* Franklin's *Pennsylvania Gazette,* Zenger's *New-York Weekly Journal,* the *Maryland Gazette,* the *Virginia Gazette,* and the *South Carolina Gazette.* A thorough piece of work.

33. Crozier, Emmet. *Yankee Reporters, 1861–65.* New York: Oxford University Press, 1956. xii + 441pp.

The latest of a series of books on northern reporting of the Civil War and the one most closely approaching the story as a newspaperman would write it. Correspondents most fully considered are Junius Henri Browne, Charles Carleton Coffin, Thomas Wallace Knox, Whitelaw Reid, Albert D. Richardson, George W. Smalley, Edmund C. Stedman, George Alfred Townsend, Henry Villard, and Franc B. Wilkie. The book is heavy on the 1861–1863 period and light on 1863–1865.

34. Dickerson, Oliver Morton, comp. *Boston under Military Rule, 1768–1769, as Revealed in a Journal of the Times.* Boston: Chapman and Grimes, 1936. xiii + 137pp.

A description of daily events in beleaguered Boston. The accounts of these events, supplied secretly to newspapers — principally the Boston *Evening Post,* the New York *Journal,* and the *Pennsylvania Chronicle* — at the time, were reportedly the most widely circulated pre-Revolutionary writings after John Dickinson's *Letters from a Farmer in Pennsylvania.* An editorial introduction provides historical background.

35. *Documents Relative to the Colonial History of the State of New York.* Albany, N.Y.: Weed, Parsons and Co., 1853–1887. 15 vols. (Edited by J. B. O'Callaghan.)

Offers vast amounts of original source material on New York history. For journalistic purposes, the London background on the Zenger conflict is particularly valuable. The Zenger story is scattered through volumes 5, 6, and 7.

36. Dumond, Dwight L., ed. *Southern Editorials on Secession.* New York and London: The Century Co., 1931. xxxiii + 529pp.

Dumond brought together 183 editorials published in 31 southern newspapers during the year immediately preceding the Civil War, but made little analysis of the character of the newspapers.

37. Fay, Bernard. *Notes on the American Press at the End of the Eighteenth Century.* New York: The Grolier Club, 1927. 29pp. + 25 facsimiles of Revolution and post-Revolution newspapers.

This limited-edition summary of a longer paper by Professor Fay on the early press of America includes a discussion of the general conditions of the American press, 1775–1800, the role of the press during the period, and the sources from which the press derived its information.

HISTORY

38. Ford, Worthington C. "Jefferson and the Newspaper," in *Records of the Columbia Historical Society*, vol. 8, pp. 78–111. Washington, D.C.: The Society, 1905.

39. Harper, Robert S. *Lincoln and the Press*. New York: McGraw-Hill Book Co., 1951. xii + 418pp.

   A thorough, well-documented study of Lincoln's press relations, roughly from the debates with Douglas in 1858 to the President's assassination. Harper used newspaper sources in all the states, England, and France. He emphasizes the threat to constitutional guarantees of press freedom during the period.

40. Knauss, James Owen. *Social Conditions among the Pennsylvania Germans in the Eighteenth Century, as Revealed in Newspapers Published in America*. Lancaster, Pa.: Press of the New Era Printing Co., 1922. x + 217pp. (Reprinted from Pennsylvania German Society *Proceedings*, vol. 29.)

   Includes material on the German newspapers and their publishers, with references to 48 specific sheets from 1732 to 1800. There is a useful bibliography, as well as a listing of libraries in which the papers can be found.

41. Kobre, Sidney. *The Development of the Colonial Newspaper*. Pittsburgh: Colonial Press, 1944. xi + 188pp.

   Aims to place the development of the early press, 1690–1783, in a social background.

42. McMurtrie, Douglas C. *The Beginnings of the American Newspaper*. Chicago: Black Cat Press, 1935. 36pp.

   A private press publication giving a few facsimiles and a short description of Colonial newspapers from 1689 to the Revolution. It includes an account of a broadside, *The Present State of New-English Affairs*, printed by Samuel Green in 1689, as the earliest attempt in the Colonies at anything resembling a newspaper.

43. Martin, Charlotte M., and Benjamin Ellis Martin. *The New York Press and Its Makers in the Eighteenth Century*. New York: New York City History Club, 1897–1898. (Appears in Half Moon Series, vol. 2, no. 4, pp. 121–162.)

   A collector's item. It surveys the work of major editors and the lives of their papers, from Bradford's New York *Gazette* to the *Federalist*. There are distinctive marginal notes.

44. Morse, Jarvis Means. *Connecticut Newspapers in the Eighteenth Century*. New Haven: Yale University Press, for the Tercentenary Commission of the State of Connecticut, 1935. 31pp. (Issued as pamphlet no. 36 of the Committee on Historical Publications.)

   Strong on the *Connecticut Gazette*, the *New-London Summary* (or *Weekly Advertiser*), and the *Connecticut Courant*.

45. Mott, Frank Luther. *Jefferson and the Press*. Baton Rouge: Louisiana State University Press, 1943. 65pp.

   Recounts Jefferson's experiences with newspapers and notes that the President "saw and stated more clearly than any other writer the importance of the press in a democratic society."

46. "A Narrative of the Newspapers Printed in New-England — in a Letter to the President of the Historical Society, from One of the Members," and "A Continuation of the Narrative," in Massachusetts Historical Society *Collections*, vols. 5 and 6, first series, pp. 208–216 and 64–77, respectively. Boston: The Society, 1798 and 1800.

Anonymous accounts. The first piece corrects "some errors" of Benjamin Franklin in attributing to the *New-England Courant* the place of being the second newspaper in Massachusetts. The second carries the account forward to the American Revolution and includes a list of 16 Connecticut newspapers.

47. Norcross, Grenville H. "Southern Newspapers Printed on Wallpaper," in Massachusetts Historical Society *Proceedings*, vol. XLVI, pp. 241ff. Boston: The Society, 1913.

In presenting to the Massachusetts Historical Society a copy of the Opelousas (La.) *Courier* of April 25, 1863, Norcross took the occasion to record its history as well as that of other wallpaper sheets.

48. Perkins, Howard Cecil, ed. *Northern Editorials on Secession*. New York and London: D. Appleton-Century Co., 1942. 2 vols. 1107pp., total.

A compilation of 495 editorials from 190 northern newspapers on the Civil War crisis, 1860–1861, forming a sequel to Dumond's *Southern Editorials on Secession* (see 36 above). An excellent introduction discusses the politics of the secession crisis and describes the northern press of 1860.

49. Regier, C. C. *The Era of the Muckrakers*. Chapel Hill: University of North Carolina Press, 1932. 254pp.

An excellent treatment, based in large part on material obtained from the muckrakers themselves. Regier takes up the background of the "literature of exposure" and discusses in turn the attacks of the movement on major cities, state politics, the federal government, big business, the church, and the press. Biographies of leading journalists are woven into the topical treatment. There is an extensive bibliography.

50. Sandburg, Carl. *Abraham Lincoln: The War Years*. New York: Harcourt, Brace and Co., 1939. 4 vols.

Splendid sketches of Civil War newspapers and editors and of Lincoln's relations with them are scattered throughout the four volumes. The best are those on Greeley, Bennett, Dana, Raymond, Bryant, and New York, Washington, and Chicago newspapers.

51. Schlesinger, Arthur M. *Prelude to Independence: The Newspaper War on Britain, 1764–1776*. New York: Alfred A. Knopf, 1958. ix + 318 + xvi pp.

An assessment, thoroughly buttressed by study of contemporary sources, of the "role of the newspaper in undermining loyalty to the mother country and creating a demand for separation." The author discusses conditions which bred colonial discontent, reviews American journalism before the Revolutionary crisis, and records step by step press activities over the 12 years surveyed. There are useful appendixes on newspaper circulations, politics, the manufacturing of paper, and British overseas policy on freedom of the press.

52. Smith, William. *The History of the Late Province of New York from Its Discovery to the Appointment of Governor Colden in 1762*. New York: New York Historical Society, 1829. 2 vols. xvi + 780pp., total.

One of the most useful sources on the Cosby administration and the subsequent Zenger trial. See particularly vol. 1, part V, pp. 247–294; and vol. 2, chapter 1, pp. 1–81. In the original publication, William Smith, Sr., attorney, historian, and member of the pro-Zenger party, ended his history with 1732; his son, William, Jr., carried it forward 30 years. The work is highly subjective, but it offers a broad picture of the political corruption of Cosby's time.

53. Starr, Louis M. *Bohemian Brigade: Civil War Newsmen in Action*. New York: Alfred A. Knopf, 1954. xvii + 367pp.

Among the better contributions to the story of Civil War journalism. Starr considers the complexity of war coverage, the volume of copy handled, press relations with the military, and the impact of the war upon the newspaper as an institution; he also lists the newspapers with war correspondents. The work of managing editors — chiefly Charles A. Dana and Sydney Gay of the New York *Tribune* and Frederic Hudson of the *Herald* — is emphasized as well as that of reporters.

54. Tyler, Moses Coit. *The Literary History of the American Revolution, 1763–1783*. New York and London: G. P. Putnam's Sons, 1897. 2 vols. 1048pp., total.

A classic study of the writing done during the Revolution, including journalistic output. Considered in detail are Philip Freneau, Thomas Paine, Thomas Jefferson, Samuel Adams, John Dickinson, Benjamin Franklin, and the major Tory writers. Exhaustive bibliography and index.

55. Weisberger, Bernard A. *Reporters for the Union*. Boston: Little, Brown and Co., 1953. xi + 316pp.

Of the books on Civil War coverage, this is perhaps the least serviceable. It is based upon the premise that Kansas in the 1850s was a proving ground for Civil War reporting later. The author does discuss thoughtfully the significance of the Correspondents Memorial on South Mountain, Md.

C. General Histories of British Journalism

56. Andrews, Alexander. *The History of British Journalism from the Foundation of the Newspaper Press in England to the Repeal of the Stamp Act in 1855*. London: Richard Bentley, 1859. 2 vols. 704pp., total.

A comprehensive record, including biographical sketches of leading personalities. The treatment is mainly topical. Vol. 1 carries through the 18th century and vol. 2 to 1855. One of the best features is a discussion of nearly 75 British press trials. There is also an extensive discussion of the Colonial press in America.

57. Bundock, Clement J. *The National Union of Journalists: A Jubilee History, 1907–1957*. Oxford: Oxford University Press, for the National Union of Journalists, 1957. x + 254pp.

Bundock was the first national organizer of the National Union of Journalists and later was national secretary. His history relies on Mansfield's *Gentlemen, the Press!* (see 77 below), but he also draws on official union records.

58. Burton, K. G. *The Early Newspaper Press in Berkshire (1723–1855).* Reading, England: The Author, 1953. x + 290pp., mimeographed.

Covers the period from the founding of the Reading *Mercury* in 1723 to the abolition of newspaper stamp duties. It is useful as a study of the development of the regional press. The chief papers discussed are the *Mercury*, Reading *Journal*, Windsor and Eton *Express*, and *Berkshire Chronicle* (of Reading).

59. *The Cambridge History of English Literature.* Cambridge, England: Cambridge University Press; New York: The Macmillan Co., 1907–1933. 15 vols.

See "Milton," VII:108–161; "The Beginnings of English Journalism," VII:389–415; "The Advent of Modern Thought in Popular Literature," VII:416–450; "Defoe — the Newspaper and the Novel," IX:1–28; "Steele and Addison," IX:29–72; "Political Literature, 1755–1775," X:438–463; "Reviews and Magazines in the Early Years of the Nineteenth Century," XII:154–180; "The Growth of Journalism" (18th and 19th centuries), XIV:184–225; "University Journalism," XIV:226–233; and "Caricature and the Literature of Sport," XIV:234–264.

60. Cruikshank, R. J. *Roaring Century, 1846–1946.* London: Hamish Hamilton, 1946. xi + 280pp.

This "reverie," a general comparison of the England of 1846 with that of a century later, was issued on the occasion of the centenary of the London *Daily News*. There is an extensive discussion of the brief editorship of Charles Dickens on the *Daily News*; the rise of the 19th-century press and trends in industry, society, amusement, sport, and war. The *Daily News* is the focal point throughout.

61. Escott, T. H. S. *Masters of English Journalism: A Study of Personal Forces.* London and Leipzig: T. Fisher Unwin, 1911. 368pp.

A general history of journalism emphasizing biography. Chapters discuss journalists and journals from the earliest days up to Roger L'Estrange; fathers of English journalism (Defoe and Addison); the middle 18th century (Philip Francis, John Wilkes, and Henry Sampson Woodfall); the work of William Cobbett, Leigh Hunt, and the Walter family; the builders of the penny papers (Frederick Greenwood, Henry Labouchere, and the Harmsworths); regional journalists and journalists in Ireland; and "sub-editors."

62. Ewald, William Bragg, comp. *Rogues, Royalty, and Reporters: The Age of Queen Anne through Its Newspapers.* Boston: Houghton Mifflin Co., 1956. xi + 243pp. (Published in England under the title *Newsmen of Queen Anne.* Oxford: B. Blackwell.)

As part of a study of life in early 18th-century England, this book discusses the origin and growth of a free press and tells how newspapers were written and what they looked like. The appendix lists periodicals, authors, and printers of the time.

63. Fox-Bourne, H. R. *English Newspapers: Chapters in the History of Journalism.* London: Chatto and Windus, 1887. 2 vols. 814pp., total.

A readable, well-documented study of 260 years of the English press by a scholar-author of note who had had years of experience on the *Examiner* and

Weekly Dispatch. Vol. 1 covers 1621–1820 and vol. 2, 1820–1887. There is good detail on Wilkes, Junius, the Woodfall family, the libel acts before and after 1792, the Napoleonic period, Reform journalism from 1826 to 1836, the London *Times* under Barnes and Delane, and the rise of the London *Daily News*.

64. Gerald, J. Edward. *The British Press under Government Economic Controls*. Minneapolis: University of Minnesota Press, 1956. xiv + 235pp.

A well-documented study on the period 1939–1955, during which intensified regulation of business affected mass-communication agencies. There is considerable emphasis on newsprint controls, wages, income, newspaper markets, advertising, circulation, and British efforts to improve press performance.

65. Gibbs, Sir Philip Hamilton. *The Journalist's London*. London: Wingate, 1952. 175pp. (In Londoner's Library.)

66. Grant, James. *The Newspaper Press: Its Origin, Progress, and Present Position*. London: Tinsley Brothers, 1871–1872. 3 vols. (Vol. 3 published under the title *The Metropolitan Weekly and Provincial Press*.)

67. Harris, [Henry] Wilson. *The Daily Press*. Cambridge, England: Cambridge University Press, 1943. x + 146pp.

68. Herd, Harold. *The Making of Modern Journalism*. London: George Allen and Unwin, Ltd., 1927. 118pp.

A popular history of the rise of the sensational press in Great Britain. There is some emphasis on George Newnes and William T. Stead, but the book deals more fully with Alfred Harmsworth and C. A. Pearson, the *Daily Mail*, pictorial journalism, and the renaissance of the *Times*. Capsule biographies of Lord Beaverbrook, the Berry Brothers, Sir Edward Cook, Geoffrey Dawson, J. L. Garvin, Sir Edward Hulton, Kennedy Jones, T. P. O'Connor, Viscount Rothermere, J. A. Spender, and Charles W. Starmer are included.

69. ———. *The March of Journalism: The Story of the British Press from 1622 to the Present Day*. London: George Allen and Unwin, Ltd., 1952. 352pp.

A good condensation of a mass of newspaper and periodical history. Chapters on the Royal Commission investigation of 1947–48 are included. However, bibliography and appendixes are limited and references to sources are few.

70. Hudson, Derek. *British Journalists and Newspapers*. London: Collins, 1945. 48pp.

An artistic booklet giving a brief general history of journalism from the news letters of Nicholas Bourne and Thomas Archer through World War II. It includes color illustrations of the greats of the press, some caricatures, and a fascinating forecast of air-raid defense as published in the *Illustrated London News* in 1924.

71. Hunt, F. Knight. *The Fourth Estate: Contributions toward a History of Newspapers, and of the Liberty of the Press*. London: David Bogue, 1850. 2 vols. 600pp., total.

Knight was one of the first writers to gather together materials on newspaper history. The first volume carries to 1800, the second from 1800 to 1850.

72. Jackson, Mason. *The Pictorial Press: Its Origin and Progress.* London: Hurst and Blackett, 1885. xii + 363pp.

A history of pictorial journalism from early broadsides to the *Illustrated London News.* About 150 line drawings augment the text.

73. Jones, Kennedy. *Fleet Street and Downing Street.* London: Hutchinson and Co., 1920. 363pp.

An associate of Lord Northcliffe wrote here in part a general history of British journalism and in part a hard-hitting plea for the press in its struggle with government. After tracing the rise of the press, 1695–1855, Jones gives more detailed treatment to growing newspaper influence in the mid- and late-Victorian era. The "romance of the *Times*" and the Northcliffe purchase in 1908 are well treated.

74. Kellett, E. E. "The Press," in vol. 2 of *Early Victorian England, 1830–1865.* London: Oxford University Press, H. Milford, 1934.

75. London Times. *Fifty Years — Memories and Contrasts: A Composite Picture of the Period 1882–1932 by Twenty-Seven Contributors to the Times.* London: Thornton Butterworth, Ltd., 1932. 224pp. (Foreword by George M. Trevelyan.)

Descriptive pieces, plus dozens of rotogravure photographs, on changes in London and elsewhere in England. Political, economic, social, military, intellectual, legal, and religious aspects of the Victorian era are discussed. The sensational press is blamed for some of the changes "for the worse."

76. Lytton, Neville. *The Press and the General Staff.* London: W. Collins Sons and Co., Ltd., 1920. xvii + 232pp.

By an English military officer who organized the work of correspondents at British General Headquarters in World War I. He deals only with that portion of the press attached to the British Expeditionary Force in France.

77. Mansfield, F. J. *Gentlemen, the Press! Chronicles of a Crusade.* London: W. H. Allen and Co., Ltd., 1943. 579pp.

The official history of the British National Union of Journalists, 1906–1943. Mansfield served from 1914 to 1934 on the editorial staff of the London *Times* and was a past president of the NUJ.

78. Massingham, H. W. *The London Daily Press.* London: Oxford University Press; New York: Fleming H. Revell Co., 1892. 192pp. (Leisure Hour Library book.)

High points in the development of the *Times, Daily News, Standard, Daily Telegraph, Daily Chronicle, Pall Mall Gazette, St. James's Gazette, Globe,* and some lesser halfpenny sheets. There is a good view of the "New Journalism" in the days before the *Daily Mail.* Illustrated.

79. Morison, Stanley. *The English Newspaper: Some Account of the Physical Development of Journals Printed in London between 1622 and the Present Day.* Cambridge, England: Cambridge University Press, 1932. xii + 335pp.

A magnificent account of changes in newspaper format, with scores of page facsimiles beginning with the corantos. More than 300 newspapers are cited.

The author is concerned principally with newspaper shape, size and folding, type display, column arrangement, and headlines. The book itself is a piece of typographic art.

80. Muddiman, Joseph George [pseud., J. B. Williams]. *A History of English Journalism to the Foundation of the Gazette*. London: Longmans, Green and Co., 1908. xi + 293pp.

A well-organized story of journalism from 1622 to 1666, when the Oxford *Gazette* was established as the first official newspaper. Topics are the corantos, the Puritan quarrel with the Crown, the press under the Commonwealth, and early advertising. Useful material on Nathaniel Butter, Nicholas Bourne, Thomas Archer, Roger L'Estrange, Marchamont Nedham, and Henry Muddiman is included.

81. Pebody, Charles. *English Journalism and the Men Who Have Made It*. London: Cassell, Petter, Galpin and Co., 1882. xii + 192pp. (Shilling Library.)

Somewhat romantic and laudatory. The English press was less impure to Pebody than the American or French press, even if its worst features were taken into account.

82. Pendleton, John. *Newspaper Reporting, in Olden Times and To-day*. London: Elliot Stock, 1890. x + 245pp.

A delightful book on reporting in England. There is material on the reporter in Parliament, traditions of the British Press Gallery, reporting "today" (1890) in Commons, and personal experiences and adventures. The bibliography lists a mass of literature on reporters from 1740 to 1885.

83. Postgate, Raymond, and Aylmer Vallance. *England Goes to Press: The English People's Opinion on Foreign Affairs as Reflected in Their Newspapers since Waterloo (1815–1937)*. Indianapolis and New York: Bobbs-Merrill Co., 1937. 337pp. (Published in England under the title *Those Foreigners*.)

A popular history of foreign policy as presented to the English people in their "favourite newspapers." Postgate prepared the periods 1815–1871 and 1914–1937 and Vallance the period 1872–1914. The coverage of wars, social and economic issues, and personalities are discussed.

84. Shaaber, Matthias A. *Some Forerunners of the Newspaper in England, 1476–1622*. Philadelphia: University of Pennsylvania Press; London: Oxford University Press, 1929. xi + 368pp.

A well-documented, scholarly account, devoted almost exclusively to an examination of written news before newspapers, of tracts (ancestors of the editorial), and of printed advertisements. Shaaber discusses official proclamations, state papers, partisan religious propaganda, popular accounts of monsters, witchcraft, and plagues, ballad writing, and the corantos.

85. Simonis, H. *The Street of Ink: An Intimate History of Journalism*. London: Cassell and Co., Ltd., 1917. xx + 372pp.

The author was a Fleet Street newspaperman for many years, director of the London *Daily News*. He provides brief accounts of the *Times, Morning Post, Daily Telegraph, Daily Mail* and *Evening News, Daily Chronicle* and *Lloyd's*

Weekly News, Daily Express, the E. Hulton firm, picture newspapers, evening and Sunday newspapers, financial and sporting papers, the provincial press, news agencies, specialty papers (*Punch, Truth, Athenaeum, Spectator, John Bull,* and *Passing Show*), the religious press, and the trade press. There is also a treatment of the major publishing ventures of Cassell, Newnes, Pearson, and Amalgamated Press.

86. Stevens, David Harrison. *Party Politics and English Journalism, 1702–1742.* Menasha, Wis.: George Banta Publishing Co., 1916; Chicago: University of Chicago Press, 1916. xii + 156pp.

Originally prepared as a Ph.D. thesis, University of Chicago.

87. Storey, Graham. *Reuters: The Story of a Century of News-Gathering.* London: William Clowes and Sons, Ltd.; New York: Crown Publishers, 1951. xii + 276pp. (Foreword by Lord Layton.)

A centennial history of the British world press association, based upon Reuters archives. The account is divided into three eras — 1851–1915 under Barons Julius and Herbert Reuter; 1915–1941, under Sir Roderick Jones; and since 1941 under Christopher Chancellor. There is considerable material on the Press Association and its relations with Reuters in the 20th century.

88. Stutterheim, Kurt von. *The Press in England.* London: George Allen and Unwin, Ltd., 1934. 223pp. (Translated by W. H. Johnston.)

A German author's historical analysis; von Stutterheim had represented a German newspaper in London for 10 years. Except for the German perspective, there is little material not covered elsewhere.

89. Symon, James D. *The Press and Its Story: An Account of the Birth and Development of Journalism up to the Present Day, with the History of All the Leading Newspapers — Daily, Weekly, or Monthly, Secular and Religious, Past and Present; Also the Story of Their Production from Wood-Pulp to the Printed Sheet.* London: Seeley, Service and Co., Ltd., 1914. xi + 328pp.

Relies upon Andrews (56), Escott (61), Fox-Bourne (63), Grant (66), and Hunt (71). There is excessive emphasis upon the picture press.

90. Symonds, R. V. *The Rise of English Journalism.* Exeter: A. Wheaton and Co., Ltd., 1952. 191pp.

Covers printed news from Elizabeth I through Daniel Defoe. There are essays on and selections from John Chamberlain, professional writer of "letters of news," 1597–1627; John Cleiveland, contemporary of Milton and author of the "Character of a London Diurnall"; Marchamont Nedham of *Mercurius Britanicus,* an abusive sheet suppressed by Charles I; Ned Ward of the London *Spy* and Tom Brown, both satirists at the turn of the 18th century who scavenged for news in London streets; and four who are better known — Henry Muddiman, Roger L'Estrange, Ichabod Dawks, and Defoe.

D. Histories of Individual Newspapers and Associations in the United States and Canada

91. Acheson, Sam. *35,000 Days in Texas: A History of the Dallas News and Its Forebears.* New York: The Macmillan Co., 1938. xi + 337pp.

The house history of the Dallas *Morning News*, which grew from the Galveston *News*, founded in 1842. Considerable space is devoted to Col. Alfred H. Belo and Belo's successor, George B. Dealey. Acheson used *News* files almost exclusively.

92. Ainsworth, Edward M. *History of the Los Angeles Times*. Los Angeles: The Times, 1940. 48pp.

A *Times*-sponsored pamphlet which merely summarizes important events in the newspaper's history and gives an account of the bombing episode of 1910.

93. *The American Weekly Mercury, Nos. 1–212*. Philadelphia: Republished in Facsimile by Colonial Society of Pennsylvania, 1898–1907. 4 vols.

This was the first newspaper published in the Middle Colonies and the fourth in America. The first number was issued December 22, 1719, by Andrew Bradford; the file runs to January 7, 1723.

94. Andrews, J. Cutler. *Pittsburgh's Post-Gazette: First Newspaper West of the Alleghenies*. Boston: Chapman and Grimes, 1936. viii + 324pp.

Published on the occasion of Pittsburgh's sesquicentennial; based on files of the newspaper and other original sources. It provides good glimpses of pioneer Pittsburgh and of John Scull and Joseph Hall, founders of the *Gazette*, and H. H. Brackenridge, an early writer for it. The final chapter gives the story of mergers whereby the *Post* and *Gazette* in 1927 came under the control of Paul Block.

95. Ashton, Wendell J. *Voice in the West: Biography of a Pioneer Newspaper*. New York: Duell, Sloan and Pearce, 1950. xv + 424pp.

The 100th anniversary history of the Salt Lake City *Deseret News*. The volume adds materially to journalistic literature of the Rocky Mountain West. There are good notes on sources, as well as an adequate bibliography and a chronology starting with Brigham Young's arrival in 1847.

96. Atlanta Journal. *This Is the Story of the Atlanta Journal*. Atlanta, Ga.: The Journal, 1944. Unpaged.

A promotional brochure; gives some history of the newspaper.

97. Baehr, Harry W., Jr. *The New York Tribune since the Civil War*. New York: Dodd, Mead and Co., 1936. xiii + 420pp.

A documented history of the *Tribune* and *Herald Tribune* from Horace Greeley's day to that of Helen Rogers Reid. Much information was obtained from the Whitelaw Reid papers. The purchase of the *Herald* from Munsey in 1924 is detailed.

98. Baltimore Sunpapers. *A New Home for the Sunpapers*. Baltimore: A. S. Abell Co., 1951. 64pp.

An illustrated promotional brochure. Thumbnail biographical sketches of Arunah Shepardson Abell (founder of the *Sun* in 1837), George William Abell, Van-Lear Black, Charles H. Grasty, Paul Patterson, H. C. Black, and H. L. Mencken are given.

99. Bankson, Russell A. *The Klondike Nugget*. Caldwell, Idaho: Caxton Printers, Ltd., 1935. 349pp.

The story of the newspaper of the Yukon, published in Dawson City in the gold-rush days of 1898, and of the newspaper's founder, Eugene C. Allen. The material is weighted too heavily with long, direct quotations from old news stories.

100. Barrett, James W., ed. *The End of the World: A Post-Mortem of Its Intangible Assets.* New York: Harper and Brothers, 1931. 273pp.

An emotional account, by Barrett and 25 others of the *World's* last staff, of the unhappy days preceding the newspaper's sale to Scripps-Howard in 1931. While extremely biased, the book does reveal the deep affection which the *World's* employees felt for the paper and its ideals.

101. ———. *The World, the Flesh and Messrs. Pulitzer.* New York: Vanguard Press, 1931. 117pp.

The last city editor of the *World* tells the story of what he regarded as an unnecessary sacrifice. The book is saturated with criticisms of the newspaper's management, particularly under Ralph Pulitzer.

102. Beebe, Lucius. *Comstock Commotion: The Story of the Territorial Enterprise and Virginia City News.* Stanford, Calif.: Stanford University Press, 1954. 129pp.

The owner (with Charles Clegg) of the *Enterprise* records the history of this raucous Nevada sheet. The format is well suited to the subject, with circus-poster type on the title page, line drawings from such sources as the Bancroft Library and Harold's Club, and no footnotes or bibliography.

103. Benét, Stephen Vincent. "The United Press," in *Fortune*, vol. 7, no. 5 (May 1933), pp. 67–72, 94+.

A compact treatment of the United Press Associations.

104. Berger, Meyer. *The Story of the New York Times.* New York: Simon and Schuster, 1951. xv + 589pp. (Foreword by Arthur Hays Sulzberger.)

The official history, issued on the *Times's* 100th anniversary, by a Pulitzer-prize-winning staff member. Only 6 of 47 chapters concern the pre-Ochs era. The most useful portion covers the 25 years preceding publication. Material on recent personalities in *Times* history is extensive: Ochs and Sulzberger, Edwin L. James, Julius Ochs Adler, Arthur Krock, Charles Ransom Miller, Charles Merz, and Carr Van Anda. Factual, like the *Times* itself.

105. Bessie, Simon Michael. *Jazz Journalism: The Story of the Tabloid Newspapers.* New York: E. P. Dutton and Co., 1938. 247pp.

A readable history of small-format newspapers, with particular reference to the New York *Daily News* and a lesser treatment of the New York *Evening Graphic*. Bessie presents a relatively unbiased picture of the way in which the tabloids mirrored "the gay years" of the 1920s.

106. Bonelli, William G. *Billion Dollar Blackjack.* Beverly Hills, Calif.: Civic Research Press, 1954. xii + 230pp.

An indictment of the Los Angeles *Times* and the Chandler family. The author, once a member of the California State Board of Equalization, claims to substantiate charges that the *Times's* owners "twist and torture the law to make it subservient to their interests." Such history as the book contains is strongly biased.

HISTORY

107. Boston Herald. *The Boston Herald and Its History*. Boston: The Herald, 1878. 93pp. (Prepared by Edwin A. Perry.)

A dedication booklet issued upon the opening of a new *Herald* building. It covers the period 1846–1878, with a description of how the newspaper was founded, its early struggles, leading events of the period, and the building.

108. Brooklyn Daily Eagle. *The Eagle and Brooklyn: The Record of the Progress of the Brooklyn Daily Eagle, Issued in Commemoration of Its Semi-Centennial and Occupancy of Its New Building*. Brooklyn, N.Y.: The Eagle, 1893. xvii + xxxi + 1195pp.

Includes a history of Brooklyn as well as of the *Daily Eagle*. The volume was prepared by Henry W. B. Howard, with the assistance of Arthur N. Jervis. It contains nearly 1,300 illustrations.

108a. Bryan, Wilhelmus Bogart. *A History of the National Capital*. New York: The Macmillan Co., 1914 and 1916. 2 vols. 1374pp., total. (Vol. I, 1790–1814; vol. II, 1815–1878.)

A scholarly, thorough history of the American seat of government, principally the city of Washington during its first 88 years, by a reporter for the Washington *Star* for 40 years. There is considerable detail on newspapers in general and, in particular, on the *National Intelligencer* of Gales and Seaton, Duff Green, the Blairs, and John C. Rives.

109. Canadian Press Association. *A History of Canadian Journalism in the Several Portions of the Dominion*. Toronto: The Association, 1908. xv + 242pp.

A 50th anniversary publication, with sections on the CPA and on journalism from its earliest beginnings (1752) in the Maritime Provinces and Quebec. Lists all officers of the Press Association from 1859 to 1908.

110. Canham, Erwin D. *The Christian Science Monitor: To Injure No Man, but to Bless All Mankind, 1908–1954*. New York: Newcomen Society of North America, 1954. 28pp.

An account of the *Monitor's* founding, early and contemporary staff members, and the paper's ideals, delivered as an address by the *Monitor's* editor at the invitation of the Newcomen Society.

110a. Canham, Erwin D. *Commitment to Freedom: The Story of the Christian Science Monitor*. Boston: Houghton Mifflin Co., 1958. xxiv + 454pp.

A 50th anniversary history by the *Monitor's* editor. The account shows journalism at the highest level. Canham includes details on the religious foundations of the *Monitor*. Illustrated.

111. Chamberlin, Joseph Edgar. *The Boston Transcript: A History of Its First Hundred Years*. Boston and New York: Houghton Mifflin Co., 1930. xii + 241pp.

A staff member's history of a distinguished journal, in 1930 still in the hands of its founding family (Dutton) but destined to succumb within a decade. This excellent book includes a detailed account of the Bixby letter of Abraham Lincoln, which the *Transcript* first published.

112. Chappell, Fred A. *The Daily News Building Yesterday and Today.* Chicago: Chicago Daily News, December 30, 1927. 11pp.

A story full of tradition and sentiment, woven around the "old building" that the *Daily News* had occupied for a half century on Wells Street. This pamphlet was issued when the present *Daily News* building on West Madison Street was under construction.

113. Chicago Tribune. *Pictured Encyclopedia of the World's Greatest Newspaper.* Chicago: The Tribune Co., 1928. 790pp.

An 80th anniversary promotion piece, but grandiose enough in scale to have permanent value despite its blatancy. In encyclopedia format, it starts with "ABC" (Audit Bureau of Circulations) and winds up with "Zone 7" (trading area of the *Tribune*).

114. Christian Science Publishing Society. *Then the Full Grain in the Ear.* Boston: The Society, 1915. 31pp.

Expresses the purpose of the *Monitor* and its goal of universal good will.

115. Cohen, Hennig. *The South Carolina Gazette, 1732–1775.* Columbia: University of South Carolina Press, 1953. xv + 273pp.

Of high historical and bibliographical value, this account of the *Gazette* is based upon its contents. It pictures South Carolina teachers, doctors, artists, architects and engineers, musicians, booksellers, and poets and essayists as their notices in the *Gazette* revealed them. There are also sketches of five Colonial editors — Thomas Whitmarsh; Lewis, Elizabeth, and Peter Timothy; and Thomas Powell.

116. Copley Press. *The Copley Press.* Aurora, Ill.: Copley Press, 1953. 460pp.

An illustrated history of the Copley publishing operation, issued on its 25th anniversary. A biography of Col. Ira Clifton Copley, purchaser of the Aurora (Ill.) *Beacon* in 1905 and years later founder of the Copley group, is included. There are histories of varying lengths on these newspapers: in Illinois, Aurora *Beacon-News*, Elgin *Daily Courier-News*, Joliet *Herald-News*, *Illinois State Journal* and *Illinois State Register*, both of Springfield; in California, San Diego *Union* and *Evening Tribune*, Southern California Associated Newspapers, Alhambra *Post-Advocate*, Burbank *Daily Review*, Culver City *Evening Star-News*, Glendale *News-Press*, Monrovia *Daily News-Post*, Redondo Beach *South Bay Daily Breeze*, and San Pedro *News-Pilot*. Also included are accounts of Copley Press bureaus, radio associations, and advertising and newsprint connections.

117. Crittenden, Charles Christopher. *North Carolina Newspapers before 1790.* Chapel Hill: University of North Carolina Press, 1928. (Published as vol. 20, no. 1, The James Sprunt Studies in History and Political Science.)

118. Dabney, Thomas Ewing. *One Hundred Great Years: The Story of the Times-Picayune from Its Founding to 1940.* Baton Rouge: Louisiana State University Press, 1944. xii + 552pp.

An account of the newspaper that is perhaps the South's most famous, and an extensive history of New Orleans as well. Dabney, a staff member, first obtained much of his material for publication in the 100th anniversary issue in 1937. There is some material on the New Orleans *Bee*, which was eventually consolidated with the *Times-Picayune*. Of the *Picayune* founders, only George W. Kendall has had a separate biography written about him; hence Dabney's accounts of Kendall's partners, Francis Asbury Lumsden and Alva Morris Holbrook, are exceedingly helpful.

119. Dana, Marshall N. *Newspaper Story: Fifty Years of the Oregon Journal, 1902–1952*. Portland, Ore.: The Journal, 1951. 229pp.

Heroes of this staff history are C. S. (Sam) Jackson and his son Phil, only publishers of the *Journal* up to the time of Dana's writing, and Sam's widow Maria. The deeply affectionate account is based upon personal experience.

120. Davis, Elmer. *History of the New York Times, 1851–1921*. New York: The New York Times Co., 1921. xxii + 434pp.

An excellent standard history, issued on the *Times*'s 70th anniversary. It has since been supplemented by Berger's 100th anniversary history (see 104).

121. Detroit News. *The Detroit News, 1873–1917: A Record of Progress*. Detroit: Evening News Assn., 1918. 88pp. (Prepared by Lee A. White.)

A color booklet describing the *News*, recording in detail its founding by James E. Scripps, and giving an account of its new building.

122. Dunn, Arthur Wallace. *Gridiron Nights: Humorous and Satirical Views of Politics and Statesmen as Presented by the Famous Dining Club*. New York: Frederick A. Stokes Co., 1915. xvi + 371pp. + 125 illustrations.

A readable history of the first 30 years of the Gridiron Club of Washington, by a past-president. There is particularly interesting material on presidents as guests, with cartoons and caricatures.

123. Dyar, Ralph E. *News for an Empire: The Story of the Spokesman-Review of Spokane, Washington, and of the Field It Serves*. Caldwell, Idaho: Caxton Printers, Ltd., 1952. xlix + 494pp.

Full accounts of the William H. Cowles family, publishers for more than half a century in Spokane. The prologue dips back to 1805 and the Lewis and Clark expedition, although the newspaper history proper begins with founding of the Spokane *Review* in Washington Territory in 1883. The author is a member of the newspaper's promotion staff. There is some bibliography of Northwest Americana.

124. Elliott, Robert Neal, Jr. *The Raleigh Register, 1799–1863*. Chapel Hill: University of North Carolina Press, 1955. vii + 133pp. (Published as vol. 36, The James Sprunt Studies in History and Political Science.)

A history of the Raleigh newspaper founded by Joseph Gales, later purchaser of the *National Intelligencer* in Washington, D.C. Included are biographies of Gales; his son, Weston, Joseph's successor in 1833; and his grandson, Seaton, successor to Weston in 1848. The study was based upon the family's personal papers and upon files of the *Register*. There is a good bibliography.

125. Emery, Edwin. *History of the American Newspaper Publishers Asso-*

ciation. Minneapolis: University of Minnesota Press, 1950. vii + 263pp.

A well-documented account of the development since the 1880s of the publishers' group organized to promote the interests of American newspapers, particularly with regard to economic problems. The study goes also into legal matters, especially ANPA efforts to protect the press from unfair legislation. There is a good account of publishers' attitudes toward the American Newspaper Guild and ANPA relations with the New Deal.

126. Freeman, Legh R. *The History of the Frontier-Index (the "Press on Wheels"), the Ogden Freeman, the Inter-Mountains Freeman and the Union Freeman.* Evanston, Ill., 1943. 13pp., mimeographed. (Introduction by Douglas C. McMurtrie.)

Notes on pioneer printing and newspaper publishing in Nebraska, Colorado, Wyoming, Utah, and Montana during the post-Civil War railroad construction period. Freeman began the *Frontier-Index* in Julesburg, Colo., July 26, 1867, and moved west with the railroad, continuing publication until 1890.

127. Glenn, William Meharry. *The Sigma Delta Chi Story (1909–1949).* Coral Gables, Fla.: Glade House, 1949. 202pp.

An anniversary history of the national professional journalism fraternity, by a charter member. Intensely idealistic. There is helpful information on Glenn's co-founders, past officers, national conventions, and the *Quill.*

128. Goddard, Delano A. *Newspapers and Newspaper Writers in New England, 1787–1815.* Boston: A. Williams and Co., 1880. 39pp.

Book publication of a paper read before the New England Historic Genealogical Society. It sketches these distinguished newspapers: *Columbian Centinel* (Benjamin Russell); pre-Revolutionary Boston *Gazette* (Benjamin Edes); *Massachusetts Spy* (Isaiah Thomas); *Independent Chronicle* (Capt. Thomas Adams); *New England Palladium* (Alexander Young and Samuel Ethridge); *New England Repertory* (John Barnard and John Park); Boston *Patriot* (Everett and Munroe); Salem *Gazette* (Thomas C. Cushing); Salem *Register* (William Carleton); and *Farmers' Weekly Museum* (Joseph Dennie). Both sides of the Jefferson-Hamilton conflict are cursorily covered.

128a. Goddard, William. *The Partnership.* Philadelphia: Printed by William Goddard, 1770. 72pp.

A history of the rise of the *Pennsylvania Chronicle*, outlining the activities of Joseph Galloway, Thomas Wharton, Sr., and Benjamin Towne. Goddard seeks to refute their calumnies against him.

129. Gramling, Oliver. *AP: The Story of News.* New York and Toronto: Farrar and Rinehart, 1940. x + 506pp. (Illustrated by Henry C. Barrow.)

The Associated Press is cast in heroic mold in this history, which is based to a considerable extent on newspaper files and AP records dating back nearly a century. The book has useful information, and its tendency to rely on the "flash" technique and to glorify the AP can be forgiven.

130. Harrison, Richard Edes. "Associated Press," in *Fortune*, vol. 15, no. 2 (February 1937), pp. 89–93, 148+.

A compact treatment of all aspects of the AP.

HISTORY

131. Hobson, Dorothy Anne. *The Valsetz Star*. Portland, Ore.: Creation House, 1942. xi + 165pp.

Valsetz, an Oregon coast-range town, was without a newspaper in 1938 when a nine-year-old child began to edit and mimeograph a sheet giving the sort of county and local news she thought Valsetz deserved. After Pearl Harbor, at age 12, she "retired," but not before her achievement had gained international recognition. This book carries the file of Dorothy Hobson's newspaper.

132. Hooker, Richard. *The Story of an Independent Newspaper*. New York: The Macmillan Co., 1924. xii + 237pp.

A staff member chronicles the Springfield *Republican*, 1824–1924. The material was taken chiefly from files of the *Republican* and from Merriam's life of Bowles (see 406 below). Hooker goes into more detail on the *Republican's* first years, 1824–1844, than did Merriam, and fills in the period 1878–1924, after Bowles's death.

133. Hutton, Bud, and Andy Rooney. *The Story of the Stars and Stripes*. New York and Toronto: Farrar and Rinehart, 1946. xi + 240pp.

A history of the United States Army newspaper of World War II — "an attempt at a free press in a part of the world where most of the free press had ceased to exist." There are numerous reprints of *Stars and Stripes* stories. Good reading.

134. Independent Reporter. *Concerning the Independent Reporter and Its Newspaper and Job-Printing Equipment*. Skowhegan, Maine, 1923. 24 unnumbered pages.

A 100th anniversary tribute to a little newspaper in Somerset County, Maine (Skowhegan).

135. Johnson, Gerald W., Frank R. Kent, H. L. Mencken, and Hamilton Owens. *The Sunpapers of Baltimore, 1837–1937*. New York: Alfred A. Knopf, 1937. xi + 430pp.

The centennial history of the *Sun* and *Evening Sun*, by four staff members. Johnson wrote chapters 1–6, to the death of Arunah S. Abell, founder; Kent, 7–10, chiefly political history of the Cleveland period and the three Bryan campaigns; Mencken, 11–18, the *Sun* under Abell's heirs, Baltimore at turn of the century, birth of the *Evening Sun*, and service of Charles H. Grasty; and Owens, 19–21, the Sunpapers in the modern day. This is probably the best source of biographical material on the first Abell.

136. Johnson, Walter C., and Arthur T. Robb. *The South and Its Newspapers: The Story of the Southern Newspaper Publishers Association and Its Part in the South's Economic Rebirth*. Chattanooga, Tenn.: Southern Newspaper Publishers Assn., 1954. ix + 386pp.

This staff history covers the period 1903–1953. There are only limited notes to sources and the approach is uncritical. Johnson was for 15 years secretary of the SNPA; Robb is editor of *Editor & Publisher*.

137. Kansas City Star Co. *The Story of the Kansas City Star*. Kansas City: The Star, 1948. 48pp.

This souvenir booklet includes also an account of WDAF, the *Star's* radio station, and of the newspaper's privately owned paper mill in Park Falls, Wis. Illustrated.

138. Kauffmann, Samuel H. *The Evening Star (1852–1952): A Century at the Nation's Capital.* New York: Newcomen Society of North America, 1952. 28pp.

An address to the Newcomen Society by the president of the *Evening Star*, given in Washington on March 28, 1952. Kauffmann memorializes the newspaper's centennial and the men associated with its growth, especially Theodore, Frank, and Newbold Noyes.

139. Kinsley, Philip. *The Chicago Tribune: Its First Hundred Years.* Vol. I, New York: Alfred A. Knopf, 1943. xv + 381pp. Vols. II and III, Chicago: The Tribune Co., 1945 and 1946. xv + 349pp.; xiv + 359pp.

A still incomplete staff history, carrying so far only to the death of Joseph Medill. The first volume covers the period from 1847 to 1860, the second 1860–1880, and the third 1880–1900. The volumes are patently biased and are actually a bringing together of various unconnected episodes in *Tribune* history. However, they do give considerable factual information.

140. Kolehmainen, John I. *Sow the Golden Seed.* Fitchburg, Mass.: The Raivaaja Publishing Co., 1955. xi + 150pp.

A history of the Fitchburg Finnish-American Socialist newspaper *Raivaaja* (the Pioneer), founded in 1905. The author used *Raivaaja* files, records of stockholders' meetings, and manuscript sources. The bibliography is of value in tracing other Finnish-American newspapers. Kolehmainen, on the staff of Heidelberg College, Tiffin, Ohio, was not associated with the newspaper.

141. Laney, Al. *Paris Herald: The Incredible Newspaper.* New York and London: D. Appleton-Century Co., 1947. x + 334pp.

A free-wheeling history of the Paris edition of the New York *Herald Tribune* by a one-time staff member. The volume concerns principally the period from World War I to the liberation of Paris and the *Herald's* resumption of publication in 1944. There are 50 fascinating pages on the paper's early years as a toy of James Gordon Bennett, Jr.

142. Lee Newspapers. *The Lee Papers: A Saga of Midwestern Journalism.* Kewanee, Ill.: Star Courier Press, 1947. 418pp.

Histories of various Lee newspapers and personalities associated with them, including Ottumwa (Iowa) *Courier*, the parent paper; Davenport (Iowa) *Times*; Muscatine (Iowa) *Journal*; Hannibal (Mo.) *Courier-Post*; La Crosse (Wis.) *Tribune*; Madison (Wis.) *Wisconsin State Journal*; Davenport (Iowa) *Democrat*; Mason City (Iowa) *Globe-Gazette*; Kewanee (Ill.) *Star-Courier*; and Lincoln (Neb.) *Star*. There is also an account of the Lee Syndicate and of the Lee radio stations.

143. Lockley, Fred. *The Story of the Journal.* Portland, Ore.: Oregon Journal, n.d. 48pp.

A promotion piece, of regional value, on how a newspaper is made, along with some history.

144. Los Angeles Times. *Midwinter 1956: Los Angeles Times 75th Anni-*

HISTORY

versary. Los Angeles: The Times, Jan. 3, 1956. 216pp., rotogravure magazine section.

A staff-prepared history of the *Times* and the city of Los Angeles. Well illustrated and choked with advertising.

145. Mallen, Frank. *Sauce for the Gander*. White Plains, N.Y.: Baldwin Books, 1954. 243pp.

A history of the New York *Evening Graphic*, together with some autobiography of a one-time staff member and considerable collected biography of *Graphic* alumni. Flippant in tone. Sources were "friends in the newspaper trade" and Mallen's old *Graphic* associates.

146. Martin, Douglas D. *Tombstone's Epitaph*. Albuquerque, N.M.: University of New Mexico Press, 1951. xii + 272pp.

Much of this worthwhile book is reproduction of stories the *Epitaph* carried in the days from its founding in Arizona by John P. Clum (1880) to the early 1900s. Martin, a former newspaperman in Detroit, became head of the University of Arizona Department of Journalism.

147. Martin, Lawrence Crawford. *So the People May Know*. Denver: The Post, 1950. 79pp. (Written in collaboration with Elvon L. Howe and members of the *Post* staff.)

A brochure issued in connection with the Denver *Post*'s dedication of a new building. Emphasizes in a manner restrained for this paper "the future of Denver, Colorado, and the Rocky Mountain Empire." Its favorable view of Fred G. Bonfils and Harry Tammen is an antidote to most published criticism of them.

148. Miller, Orlo. *A Century of Western Ontario: The Story of London, the Free Press, and Western Ontario, 1849–1949*. Toronto: Ryerson Press, 1949. xi + 289pp.

The author emphasizes the "unique" nature of this newspaper, in the hands of Josiah Blackburn and his descendants since 1852. The book is weighted heavily on the early period of the *Free Press*.

149. Milwaukee Journal. *Portrait of a Paper*. Milwaukee, Oct. 6, 1957–Feb. 2, 1958. 20 unbound leaves.

A reprint in brochure form of a series of articles in the *Journal* depicting in news stories and pictures the history of the newspaper over 75 years.

150. Morris, Joe Alex. *Deadline Every Minute: The Story of the United Press*. Garden City, N.Y.: Doubleday and Co., 1957. 356pp.

A 50th anniversary history of the United Press Associations, by a former foreign editor of UP. Highly readable and fast-moving, the volume is particularly useful for its information on UP executives: Hugh Baillie, Karl Bickel, William W. Hawkins, and Roy W. Howard.

151. Nevins, Allan. *The Evening Post: A Century of Journalism*. New York: Boni and Liveright, 1922. 590pp.

Among the best books on individual newspapers. Nevins treats fully *Post* history from 1801 through 1900, with a concluding chapter on 1900–1922. The

25

volume performs a useful service in tying together the careers of many editors whose lives in separate biographies tend to be isolated. See particularly the material on Alexander Hamilton's part in the paper's founding, and that on William Coleman, William Leggett, William Cullen Bryant, John Bigelow, Parke Godwin, Henry Villard and Oswald Garrison Villard, Carl Schurz, Horace White, Edwin Lawrence Godkin, and Rollo Ogden.

152. New York Evening Journal. *What's in the New York Evening Journal, America's Greatest Evening Newspaper.* New York: The Evening Journal, 1928. 84pp.

Sketches of several dozen *Journal* "stars" from Arthur Brisbane on. A brochure of some curio value.

153. *New York Evening Post, a Distinguished Newspaper.* New York: The Evening Post, n.d. 24 unnumbered pages.

A leatherette-bound collector's item, embossed in gold leaf. It sets forth the historic ideal voiced by Alexander Hamilton in 1801 that the *Post* be "a national institution" and pays tribute to William Cullen Bryant and Henry Villard.

154. New York Evening Post. *The Evening Post: 100th Anniversary Supplement.* New York, Nov. 16, 1901. 142pp.

155. ———. *Forward March! A Century of Journalism.* New York: Literary Classic, Inc., 1943. viii + 245pp.

An anthology of articles from the *Evening Post* over 140 years. Included among 34 pieces are 9 editorials. Selections are devoted to New York City, the Civil War, and world affairs. One of the three sections in the book is wholly contemporary — pre-World War II and the World War II period.

156. ———. *The New York Evening Post, Founded by Alexander Hamilton, 1801–1925.* New York: The Evening Post, 1925. 45pp.

A promotional brochure issued in connection with a forthcoming new building in 1926 and the newspaper's 125th anniversary. Color pictures of noted editors, facsimiles of selected issues, and descriptive text are included.

157. ———. *Press Time: A Book of Post Classics.* New York: Books, Inc., 1936. xii + 383pp.

158. New York Herald Tribune. *Every Morning: Why the New York Herald Tribune Is One of the Leading Newspapers of the World.* New York: The Herald Tribune, 1948. 60pp.

A behind-the-scenes promotional brochure.

159. New York Sun. *One Hundredth Anniversary, 1833–1933.* New York: The Sun, Sept. 2, 1933. 108pp.

The centennial issue of Benjamin Day's penny paper of 1833 includes a reprint of the 4-page, 7 × 10-inch issue of vol. 1, no. 1, and a historical account.

160. New York Times. *The New York Times, 75th Anniversary, 1851–1926.* New York: The Times, 1926. 63pp.

161. ———. *One Hundred Years of Famous Pages from the New York*

Times, 1851–1951. New York: Simon and Schuster, 1951. xii + 100pp. (Introduction by Henry Steele Commager.)

A centennial brochure reproducing historic pages on news events from Henry J. Raymond's first issue, September 18, 1851, to Harry Truman's discharge of Gen. Douglas MacArthur, April 11, 1951. Two thirds of the content is devoted to 20th-century news events.

162. Nichols, M. E. *(CP): The Story of the Canadian Press.* Toronto: Ryerson Press, 1948. xvi + 327pp. (Foreword by Leonard W. Brockington.)

A former president of Canada's leading press association records its history. Although based largely on official association records, 1906–1948, the book includes biographical material on CP personalities as well as institutional data. There are sketches of E. H. Macklin, John Ross Robertson, John W. Dafoe and J. F. B. Livesay. Most of the emphasis is on the Winnipeg area, where the CP got its start.

163. O'Brien, Frank M. *The Story of the Sun, 1833–1928.* New York: George H. Doran Co., 1918; new edition, New York: D. Appleton and Co., 1928. xiii + 305pp.

Read along with biographies of Charles A. Dana and Edward P. Mitchell, this book fills out the *Sun* story through its purchase by William T. Dewart. O'Brien, an editorial writer when the book was first written and editor at the time of the revision, presents a glowing account of the newspaper. There are useful chapters on Frank A. Munsey and Dewart.

164. Palmer, Lincoln B. "The American Newspaper Publishers' Association," in *Publishers' Guide,* May 1913.

165. Philadelphia Evening Bulletin. *One Day.* Philadelphia: The Bulletin, 1929. iv + 307pp.

A promotional book to show how one copy of the *Evening Bulletin* would appear in book form. The issue is that of June 4, 1928.

166. ———. *100 Years in Philadelphia: The Evening Bulletin's Anniversary Book.* Philadelphia: The Bulletin, 1947. 160pp.

A pictorial book, with some explanatory text, issued in commemoration of the newspaper's centennial.

167. Philadelphia Inquirer. *A Great Newspaper Is Re-Born.* Philadelphia: The Inquirer, n.d. 52 unnumbered pages.

A promotional piece to publicize publisher M. L. Annenberg and his "amazing revitalization" of the *Inquirer* in the 1930s. There is a cursory history of the paper, plus a biography of Annenberg.

168. Philadelphia Record. *Backstage with a Great Newspaper.* Philadelphia: The Record, 1936. 63pp.

An account of news-gathering activities of the now-deceased *Record.* It gives a brief history of the paper not readily obtainable elsewhere.

169. Portland Oregonian. *The Oregonian Goes to Press.* Portland, Ore.: The Oregonian, 1948. 21pp.

170. Providence Journal. *Half a Century with the Providence Journal.* Providence, R.I.: The Journal Co., 1904. xiii + 235pp.

Chiefly a biography of Henry R. Davis, long-time secretary of the Journal Co., with some history of the newspaper and of Providence. There are also accounts of *Journal* editors.

171. Radder, Norman J. *Through Twenty Years: A History of the Sheboygan Press, 1907–1927.* Sheboygan, Wis.: The Press, 1927. 47pp.

An account of the early years of one of Wisconsin's leading small-city daily newspapers.

172. Rice, William B. *The Los Angeles Star, 1851–1864: The Beginnings of Journalism in Southern California.* Berkeley and Los Angeles: University of California Press, 1947. xvi + 315pp.

The bulk of this study concerns an early *Star* editor, Henry Hamilton (1856–1860), and the Civil War years up to the newspaper's suspension in 1864. It treats principally the *Star's* editorial opinions and not news. Considerable detail on the early years of southern California is included, and there is an extensive bibliography of southern California history.

173. ———. *Southern California's First Newspaper: The Founding of the Los Angeles Star.* Los Angeles: Glen Dawson, 1941. 54pp.

An earlier, limited issue of Rice's full study of the *Star* (172).

174. Rosewater, Victor. *History of Co-operative News-Gathering in the United States.* New York and London: D. Appleton and Co., 1930. xiv + 430pp.

Rosewater begins with news-gathering in the early coffee-house exchange days and carries the story through to the contemporary period of AP, UP, and INS. There is good detail on the crisis at the turn of the 20th century that gave rise to the modern Associated Press. Included also is an account of press use of the pony express, oceanic steamers, and modern supplemental news services.

175. St. Louis Post-Dispatch. *The Story of the St. Louis Post-Dispatch.* St. Louis: Pulitzer Publishing Co., 1954. 60pp.

The sixth edition of an excellent promotional publication; it gives highlights of the *Post-Dispatch's* history and accounts of its crusading accomplishments. First issued in 1928 on the newspaper's fiftieth anniversary under Pulitzer ownership and prepared then by Charles G. Ross of the Washington Bureau, it was revised in 1940, 1944, 1949, and 1953.

176. St. Louis Republic. *Century Club of American Newspapers.* St. Louis: George Knapp and Co., 1909. 36 unnumbered pages.

Brief accounts of the history and ownership of 82 United States newspapers in 18 states that constituted the 100-year-old group in 1909. Of the 82, 34 still were publishing nearly another half century later (1957) in one form or another, 14 with the original name and 20 with a combination name as the result of a consolidation.

177. Sass, Herbert Ravenel. *Outspoken: 150 Years of the News and Courier.* Columbia: University of South Carolina Press, 1953. 120pp.

Little more than a 150th anniversary account prepared for a special edition of January 10, 1953. Nearly half of the book is a collection of biographies of staff members. Sass is a South Carolina novelist who started his career on the *News and Courier.*

178. Scanlon, John J. *The Passing of the Springfield Republican.* Amherst, Mass.: Amherst College, 1950. 82pp.

A former staff member attempts to analyze the economic developments that led to the death of the *Republican* in 1946, mainly competition, price wars, and labor trouble. Tables show the changes in Springfield newspaper circulation, 1885–1948, and advertising linage, 1923–1945, and the decline in number of U.S. newspapers.

179. Scharf, J. Thomas. *The Chronicles of Baltimore: Being a Complete History of the Baltimore Town and Baltimore City from the Earliest Period to the Present Time.* Baltimore: Turnbull Brothers, 1874. viii + 756pp.

A poorly organized general history which does contain, however, a reasonably adequate account of Baltimore newspapers. Dates of founding and ending are included for almost all papers.

180. ———— and Thompson Westcott. "The Press of Philadelphia," in their *History of Philadelphia,* vol. III, pp. 1958–2062. Philadelphia: L. H. Everts & Co., 1884.

An encyclopedic history of Philadelphia newspapers, general and specialized, from Andrew Bradford's *American Weekly Mercury* (1719) to the date of publication. See particularly the accounts of the *Pennsylvania Packet or General Advertiser; Gazette of the United States; North American; Port Folio; Saturday Evening Post; Inquirer; Godey's Lady's Book; Public Ledger; Graham's Magazine; Evening Bulletin; Record; Press;* and *Times.*

181. E. W. Scripps Company. *A Handbook of Scripps-Howard.* Memphis: Memphis Publishing Co., 1948. 310pp.

A picture of the Scripps national structure "in proper perspective." Most of the work for this handbook was done by the late John H. Sorrells, executive editor. It includes a discussion of aims, methods, and purposes; sketches of Scripps-Howard personalities, including 17 biographies of past and present executives; and accounts of the United Press Associations and Newspaper Enterprise Association. Exceptionally valuable material.

182. Shaw, Archer H. *The Plain Dealer: One Hundred Years in Cleveland.* New York: Alfred A. Knopf, 1942. xv + 402pp.

Like most house histories, this one, written by the chief editorial writer of the *Plain Dealer* for 32 years, is generally laudatory in tone and unexciting. It has useful information on the history of Cleveland and is well illustrated.

183. Smith, J. Eugene. *One Hundred Years of Hartford's Courant: From Colonial Times through the Civil War.* New Haven: Yale University Press, 1949. 342pp.

A scholarly history, heavy in spots. Unfortunately there is no preface offering a general interpretation of the importance of the *Courant* in the development of New England.

184. Stars and Stripes. *Squads Write! A Selection of the Best Things in Prose, Verse and Cartoon from the Stars and Stripes.* New York: Harper and Brothers, 1931. x + 335pp. (Edited by John T. Winterich.)

This anthology of the official newspaper of the AEF in World War I provides a useful historical record, with 60 illustrations, of the paper's 71 weeks (February 8, 1918, to June 13, 1919). Among writers were Franklin P. Adams, Stephen T. Early, Grantland Rice, Harold Ross, and Alexander Woollcott.

185. Talley, Robert. *One Hundred Years of the Commercial Appeal: The Story of the Greatest Romance in American Journalism.* Memphis: The Commercial Appeal, 1940. 71pp.

A souvenir prepared from the centennial issue of the newspaper, January 1, 1940.

186. Warner, Henry Edward. *Seeing the Sun: A Visitor's Description of the Making of a Newspaper.* Baltimore: A. S. Abell Co., 1922. 40pp.

187. Yank. *The Best from Yank, the Army Weekly.* Cleveland and New York: World Publishing Co., 1945. 256pp. + 48 full-page illustrations.

Representative selections originally appearing in *Yank* from the summer of 1942 to the fall of 1944. The contents are divided almost evenly among war reports from all fronts, fiction and humor, poems, cartoons, and photographs. *Yank's* staff members are listed.

E. Histories of Individual Newspapers in Great Britain

188. Berrey, R. Power. *The Romance of a Great Newspaper.* London: News of the World, n.d. 57pp.

A history of the first large Sunday newspaper in England, *Bell's Weekly Messenger* (1796), which later became the *New Weekly Messenger* (1832) and finally the *News of the World* (1843). The account includes biographies of John Browne Bell, and, in the contemporary period, of Sir Emsley Carr and Lascelles Carr.

189. Blunden, Edmund. *Leigh Hunt's Examiner Examined.* London: Cobden-Sanderson, 1928. xi + 263pp.

An account of the *Examiner's* contents, 1808 to 1825, with selections by Hunt, Lamb, Keats, Shelley, and Byron. The author discusses Hunt's involvement in libel prosecutions, 1808–1809, famous in literary history.

190. Booth, J. B. *Old Pink 'Un Days.* New York: Dodd, Mead and Co., 1925. 413pp.

A history of British sporting journalism, particularly of the *Sporting Times,* founded in 1865, and John Corlett, who was associated with the paper from 1865 to 1913.

191. ———. *Sporting Times, The "Pink 'Un" World.* London: T. W. Laurie, 1938. xx + 284pp. (Foreword by the Earl of Lonsdale, K.G.)

192. Bowman, William Dodgson. *The Story of the Times.* London: But-

ler and Tanner, Ltd., 1931; New York: Lincoln MacVeagh, Dial Press, 1931. ix + 342pp.

Though superseded by the *Times*'s own four-volume history, Bowman's book is a useful single-volume account. It ends when the *Times* passed into the hands of John Jacob Astor after the death of Lord Northcliffe.

193. Burnham, Edward Frederick Lawson [Lord]. *Peterborough Court: The Story of the Daily Telegraph*. London: Cassell and Co., Ltd., 1955. 225pp.

Burnham traces the growth of a quality London newspaper from its start as a precursor of the yellow press to a position as one of the most widely read newspapers in England.

194. Clive, John. *Scotch Reviewers: The Edinburgh Review, 1802–1815*. Cambridge, Mass.: Harvard University Press, 1957. 224pp.

A scholarly history based on contemporary material. The author includes a brief biography of Francis Jeffrey as editor and accounts of the Whig party and its relation to the Edinburgh reviews. There is an extensive bibliography.

195. Cudlipp, Hugh. *Publish and Be Damned: The Astonishing Story of the Daily Mirror*. London: Andrew Dakers, Ltd., 1953. xi + 292pp.

A lively history of Northcliffe's original tabloid — 50 years old in 1953. Cudlipp, who has been with the *Mirror* and *Sunday Pictorial* since 1935, does not apologize for England's sensational press.

196. Desmond, R. G. C. *Our Local Press: A Short Historical Account of the Newspapers of Walthamstow*. Walthamstow (London): Walthamstow Antiquarian Society, 1955. 82pp.

A review of newspapers in a residential and industrial suburb nine miles northeast of London. It covers the period from the establishment of the *Walthamstow Chronicle and Leyton Intelligence* in 1870 to the present. A fine contribution to an understanding of the problems of journalism in the shadow of London.

197. Facsimile Text Society. *Defoe's Review*. Facsimile Book 1–22 of vol. I–IX, 1704–1713. New York: Columbia University Press, 1938.

198. Fielding, Henry. *The Covent Garden Journal*. New Haven: Yale University Press, 1915. 2 vols. xii + 661pp., total. (Edited by Gerard Edward Jensen.)

199. Gibb, Mildred A., Frank Beckwith, and Members of the Editorial Staff of the Yorkshire Post. *The Yorkshire Post: Two Centuries*. Yorkshire: Yorkshire Conservative Newspaper Co., Ltd., 1954. xi + 112pp.

A staff history of the distinguished provincial newspaper of Leeds, one of the few surviving papers that date from the mid-18th century.

200. Hatton, Joseph. *Journalistic London*. London: Sampson Low, Marston, Searle & Rivington, 1882. viii + 249pp.

An interesting old book, with pictures of many early editors and newspaper buildings. There is a highly readable sketch of Charles Dickens during his short tenure as editor of the London *Daily News* in 1846. Full chapters on the London *Times*, the London *Daily Telegraph*, the *Illustrated London News*, and other leading newspapers are included.

201. Hindle, Wilfrid. *The Morning Post, 1772–1937: Portrait of a Newspaper*. London: George Routledge & Sons, Ltd., 1937. xi + 260pp.

When it merged with the London *Telegraph* in 1937, the *Post* was the oldest continuously published British newspaper. Hindle attributes its distinction to a peculiar English trait: "staunch and strong, upright and downright, scorning wrong." There are excellent biographical accounts of Algernon Borthwick (Lord Glenesk) and H. A. Gwynne.

202. Jewish Chronicle. *The Jewish Chronicle, 1841–1941: A Century of Newspaper History*. London: The Jewish Chronicle, 1949. xv + 187pp.

203. London Daily Mail. *News in Our Time, 1896–1946: Golden Jubilee Book of the Daily Mail*. London: Associated Newspapers, Ltd., 1946. 176pp.

204. London Times. *History of the London Times, 1785–1948*. London: The Times; New York: The Macmillan Co., 1935–1948. 4 vols., with vol. IV in two parts.

Perhaps the most outstanding staff-prepared, newspaper-published history that has ever been issued. Thoroughly detailed and well written, the volumes reveal how and why the *Times* became a national institution. Publication was begun on the occasion of the *Times*'s 150th anniversary in 1935. The separate volumes carry these subtitles: I. *The Thunderer in the Making, 1785–1841*; II. *The Tradition Established, 1841–1884*; III. *The Twentieth Century Test, 1884–1912*; and IV. *The 150th Anniversary and Beyond, 1912–1948*. An exceptionally detailed appendix at the close of the last volume has a full account of press handling of the Abdication crisis of 1936, including the *Times*'s own considerable role.

205. ———. *The London Times: A Newspaper History, 1785–1935*. London: The Times, 1935. 213pp.

Reprinted from the 150th Anniversary Number, January 1, 1935.

206. ———. *Printing The Times since 1785: Some Account of the Means of Production and Changes of Dress of the Newspaper*. London: The Times, 1953. x + 195pp., illustrated.

207. McKenzie, F. A. *The Mystery of the Daily Mail*. London: Associated Newspapers, Ltd., 1921. 128pp.

A promotion piece aimed at explaining the "astounding development of the *Mail* during its first quarter-century." The volume covers the paper's founding by Alfred Harmsworth, its early campaigns and popular appeals, its interest in aviation and photography, its propaganda activities in World War I, and its business activities.

208. Mills, William Haslam. *The Manchester Guardian: A Century of History*. London: Chatto and Windus, 1921; New York: Henry Holt and Co., 1922. vi + 146pp. (Preface by Charles P. Scott.)

Contains the *Guardian*'s history as published in its centennial number of May 5, 1921.

209. Nobbe, George. *The North Briton: A Study in Political Propaganda.* New York: Columbia University Press, 1939. ix + 274pp.

An account of John Wilkes's newspaper and, in effect, a biography of Wilkes. The authorship of individual issues of the *North Briton* is indicated.

210. Robertson-Scott, John William. *The Life and Death of a Newspaper.* London: Methuen and Co., Ltd., 1952. xii + 417pp.

An account principally of the "temperaments, perturbations and achievements" of John Morley, W. T. Stead, E. T. Cook, Harry Cust, and J. L. Garvin as editors of the *Pall Mall Gazette.*

211. ————. *The Story of the Pall Mall Gazette, of Its First Editor Frederick Greenwood, and of Its Founder George Murray Smith.* London: Oxford University Press, 1950. ix + 470pp.

A member of the *Pall Mall* staff tells here (at age 84) one of the most fascinating of British newspaper history-biographies. Besides the story of Greenwood, Smith, and the newspaper, Robertson-Scott relates the parts played in 19th-century journalism by literary-press figures such as Charlotte Brontë, William Makepeace Thackeray, Anthony Trollope, and Harriet Martineau, and political figures like Gladstone, Lord Salisbury, and Disraeli. The author records also Greenwood's services with the *St. James's Gazette.* An informative chapter deals with George Smith's founding of Britain's *Dictionary of National Biography.*

212. Rust, William. *The Story of the Daily Worker.* London: People's Press Printing Society, 1949. 127pp.

213. Wright, Frederic Victor. *The West Sussex Gazette, 1853–1953.* Arundel, Sussex: The West Sussex Gazette, private publication, 1953. 43pp.

F. Histories of the Regional and Specialized Press in the United States

214. Allsopp, Fred W. *History of the Arkansas Press for a Hundred Years and More.* Little Rock, Ark.: Parke-Harper Publishing Co., 1922. 684pp.

An illustrated chronicle of Arkansas journalism dating from 1819, when the first newspaper was started by William E. Woodruff — the *Arkansas Gazette.* The bulk of the book is a mere alphabetizing of state newspapers by counties. There are short sketches of dozens of Arkansas editors and a short history of the Arkansas Press Association.

215. Alter, J. Cecil. *Early Utah Journalism: A Half Century of Forensic Warfare, Waged by the West's Most Militant Press.* Salt Lake City: Utah State Historical Society, 1938. 405pp.

A history of every Utah newspaper, listed alphabetically by city, with sketches of editors from 1850 to 1900. The author states that he examined "every column of every Utah newspaper still preserved." The work tends to bog down in a dull presentation.

216. Andersen, Arlow William. *The Immigrant Takes His Stand: The*

Norwegian-American Press and Public Affairs, 1847–1872. Northfield, Minn.: Norwegian-American Historical Assn., 1953. vii + 176pp.

The history of this press from its beginnings in Norway, Wis., through its first quarter-century. Andersen analyzes editorials from Norwegian-American journals for views on foreign policy, slavery, Abraham Lincoln, social reforms, and Reconstruction. A table shows the founding dates of the first 32 Norwegian-American newspapers.

216a. Bass, Althea. *Cherokee Messenger.* Norman: University of Oklahoma Press, 1936. 348pp.

Although basically a biography of the Reverend Samuel A. Worcester, missionary to the Cherokee Nation in the 1820s and 1830s, this book includes helpful information on the *Cherokee Phoenix* and the Indian Press as a whole. This scholarly work is based on manuscript collections of the American Board of Commissioners for Foreign Missions.

217. Baumgartner, Apollinaris W. *Catholic Journalism: A Study of Its Development in the United States, 1789–1930.* New York: Columbia University Press, 1931. xvi + 113pp.

Includes a tabulation of Catholic newspapers existing in 1930 and a limited bibliography of Catholic periodical literature.

218. Bruce, John. *Gaudy Century: The Story of San Francisco's Hundred Years of Robust Journalism.* New York: Random House, 1948. xvii + 302pp. (Introduction by Joseph Henry Jackson.)

Robust enough, but not quite a history of the full century from the Gold Rush to 1948 since there is little that extends beyond the Preparedness Day bombing of 1916. The author, who lived most of his life in San Francisco and was a city editor of the *Chronicle*, used old newspaper reports as background.

219. Bunje, E. T. H., F. Schmitz, and H. Penn. *Journals of the Bay Cities, 1854–1936.* Berkeley, Calif.: California Cultural Research, sponsored by University of California, 1936. 93 numbers.

220. ———. *Journals of the Golden Gate, 1846–1936.* Berkeley, Calif.: California Cultural Research, 1936. 134 numbers.

Bunje's two regional journalistic surveys of San Francisco and vicinity were carried out under the auspices of the Works Progress Administration.

220a. Cameron, Kenneth Walter. *Emerson, Thoreau and Concord in Early Newspapers: Biographical and Historical Lore for the Scholar and General Reader.* Hartford: Transcendental Books, 1958. 355pp.

Contains photographic reproductions of about 300 articles from various newspapers and magazines, most of them from New England and New York, about the Concord literary figures of the mid-19th century.

221. Carmony, Donald F. "The Pioneer Press in Indiana," in *Indiana History Bulletin*, vol. 31, no. 10 (October 1954), pp. 187–232.

Issued in commemoration of the 150th anniversary of Indiana's first newspaper.

HISTORY

222. Clark, Thomas D. *The Rural Press and the New South*. Baton Rouge: Louisiana State University Press, 1948. 111pp.

This supplement to *The Southern Country Editor* (223) includes three lectures on southern history under the title "The People's Press," and two on "News and the Editor's Relationships to the 'New South.'"

223. ———. *The Southern Country Editor*. Indianapolis and New York: Bobbs-Merrill Co., 1948. 365pp.

A study of the weekly rural press of the South from Reconstruction to the present. Clark places the country press among the South's most vigorous institutions — along with the country store and the small-town church and school. The bibliography lists nearly 200 small newspapers, most of them from Kentucky, Tennessee, Mississippi, Alabama, North and South Carolina, and Georgia; there are none from Florida, Arkansas, Louisiana, or Texas, and only one from Virginia.

224. Demaree, Albert Lowther. *The American Agricultural Press, 1819–1860*. New York: Columbia University Press, 1941. xvi + 272pp. (Columbia University Studies in History of American Agriculture, No. 8.)

Demaree regards the agricultural press of the pre-Civil War period as an unrivaled means for exchange of ideas among 80 per cent of the population. There are special studies of particular farm papers, chief among these being John Skinner's *American Farmer* (1819).

225. Detwiler, Frederick G. *The Negro Press in the United States*. Chicago: University of Chicago Press, 1922. x + 274pp.

This early and careful study includes material on the size and influence of the Negro press; on its history in slavery days and under freedom; on favorite Negro-press themes; on techniques; on demands for Negro rights; and on the press as both reflector and critic of Negro life.

226. Emrich, Duncan, ed. *Comstock Bonanza*. New York: Vanguard Press, 1950. 363pp.

A valuable anthology of forgotten news stories and articles gleaned from magazines, newspaper files, and out-of-print books referring to silver-rush days in Virginia City, Nev. Writers include Dan De Quille, Bret Harte, and Mark Twain. Emrich adds a short biographical sketch of each writer whose work is included.

227. Foik, Paul J. *Pioneer Catholic Journalism*. New York: United States Catholic Historical Society, 1930. x + 221pp.

Father Foik traces the origin, scope, progress, and design of Catholic newspapers and magazines from their beginnings to 1840. The first paper analyzed is the *Michigan Essay*. A chronological list of the periodicals gives beginning dates only and unfortunately does not indicate the length of each publication's life.

228. Griffith, Louis Turner, and John Erwin Talmadge. *Georgia Journalism, 1763–1950*. Athens: University of Georgia Press, 1951. x + 413pp. (Introduction by John E. Drewry.)

The bulk of this account covers the press in the 19th century; there is one chapter on the Colonial Georgia printer and one on the press since 1900. It includes a chronological history (based upon official minutes) of the Georgia Press Association, which sponsored the publication, and an annotated listing of state newspapers as of 1950. There is an extensive treatment of Henry W. Grady.

229. Herrick, John P. *Founding a Country Newspaper Fifty Years Ago.* Olean, N.Y.: Privately printed, 1938. 47pp.

An interesting view of old-time country journalism on the *Oswayo Valley Mail* (Pennsylvania).

230. History of San Francisco Journalism Project. *History of Journalism in San Francisco.* San Francisco, 1939–1944. 7 vols., mimeographed. (Vols. 1–6 by the project writers; vol. 7 by the Writers' Program, Works Projects Administration in Northern California.)

231. Hooper, Osman Castle. *History of Ohio Journalism, 1793–1933.* Columbus, Ohio: Spahr and Glenn Co., 1933. ix + 190pp.

A brief account beginning with the *Centinel of the North-Western Territory.* It is based chiefly upon various Ohio county newspaper histories, state almanacs, and printing trade books and files. No footnotes and no detailed bibliography.

232. Janowitz, Morris. *The Community Press in an Urban Setting.* Glencoe, Ill.: The Free Press, 1952. 256pp.

Careful social research on urban small newspapers. Janowitz studied 82 community newspapers with a weekly circulation of 983,000 within the city limits of Chicago, analyzing attributes of readership, impact of readership, the social role of the small publisher, and the social purpose of the community press. There is excellent material on small-newspaper growth and economic organization, the likely future of this type of press, and content analysis and readership surveys.

233. *The Jewish Encyclopedia,* vol. IX. New York and London: Funk and Wagnalls Co., 1905. (Isidore Singer, managing editor.)

This volume gives a history of Jewish periodicals and newspapers from earliest times to 1905 and includes a list of Jewish papers published throughout the world at that time, including language of publication, place of publication, and date of founding.

234. Kansas State Historical Society and Department of Archives. *History of Kansas Newspapers.* Topeka: Kansas State Printing Plant, 1916. 368pp. (Compiled by William E. Connelley.)

Contains considerable material on newspapers from Kansas territorial organization in 1854 to 1916. The organization is poor, however, as is the writing style.

235. King, William L. *The Newspaper Press of Charleston, S.C.: A Chronological and Biographical History, Embracing a Period of One Hundred and Forty Years.* Charleston, S.C.: Edward Perry Book Press, 1872. xi + 192pp.

This volume has no literary merit, but it has value as a factual record. Some history of Charleston is included, and the *News and Courier* and the *Mercury* are treated. The account of the press during the Reconstruction fails to come to grips with the problem.

236. Knauss, James Owen. *Territorial Florida Journalism.* Deland, Fla.: Florida State Historical Society, 1926. x + 250pp. (Publication No. 6 of the Society.)

Contains facsimiles of the first pages of Florida newspapers and includes a bibliography of the works consulted.

237. Ludington, Flora Belle. *The Newspapers of Oregon, 1846–1870.* Eugene, Ore.: Koke-Tiffany Co., 1925. 34pp.

Originally prepared as a thesis at Mills College, California. There is some value in its account of dates of the founding of Oregon's first newspapers.

238. McMurtrie, Douglas C. *A California Broadside of 1849.* Chicago: Privately printed, 1935. 8pp.

A reproduction of a mass-meeting broadside of June 11, 1849, which McMurtrie states had escaped recording as one of the first issues of the San Francisco press. The broadside called for action against the "dilatoriness" of Washington in providing for California statehood.

239. Mellen, George Frederick. "Southern Editors," in *The South in the Building of the Nation,* vol. 7, pp. 470–483. Richmond, Va.: Southern Historical Publication Society, 1909.

Sketches of southern editors, 1727 to 1900. Most thorough are those on Thomas Ritchie (Richmond *Enquirer*); John Hampden Pleasants (Richmond *Whig*); John M. Daniel (Richmond *Examiner*); many editors, including Henry Watterson, are covered only cursorily.

240. Morse, Lucius B. *The Daily Court Newspapers of the United States.* Philadelphia: University of Pennsylvania Wharton School, 1929. 56pp.

A compendium on legal newspapers: history, analysis, business problems, and techniques. It covers 55 legal newspapers beginning with 1853, when the Pittsburgh *Legal Journal* was founded. The bibliography is sketchy.

241. Oak, Vishnu V. *The Negro Newspaper.* Xenia, Ohio: Antioch Press, printed privately for the author, 1948. 170pp.

Presented as vol. 1 of a projected series by Oak on "The Negro Entrepreneur." Oak makes outspoken evaluations, favorable and unfavorable, of Negro newspapers — with fair balance. There is good detail on both business and editorial aspects of the Negro press. The bibliography includes books and articles on the Negro press and a general directory of Negro publications in the United States.

242. Olszyk, Edmund G. *The Polish Press in America.* Milwaukee: Marquette University, 1939. 146pp.

A master of arts thesis of exceptionally high quality. It brings together otherwise scattered information on Polish-language newspapers from 1863 on and examines their part in preserving a spirit of nationalism and in orienting immigrants to customs and practices in America, as well as the waning trend in this press.

243. Park, Robert E. *The Immigrant Press and Its Control.* New York and London: Harper and Brothers, 1922. xx + 488pp. (Harper's Series on Americanization.)

One of the best studies ever made of the foreign-language press and its influence upon newcomers in the United States. Park used original sources, including foreign-language newspaper files of the Post Office Department.

244. Penn, Irvine Garland. *The Afro-American Press and Its Editors.* Springfield, Mass.: Willey and Co., 1891. 565pp.

Excellent for information on the beginnings of the Negro press. Penn provides background on the *Freedom's Journal* (first Afro-American newspaper in New York, 1827); Frederick Douglass's *North Star* (Rochester, N.Y., 1847–1865); the *Colored American* of Augusta, Ga. (first Negro newspaper in the South); and lesser Negro newspapers and Afro-American magazines. Penn was a former editor of the Lynchburg (Va.) *Laborer*.

245. Perrin, William Henry. *The Pioneer Press of Kentucky, from the Printing of the First Paper West of the Alleghanies, August 11, 1787, to the Establishment of the Daily Press in 1830.* Louisville: John P. Morton Co., printers to the Filson Club, 1888. 93pp.

A piece marking 100 years of journalism in Kentucky. It includes facsimiles of early papers, including that of John Bradford — the *Kentucke Gazette*, 1788; a sketch of Matthew Lyon's experiences in Kentucky, 1801–1811; and an account of the establishment of the *Argus of Western America* in Frankfort, 1806, and of the Louisville *Journal* by George D. Prentice, 1830.

246. Purcell, George W. "A Survey of Early Newspapers in the Middle Western States," in *Indiana Magazine of History*, vol. XX (December 1924), pp. 347–363.

247. Ray, Grace E. *Early Oklahoma Newspapers.* Norman: University of Oklahoma Press, 1928. 119pp.

A history and description of Oklahoma publications from their beginnings to the opening of the territory to settlement in 1889.

248. Schappes, Morris U. *The Daily Worker: Heir to the Great Tradition.* New York: The Daily Worker, 1944. 32pp.

Communist party propaganda. Schappes commemorates 20 years of the *Worker* and tries to tie its "tradition" to that of other oppositionist journals of distinction: Colonial gazettes, Garrison's *Liberator*, women's rights papers, and the labor press in general.

249. Schlebecker, John T., and Andrew W. Hopkins. *A History of Dairy Journalism in the United States, 1810–1950.* Madison: University of Wisconsin Press, 1957. 416pp.

An account of the changing attitudes and activities of editors of more than 100 dairy journals; in effect also a history of the dairy industry. The notes, bibliography, and appendixes are useful for tracing dates of publication and changes of title of these periodicals.

250. Simpson, George E. *The Negro in the Philadelphia Press.* Philadelphia: University of Pennsylvania Press, 1936. xix + 158pp.

251. Smith, Amelie de Fonfride. *Oregon Press and Autograph Souvenir.* Portland, Ore.: C. H. Crocker, 1899. 88pp.

Compiled for and dedicated to the National Editorial Association, which held its 1899 convention in Oregon. Portraits, maps, and facsimiles are included.

252. Soltes, Mordecai. *The Yiddish Press: An Americanizing Agency.* New York: Teachers College, Columbia University, 1925. 242pp.

A history of Yiddish daily newspapers in New York City, including a discussion of readership, editorial development, scope, subject matter, and specific Americanizing efforts. Numerous statistical tables, appendixes, and an extensive bibliography are provided.

253. Stevens, Daniel G. *The First Hundred Years of the American Baptist Publication Society.* Philadelphia: The Society, 1925. 120pp.

254. Thwaites, Reuben G. "The Ohio Valley Press before the War of 1812," in American Antiquarian Society *Proceedings,* new series, vol. XIX, pp. 308–368. Worcester, Mass.: The Society, 1909.

255. Tinker, Edward L. "Two-Gun Journalism in New Orleans," in American Antiquarian Society *Proceedings,* new series, vol. LXI, part 2, pp. 239–266. Worcester, Mass.: The Society, 1951.

256. Turnbull, George S. *History of Oregon Newspapers.* Portland, Ore.: Binfords and Mort, 1939. 568pp.

As state journalism histories go, this one is unusual in its thoroughness. There is a good narrative of the pioneer and statehood periods, with the minor data separated from the general account. Since there is no formal history of the Portland *Oregonian,* this book is highly useful for the background it provides on Henry Pittock and Harvey W. Scott.

257. ———. *Influences of Newspapers on the Economic, Social, Cultural, and Political History of Pioneer Oregon to 1859.* Seattle: University of Washington, 1932. 140 leaves.

258. Walker, Norman. "The Southern Press," in *The South in the Building of the Nation,* vol. 7, pp. 402–436. Richmond, Va.: Southern Historical Publication Society, 1909.

A summary by an associate editor of the New Orleans *Times-Democrat* of the characteristics of the press in the Colonial period; dates of founding of the principal newspapers; and the relation between the southern press and literature and between the press and industry.

259. Wittke, Carl. *The German-Language Press in America.* Lexington: University of Kentucky Press, 1957. vi + 311pp.

A much-needed history of this press, from 1732 to the present. More emphasis is placed upon the importance of the German-language press in the history of German immigration than upon individual newspapers, but major newspapers are considered in some detail. The author points out practical problems which publishers of foreign-language newspapers have had to face: in circulation, advertising, format, and mechanical production. Only a minor portion of the book deals with World War I and the contemporary period.

260. Woody, Robert H. *Republican Newspapers of South Carolina.* Charlottesville, Va.: Historical Publishing Co., 1936. 60pp. (In Southern Sketches, No. 10, first series.)

A well-documented monograph on Republican military and political newspapers in South Carolina, 1861 to the close of Reconstruction. An interesting account of *The New South*, published at Beaufort on November 7, 1861, after federal seizure of Port Royal, is included.

261. Young, John Philip. *Journalism in California*. San Francisco: Chronicle Publishing Co., 1915. x + 362pp.

Published in commemoration of the 50th anniversary of the San Francisco *Chronicle*. The volume is inadequate as a general history of California journalism, for the *Chronicle* material bulks disproportionately. There is some helpful information on Charles and M. H. De Young and M. H. De Young's son, Charles.

G. General Printing History

262. Butler, Pierce. *The Origin of Printing in Europe*. Chicago: University of Chicago Press, 1940. xv + 154pp.

263. Carter, Thomas Francis. *The Invention of Printing in China and Its Spread Westward*. New York: Ronald Press Co., 1955. 2nd edition. xxiv + 293pp. (Revised by L. Carrington Goodrich.)

A scholarly work on printing from its Chinese source to Gutenberg; includes also the story of the invention of paper. Carter's first edition appeared in 1925, when the author was a professor of Chinese at Columbia; the revision, by a successor in the same department, is essentially the original book except for minor changes required by later scholarship.

264. Dreier, Thomas. *The Power of Print — and Men: Commemorating the Fifty Years of Linotype's Contribution to Printing and Publishing*. Brooklyn, N.Y.: Mergenthaler Linotype Co., 1936. xiv + 165pp.

A romanticized history of mechanical achievement, including brief biographical accounts of Ottmar Mergenthaler and James O. Clephane and their effort to perfect a workable composing machine. It includes a transcript of a National Broadcasting Co. nationwide salute (June 29, 1936) to the modern newspaper and the invention of the Linotype.

265. Forkert, Otto Maurice. *From Gutenberg to the Cuneo Press: An Historical Sketch of the Printing Press*. Chicago: Cuneo Press, 1933. 30pp.

266. Fuhrmann, Otto W. *The 500th Anniversary of the Invention of Printing*. New York: Philip C. Duschnes, 1937. 34pp.

267. Gentry, Helen, and David Greenhood. *Chronology of Books and Printing*. New York: The Macmillan Co., 1936. Revised edition. viii + 186pp.

268. Goodwin, Rutherfoord. "The Williamsburg Paper Mill of William Parks, the Printer," in *Papers of the Bibliographical Society of America*, vol. 31, part 1, pp. 21–44. Chicago: University of Chicago Press, 1937.

A paper read at a Bibliographical Society meeting by the director of the Department of Education of Colonial Williamsburg. Parks's mill, established in 1744, was the first and, so far as is known, the only paper mill in Colonial Virginia; Parks also was founder of the *Virginia Gazette* in 1736.

269. Hamilton, Frederick W. *A Brief History of Printing in America*.

HISTORY

Chicago: Committee on Education, United Typothetae of America, 1918. 89pp. (Typographical Technical Series for Apprentices, no. 54.)

Contains a brief sketch of the development of the newspaper and some notes on publishers who have especially contributed to printing.

270. Haynes, Merritt Way. *The Student's History of Printing*. New York: McGraw-Hill Book Co., 1930. 118pp. (McGraw-Hill Vocational Series.)

Principal dates, personages, and events in the development of typography from the earliest times to the present are given in chronological order.

271. Isaacs, George A. *The Story of the Newspaper Printing Press*. London: Co-operative Printing Society, 1931. 287pp.

Book issue of a series of articles from the journal of the society.

272. London Times. *Printing in the Twentieth Century, A Survey*. London: Times Publishing Co., Ltd., 1930. xvi + 298 + xxviii pp.

An artistic reprint of the text of the printing number of the *Times*, October 29, 1929. It summarizes the history of printing, typographic design, and bookmaking, and the development of the mechanics of the newspaper and periodical press. The volume covers printing in Western Europe and the United States as well as in England.

273. McMurtrie, Douglas C. *The Book: The Story of Printing and Bookmaking*. New York: Oxford University Press, 1943. xxx + 676pp.

Among McMurtrie's last works, this is one of his finest. In a sense, it is a seventh and final revision of *The Golden Book* (first published by P. Covici, Chicago, 1927), using basically the same information but expanding upon it to include later findings. The contents start with primitive human records and origins of the alphabet and paper; the Gutenberg story is told in full, along with an account of early modern-day dissemination of printing. Although fundamentally European in background, the book covers the careers of American Colonial journalist-printers and the spread of printing in the New World. Extensive bibliography on printing.

274. ———. *Commemoration of the Achievement of Johann Gutenberg*. Chicago: Chicago Club of Printing House Craftsmen, Printing Division, Washburn Trade School, 1942. 46pp.

275. ———. *A History of Printing in the United States: The Story of the Introduction of the Press and of Its History and Influence during the Pioneer Period in Each State of the Union*. New York: R. R. Bowker Co., 1936. Vol. 2. xxvi + 462pp.

This projected four-volume work was to have been the first complete history of printing since Isaiah Thomas's publication in 1810. Vol. 2 (on the Middle and South Atlantic states) was issued first and was the only volume completed. There is a separate treatment of Benjamin Franklin, Philadelphia printers of the Revolution, and the early German press in Pennsylvania. The volume is illustrated with reproductions of scores of laws, newspaper pages, and covers of early almanacs.

276. ———. *Wings for Words: The Story of Johann Gutenberg and His*

Invention of Printing. New York: Rand McNally and Co., 1940. 175pp.

277. Morison, Stanley, and Holbrook Jackson. *A Brief Survey of Printing: History and Practice.* New York: Alfred A. Knopf, 1923. 87pp.

278. Munsell, Joel. *The Typographical Miscellany.* Albany, N.Y.: Joel Munsell, 1850. 267pp.

A noted Albany printer and antiquarian of the 19th century attempted here to "garner up whatever could be collected of the unpublished history of printing in our cities and counties." The work remains, more than a century later, a mine of information about early printers and printing. Particularly useful are sections devoted to printers and printing in eastern New York. There are also sketches of the contemporary newspaper press in Germany, France, England, and the United States.

279. Oswald, John Clyde. *A History of Printing: Its Development through Five Hundred Years.* New York: D. Appleton and Co., 1928. 403pp.

280. Plomer, Henry Robert. *A Short History of English Printing, 1476–1900.* London: K. Paul, Trench, Truebner and Co., Ltd., 1915. xii + 276pp.

281. Rossiter, William S. "Printing and Publishing," in *Census Reports, Twelfth Census of the United States,* 9 Part III, pp. 1039–1119. Washington, D.C.: Government Printing Office, 1902.

282. *A Short History of the Printing Press and of the Improvements in Printing Machinery from the Time of Gutenberg up to the Present Day.* New York: Published for Robert Hoe, 1902. 89pp.

A company publication as valuable for its extensive illustrations as for its text. Presses pictured range from those of medieval days to the double sextuple press built at the turn of the century.

283. Tapley, Harriet Silvester. *Salem Imprints, 1768–1825.* Salem, Mass.: The Essex Institute, 1927. x + 512pp.

A history of the first half-century of printing in Salem, plus an account of bookshops, booksellers, bookbinders, and libraries.

284. Thomas, Isaiah. *The History of Printing in America.* Albany, N.Y.: Joel Munsell, 1874. 2 vols. lxxxvii + 423pp.; viii + 666 + 47pp. (Republication of Thomas's original work of 1810.)

One of the classics of American journalistic literature. Thomas's work includes biographies of early printers and accounts of newspapers in all the Colonies and in some of the new states after independence. In addition there are accounts of printing in Spanish, French, Dutch, and Portuguese America. Munsell in the reissue added some of Thomas's own corrections and some new material, including a catalogue of American publications before 1776 and a memoir of Isaiah by his grandson, Benjamin Franklin Thomas. With Frederic Hudson's work (see 12) this is the only effective general history of the press written before the 20th century.

285. Wheeler, Joseph Towne. *The Maryland Press, 1777–1790.* Balti-

more: Maryland Historical Society, 1938. xvi + 226pp. (Introduction by Lawrence C. Wroth.)

A continuation of Wroth's *History of Printing in Colonial Maryland* (290). There are biographical accounts of printers who worked in Maryland during the Revolution and a record of Maryland newspapers, almanacs, resolutions and laws, pamphlets, and tracts on slavery. The bibliography lists 550 titles.

286. Winship, George Parker. *The Cambridge Press, 1638–1692: A Re-examination of the Evidence Concerning the Bay Psalm Book and the Eliot Indian Bible, as Well as Other Contemporary Books and People.* Philadelphia: University of Pennsylvania Press, 1945. ix + 385pp.

287. ————. *Printing in the Fifteenth Century.* Philadelphia: University of Pennsylvania Press, 1940. xi + 158pp.

288. Winterich, John T. *Early American Books and Printing.* Boston: Houghton Mifflin Co., 1935. 252pp.

289. Wroth, Lawrence C. *The Colonial Printer.* New York: Grolier Club, 1931; Portland, Maine: Southworth-Anthoensen Press, 1938. xxiv + 368pp.

An excellent, scholarly study, covering all aspects of Colonial printing, including newspapers. There are 24 plates and 6 drawings, and more than 60 pages of textual notes, bibliographical references, and index. The work shows clearly the close connections among journalism, religious printing, almanac publication, legal and medical texts, handbills, and politics.

290. ————. *A History of Printing in Colonial Maryland.* Baltimore: Typothetae of Baltimore, 1922. xiv + 275pp.

A scholarly contribution, of which nearly half is annotated bibliography of Maryland books, broadsides, and newspapers, 1689–1776. Wroth includes biographical material on William Parks, William and Mary Goddard, and John Peter Zenger during his interlude as public printer of Maryland.

II

Biography

The collected biographies in section A are alphabetized by author or title entry. In sections B, C, and D biographies of individual journalists are entered under the biographee's name, alphabetically listed. Where there is more than one volume on a journalist, autobiographies are listed first and then biographies alphabetized by author. Thus if the user of this bibliography is searching for material on a particular journalist, he can find it directly by looking under that journalist's name. But if he is seeking biographical material on journalists in various categories — newspaper editors, magazine editors, columnists, or war correspondents, for example — it will be necessary for him to use the index, which provides a guide under the subheadings of the entry "Biographies."

The great majority of biographies listed here are about men and women whose careers were devoted primarily to journalism or who practiced journalism in one form or another at some time. There are also, however, a few books on persons who were primarily engaged in other fields but whose activities touched importantly on some phase of journalism.

General reference works of collected biography for the most part have not been included, but the reader is reminded that they frequently can be exceptionally helpful. Chief among these are the multi-volume *Dictionary of American Biography*, *Dictionary of Canadian Biography*, and *Dictionary of National Biography*. Other useful works, particularly for contemporary figures in journalism, are *Current Biography* (H. W. Wilson Co., monthly since 1940), *Who's Who in America*, and *Who's Who* (Great Britain).

A. Collected Biographies

291. *America's Greatest Men and Women*. Indianapolis and St. Louis: Ward Publishing Co., 1894. 256pp. (Edited by Stanley Waterloo.)

Presents 256 photographs and brief biographies of "the most famous living people on the continent." An exceptionally high percentage are newspapermen, from the venerable Dana to the still-to-become-famous Richard Harding Davis.

292. Beard, Annie E. S. *Our Foreign-Born Citizens: What They Have Done for America*. New York: Thomas Y. Crowell Co., 1929 and 1932. ix + 396pp.

Of 43 naturalized Americans singled out by the author for their achievements, 7 were journalists: James Gordon Bennett, Sr., Edward Bok, Samuel S. McClure, Ottmar Mergenthaler, Joseph Pulitzer, Jacob A. Riis, and Carl Schurz.

BIOGRAPHY

293. Benjamin, S. G. W. "A Group of Pre-Revolutionary Editors: Beginnings of Journalism in America," and "Notable Editors between 1776 and 1800: Influences of the Early American Press," in *Magazine of American History*, vol. 17, nos. 1 and 2 (1887), pp. 1–29 and 97–127.

Useful, brief, illustrated articles on 18th-century American journalists. Included are facsimiles of famous front pages and portraits of noted editors.

294. Bent, Silas. *Newspaper Crusaders: A Neglected Story.* New York: Whittlesey House, McGraw-Hill Book Co., 1939. xiii + 313pp.

Bent records the accomplishments of newspaper editors as crusaders: Pulitzer, Hearst, Scripps, James Franklin, Isaiah Thomas, John Fenno, Philip Freneau, editors during the slavery controversy, New York *Times* editors against Boss Tweed, Chicago editors, and Bovard of the St. Louis *Post-Dispatch.* The book lacks thoroughness, being only a series of short biographies with no notes and a scanty bibliography of the most obvious secondary sources.

295. British Broadcasting Corp. *A Portrait Gallery of BBC People.* London: The BBC, 1951. 94pp.

296. Bullard, F. Lauriston. *Famous War Correspondents.* Boston: Little, Brown and Co., 1914. xii + 437pp.

Excellent biographies of war correspondents from different periods and different geographical areas, with emphasis on their picturesque experiences. The correspondents are Sir William H. Russell, Archibald Forbes, Januarius Aloysius MacGahan, Frederick Villiers, Bennet Burleigh, Edmond O'Donovan, the five Vizetellys, Edward Frederick Knight, George Warrington Steevens, Winston Spencer Churchill, James Creelman, and George Wilkins Kendall. An introduction traces the rise of war-news coverage; concluding chapters, on Civil War coverage in America and the Spanish-American War, provide shorter biographies of Charles Carleton Coffin, Whitelaw Reid, George W. Smalley, Henry Villard, Stephen Crane, and Richard Harding Davis. Bullard was on the staff of the Boston *Herald.*

297. Bulman, David, ed. *Molders of Opinion.* Milwaukee: Bruce Publishing Co., 1945. viii + 166pp.

Biographies of newspaper and radio commentators: Paul Mallon, Dorothy Thompson, Gabriel Heatter, Walter Lippmann, H. V. Kaltenborn, Westbrook Pegler, Fulton Lewis, Jr., Sumner Welles, Raymond Gram Swing, Drew Pearson, David Lawrence, John B. Kennedy, George E. Sokolsky, and Walter Winchell. Authors of the biographies are mostly journalists themselves.

298. Bungay, George W. *Off-Hand Takings: Or, Crayon Sketches of the Noticeable Men of Our Age.* New York: De Witt and Davenport, 1854. viii + 408pp.

Includes a piece on Horace Greeley, one of the few studies of Greeley antedating Parton's biography. Also treated are Nathaniel P. Willis, P. T. Barnum, George W. Kendall, Theodore Parker, Wendell Phillips, William Cullen Bryant, James Gordon Bennett, and James Watson Webb.

299. Camrose, Viscount. *British Newspapers and Their Controllers.* London: Cassell and Co., Ltd., 1948. Revised edition. ix + 178pp.

Gives details on the ownership and control of every morning, evening, and Sunday newspaper in Great Britain; includes also brief accounts of individual newspapers and short biographies of their owners. It is most helpful for its details on lesser known proprietors, particularly in the provinces. This work by a "press lord" gave support to newspaper publishers at a time when they were under attack (1947–1948) in the investigation by the Royal Commission on the Press.

300. Filler, Louis. *Crusaders for American Liberalism*. New York: Harcourt, Brace and Co., 1939. viii + 422pp.

Includes biographies of most editors and writers of the muckraking period. Treated at some length are Lincoln Steffens and "The Shame of the Cities," Ida M. Tarbell and Standard Oil, Tom Lawson and finance, Upton Sinclair and "The Jungle," David Graham Phillips and "The Treason of the Senate," and William Randolph Hearst. Outstanding muckraking cartoons are reproduced.

301. Fisher, Charles. *The Columnists*. New York: Howell, Soskin Publishers, 1944. 317pp.

Somewhat tongue-in-cheek sketches of 20 columnists of the World War II era: Dorothy Thompson, Walter Lippmann, Ernie Pyle, Maj. George Fielding Eliot, Fletcher Pratt, Hanson W. Baldwin, Mark Sullivan, Raymond Clapper, Westbrook Pegler, Frank R. Kent, Drew Pearson, Robert S. Allen, Sam Grafton, Leonard Lyons, Danton Walker, Charles B. Driscoll, David Lawrence, Paul Mallon, Ernest K. Lindley, and Walter Winchell. A beginning chapter discusses the rise of the column.

302. Hamilton, Milton W. *The Country Printer, New York State, 1785-1830*. New York: Columbia University Press, 1936. xiii + 360pp. (New York State Historical Association Series No. 4; edited by Dixon Ryan Fox.)

Defines the contributions to journalism of nearly 700 printers who pushed into rural New York and kept "the diary of the communit[ies]." Over all, an outline of country journalism in all its phases.

303. Hanazono, Kanesada. *Journalism in Japan and Its Early Pioneers*. Osaka: Osaka Mainichi, 1926. ix + 82pp.

The life and work of 10 prominent leaders of the Japanese press in the generation before Japan became a constitutional empire in 1889. The author served on the *Japan Times* and the Tokyo *Nichi-Nichi*.

304. Hansen, Harry. *Midwest Portraits: A Book of Memories and Friendships*. New York: Harcourt, Brace and Co., 1923. 357pp.

Considers Chicago literary journalists of the early years of the 20th century: Carl Sandburg, Sherwood Anderson, Robert Herrick, Edgar Lee Masters, and Ben Hecht. Hansen was at the time literary editor of the Chicago *Daily News*.

305. Herd, Harold. *Seven Editors*. London: George Allen and Unwin, Ltd., 1955. 126pp.

Sketches along the bypaths of British journalism, with one excursion to the United States. Five of the seven are today little more than historical footnotes, but Herd treats them fascinatingly: Eustace Budgell, tragic figure in Grub Street in the early 18th century (the *Bee*); Dr. John Hill, portrayed as the first columnist, for the London *Advertiser* and *Literary Gazette* in 1751; Nicholas Byrne, editor of the London *Morning Post*, who was assassinated in his office in 1832; William Maginn, early editor of *Fraser's Magazine* (1830s); and Albany Fonblanque, Radical editor of the *Examiner* in the Reform Bill era. Better known are William Hone, the bookseller, thrice tried in post-Waterloo days for his parodies; and the American, James Gordon Bennett, whom Herd "introduces" to Englishmen as the inventor of sensational journalism.

306. Hildeburn, Charles R. *Sketches of Printers and Printing in Colonial New York (with Numerous Illustrations)*. New York: Dodd, Mead and Co., 1895. xiv + 189pp.

Provides useful information on the Parkers (James and Samuel); the *New-York Weekly Post-Boy*; Henry De Forest, New York's first native printer; John Holt, first printer of the *Laws of the City of New York*; James Robertson, a Loyalist, of the New York *Chronicle* and Albany *Gazette*; and others of lesser stature; as well as more detailed material on William Bradford, John and Anna Zenger, Hugh Gaine, and James Rivington. A chapter on Loyalist printers of the Revolution is especially good.

307. Howe, Mark Antony De Wolfe. *The Atlantic Monthly and Its Makers*. Boston: Atlantic Monthly Press, 1919. 106pp.

Biographies of the eight editors of the *Atlantic* from its founding in 1857 to 1910: James Russell Lowell, James Thomas Fields, William Dean Howells, Thomas Bailey Aldrich, Horace Elisha Scudder, Walter Hines Page, Bliss Perry, and Ellery Sedgwick.

308. Howey, Walter, ed. *Fighting Editors*. Philadelphia: David McKay Co., 1948. viii + 163pp.

Entertaining sketches of noted editors and of press struggles against authority and/or corruption. These had appeared first as feature articles in the *American Weekly*. Pieces on Zenger, Henry Grady in Atlanta, the heroic James King of William in early San Francisco, Joseph Pulitzer, and Hearst are included.

309. Lyons, Eugene, ed. *We Cover the World*. New York: Harcourt, Brace and Co., 1937. 413pp.

Foreign correspondents of the period from World War I to the middle 1930s recount personal experiences. Biographical background is included. Contributors are James A. Mills, Karl von Wiegand, Frazier Hunt, Linton Wells, Negley Farson, Hallet Abend, Junius B. Wood, William Henry Chamberlin, George Seldes, Mary Knight, Frank H. Hedges, Randall Gould, Jack Starr-Hunt, H. R. Ekins, Webb Miller, and Eugene Lyons.

310. Madison, Charles A. *Critics and Crusaders: A Century of American Protest*. New York: Henry Holt and Co., 1947. xii + 572pp.

Four of these 18 American rebels had a journalistic background: William Lloyd Garrison, Margaret Fuller, Albert Brisbane, and Lincoln Steffens. Several others were associated with journalism in one way or another: Wendell Phillips, Edward Bellamy, Henry Thoreau, and Randolph Bourne.

311. Martin, Benjamin Ellis. "Transition Period of the American Press," in *Magazine of American History*, vol. 17, no. 4 (1887), pp. 273–294. New York Publication Co.

Martin considers these editors of the early 19th century: William Coleman,

William Cobbett, James Cheetham, James T. Callender, Noah Webster, and Joseph Gales.

312. "The Men Who Advertise," in *Rowell's American Newspaper Directory, 1870,* pp. 1–209. New York: George P. Rowell Co., 1870.

Valuable accounts of nearly 125 "successful advertisers" and their firms, along with hints on good advertising methods.

313. Miller, E. Morris. *Pressmen and Governors: Australian Editors and Writers in Early Tasmania.* Sydney and London: Angus and Robertson, 1952. viii + 308pp.

Biographical sketches of 12 journalistic leaders in the period 1818–1846. Particular reference is made to the *Colonial Times,* the Hobart *Town Gazette,* the Hobart *Town Magazine,* and the *Tasmanian.*

314. Milne, James. *A Window in Fleet Street.* New York: Holborn House, 1932. xiv + 319pp.

Recollections of people whom the author, literary editor of the London *Daily Chronicle,* met in the course of his years in Fleet Street from the 1880s on. Many were English journalists or foreign journalists stationed in Britain: Archibald Forbes, J. L. Garvin, Sir Philip Gibbs, Henry Labouchere, H. W. Massingham, John Morley, Lord Northcliffe, T. P. O'Connor, George A. Sala, George W. Smalley, and W. T. Stead.

315. Moore, John Weeks, ed. *Moore's Historical Biographical and Miscellaneous Gatherings.* Concord, N.H.: Republican Press Assn., 1886. 604pp.

Brief biographical notes on authors, publishers, editors, printers, and inventors, in addition to notes on the printing, publishing, and editing of books, newspapers, and magazines and literary publications (1420 to 1886).

316. Mowry, George Edwin. *The California Progressives.* Berkeley: University of California Press, 1951. xi + 349pp. (Chronicles of California Series.)

This general history of the Progressive movement, 1910–1916, contains some biographical material on editors who supported and opposed the program: Chester Rowell (Fresno *Morning Republican*); Fremont Older (San Francisco *Bulletin*); E. T. Earl (Los Angeles *Express*); and Harrison Gray Otis (Los Angeles *Times*).

317. Neal, John. *American Writers: A Series of Papers Contributed to Blackwood's Magazine (1824–1825).* Durham, N.C.: Duke University Press, 1937. 255pp. (Edited by Fred Lewis Pattee.)

In this heavily prejudiced series of articles, which appeared originally over the signature XYZ, Neal portrayed the early American editors William Coleman, Joseph Dennie, Mordecai Noah, Benjamin Franklin, John Hall, Hezekiah Niles, Thomas Paine, Noah Webster, and himself (to whom he gives considerable space and whom he artfully assails). Neal's work was perhaps the first American literary product to appear in a British review.

318. Ogilvie, William Edward. *Pioneer Agricultural Journalists: Brief Biographical Sketches of Some of the Early Editors in the Field of*

BIOGRAPHY

Agricultural Journalism. Chicago: Arthur G. Leonard, 1927. xii + 128pp.

The author discusses John Stuart Skinner, the *American Farmer*, 1819; Jesse Buel, the *Cultivator*, Albany, 1834; Luther Tucker, the *Genesee Farmer*, Rochester, N.Y., 1834; Orange Judd, the *Orange Judd Farmer*, Chicago, 1880s; Norman J. Colman, *Colman's Rural World*, St. Louis, 1864; William Dempster Hoard, *Hoard's Dairyman*, Fort Atkinson, Wis., 1870; Wilmer Atkinson, *Farm Journal*, Philadelphia, 1877; James Harvey Sanders and Alvin H. Sanders, *National Livestock Journal*, Chicago, 1870; William Ransdell Goodwin, *Breeder's Gazette*, Kansas City, 1885; Joseph E. Wing, *Breeder's Gazette*, 1898; Herbert Quick, *Farm and Fireside*; Henry Wallace, *Wallace's Farm and Dairy*, Ames, Iowa, 1895; James Melville Pierce, the *Iowa Homestead*, Des Moines, 1893; and Herbert W. Collingwood, the *Rural New Yorker*, 1899. All the sketches fill in the essential background and the circumstances under which each paper was established.

319. Overseas Press Club of America. *Who's Who in Foreign Correspondence.* New York: The Press Club, 1948. 104pp. Supplements issued in 1951 and 1957. (Introduction by Robert B. Considine.)

This history of the Overseas Press Club, founded in 1939, gives considerable attention to "case histories" (biographies) of members. The club's constitution and by-laws are included.

320. Parton, James. *Captains of Industry: Or, Men of Business Who Did Something besides Making Money.* Boston and New York: Houghton Mifflin Co., 1884 and 1891. 2 vols. 790pp., total.

See I:254ff, "Horace Greeley's Start"; I:264ff, "James Gordon Bennett and How He Founded His *Herald*"; I:275ff, "Three John Walters and Their Newspaper"; and II:288ff, "Charles Knight, Publisher" (*British Penny Magazine*). Vol. I contains a short biographical sketch of Parton.

321. ———, ed. *Sketches of Men of Progress.* New York: New York and Hartford Publishing Co.; Cincinnati: Greer and Co., 1870–1871. 736pp.

The best of Parton's collected biographies for journalistic purposes. See the material on William Cullen Bryant (New York *Evening Post*), pp. 7–12; George W. Childs (Philadelphia *Public Ledger*), pp. 75–90; Thurlow Weed (Albany *Evening Journal*), pp. 221–226; James Watson Webb (New York *Courier and Enquirer*), pp. 349–404; and Cassius Marcellus Clay, pp. 447–452.

322. Poole, Ernest. *Giants Gone: Men Who Made Chicago.* New York and London: Whittlesey House, McGraw-Hill Book Co., 1943. 353pp.

Poole tries to picture Chicago's growth through the lives of its builders, among them editors Long John Wentworth, Joseph Medill, Victor Lawson, and Herman Kohlsaat.

323. Rayfield, Stanley. *Life Photographers, Their Careers and Favorite Pictures.* New York: Doubleday and Co., 1957. 89pp.

Forty capsule biographies of staff members of *Life*, plus short accounts of photographers' problems and a discussion of photographic techniques.

324. Ross, Ishbel. *Ladies of the Press: The Story of Women in Journalism by an Insider.* New York and London: Harper and Brothers, 1936. xii + 622pp. (Foreword by Stanley Walker.)

Discusses dozens of women in journalism, from Anne Royall to Anne O'Hare McCormick. The volume is not well organized, however. Nelly Bly and Nixola Greeley-Smith (Horace Greeley's granddaughter) get full chapters. Miss Ross was a reporter for the New York *Tribune* and *Herald Tribune*.

325. Saturday Evening Post. *Post Biographies of Famous Journalists.* Athens: University of Georgia Press, 1942. x + 518pp. (Edited by John E. Drewry.)

Twenty-two sketches of newspaper and magazine writers and publishers, collected from *Post* issues between 1928 and 1942. There are articles on Arthur Brisbane, Dorothy Dix, Silliman Evans, Clifton Fadiman, Marshall Field III, George Gallup, Edgar A. Guest, William Randolph Hearst, Roy Howard, Ed Howe, Sir Willmott Lewis, Robert R. McCormick, Bernarr Macfadden, O. O. McIntyre, Don Marquis, Eleanor Patterson, Westbrook Pegler, Joseph Pulitzer, Jr., Herbert Bayard Swope, Dorothy Thompson, Henry Watterson, and Walter Winchell. Editor Drewry includes a general introduction and biographical notes.

326. ———. *More Post Biographies.* Athens: University of Georgia Press, 1947. xii + 392pp. (Edited by John E. Drewry.)

A sequel to *Post Biographies*, with an additional 22 sketches compiled from *Post* articles between 1937 and 1946. Subjects are Hugh Baillie, Helen Bonfils, Mary Coyle Chase, the *Christian Science Monitor* (a composite biography), Raymond Clapper, Jay N. Darling, Gene Howe, John S. Knight, Arthur Krock, Sgt. William M. Mauldin, William L. McLean, Eugene Meyer, "Paper Dolls" (women in journalism), Drew Pearson, "Sports Editor" (a composite biography), Emily Post, Ernie Pyle, Helen Rogers Reid, Wheeler Sammons (*Who's Who in America*), Taylor Spink (*Sporting News*), Walter Yust (*Encyclopaedia Britannica*), and "Headlines in Celluloid" (newsreels).

327. Seldes, George. *Lords of the Press.* New York: Julian Messner, 1938. viii + 408pp.

Perhaps Seldes's best known work attacking the press. The "Lords" are the members of the American Newspaper Publishers Association, to which "nothing is sacred . . . but itself" as guardian of the press. Seldes specifically attacks Joseph Medill Patterson, Robert R. McCormick, Paul Block, Harry Chandler, Roy Howard, Abraham Cahan, William T. Dewart, Frank Gannett, William Randolph Hearst, and others in lesser positions of newspaper power. He praises J. David Stern, William Allen White, and a scattering of others.

328. Smith, Henry Justin. *A Gallery of Chicago Editors.* Chicago: The Daily News, 1930. 20pp. (Reprint no. 44.)

Sketches of seven influential editors: John Calhoun, John Wentworth, Joseph Medill, Wilbur F. Storey, Melville E. Stone, Herman Kohlsaat, and Victor F. Lawson.

329. Truman, Benjamin Cummings. "Old Time Editors and Newspapermen I Have Known," in *Pacific Printer, Publisher and Lithographer*, vol. VI (December 1911), pp. 338ff.

330. Ulmann, Doris. *A Portrait Gallery of American Editors: Being a Group of XLIII Likenesses, with Critical Essays by the Editors and*

an Introduction by Louis Evan Shipman. New York: William Edwin Rudge, 1925. xii + 177pp.

A volume of fine printing which sketches 43 magazine editors of the early 20th century. Every piece includes a photograph of the editor and descriptive matter outlining the principles of editing held by each. Most of the major "slick" magazines and organs of opinion are represented.

331. Wilson, James Grant. *Bryant and His Friends: Some Reminiscences of the Knickerbocker Writers.* New York: Fords, Howard and Hulbert, 1886. 443pp.

Chiefly devoted to William Cullen Bryant but includes also a number of sketches of his colleagues, some of them journalists.

332. Wright, Richardson. *Forgotten Ladies: Nine Portraits from the American Family Album.* Philadelphia and London: J. B. Lippincott Co., 1928. 307pp.

Two of these ladies were journalists: Anne Royall, "the widow with the serpent's tongue"; and Sarah Josepha Hale, "the madonna in bustles." There is a fair bibliography on each.

B. United States and Canadian Journalists

WILLIS J. ABBOT

333. Abbot, Willis J. *Watching the World Go By.* Boston: Little, Brown and Co., 1933. xii + 358pp.

The autobiography of the editor of the *Christian Science Monitor* in the 1920s and 1930s. Much of the book deals with Abbot's career before his service on the *Monitor*: in New Orleans, Kansas City, New York, and Chicago.

LYMAN ABBOTT

334. Abbott, Lyman. *Reminiscences.* Boston and New York: Houghton Mifflin Co., 1915. ix + 509pp.

The autobiography of a nationally famous clergyman, author, and editor in the half century after the Civil War. There is an excellent chapter on Abbott's service to journalism through the *Christian Union* and its successor, the *Outlook*, which Abbott edited from 1881 to 1922.

335. Brown, Ira V. *Lyman Abbott, Christian Evolutionist: A Study in Religious Liberalism.* Cambridge, Mass.: Harvard University Press, 1953. ix + 303pp.

An analysis of Abbott's contribution to American intellectual life as editor of the *Outlook*. It is based on *Outlook* files, Abbott's books, family letters and papers, and the Theodore Roosevelt manuscripts. The book discusses at length the negotiations leading to Roosevelt's joining the *Outlook* after his presidency. There is also a fine chapter on "Mr. Beecher's Paper," concerning the transfer of the *Christian Union* to Abbott.

ROBERT S. ABBOTT

336. Ottley, Roi. *The Lonely Warrior: The Life and Times of Robert S. Abbott.* Chicago: Henry Regnery Co., 1955. 381pp.

On the founder of a Negro newspaper, the Chicago *Defender*. The study is built upon scattered sources, including Abbott's fragmentary papers and writings and the *Defender*'s columns. The author is editor of another Negro newspaper, the Amsterdam (N.Y.) *News*.

HALLETT ABEND

337. Abend, Hallett. *My Life in China, 1926–1941*. New York: Harcourt, Brace and Co., 1943. 396pp.

The memoirs of a correspondent for the New York *Times* during the period in which Chiang Kai-shek rose to power. There is considerable material on Chiang and the early period of Chinese communism.

FRANKLIN PIERCE ADAMS

338. Adams, Franklin Pierce. *The Diary of Our Own Samuel Pepys.* New York: Simon and Schuster, 1935. 2 vols. 1305pp., total.

Autobiographical extracts from F. P. A.'s columns, 1911–1934. Adams wrote "The Conning Tower" for the New York *Mail, Tribune, World,* and *Herald Tribune.*

SAMUEL ADAMS

339. Harlow, Ralph Volney. *Samuel Adams, Promoter of the American Revolution: A Study in Psychology and Politics.* New York: Henry Holt and Co., 1923. x + 363pp.

This biography, with its subjective, psychological slant, is inferior to Miller's. Adams's relations with the Committees of Correspondence are only slightly dealt with.

340. Miller, John C. *Sam Adams: Pioneer in Propaganda.* Boston: Little, Brown and Co., 1936. 437pp.

A standard biography of the Colonial firebrand by a widely known historian of the Independence period. There are extensive chapters on the Stamp Act and the Committees of Correspondence.

GEORGE ADE

341. Kelly, Fred C. *George Ade, Warmhearted Satirist.* Indianapolis: Bobbs-Merrill Co., 1947. 282pp.

Ade was a leading figure among the literary-journalistic fraternity at the turn of the century. Kelly, an admirer for 40 years, tells of Ade's varied activities, including column-writing for the Chicago *Daily News* at the time of the World's Fair in 1893.

THOMAS BAILEY ALDRICH

342. Greenslet, Ferris. *The Life of Thomas Bailey Aldrich.* Boston and New York: Houghton Mifflin Co., 1908. 303pp.

Aldrich was editor of the *Atlantic Monthly*, 1881–1890, but he was more distinguished as a writer. There is only a brief account of his *Atlantic* editorship.

BIOGRAPHY

FRED W. ALLSOPP

343. Allsopp, Fred W. *Twenty Years in a Newspaper Office*. Little Rock, Ark.: Central Printing Co., 1907. 266pp.

Allsopp soliloquizes about his experiences on the *Arkansas Gazette* of Little Rock. Despite the title, the book is the work of a young man (Allsopp was 39). A portion deals with the Heiskell family, who took over a controlling interest in the *Gazette* in 1902. A fine regional book.

344. ———. *Little Adventures in Newspaperdom*. Little Rock, Ark.: Arkansas Writer Publishing Co., 1922. 239pp.

A continuation of Allsopp's *Twenty Years in a Newspaper Office*. The book is simple, kind, and sentimental.

OSCAR AMERINGER

345. Ameringer, Oscar. *If You Don't Weaken: The Autobiography of Oscar Ameringer*. New York: Henry Holt and Co., 1940. xviii + 476pp. (Foreword by Carl Sandburg.)

Ameringer was a labor-newspaper editor in Cleveland, Cincinnati, Milwaukee, and Oklahoma City; and, at the time of writing, editor of the *American Guardian* in Oklahoma City. He describes his early years in Germany and his experiences as a radical and labor agitator with a marked sense of humor, despite considerable heartbreak in his life.

MARGARET ANDERSON

346. Anderson, Margaret. *My Thirty Years' War*. New York: Covici-Friede, 1930. 274pp.

The first volume of a two-part autobiography by the founder of the *Little Review* (1914). Included are anecdotes about Ernest Hemingway, Gertrude Stein, and others. There is somewhat excessive exploitation of Miss Anderson's ego.

347. ———. *The Fiery Fountains*. New York: Hermitage House, 1951. ix + 242pp.

The continuation of *My Thirty Years' War*, covering the years 1925–1945.

SHERWOOD ANDERSON

348. Anderson, Sherwood. *Sherwood Anderson's Memoirs*. New York: Harcourt, Brace and Co., 1942. x + 507pp.

Like many of his contemporaries, Anderson had a newspaper background in Chicago during the "literary revival" period early in the 20th century. But there is little in this volume on the journalistic phase of Anderson's career.

NORMAN ANTHONY

349. Anthony, Norman. *How to Grow Old Disgracefully*. New York: Duell, Sloan and Pearce, Eagle Books, 1946. 247pp.

Autobiography combined with humor. Anthony was editor of *Judge* in the 1920s, later of the old *Life*, and founder of *Ballyhoo* in 1931. The book includes choice illustrations from *Ballyhoo*. Readers may need an appreciation of crude humor.

PHYLLIS ARGALL

350. Argall, Phyllis. *My Life with the Enemy*. New York: The Macmillan Co., 1944. viii + 290pp.

The experiences of a Canadian woman who lived for more than 20 years in Japan as missionary, educator, and editor of anti-Axis newspapers. She was managing editor of *Japan News-Week* at the time of Pearl Harbor and correspondent for the London *News-Chronicle*. Her book is highly critical of the Japanese, by whom she was imprisoned.

WILMER ATKINSON

351. Atkinson, Wilmer. *Wilmer Atkinson: An Autobiography*. Philadelphia: Wilmer Atkinson Co., 1920. xviii + 375pp.

The author founded the *Farm Journal* in 1877. He died while writing this simple but detailed story of his life.

BENJAMIN FRANKLIN BACHE

352. Fay, Bernard. *The Two Franklins: Fathers of American Democracy*. Boston: Little, Brown and Co., 1933. xvi + 397pp.

The life of Benjamin Franklin's grandson by a Frenchman who is also a biographer of the grandfather. Based on original sources. Fay took most of his newspaper material from files of Bache's pro-Jefferson *Aurora* and the Federalist *Gazette of the United States* and *Porcupine's Gazette*.

RAY STANNARD BAKER

353. Baker, Ray Stannard. *Native American*. New York: Charles Scribner's Sons, 1941. viii + 336pp.

Limited to Baker's first 22 years; ends with his departure for Chicago in 1892 to work for the *Record*.

354. ———. *American Chronicle*. New York: Charles Scribner's Sons, 1945. vii + 531pp.

Continuation of *Native American*, covering the period from 1892 through the death of Woodrow Wilson in 1924. This is an excellent addition to autobiographies of muckraking reporters. The first half of the book is most heavily devoted to journalism; after World War I, Baker writes primarily of politics.

WILLIAM WATTS BALL

355. Ball, William Watts. *The Editor and the Republic: Papers and Addresses of William Watts Ball*. Chapel Hill: University of North Carolina Press, 1954. xxii + 209pp. (Edited by Anthony Harrigan.)

Harrigan provides a biographical introduction on the extremely conservative editor of the Charleston *News and Courier*, 1927–1941, and follows this with 17 articles and speeches by Ball on South Carolina, regional, and national sub-

BIOGRAPHY

jects. Three of the pieces are on newspapers. The book makes an effort to put into perspective an articulate, outspoken southern editor of the "old school."

JOHN KENDRICK BANGS

356. Bangs, Francis Hyde. *John Kendrick Bangs, Humorist of the Nineties: The Story of an American Editor — Author — Lecturer and His Associations.* New York: Alfred A. Knopf, 1941. 300 + xv pp.

Covers principally Bangs's literary career but treats also of his activity as one of the founders of the old *Life* (1883) and as editor of *Harper's Weekly* (1899–1901), the *New Metropolitan Magazine* (1903), and *Puck* (1904–1905). Bangs's relations with W. D. Howells, Richard Harding Davis, Mark Twain, Bill Nye, Charles Dudley Warner, and George Harvey are discussed.

ELIZABETH L. BANKS

357. Banks, Elizabeth L. *The Autobiography of a "Newspaper Girl."* New York: Dodd, Mead and Co., 1902. viii + 317pp.

The story of a Milwaukee reporter who gained some newspaper fame and fortune in London and New York in the days when a woman in journalism was an oddity. Her book is most interesting for its accounts of the stunts she used to attract the attention of metropolitan editors.

358. ———. *Campaigns of Curiosity: Journalistic Adventures of an American Girl in London.* Chicago and New York: F. Tennyson Neely, 1894. xvi + 208pp.

Concerns Miss Banks's early career and adventures.

359. ———. *The Remaking of an American.* Garden City, N.Y.: Doubleday, Doran and Co., 1928. 297pp.

In the third of her autobiographies, the mature Miss Banks returns to the United States after many years in England and writes of what her American citizenship means to her. Not particularly journalistic, this book deals at length with her work for the Allies during World War I.

INMAN BARNARD

360. Barnard, Inman. *Cities and Men.* New York: E. P. Dutton and Co., 1940. x + 256pp. (Introduction by Sisley Huddleston.)

Recollections of a foreign correspondent in his 90th year. Barnard deals almost wholly with pre-1900 Europe, when he was with the New York *Herald*, for years the private secretary and confidant of James Gordon Bennett, Jr. It is difficult to tell how much of Barnard's story is accurate and how much is romance, for he wrote mostly from memory; over all, however, this is a sophisticated autobiography of a well-preserved *grand seigneur*.

PHINEAS T. BARNUM

361. Barnum, Phineas T. *Life of P. T. Barnum, Written by Himself.* New York: L. S. Redfield, 1855. viii + 404pp.

Barnum worked closely with the press, knew how to use it, and ran newspapers for short times. His autobiography is particularly helpful on his experiences with the *Herald of Freedom* in Connecticut, 1831–1834, and with the *Illustrated Weekly News* in New York in 1853. See also "Barnum's Rules for Success in Business."

362. Root, Harvey W. *The Unknown Barnum.* New York: Harper and Brothers, 1927. vii + 376pp.

A 20th-century study of Barnum. This volume includes a description of Barnum's publication, at age 21, of the *Herald of Freedom.* Also of interest to journalism is "An Object Lesson in Publicity," or how Barnum in 1878–1879 put on a drive to raise funds to beautify a cemetery in Bridgeport. The rest is mostly on show-business personalities.

DAVID S. BARRY

363. Barry, David S. *Forty Years in Washington.* Boston: Little, Brown and Co., 1924. xi + 349pp.

Barry served from 1879 to 1919 as Washington correspondent for the Detroit *Post* and *Tribune,* New York *Sun,* and Providence *Journal,* later becoming sergeant-at-arms of the U.S. Senate. He deals heavily in political recollections from the Hayes-Tilden campaign to Woodrow Wilson.

GEORGE A. BARRY

364. Barry, Richard. *Father and His Town.* Boston: Houghton Mifflin Co., 1941. viii + 299pp.

A worshipful story about a small-town newspaperman who went to Santa Ybel, Calif., at age 59, took over the faltering *Independent,* and in the next 25 years made a success of this weekly. The period is the first quarter of the 20th century. Before going to California, George Barry had had a generation of experience in Wisconsin, where he had been one of the founders of the Eau Claire *Telegram.*

GEORGE A. BARTON

365. Barton, George A. *My Lifetime in Sports.* Minneapolis: The Olympic Press, 1957. ix + 340pp.

The autobiography of a sports writer who served for 53 years with Minneapolis newspapers, particularly the *Tribune.* The emphasis is largely regional, but there is extensive material on Barton's associations with national sport figures.

CHARLES J. BAYNE

366. Bayne, Charles J. *Coming of the Crow's Feet.* Atlanta, Ga.: Tupper and Love, 1949. 455pp.

Reminiscences of more than 50 years dating back to the second Cleveland administration, by an editorial writer and columnist for the Macon (Ga.) *News* and *Telegraph.* The volume is heavily anecdotal, with lengthy reference to Bayne's friendship with Don Marquis.

NIVER W. BEAMAN

367. Beaman, Niver W. *Fat Man in a Phone Booth: Notes off a News-*

paperman's Cuff. Chicago: Cloud, 1947. 247pp. (Foreword by Clare Boothe Luce.)

More serious than its flippant title would indicate, this is a romantic story of reporting, chiefly on small newspapers in Waterbury and Greenwich, Conn. In 1946 the author became editor of *Moose Magazine*.

HENRY WARD BEECHER

368. Abbott, Lyman. *Henry Ward Beecher: A Sketch of His Career*. New York: Funk and Wagnalls, 1883; London: F. Bordon Hunt, 1883. xi + 604pp.

Includes extensive treatment of "Mr. Beecher as a Journalist": as editor of the Cincinnati *Journal*, a Presbyterian organ; as founder of the antislavery *Independent*; and as editor of the *Christian Union*.

ROBERT BENCHLEY

369. Benchley, Nathaniel. *Robert Benchley*. New York, Toronto, and London: McGraw-Hill Book Co., 1955. 258pp. (Foreword by Robert E. Sherwood.)

Benchley's eldest son offers a picture of his father (who was with *Vanity Fair*, the old *Life*, and the *New Yorker*) as a fighter for civil rights, a literary legend, a comedian, and an irresponsible businessman.

PARK BENJAMIN

370. Hoover, Merle M. *Park Benjamin, Poet and Editor*. New York: Columbia University Press, 1948. xiii + 229pp.

A life of one of the most important literary editors of the period 1830–1860: on the *New England Magazine*, the *American Monthly Magazine*, and Horace Greeley's *New-Yorker*. Later Benjamin established the *New World*, a widely known semiliterary weekly. The book is based on original sources.

JAMES GORDON BENNETT, SR.

371. Carlson, Oliver. *The Man Who Made News: James Gordon Bennett*. New York: Duell, Sloan and Pearce, 1942. xi + 440pp.

The best biography of the elder Bennett. The emphasis is on Bennett's changing a dull, barren, political press into a newsy, sensational press. There is an extensive bibliography. The bulk of the material was obtained from *Herald* files and from files of newspapers contemporary with Bennett's *Herald*.

372. Parton, James. "James Gordon Bennett and the New York *Herald*," in Parton's *Famous Americans of Recent Times*, pp. 259–306. Boston: Houghton Mifflin and Co., 1881.

A thorough contemporary analysis of how the exploitation of news as a commodity made possible the *Herald* founder's success. The article appeared originally in the *North American Review* in 1867.

373. Pray, Isaac C. *Memoirs of James Gordon Bennett and His Times*. New York: Stringer and Townsend, 1855. xxiv + 488pp.

A contemporary account, leaned upon heavily by subsequent writers. It was reportedly authorized by Bennett, although Pray, who worked for him, wrote that he did not consult Bennett or anyone connected with the editor.

374. Seitz, Don Carlos. *The James Gordon Bennetts: Father and Son — Proprietors of the New York Herald.* Indianapolis: Bobbs-Merrill Co., 1928. 405pp.

The third of Seitz's books on the "greats" of New York journalism (see also Seitz on Greeley, 649 below, and Pulitzer, 895). He is critical of the long Bennett dynasty. Unbalanced in spots, the book has as much space devoted to the Stanley-Livingstone story as to the elder Bennett's relations with Lincoln. Seitz makes no attribution to sources other than Pray's *Memoirs.*

JAMES GORDON BENNETT, JR.

375. Crockett, Albert S. *When James Gordon Bennett Was Caliph of Bagdad.* New York: Funk and Wagnalls Co., 1926. xvi + 414pp.

Based upon Crockett's recollections of many years. (The title was derived from the author's boyhood dreams of New York as his Bagdad and Bennett as his Caliph.) The volume is marred somewhat by being as much autobiography of Crockett as biography of Bennett, but the editor's whims and fancies are clearly brought out.

MEYER L. BERGER

376. Berger, Meyer L. *The Eight Million: Journal of a New York Correspondent.* New York: Simon and Schuster, 1942. x + 334pp.

Short, autobiographical narratives about "the queer, the quaint, and the quizzical in New York City," from Berger's apprenticeship days on the old *Morning World* to the time when he became a star reporter for the New York *Times.* There is good material on his coverage of the criminal syndicate "Murder, Inc."

AMBROSE BIERCE

377. De Castro, Adolphe. *Portrait of Ambrose Bierce.* New York: The Century Co., 1929. xvi + 351pp.

De Castro, a friend and journalistic colleague of many years, places Bierce in the tradition of Juvenal, Martial, Cervantes, Swift, and Voltaire. Detailed accounts relate to Bierce and De Young of the San Francisco *Chronicle* and to Bierce and Hearst, whom De Castro blames for "morally" compelling Bierce to go to his death in Mexico in 1913.

378. Fatout, Paul. *Ambrose Bierce, the Devil's Lexicographer.* Norman: University of Oklahoma Press, 1951. xv + 349pp.

A psychological approach toward an understanding of Bierce. Like other writers on Bierce, the author analyzes the probable reasons for Bierce's disappearance into Mexico. The book is well documented.

379. Grattan, C. Hartley. *Bitter Bierce: A Mystery of American Letters.* Garden City, N.Y.: Doubleday, Doran and Co., 1929. xi + 291pp.

In three parts: a biography, an analysis of Bierce's writings, and an analysis of his ideas. Grattan regards Bierce as more worthy of high place than Bret Harte, O. Henry, James Whitcomb Riley, or George Ade, and the equal of Frank Norris, Stephen Crane, and Jack London.

380. McWilliams, Carey. *Ambrose Bierce: A Biography*. New York: Albert and Charles Boni, 1929. ix + 358pp.

Perhaps the most thorough and well balanced of the Bierce biographies. McWilliams quotes extensively from Bierce's journalistic writings. He gives an excellent synthesis of the man he describes as "great, bitter, idealistic, cynical, morose, frustrated, cheerful, bad, sadistic, obscure, perverted, famous, brutal, kind, a fiend, a God, a Misanthrope, a poet, a realist who wrote romance, a fine satirist, and something of a charlatan."

381. Walker, Franklin. *Ambrose Bierce, the Wickedest Man in San Francisco*. San Francisco: Colt Press, 1941. 45pp.

A limited-edition, artistically designed appreciation of Bierce by a student of western Americana. Its value lies more in the fascinating method of treatment than in the substance of the material. See particularly "Bierce and the *Wasp*."

JOHN BIGELOW

382. Bigelow, John. *Retrospections of an Active Life*. New York: Baker and Taylor, 1910. 5 vols.

Autobiography, letters, and papers of one of America's amazing journalistic, literary, political, and diplomatic figures. See particularly I:73–139, Bigelow joining Bryant on the New York *Evening Post*, 1848; I:319–324, his withdrawal from that paper, 1860; IV:291–325, Bigelow's short-time editorship of the New York *Times* after the death of Raymond, 1869; and V:365–384, comments on the *Evening Post* after the death of Bryant, 1878. There are numerous references to journalistic figures of the period 1840–1878.

383. Century Association. *John Bigelow: Memorial Addresses Delivered before the Century Association, March 9, 1912*. New York: The Association, 1912. 53pp.

384. Clapp, Margaret. *Forgotten First Citizen: John Bigelow*. Boston: Little, Brown and Co., 1947. x + 390pp.

Covers thoroughly Bigelow's career as a partner of William Cullen Bryant's on the New York *Evening Post* in the 1850s. There is a significant account also of his unhappy experience as managing editor of the New York *Times*. Based upon original sources, with complete notes.

PAUL BILKEY

385. Bilkey, Paul. *Persons, Papers and Things: Being the Casual Recollections of a Journalist, with Some Flounderings in Philosophy*. Toronto: Ryerson Press, 1940. xii + 235pp.

The autobiography of the editor-in-chief of the Montreal *Gazette*. It covers chiefly the period 1896–1938, with extended comments on Sir Wilfrid Laurier, Canadian development, and Canadian problems of unity among the widely separated provinces.

THE LITERATURE OF JOURNALISM

MALCOLM W. BINGAY

386. Bingay, Malcolm W. *Detroit Is My Own Home Town.* Indianapolis and New York: Bobbs-Merrill Co., 1946. 360pp.

Records the unbounded affection of an editor (Detroit *Free Press*) for his city.

387. ———. *Of Me I Sing.* Indianapolis: Bobbs-Merrill Co., 1949. 300pp.

The brash story of Bingay's happy life with the Detroit *News* and the Detroit *Free Press.* Many illustrations show the author with big-time celebrities.

HARRY LEWIS BIRD

388. Bird, Harry Lewis. *This Fascinating Advertising Business.* New York: Bobbs-Merrill Co., 1947. 405pp.

Behind-the-scenes accounts, with a discussion of some leading personalities in advertising.

RUSSELL BIRDWELL

389. Birdwell, Russell. *I Ring Doorbells.* New York: Julian Messner, 1939. 253pp.

A superficial book by a Hearst reporter about "old-time reporting." The foreword by Gene Fowler is as good as the text. There is one useful chapter on the Lindbergh flight of 1927.

JAMES GILLESPIE BIRNEY

390. Birney, James G. *The Letters of James G. Birney, 1831–1857.* New York and London: D. Appleton-Century Co., 1938. 2 vols. xxxvi + 1189pp., total. (Edited by Dwight L. Dumond.)

An invaluable Birney collection containing source material on his American Anti-Slavery Society work and on his abolitionist newspaper ventures.

391. Birney, William. *James G. Birney and His Times: The Genesis of the Republican Party, with Some Account of Abolition Movements in the South before 1828.* New York: D. Appleton and Co., 1890. xii + 444pp.

Written by Birney's son more than 30 years after the death of this moderate abolitionist editor. The volume treats in detail the crisis that Birney went through in 1835–1836 in trying to establish the *Philanthropist* in Danville, Ky., and Cincinnati. Appendixes give material on antislavery literature before 1831 and a sketch of the life of Benjamin Lundy, founder of the *Genius of Universal Emancipation.*

392. Fladeland, Betty. *James Gillespie Birney: Slaveholder to Abolitionist.* Ithaca, N.Y.: Cornell University Press, 1955. ix + 323pp.

A documented study, with an extensive bibliography. The material on Birney's journalistic career is subordinated to a political account.

393. Green, Beriah. *Sketches of the Life and Writings of James G. Birney.* Utica, N.Y.: Jackson and Chaplin, 1844. 119pp.

A contemporary biography written at the time of Birney's candidacy for the presidency. It includes an account of Birney's experience with the *Philanthropist* in 1836.

ALEXANDER BLACK

394. Black, Alexander. *Time and Chance: Adventures with People and Print*. New York: Farrar and Rinehart, 1937. x + 338pp.

The autobiography of an editor of many talents and author of novels, essays, and historical and technical works. An artist and photographer as well, Black prepared his own illustrations for this fascinating story of his life. Once Sunday editor of the New York *World*, he gives a good picture of Joseph Pulitzer.

THE BLAIRS

395. Smith, William Ernest. *The Francis Preston Blair Family in Politics*. New York: The Macmillan Co., 1933. 2 vols. 1039pp., total.

On Francis P. Blair and his sons Francis P., Jr., and Montgomery, leaders in politics and journalism from the 1820s to 1880s. Smith had access to previously unpublished Blair family papers. Vol. I takes up the journalistic background, including establishment of the Washington *Globe* in Jackson's administration and *Globe* policies during its period of supremacy; and the succession to journalistic power in Washington of Thomas Ritchie's *Union*. Vol. II includes a discussion of the younger Blairs' activities in the Greeley-Brown campaign of 1872.

SAMUEL G. BLYTHE

396. Blythe, Samuel George. *The Making of a Newspaperman*. Philadelphia: Henry Altemus Co., 1912. 239pp.

An inspirational autobiography by a staff writer and editor for the *Saturday Evening Post* early in the century, told in simple language to attract youngsters.

EDWARD W. BOK

397. Bok, Edward William. *The Americanization of Edward Bok: The Autobiography of a Dutch Boy Fifty Years After*. New York: Charles Scribner's Sons, 1921. 462pp.

The widely read autobiography of the editor of the *Ladies' Home Journal*, 1889–1919. Throughout there runs a note of idealism and inspiration, with Bok stressing the opportunity of America. Bok's use of the third person in referring to himself makes the book stilted in tone.

398. ———. *Twice Thirty: Some Short and Simple Annals of the Road*. New York: Charles Scribner's Sons, 1925. vi + 539pp.

A sequel to *Americanization*. Filled with little experiences and advice.

JOSHUA A. BOLLES

399. Bolles, Joshua K. *Father Was an Editor*. New York: W. W. Norton Co., 1940. 284pp. (Etchings by Arthur D. Fuller.)

Life of the editor of the New Milford (Conn.) *Gazette* at the turn of the century, by his son. This was a man completely wrapped up in his little weekly.

FRED G. BONFILS and HARRY TAMMEN

400. Fowler, Gene. *Timber Line: A Story of Bonfils and Tammen*. New York: Covici-Friede, 1933; Garden City, N.Y.: Garden City Publishing Co., reprint, 1947. 480pp.

The history of the Denver *Post* of an earlier day as seen through the careers of its builders, Bonfils the gambler and Tammen the barkeeper, who created what became a legend in Denver. Fowler gives a highly colored picture — but probably it cannot be overpainted. Despite the free-and-easy treatment, the book has substance and can be read for enjoyment and a view of journalism engaged in for fun, "for justice," and of course for profit.

STEPHEN BONSAL

401. Bonsal, Stephen. *Heyday in a Vanished World*. New York: W. W. Norton and Co., 1937. 445pp.

The memoirs over a half-century of a distinguished reporter on the New York *Herald* who in World War I served the United States in important diplomatic missions. An early chapter deals with the Parnell-Kitty O'Shea story in Ireland; the bulk of the book concerns the Balkans, on which Bonsal became a political expert.

402. ———. *Unfinished Business*. New York: Doubleday, Doran and Co., 1944. xi + 313pp.

Excerpts from Bonsal's diary, written when Bonsal was Woodrow Wilson's confidential interpreter at the Versailles Peace Conference in 1919.

OLIVER K. BOVARD

403. Markham, James W. *Bovard of the Post-Dispatch*. Baton Rouge: Louisiana State University Press, 1954. xxii + 226pp.

Markham, who regards Bovard as "the greatest managing editor," covers his career for 40 years, until his retirement from the St. Louis *Post-Dispatch* in 1938. The study is based upon original documents, private papers and newspaper records, and articles about the *Post-Dispatch*.

RICHARD R. BOWKER

404. Fleming, E. McClung. *R. R. Bowker: Militant Liberal*. Norman: University of Oklahoma Press, 1952. xv + 395pp.

A biography of an important figure in journalism, literature, and libraries during more than half a century. Bowker was city editor and literary critic of the old New York *Evening Mail*, 1868–1875, and editor and owner of the booktrade journal, *Publishers' Weekly*, almost continuously from 1872 to 1933. There is good detail on his association with Melvil Dewey in the founding of the American Library Association and the *Library Journal* and on his extensive activities on behalf of an international copyright law. The book is thoroughly documented.

BIOGRAPHY

SAMUEL BOWLES III

405. Bradford, Gamaliel. "Samuel Bowles," in *Union Portraits*, pp.263–295. Boston and New York: Houghton Mifflin Co., 1916.

Among nine Civil War leaders, chiefly military men, Bradford included one journalist, Bowles.

406. Merriam, George S. *The Life and Times of Samuel Bowles*. New York: The Century Co., 1885. 2 vols. 938pp., total.

Still the best account available on the founder of the *Daily Springfield Republican*. Vol. I covers Bowles's career to 1864 and vol. II the last 13 years of his life. The stress throughout is on Bowles's political views, although the last six chapters of vol. II discuss characteristics of the *Republican* and Bowles's concepts of journalistic ethics, and provide personal glimpses.

ANDREW BRADFORD

407. De Armond, Anna Janney. *Andrew Bradford: Colonial Journalist*. Newark: University of Delaware Press, 1949. ix + 272pp.

A documented biography of the founder of the first newspaper in Philadelphia, the *American Weekly Mercury* (1719). There is a chapter on Bradford's *American Magazine* (1740–1741), material on foreign and Colonial affairs, a discussion of Bradford's controversies with Andrew Hamilton, and an index of the *American Weekly Mercury*, 1719–1746.

JOHN BRADFORD

408. Wilson, Samuel M. "The *Kentucky Gazette* and John Bradford, Its Founder," in *Papers of the Bibliographical Society of America*, vol. 31, part 2, pp. 102–132. Chicago: University of Chicago Press, 1937.

Sketches the life of the first printer in Kentucky, who founded the state's first newspaper in 1787.

MATHEW BRADY

409. Horan, James D. *Mathew Brady: Historian with a Camera*. New York: Crown Publishers, 1955. xix + 244pp. (Picture collation by Gertrude Horan.)

An effective biographical-pictorial study of Brady, whose sense of news and history contributed extensively to the development of journalism and to an understanding of the Civil War. The book includes Horan's report on his search into materials on Brady's life; a listing of picture sources from 23 collections; a biography of Brady; 453 reproductions of Brady's work or the work of his assistants; and a bibliography.

410. Meredith, Roy. *Mr. Lincoln's Camera Man: Mathew B. Brady*. New York: Charles Scribner's Sons, 1946. xiii + 368pp.

An excellent pictorial study of the Civil War, with commentary accompanying several hundred prints taken by Brady or by men under assignment to him. Dozens of these were spot-news pictures. The book includes a running account of Brady's life, from the 1840s to the 1890s.

THE LITERATURE OF JOURNALISM

WILLIAM COWPER BRANN

411. Carver, Charles. *Brann and the Iconoclast*. Austin: University of Texas Press, 1957. xvii + 196pp. (Introduction by Roy Bedichek.)

Life of the tempestuous, vitriolic editor of a monthly newspaper in Waco, Texas, who was horsewhipped and kidnaped by mobs and finally shot to death in 1898. Carver had access to the complete files of the *Iconoclast*, 1894–1898, and drew upon the 12-volume *Works of Brann*. Most attention is paid to Brann's attacks upon the administration of Baylor University.

ARTHUR BRISBANE

412. Carlson, Oliver. *Brisbane: A Candid Biography*. New York: Stackpole and Sons, 1937. 373pp.

Censures Brisbane, attributing to him all the elements of success except truth, integrity, consistency, and humanity. Writing within a year of Brisbane's death, Carlson leaned heavily upon secondary sources.

BEMAN BROCKWAY

413. Brockway, Beman. *Fifty Years in Journalism: Embracing Recollections and Personal Experiences, with an Autobiography*. Watertown, N.Y.: Daily Times Printing and Publishing House, 1891. xii + 426 + 67pp.

Brockway was editor of the Watertown (N.Y.) *Times and Reformer* through the latter third of the 19th century; he also had had earlier experience on Horace Greeley's staff and had served in the New York Legislature. This book is a rambling collection of 70 chapters that give personal reminiscences unavailable elsewhere. Francis P. Blair, Greeley and the campaign of 1872, Charles A. Dana, Thurlow Weed, and other Albany editors are dealt with extensively.

ISAAC H. BROMLEY

414. Osborn, Norris G. *Isaac H. Bromley*. New Haven: Yale University Press, 1920. 43pp. (Introduction by Hart Lyman.)

A lecture in biographical form given as part of a series endowed at Yale by Bromley's widow. Bromley was from the early 1870s to his death in 1898 a penetrating editorial writer for the New York *Tribune*.

NOAH BROOKS

415. Blackmon, Robert E. "Noah Brooks: Sometime 'John Riverside,' 'Castine,' *Alta* Editor, Etc.," in *California Historical Society Quarterly*, vol. XXXIII, no. 3 (September 1954), pp. 193–216.

HEYWOOD BROUN

416. *Heywood Broun as He Seemed to Us*. New York: Random House, 1940. 48pp.

A stenographic record of the Heywood Broun Memorial Meeting held under American Newspaper Guild auspices on February 12, 1940. There are 23 commentaries on Broun's career as man and journalist.

BIOGRAPHY

417. Kramer, Dale. *Heywood Broun: A Biographical Portrait*. New York: A. A. Wyn, Current Books, 1949. 316pp. (Foreword by Herbert Bayard Swope.)

Includes a good account of Broun's struggle to establish the American Newspaper Guild in 1933. Through the book runs a thread of deep personal sympathy for the huge, shuffling columnist who sought ever to improve the lot of newspapermen in the face of difficulties and personal hardship.

GEORGE BROWN

418. Lewis, John. *George Brown*. Toronto: Morang and Co., Ltd., 1909. xv + 281pp. (Vol. XIX in The Makers of Canada, Parkman edition.)

George Brown established the Toronto *Globe* in 1844 and built it into a newspaper of greater influence in Upper Canada than any theretofore. He was active in political affairs throughout the Confederation period. The political material outweighs the journalistic, but the early years of the *Globe* are adequately covered.

CHARLES FARRAR BROWNE (ARTEMUS WARD)

419. Seitz, Don C. *Artemus Ward: A Biography and Bibliography*. New York and London: Harper and Brothers, 1919. 338pp.

The life of Charles Farrar Browne, wit and paragrapher who helped lighten the burden of the Civil War. Seitz traces his career from Maine through service with the Cleveland *Plain Dealer* in the 1850s and with *Vanity Fair*. The bibliography lists Browne's contributions to the *Carpet-Bag*, *Plain Dealer*, *Vanity Fair* and London *Punch*, as well as his miscellaneous writings.

LOUIS BROWNLOW

420. Brownlow, Louis. *A Passion for Politics: The Autobiography of Louis Brownlow*. Chicago: University of Chicago Press, 1955. xii + 605pp.

The first part of a projected two-volume autobiography of a southern journalist-politician for half a century who was related to "Parson" William G. Brownlow. A good portion of Louis Brownlow's account deals with personal journalism in Tennessee and Kentucky and with Washington correspondence.

WILLIAM G. BROWNLOW

421. Brownlow, William G. *Sketches of the Rise, Progress, and Decline of Secession*. Philadelphia: George W. Childs; Cincinnati: Applegate and Co., 1862. 458pp.

The famous "Parson Brownlow's Book." Brownlow was the belligerent pro-Union editor of the Knoxville *Whig*. About 50 pages are autobiographical; much of the remainder of the book is merely a compilation of editorials from the *Whig*, quotations from other newspapers, and a series of diatribes against enemies. Valuable, nevertheless.

422. Coulter, E. Merton. *William G. Brownlow: Fighting Parson of the Southern Highlands*. Chapel Hill: University of North Carolina Press, 1937. vii + 431pp.

An account of Parson Brownlow's personal journalism with the Knoxville *Whig and Independent Journal* and later with the Knoxville *Whig and Rebel Ventilator.* Coulter attributes to Brownlow Radical excesses unequaled even by imported Carpetbaggers. The book is carefully documented.

423. Temple, Oliver Perry. "William Gannaway Brownlow," in his *Notable Men of Tennessee from 1833 to 1875*, pp. 271–356. New York: Cosmopolitan Press, 1912.

A eulogistic short biography by a one-time Tennessee lawyer and judge. The study has since been superseded by Coulter's.

WILLIAM CULLEN BRYANT

424. Bigelow, John. *William Cullen Bryant.* Boston and New York: Houghton Mifflin Co., 1890. vi + 355pp.

Bryant's associate for many years considers the life of the editor of the New York *Evening Post* in its numerous phases: barrister, adventurer, journalist, poet, tourist, and auditor. Most attention is given to him as journalist and poet.

425. Godwin, Parke. *A Biography of William Cullen Bryant, with Extracts from His Private Correspondence.* New York: D. Appleton and Co., 1883. 2 vols. 869pp., total.

By an *Evening Post* associate. Much of the material was obtained from Julia S. Bryant, a daughter.

426. ———. *Commemorative Addresses.* New York: Harper and Brothers, 1895. 239pp.

Five addresses by Godwin, two of which honor Bryant and George William Curtis of *Harper's.* Both are excellent presentations of the views of one editor on the contributions of two esteemed colleagues.

JOSEPH TINKER BUCKINGHAM

427. Buckingham, Joseph Tinker. *Personal Memoirs and Recollections of Editorial Life.* Boston: Ticknor, Reed, and Fields, 1852. 2 vols. 511pp., total.

Slow reading, but valuable for views of the journalistic scene during the generation before the Civil War. Buckingham was editor of the *New England Galaxy,* 1817–1828, and founder of the Boston *Courier,* 1824. Vol. II, devoted wholly to the *Courier,* is the more valuable. Especially useful are an excellent contemporary view of the murder of Elijah Lovejoy in 1837; comments on freedom of the press during that period; and selections from James Russell Lowell, whose *Biglow Papers* first appeared in the *Courier.*

428. ———. *Specimens of Newspaper Literature, with Personal Memoirs, Anecdotes, and Reminiscences.* Boston: Redding and Co., 1852. 2 vols. 704pp., total.

Among the earliest efforts of an American newspaperman to combine newspaper history with autobiography. Buckingham relied heavily upon Thomas's *History of Printing.* The volumes contain accounts of 45 early American papers; see particularly the review of Benjamin Russell's *Massachusetts Cen-*

tinel, John Campbell's Boston *News-Letter*, Edes and Gill's Boston *Gazette*, and Thomas's *Massachusetts Spy*.

LOUIS F. BUDENZ

429. Budenz, Louis Francis. *This Is My Story*. New York: Whittlesey House, McGraw-Hill Book Co., 1947. xv + 379pp.

Budenz was managing editor of the *Daily Worker* (June 1940 to October 1945). He deals mostly with his activities in the Communist party and with his reasons for breaking with it and re-entering the Catholic Church. There is a short account of the organization of the *Daily Worker*.

HENRY CUYLER BUNNER

430. Jensen, Gerard E. *The Life and Letters of Henry Cuyler Bunner*. Durham, N.C.: Duke University Press, 1939. xi + 247pp.

Bunner was the widely respected editor of the humor magazine *Puck*. This volume covers the history of the magazine from its founding in 1877 to Bunner's death in 1896.

ROBERT J. BURDETTE

431. Burdette, Clara B. *Robert J. Burdette: His Message*. Pasadena, Calif.: Clara Vista Press; Philadelphia: John C. Winston Co., 1922. 460pp.

A biography interwoven with edited versions of Burdette's writings. Burdette was a 19th- and early 20th-century humorist, newspaper editor, lecturer, and clergyman; he is noted chiefly for his "Hawkeyetems," written for the Burlington (Iowa) *Hawkeye*.

EDWARD H. BUTLER

432. Harriman, Lewis G. *Buffalo Evening News and Its Courageous Leader Edward H. Butler*. New York: Newcomen Society of North America, 1955. 28pp.

An address in commemoration of the 105th anniversary of the birth of the founder of the *Evening News*. Harriman gives an account of Butler's life and of *News* history as factors in the development of New York State's Niagara frontier in the Buffalo-Niagara Falls area.

SYLVANUS CADWALLADER

433. Cadwallader, Sylvanus. *Three Years with Grant, as Recalled by War Correspondent Sylvanus Cadwallader*. New York: Alfred A. Knopf, 1955. xiv + 353pp. (Edited by Benjamin P. Thomas.)

Recollections of a correspondent of the Chicago *Times* who was later correspondent-in-chief for the New York *Herald*. Editor Thomas, a Lincoln scholar, who pieced together the long-unpublished Cadwallader manuscript after it had been acquired by the Illinois Historical Society, provides a biography of Cadwallader. There are extensive references to Cadwallader's relations with Grant, Sherman, Sheridan, E. M. Stanton, and John A. Rawlins.

JAMES T. CALLENDER

434. Ford, Worthington C., ed. *Thomas Jefferson and James Thomson Callender, 1798–1802*. Brooklyn, N.Y.: Historical Printing Club, 1897. 45pp. (Reprinted from *New-England Historical and Genealogical Register, 1896–1897*.)

A pamphlet giving some detail on an amazing personality in the journalism of the Jeffersonian period, principally through 40 to 50 personal letters, mostly from Callender to Jefferson, and a report of Callender's trial for violation of the Sedition Act as carried in the *Virginia Gazette* in June 1800. Callender was associated principally with the Richmond *Examiner* and Philadelphia *Gazette*.

JAMES CANNON

435. Cannon, Jimmy. *Nobody Asked Me*. New York: Dial Press, 1951. 339pp.

Light stuff, mostly on sports, by a writer for the New York *Post* who earlier had served an array of New York City newspapers, Hearst press associations, and during World War II *Stars and Stripes*. In the introduction Cannon tells of his coverage of the Korean War in 1950.

MATHEW CAREY

436. Carey, Mathew. *Autobiography*. Brooklyn, N.Y.: Eugene L. Schwaab, 1942. ix + 133pp. (No. 1 of Research Classics.)

Carey's *Autobiography*, which first appeared as a series of 32 letters in the *New-England Magazine*, October 4, 1833, to October 21, 1837, is a valuable work for literary and journalistic history, 1785–1835.

437. Bradsher, Earl L. *Mathew Carey: Editor, Author and Publisher, a Study in American Literary Development*. New York: Columbia University Press, 1912. x + 144pp.

Bradsher considers Carey's career as editor of the *Pennsylvania Herald* in 1785, conditions in publishing in the late 18th and early 19th centuries, and Carey's work to free America from journalistic dependence on Europe. A scholarly work.

438. Rowe, Kenneth Wyer. *Mathew Carey: A Study in American Economic Development*. Baltimore: Johns Hopkins Press, 1933. 137pp. (Johns Hopkins Studies in Historical and Political Science, LI, no. 4.)

A short biography is included, but most of this study concerns Carey's activities in focusing public opinion upon protectionism. There is an extensive bibliography.

BOAKE CARTER

439. Carter, Boake. *This Is Life*. New York: Dodge Publishing Co., 1937. viii + 245pp.

This "mirror of emotions" of a columnist and broadcaster shows some 35 reflections over four years.

BIOGRAPHY

HODDING CARTER

440. Carter, Hodding. *Where Main Street Meets the River*. New York: Rinehart and Co., 1953. 339pp.

The autobiography of a liberal southern editor, of the *Delta Democrat-Times*, Greenville, Miss., is a readable account of a growing South. It goes somewhat beyond Mississippi into Carter's account of his experience with *PM* in the 1940s.

JOHN FRANKLIN CARTER (JAY FRANKLIN)

441. Carter, John Franklin. *The Rectory Family*. New York: Coward McCann, 1937. 275pp. (Etchings by Oscar Howard.)

Carter, news commentator, columnist, and author, wrote under the pseudonym of Jay Franklin. This autobiography of his youth in the years before World War I gives a good picture of "the snug little world of New England" before the great changes of the 20th century.

ROBERT J. CASEY

442. Casey, Robert J. *Such Interesting People*. Indianapolis: Bobbs-Merrill Co., 1943. 347pp.

With humor and some irreverence, Casey tells about people he met in many years as a reporter, chiefly with the Chicago *Daily News*. Two of the more interesting chapters are on "Life among the Multiple Managing Editors" and "Mr. Lawson's Newspaper."

443. ———. *More Interesting People*. Indianapolis: Bobbs-Merrill Co., 1947. 349pp.

More of raconteur Casey's recollections of newspaper zanies. See particularly "The Rise of the Asterisk," Casey's caustic attack upon "editorial fix-it-up men" who seek to improve upon news writing.

WILLIAM HENRY CHAMBERLIN

444. Chamberlin, William Henry. *The Confessions of an Individualist*. New York: The Macmillan Co., 1940. x + 320pp.

The autobiography of a foreign correspondent for the *Christian Science Monitor* in Moscow, Tokyo, Berlin, and Paris. Important chapters are those on "The Red and the Brown" and on comparisons between Russia and Germany in the mid-1930s.

(JAMES) JULIUS CHAMBERS

445. Chambers, [James] Julius. *The Book of New York: Forty Years' Recollections of the American Metropolis*. New York: The Book of New York Co., 1912. 448pp., illustrated.

A combination of personal narrative and history of New York City, 1870–1910, by a former managing editor of the *Herald* and the *World*. This is mainly a municipal promotion piece, but much of the content concerns New York newspapers. Some of the biographical material later was incorporated in Chambers's *News Hunting on Three Continents*.

446. ———. *A Mad World and Its Inhabitants*. New York: D. Appleton and Co.; London: Sampson Low, Marston, Searle and Rivington, 1877. 228pp.

A reporter's experiences during incarceration in Baldric's Asylum, a private institution for lunatics in New York. The material was first published in New York newspapers. Chambers's methods were sufficiently scientific to warrant the attention of medical authorities, and his findings were instrumental in bringing about changes in New York State lunacy laws.

447. ———. *News Hunting on Three Continents*. New York: Mitchell Kennerley, 1921. xii + 405pp.

Chambers's life from 1870 to about 1900, in which period he rose from cub reporting for the New York *Tribune* and the *Herald* to managing editorships under the younger Bennett and under Pulitzer on the *World*. The story of his establishing the Paris *Herald* for Bennett is included. Unfortunately, Chambers did not carry his autobiography through his later years.

CHARLES CHAPIN

448. Chapin, Charles. *Charles Chapin's Story, Written in Sing Sing Prison*. New York and London: G. P. Putnam's Sons and Knickerbocker Press, 1920. xxiii + 334pp. (Introduction by Basil King.)

The autobiography of a city editor of the New York *Evening World* for more than 25 years, who was sentenced to life in prison for the murder of his wife in 1918. The sensational circumstance that made this newspaperman's life notorious has interest, but the book itself is filled with rationalizations and maudlin explanations.

449. ———. *The Constance Letters of Charles Chapin*. New York: Simon and Schuster, 1931. xi + 355pp. (Edited by Eleanor Early and Constance.)

Exchanges between Chapin and an anonymous woman, "Constance," who had sought the imprisoned editor's advice in connection with the editing of a trade magazine. In publishing these letters, Constance's expressed purpose was to reveal Chapin as "a great and gallant man who even in tragedy never dipped his colors." The letters run from February 15, 1924, to March 17, 1929. More useful is a "History of Charles Chapin," by Miss Early, International News Service correspondent, who describes factually the fallen city editor's career.

450. ———. *The Uncensored Letters of Charles Chapin*. New York: Rudolph Field, 1931. 208pp. (Edited by Viola Irene.)

Letters written from Sing Sing between Thanksgiving Day 1920 and January 28, 1921, by Chapin to Miss Irene. There is only a bit on Chapin's editing of the prison newspaper, the *Bulletin*.

EARL V. CHAPIN

451. Chapin, Earl V. *Long Wednesdays*. New York: Abelard Press, 1953. 268pp.

Trials of a weekly newspaper editor in far northern Minnesota in the latter days of the Depression. How to edit a newspaper and to maintain integrity without an adequate plant or financial capital is the theme.

BIOGRAPHY

HECTOR CHARLESWORTH

452. Charlesworth, Hector. *Candid Chronicles: Leaves from the Note Book of a Canadian Journalist.* Toronto: The Macmillan Co. of Canada, Ltd., 1925. xv + 404pp.

Memoirs of a Toronto newspaperman (Toronto *World* and Toronto *Empire*), who seeks to portray Canada's social and economic development in the years before 1900. There are good chapters on Canadian newspapers in the 1890s, with considerable material on W. F. Maclean of the Toronto *World*.

453. ———. *More Candid Chronicles: Further Leaves from the Note Book of a Canadian Journalist.* Toronto: The Macmillan Co. of Canada, Ltd., 1928. xv + 429pp.

454. ———. *I'm Telling You: Being the Further Candid Chronicles.* Toronto: The Macmillan Co. of Canada, Ltd., 1937. xiv + 344pp.

EDNA WOOLMAN CHASE

455. Chase, Edna Woolman, and Ilka Chase. *Always in Vogue.* Garden City, N.Y.: Doubleday and Co., 1954. 381pp.

Edna Chase's distinctive story of her career as editor of *Vogue*, which she served for 56 years before her retirement in 1952, is kindly and nostalgic, and into it she weaves much of the history of the Condé Nast Publications. There is heavy emphasis on *Vogue*'s typographical excellence; dozens of pictures depict a half-century of style changes.

WILLIAM L. CHENERY

456. Chenery, William L. *So It Seemed.* New York: Harcourt, Brace and Co., 1952. xi + 300pp.

The autobiography of a newspaper and magazine editor of 40 years' experience in Chicago and New York, chiefly as editor of *Collier's Weekly*. Chenery records associations with numerous contributors to *Collier's*, among them Winston Churchill, H. G. Wells, and Franklin Roosevelt. An appealing book.

GEORGE W. CHILDS

457. Childs, George W. *Recollections.* Philadelphia: J. B. Lippincott Co., 1890. 404pp. (Preface by Melville Philips.)

Childs purchased the Philadelphia *Public Ledger* in 1864 and in the succeeding quarter-century made it one of the most famous newspapers in the country. His *Recollections* consist of four articles that first appeared in *Lippincott's Magazine*, June–September 1889. An excellent book, although rambling.

WILLIAM CONANT CHURCH

458. Bigelow, Donald Nevins. *William Conant Church and the Army and Navy Journal.* New York: Columbia University Press, 1952. viii + 266pp.

In this combination biography and newspaper history, a third is devoted to Church's life and the remainder to the military affairs paper he founded in

1863 and edited for 54 years. Bigelow is particularly thorough on the Civil War. There is a good selected bibliography of primary sources.

DONALD H. CLARKE

459. Clarke, Donald Henderson. *Man of the World: Recollections of an Irreverent Reporter*. New York: Vanguard Press, 1951. 304pp.

Two dozen autobiographical narratives by a novelist and one-time staff member of the New York *World*. These deal chiefly with the 1920s, although there are flashbacks to Joseph Pulitzer and the early days of the century. Herbert Bayard Swope, *World* executive editor, is analyzed.

JOSEPH I. C. CLARKE

460. Clarke, Joseph I. C. *My Life and Memories*. New York: Dodd, Mead and Co., 1925. xv + 404pp. (Introduction by Rupert Hughes.)

Among the better autobiographies of working newspapermen for the period 1875–1915, chiefly because of the high quality of the writing. Clarke served the New York *Herald*, 1871–1883 and 1903–1906; he was on Albert Pulitzer's New York *Journal* for a time; he edited a literary weekly, the *Criterion*; and he was publicity director for Standard Oil in later years. He offers useful material on Irish Republicanism, the younger Bennett, Henry M. Stanley, Albert and Joseph Pulitzer, and leaders in politics, science, and the arts.

CASSIUS MARCELLUS CLAY

461. Clay, Cassius M. *Appeal of Cassius M. Clay to Kentucky and the World*. Boston: J. M. Macomber and E. L. Pratt, 1845. 35pp.

A stirring pronouncement from the editor of the abolitionist newspaper in Lexington, the *True American*, when the Kentucky slave oligarchy refused to let his press continue.

462. ———. *The Life of Cassius Marcellus Clay: Memoirs, Writings, and Speeches, Showing His Conduct in the Overthrow of American Slavery, the Salvation of the Union, and the Restoration of the Autonomy of the States*. Cincinnati: J. Fletcher Brennan and Co., 1886. 600pp.

A rambling autobiography, written when Clay was 75 and intended as the first of two volumes; the second was never written. Most of the book concerns Clay's life through the Civil War. Scattered throughout are references to journalistic experiences involving freedom of speech, including the *True American* conflict of 1845.

463. ———. *The Writings of Cassius Marcellus Clay, Including Speeches and Addresses*. New York: Harper and Brothers, 1848. xv + 535pp. (Edited, with a preface and memoir, by Horace Greeley.)

A useful original source on the *True American* episode. The book as a whole is a compendium on civil liberties for the period 1832 to 1848. Greeley's contribution is outright eulogy of Clay as a hero who "bearded the monster [slavery] in his den, and dared him to a most unequal encounter."

SAMUEL LANGHORNE CLEMENS (MARK TWAIN)

464. Clemens, Samuel L. *Mark Twain's Autobiography*. New York and

London: Harper and Brothers, 1924. 2 vols. 733pp., total. (Introduction by Albert Bigelow Paine.)

Paine gives background material on the preparation of these volumes. The autobiography itself wanders, with incidents and comments put down according to Clemens's fancy.

465. ———. *Mark Twain in Eruption: Hitherto Unpublished Pages about Men and Events.* New York and London: Harper and Brothers, 1940. xxviii + 402pp. (Edited by Bernard De Voto.)

Significant autobiographical material not included in the two-volume Twain *Autobiography.* Clemens discusses Bret Harte, Thomas Bailey Aldrich, Murat Halstead, Bayard Taylor, James R. Osgood, and the then rising Winston Spencer Churchill of Great Britain. He also takes up the failure of the publishing house of Webster and Co., an account which should be compared with Samuel Charles Webster's work *Mark Twain, Business Man* (473).

466. Benson, Ivan. *Mark Twain in the West.* Sacramento, Calif.: State Printing Office, 1936. vii + 30pp.

467. ———. *Mark Twain's Western Years.* Stanford, Calif.: Stanford University Press; London: Oxford University Press, 1938. x + 218pp.

Discusses Clemens's development as a journalist in Nevada and California, 1861–1866. The work is based upon material previously undiscovered: selected Mark Twain items from the Virginia City *Territorial Enterprise*; from San Francisco, Sacramento, and Hawaiian newspapers; and from magazines. There are good notes and bibliography.

468. Branch, Edgar Marquess. *The Literary Apprenticeship of Mark Twain.* Urbana: University of Illinois Press, 1950. xlv + 325pp.

Includes selections from Twain's early writing.

469. De Voto, Bernard. *Mark Twain's America.* Boston: Little, Brown and Co., 1932. xvi + 353pp.

Only incidentally concerned with Clemens's journalistic career, De Voto seeks to correct some impressions of his literary achievement and to analyze America as represented only in Clemens's books. There is a useful appendix on newspaper humor of the southwestern frontier.

470. Ferguson, [John] De Lancey. *Mark Twain: Man and Legend.* Indianapolis: Bobbs-Merrill Co., 1943. 352pp.

471. Mack, Effie Mona. *Mark Twain in Nevada.* New York: Charles Scribner's Sons, 1947. xiii + 398pp.

Supplements *Mark Twain's Western Years* (467) but covers only the period 1861–1864. Nearly half is devoted to the "Washoe School of Journalism" and includes a joint analysis of Dan De Quille and Mark Twain. Well written and scholarly.

472. Paine, Albert Bigelow. *Mark Twain, a Biography: The Personal and Literary Life of Samuel Langhorne Clemens.* New York and London: Harper and Brothers, 1912. 3 vols.

Paine, Mark Twain's official biographer and literary executor, obtained his information from letters, diaries, account books, and persons who had known Clemens, from his own acquaintanceship with him, and from material Clemens dictated to Paine. Though much has been written since this biography, Paine's remains the standard work.

473. Webster, Samuel Charles, ed. *Mark Twain, Business Man.* Boston: Little, Brown and Co., 1946. 409pp.

The significant part of this work relates to Clemens's experiences in the 1880s with the Paige Typesetting Machine. Samuel Webster, the son of Clemens's associate Charles L. Webster, seeks to show that Clemens was in error when he attributed the failure of his publishing firm to Charles Webster, that the real "culprit" was the Paige Typesetter, in which Clemens invested thousands of dollars. The chapters on the composing machine provide an account of grand publishing vision mixed with poor publishing sense. (See also No. 465 above.)

JOHN P. CLUM

474. Clum, Woodworth. *Apache Agent: The Story of John P. Clum.* Boston: Houghton Mifflin Co., 1936. xv + 297pp.

Pictures late-frontier America, 1835–1886: part politics, part Indian-fighting, part journalism, part romance. Clum was the first mayor of Tombstone, Ariz., founder of the Tombstone *Epitaph*, agent among the Apaches, and captain of a Citizens' Safety Committee. The book is more on the Apache story than on journalism.

HENRY W. CLUNE

475. Clune, Henry W. *Main Street Beat.* New York: W. W. Norton and Co., 1947. 269pp.

Reminiscences of an editor of the Rochester (N.Y.) *Democrat and Chronicle,* who wrote affectionately about his city and its people. The book provides good pictures of conservative Rochester.

IRVIN S. COBB

476. Cobb, Irvin S. *Exit Laughing.* Indianapolis: Bobbs-Merrill Co., 1941. 572pp.

The autobiography of one of Kentucky's famous sons — newspaper writer, short story writer, humorist, dramatist, and Hollywood star. Cobb's full life included staff work for the *Saturday Evening Post,* New York *World,* and *Cosmopolitan.*

477. ———. *Stickfuls: Compositions of a Newspaper Minion.* New York: George H. Doran Co., 1923. 355pp.

Semi-autobiographical pieces. With *Exit Laughing,* this book gives a full picture of Cobb.

478. Neuman, Fred G. *Irvin S. Cobb: His Life and Achievements.* Paducah, Ky.: Young Publishing Co., 1934. 275pp. (Introduction by O. O. McIntyre.)

By one of Cobb's closest friends, this book gives details on his early experiences as a reporter in Paducah and on his extraordinary success as a New York newspaperman early in the century.

BIOGRAPHY

WILLIAM COBBETT (see also No. 1282)

479. Cobbett, William. *The Autobiography of William Cobbett: The Progress of a Plough-Boy to a Seat in Parliament.* London: Bowering Press, 1947. 272pp. (Edited by William Reitzel.)

Cobbett's *Autobiography* has gone through numerous editions; this recent one is useful because of its extensive notes. Cobbett's American experiences (1792–1795, 1796–1800, and 1817–1819) comprise three chapters.

480. Bowen, Marjorie [Mrs. Gabrielle Long]. *Peter Porcupine.* New York and London: Longmans, Green and Co., 1935. xii + 312pp.

A British author's biography of Cobbett written for the lay reader interested in Cobbett's whole career. His American journalistic experiences receive only limited treatment.

481. Clark, Mary Elizabeth. *Peter Porcupine in America: The Career of William Cobbett, 1792–1800.* Philadelphia: University of Pennsylvania Press, 1939. iii + 193pp.

Originally a Ph.D. thesis, this volume reconstructs in detail Cobbett's career in Philadelphia. The work is based in part on newspapers of the 1790s.

482. Cole, G. D. H. *The Life of William Cobbett.* New York: Harcourt, Brace and Co., 1924. x + 458pp.

By a British economist, the outstanding biography of this effective pamphleteer and political journalist. Relatively few pages are devoted to his work in America. The bibliography is excellent.

ELIZABETH COCHRANE (NELLIE BLY)

483. Rittenhouse, Mignon. *The Amazing Nellie Bly.* New York: E. P. Dutton Co., 1956. 254pp.

The life of Elizabeth Cochrane, who as a reporter for the New York *World* in 1889–1890 broke Jules Verne's fictional record of *Around the World in 80 Days.* Nellie did it in 72:6:11. The *World* trip around the world is presented "play-by-play." Perhaps the best biography of a stunt reporter.

CHARLES CARLETON COFFIN

484. Griffis, William Elliot. *Charles Carleton Coffin: War Correspondent, Traveler, Author, and Statesman.* Boston: Estes and Lauriat, 1898. 357pp.

A eulogistic biography by a New England clergyman of the distinguished Boston *Journal* correspondent who served that newspaper throughout the Civil War. This is one of the relatively few full-length books on reporters who saw extensive war service. Coffin was among the most competent of correspondents in the field.

HARRY J. COLEMAN

485. Coleman, Harry J. *Give Us a Little Smile, Baby.* New York: E. P. Dutton and Co., 1943. 258pp.

The "photobiography" of a Hearst cameraman who covered the San Francisco earthquake and fire in 1906. Numerous cartoons and photographs, many of bygone sports events (chiefly prize fights), newspaper family groups, and early airplanes, fill the pages.

ANTHONY COMSTOCK

486. Broun, Heywood, and Margaret Leech. *Anthony Comstock: Roundsman of the Lord.* New York: Albert and Charles Boni, 1927. 283pp.

A portrait of the 19th-century and early 20th-century reformer who battled for years to suppress vice in America, particularly with regard to keeping obscene literature from the mails. Of moment in journalistic study because of Comstock's zealous raids upon publishers of obscene and fraudulent matter and upon dishonest advertisers.

CHARLES TABER CONGDON

487. Congdon, Charles Taber. *Reminiscences of a Journalist.* Boston: James R. Osgood and Co., 1880. xii + 393pp.

Congdon's fame rests chiefly on the essays he wrote for Horace Greeley and the New York *Tribune* as a staff member from 1857 to 1882. He recalls numerous political and literary figures of pre-Civil War and post-Civil War years, and discusses training for journalism and the fascination of the newspaper. He gives stanch support to Greeley.

WINNIFRED COOLEY

488. Cooley, Winnifred Harper. *I Knew Them When . . . !* New York: The Saravan House, 1940. 250pp.

A globe-trotting reporter's accounts of famous people she had come to know.

E. D. COWEN

489. Murray, Charles A., and other contributors. *The Newspaper Career of E. D. Cowen.* Seattle: Western Printing Co., 1930. 151pp.

A volume about an extraordinary western journalist, 1875–1900. The book centers chiefly on Cowen's activities in Colorado and New Mexico; from there he went to Chicago and eventually, after service with the younger Bennett, settled in Washington State with the Seattle *Press.* In addition to two autobiographical sketches by Cowen, sixteen brief chapters are contributed by Charles A. Murray, Slason Thompson, R. E. M. Strickland, C. E. Arney, Hugh Hume, and Frank M. Dallam, Jr.

GARDNER COWLES

490. Des Moines Register and Tribune. *Gardner Cowles, 1861–1946.* Des Moines: The Register and Tribune Co., 1946. 125pp.

A memorial biography of the senior Cowles, considerably better done than most such tributes. It includes the obituary of Cowles as run in the *Register,* March 1, 1946; editorials from the *Register* and *Tribune;* tributes from Iowa editors and from national newspapers; and comments of leading citizens.

BIOGRAPHY

JAMES M. COX

491. Cox, James M. *Journey through My Years*. New York: Simon and Schuster, 1946. xi + 463pp.

Cox regarded himself more a newspaperman than a politician. The chapters most closely concerned with the press are those on his taking over of the Dayton (Ohio) *Daily News* at age 28, his entry into the Miami newspaper field in 1923 through purchase of the *Metropolis* (changed to *Daily News*), and his buying of the *Atlanta Journal*. Well written and modest.

492. Babson, Roger W. *Cox, the Man*. New York: Brentano's, 1920. iii + 128pp.

A political biography prepared for the presidential campaign of 1920.

STEPHEN CRANE

493. Beer, Thomas. *Stephen Crane: A Study in American Letters*. New York: Alfred A. Knopf, 1923. 248pp. (Introduction by Joseph Conrad.)

The standard biography of the author of *The Red Badge of Courage*, who reported the Spanish-American War for New York newspapers. The book describes Crane's Cuban experiences.

494. Berryman, John. *Stephen Crane*. New York: William Sloane Associates, 1950. xv + 345pp. (American Men of Letters Series.)

A critical biography of Crane analyzing the decline in his reputation after 1898 and its revival after Beer's biography appeared in 1923. Berryman leans heavily on Beer, although he treats Crane's war reporting much more extensively and makes frequent reference to other journalists of Crane's day.

J. H. CRANSTON

495. Cranston, James Herbert. *Ink on My Fingers*. Toronto: Ryerson Press, 1953. x + 188pp. (Edited by William H. Cranston.)

The autobiography of the editor for 21 years of the Toronto *Weekly Star*. Cranston was later publisher of the Midland (Ont.) *Free Press-Herald*, a weekly on Georgian Bay, but this volume is concerned mostly with the years he served the *Star*. There is an excellent analysis of J. E. Atkinson, who built the Toronto *Star* into a leading Canadian daily.

GEORGE CREEL

496. Creel, George. *Rebel at Large: Recollections of Fifty Crowded Years*. New York: G. P. Putnam's Sons, 1947. viii + 384pp.

A delightful book, by a man of strong loves and strong hates. Director of the Committee on Public Information in World War I, Creel covers that story in detail as well as his long journalistic experience in Kansas City and Denver. The book rings throughout with tones of Creel's crusading fervor.

WILLIAM A. CROFFUT

497. Croffut, William A. *An American Procession, 1855–1914: A Personal*

Chronicle of Famous Men. Boston: Little, Brown and Co., 1931. 321pp.

Reminiscences of a journalist, 1835–1915, who reportedly knew every president from Millard Fillmore to Woodrow Wilson. Despite some excusable "stretching" at the extremes, this is a useful book. In addition to politicians and military figures Croffut sketches Bennett the elder, N. P. Willis, Horace Greeley and Mrs. Greeley, Mark Twain, Henry Ward Beecher, Theodore Tilton, Wendell Phillips, Walt Whitman, Edmund C. Stedman, Joseph Pulitzer, William Cullen Bryant, David Dudley Field, James Watson Webb, P. T. Barnum, and Thurlow Weed.

CYRUS H. K. CURTIS

498. Bok, Edward W. *A Man from Maine.* New York: Charles Scribner's Sons, 1923. xv + 278pp.

A simple, worshipful account of the life of the owner of the *Saturday Evening Post, Ladies' Home Journal,* and Philadelphia newspapers.

GEORGE WILLIAM CURTIS (see also No. 426)

499. Cary, Edward. *George William Curtis.* Boston and New York: Houghton Mifflin Co., 1894. ix + 343pp.

The life of an editor of *Harper's Weekly,* who was also a literary figure, scholar, and orator, and editor of Harper's "Easy Chair" department. Goes considerably beyond Curtis's journalistic work into the politics of the years 1856–1880.

JOHN WESLEY DAFOE

500. Ferguson, George V. *John W. Dafoe.* Toronto: Ryerson Press, 1948. 127pp.

A study in greatness as represented in the editor of the Winnipeg *Free Press,* 1901–1944. This is chiefly an impressionistic profile by one journalist of another. Ferguson is editor of the Montreal *Star.* The book contains much contemporary Canadian history and analyzes the relationship between Dafoe as editor and Sir Clifford Sifton as owner of the *Free Press.*

501. Hutchinson, Bruce. "The Greatest Man in Canada," in *Fortune,* vol. XXV, no. 6 (June 1942), pp. 107–111 + 114–120.

Another tribute to Dafoe, this by a distinguished western Canadian journalist, editor of the Victoria *Times.* Illustrated.

CHARLES ANDERSON DANA

502. Dana, Charles A. *Proudhon and His "Bank of the People"* . . . *by Charles A. Dana, Editor of the New York Sun.* New York: Benjamin R. Tucker, 1896. vii + 67pp.

Publisher Tucker uses Dana's own words against him nearly a half-century after they were written. The pieces were originally submitted by Dana in 1849 to the New York *Tribune* and a weekly in New York (the *Spirit of the Age*) as a defense of the French socialist Pierre Proudhon. Tucker in 1896 found Dana's editorials against liberalism a contrast to his one-time revolutionary spirit. The calling up of Dana's past gives a fascinating insight into the editor's cynicism and change in economic views. Tucker was editor of *Liberty*, a fortnightly devoted to anarchism.

503. ———. *Recollections of the Civil War: With the Leaders at Washington and in the Field in the Sixties.* New York: D. Appleton and Co., 1898. xiii + 296pp.

Limited wholly to Dana's service as assistant secretary of war under Edwin M. Stanton, 1862–1865. There is a brief mention of disagreements with Horace Greeley and troubles with Civil War correspondents. Good as a military account.

504. Fenton, Alfred H. *Dana of The Sun.* New York and Toronto: Farrar and Rinehart, 1941. viii + 278pp.

An inadequate life of Dana, apparently written for young readers. No preface and no index.

505. Rosebault, Charles J. *When Dana Was the Sun: A Story of Personal Journalism.* New York: Robert M. McBride and Co., 1931. xiv + 294pp.

A eulogistic biography by a staff member of the *Sun*, 1884–1907. It opens with Eugene Field's poem, "But bless ye, Mr. Dana," and closes with the words of one of his reporters, "I'd rather be Charles A. Dana than President of the United States." This is superseded by the work of Candace Stone.

506. Stone, Candace. *Dana and the Sun.* New York: Dodd, Mead and Co., 1938. xiii + 431pp. (Introduction by William T. Dewart.)

An analysis of *Sun* editorial policies under Dana's influence, 1868–1897. A critical book, more useful than full-life biographies of Dana or reminiscences of his colleagues.

507. Wilson, James Harrison. *The Life of Charles A. Dana.* New York and London: Harper and Brothers, 1907. xii + 534pp.

An authorized biography based upon letters and documents given to Wilson by the Dana family. A major general in the army, Wilson had had a long association with Dana and had been assisted by the editor in preparing a biography of Ulysses S. Grant in 1868. There is heavy emphasis on Dana's War Department work during the Civil War. Little critical judgment is displayed.

JOSEPHUS DANIELS

508. Daniels, Josephus. *Tar Heel Editor.* Chapel Hill: University of North Carolina Press, 1939. xix + 544pp.

The first of five volumes of the elder Daniels's memoirs covers his boyhood and youth and entry into North Carolina politics in the 1880s up to 1893, when Daniels first went to Washington as chief of the Appointments Division under Grover Cleveland. Daniels's books all are long and detailed, but a great contribution to journalistic-political literature. He was owner of the Raleigh *News and Observer*.

509. ———. *Editor in Politics.* Chapel Hill: University of North Carolina Press, 1941. xix + 644pp.

The second volume of memoirs, covering 1893–1912, includes views of the second Cleveland administration, discussion of politics in North Carolina and the fight for free silver, and considerable attention to journalism. It closes with Daniels's appointment as secretary of the navy under Woodrow Wilson.

510. ———. *The Wilson Era: Years of Peace, 1910–1917*. Chapel Hill: University of North Carolina Press, 1944. xvi + 615pp.

The memoirs now become more political than journalistic, as Daniels devotes himself to foreign affairs, the navy, and problems of neutrality. There are numerous cartoons from metropolitan newspapers.

511. ———. *The Wilson Era: Years of War and After, 1917–1923*. Chapel Hill: University of North Carolina Press, 1946. xviii + 654pp.

Concerns Daniels's concept of Wilsonian statesmanship and his belief that the Covenant of the League of Nations "would one day bless mankind." There is a brief discussion of World War I propaganda in "Public Information, Not Censorship."

512. ———. *Shirt-Sleeve Diplomat*. Chapel Hill: University of North Carolina Press, 1947. xix + 547pp.

Covers the years 1933–1942, when Daniels was Franklin D. Roosevelt's ambassador to Mexico.

513. Daniels, Jonathan. *The End of Innocence*. Philadelphia: J. B. Lippincott Co., 1954. 351pp.

The son of Josephus Daniels and his successor on the Raleigh *News and Observer* writes here a somewhat emotional recollection of youthful years. This concerns chiefly the father's connections with the Wilson administration.

HOMER DAVENPORT

514. Davenport, Homer. *The Country Boy: The Story of His Own Early Life*. New York: G. W. Dillingham Co., 1910. 191pp. (Illustrated with 62 Davenport cartoons.)

A famous newspaper cartoonist looks back fondly at his boyhood home in Silverton, Ore., in the 1880s. Davenport concludes the story with his departure for San Francisco; he includes nothing of his subsequent journalistic activities.

RUSSELL DAVENPORT

515. Davenport, Russell W. *The Dignity of Man*. New York: Harper and Brothers, 1955. viii + 338pp. (Foreword by John Knox Jessup.)

A philosophical inquiry by the late editor of *Fortune* into the nature of the human spirit, in an effort to find a free-world answer to communism. In a biographical introduction Jessup traces Davenport's journalistic career with *Time* and *Fortune* and his Willkie-for-President activities in 1940.

OSCAR KING DAVIS

516. Davis, Oscar King. *Released for Publication: Some Inside Political History of Theodore Roosevelt and His Times, 1898–1918*. Boston and New York: Houghton Mifflin Co., 1925. viii + 468pp.

Reminiscences of the first Roosevelt's era by a Washington correspondent of the New York *Times*. His attitude toward Roosevelt is completely admiring.

BIOGRAPHY

RICHARD HARDING DAVIS

517. Davis, Richard Harding. *Adventures and Letters of Richard Harding Davis*. New York: Charles Scribner's Sons, 1918. viii + 417pp. (Edited by Charles Belmont Davis.)

A well-organized book, with Charles Davis's notes interposed to provide continuity. Numerous illustrations are included, principally from Richard Harding Davis's last 20 years. Almost all the letters are to the Davis family; they cover the period from age 16 almost to the journalist's death.

518. Downey, Fairfax. *Richard Harding Davis: His Day*. New York and London: Charles Scribner's Sons, 1933. x + 322pp.

The author continues to play up the aura of romance that surrounded Davis as a reporter early in the century. Downey includes a chapter on Davis's mother, Rebecca Harding Davis, herself a writer of note. His sources included Charles Belmont Davis's edited letters and the Talcott Williams collection of Davis clippings in the Columbia University School of Journalism.

ROBERT H. DAVIS

519. Davis, Robert H. *Bob Davis Recalls: Sixty True Stories of Love and Laughter and Tears*. New York: D. Appleton Century Co., 1927. x + 314pp.

Brief autobiographical accounts, laden with human interest. Davis first wrote the pieces for the editorial page of the New York *Sun*.

520. Mathias, Fred S. *The Amazing Bob Davis: His Last Vagabond Journey*. New York and Toronto: Longmans, Green and Co., 1944. ix + 326pp.

A sympathetic portrayal of a journey Davis took a short time before his death, from New York into Mexico. In a thumbnail biography, Mathias traces Davis's career as a reporter for New York newspapers, fiction editor for Frank A. Munsey, and columnist for the *Sun* for many years.

JAMES D. B. DE BOW

520a. Skipper, Ottis Clark. *J. D. B. De Bow: Magazinist of the Old South*. Athens: University of Georgia Press, 1958. x + 269pp.

This careful biography goes into extended detail on De Bow's championship of southern economic and cultural development, his defense of slavery and secession, and *De Bow's Review* during wartime and Reconstruction. Skipper provides a thorough bibliography of manuscript sources, letters, public documents, and newspapers.

521. Weatherford, W. D. *James Dunwoody Brownson De Bow*. Charlottesville, Va.: Historical Publishing Co., 1935. 49pp. (Southern Sketches No. 3.)

A scholarly monograph; Part I presents a life of De Bow and Part II his writings and influence from 1846 to 1867. The book contributes materially to an understanding of pre-Civil War southern journalism.

THE LITERATURE OF JOURNALISM

CHARLES DE MORSE

522. Wallace, Ernest. *Charles De Morse: Pioneer Editor and Statesman.* Lubbock, Texas: Texas Tech Press, 1943. v + 271pp.

De Morse founded the *Northern Standard* of Clarksville, Texas, in 1842 and was editor for 45 years, during which period he played a role in the annexation of Texas, the Mexican War, secession, and the framing of the Texas Constitution of 1876. There is an extensive bibliography of original materials and of Texas newspapers of the period.

GEORGE B. DEALEY

523. Sharpe, Ernest. *G. B. Dealey of the Dallas News.* New York: Henry Holt and Co., 1955. xiii + 304pp. (Preface by Harry C. Withers.)

A sympathetic account of the builder of an outstanding Texas newspaper, whose years of service extended from 1874 to 1946. Sharpe, though not a staff member, was assisted by Dealey family collections covering the period 1885–1940. The work leans heavily on Acheson's *35,000 Days in Texas* (see 91) and on the *Texas Almanac.*

WILLIAM CHAPIN DEMING

524. Deming, William Chapin. *Collected Writings and Addresses of William Chapin Deming.* Glendale, Calif.: Arthur H. Clark Co., 1946. 4 vols. (Edited by Agnes Wright Spring.)

Comments, over 45 years, of a lawyer, businessman, member of the Wyoming Legislature, president of the United States Civil Service Commission in 1920s, and editor and publisher of the *Wyoming State Tribune-Leader* (Cheyenne). The pieces cover an immense variety of subjects, many of them journalistic problems; some were from Deming's newspaper columns.

525. Spring, Agnes Wright. *William Chapin Deming of Wyoming: Pioneer Publisher, and State and Federal Official.* Glendale, Calif.: Arthur H. Clark Co., 1944. 531pp.

A lengthy tribute to Deming. Woven throughout are helpful accounts of various newspapers of Wyoming rarely mentioned in general or regional histories. There is a useful regional bibliography of Deming's published writings, magazine and newspaper articles, and addresses. The volume covers the years 1890–1940.

JOSEPH DENNIE

526. Dennie, Joseph. *The Lay Preacher.* New York: Scholars' Facsimiles and Reprints, 1943. ix + 184pp. (Edited by Milton Ellis.)

Dennie's reputation as a literary figure and journalist rests heavily on his "Lay Preacher" essays (1795–1801). Two sets are reprinted here: one of 36 items from a Dennie edition of 1796 and another of 28 items from an edition of 1817.

527. Ellis, Harold M. *Joseph Dennie and His Circle: A Study in American Literature from 1792 to 1812.* Austin: University of Texas, 1915. vii + 285pp. (Bulletin of the University of Texas, No. 40.)

BIOGRAPHY

JOHN DICKINSON

528. Stille, Charles J. *The Life and Times of John Dickinson, 1732–1808*. Philadelphia: Historical Society of Pennsylvania, 1891. xi + 437pp. (In vol. XIII of *Memoirs* of the Society.)

This still remains a useful discussion of Dickinson. Unlike Franklin and Samuel Adams, Dickinson has not been the subject of extensive biographies.

CHARLES SANFORD DIEHL

529. Diehl, Charles Sanford. *The Staff Correspondent: How the News of the World Is Collected and Dispatched by a Body of Trained Press Writers*. San Antonio, Tex.: Clegg Co., 1931. 297pp.

An autobiography, plus a report on the organization and development of the Associated Press, 1883–1911. Diehl was an assistant general manager of AP. Also treated are Diehl's 10 years of service before 1883 with the Chicago *Times*. A portrait of Wilbur F. Storey is included. Diehl does not go into his own career as owner of the San Antonio *Light*.

J. M. DIXON

530. Dixon, J. M. *The Valley and the Shadow: Comprising the Experiences of a Blind Ex-Editor, a Literary Biography, Humorous Autobiographical Sketches, a Chapter on Iowa Journalism, and Sketches of the West and Western Men*. New York: Russell Bros., 1868. 336pp.

By an early associate editor of the *Iowa State Register*. About a sixth of the content deals with the Iowa press in the years immediately after statehood (1846) and with early-day Des Moines.

EDDIE DOHERTY

531. Doherty, Edward. *Gall and Honey: The Story of a Newspaperman*. New York: Sheed and Ward, 1941. 300pp.

Doherty writes a confessional-type autobiography in telling the story of his experiences with Hearst, Joseph Patterson, and *Liberty Magazine*. His forte was human interest stories.

GEORGE H. DORAN

532. Doran, George H. *Chronicles of Barabbas*. New York and Toronto: Rinehart and Co., 1935 and 1952. xiii + 446pp.

Observations of a book publisher who knew personally and in a business capacity dozens of the nation's authors, editors, and publishers. The 1952 edition includes additional recollections but does not change the 1935 text. Only 50 pages are personal; then follow fascinating descriptions of people of all classes who trafficked in publishing. There are fine thumbnail sketches of George Horace Lorimer, Irvin S. Cobb, H. L. Mencken, Christopher Morley, and others.

FREDERICK DOUGLASS

533. Douglass, Frederick. *Life and Times of Frederick Douglass, Written by Himself*. Hartford, Conn.: Park Publishing Co., 1882. 564pp.

The autobiography of a Negro slave who became one of the leaders in the antislavery movement. Most useful journalistically is the chapter in which Douglass tells of disagreements with the Garrisonians and of his decision to found an antislavery newspaper of his own in Rochester, N.Y. Most biographies of Douglass are more useful than his own story.

534. Chesnutt, Charles W. *Frederick Douglass*. Boston: Small, Maynard and Co., 1899. xix + 141pp. (Beacon Biographies of Eminent Americans.)

Chesnutt was a prominent Negro author and lawyer in North Carolina and Ohio.

535. Holland, Frederic May. *Frederick Douglass, the Colored Orator*. New York: Funk and Wagnalls, 1891. vi + 424pp. (American Reformers Series.)

Not equal to other works on Douglass, despite extensive material on Douglass's *North Star* and Douglass's relations with William Lloyd Garrison.

536. Quarles, Benjamin. *Frederick Douglass*. Washington, D.C.: Associated Publishers, 1948. xi + 378pp.

A scholarly approach to Douglass's career, written originally as a Ph.D. thesis. The volume centers on the *North Star* and *Frederick Douglass' Paper*. The author consulted more than 40 newspapers and periodicals of the Civil War period, many of them abolitionist papers, plus contemporary broadsides.

537. Washington, Booker T. *Frederick Douglass*. Philadelphia and London: George W. Jacobs and Co., 1906. 365pp. (American Crisis Biographies.)

A great Negro of the post-Civil War period writes of the earlier hero of his race. References to the antislavery press are scattered.

THEODORE DREISER

538. Dreiser, Theodore. *A Book about Myself*. New York: Boni and Liveright, 1922. 502pp.

Dreiser's intense self-analysis of his unhappy years as a newspaper reporter in the 1890s in Chicago and elsewhere.

539. Elias, Robert H. *Theodore Dreiser: Apostle of Nature*. New York: Alfred A. Knopf, 1949. xi + 354pp.

Seeks to analyze the apparent contradictions in Dreiser's character and interpret them in relation to his whole career. See Chapter VIII for material on Dreiser's "Editorial Days," particularly with the *Delineator*. The documentation is extensive.

540. Matthiessen, F. O. *Theodore Dreiser*. New York: William Sloane Associates, 1951. vi + 267pp. (American Men of Letters Series.)

Contains a chapter on Dreiser's newspaper days. See also "Ten Years in the Desert," an account of Dreiser's work with Butterick Publications. There are helpful bibliographical notes.

CHARLES B. DRISCOLL

541. Driscoll, Charles B. *Country Jake*. New York: The Macmillan Co., 1946. 256pp.

The successor to O. O. McIntyre in writing the column "New York Day by Day" writes his own autobiography.

WELLS DRURY

542. Drury, Wells. *An Editor on the Comstock Lode*. New York: Farrar and Rinehart, 1936. xx + 343pp. (Foreword by Ella Bishop Drury.)

Reminiscences of a famous editor of the silver-rush days in Virginia City, Nev. Drury tells of his experiences in mining camps, associations with bonanza kings, and impressions of other writers of his time. Mrs. Drury provides a brief biography that includes information on her husband's career in pioneer Oregon and as an editor for Hearst in San Francisco.

WILLIAM DUANE

543. Ford, Worthington C. "Letters of William Duane," in Massachusetts Historical Society *Proceedings*, 2nd Series vol. XX, pp. 257–394. Boston: The Society, 1906–1907.

Exchanges between Duane, from 1798 to 1822 editor of the pro-Jeffersonian *Aurora*, and, principally, Thomas Jefferson and James Madison.

ARTHUR WALLACE DUNN

544. Dunn, Arthur Wallace. *From Harrison to Harding: A Personal Narrative Covering a Third of a Century, 1888–1921*. New York and London: G. P. Putnam's Sons, 1922. 2 vols. 864pp., total.

Dunn was long active in the Gridiron Club of Washington and was one of its past presidents.

FINLEY PETER DUNNE

545. Ellis, Elmer. *Mr. Dooley's America: A Life of Finley Peter Dunne*. New York: Alfred A. Knopf, 1941. x + 310pp.

Dunne, satirically humorous philosopher of American life, captured the nation's attention with his penetrating wit and effective use of dialect early in the century. There is considerable background on Dunne's early career in Chicago.

MAX EASTMAN

546. Eastman, Max. *Enjoyment of Living*. New York and London: Harper and Brothers, 1948. xv + 603pp.

This autobiography of a radical editor, essayist, and poet covers chiefly Eastman's first 40 years. Journalistically most useful is Part VI: "Editor and Revolutionist," in which Eastman discusses his editorship of the *Masses* (1913–1917) and the *Liberator* (1918–1922).

MARY BAKER EDDY

547. Bates, Ernest Sutherland, and John V. Dittemore. *Mary Baker*

Eddy: The Truth and the Tradition. New York: Alfred A. Knopf, 1932. v + 476pp.

Comparatively little of this book gives much information on Mrs. Eddy's publishing activities. The discussion of the Christian Science Publishing Society, *Christian Science Journal,* and *Christian Science Sentinel* is more extensive than that of the *Christian Science Monitor.*

548. Dakin, Edwin Franden. *Mrs. Eddy: The Biography of a Virginal Mind.* New York and London: Charles Scribner's Sons, 1930. x + 563pp.

A painstaking biography of Mrs. Eddy, carefully documented by appendixes and bibliography. The volume is of more than average journalistic value, for it was the center of a "freedom of speech" controversy; publication of Dakin's book was effected in the face of pressures by what Scribner's called an "organized minority" to suppress some of the author's findings. There is extensive material on Mrs. Eddy and the press, in which the "pressure-promotional activities" of the Christian Science Board of Lectureship and its Committee on Publication are described. There is also detail on the investigation into Mrs. Eddy's health by the New York *World* in 1906 and the subsequent sensational human interest story.

549. Powell, Lyman P. *Mary Baker Eddy: A Life-Size Portrait.* New York: The Macmillan Co., 1930. xv + 364pp.

The official biography, approved by the Christian Science Board of Directors. It was prepared by a minister of another denomination. Powell gives more detail on the *Christian Science Monitor* than either Bates and Dittemore or Dakin.

PETER EDES

550. Boardman, Samuel Lane, ed. *Peter Edes, Pioneer Printer in Maine: A Biography.* Bangor, Maine: Printed for the De Burians, 1901. 159pp.

Peter Edes in 1795 printed the first newspaper in what became Augusta, Maine — the *Kennebeck Intelligencer* — and later in Bangor the *Weekly Register.* The book also includes an account of the newspapers of Boston in 1797.

EDWIN FRANCIS EDGETT

551. Edgett, Edwin Francis. *I Speak for Myself: An Editor in His World.* New York: The Macmillan Co., 1940. xi + 385pp.

Edgett spent virtually his whole career on the Boston *Transcript,* as dramatic editor from 1894 to 1899 and as literary editor for 40 years after 1901. He deals widely with literature, art, music, and the theater.

GEORGE CARY EGGLESTON

552. Eggleston, George Cary. *A Rebel's Recollections.* New York: Hurd and Houghton, 1875. lxxv + 260pp.

Eggleston was literary editor of the New York *Evening Post* in Bryant's last years and later an editorial writer on the New York *World*. He had served in the Confederate Army during the Civil War. One of the first of numerous Eggleston books on history and biography, novels, and boys' books, this was directed toward burying animosities between North and South.

553. ———. *Recollections of a Varied Life*. New York: Henry Holt and Co., 1910. viii + 354pp.

A loosely organized autobiography. Dozens of press personalities of the period 1870–1910 are referred to. There is good detail on how Eggleston handled the *World*'s editorials during the second Cleveland administration.

NEGLEY FARSON

554. Farson, Negley. *The Way of a Transgressor*. New York: Harcourt, Brace and Co., 1936. x + 602pp.

A romantic narrative of adventure. At one time or another Farson was an engineer, seller of army and navy supplies to the Russian government, lieutenant in the British Royal Flying Corps, sales manager for Mack Truck, and European correspondent for the Chicago *Daily News*. His story shows little critical perspective.

555. ———. *A Mirror for Narcissus*. New York: Doubleday and Co., 1956. 330pp. London: Victor Gollancz, Ltd., 1956. 302pp.

A continuation of the autobiography begun with *The Way of a Transgressor*. Farson tells of travels through Africa, South America, the United States, and much of Europe.

556. ———. *Transgressor in the Tropics*. New York: Harcourt, Brace and Co., 1938. 305pp.

DEXTER W. FELLOWS

557. Fellows, Dexter W., and Andrew A. Freeman. *This Way to the Big Show: The Life of Dexter Fellows*. New York: Viking Press, 1936. 362pp.

Fellows gives a practical background in public relations — circus style. As a press agent for Ringling Brothers, Barnum and Bailey Combined Shows, he dazzled newspapermen and was dazzled by them.

EDNA FERBER

558. Ferber, Edna. *A Peculiar Treasure*. New York: Doubleday, Doran and Co., 1939. 398pp.

The autobiography of the author of *Show Boat*, *Cimarron*, and other best sellers of the 1920s and 1930s. Miss Ferber, who began her career on the Appleton (Wis.) *Post-Crescent* and Milwaukee *Journal*, provides excellent reading on the *Journal* in a period before it became a nationally famous newspaper.

NAT FERBER

559. Ferber, Nat. *I Found Out: A Confidential Chronicle of the Twenties*. New York: Dial Press, 1939. viii + 351pp.

A Hearst reporter's story. This glib account of an "easy age" in American moral principles deals largely with murders and swindles, jury fixing, and bankruptcies. There is material on Mayor Jimmy Walker of New York and the Seabury inquiry of the late 1920s and early 1930s.

EUGENE FIELD

560. Dennis, Charles H. *Eugene Field's Creative Years*. Garden City, N.Y.: Doubleday, Page and Co., 1924. viii + 339pp.

A sympathetic biography by Field's managing editor on the Chicago *Daily News*. Most of the book concerns Field's *Daily News* activity, 1883–1895, including accounts of his column, "Sharps and Flats," and his relations with publishers.

561. Thompson, Slason. *Eugene Field: A Study in Heredity and Contradictions*. New York: Charles Scribner's Sons, 1901. 2 vols. 695pp., total.

Field's life as told a few years after his death by a close friend and associate on the Chicago *Daily News*. Thompson writes of two Fields: the author and the man.

562. ———. *Life of Eugene Field, the Poet of Childhood*. New York: D. Appleton and Co., 1927. xv + 407pp.

563. Wilson, Francis. *The Eugene Field I Knew*. New York: Charles Scribner's Sons, 1898. 128pp.

Wilson knew Field through association in dramatic activities.

MARSHALL FIELD III

564. Tebbel, John. *The Marshall Fields: A Study in Wealth*. New York: E. P. Dutton and Co., 1947. 320pp.

Tebbel deals chiefly with Marshall Field I and Marshall Field III, who sought to follow liberal courses in journalism with *PM* and the Chicago *Sun*. Approximately half concerns "The Store," or the Fields as builders of wealth; the remainder is on "How to Spend a Fortune," or the third Field's concepts. Tebbel regards Marshall Field III highly. The bibliography lists magazine and newspaper articles on the *Sun* and *PM*, 1940–1945.

JAMES T. FIELDS

565. Austin, James C., ed. *Fields of the Atlantic Monthly: Letters to an Editor, 1861–1870*. San Marino, Calif.: The Huntington Library, 1953. xi + 445pp.

A fine contribution to biography and to magazine history, portraying the life of James T. Fields as publisher (Ticknor and Fields), poet, editor, and essayist. For each sequence of correspondence between Fields and contributors to the *Atlantic* Austin fills in the necessary background. The book is well written and carefully footnoted.

LOUIS FISCHER

566. Fischer, Louis. *Men and Politics: An Autobiography*. New York:

Duell, Sloan and Pearce, 1946. ix + 672pp. (Introduction by Sumner Welles.)

An excellent personal memoir covering Fischer's life as a foreign correspondent, 1921–1939. The emphasis is heaviest on the Soviet Union.

GEORGE FITZHUGH

567. Wish, Harvey. *George Fitzhugh, Propagandist of the Old South.* Baton Rouge: Louisiana State University Press, 1943. ix + 360pp. (Southern Biography Series.)

A competent analysis of a leading proslavery advocate of the 1850s. Fitzhugh was an editorial writer for the Richmond *Examiner*, 1854–1856, and the Richmond *Enquirer*, 1856–1857, and a contributor to *De Bow's Review* and the *Southern Literary Messenger*. The author discusses Fitzhugh's editorial conflicts with the northern press, particularly with Horace Greeley. The book is based upon unpublished manuscripts and contemporary newspapers.

FRANK I. FLETCHER

568. Fletcher, Frank Irving. *Lucid Interval: Confessions of a Custodian of the Convictions of Others.* New York: Harper and Brothers, 1938. xiii + 272pp.

The capricious autobiography of a free-lance advertising copywriter who rebels against the strictures of brevity imposed by his profession. He tells his story as he wants to tell it: he is contrarily verbose and meditative according to his moods.

ARTHUR R. FORD

569. Ford, Arthur R. *As the World Wags On.* Toronto: Ryerson Press, 1950. x + 228pp.

Ford was a prominent Canadian journalist for 50 years, and after 1920 successively managing editor, editor-in-chief, and vice president of the London (Ont.) *Free Press.* He writes also of his extensive experience in Winnipeg, in Ottawa, and as president of Canadian Press, Ltd. He gives a general view of Canadian politics, economic problems, and over-all press developments, and discusses these noted editors: Sir John Willison, John W. Dafoe, M. E. Nichols, and E. H. Macklin.

JOHN W. FORNEY

570. Forney, John W. *Anecdotes of Public Men.* New York: Harper and Brothers, 1873 and 1881. 2 vols. 881pp., total.

Reminiscences of the editor of the Philadelphia *Press* and Washington *Daily Union* during the Civil War. The story is unorganized and wanders widely, yet Forney offers a mine of information involving almost every political, business, and journalistic figure of the period after 1851.

571. Philadelphia Press. *Forty Years of American Journalism: Retirement of Mr. J. W. Forney from the Philadelphia Press.* Philadelphia: Vallette, Haslam and Co., 1877. 80pp.

This pamphlet was issued on the occasion of Forney's sale of the *Press* and is basically a tribute from his staff. More than half of the content consists of editorial praise, mostly from newspapers in Pennsylvania.

WILBUR FORREST

572. Forrest, Wilbur. *Behind the Front Page: Stories of Newspaper Stories in the Making.* New York and London: D. Appleton-Century Co., 1935. viii + 350pp.

A reporter and chief editorial writer for the New York *Herald Tribune* writes of the period from his assignment to Europe in 1915 through the 1920s. Good, but not distinguished work.

GRANVILLE FORTESCUE

573. Fortescue, Granville. *Front Line and Deadline: The Experiences of a War Correspondent.* New York: G. P. Putnam's Sons, 1937. 310pp.

In the Richard Harding Davis tradition, but not equal to Davis in quality. Fortescue, a correspondent for the London *Daily Telegraph* during World War I, writes more about military events themselves than about the reporting of them. There are two chapters on the Spanish Civil War.

GENE FOWLER

574. Fowler, Gene. *A Solo in Tom-Toms.* New York: Viking Press, 1946. 390pp.

This autobiography of the author of *Timber Line* and *Good Night, Sweet Prince* deals almost wholly with Fowler's early years and with his experiences in the Old West; there is interesting material on his service with the Denver *Post.*

BENJAMIN FRANKLIN

575. Franklin, Benjamin. *Autobiography.* ("The Unmutilated and Correct Version," compiled and edited, with notes, by John Bigelow.) New York and London, 1868; new issue, G. P. Putnam's Sons, 1909. v + 325pp.

This work was edited by Bigelow for his collected edition of Franklin's works. At the time, it was presented as the only text based upon Franklin's original manuscript. The *Autobiography,* of course, is among the all-time classics of journalistic literature.

576. ———. *Autobiography of Benjamin Franklin: A Restoration of a "Fair Copy."* Berkeley and Los Angeles: University of California Press, in cooperation with Huntington Library, San Marino, Calif., 1949. xxvii + 210pp. (Preface by Godfrey Davis; introduction and preparation of the restored copy by Max Farrand.)

A scholarly edition of Franklin's *Autobiography* based on four sources: the French translation by Buisson (1791); the edition of Franklin's works edited by a grandson, William Temple Franklin (1817–1818); the John Bigelow edition (1868); and a French translation by Le Veillard in the Library of Congress. The Farrand version probably is the best Franklin text available today.

BIOGRAPHY

577. ———. *Benjamin Franklin's Letters to the Press, 1758–1775.* Chapel Hill: University of North Carolina Press, for the Institute of Early American History and Culture, Williamsburg, Va., 1950. lxv + 308pp. (Collected and edited by Verner W. Crane.)

Eight of these letters to newspapers were written in London on a mission from 1758 to 1761; six in Philadelphia in 1764; and 127 in London on a second mission, 1765–1775. An extensive introduction considers Franklin as a journalist, London newspapers of the pre-Revolutionary period, Franklin's relations with newspaper proprietors, and his use of pseudonyms. Well documented.

578. ———. *Mr. Franklin: A Selection from His Personal Letters.* New Haven: Yale University Press; London: Geoffrey Cumberlege, Oxford University Press, 1956. xxii + 61pp. (Edited by Leonard W. Labaree and Whitfield J. Bell, Jr.)

A commemorative booklet issued on January 17, 1956, the 250th anniversary of Franklin's birth. There are 27 selections from *The Papers of Benjamin Franklin,* a work in progress under the auspices of the American Philosophical Society. The letters include a number on typography.

579. McMaster, John Bach. *Benjamin Franklin as a Man of Letters.* Boston: Houghton Mifflin Co., 1887. ix + 293pp. (American Men of Letters Series.)

The first four chapters, carrying through 1748, give a quick survey of Franklin's journalistic career in Pennsylvania.

580. *New-England Courant, A Selection of Certain Issues Containing Writings of Benjamin Franklin.* Boston: American Academy of Arts and Sciences, 1956. 120pp. of collotypes. (Introduction by Perry Miller.)

Published in honor of the 250th anniversary of Franklin's birth, this includes in addition to Franklin's own issues of the *Courant* those published by him during the imprisonment of his brother James and also all numbers containing Franklin's *Silence Dogood* papers.

581. Oswald, John Clyde. *Benjamin Franklin, Printer.* New York: Doubleday, Page and Co., for Associated Advertising Clubs of the World, 1917. xv + 243pp.

Limited to Franklin's printing activity, as printing was known in the 18th century — printing, editing, publishing, and advertising. There are separate chapters on Franklin as type founder, advertiser, and propagandist, his style and literary works, and the *Pennsylvania Gazette.* Oswald, a recognized historian of printing, was editor of the *American Printer.*

582. Parton, James. *Life and Times of Benjamin Franklin.* Boston: James R. Osgood and Co., 1864. 2 vols. 1334pp., total.

The appendix contains a manuscript record from the General Court of Massachusetts (1722) of proceedings against James Franklin in connection with the activities of Benjamin's half-brother on the *New-England Courant.*

583. Van Doren, Carl. *Benjamin Franklin.* New York: Viking Press, 1938. xix + 845pp.

Still the definitive Franklin biography. Van Doren gives information on James Franklin's *New-England Courant* from a file almost certainly kept by Benjamin and, in addition, includes new material from the *Pennsylvania Gazette*. An extensive general bibliography and notes are exceptionally valuable.

JOSEPH FREEMAN

584. Freeman, Joseph. *An American Testament: A Narrative of Rebels and Romantics.* New York: Farrar and Rinehart, 1936. x + 678pp.

The autobiography of a newspaper reporter and magazine writer associated with liberal organizations. Freeman was a co-founder of the *New Masses* (1926).

PHILIP FRENEAU

585. Austin, Mary S. *Philip Freneau: The Poet of the Revolution.* New York: Wessels, 1901. 285pp. (Edited by Helen Kearny Vreeland.)

Deals more with Freneau's poetry than with his activity as a journalist. The editor was the poet's great-granddaughter.

586. Forman, Samuel E. *The Political Activities of Philip Freneau.* Baltimore: Johns Hopkins Press, 1902. 105pp. (Johns Hopkins Studies in Historical and Political Science, Series XX, nos. 9–10.)

587. Leary, Lewis. *That Rascal Freneau: A Study in Literary Failure.* New Brunswick, N.J.: Rutgers University Press, 1941. x + 501pp.

A comprehensive, probably definitive study on Freneau. Careful attention is given to his association with the *National Gazette*, 1791–1793, and with the *Freeman's Journal*, the *Daily Advertiser*, the *Country Printer*, and the *Time-Piece*. Extensive notes and index.

588. Pattee, Fred Lewis, ed. *The Poems of Philip Freneau, Poet of the American Revolution.* Princeton, N.J.: Princeton University Library, 1902–1907. 3 vols. (Edited for Princeton Historical Assn.)

Pattee footnotes the original sources for Freneau's poems, many of which first appeared in Revolutionary newspapers. Pages xiii–cxii of vol. 1 provide a brief biography.

WILLIAM HENRY FRY

589. Upton, William Treat. *William Henry Fry: American Journalist and Composer-Critic.* New York: Thomas Y. Crowell Co., 1954. xv + 346pp.

The life of the composer of the opera *Leonora* — a composer by preference and a newspaperman by inheritance and training. Fry was a correspondent for the New York *Tribune* and Philadelphia *Public Ledger*, 1852–1864, and was music editor of the *Tribune*. This book is weighted heavily on the music side, although its journalistic value is high, particularly for excerpts from Fry's critiques.

MARGARET FULLER (OSSOLI)

590. Higginson, Thomas Wentworth. *Margaret Fuller Ossoli.* Boston: Houghton Mifflin Co., 1884. 323pp. (Men of Letters Series.)

BIOGRAPHY

Deals chiefly with Miss Fuller's literary life.

591. Stern, Madeleine B. *The Life of Margaret Fuller*. New York: E. P. Dutton and Co., 1942. xvi + 549pp.

A biography of the American feminist of the 1840s who was associated with the Brook Farm group, editor of the *Dial*, and literary critic for Horace Greeley. An outstanding piece of research, the volume is based upon the author's study of Fuller manuscripts.

BESS FURMAN

592. Furman, Bess. *Washington By-Line: The Personal History of a Newspaperwoman*. New York: Alfred A. Knopf, 1949. x + 348pp.

Miss Furman, an Associated Press and New York *Times* reporter in Washington, 1928–1948, tells of White House coverage of the Roosevelts and Trumans, diplomacy, conventions —and more conventions. She emphasizes the excitement and glitter of Washington reporting.

HUGH GAINE

593. Gaine, Hugh. *The Journals of Hugh Gaine, Printer*. New York: Dodd, Mead and Co., 1902. 2 vols. xii + 240pp.; xii + 235pp. (Edited by Paul Leicester Ford.)

Vol. I contains biographical material on this editor of the New York *Mercury* during the Revolutionary period, who was at one time public printer of New York. Emphasized particularly are Gaine's writings on the French and Indian War, the Revolution, and two years of the John Adams administration.

PAUL GALLICO

594. Gallico, Paul. *Confessions of a Story Writer*. New York: Alfred A. Knopf, 1946. x + 576pp.

Partly autobiographical, partly a collection of Gallico's fiction from the *Saturday Evening Post*. The volume includes an explanation of how Gallico came to develop his fiction ideas after 14 years as a newspaperman.

595. ———. *Farewell to Sport*. New York and London: Alfred A Knopf, 1938. 346pp.

Gallico, in leaving sports writing for wider literary pursuits, recalls his years in "this dizzy, spinning, golden world" with nostalgia and affection; at the same time there is a penetrating dissection of hypocrisy and fraud in sports — particularly in college football. Sketches of Babe Ruth, Jack Dempsey, Bobby Jones, and other greats are included.

FRANK GANNETT

596. Williamson, Samuel T. *Imprint of a Publisher: The Story of Frank Gannett and His Independent Newspapers*. New York: Robert M. McBride and Co.; Toronto: George J. McLeod, Ltd., 1948. x + 308pp. (Published earlier as *Frank Gannett: A Biography*. New York: Duell, Sloan and Pearce, 1940. vi + 250pp.)

THE LITERATURE OF JOURNALISM

The authorized life of the publisher of the Gannett newspapers. Clearly eulogistic, although Williamson says, "No restrictions were placed on either subject matter or its handling."

GUY P. GANNETT

597. Zuver, Dudley. *The Lengthened Shadow of a Maine Man: A Biography of Guy P. Gannett.* Freeport and Portland, Maine: Guy P. Gannett Publishing Co. and Bond Wheelwright Co., 1956. 128pp. (American Saga Series.)

Considers Gannett's career with newspapers, in banking and finance, with power companies and utilities, and in public and civic affairs. Gannett's journalistic career centered around three newspapers in Portland, one in Waterville, and one in Augusta. Author Zuver has been an editor for *Harper's.*

WENDELL PHILLIPS GARRISON

598. Garrison, Wendell Phillips. *Letters and Memorials of Wendell Phillips Garrison, Literary Editor of the Nation, 1865–1906.* Cambridge, Mass.: Riverside Press, 1908. xvi + 297pp.

WILLIAM LLOYD GARRISON

599. Garrison, William Lloyd. *Selections from the Writings and Speeches of William Lloyd Garrison.* Boston: R. F. Wallcut, 1852. xii + 416pp.

600. Chapman, John Jay. *William Lloyd Garrison.* New York: Moffatt, Yard and Co., 1913. 278pp.

601. Garrison, Wendell Phillips, and Francis Jackson Garrison. *William Lloyd Garrison, 1805–1879: The Story of His Life Told by His Children.* New York: The Century Co., 1885. 4 vols.

Garrison's sons tried to "co-ordinate materials to serve posterity in forming that judgment of him which we have no desire to forestall." Vols. II and III are most serviceable for Garrison's antislavery crusades. Footnotes and marginal notes are a distinct help.

602. Grimke, Archibald H. *William Lloyd Garrison, the Abolitionist.* New York: Funk and Wagnalls, 1891. ix + 405pp. (American Reformers Series.)

Interesting chiefly because of its authorship, by one of the distinguished Grimke family whose activity in the antislavery movement was in many ways as effective as Garrison's. The volume is based heavily on the life of Garrison by his sons.

603. Johnson, Oliver. *William Lloyd Garrison and His Times: Or, Sketches of the Anti-Slavery Movement in America, and of the Man Who Was Its Founder and Moral Leader.* Boston and New York: Houghton Mifflin Co., 1879. 490pp. (Foreword by John Greenleaf Whittier.)

A biography of considerable value because of the detail with which it treats Garrison's early years. Johnson considers Garrison's relations with Benjamin Lundy; the founding of the *Liberator*; his association with Arthur Tappan;

hostility of the general press toward Garrison; the Lovejoy martyrdom; persecution of James G. Birney; various antislavery editors; and Garrison's religious-society and non-press relationships. Johnson had been associated with Garrison for years as a temporary editor of the *Liberator* and as editor of the *National Anti-Slavery Standard.*

604. Korngold, Ralph. *Two Friends of Man: The Story of William Lloyd Garrison and Wendell Phillips and Their Relationship with Abraham Lincoln.* Boston: Little, Brown and Co., 1950. xii + 425pp.

A joint biography, principally political and social, but the importance of the *Liberator* and other antislavery newspapers is made clear throughout.

605. Nye, Russel B. *William Lloyd Garrison and the Humanitarian Reformers.* Boston and Toronto: Little, Brown and Co., 1955. vi + 215pp. (Library of American Biography, edited by Oscar Handlin.)

Nye sees Garrison's work as symbolic of the moral and ideological conflict in his generation that led to civil war. Garrison's editorial career is subordinated.

606. Phillips, Wendell. *William Lloyd Garrison: Eulogy at the Funeral of Garrison, May 28, 1879.* Boston, 1897. 16pp. (Old South Leaflets, General Series, no. 79, vol. 4.)

Contains also "The Murder of Lovejoy," Phillips's first speech in Faneuil Hall, December 8, 1837.

607. Swift, Lindsay. *William Lloyd Garrison.* Philadelphia: George W. Jacobs Co., 1911. 412pp. (American Crisis Biographies.)

Based principally on secondary sources, with heavy reliance upon the life of Garrison by his sons. Some material is included on Garrison as editor and pamphleteer in the days before the establishment of the *Liberator.*

608. Villard, Fanny Garrison. *William Lloyd Garrison on Non-Resistance.* New York: Nation Press Printing Co., 1924. 79pp.

Five short sketches: Garrison in his daughter's eyes; Garrison's views on non-resistance as expressed in 1838; a review of the *Non-Resistant*, a semimonthly published from 1838 to 1849; a piece by Leo Tolstoi (1904) on "What I Owe to Garrison"; and a tribute to Garrison by his grandson, Oswald Garrison Villard.

EMILE GAUVREAU

609. Gauvreau, Emile. *My Last Million Readers.* New York: E. P. Dutton and Co., 1941. 488pp.

A readable autobiography of the editor of Bernarr Macfadden's New York *Graphic* in the 1920s who, after its demise, became an executive for Hearst on the *Mirror.* Gauvreau has been held in somewhat lower esteem than he perhaps deserves. His life story is more moderate than a reader might expect and contains abundant useful information.

EDWIN F. GAY

610. Heaton, Herbert. *A Scholar in Action: Edwin F. Gay.* Cambridge, Mass.: Harvard University Press, 1952. vi + 260pp.

The life of an educator who was in addition a public official, newspaper president, and research scholar. After serving as the first dean of the Harvard

Graduate School of Business Administration, 1908–1917, Gay was president of the New York *Evening Post*, 1919–1923. The material is of value for the background it gives on the *Post* under Thomas W. Lamont. There is also some information on the launching of the magazine *Foreign Affairs* in 1922, in which Gay had a hand.

MARK J. GAYN

611. Gayn, Mark J. *Journey from the East: An Autobiography*. New York: Alfred A. Knopf, 1944. 426 + viii pp.

The life of a Chinese-born journalist of Russian parents who was educated in Soviet schools, Pomona College (California), and the Columbia School of Journalism. Gayn was a correspondent for the Washington *Post*, for Rengo and Domei, and for the anti-Japanese *China Press* in Shanghai. His book covers chiefly his youth and early career.

FLOYD GIBBONS

612. Gibbons, Edward. *Floyd Gibbons, Your Headline Hunter*. New York: Exposition Press, 1953. xii + 350pp.

In a worshipful book his brother presents Floyd Gibbons as an explorer of the unknown, a prophet who early foresaw Communist plans, and a patriot.

613. Gilbert, Douglas. *Floyd Gibbons: Knight of the Air*. New York: Robert M. McBride Co., 1930. 96pp. (Edited by Burton Rascoe.)

This biography of the World War I correspondent later turned radio reporter moves in staccato style with glimpses of desert sheiks and broadcasting among the Riffs.

CHARLES DANA GIBSON

614. Downey, Fairfax. *Portrait of an Era, as Drawn by C. D. Gibson: A Biography*. New York and London: Charles Scribner's Sons, 1936. xxii + 391pp.

An effort to portray in text and pictures the "magic" of Gibson's pen that made "Gibson illustrations in books and magazines [step] out of *Life* into life." There are more than 200 line-reproductions of Gibson characters, mostly from *Life* and *Collier's*. Gibson's biography is largely a story of the old *Life*.

FRANK B. GILBRETH

615. Gilbreth, Frank Bunker, Jr. *I'm a Lucky Guy*. New York: Thomas Y. Crowell Co., 1951; London: Heinemann, 1952. 239pp.

Gilbreth, author of *Cheaper by the Dozen*, served on the New York *Herald Tribune*, with the Associated Press, and on the Charleston (S.C.) *News and Courier*.

MRS. ELIZABETH GILMER (DOROTHY DIX)

616. Kane, Harnett T., with Ella Bentley Arthur. *Dear Dorothy Dix: The Story of a Compassionate Woman*. Garden City, N.Y.: Doubleday and Co., 1952. 314pp.

BIOGRAPHY

A biography of Elizabeth Meriwether Gilmer, the New Orleans woman who started on the *Picayune* in 1894 by covering vital statistics and writing a salad column and rose to become the most famous lovelorn columnist in the nation. Kane covers Miss Dix's career as one of continuous struggle alternating between anxiety and despair.

EDDY GILMORE

617. Gilmore, Eddy. *Me and My Russian Wife*. New York: Doubleday and Co., 1954. 313pp.

Gilmore, the Associated Press correspondent in Moscow for more than a decade, refuses to pose as a "Russian expert" and offers his autobiography only as one reporter's commentary. His story spans World War II and carries through the period of Joseph Stalin's death.

CARTER GLASS

618. Palmer, James E. *Carter Glass, Unreconstructed Rebel.* Roanoke, Va.: Institute of American Biography, 1938. 320pp.

619. Smith, Rixey, and Norman Beasley. *Carter Glass: A Biography.* New York and Toronto: Longmans, Green and Co., 1939. xv + 519pp. (Preface by Douglas Southall Freeman.)

Glass owned the Lynchburg (Va.) *Daily News* and *Daily Advance*. However, his career was almost wholly political, and there is little in this biography that refers to his journalistic connections.

LAWRENCE A. GOBRIGHT

620. Gobright, Lawrence A. *Recollections of Men and Things at Washington during a Third of a Century*. Philadelphia: Claxton, Remsen, and Haffelfinger, 1869. xi + 420pp.

Gobright was one of the first press association correspondents in the capital. While autobiographical, his account is centered chiefly on the Washington scene, from Jackson-era fisticuffs to the Johnson impeachment. The best material perhaps is Gobright's report of his personal coverage of Lincoln's assassination.

EDWIN LAWRENCE GODKIN

621. Armstrong, William M. *E. L. Godkin and American Foreign Policy, 1865–1900*. New York: Bookman Associates, 1957. 268pp.

A well-documented study of Godkin's attitudes based on a selection of his editorials in the *Nation* and the New York *Evening Post*. Some biographical material is included.

622. Bryce, James. "Edwin Lawrence Godkin," in *Studies in Contemporary Biography*, pp. 363–382. New York and London: The Macmillan Co., 1903.

A penetrating, brief sketch of Godkin's career as founder of the *Nation* and, after 1881, editor of the New York *Evening Post*, written by Britain's noted historian and diplomat.

623. Ogden, Rollo, ed. *Life and Letters of Edwin Lawrence Godkin (with Portraits).* New York and London: The Macmillan Co., 1907. 2 vols. 600pp., total.

Still the best material on the life of Godkin. Ogden, long a colleague of Godkin's, later became editor of the New York *Times*. This is a book worth reading by all who are concerned with the qualities that make for excellence in journalism.

624. Rhodes, James Ford. "Edwin Lawrence Godkin," in *Historical Essays*, pp. 267–297. New York: The Macmillan Co., 1909.

A lecture given at Harvard, April 13, 1908; also published in the *Atlantic Monthly*, September 1908. Rhodes assesses Godkin's contributions to journalism, for the most part favorably.

HYMAN GOLDBERG

625. Goldberg, Hyman. *How I Became a Girl Reporter.* Garden City, N.Y.: Doubleday and Co., 1950. 215pp.

JAMES M. GOODHUE

626. Berthel, Mary Wheelhouse. *Horns of Thunder: The Life and Times of James M. Goodhue, Including Selections from His Writings.* St. Paul: Minnesota Historical Society, 1948. xii + 276pp.

A story of early Minnesota and its prophet, the builder of the *Minnesota Pioneer*, precursor of the present St. Paul *Pioneer Press*. The period is 1848–1852. Among the better regional journalistic histories.

HENRY W. GRADY

627. Grady, Henry W. *The Complete Orations and Speeches of Henry W. Grady.* New York: Hinds, Noble and Eldredge, 1910. v + 233pp. (Edited by Edwin D. Shurter.)

Addresses taken from the files of the Atlanta *Constitution*, and a short biographical account of Grady as an orator. The volume includes the famous speech on "The New South," delivered before the New England Society in 1886.

628. ⸻. *The New South and Other Addresses.* New York: Charles E. Merrill Co., 1904. 136pp. (Edited by Edna Henry Lee Turpin.)

Another issuance of Grady's major speeches. A brief biography and some critical opinions are included.

629. Harris, Joel Chandler. *Life of Henry W. Grady: His Writings and Speeches — a Memorial Volume Compiled by Mr. Henry W. Grady's Co-Workers on the Constitution.* New York: Cassell Publishing Co., 1890. xiii + 628pp.

An uncritical tribute. Henry Watterson wrote the "In Memoriam" and Harris a biographical sketch. The bulk of the work is a compilation of comments on the occasion of Grady's death.

630. Nixon, Raymond B. *Henry W. Grady: Spokesman of the New South.* New York: Alfred A. Knopf, 1943. x + 366 + xiv pp.

The most important and conclusive work on Grady's building of the Atlanta *Constitution*. There is an extensive bibliography of Grady manuscripts, Georgia newspapers of the period of the 1870s and 1880s, and books and articles by and about Grady. Grady's speech on "The New South" is given in full.

631. Terrell, Russell Franklin. *A Study of the Early Journalistic Writings of Henry W. Grady*. Nashville, Tenn.: George Peabody College for Teachers, 1927. 177pp. (Contributions to Education No. 39.)

Sixty-seven selections of Grady's work from the Atlanta *Constitution* and *Herald*, 1869–1883. Terrell analyzes Grady's literary style, his ability as an editorial writer, and his national position in journalism, and reviews his relations with Henry Watterson, Charles A. Dana, and Samuel Bowles III.

JERRY B. GRAHAM

632. Graham, Jerry B. *Handset Reminiscences: Recollections of an Old-Time Printer and Journalist*. Salt Lake City, Utah: Century Printing Co., 1915. 307pp.

A nostalgic narrative of a wandering editor in the half-century before and after the Civil War: from devil in Rochester, N.Y., in the 1850s to composing room work for the elder Bennett's *Herald*; to Nevada silver towns and California; back to New York and Savannah in the Reconstruction; to Michigan in the 1870s and Colorado in the eighties; and finally to his last venture with the Bingham (Utah) *Bulletin* in 1895.

SHEILAH GRAHAM

632a. Graham, Sheilah, and Gerald Frank. *Beloved Infidel: The Education of a Woman*. New York: Henry Holt and Co., 1958. iii + 338pp.

Miss Graham rose from poverty in England and an early career in musical comedy to become a Hollywood correspondent. Primarily, however, this book is concerned with her deep friendship with the writer F. Scott Fitzgerald. Frank, her collaborator, is a newspaperman, magazine editor, and ghost writer.

HORACE GREELEY

633. Greeley, Horace. *Recollections of a Busy Life*. New York: J. B. Ford and Co., 1868. 624pp.

Horace Greeley's own story — rambling, disorganized, utterly honest, completely delightful. Everyone interested in journalism should read it in full. The subtitle covers the book: *Reminiscences of American Politics and Politicians, from the Opening of the Missouri Contest to the Downfall of Slavery; to Which Are Added Miscellanies* — "*Literature as a Vocation,*" "*Poets and Poetry,*" "*Reforms and Reformers,*" "*A Defence of Protection,*" *etc., etc.; Also, a Discussion with Robert Dale Owen of the Law of Divorce.* This is Greeley as he was, and as no one since has pictured him.

634. Bradford, Gamaliel. *As God Made Them: Portraits of Some Nineteenth Century Americans*, pp. 129–167. Boston and New York: Houghton Mifflin Co., 1929.

Fourth among these seven portraits is a sketch of Greeley. The vignette is based almost wholly on works of Parton and Linn and on Greeley's own *Recollections*.

635. Chamberlin, Everett. *The Struggle of '72: The Issues and Candidates of the Present Political Campaign*. Chicago: Union Publishing Co., 1872. 568pp.

Campaign literature, anti-Greeley and pro-Ulysses S. Grant. Subsequent studies have not upheld this negative view of Greeley.

636. Cornell, William M. *The Life and Public Career of Hon. Horace Greeley*. Boston: Lee and Shepard, 1872. 312pp.

A campaign biography based largely on Greeley's *Recollections* and on Parton. Today it is among the least serviceable of books on Greeley. A sketch of B. Gratz Brown, Greeley's vice-presidential running mate, is included.

637. Fahrney, Ralph Ray. *Horace Greeley and the Tribune in the Civil War*. Cedar Rapids, Iowa: Torch Press, 1936. 229pp.

A good specialized study on Greeley's and the *Tribune*'s war influence. Attention is paid to Greeley's break in 1860 with Seward and Weed, to the editor's views on secession and war, on emancipation, on the military struggle from Fredericksburg to Petersburg, and to his connection with the abortive Niagara Peace episode. The volume is based upon unprinted letters and manuscripts, official documents, diaries of contemporaries, and Civil War newspaper files.

638. Hale, William Harlan. *Horace Greeley: Voice of the People*. New York: Harper and Brothers, 1950. xiii + 377pp.

One of many recent books on Greeley, by a working journalist for various magazines and in government service who has been interested in Greeley since childhood. Competently but not inspiringly written.

639. Hall, A. Oakey. *Horace Greeley, Decently Dissected*. New York: Ross and Tousey, 1862. 38pp.

The author takes Greeley apart by turning the *Tribune*'s own words against him. This is valuable today as an example of articulate Democratic opposition to Greeley. Hall, a New York politician, was mayor during the Tweed Ring period.

640. Horner, Harlan H. *Lincoln and Greeley*. Urbana: University of Illinois Press, 1953. vii + 432pp.

A documented study of relations between Lincoln and Greeley, by one who had studied both for more than 40 years. Such hero-worship as there is goes to Lincoln, but affection for Greeley is evident.

641. Ingersoll, L. D. *The Life of Horace Greeley, Founder of the New York Tribune*. Chicago: Union Publishing Co., 1873. 688pp.

A memorial biography, valuable today for its extensive appendix including testimonials of Congress and other public bodies, obituary editorials from metropolitan newspapers, and reprints of numerous public addresses by Greeley. Profusely illustrated.

642. Isely, Jeter Allen. *Horace Greeley and the Republican Party, 1853–1861: A Study of the New York Tribune*. Princeton, N.J.: Princeton University Press, 1947. xiii + 368pp.

An excellent period study. Isely sought to examine everything Greeley wrote in the eight years 1853–1861. He regards the editor as one who must assume a great responsibility for bringing on the Civil War. There are charts on *Tribune* circulation and an extensive bibliography.

643. Johnson, Oliver. *What I Know of Horace Greeley.* New York: Golden Age, 1872. 12pp. (In Golden Age Campaign Tracts.)

Praise of Greeley issued during the campaign of 1872. Johnson was an associate of Garrison's in the abolitionist movement for 30 years. This pamphlet is worth journalistic consideration because of a quarrel surrounding its publication: Johnson had written it for the *Independent*; after acceptance by the managing editor, the piece was rejected by higher authority and then issued by *Golden Age*.

644. Linn, William Alexander. *Horace Greeley: Founder and Editor of the New York Tribune.* New York and London: D. Appleton and Co., 1903; reissued 1912. xiii + 267pp. (Appleton's Historic Lives Series.)

A lesser contribution. Linn worked for Greeley for a time, but his broader service was as news and managing editor of the *Evening Post* under Godkin.

645. Myers, Joseph S. *The Genius of Horace Greeley.* Columbus: Ohio State University Press, 1929. 40pp. (Journalism Series No. 6.)

Seeks to explain Greeley's extraordinary qualities. Entering on the study with an anti-Greeley bias, Myers ended by expressing a certain degree of respect for Greeley.

646. New York Tribune Association. *A Memorial of Horace Greeley.* New York: The Tribune, 1873. 268pp.

Includes obituaries and editorials from the *Tribune*; resolutions and proceedings of public bodies, pulpit, and press; a 14-page biography from the *Tribune Almanac*; and poems dedicated to Greeley. These publications, mostly anonymous, were put into permanent form as a "universal expression of sympathy and homage."

647. Parton, James. *The Life of Horace Greeley, Editor of the New York Tribune.* New York: Mason Brothers, 1855. 442pp.

First of the Greeley biographies, Parton's remains today as good as it was when it appeared more than a century ago. Parton was thorough in interviewing scores of persons then alive who knew Greeley; and he refrained from going to the editor himself and running the danger of losing his objectivity. For a record of Greeley's early years almost every biographer since has leaned on Parton. Considering that the author wrote when Greeley's Civil War influence still lay in the future, the final judgment is significant: "Reader, if you like Horace Greeley, do as well in your place, as he has in his. If you like him not, do better."

648. Reavis, L. U. *A Representative Life of Horace Greeley.* New York: G. W. Carleton and Co.; London: Low and Son, 1872. 579pp. (Introduction by Cassius M. Clay.)

With Parton's, the best contemporary biography. Treats Greeley's career topically: as editor, politician, statesman, man of letters, reformer, and self-made man. Reavis quotes extensively from Greeley's own work and from the *Tribune*. Special attention is paid to the relations between Greeley and Henry

Clay and Margaret Fuller and to Greeley's action in supporting bail bond for Jefferson Davis. Reavis was a St. Louis journalist.

649. Seitz, Don C. *Horace Greeley, Founder of the New York Tribune.* Indianapolis: Bobbs-Merrill Co., 1926. 433pp.

The more recent biographies by Hale and Van Deusen are superior to Seitz's, which also does not match the earlier Parton and Reavis works. Generally Seitz is fair to Greeley.

650. Sotheran, Charles. *Horace Greeley and Other Pioneers of American Socialism.* New York: Humboldt Publishing Co., 1892; reissued, Mitchell Kennerley, 1915. xlviii + 349pp.

The work of an early American socialist who used Greeley as his central figure "to show Socialism in its true colors and as being constructive in its economic philosophy and constitutional in its political action." Sotheran discusses, besides Greeley, Robert Dale Owen, Albert Brisbane, Parke Godwin, and Charles A. Dana.

651. State of New York, Division of Archives and History. *Proceedings at the Unveiling of a Memorial to Horace Greeley at Chappaqua, N.Y., February 3, 1914.* Albany, N.Y., 1915. 263pp.

A centennial book on Greeley published under the auspices of the state historian. It includes material on plans for a statue to Greeley at Chappaqua and the dedication of it; exercises at Greeley's birthplace in New Hampshire; honors to him in Greeley, Colo.; commemorative exercises of Typographical Union No. 6; facsimiles of Greeley manuscripts; extracts of addresses; and a Greeley bibliography.

652. Stoddard, Henry Luther. *Horace Greeley: Printer, Editor, Crusader.* New York: G. P. Putnam's Sons, 1946. xiv + 338pp.

Stoddard portrays Greeley idealistically and persuasively. This is among the more interesting accounts, if not the most authentic.

653. Trietsch, James H. *The Printer and the Prince: A Study of the Influence of Horace Greeley upon Abraham Lincoln as Candidate and President.* New York: Exposition Press, 1955. 332pp.

The author maintains that Lincoln's place in history was established to a great extent as a result of the pressure Greeley exerted on the President, which forced Lincoln to defend administration positions. The book is based upon published writings and Lincoln correspondence; the author lacked access to Greeley manuscripts and copies of the New York *Tribune.*

654. Van Deusen, Glyndon G. *Horace Greeley: Nineteenth Century Crusader.* Philadelphia: University of Pennsylvania Press, 1953. 445pp. (Prepared under the auspices of the American Historical Assn.)

Best by far of recent Greeley biographies. It is adequately illustrated with cartoons of the day and extensively annotated.

655. Wingate, Charles F., ed. *H. G.: 1811–1872. Sketch of the Celebration of the Sixty-First Birthday of the Hon. Horace Greeley, Ll.D., at the Residence of His Intimate Friend, Mr. Alvin J. Johnson, 323 West Fifty-Seventh Street, New York, February 3, 1872; With a Selection*

BIOGRAPHY

*of the Letters Received on That Occasion, Comments of the Press,
Etc.* New York: Privately printed. 1872. 83pp.

Greeley was lionized on his 61st birthday in a great affair undoubtedly tied
to his prospective presidential candidacy.

656. Zabriskie, Francis Nicoll. *Horace Greeley, the Editor.* New York
and London: Funk and Wagnalls Co., 1890. vii + 398pp. (American
Reformers Series.)

A condensed account, in small format. It is based mainly on Greeley's *Recollections*, Parton, and estimates of Greeley issued at the time of his death.

ELIZABETH HIATT GREGORY

657. Gregory, Elizabeth Hiatt. *Show Window of Life.* Los Angeles: Wayside Press, 1944. 160pp.

Recollections of a relatively unknown journalist who was one of the first
women to write aviation stories.

FREDERICK GRIFFIN

658. Griffin, Frederick. *Variety Show: Twenty Years of Watching the
News Parade.* Toronto: The Macmillan Co. of Canada, Ltd., 1936.
xi + 359pp.

Personal reminiscences of a reporter for the Toronto *Star*.

SOLOMON BULKLEY GRIFFIN

659. Griffin, Solomon Bulkley. *People and Politics: Observed by a Massachusetts Editor.* Boston: Little, Brown and Co., 1923. xi + 510pp.

Griffin was a staff member of the Springfield *Daily Republican* all his adult
life, managing editor for 41 years after the death of Samuel Bowles III.

RUFUS W. GRISWOLD

660. Griswold, Rufus W. *Passages from the Correspondence and Other
Papers of Rufus W. Griswold.* Cambridge, Mass.: W. M. Griswold,
1898. 308pp.

This volume is composed mostly of letters covering the period 1841–1857. Griswold was Edgar Allan Poe's literary executor, and the correspondence regarding Poe is most useful. Griswold became editor, after Poe, of *Graham's Lady's
and Gentleman's Magazine*, and later of the *International Magazine*. There
are exchanges between Griswold and Greeley, Raymond, James T. Fields, and
Nathaniel P. Willis. Without prior background on Griswold it is difficult to
put the letters into context.

661. Bayless, Joy. *Rufus Wilmot Griswold: Poe's Literary Executor.*
Nashville, Tenn.: Vanderbilt University Press, 1943. x + 320pp.

A scholarly biography, of which a significant portion relates to Griswold's
antagonistic obituary of Edgar Allan Poe in the New York *Tribune* and to his
subsequent publication and unsympathetic interpretation of Poe's writings.

THE LITERATURE OF JOURNALISM

BEN GROSS

662. Gross, Ben. *I Looked and I Listened.* New York: Random House, 1954. vii + 344pp.

Gross, radio editor of the New York *Daily News*, writes with gusto and joy on how he rose from cub reporter in the early 1920s to become an authority in his field. Woven into the book is a solid portion of radio news history, with helpful accounts of the birth of the networks and "TV and the Future."

BRITON HADDEN

663. Busch, Noel F. *Briton Hadden: A Biography of the Co-Founder of Time.* New York: Farrar, Straus and Co., 1949. 236pp.

An account by Hadden's cousin of the part Henry R. Luce's colleague played in *Time's* first years, from its founding in 1923 to Hadden's death in 1929. The book lacks a table of contents and an index.

DAVID HALE

664. Thompson, Joseph P. *Memoir of David Hale, Late Editor of the Journal of Commerce: With Selections from His Miscellaneous Writings.* New York: John Wiley, 1850. 520pp.

Emphasizes Hale's effort to bring to the *Journal of Commerce* "the principles of sound morality and true independence." A fourth of the book is biography of Hale; the bulk of the remainder consists of Hale's own writings, mostly taken from the *Journal.* The abolitionist issue is treated fully.

SARAH JOSEPHA HALE

665. Entrikin, Isabelle Webb. *Sarah Josepha Hale and Godey's Lady's Book.* Philadelphia: University of Pennsylvania, 1946. vi + 160pp.

Treats of Mrs. Hale's solid contribution to American literary history during her years with *Godey's Lady's Book.*

666. Finley, Ruth E. *The Lady of Godey's: Sarah Josepha Hale.* Philadelphia and London: J. B. Lippincott Co., 1931. 318pp.

Some consideration is given to Louis Antoine Godey, the publisher who made Mrs. Hale's magazine work possible.

JAMES HALL

667. Flanagan, John T. *James Hall: Literary Pioneer of the Ohio Valley.* Minneapolis: University of Minnesota Press, 1941. vii + 218pp.

The life of an early 19th-century lawyer, politician, poet, historian, romancer, literary critic, editor, and banker. Hall, a sincere propagandist for the early Ohio Valley, was editor, among other papers, of the *Illinois Gazette* (Shawneetown), *Illinois Intelligencer* (Vandalia), and *Western Monthly Magazine* (Cincinnati). A well-documented book, with an extensive bibliography of Hall's works.

GERARD HALLOCK

668. Hallock, William H. *Life of Gerard Hallock, Thirty-Three Years*

Editor of the New York Journal of Commerce. New York: Oakley, Mason and Co., 1869. 287pp.

An unintegrated treatment of the life of an associate of David Hale's from the 1820s to 1861. Hallock also was one of the founders of the early Associated Press. There is a highly useful picture of the U.S. press as of 1827, preceding the establishment of the *Journal of Commerce*; also interesting is Hallock's own account of the Civil War controversy that led to his paper's exclusion from the mails.

ANDREW HAMILTON

669. Konkle, Burton Alva. *The Life of Andrew Hamilton, 1676–1741: "The Day-Star of the American Revolution."* Philadelphia: National Publishing Co., 1941. 168pp.

A eulogistic biography of the attorney who defended John Peter Zenger, by an author of numerous monographs on Colonial history. A fifth of the book is devoted to the Zenger trial. The approach is legal rather than journalistic.

670. Loyd, William Henry, Jr. "Andrew Hamilton," in *Great American Lawyers*, vol. I, pp. 1–48. Philadelphia: John C. Winston Co., 1907. (Edited by William Draper Lewis.)

A competent sketch of Hamilton, with about a third of this brief account devoted to the lawyer's part in the Zenger trial. The bulk of the sketch gives material on Hamilton's life not generally included in accounts of the trial.

HUTCHINS HAPGOOD

671. Hapgood, Hutchins. *A Victorian in the Modern World.* New York: Harcourt, Brace and Co., 1939. xiv + 604pp.

An autobiography of the brother of the more widely known Norman Hapgood. Hutchins was a contributor to numerous magazines and reviews, a dramatic critic, and an editorial writer for New York newspapers.

NORMAN HAPGOOD

672. Hapgood, Norman. *The Changing Years: Reminiscences of Norman Hapgood.* New York: Farrar and Rinehart, 1930. ix + 321pp.

A philosophical, essay-type autobiography of a crusading magazine editor, who was with *Collier's Weekly*, 1903–1912, *Harper's*, 1913–1916, and *Hearst's International Magazine*, 1923–1925. There is a significant chapter on Hapgood's interlude with Hearst.

WARREN G. HARDING

673. Cuneo, Sherman A. *From Printer to President: The Story of Warren G. Harding.* Philadelphia: Dorrance, 1922. 153pp.

A simple, worshipful narrative of Harding's life by another Ohio editor who had been his friend for years. Helpful information is given on Harding's small-city newspaper background with the Marion *Star*.

JAMES H. HARE

674. Carnes, Cecil. *Jimmy Hare, News Photographer: Half a Century with a Camera.* New York: The Macmillan Co., 1940. xiii + 304pp.

A biography of a news cameraman who covered the world scene between the Spanish-American War and World War I for *Collier's, Leslie's,* and other publications. The book contains more than 60 of Hare's pictures, the bulk of them war shots.

JEANNE PERKINS HARMAN

675. Harman, Jeanne Perkins. *Such Is Life.* New York: Thomas Y. Crowell Co., 1956. 210pp.

Seven years in the life of a reporter-researcher for *Life.* The author analyzes the grand-scale internal politics of a big magazine, with enough humor to take the edge off her comments. There is a good account of Communist operations within the American Newspaper Guild of New York and the author's part in helping to break up attempts at Communist domination.

J. HENRY HARPER

676. Harper, J. Henry. *I Remember.* New York and London: Harper and Brothers, 1934. 281pp.

Happy, random reminiscences of the grandson of one of the founders of Harper and Brothers. Henry Harper, 84 when he wrote, based his story wholly upon memory.

JOEL CHANDLER HARRIS

677. Wiggins, Robert Lemuel. *The Life of Joel Chandler Harris.* Nashville, Tenn.: Publishing House, Methodist Episcopal Church, South, 1918. iii + 447pp.

The life of the creator of the "Uncle Remus" stories who served for a quarter-century with the Atlanta *Constitution.* A third of the book is biography; the remainder includes Harris's earliest literary efforts and short stories and literary criticisms in the *Constitution,* 1876–1881. There is also a bibliography of articles by Harris in newspapers and periodicals and of books containing sketches of Harris.

CARTER HARRISON

678. Harrison, Carter. *Stormy Years.* Indianapolis and New York: Bobbs-Merrill Co., 1935. 361pp.

Carter Harrison was mayor of Chicago for five terms between 1897 and 1915, while earlier in the 1890s he had been publisher of the Chicago *Times.* References to this newspaper provide helpful background on a phase of Chicago journalism usually overshadowed by the more prominent papers of that day.

MARGUERITE HARRISON

679. Harrison, Marguerite. *There's Always Tomorrow: The Story of a Checkered Life.* New York: Farrar and Rinehart, 1935. viii + 664pp.

The autobiography of a Baltimore newspaperwoman, music and dramatic critic for the *Sun*. It includes an account of her service as agent for an American military intelligence division, of reporting in Germany at the time of the Versailles Treaty, and of the early days of Soviet Russia.

WALTER MUNFORD HARRISON

680. Harrison, Walter Munford. *Me and My Big Mouth*. Oklahoma City: Britton Printing Co., 1954. 415pp.

By a managing editor for 30 years of the Oklahoma City *Daily Oklahoman* and *Times*; more recently Harrison has been editor of an Oklahoma City community journal, the *North Star*. Harrison is enthusiastic, outspoken, intellectually aggressive, and interesting. He gives considerable background on the organization of the Oklahoma Publishing Co., owners of the *Oklahoman* and *Times*, and its publisher, Edward K. Gaylord. Accounts of a generation of Oklahoma political battles are included as well.

ERNEST W. HARROLD

681. Harrold, Ernest W. *The Diary of Our Own Pepys: E. W. Harrold's Record of Canadian Life*. Toronto: The Ryerson Press, 1947. vii + 296pp. (Edited by I. Norman Smith.)

A condensation of a Pepys-style diary run in the Ottawa *Citizen*, 1930–1945. Harrold was associate editor from 1923 to his death in 1945 and had been on the staff since 1913. The author principally reflects upon life in Ottawa.

BRET HARTE

682. Harte, Bret. *The Letters of Bret Harte*. Boston and New York: Houghton Mifflin Co., 1926. xviii + 515pp. (Assembled and edited by Geoffrey Bret Harte.)

The letters cover the period 1866–1902. Most of these are from Harte's post-California years and have little bearing on journalism.

683. Merwin, Henry Childs. *The Life of Bret Harte: With Some Account of the California Pioneers*. London: Chatto and Windus, 1912. xii + 362pp.

More than half of this book concerns Harte's early life in California. There is a good discussion of Harte's work as first editor of the *Overland Monthly* and of newspapermen in early California.

GEORGE B. HARVEY

684. Harvey, George B. *Women, Etc.: Some Leaves from an Editor's Diary*. New York: Harper and Brothers, 1908. 231pp.

The editor of *Harper's Weekly* and owner of the *North American Review* writes about women and their attributes: friendship, loquacity, obstinacy, etc. Light reading.

685. Johnson, Willis Fletcher. *George Harvey: A Passionate Patriot*.

THE LITERATURE OF JOURNALISM

London: George Allen and Unwin, Ltd., 1930. x + 436pp. (Introduction by Calvin Coolidge.)

In the first quarter of the 20th century Harvey as editor of *Harper's Weekly* was one of the nation's most active political-magazine journalists. Eventually he became Warren G. Harding's ambassador to Great Britain. Politics and journalism are evenly balanced in this biography.

T. N. HASSELQUIST

686. Ander, Oscar Fritiof. *T. N. Hasselquist*. Rock Island, Ill., 1931. 260pp. (Augustana Library Publications No. 14.)

The life of a clergyman who while taking a leading role in developing the Swedish Lutheran Church in the United States, 1852–1891, was associated with several newspapers. He founded *Hemlandet* in Galesburg, Ill., in 1855, and later was active on *Det Ratta Hemlandet*.

JACK HASTY

687. Hasty, Jack. *Done with Mirrors: Admissions of a Free-Lance Writer*. New York: Ives Washburn, 1943. xiii + 337pp. (Foreword by Sheila Barrett.)

Hasty deals mostly with radio and movie-script writing and with directing and producing, but he also did free-lance work for advertising agencies, magazines, and newspapers.

ANTHONY HASWELL

688. Spargo, John. *Anthony Haswell: Printer, Patriot, Ballader; A Biographical Study with a Selection of His Ballads and an Annotated Bibliographical List of His Imprints*. Rutland, Vt.: The Tuttle Co., 1925. xv + 293pp.

A beautiful collector's item by the president of the Bennington Battle Monument Association, containing the full story of Haswell as pamphleteer and editor of the *Vermont Gazette*. There is a thorough discussion of his trial and conviction of violating the Sedition Act of 1798. The bibliography is impressive.

VIOLET SWEET HAVEN

689. Haven, Violet Sweet. *Many Ports of Call*. New York and Toronto: Longmans, Green and Co., 1940. v + 250pp.

A Washington State and Idaho girl's experiences as a teacher and newspaperwoman, from "shoe-string travel and reporting" to fashion writing on the *Japan Times and Mail* and a press flight on the Atlantic Clipper in 1939.

JOHN HAY

690. Thayer, William Roscoe. *The Life and Letters of John Hay*. Boston and New York: Houghton Mifflin Co., 1915. 2 vols. 904pp., total.

A biography of Abraham Lincoln's personal secretary who became secretary of state under Theodore Roosevelt. Vol. I contains accounts of Hay's experience in journalism, 1870–1874, as an editorial writer for the New York *Tribune*. A good index lists other connections of Hay with journalism and literature.

LAFCADIO HEARN

691. Lawless, Ray McKinley. *Lafcadio Hearn: Critic of American Life and Letters*. Chicago: University of Chicago, 1942. 148pp. (Ph.D. Dissertations on Literature and Art, No. 4.)

Examines Hearn's comments on American men of letters. There is a useful bibliography of Hearn's magazine articles and newspaper pieces for the Cincinnati *Commercial*, Cincinnati *Enquirer*, New Orleans *Item*, and New Orleans *Times-Democrat*.

692. McWilliams, Vera. *Lafcadio Hearn*. Boston: Houghton Mifflin Co., 1946. ix + 465pp.

Considerable research went into this comprehensive treatment of Hearn. The author includes a mass of Hearn's journalistic material. His New York, New Orleans, and Cincinnati experiences are recorded in full.

693. Tinker, Edward L. *Lafcadio Hearn's American Days*. New York: Dodd, Mead and Co., 1924. xiv + 374pp.

GEORGE HEARST

694. Older, Mr. and Mrs. Fremont. *The Life of George Hearst, California Pioneer*. San Francisco: Privately printed for William Randolph Hearst by John Henry Nash, 1933. 238pp.

A eulogistic biography of William Randolph Hearst's father, with the book's chief merit being its artistic gold-leaf, deckle-edged format. However, it does give necessary background on W. R. Hearst's heritage and an account of George Hearst's purchase of the San Francisco *Examiner* and his installation of the son as editor.

WILLIAM RANDOLPH HEARST

695. Hearst, William Randolph. *William Randolph Hearst: A Portrait in His Own Words*. New York: Simon and Schuster, 1952. x + 309pp. (Edited by Edmond D. Coblentz.)

Hearst's views on many subjects as evidenced in his writings and messages. Edited by a Hearst executive of many years, this is a frank vindication of "The Chief." Coblentz contributed necessary interpolations for background and sequence but the bulk is Hearst — on such diverse topics as politics, economics, philosophy, sociology, and religion.

696. ———. *Selections from the Writings and Speeches of William Randolph Hearst*. San Francisco: Privately published, 1948. xxxi + 765pp. (Compiled by E. F. Tompkins.)

About 400 extracts, arranged topically, but with no explanations to give background to Hearst's subject matter. Hearst on agriculture, Americanism, anti-Semitism, business, censorship, communism, democracy, education, fascism, foreign affairs, immigration, journalism, labor relations, national defense and security, politics, public morals, religion, tariff, taxation, two world wars, and youth. Editor Tompkins is a Hearst editorial writer.

697. Carlson, Oliver, and Ernest Sutherland Bates. *Hearst: Lord of San Simeon.* New York: Viking Press, 1936. xv + 332pp.

The most useful of the Hearst biographies prepared during the publisher's lifetime. Carlson and Bates attribute a "feudal" nature to Hearst, but the treatment in general is fair. Hearst is considered as capitalist, journalist, and politician; his private life is also discussed.

698. Lundberg, Ferdinand. *Imperial Hearst: A Social Biography.* New York: Equinox Co-operative Press, 1936. xvi + 406pp. (Preface by Charles A. Beard.)

Severest of the contemporary indictments of Hearst. Beard too was harsh, advocating "ostracism" and "oblivion." The book is detailed as to the financial, political, and social effects of Hearst.

699. Older, Mrs. Fremont. *William Randolph Hearst: American.* New York and London: D. Appleton-Century Co., 1936. xiii + 581pp.

The most favorable and, likewise, most uncritical of the Hearst biographies. It is based for the most part on family friendships, for Mrs. Older's husband was employed by Hearst, and on material from numerous persons within the Hearst organization.

700. Tebbel, John. *The Life and Good Times of William Randolph Hearst.* New York: E. P. Dutton and Co., 1952. 386pp.

Published a year after Hearst's death, this is perhaps the best balanced treatment. Although he confirms the view that Hearst worked incalculable harm to the press, Tebbel considers good with bad. There is a full discussion of all facets of Hearst's life — how he ran his businesses, his relations with women, his presidential ventures — and an interpretation of the works of earlier biographers.

701. Winkler, John K. *W. R. Hearst: An American Phenomenon.* New York: Simon and Schuster, 1928. 355pp.

First of the biographies issued during the publisher's lifetime; now superseded by Winkler's own revision (702).

702. ———. *William Randolph Hearst: A New Appraisal.* New York: Hastings House, 1955. viii + 325pp.

The most recent Hearst biography, although in effect a bringing up to date of Winkler's earlier work. The appraisal is favorable, with Hearst characterized as "an individual of such towering ability and diversified talents as to assume not only leadership but domination of his chosen field." Winkler fails to match the work of the more critically minded Tebbel. Typographically attractive, the book is illustrated with a "Hearst Family Album." Only about 20 per cent of the text is new material.

S. BURTON HEATH

703. Heath, S. Burton. *Yankee Reporter.* New York: Wilfred Funk, 1940. 391pp.

BIOGRAPHY

Heath won a Pulitzer Prize in 1940 for reportorial investigations resulting in the conviction of a federal circuit judge in New York on criminal charges. Out of his years as a reporter for the New York *World-Telegram* come good descriptions of Fiorello La Guardia, Thomas E. Dewey, and Gov. Franklin D. Roosevelt, plus an analysis of freedom of the press at the local level.

BEN HECHT

704. Hecht, Ben. *A Child of the Century*. New York: Simon and Schuster, 1954. 654pp.

> The autobiography of one of the reporters who came out of the Chicago of the 1910s and 1920s. The meat of the book lies in 247 pages devoted to "Chicago" and "I Was a Reporter." A long discussion of Sherwood Anderson, Theodore Dreiser, Carl Sandburg, and Charles MacArthur is interesting.

KARL HEINZEN

705. Wittke, Carl. *Against the Current: The Life of Karl Heinzen (1809–1880)*. Chicago: University of Chicago Press, 1945. x + 342pp.

> A scholarly study of a radical German-American editor who came to the United States after the Revolution of 1848. Heinzen never became prosperous running his newspapers, of which *Der Pionier* was the most important, but he fought for 25 years against slavery and militarism, and for political and social reform.

MARK HELLINGER

706. Bishop, Jim. *The Mark Hellinger Story: A Biography of Broadway and Hollywood*. New York: Appleton-Century-Crofts, 1952. xv + 367pp.

> An oversentimentalized biography of a New York *Mirror* and King Features Syndicate columnist and Hollywood producer. There are vivid pictures of razzle-dazzle journalism in the 1920s and 1930s.

ERNEST HEMINGWAY

707. Fenton, Charles A. *The Apprenticeship of Ernest Hemingway: The Early Years*. New York: Farrar, Straus and Young, 1954. xi + 302pp.

> The author traces Hemingway's literary apprenticeship, 1916–1925, which included long periods as a working newspaperman in Oak Park, Ill., Kansas City, Toronto, Chicago, and Western Europe.

R. H. HENRY

708. Henry, R. H. *Editors I Have Known since the Civil War*. Jackson, Miss.: Jackson Clarion Ledger, 1922. 434pp.

> For 50 years the author owned and edited the *Clarion-Ledger* in Jackson. He knew dozens of southern editors, and he fills his pages with all their names. The book is little more than a collection of miscellany.

THE LITERATURE OF JOURNALISM

MARGUERITE HIGGINS

709. Higgins, Marguerite. *News Is a Singular Thing*. Garden City, N.Y.: Doubleday and Co., 1955. 256pp.

Miss Higgins has been perhaps the most successful woman reporter of the World War II and postwar period. She emphasizes the latter days of the war against Germany and then the Korean War; how she became a bureau chief for the New York *Herald Tribune* in Berlin; and how generals and political leaders can get along with the press. She is blunt and forthright.

SIR FRANCIS HINCKS

710. Hincks, Sir Francis. *Reminiscences of His Public Life*. Montreal: William Drysdale and Co., 1884. 450pp.

In 1839, as an aftermath of political crisis in Canada, Hincks established the Toronto *Examiner* on the principle of moderate liberalism and "responsible government." He deals mostly with political and economic issues; for a short time in the 1850s he was prime minister and in 1869 was Canada's finance minister. In his last years he was editor of the Montreal *Journal of Commerce*.

MARY EVELYN HITCHCOCK (MARY DOYLE)

711. Hitchcock, Mary Evelyn [pseud. Mary Doyle]. *Life Was Like That*. Boston: Houghton Mifflin Co., 1936. 256pp.

The entertaining autobiography of a woman who started with the Floradora Company early in the century and later became a reporter for the New York *World*.

LAWRENCE K. HODGES

712. Hodges, Lawrence Kaye. *Twenty Eventful Years*. New York: Wilson-Erickson, 1937. xiv + 523pp.

Of high regional value. Hodges was chief editorial writer of the Portland *Oregonian*, 1913–1933. The book is mainly a compilation of his editorials. Paul Kelty, editor of the *Oregonian*, sketches Hodges's career.

HENRY HOLT

713. Holt, Henry. *Garrulities of an Octogenarian Editor: With Other Essays Somewhat Biographical and Autobiographical*. Boston and New York: Houghton Mifflin Co., 1923. viii + 460pp.

For the most part this volume reprints material that Holt had written about himself for periodicals. Commentary on E. L. Godkin is included. The author was the founder of Henry Holt and Co.

CLAUDE HOPKINS

714. Hopkins, Claude. *My Life in Advertising*. New York and London: Harper and Brothers, 1936. 9th edition. 206pp. (First issued in 1927.)

"Helpful suggestions to those who will follow me," by a national advertising agent once associated with Lord and Thomas. He tells of activities on behalf of automobiles and tires, Palmolive, mail order houses, puffed grains and Quaker Oats, and Pepsodent. Full of braggadocio.

HENRY BEETLE HOUGH

715. Hough, Henry Beetle. *Country Editor*. New York: Doubleday, Doran and Co., 1940. viii + 325pp.

On the joys and problems of publishing a small newspaper in Massachusetts. Hough was editor of the *Martha's Vineyard Gazette* after 1920; the paper had a history dating from 1846.

716. ———. *Once More the Thunderer*. New York: Ives Washburn, 1950. 316pp.

Second of the author's accounts of life on the *Martha's Vineyard Gazette*, this one dealing with memories after Hough had completed 30 years with the newspaper.

BOYCE HOUSE

717. House, Boyce. *Cub Reporter: Being Mainly about Mr. Mooney and the Commercial Appeal*. Dallas, Tex.: Hightower Press, 1947. 175pp.

Recollections of a period in southern journalism "now gone forever." House pays unbounded tribute to Charles Patrick Joseph Mooney, editor of the Memphis *Commercial Appeal*. Police reporting is treated at length.

EDGAR WATSON HOWE

718. Howe, E. W. *Plain People*. New York: Dodd, Mead and Co., 1929. 317pp.

By the editor of the Atchison (Kan.) *Globe*, 1877–1911, and of Howe's *Monthly*, 1911–1937. Although outwardly a simple story of a small-city editor, the book has philosophical depth and reveals Howe's feeling of discontent with the world as it is.

JOSEPH HOWE

719. Grant, William Lawson. *The Tribune of Nova Scotia: A Chronicle of Joseph Howe*. Toronto: Glasgow, Brook and Co., 1935. xi + 163pp. (Vol. 26 of The Chronicles of Canada.)

The life of a mid-19th-century Nova Scotian — politician, editor, and governor of the province at the time of his death in 1873. Howe as a young man in 1827 purchased the *Acadian* in Halifax and a year later bought the larger *Nova Scotian*.

720. Longley, J. W. *Joseph Howe*. Toronto: Morang and Co., Ltd., 1909. 307pp. (Vol. XII in The Makers of Canada, Parkman edition.)

A political biography, with only limited reference to Howe's journalistic activities.

WILLIAM DEAN HOWELLS

721. Howells, William D. *My Mark Twain: Reminiscences and Criticisms*. New York and London: Harper and Brothers, 1910. 187pp.

The first half of this book is biography-autobiography, a record of 44 years of friendship between Howells and Samuel L. Clemens. The second half consists of reviews of Mark Twain's books in the *Atlantic, Century, Harper's,* and *North American Review,* 1869–1901.

722. ———. *Years of My Youth.* New York and London: Harper and Brothers, 1916. 239pp.

This autobiography covers Howells's experiences from childhood (born 1837), through his active newspaper career in Ohio as a young man, to the 1860s. Much is on Columbus and the *Ohio State Journal.*

723. Firkins, Oscar W. *William Dean Howells: A Study.* Cambridge, Mass.: Harvard University Press, 1924. viii + 356pp.

Contains a helpful, brief sketch of Howells's life, with separate studies relating to his novels, plays, poems, criticism, style, and humor. There is little on his journalistic activities.

FRANK McKINNEY HUBBARD

724. Kelly, Fred C. *Life and Times of Kin Hubbard, Creator of Abe Martin.* New York: Farrar, Straus and Young, 1952. 179pp.

Frank McKinney Hubbard spent almost his whole journalistic career as caricaturist and paragrapher on the Indianapolis *News,* 1891–1930. His "Abe Martin's Sayings" were widely syndicated and were published annually in book form.

WILLIAM CADWALADER HUDSON

725. Hudson, William Cadwalader. *Random Recollections of an Old Political Reporter.* New York: Cupples and Leon Co., 1911. 271pp. (Introduction by St. Clair McKelway.)

Hudson was with the Brooklyn *Eagle* for 44 years. His reminiscences run from 1868 to 1886 and include views of "Boss" Tweed, William T. Tilden, Roscoe Conkling, James A. Garfield, Chester A. Arthur, Theodore Roosevelt, James G. Blaine, and David B. Hill.

FRAZIER HUNT

726. Hunt, Frazier. *One American and His Attempt at Education.* New York: Simon and Schuster, 1938. viii + 400pp.

The autobiography of a foreign correspondent who went to France and Russia for the New York *Sun* in World War I and was also a correspondent for the Chicago *Tribune.* He gives accounts of the Bolshevik Revolution and the postwar period down to the early 1930s.

RALPH INGERSOLL

727. Gibbs, Wolcott. "A Very Active-Type Man," in *New Yorker,* vol. 18, nos. 11 and 12 (May 2 and May 9, 1942), pp. 21–30 and 21–30.

A profile of the editor of *PM.*

BIOGRAPHY

WASHINGTON IRVING

728. Irving, Washington. *Letters of Jonathan Oldstyle*. New York: Columbia University Press, for Facsimile Text Society, 1941. xx + x + 67pp.

Irving early in the 19th century wrote for the New York *Morning Chronicle*. The Jonathan Oldstyle letters were satirical pieces on social and theatrical New York which gained him some distinction, despite his youth and the amateurishness of the writing. This publication is from an edition of 1824.

WILL IRWIN

729. Irwin, Will. *The Making of a Reporter*. New York: G. P. Putnam's Sons, 1942. 439pp.

The life of a newspaperman–magazine writer in the early years of the 20th century. Worth reading for its descriptions of San Francisco in the 1900s, the New York *Sun*, muckraking for *McClure's* and *Collier's*, and war correspondence in 1917–1918, and for its comments on Herbert Hoover, Irwin's lifelong friend.

DEAN S. JENNINGS

730. Jennings, Dean S. *Leg Man*. Hollywood, Calif.: George Palmer Putnam, 1940. xi + 252pp.

Ephemeral. Jennings, a reporter for the San Francisco *Bulletin* and *Chronicle* and for the Paris *Herald*, recounts stories gathered on his news beats but not previously printed.

ORRICK JOHNS and GEORGE SIBLEY JOHNS

731. Johns, Orrick. *Time of Our Lives: The Story of My Father and Myself*. New York: Stackpole Sons, 1937. 353pp.

A biography of George S. Johns, for years editor of the St. Louis *Post-Dispatch*, and an autobiography of his son, one-time editor of the *New Masses*. The treatment of the father's life is more significant than that of the son's. There is good detail on struggles of news writers during the Depression and on the Federal Writers' Project, which Orrick Johns headed in New York for a time.

ROBERT UNDERWOOD JOHNSON

732. Johnson, Robert Underwood. *Remembered Yesterdays*. Boston: Little, Brown and Co., 1923. xxi + 624pp.

Johnson was on the staff of the *Century* for 40 years, 1873–1913, and was editor from 1909 to 1913. His autobiography ranges widely: from the *Century's* accounts of the Civil War and battles for international copyright to travel sketches and views of several dozen literary figures of the time.

CHARLES and EUGENE JONES

733. Jones, Charles, and Eugene Jones. *Double Trouble: The Autobiography of the Jones Twins*. Boston: Little, Brown and Co., 1952. 317pp.

This pair of youthful photographers tell of their identification difficulties in working for different newspapers in the same city, on one occasion Charles for the New York *Mirror* and Gene for the New York *Daily News*; on another, Charles for the Washington *Daily News* and Gene for the Washington *Times-Herald*.

ELIZABETH JORDAN

734. Jordan, Elizabeth. *Three Rousing Cheers*. New York and London: D. Appleton-Century Co., 1938. xiii + 403pp.

An appealing autobiography — uncritical, gentle, and sincere — of a woman who was a reporter for the New York *World* in the 1880s and 1890s, editor of *Harper's Bazaar* early in the 20th century, critic, novelist, and playwright. Miss Jordan gives good portraits of the *World* and its staff under Joseph Pulitzer.

H. V. KALTENBORN

735. Kaltenborn, H. V. *Fifty Fabulous Years, 1900–1950: A Personal Review*. New York: G. P. Putnam's Sons, 1950. viii + 312pp.

Kaltenborn was one of the earliest radio news commentators, serving successively with CBS and NBC after 1930. He gives an account of radio's troubles in the 1920s over the voicing of opinions on the air. The first part of his book deals with his newspaper work as a reporter and editor on the Brooklyn *Eagle* for more than a quarter-century.

736. ———. *It Seems like Yesterday*. New York: G. P. Putnam's Sons, 1956. 220pp.

An illustrated personal narrative of the radio-television critic and commentator, who recalls world events since the William Jennings Bryan campaign of 1896.

JAMES KEELEY

737. Linn, James Weber. *James Keeley: Newspaperman*. Indianapolis and New York: Bobbs-Merrill Co., 1937. 286pp.

The life of the managing editor of the Chicago *Tribune* from 1900 to 1914. Linn reveals how a hard-hitting news executive became a supporter of "respectability" when he moved over to the Chicago *Herald*.

FLORENCE FINCH KELLY

738. Kelly, Florence Finch. *Flowing Stream: The Story of Fifty-Six Years in American Newspaper Life*. New York: E. P. Dutton and Co., 1939. xvi + 571pp.

A staff member of the New York *Times Book Review* for 30 years, Mrs. Kelly was also a novelist and short-story writer and analyst of America's contributions in World War I. There is much of value here on book reviewing and women in journalism and on three publishers who resurrected moribund newspapers — Taylor of the Boston *Globe*, Hearst of the San Francisco *Examiner*, and Ochs of the New York *Times*.

BIOGRAPHY

AMOS KENDALL

739. Kendall, Amos. *Autobiography of Amos Kendall*. Boston: Lee and Shepard, 1872; New York: Lee, Shepard and Dillingham, 1872. ix + 700pp. (Edited by William Stickney.)

A minutely detailed life of Andrew Jackson's postmaster-general, kitchen-cabinet adviser, newspaper supporter, and friend, who was an influence in United States affairs from Monroe's day to the Civil War. There is good detail on Jackson's quarrel with Duff Green over the *United States Telegraph* and the subsequent establishment of the Washington *Globe*. The volume also includes comments on Francis P. Blair, William Duane, James Gordon Bennett Sr., and Thomas Ritchie. Editor Stickney was Kendall's son-in-law.

GEORGE WILKINS KENDALL

740. Copeland, Fayette. *Kendall of the Picayune: Being His Adventures in New Orleans, on the Texan Santa Fe Expedition, in the Mexican War, and in the Colonization of the Texas Frontier*. Norman: University of Oklahoma Press, 1943. 351pp.

A well-written and scholarly life of the founder of the New Orleans *Picayune* (1837). Draws upon Kendall family papers covering nearly half a century, federal and Texas documents, and files of three dozen newspapers in the South, the East, and Mexico. The body of the book concerns the pre-Civil War period, but Copeland adds the story of Kendall's resurrection of the *Picayune* in the turmoil of New Orleans during Reconstruction.

MARY KNIGHT

741. Knight, Mary. *On My Own*. New York: The Macmillan Co., 1938. ix + 374pp.

Miss Knight's theme is the handicap of being a woman. Nevertheless she made her way in the newspaper world, serving abroad for the United Press and in the United States for the New York *World-Telegram*.

FRANK KNOX

742. Beasley, Norman. *Frank Knox, American: A Short Biography*. Garden City, N.Y.: Doubleday, Doran and Co., 1936. 184pp.

Issued during the Landon-Knox presidential campaign. Beasley pictures Knox as a crusader from his days as a Rough Rider through editorships in Sault Ste. Marie, Mich.; Manchester, N.H.; and Chicago (where he was owner of the *Daily News*).

MOSES KOENIGSBERG

743. Koenigsberg, Moses. *King News: An Autobiography*. Philadelphia and New York: Frederick A. Stokes Co., 1941. 511pp.

By a Hearst executive, organizer of King Features Service in 1916. The volume gives considerable background on Hearst newspapers in Boston, Chicago, and New York, as well as on syndicates and press associations. There is extensive commentary on William Randolph Hearst. One of the better books by those high in the Hearst organization.

JACK KOFOED

744. Kofoed, Jack. *Leg Man in Seven-League Boots*. Coral Gables, Fla.: Glade House, 1946. 167pp. (Illustrated by Crawford Parker.)

A good light autobiography, with sketches of the sundry creatures whom a newspaperman meets. Kofoed served on the staff of the New York *Telegram*, New York *Post*, and other newspapers.

HERMAN KOHLSAAT

745. Kohlsaat, Herman H. *From McKinley to Harding: Personal Recollections of Our Presidents*. New York and London: Charles Scribner's Sons, 1923. x + 241pp.

Kohlsaat's personal report of his influence on and friendships with presidents. Only rarely does he bring in the newspapers with which he was associated, the Chicago *Inter-Ocean* and *Record-Herald* — and then merely to give necessary news and editorial information regarding political developments. There are fascinating personal accounts of William McKinley and Theodore Roosevelt.

IRENE KUHN

746. Kuhn, Irene. *Assigned to Adventure*. Philadelphia: J. B. Lippincott Co., 1938. 432pp.

Miss Kuhn started as a cub in Syracuse, N.Y., and later handled the rewrite desk of the New York *Daily News*. In a modest fashion she gives accounts of work on the Paris edition of the Chicago *Tribune* after World War I and on the New York *World-Telegram*, and sketches of Hollywood.

GERARD LAMBERT

747. Lambert, Gerard. *All Out of Step*. New York: Doubleday and Co., 1956. 316pp.

The life of the author of "Even Your Best Friend Won't Tell You!" Lambert's advertising agency made halitosis famous. His is an extravagant book ranging in subject from Gillette razor campaigns to public opinion polling and work for the Institute for International Social Research.

RING LARDNER

748. Elder, Donald. *Ring Lardner*. Garden City, N.Y.: Doubleday and Co., 1956. 409pp.

A painstaking biography of a sports and fiction writer of the early 20th century. There are numerous and extended selections from Lardner's work and from his personal letters, plus a complete list of all his published work.

VICTOR LAWSON

749. Dennis, Charles H. *Victor Lawson: His Time and His Work*. Chicago: University of Chicago Press, 1935. xi + 471pp.

BIOGRAPHY

A semiofficial biography of the editor-owner of the Chicago *Daily News* by an editorial associate. Dennis had access to Lawson's letters and memoranda, his own files as a *News* executive, and materials from other colleagues. There are useful chapters on early *Daily News* columnists, the early days of the Linotype, the establishment of the *News* foreign service, and the organization of the modern Associated Press.

FRANK A. LEACH

750. Leach, Frank A. *Recollections of a Newspaperman: A Record of Life and Events in California.* San Francisco: Samuel Levinson, 1917. 416pp.

Reminiscences of 65 years, from pioneer days to World War I. Leach established the Napa (Calif.) *Daily Reporter*, the Vallejo *Review*, and the Vallejo *Evening Chronicle*, and held an interest in the Oakland *Enquirer*. There is much on the San Francisco earthquake and fire of 1906.

CHARLES G. LELAND

751. Leland, Charles Godfrey. *Memoirs.* New York: D. Appleton and Co., 1893. x + 439pp.

An effort at "candid autobiography," which the author rather doubted could be written. The volume covers a many-faceted career in literature, journalism, and linguistics. Leland's work included contributions to *Graham's Magazine*; assistant editorship of the Philadelphia *Bulletin*; associate editorship of P. T. Barnum's *Illustrated News*; and service on John W. Forney's Philadelphia *Press*. See particularly Leland's discussion of his career as managing editor of the Philadelphia *Press*, 1866–1869.

752. Pennell, Elizabeth Robins. *Charles Godfrey Leland.* Boston and New York: Houghton Mifflin and Co., 1906. 2 vols. 891pp., total.

The author, Leland's niece, based her biography to a considerable extent upon her uncle's memoirs.

MRS. FRANK LESLIE

753. Stern, Madeleine B. *Purple Passage: The Life of Mrs. Frank Leslie.* Norman: University of Oklahoma Press, 1953. 281pp.

A biography of the much-married, highly capable force behind the Leslie Publications. The title is appropriate, yet the book is more solid in content than it may suggest. The author dug into scores of primary sources on Frank Leslie and his wife, and she provides a full listing of Mrs. Leslie's extensive writings and a check list of Leslie magazines.

FULTON LEWIS, JR.

754. Herndon, Booton. *Praised and Damned: The Story of Fulton Lewis, Jr.* New York: Duell, Sloan and Pearce; Boston: Little, Brown and Co., 1954. 147pp. (Edited by Gordon Carroll.)

Fulsome praise of radio commentator Lewis, whose support of right-wing political thought the author calls "compelling and dynamic." There is a brief biography of Lewis that includes his distinguished family background and his early struggles as a cub reporter of the Washington scene in the 1920s and 1930s.

SINCLAIR LEWIS

755. Lewis, Sinclair. *From Main Street to Stockholm: Letters of Sinclair Lewis, 1919–1930.* New York: Harcourt, Brace and Co., 1952. xii + 307pp. (Edited, with an introduction, by Harrison Smith.)

This correspondence between Lewis and Harcourt, Brace and Co., his publishers, during the years of Lewis's greatest fame makes excellent reading as background on the business side of Lewis's publishing ventures. The full series of exchanges between Lewis and Harcourt, Brace at the time of the author's rejection of the Pulitzer Prize for *Arrowsmith* is included.

756. ———. *The Man from Main Street.* London: William Heinemann, Ltd., 1954. xiv + 294pp. (Edited by Harry E. Maule and Melville H. Cane.)

Selected essays and other writings, in part autobiographical, brought together after Lewis's death in 1951. See particularly "I'm an Old Newspaperman Myself," first published in *Cosmopolitan,* April and May 1947, and Lewis's letter to the Pulitzer Prize committee rejecting the award for *Arrowsmith* in 1926.

ALFRED (JAKE) LINGLE

757. Boettiger, John. *Jake Lingle, or Chicago on the Spot.* New York: E. P. Dutton and Co., 1931. 333pp.

A review of the gangland murder in 1930 of Alfred Lingle, police reporter for the Chicago *Tribune,* by the *Tribune* reporter assigned to cover it. Boettiger himself helped solve the case.

WALTER LIPPMANN

758. Brown, John Mason. "A Preface to Lippmann," in *Through These Men: Some Aspects of Our Passing History,* pp. 198–227. New York: Harper and Brothers, 1956.

A useful and thoughtful sketch of Walter Lippmann is included among a series of 10 articles on contemporary political, judicial, and scientific leaders.

759. Weingast, David Elliott. *Walter Lippmann: A Study in Personal Journalism.* New Brunswick, N.J.: Rutgers University Press, 1949. xx + 154pp. (Introduction by Harold L. Ickes.)

This biography is based primarily upon Lippmann's views as expressed in his column "Today and Tomorrow," 1932–1938. Lippmann's economic views, his relations with Franklin D. Roosevelt and the New Deal, the nature of his appeal as a columnist, and his bringing of scholarship into journalism are treated in detail. There is a good bibliography of Lippmann's books and articles.

J. F. B. LIVESAY

760. Livesay, J. F. B. *The Making of a Canadian.* Toronto: Ryerson Press, 1947. x + 181pp. (Edited by Florence Randal Livesay.)

Livesay, long the general manager of the Canadian Press, is regarded by many as that news agency's chief builder. In a deeply personal story he writes of the CP and gives sketches of Sir Clifford Sifton, first premier of Saskatchewan, and Walter Scott, owner of the Regina *Leader*.

HENRY DEMAREST LLOYD

761. Lloyd, Caro. *Henry Demarest Lloyd, 1847–1903: A Biography.* New York and London: G. P. Putnam's Sons, 1912. 2 vols. 698pp., total. (Introduction by Charles Edward Russell.)

A life of the political reformer who was author of *Wealth against Commonwealth*, written by his sister. Vol. I covers Lloyd's early career on the Chicago *Tribune* and his magazine writing in the 1870s and 1880s. Both volumes, however, are of interest for their material on the press.

LOUIS P. LOCHNER

762. Lochner, Louis P. *Always the Unexpected: A Book of Reminiscences.* New York: The Macmillan Co., 1956. viii + 339pp.

A valuable addition to foreign correspondents' autobiographies, by the Berlin bureau chief of the Associated Press, 1924–1942. In addition to the political recollections there is fascinating material in "Thoughts on Book Writing" (Lochner found time to write six).

DAVID ROSS LOCKE (PETROLEUM V. NASBY)

763. Locke, David Ross. *The Nasby Letters, Being the Original Nasby Letters as Written during His Lifetime.* Toledo, Ohio: The Toledo Blade, 1893. 510pp.

A short biography of Locke and a compilation by the *Blade* of scores of his Petroleum V. Nasby articles. Most of these had appeared in the *Blade*, with which Locke was associated almost continuously from 1865 to his death in 1888. The letters run from 1863 to 1887. Locke achieved fame by portraying, under the pseudonym Nasby, a corrupt, dissolute Democrat who manhandled the English language.

764. ———. *"Swingin Round the Cirkle."* Boston: Lee and Shepard, 1867. 299pp.

Petroleum V. Nasby's violently anti-Democratic satires written during the congressional campaign of 1866. Illustrations, vicious in their implications, are by Thomas Nast.

765. Clemens, Cyril. *Petroleum V. Nasby.* Webster Groves, Mo.: International Mark Twain Society, 1936. xv + 162pp. (Foreword by Irvin S. Cobb.)

A life of Locke published by the Mark Twain Society as one of a series on American humorists. There is a good bibliography of secondary materials on Locke and on American humor of his day.

WALTER LOCKE

766. Locke, Walter. *This World, My Home.* Yellow Springs, Ohio: An-

tioch Press, 1957. xiii + 171pp. (Introduction by Brooks Atkinson.)

About three dozen autobiographical sketches of a retired editor of the Dayton (Ohio) *Daily News* who became a columnist for Cox newspapers in Ohio, Georgia, and Florida. Locke early in life had been on the staff of the *Nebraska State Journal* (Lincoln).

JACK LONDON

767. London, Joan. *Jack London and His Times: An Unconventional Biography.* New York: Doubleday, Doran and Co., 1939. 387pp.

Jack London engaged in some war correspondence and wrote also for the *Atlantic Monthly* and *Overland Monthly.* This biography by his daughter, 23 years after her father's death, puts London beside Stephen Crane and Frank Norris as one of three who blazed trails into modern American literature.

768. Stone, Irving. *Sailor on Horseback: The Biography of Jack London.* Boston: Houghton Mifflin Co., 1938. 338pp.

Stone paints the London story in appropriately big strokes: its subject "had never played life 'the little way.' " There is a worthwhile account of London's business dealings with S. S. McClure, who helped him first break into an eastern magazine.

GEORGE HORACE LORIMER

769. Tebbel, John. *George Horace Lorimer and the Saturday Evening Post.* Garden City, N.Y.: Doubleday and Co., 1948. xii + 335pp.

Lorimer edited the *Post* through the first third of the 20th century and built its enormous reputation as the representative of middle-class readers. Tebbel's study is based upon private papers of Lorimer, extensive correspondence and interviews with *Post* associates and contributors, and contemporary articles on Lorimer.

ELIJAH P. LOVEJOY

770. Beecher, Rev. Edward. *Narrative of Riots at Alton in Connection with the Death of Elijah P. Lovejoy.* Alton, Ill.: Published by George Horton, 1838. 159pp.

Beecher, president of Illinois College, gave here the contemporary report of the "premeditated murder" of Lovejoy. It was he who wrote of Lovejoy as "the first martyr in America to the great principles of the freedom of speech and of the press."

771. Lovejoy, Joseph C., and Owen Lovejoy. *Memoir of the Rev. Elijah P. Lovejoy, Who Was Murdered in Defence of the Liberty of the Press, at Alton, Illinois, Nov. 7, 1837.* New York: John S. Taylor, 1838. 382pp. (Introduction by John Quincy Adams.)

The brothers of the editor of the Alton *Observer* here trace the story of Elijah's life and works. The book reveals the deep emotions of the time. Included is a full account of the riot trials from the Alton *Telegraph,* January 24, 1838.

772. Tanner, Henry. *The Martyrdom of Lovejoy: An Account of the Life, Trials, and Perils of Rev. Elijah P. Lovejoy Who Was Killed by a Pro-*

BIOGRAPHY

Slavery Mob at Alton, Ill., on the Night of November 7, 1837, by an Eye-Witness. Chicago: Fergus Printing Co., 1881. 233pp.

Tanner had worked with Lovejoy years earlier. His book is based in part upon the *Memoir* of the Lovejoy brothers and in part upon contemporary publications already out of print in 1881. Useful inclusions are a chapter of commentary from the American press after Lovejoy's death, appendixes dealing with contemporary discussion in Congress, and notes by Dr. Samuel Willard of Chicago, a witness to the scenes of 1837.

ROBERT MORSS LOVETT

773. Lovett, Robert Morss. *All Our Years: The Autobiography of Robert Morss Lovett.* New York: The Viking Press, 1948. x + 373pp.

Lovett was for a half-century an educator, author, and leader in liberal political movements. His autobiography includes background on his fringe activities in journalism, particularly his years as a reviewer and critic for the *New Republic*, 1921–1929.

JAMES RUSSELL LOWELL

774. Howard, Leon. *Victorian Knight-Errant: A Study of the Early Literary Career of James Russell Lowell.* Berkeley and Los Angeles: University of California Press, 1952. x + 388pp.

Howard seeks to discover the extent to which close observation of Lowell's literary output can improve understanding of the individual and his age. There is extensive information on the journalistic outlets that Lowell used, particularly the Boston *Courier, North American Review, Massachusetts Quarterly Review, National Anti-Slavery Standard,* and other abolitionist papers.

775. Scudder, Horace Elisha. *James Russell Lowell: A Biography.* Boston and New York: Houghton Mifflin Co., 1901. 2 vols. 937pp., total.

Useful on Lowell's relations with newspapers and periodicals. Vol. I covers Lowell's career in antislavery ranks, the start of the "Biglow Papers" in the Boston *Courier*, and his editorship of the *Atlantic Monthly*, 1857–1861. Vol. II deals principally with Lowell's political and diplomatic career. Appendixes list his writings, journalistic and literary, chronologically from 1837 to 1890.

JOAN LOWELL

776. Lowell, Joan. *Gal Reporter.* New York: Farrar and Rinehart, 1933. xi + 304pp.

The author, a stunt reporter for the Boston *Record*, writes here a lively account of the way in which she built a journalistic career after the failure of a literary career.

JAMES LUBY

777. Lee, James Melvin, ed. *James Luby, Journalist.* Washington, D.C.: Ransdell, 1930. 135pp.

A memorial to a Philadelphia and New York newspaperman, 1877–1925. Luby became managing editor of the New York *Sun* in 1913, and from 1915 to 1921 was editor of the *Evening Sun*. Besides a biography by Lee, this work includes reprints of Luby's editorials from the *Sun*.

CLARE BOOTHE LUCE

777a. Hatch, Alden. *Ambassador Extraordinary: Clare Boothe Luce*. New York: Henry Holt and Co., 1956. 254pp.

As journalist, playwright, and diplomat, Mrs. Luce receives rather exaggerated treatment: one who "carries the heavens of democracy on her slight shoulders." Illustrated.

778. Henle, Faye. *Au Clare de Luce: Portrait of a Luminous Lady*. New York: Stephen Daye, 1943. 205pp.

An early biography of the wife of the head of *Time-Life-Fortune*, herself on the staff of *Vogue* and *Vanity Fair* in the early 1930s. The book now is outdated by later developments in Mrs. Luce's career. The style places a high premium on glamour.

HENRY ROBINSON LUCE

779. Gibbs, Wolcott. "Time . . . Fortune . . . Life . . . Luce," in *New Yorker*, vol. 12, no. 41 (Nov. 28, 1936), pp. 20–25, and in *Profiles from the New Yorker*, pp. 297–311. New York: Alfred A. Knopf, 1938.

A classic among the Profiles, with penetrating satire on the co-founder of Lucenterprises. In Gibbs's portrait, "backward ran sentences until reeled the mind," and "where it all will end, knows God." Nearly a quarter century later, bigger still has grown *Time*, although style modified has become.

780. Time, Inc. *Henry R. Luce, Editor-in-Chief of Time, Life and Fortune*. New York, October 1956. 16pp., mimeographed, unbound.

Distributed on request through *Time*'s special services departments. Except for periodical articles, no readily available biographical material exists on Luce; this at least gives the official side.

CHARLES LUMMIS

781. Bingham, Edwin R. *Charles F. Lummis: Editor of the Southwest*. San Marino, Calif.: Huntington Library, 1955. x + 218pp.

A study of personal journalism in California. This volume deals as much with *Out West*, a monthly, as with its editor, Lummis. The period is 1900–1928.

BENJAMIN LUNDY

782. Landon, Fred. "Benjamin Lundy, Abolitionist," in *Dalhousie Review*, vol. 7 (July 1927), pp. 189–197.

This short article sets forth the main facts of Lundy's life, emphasizing his extensive travels (to Haiti, Canada, and Texas) in sponsoring the cause of the Negro. Landon regards Lundy as the inspiration for Garrison and others.

783. Lawrence, George A. *A Pioneer of Freedom: An Address before the Illinois Historical Association at Springfield, Illinois*. Galesburg, Ill.: Wagoner Printing Co., 1913. 46pp.

A tribute to the founder of the *Genius of Universal Emancipation*.

BIOGRAPHY

MATTHEW LYON

784. Campbell, Tom W. *Two Fighters and Two Fines: Sketches of the Lives of Matthew Lyon and Andrew Jackson*. Little Rock, Ark.: Pioneer Publishing Co., 1941. 557pp.

Matthew Lyon was active in journalism in Vermont and later in Kentucky and Arkansas and was the hero of the Alien and Sedition Act controversy. Both he and Andrew Jackson were victims of unjustified fines, Lyon after his sedition trial in 1798 and Jackson by a federal court as a result of his actions during the defense of New Orleans in 1814–1815. The Lyon sketch comprises the first 163 pages.

785. McLaughlin, J. Fairfax. *Matthew Lyon: The Hampden of Congress*. New York: Wynkoop Hallenbeck Crawford Co., 1900. xi + 531pp.

A eulogistic life of Lyon; useful for the information it adds to the Alien and Sedition Act story.

EUGENE LYONS

786. Lyons, Eugene. *Assignment in Utopia*. New York: Harcourt, Brace and Co., 1937. ix + 658pp.

An account of disillusionment with utopian dreams of the "better world" of Soviet Russia, which Lyons covered for the United Press, 1928 to 1934.

CHARLES K. McCLATCHY

787. McClatchy, Charles K. *Private Thinks by C. K.* New York: Scribner Press, 1936. xv + 342pp. (Foreword by Hiram W. Johnson.)

Comments over a period of more than 30 years by the editor of the Sacramento *Bee*, including selected editorials, travel sketches, and recollections of political conventions. The first 40 pages are devoted to C. K.'s views about newspapers and newspapermen.

ALEXANDER KELLY McCLURE

788. McClure, Col. Alexander Kelly. *Recollections of Half a Century*. Salem, Mass.: Salem Press Co., 1902. vii + 502pp.

McClure founded the Philadelphia *Times* in 1873 as a crusading reform paper and was editor until 1901. His rambling autobiography pays little attention to chronology and is mostly about politicians, Union and Confederate generals, other celebrities, and passing events, but there is good detail on Gales and Blair, Parson Brownlow, Henry W. Grady, and George D. Prentice.

SAMUEL S. McCLURE

789. McClure, S. S. *My Autobiography*. New York: Magazine Publishers, 1913; Frederick A. Stokes Co., 1914. xii + 266pp.

A dull and superficial autobiography of the founder of *McClure's Magazine*. Largely concerned with McClure's early struggles, it gives little significant material on the founding of *McClure's* or on muckraking although there are some helpful facts on McClure's dealings with Ida M. Tarbell, Rudyard Kipling, George Meredith, and Lincoln Steffens.

ROBERT R. McCORMICK and JOSEPH PATTERSON

790. Tebbel, John. *An American Dynasty*. Garden City, N.Y.: Double-day and Co., 1947. x + 363pp.

Covers the McCormicks, Medills, and Pattersons. In five parts: Joseph Medill and the Chicago *Tribune* through last half of the 19th century; the transition period during which James Keeley was a *Tribune* force; the Robert R. McCormick era; the "world of the Pattersons" (Joseph and Eleanor of the New York *Daily News* and Washington *Times-Herald*); and the family's concept of freedom of the press. Tebbel's assessment is negative — that the family eventually will sink into obscurity, although its newspapers may continue to prosper.

JOHN T. McCUTCHEON

791. McCutcheon, John T. *Drawn from Memory*. Indianapolis: Bobbs-Merrill Co., 1950. 459pp. (Foreword by Evelyn Shaw McCutcheon.)

The autobiography of a Chicago *Tribune* cartoonist for most of the first half of the 20th century. The volume covers principally the pre-World War II period. Excellent typography, with many McCutcheon cartoons and sketches inset with the text.

JAMES A. MacDONALD

792. Liebling, A. J. *The Honest Rainmaker: The Life and Times of Colonel John R. Stingo*. Garden City, N.Y.: Doubleday and Co., 1953. 317pp.

A tongue-in-cheek, jargon-filled account, entertaining but of no importance as a biography. The hero is James A. MacDonald — nom de plume Col. Stingo, otherwise "The Honest Rainmaker" — in actuality a writer on horse racing. The story goes back half a century to the New York *Evening Journal* and then takes in something of Los Angeles, where Col. Stingo once was sports editor of the *Examiner*.

WALT McDOUGALL

793. McDougall, Walt. *This Is the Life*. New York: Alfred A. Knopf, 1926. x + 330pp.

A light autobiography of one of the first newspaper staff-cartoonists. McDougall worked for Pulitzer "when the *World* was young" and for Hearst on the *Journal*, and later failed with *McDougall's Magazine* (designed to muck-rake the muckrakers).

BERNARR MACFADDEN

794. Macfadden, Mary, and Emile Gauvreau. *Dumbbells and Carrot Strips: The Story of Bernarr Macfadden*. New York: Henry Holt and Co., 1953. 405pp.

The wife of the "Father of Physical Culture" and a one-time editor of the New York *Daily Graphic* tell an intimate story in rather excessive detail. There is a full section on "The *True Story* Goldmine," but the authors disavow any intent to give an account of Macfadden Publications, Inc. Over all, this has little merit.

795. Oursler, Fulton. *The True Story of Bernarr Macfadden*. New York: Lewis Copeland Co., 1929. vi + 281pp.

A eulogy on the physical-culture strong man, replete with pictures of Macfadden at all ages and in all stages. Chapters treat the "strange story of *Physical Culture*," "the true story of *True Story*," and "the story of the *Graphic*."

796. Wood, Clement. *Bernarr Macfadden: A Study in Success*. New York: Lewis Copeland Co., 1929. 316pp.

Another eulogy, this one emphasizing Macfadden's battle for sound health policies against prudery. Macfadden's press activities are related to his over-all purpose of "conquering for sane living."

JAMES H. McGRAW

797. McGraw, James H. *Teacher of Business: The Publishing Philosophy of James H. McGraw*. Chicago: Advertising Publications, 1944. 91pp. (Edited by G. D. Crain, Jr.)

On the founder of the McGraw-Hill Publishing Co. However, less than a fourth of these pages are devoted to McGraw as an industrial publications editor; the remainder consists of his papers and addresses, chiefly on his ideals for industrial journalism.

JANE and ROBINSON McILVAINE

798. McIlvaine, Jane S. *It Happens Every Thursday*. Philadelphia: Macrae Smith Co., 1951. 231pp. (Foreword by Arthur Krock.)

Jane and Robinson McIlvaine resurrected the down-at-the-heel Downingtown (Pa.) *Archive* after World War II. This is Mrs. McIlvaine's account of their trials, or, How to Survive under the Shadow of Philadelphia.

O. O. McINTYRE

799. Driscoll, Charles B. *The Life of O. O. McIntyre*. New York: Greystone Press, 1938. 344pp.

Oscar Odd McIntyre was the "model" New York columnist — the Gallipolis boy from Ohio who made good in the Big Town and remained untouched by it. This highly eulogistic biography cannot be taken too seriously, but there is good material in it. Upon McIntyre's death in 1938 Driscoll succeeded him as author of the column "New York Day by Day."

ST. CLAIR McKELWAY

800. University of the State of New York. *St. Clair McKelway*. Albany, N.Y.: Regents of the University, 1915. 50pp.

A memorial adopted by the university's regents on the death of Chancellor McKelway, editor of the Brooklyn *Eagle*, who had been a regent for 33 years. A formal document, of course, but it includes a valuable tribute to McKelway as a journalist by Oswald Garrison Villard of the *Evening Post* and as an educator by Chester S. Lord of the *Sun*.

HENRY McLEMORE

801. McLemore, Henry. *One of Us Is Wrong*. New York: Henry Holt and Co., 1953. 242pp.

A truly humorous book, semi-autobiographical, by a nationally known sports columnist.

MILTON A. McRAE

802. McRae, Milton A. *Forty Years in Newspaperdom: The Autobiography of a Newspaperman*. New York: Brentano's, 1924. xviii + 496pp. (Preface by Arthur H. Vandenberg.)

McRae was the partner of Edward W. Scripps and was associated with him in the Scripps-McRae League of Newspapers. Most of his book concerns the formation of the league (1894–1896) and McRae's activities up to 1914. There is interesting material also on Lawson, Watterson, Murat Halstead, James M. Cox, and George G. Booth.

MARIE MANNING (BEATRICE FAIRFAX)

803. Manning, Marie. *Ladies Now and Then*. New York: E. P. Dutton Co., 1944. 254pp.

The autobiography of a sob sister. Marie Manning was a New York *World* and later Hearst and International News Service reporter and columnist. Herein she moves about through most of the first half of the 20th century, from the birth of "Beatrice Fairfax" (Arthur Brisbane's idea) to Mrs. Franklin D. Roosevelt ("God's gift to newspaper women").

ISAAC F. MARCOSSON

804. Marcosson, Isaac F. *Adventures in Interviewing*. New York: Dodd, Mead and Co., 1923. 314pp.

Recollections of a *Saturday Evening Post* writer. There are portraits of military and political figures and, among journalists, Henry Watterson, Lord Northcliffe, and Walter Hines Page. A good account of Marcosson's editing activities during a period with *World's Work* is included.

805. ———. *Turbulent Years*. New York: Dodd, Mead and Co., 1938. xi + 497pp.

A sequel to *Adventures in Interviewing*, covering Marcosson's career as *Saturday Evening Post* correspondent from 1919 to 1936. As in the earlier book, there are numerous sketches of political and military men whom the author knew.

HERBERT L. MATTHEWS

806. Matthews, Herbert L. *The Education of a Correspondent*. New York: Harcourt, Brace and Co., 1946. 550pp.

BIOGRAPHY

The life of a New York *Times* correspondent, chiefly from the Ethiopian war through World War II. Matthews writes as a pupil receiving schooling in totalitarianism and its evils. There are "courses" in Abyssinia, Spain, and Italy, with additional "lessons" on India and Afghanistan. This is a book by one inclined more to scholarly investigation than to rapid-fire reporting.

JOSEPH MEDILL (see also ROBERT R. McCORMICK)

807. Bennett, James O'Donnell. *Joseph Medill: A Brief Biography and an Appreciation*. Chicago: The Tribune Co., 1947. 42pp.

A commemoration booklet issued on the occasion of the 100th anniversary of the Chicago *Tribune*.

HENRY LOUIS MENCKEN

808. Mencken, H. L. *Happy Days, 1880–1892*. New York: Alfred A. Knopf, 1940. xi + 313pp.

The first of Mencken's series of memoirs covers "the Menckenesque universe" through age 12. As Mencken says, "excessively subjective and chaotic."

809. ———. *Newspaper Days, 1899–1906*. New York: Alfred A. Knopf, 1941. xi + 313pp.

Mencken describes his early years as a newspaperman in Baltimore, where he started on the old *Herald*. The recollections deal chiefly with reporting experiences, including coverage of the great Baltimore fire of 1904.

810. ———. *Heathen Days, 1890–1936*. New York: Alfred A. Knopf, 1943. x + 299pp.

Mencken moves more rapidly here, and his third volume telescopes the years. Among 20 dips into his memory, he discusses "the educational process" (1896); political conventions (1912); the "noble experiment" (1924); and the Dayton monkey trial (1925).

811. ———. *The Days of H. L. Mencken*. New York: Alfred A. Knopf, 1947. 946pp.

An omnibus volume of the three autobiographies listed above.

812. ———. *Minority Report: H. L. Mencken's Notebooks*. New York: Alfred A. Knopf, 1956. vi + 293pp.

Some 432 notes, offered as samples of Mencken's "raw materials" that "might enkindle an occasional reader to more orderly and profitable lucubrations." The comments were found among Mencken's papers by a secretary some time after his death.

813. ———. *The Vintage Mencken*. New York: Vintage Books, 1956. xiv + 240pp. (Gathered by Alistair Cooke.)

814. Angoff, Charles H. *H. L. Mencken: A Portrait from Memory*. New York: Thomas Yoseloff, 1956. 244pp.

Impressionistic recollections by a one-time colleague who claims to have known Mencken better in the years 1925–1935 than almost anyone else. Much of the book is in the form of conversation. Angoff deals in detail with the democratizing of American journalism through Mencken's *American Mercury.* The content is topical, across the broad range of Mencken's interests.

815. Goldberg, Isaac. *The Man Mencken: A Biographical and Critical Survey.* New York: Simon and Schuster, 1925. xiv + 388pp.

Goldberg, literary editor of the *American Freeman,* 1923–1932, based his book upon acquaintanceship with Mencken's writings over a period of more than 10 years. He expresses fundamental sympathy with the "Bad Boy of Baltimore."

816. Kemler, Edgar. *The Irreverent Mr. Mencken.* Boston: Little, Brown and Co., 1950. x + 317pp.

Mencken is pictured as an American Rabelais, Swift, or Shaw who abused his gifts and whose only enduring work will be *The American Language.* The author obtained much of his material from Mencken himself. The book carries useful notes and a Mencken chronology.

817. Manchester, William. *Disturber of the Peace: The Life of H. L. Mencken.* New York: Harper and Brothers, 1950. xiv + 336pp. (Introduction by Gerald W. Johnson.)

Based upon materials from many of Mencken's friends and associates and from Mencken himself. Manchester praises Mencken's contributions as a philologist. Detailed treatment is given to Mencken's association with George Jean Nathan, to the Scopes trial, and to the "Banned in Boston" episode.

EDWIN T. MEREDITH

818. Meredith Publishing Co. *Edwin T. Meredith, 1876–1928: A Memorial Volume.* Des Moines, Iowa: Meredith Publishing Co., 1931. 66pp.

A tribute to a distinguished agricultural journalist, founder of *Successful Farming,* who for a short period was Woodrow Wilson's secretary of agriculture. The book includes a brief biography, comments from Meredith's magazines, press opinions, and testimonials.

OTTMAR MERGENTHALER

819. Mengel, William. *Ottmar Mergenthaler and the Printing Revolution.* Brooklyn, N.Y.: Mergenthaler Linotype Co., 1954. 63pp. (Introduction by Lin Yutang.)

A centenary book commemorating Mergenthaler's birth. It supplements Drier's work of 1937 on the linotype (264 above). A helpful chronology of the linotype is included.

AGNES E. MEYER

820. Meyer, Agnes E. *Out of These Roots: The Autobiography of an American Woman.* Boston: Little, Brown and Co., 1953. x + 385pp.

Mrs. Meyer, wife of Eugene Meyer, owner of the Washington *Post* since 1933, and herself a journalist, tells of her husband's rebuilding of the *Post.* However, she goes far beyond journalism in writing of a life that included a book on Chinese painting, translation of Thomas Mann, and contributions to public recreation, public health, and public education. The volume shows intellectual depth.

BIOGRAPHY

ALEXANDER QUINTELLA MILLER

821. Miller, Alexander Quintella, Sr. *Jayhawk Editor*. Los Angeles: Sterling Press, 1955. 256pp. (Compiled and edited by James D. Callahan.)

The autobiography of a Kansas editor for more than 60 years — publisher of the Belleville *Telescope* and interpreter of the Kansas scene. Included are sub-biographies of outstanding Kansas and western personalities who were Miller's friends and associates: Arthur Capper, William Rockhill Nelson, Henry J. Allen, William Allen White, and Palmer Hoyt.

CHARLES R. MILLER

822. Bond, F. Fraser. *Mr. Miller of the Times: The Story of an Editor*. New York and London: Charles Scribner's Sons, 1931. x + 264pp.

Miller's 47-year career with the New York *Times* extended from the last years of the Jones ownership through the first quarter-century under Adolph S. Ochs. Valuable material relates to the part played by Miller at the time of the Ochs purchase.

JOAQUIN MILLER

823. Marberry, M. M. *Splendid Poseur: Joaquin Miller — American Poet*. New York: Thomas Y. Crowell Co., 1953. 310pp.

Although the author takes an unsympathetic view of Miller, this is a useful volume for its information on Miller's early journalistic experiences in the West, his relations with Mrs. Frank Leslie, and views of him by his contemporaries, particularly Ambrose Bierce.

824. Peterson, Martin Severin. *Joaquin Miller: Literary Frontiersman*. Stanford, Calif.: Stanford University Press, 1937. ix + 198pp.

This is a more favorable analysis of Miller than Marberry's but material on his newspaper activities is scattered throughout the book. There is an extensive bibliography.

MAX MILLER

825. Miller, Max. *I Cover the Waterfront*. New York: E. P. Dutton and Co., 1932. 204pp.

A reporter for the San Diego *Sun* who later became a well-known literary figure writes about the marine beat: tuna clippers, sardine boats, elephant seals, and people. Humorous, refreshing, and well written.

WEBB MILLER

826. Miller, Webb. *I Found No Peace: The Journal of a Foreign Correspondent*. New York: Simon and Schuster, 1936. xiii + 332pp.

A best seller in its day, by a reporter for the United Press who died in London in 1940. See particularly an inserted chapter by Roy W. Howard in which Howard gives his version of the "premature Armistice" of 1918.

EDWARD P. MITCHELL

827. Mitchell, Edward P. *Memoirs of an Editor: Fifty Years of American*

Journalism. New York and London: Charles Scribner's Sons, 1924. xii + 458pp.

The autobiography of a New York *Sun* editor under Dana, who succeeded Dana as editor-in-chief after 1897. It is helpful for details on control of the *Sun* between Dana's death and the Munsey purchase, and on Mitchell's position in connection with these changes. Mitchell praises Frank A. Munsey, one of the few to render such a verdict.

WILLIAM B. MOORHEAD

828. Moorhead, William B. *Police Reporter.* Kansas City, Mo.: Printed for the author by Allis Press, 1955. vii + 204pp. (Foreword by Ralph H. Eades.)

Recollections of incidents over 40 years, during which period Moorhead covered the police beat for the Kansas City *Star.*

FREDERIC COOK MOREHOUSE

829. Stevens, W. Bertrand. *Editor's Quest: A Memoir of Frederic Cook Morehouse.* New York: Morehouse-Gorham Co., 1940. 240pp. (Foreword by Clifford P. Morehouse.)

Morehouse was editor of the *Living Church,* an Episcopal organ published for many years in Milwaukee. Author Stevens, the Episcopal bishop of Los Angeles, writes simply and straightforwardly about Morehouse's career during the first 30 years of the 20th century.

WARD MOREHOUSE

830. Morehouse, Ward. *Just the Other Day: From Yellow Pines to Broadway.* New York: McGraw-Hill Book Co., 1953. 240pp.

The autobiography of a Georgia-born dramatic critic for the Atlanta *Journal,* the New York *Tribune,* and, for more than 20 years, the New York *Sun.* There is an excellent review of the sale of the *Sun* in 1950 to the New York *World-Telegram.*

THOMAS B. MORGAN

831. Morgan, Thomas B. *The Listening Post: Eighteen Years on Vatican Hill.* New York: G. P. Putnam's Sons, 1944. v + 242pp.

In part autobiographical, but chiefly an account of how a reporter obtains news of the Vatican. Morgan spent most of his career in Rome with the United Press. This is a useful book in its journalistic approach to Vatican history, particularly the pontificates of Pius XI and Pius XII.

832. ———. *A Reporter at the Papal Court: A Narrative of the Reign of Pope Pius XI.* New York and Toronto: Longmans, Green and Co., 1938. 302pp.

Morgan gives excellent material on news-gathering in the Vatican, plus descriptive accounts of distinguished reporters who at one time or another had the Roman assignment.

BIOGRAPHY

LILIAN T. MOWRER

833. Mowrer, Lilian T. *Journalist's Wife.* New York: William Morrow and Co., 1937. viii + 414pp.

The autobiography of the wife of Edgar Ansel Mowrer, foreign correspondent for the Chicago *Daily News.* Mrs. Mowrer tells of their joint experiences in Europe between World Wars I and II, with good portraits of numerous leaders and analyses of changing world conditions.

PAUL SCOTT MOWRER

834. Mowrer, Paul Scott. *The House of Europe.* Boston: Houghton Mifflin Co., 1945. 647pp.

By the elder of the Mowrer brothers, foreign correspondents for the Chicago *Daily News.* The title is incomplete, this book being in part the autobiography of an Illinois youth in the quiet days early in the century and in part an analysis of world affairs into which the small-town reporter later moved. Mowrer discusses his work as a Paris correspondent and as a World War I correspondent in the Balkans and North Africa. Also, he provides considerable material on Edgar Ansel Mowrer, a tribute to Victor Lawson, and an excellent analysis of the Chicago *Daily News* foreign service. He does not go beyond 1933, when he returned to Chicago as editor of the *Daily News.* The book is interesting and thoughtful.

FLORABEL MUIR

835. Muir, Florabel. *Headline Happy.* New York: Henry Holt and Co., 1950. 248pp.

Reporter Muir records many of her escapades in covering the famous and infamous of California — among them Errol Flynn, Bugs Siegel, Mickey Cohen, Charlie Chaplin, and Ruth Snyder. She worked also in Salt Lake City and for the New York *Daily News.*

JOEL MUNSELL

836. Edelstein, David S. *Joel Munsell: Printer and Antiquarian.* New York: Columbia University Press, 1950. 420pp.

A valuable contribution to typographical history. Munsell operated the Munsell Press in Albany, one of the leading printing houses in mid-19th-century America. His life story is that of a practical printer, scholar, publisher, and bookseller.

FRANK A. MUNSEY

837. Britt, George. *Forty Years — Forty Millions: The Career of Frank A. Munsey.* New York: Farrar and Rinehart, 1935. vi + 309pp.

Written without rancor, but nevertheless a severe indictment of the newspaper consolidator. Britt never knew Munsey but obtained his data from men who had been the publisher's employees and verified these reports through newspaper and library files. Munsey is portrayed as "lonesome and frostbitten, a killer who wanted to be a creator."

EMILY MURPHY

838. Sanders, Byrne Hope. *Emily Murphy: Crusader ("Janey Canuck").* Toronto: The Macmillan Co. of Canada, Ltd., 1945. xviii + 355pp.

Emily Ferguson Murphy was one of the outstanding women of western Canada early in the 20th century: newspaperwoman, author, public health and welfare leader, worker for political rights for women, and police magistrate in Edmonton. She was literary editor of the Winnipeg *Telegram* (1904–1912) and president of the Canadian Women's Press Club (1913–1920).

THOMAS NAST

839. Paine, Albert Bigelow. *Th. Nast: His Period and His Pictures.* New York and London: Harper and Brothers, 1904. xxi + 583pp.

Includes about 400 reproductions of Nast's cartoons in *Harper's Weekly* over 40 years, from the 1850s to the McKinley administration. Paine places Nast with Lincoln and Grant as a benefactor of the people.

WILLIAM ROCKHILL NELSON

840. Johnson, Icie F. *William Rockhill Nelson and the Kansas City Star.* Kansas City: Burton Publishing Co., 1935. 208pp. (Introduction by William Allen White.)

The life of an editor who "found his city in mud and left it marble." Johnson emphasizes Nelson's civic interests as well as his journalistic power. There is no indication of sources.

841. Kansas City Star Staff. *William Rockhill Nelson: The Story of a Man, a Newspaper, and a City.* Cambridge, Mass.: Riverside Press, 1915. 274pp.

There are chapters on Nelson's founding of the *Star*, his fight for good government, his service to Kansas City in building parks and boulevards, his national reputation, and the esteem of his staff for him. The appendix carries comments of American newspapers on Nelson's death.

RICHARD L. NEUBERGER

842. Neuberger, Richard L. *Adventures in Politics: We Go to the Legislature.* New York: Oxford University Press, 1954. xi + 210pp.

Dick Neuberger — newspaperman, magazine writer, author, and politician — went from the Oregon Legislature to the United States Senate in 1954. His story covers primarily his Oregon political career, along with that of his wife Maurine, also active in politics. Much of the material in the book had been written first for newspapers and national periodicals.

THOMAS LOW NICHOLS

843. Nichols, Thomas Low. *Forty Years of American Life, 1821–1861.* New York: Stackpole Sons, 1937. 421pp. (Republication of work originally issued in 1864 and revised in 1874.)

Part autobiography and part descriptive narrative of American institutions.

Nichols was a novelist, journalist, social reformer, and physician. His intensely interesting book is caustic in its attacks on the northern press; there are separate chapters on the periodical press and Horace Greeley.

ELIZA JANE NICHOLSON

844. Harrison, James Henry. *Pearl Rivers, Publisher of the Picayune.* New Orleans: Tulane University of Louisiana, 1932. 63pp. (Edited by G. E. Simmons.)

A biography of Mrs. Eliza Jane Nicholson, who took over the near-bankrupt New Orleans *Picayune* during Reconstruction days and restored it in 20 years to a position of prominence in metropolitan journalism. Included is an account of how Mrs. Nicholson gave Dorothy Dix a start in journalism.

HEZEKIAH NILES

845. Stone, Richard Gabriel. *Hezekiah Niles as an Economist.* Baltimore: Johns Hopkins Press, 1933. 137pp. (Johns Hopkins University Studies in Historical and Political Science, Vol. LI, no. 5.)

A well-documented study of the man who founded *Niles' Weekly Register* and of the American economic scene, 1780–1815.

MORDECAI M. NOAH

846. Goldberg, Isaac. *Major Noah: American-Jewish Pioneer.* Philadelphia: Jewish Publication Society of America, 1936. xvii + 316pp.

Portrays Noah as a prototype of the early American Jew who identified himself with the fortunes of the United States in politics, journalism, diplomacy, oratory, drama, philanthropy, civic affairs, and Utopian projects. Noah's aggressive career in journalism (New York *National Advocate* and New York *Enquirer,* plus other newspapers from the 1820s to the 1840s) is interwoven with his other activities. An extensive bibliography is given.

ALEXANDER DANA NOYES

847. Noyes, Alexander Dana. *The Market Place: Reminiscences of a Financial Editor.* Boston: Little, Brown and Co., 1938. xii + 384pp.

Noyes, a financial editor of the New York *Times,* gives background on the speculation of the 1920s, the Panic of 1929, and economic effects of the Depression through 1937. Earlier, he had had a career of almost 50 years in New York journalism; he gives a good account of business news coverage from 1883 on.

EDGAR WILSON NYE (BILL NYE)

848. Nye, Frank Wilson. *Bill Nye: His Own Life Story.* New York and London, 1926. xx + 412pp. (Foreword by Melville E. Stone.)

Edgar Wilson Nye gained a wide reputation in the 1880s as editor of the Laramie (Wyo.) *Boomerang* and was regarded by many as America's "national humorist." In this biography (essentially autobiographical), Nye's eldest son fills in the continuity and lets the father tell his own story from his writings. After 1887 Bill Nye was on the New York *World*.

HOWARD VINCENT O'BRIEN

849. O'Brien, Howard Vincent. *All Things Considered: Memories, Experiences and Observations of a Chicagoan*. Indianapolis: Bobbs-Merrill Co., 1948. xix + 345pp.

This volume by a Chicago *Daily News* columnist was published posthumously. The first quarter is a memoir; the remainder includes selections from O'Brien's columns on family life, travel, and people. The period covered is 1932–1947. Well worth reading.

ADOLPH S. OCHS

850. Hinkel, John V. *The Contributions of Adolph S. Ochs to Journalism*. New York: Privately printed, 1931. 86pp.

Issued in a limited edition on the 35th anniversary of Ochs's acquiring the New York *Times*. The material was originally submitted as a master's thesis in the Columbia University School of Journalism. Hinkel includes some original material in comments of 17 persons in personal letters to the author in which they discuss Ochs.

851. Johnson, Gerald W. *An Honorable Titan: A Biographical Study of Adolph S. Ochs*. New York and London: Harper and Brothers, 1946. ix + 313pp.

A tribute by a Baltimore *Sun* writer to the publisher of the New York *Times*, this is the only effective full-length treatment of Ochs's career. Documentary sources are cited.

FREMONT OLDER

852. Older, Fremont. *Growing Up*. San Francisco: San Francisco Call-Bulletin, 1931. viii + 168pp.

853. ———. *My Own Story*. San Francisco: The Call Publishing Co., 1919. 197pp. (Reissued, Oakland, Calif.: Post-Enquirer Publishing Co., 1925.)

The managing editor of the San Francisco *Bulletin* for nearly a quarter of a century after 1895 tells of his struggles for good government amid numerous obstacles created by entrenched interests. The book was written after Older had broken with the *Bulletin* management and had moved to the *Call*.

854. Wells, Evelyn. *Fremont Older*. New York: D. Appleton-Century Co., 1936. xi + 407pp.

Panegyric by an employee to whom Older gave her first newspaper assignment. Based mostly upon memory and Older's *My Own Story*.

FREDERICK L. OLMSTED

855. Mitchell, Broadus. *Frederick Law Olmsted: A Critic of the Old South*. Baltimore: Johns Hopkins University, 1924. (Studies in Historical and Political Science, Vol. 42, pp. 161–318.)

BIOGRAPHY

A three-part study: biography of Olmsted, analysis of his criticisms of the antebellum South, and discussion of his interpretations of the economic effects of slavery. Mitchell discusses in some detail Olmsted's relations with Henry J. Raymond of the New York *Times* while he was a reporter for that newspaper. Of high journalistic value.

CHARLES J. O'MALLEY

856. O'Malley, Charles J. *It Was News to Me.* Boston: Bruce Humphries, 1939. 407pp.

Reminiscences, mostly of world tours between 1883 and 1939, of an Irish-born reporter whose principal association was with Boston newspapers. Gracious and intimate in tone. Well illustrated.

BRADLEY SILLICK OSBON

857. Osbon, Capt. Bradley Sillick. *A Sailor of Fortune: Personal Memoirs of Captain B. S. Osbon.* New York: McClure, Phillips and Co., 1906. ix + 332pp. (Edited by Albert Bigelow Paine.)

Osbon, a distinguished naval reporter of the Civil War who achieved a scoop in reporting the fall of Fort Sumter for the New York *World*, told his life story to Paine when he was nearly 80. It is a simple narrative, with the bulk of it limited to the Civil War. Most of Osbon's life was more naval than journalistic, although in 1871 he established the *Nautical Gazette*, a weekly, which he edited for 13 years; later he was associate editor of the *American Shipbuilder*.

JAMES OTIS

858. Tudor, William. *The Life of James Otis of Massachusetts: Containing Also, Notices of Some Contemporary Characters and Events from the Year 1760 to 1775.* Boston: Wells and Lilly, 1823. xx + 508pp.

A detailed life of the Colonial pamphleteer by the founder of the *North American Review*. Three chapters deal with Otis's relation to the Stamp Act controversy.

WALTER HINES PAGE

859. Hendrick, Burton J. *The Life and Letters of Walter H. Page, 1855–1918.* Garden City, N.Y.: Doubleday, Page and Co., 1921–1925. 3 vols.

Although Page's greatest fame came as ambassador to Great Britain during World War I, he had had a distinguished career as editor of *World's Work* and as founder of Doubleday, Page and Co. Hendrick records this service, as well as Page's editorship of the *Atlantic Monthly*, 1898–1899. Vol. III includes Page's letters to Woodrow Wilson.

860. ———. *The Training of an American: The Earlier Life and Letters of Walter H. Page, 1855–1913.* Boston and New York: Houghton Mifflin Co., 1928. xii + 444pp.

A companion book to *The Life and Letters*. Hendrick considers fully Page's formative years in the post-Civil War South as a literary man and journalist.

He gives separate treatment to Page's apprenticeship in journalism, his work as business manager and editor of the *Forum*, and his editorship of the *Atlantic Monthly*.

RALPH D. PAINE

861. Paine, Ralph D. *Roads of Adventure*. Boston and New York: Houghton Mifflin Co., 1922. xiii + 452pp.

Romance in the Richard Harding Davis and James Creelman pattern. Paine, at one time a reporter for the New York *Herald*, deals chiefly with his correspondence during the Spanish-American War, his subsequent experiences in the Far East, and his special work for the Creel Committee on Public Information during World War I.

THOMAS PAINE

862. Berthold, S. M. *Thomas Paine: America's First Liberal*. Boston: Meador Publishing Co., 1938. 264pp.

Readable, but uncritical. No listing of sources or bibliography.

863. Best, Mary Agnes. *Thomas Paine: Prophet and Martyr of Democracy*. New York: Harcourt, Brace and Co., 1927. viii + 413pp.

Treats Paine sympathetically, but not so exhaustively as Moncure Conway's work. No reference to sources.

864. Conway, Moncure D. *The Life of Thomas Paine: With a History of His Literary, Political, and Religious Career in America, France, and England*. London: G. P. Putnam's Sons, 1892. 2 vols. (Single-volume edition: London: Watts and Co., 1909. xvi + 351pp.)

A defense of Paine by a noted author and editor who in the 1860s had edited the *Dial*. This was among the first studies to depart from the stands of early biographers, who were "malignantly hostile" to Paine. The author investigated original documents. He included a sketch of Paine by William Cobbett.

865. ———, ed. *The Writings of Thomas Paine*. New York: G. P. Putnam's Sons, 1894–1896. 4 vols.

866. Woodward, W. E. *Tom Paine: America's Godfather*. New York: E. P. Dutton and Co., 1945. 359pp.

A popular biography, by a prolific historian. Woodward intended to present "a true picture of one who was for nearly 150 years a target for abuse."

FREDERICK PALMER

867. Palmer, Frederick. *With My Own Eyes: A Personal Story of Battle Years*. Indianapolis: Bobbs-Merrill Co., 1932. 396pp.

Palmer was a correspondent in the period from the Spanish-American War to World War I. He represented *Collier's* during the Russo-Japanese War; in 1914–1916 he was accredited to the British forces and later was an American press censor. Although the book ranges widely, it is solidly based. There is good material on censorship, John J. Pershing, and Palmer's association with other generals.

BIOGRAPHY

LOUELLA O. PARSONS

868. Parsons, Louella O. *The Gay Illiterate*. Garden City, N.Y.: Doubleday, Doran and Co., 1944. 194pp.

> A Hollywood gossip columnist for the Hearst newspapers, regarded as the most powerful woman in Hollywood, tells of the movie colony and Hollywood legends; Miss Parsons also describes other cities in which she worked, particularly New York and Chicago.

JAMES PARTON

869. Flower, Milton E. *James Parton: The Father of Modern Biography*. Durham, N.C.: Duke University Press, 1951. ix + 253pp.

> A competent work on an author, journalist, and crusader, who was perhaps America's first professional biographer. There is full detail on Parton's work in preparing his *Life of Horace Greeley* in 1855, plus extensive information on Parton's associations with newspaper and magazine editors. The book is based on family papers and unpublished materials in libraries.

GROVE PATTERSON

870. Patterson, Grove. *I Like People*. New York: Random House, 1954. vii + 300pp.

> The editor-in-chief of the Toledo *Blade* expresses the philosophy of his life in the title of his book, which is rambling, and has Pollyanna overtones. There is good material on Patterson's association with the American Society of Newspaper Editors.

JOSEPH PATTERSON (see ROBERT R. McCORMICK)

CHARLOTTE PAUL

871. Paul, Charlotte. *Minding Our Own Business*. New York: Random House, 1955. 309pp.

> The experiences of the author and her family who, after World War II, obtained the Snoqualmie (Wash.) *Valley Record*, a weekly, and eventually made a success of it. Mrs. Paul and her husband were former members of the foreign news staff of the Chicago *Times*.

MAURY H. B. PAUL

872. Harriman, Margaret Case, "Dolly and Polly, Billy and Cholly," in *New Yorker*, vol. 13 (Oct. 16 and Oct. 23, 1937), pp. 23–27 and 22–27.

> The Profile of Maury Paul, who wrote under the pen names "Dolly Madison," "Polly Stuyvesant," "Billy Benedick," and "Cholly Knickerbocker." The author relates how Paul's coy approach and adeptness at personal badgering combined with a change in society standards to produce a circulation-building type of journalism for Hearst.

873. Nichols, Mary E. [pseud. Eve Brown]. *Champagne Cholly: The Life and Times of Maury Paul*. New York: E. P. Dutton and Co., 1947. 324pp.

The life of a male New York society editor for Hearst who was known as "Cholly Knickerbocker." Worth reading only for such "inside dope" on New York society as the curious may crave.

ANDREW P. PEABODY

874. Young, Edward J. "Memoir of Andrew P. Peabody," in Massachusetts Historical Society *Proceedings*, 2nd series, vol. XI, pp. 25–46. Boston: the Society, 1896–1897.

A brief sketch of an American Unitarian clergyman, educator, and editor. Young discusses Peabody's contributions, 1837–1859, to religious newspapers, to the *New England Magazine* and other periodicals, and his proprietorship and editorship of the *North American Review*, 1853–1863.

CHARLES PEDEN

875. Peden, Charles. *Newsreel Man*. Garden City, N.Y.: Doubleday, Doran and Co., 1932. x + 126pp.

An autobiographical narrative of a reporter-photographer for Movietonews, Inc. Wholly popular in content and breezy in style. The final chapter is on the Lindbergh kidnapping case.

DAVID GRAHAM PHILLIPS

876. Marcosson, Isaac F. *David Graham Phillips and His Times*. New York: Dodd, Mead and Co., 1932. ix + 308pp.

A fairly useful although undistinguished biography of a novelist-journalist-political writer of the first decade of the century. Marcosson fails to provide essential reference material on Phillips, and his account of Phillips's muckraking work on *The Treason of the Senate* is inadequate, as is his treatment of Phillips's literary career.

WENDELL PHILLIPS (see WILLIAM LLOYD GARRISON)

DONN PIATT

877. Miller, Charles Grant. *Donn Piatt: His Work and His Ways*. Cincinnati: Robert Clarke and Co., 1893. 381pp.

The life of a versatile and conspicuous journalist of the middle and late 19th century. Piatt was Washington correspondent of the Cincinnati *Commercial* after the Civil War and later a founder of the Washington *Capital*, a weekly devoted to uncovering corruption. Before the day of the sensational press, Piatt discovered the value of stressing personalities in news features.

WALTER B. PITKIN

878. Pitkin, Walter B. *On My Own*. New York: Charles Scribner's Sons, 1944. vii + 526pp.

Pitkin, best known as the author of *Life Begins at Forty*, was with the New York *Tribune* and the New York *Post* early in the century and for many years was a professor of journalism at Columbia University. *On My Own* is somewhat egotistical in style and deals insufficiently with Pitkin's journalistic experiences.

EDGAR ALLAN POE

879. Phillips, Mary E. *Edgar Allan Poe, the Man.* Chicago: John C. Winston Co., 1926. 2 vols. 1685pp., total.

Although considerably longer than the other biographies of Poe, this work does not treat as critically the magazine controversies in which Poe was involved.

880. Pope-Hennessy, Una. *Edgar Allan Poe, 1809–1849: A Critical Biography.* London: The Macmillan Co., Ltd., 1934. xii + 342pp.

A British author's comprehensive study of Poe includes detailed material on his editorships in Richmond and Philadelphia and his experience in New York journalism.

881. Woodberry, George E. *Edgar Allan Poe.* Boston: Houghton Mifflin Co., 1885. ix + 354pp. (American Men of Letters Series.)

Principally a literary biography, but there are useful interpretations of Poe's relations with Rufus W. Griswold and of Poe's editorship of *Graham's Magazine.*

MARCUS M. POMEROY

882. Pomeroy, Marcus M. *Journey of Life: Reminiscences and Recollections of "Brick" Pomeroy.* New York: Advance Thought Co., 1890. 251pp. (Birch Bark Series, vol. 2, no. 3.)

The autobiography of the controversial editor of the La Crosse (Wis.) *Democrat* and later the New York *Democrat* covers in the main Pomeroy's first 37 years, to 1870. It was written, as Pomeroy says, at the request of many persons who wanted for the edification of poor boys a story of success achieved in spite of struggle, temptation, and abuse and criticism.

883. Tucker, Mary E. *Life of Mark M. Pomeroy: A Representative Young Man of America.* New York: G. W. Carleton Co., 1868. 230pp.

A justification of "Brick" Pomeroy's career up to 1868. As editor of the La Crosse *Democrat,* Pomeroy had been among the more vitriolic Copperheads during the Civil War.

ERNEST POOLE

884. Poole, Ernest. *The Bridge: My Own Story.* New York: The Macmillan Co., 1940. 422pp.

The autobiography of a Chicago novelist, crusader for the betterment of New York slums early in the 1900s, and correspondent in Russia in 1905 and in World War I. There are interesting chapters on Poole's journalistic interludes.

BENJAMIN PERLEY POORE

885. Poore, Benjamin Perley. *Perley's Reminiscences of Sixty Years in the National Metropolis.* Philadelphia: Hubbard Brothers, 1886. 2 vols. 1087pp., total.

THE LITERATURE OF JOURNALISM

One of the most fascinating of autobiographical narratives by Washington reporters. "Perley" (a pen name used for more than 30 years) is long-winded but full of wit and memories reaching from Andrew Jackson to Grover Cleveland. He was a correspondent for the Boston *Journal*, first editor of the *Congressional Record* in 1869, and one of the founders of the Gridiron Club. The accuracy of his early "memories" is open to some question — he was born in 1820 and died in 1887.

ZELDA POPKIN

886. Popkin, Zelda. *Open Every Door*. New York: E. P. Dutton Co., 1956. 379pp.

The delightful autobiography of a journalist-novelist who started in Wilkes-Barre, Pa., and achieved moderate success.

WILLIAM SYDNEY PORTER (O. HENRY)

887. Davis, Robert H., and Arthur B. Maurice. *The Caliph of Bagdad: Being "Arabian Nights" Flashes of the Life, Letters, and Work of O. Henry*. New York and London: D. Appleton and Co., 1931. vii + 411pp.

A sympathetic account giving the essential details of Porter's newspaper career as well as of his short-story writing. See especially Davis's story of his search for Porter in 1903 on assignment from the New York *World*.

888. Williams, William Wash. *The Quiet Lodger of Irving Place*. New York: E. P. Dutton and Co., 1936. 251pp.

Williams, a reporter for the New York *World* when Porter came to New York in 1902, is said to have been the short-story writer's closest friend and confidant. The author tells of his first meeting with Porter, life in Irving Place, and the methods by which Porter worked and wrote.

WILLIAM TROTTER PORTER

888a. Yates, Norris W. *William T. Porter and the Spirit of the Times: A Study of the "Big Bear" School of Humor*. Baton Rouge: Louisiana State University Press, 1957. xi + 222pp.

A life of the founder of an early sporting journal of the turf and its editor, 1831–1856. Porter's paper gave an important impetus to the writing of literature about the American back country.

E. ALEXANDER POWELL

889. Powell, E. Alexander. *Adventure Road*. London: Cape, 1955. 312pp.

Reminiscences over a half-century of a round-the-world reporter, chiefly remembrances of an age gone by.

890. ———. *Free Lance*. New York: Harcourt, Brace and Co., 1937. xii + 514pp.

Powell was a newspaper and magazine correspondent, foreign-service official, army officer, author of numerous books, and correspondent for the New York *World* and London *Daily Mail* in World War I. He correctly calls his recollections "speed-boat skimming along the surface in a smother of foam."

BIOGRAPHY

TED PRAGER

891. Prager, Ted. *Police Reporter*. New York: Duell, Sloan and Pearce, 1957. vii + 212pp. (In collaboration with Donald D. McLennan.)

Autobiographical recollections of incidents in the life of a New York reporter of 40 years' service who became an assistant city editor of the New York *Daily News*. There are dramatic episodes relating to "cops," "scoops," and "characters," together with some material on the mechanics of police reporting.

ORVILLE PRESCOTT

892. Prescott, Orville. *The Five-Dollar Gold Piece*. New York: Random House, 1956. xi + 243pp. (Illustrated by Vasiliu.)

The autobiography of a "bookish" editor-critic for the New York *Times* since 1942.

JOSEPH PULITZER

893. Barrett, James Wyman. *Joseph Pulitzer and His World*. New York: Vanguard Press, 1941. xvi + 449pp.

By the *Morning World*'s last city editor, a book of deep appreciation matched by deeper sadness. Barrett's own involvement in the sale of the *World* is shown in his bias against Scripps-Howard. Probably the best written of the Pulitzer biographies.

894. Ireland, Alleyne. *An Adventure with a Genius: Recollections of Joseph Pulitzer*. New York: E. P. Dutton and Co., 1920. 236pp. (Reissue of the author's *Joseph Pulitzer: Reminiscences of a Secretary*. New York: Mitchell Kennerley, 1914.)

Pulitzer's last year of life, 1910–1911, as told by his secretary. The volume reveals the intensity of Pulitzer's demands upon men.

895. Seitz, Don C. *Joseph Pulitzer: His Life and Letters*. New York: Simon and Schuster, 1924. xvi + 478pp.

Still among the good studies of Pulitzer; also the best of Seitz's three biographies, of Pulitzer, Greeley, and Bennett. Seitz served Pulitzer on the *World* for nearly 20 years and became business manager. Half of the book covers in detail the publisher's last 15 years. There is excellent material on the Panama Canal case and the subsequent criminal libel prosecution against the *World*.

GEORGE PUTNAM

896. Turnbull, George. *An Oregon Editor's Battle for Freedom of the Press*. Portland: Binfords and Mort, 1952. 91pp.

A tribute to the editor of the Medford (Ore.) *Tribune* who early in the 20th century won his case in the state supreme court after arrest on a charge of criminal libel.

897. ———. *An Oregon Crusader*. Portland: Binfords and Mort, 1955. xxviii + 246pp.

An expansion of Turnbull's earlier study. The author adds accounts of Putnam's crusades in Salem, Ore., against the Ku Klux Klan in the early 1920s and against labor "goons" in the 1930s. In these years Putnam was editor of the Salem *Capital Journal*.

ERNEST PYLE

898. Miller, Lee G. *The Story of Ernie Pyle*. New York: The Viking Press, 1950. viii + 439pp.

All who appreciate the greatness of honest reporters should read this, Pyle's life as told by a friend and former associate. Miller draws, from Pyle's correspondence, a story of soul-searching that made the latter so remarkable an observer and reporter of the feelings of the average soldier in World War II. Pyle's own writings are treated only slightly.

CLAYTON RAND

899. Rand, Clayton. *Ink on My Hands*. New York: Carrick and Evans, 1940. xix + 348pp. (Preface by William Allen White.)

Reminiscences of a weekly editor who helped the Negro, struggled for schools, fought the Ku Klux Klan, headed the Mississippi Press Association, and became president of the National Editorial Association. He edited the *Neshoba Democrat* in Philadelphia, Miss., and later three other Mississippi newspapers: De Kalb *Democrat*, Tunica *Times*, and Gulfport *Dixie Guide*.

BURTON RASCOE

900. Rascoe, Burton. *Before I Forget*. New York: Doubleday, Doran and Co., 1937. xix + 442pp.

Rascoe, a nationally known literary critic, writes here principally of his childhood in Kentucky and Oklahoma and his early journalistic career in Chicago as literary editor of the *Tribune*, 1912–1920. The book is most useful for recollections of the great *Tribune* staff of James Keeley, Joseph Patterson, and Joseph Beck. See also the material on Sherwood Anderson, Carl Sandburg, and H. L. Mencken as they were in the 1920s.

901. ———. *We Were Interrupted*. Garden City, N.Y.: Doubleday and Co., 1947. 342pp.

A companion volume to *Before I Forget*, covering Rascoe's activities with the Newspaper Enterprise Association, *McCall's*, and the New York *Tribune* during the 1920s. There are views of W. Somerset Maugham, Joseph Conrad, Theodore Dreiser, Ellen Glasgow, Bertrand Russell, AE (George) Russell, Willa Cather, John Galsworthy, and Amy Lowell.

CHARLES RAY

902. Monaghan, Jay. *The Man Who Elected Lincoln*. Indianapolis and New York: Bobbs-Merrill Co., 1956. x + 334pp.

About Dr. Charles Ray, editor-in-chief of the Chicago *Tribune* during the years between the Kansas-Nebraska Act and the Civil War. The book is based upon Ray's personal papers, the Lincoln papers in the Library of Congress, files of the *Tribune*, and memoirs of Ray's associates.

BIOGRAPHY

HENRY J. RAYMOND

903. Brown, Francis. *Raymond of the Times.* New York: W. W. Norton and Co., 1951. 345pp.

Makes available new findings on Raymond's life. The author searched out Raymond's papers in libraries throughout the United States and obtained additional information from private collections; he was also assisted by materials provided by the New York *Times.* Excellent notes and bibliography add to the book's value.

904. Dodd, Dorothy. *Henry J. Raymond and the New York Times during Reconstruction.* Chicago: University of Chicago, 1936. 90pp.

Ph.D. thesis, University of Chicago.

905. Maverick, Augustus. *Henry J. Raymond and the New York Press for Thirty Years: Progress in American Journalism from 1840 to 1870.* Hartford, Conn.: A. S. Hale and Co., 1870. xx + 501pp.

A private-subscription biography published after Raymond's death; until recent years the only full-length treatment of the founder of the New York *Times.* Heavy on the editor's political career and influence during the Civil War. About a third of the volume concerns New York City newspapers (24 dailies) in 1870. The appendix carries addresses and letters of Raymond. A slow-moving book, but invaluable.

OPIE READ

906. Read, Opie. *I Remember.* New York: Richard R. Smith, 1930. vi + 335pp.

Read wrote novels, edited newspapers, and was chiefly a humorist. His autobiography consists merely of strung-out recollections, among them those relating to the *Arkansaw Traveler,* a humor sheet which he founded in Little Rock in 1882 and moved to Chicago in 1888. There are some good portraits of the old Chicago Press Club. Romantic and full of anecdotes.

HARRY REICHENBACH

907. Reichenbach, Harry. *Phantom Fame: The Anatomy of Ballyhoo, as Told to David Freedman.* New York: Simon and Schuster; London: Noel Douglas, 1932. 258pp. (Introduction by Walter Winchell.)

A show-business promoter, Reichenbach was a master at cooking up stories that newspapers would be forced to publish as news. He played a part in building the movies from early nickel-store shows to a national industry.

WHITELAW REID

908. Reid, Whitelaw. *American and English Studies.* New York: Charles Scribner's Sons, 1913. 2 vols. 658pp., total.

Twenty-three addresses and articles by the editor of the New York *Tribune,* 1872–1912. See vol. II, pp. 193–343, for "An Editor's Reflections," Reid's views on journalism as a career, practical office problems, changes in the press, and journalistic duties and responsibilities.

THE LITERATURE OF JOURNALISM

909. Cortissoz, Royal. *The Life of Whitelaw Reid*: Vol. I, *Journalism, War, Politics*; Vol. II, *Politics, Diplomacy*. New York: Charles Scribner's Sons, 1921. 2 vols. 896pp., total.

A sound biography of Horace Greeley's successor on the New York *Tribune*. Cortissoz was art editor under Reid for many years.

QUENTIN REYNOLDS

910. Rechnitzer, F. E. *War Correspondent: The Story of Quentin Reynolds*. New York: Julian Messner, 1943. 214pp.

Paints Reynolds in heroic lines and carries several dozen illustrations of the news-gathering Quentin in various battle scenes in the early days of World War II. Actually an interesting piece of Allied propaganda.

ROBERT BARNWELL RHETT

911. White, Laura A. *Robert Barnwell Rhett: Father of Secession*. New York: The Century Co., 1931. 264pp.

A life of the South Carolina "fire-eater," editor of the Charleston *Mercury*. The material is substantial and the scholarship sound; the writing is plebian. The author relied upon the *Mercury* as her most valuable source, but the book is mostly political biography.

GRANTLAND RICE

912. Rice, Grantland. *The Tumult and the Shouting: My Life in Sport*. New York: A. S. Barnes and Co., 1954. xvi + 368pp.

Perhaps the best of the autobiographies of sports writers, published a few months after Rice's death. In addition to being an account of "Granny" Rice's career, this is also a history of 20th-century baseball, boxing, golf, tennis, football, horse racing, and track, and of the athletes who participated in these sports.

ALBERT DEANE RICHARDSON

913. Richardson, Abby Sage. *Garnered Sheaves from the Writings of Albert D. Richardson, Collected and Arranged by His Wife, to Which Is Added a Biographical Sketch of the Author*. Hartford, Conn.: Columbian Book Co., 1871. 430pp.

The biography of the Civil War correspondent for the New York *Tribune* is the most useful part of this book; it gives helpful material on Richardson's early career which the reporter's own Civil War narratives do not offer. The articles by Richardson are political and travel pieces, chief of which are commentaries on "Free Missouri," accounts of Washington, D.C., and a sketch of a transcontinental journey to San Francisco.

FRANCIS ASBURY RICHARDSON

914. Richardson, Francis A. "Recollections of a Washington Newspaper Correspondent," in *Records of the Columbia Historical Society*, vol. 6, pp. 24–42. Washington, D.C.: The Society, 1903.

An account of post-Civil War reporting, by a long-time member of the Baltimore *Sun* staff. Richardson discusses the increase in the size of the capital press corps, growth in telegraphic reporting, and changes in the interview technique.

JAMES H. RICHARDSON

915. Richardson, James H. *For the Life of Me: Memoirs of a City Editor.* New York: G. P. Putnam's Sons, 1954. 312pp.

A city editor of the Los Angeles *Examiner* gives an account of crime-hunting metropolitan journalism. For quick, entertaining reading.

JACOB A. RIIS

916. Riis, Jacob A. *The Making of an American.* New York: The Macmillan Co., 1901. xiii + 442pp.

The simply told, idealistic autobiography of a police reporter whose work led him to do much to help improve conditions in the tenement districts of New York City. Riis was on the staff of the New York *Tribune*, 1877–1888, and of the New York *Evening Sun*, 1888–1899.

917. Ware, Louise. *Jacob A. Riis: Police Reporter, Reformer, Useful Citizen.* New York: D. Appleton-Century Co., 1938. xix + 335pp. (Introduction by Allan Nevins; foreword by Roger W. Riis.)

Portrays Riis as one who awakened the whole country to the worst evils of slums. The book is based upon extensive research into the Riis family papers, Riis's own books, and contemporary pamphlets, reports, and public documents.

GEORGE RIPLEY

918. Frothingham, Octavius Brooks. *George Ripley.* Boston: Houghton Mifflin Co., 1882. 321pp. (American Men of Letters Series.)

Ripley, called the father of literary criticism in the American press, contributed to the New York *Tribune*. About a third of the book is devoted to Brook Farm, with which he was associated. There are numerous references to Horace Greeley, Charles A. Dana, and other journalists of the day.

THOMAS RITCHIE

919. Ambler, Charles Henry. *Thomas Ritchie: A Study in Virginia Politics.* Richmond, Va.: Bell Book and Stationery Co., 1913. vii + 303pp.

A competent analysis of a Virginian who dominated Old Dominion journalism from 1804 to 1845 and did much in a day of low-level journalism to raise editorial ethics. The volume relies heavily on the files of Ritchie's Richmond *Enquirer*. Ambler records how Ritchie influenced major issues in the Jackson-Calhoun-Benton era, and gives a detailed analysis of Ritchie's move from Richmond to Washington in 1845 to become a Polk administration editor with the Washington *Union*.

KENNETH ROBERTS

920. Roberts, Kenneth. *I Wanted to Write.* Garden City, N.Y.: Doubleday and Co., 1949. 471pp.

The autobiography of the author of *Northwest Passage, Oliver Wiswell,* and other novels of early America. Much of the first 100 pages is devoted to Roberts's newspaper experience in Boston, with portraits of Edwin A. Grozier and other editors of the Boston *Post.* There is also considerable material on George Horace Lorimer and the *Saturday Evening Post,* to which Roberts contributed. The appendix includes selected Roberts articles, letters, and comments on Pulitzer Prizes, as well as reviews of the author's books.

ERNEST ROGERS

921. Rogers, Ernest. *Peachtree Parade.* Atlanta, Ga.: Tupper and Love, 1956. 221pp. (Introduction by James Saxon Childers.)

More a series of personal recollections than a formal autobiography, by a staff member of the Atlanta *Journal* since 1920. In many ways a "biography" of contemporary Atlanta and an account of famous personages who have trod Peachtree Street, including Bobby Jones and Margaret Mitchell. A sketch of Miss Mitchell is excellent.

WILL ROGERS

922. Croy, Homer. *Our Will Rogers.* Boston: Little, Brown and Co.; New York: Duell, Sloan and Pearce, 1953. xii + 377pp.

This biography by a newspaperman and novelist who knew Rogers includes the story of the newspaper column Rogers began to write in 1922.

923. Rogers, Betty Blake. *Will Rogers: His Wife's Story.* Indianapolis: Bobbs-Merrill Co., 1941. 312pp.

Much of Mrs. Rogers' biography of her husband appeared first in serial form in the *Saturday Evening Post.* See Chapter XI for her account of how Will started to write a newspaper column.

NICHOLAS ROOSEVELT

924. Roosevelt, Nicholas. *A Front Row Seat.* Norman: University of Oklahoma Press, 1953. xi + 304pp.

The author, from the Theodore Roosevelt branch of the family, served the New York *Times* and *Herald Tribune,* 1921–1946. He stresses the interrelations between journalism and history. The book offers a critical view of Franklin Roosevelt and penetrating glimpses into the New York *Times.*

ALBION ROSS

925. Ross, Albion. *Journey of an American.* Indianapolis: Bobbs-Merrill Co., 1957. 346pp.

On the wanderings during a quarter-century of a New York *Times* foreign correspondent who sought to comprehend the restlessness and rootlessness of modern mankind.

HAROLD ROSS

926. Kramer, Dale. *Ross and the New Yorker.* Garden City, N.Y.: Doubleday and Co., 1951. 306pp.

BIOGRAPHY

An appreciative biography of the individualist who founded the most sophisticated magazine of the first half of the 20th century. Kramer includes detailed accounts of many of the *New Yorker*'s staff, particularly E. B. White, James Thurber, Katharine Angell, and Wolcott Gibbs.

GEORGE P. ROWELL

927. Rowell, George P. *Forty Years an Advertising Agent, 1865–1905.* New York: Printers' Ink Publishing Co., 1906. 517pp.

Rowell in 1869 established the first authentic directory of newspapers and included circulations, advertising rates, and the nature of the publications. His autobiography was written for *Printers' Ink.* There is a good account of his establishment of the *American Newspaper Directory* and a picture of journalism at the time of the Philadelphia Centennial in 1876.

ANNE ROYALL

928. Jackson, George Stuyvesant. *Uncommon Scold: The Story of Anne Royall.* Boston: Bruce Humphries, 1937. 161pp.

A life of the feminine scourge of politicians and editors in Andrew Jackson's time. Mrs. Royall edited newspapers in Washington (1831–1854) under the titles of "Paul Pry" and "The Huntress." Jackson steers midway between the newspaper-supplement type of biography about an obscure newspaperwoman and the opinionated vindication of Mrs. Royall by Mrs. Sarah Harvey Porter. The book is based on primary sources.

929. Porter, Sarah Harvey. *The Life and Times of Anne Royall.* Cedar Rapids, Iowa: Torch Press, 1909. 292pp.

An effort to redeem Mrs. Royall's reputation from the effects of "ridicule, injustice, and vilifying persecution." Mrs. Porter discounts Mrs. Royall's bitter attacks on enemies through her newspapers and praises her battles in behalf of sound money, liberal immigration laws, racial advancement, and Free Masonry. The book also contains "pen portraits" by Mrs. Royall of Andrew Jackson and John Quincy Adams.

DAMON RUNYON

930. Weiner, Ed. *The Damon Runyon Story.* New York and London: Longmans, Green and Co., 1948. xiv + 258pp. (Prelude by Walter Winchell.)

A sympathetic biography by a friend of this sports and short-story writer. Weiner stresses Runyon's personality rather than his professional career.

DAMON RUNYON, JR.

931. Runyon, Damon, Jr. *Father's Footsteps.* New York: Random House, 1954. 180pp.

This is merely a review of family relations, with the long estrangement between father and son and the drinking problems of both being considered in excessive detail. There is almost nothing about the professional career of Runyon senior or junior.

THE LITERATURE OF JOURNALISM

CHARLES EDWARD RUSSELL

932. Russell, Charles Edward. *Bare Hands and Stone Walls: Some Recollections of a Side-Line Reformer.* New York: Charles Scribner's Sons, 1933. x + 441pp.

933. ———. *These Shifting Scenes.* New York: George H. Doran Co., 1914. 311pp.

Reminiscences of a newspaperman whose reputation became broader in his later life as a Pulitzer Prize winning biographer and a socialist political leader. The volume records his experiences with tramp printers in post-Civil War days; his coverage of the Haymarket Riot of 1886 and political campaigns; and his views on "the high art of reporting." Russell was city editor of the New York *World* in the 1890s.

EDWARD RUSSELL

934. Russell, Charles Edward. *A Pioneer Editor in Early Iowa: A Sketch of the Life of Edward Russell.* Washington, D.C.: Ransdell, 1941. 78pp.

A tribute to a father by his son many years after the father's death. Edward Russell, who edited the Davenport *Gazette* in Civil War and post-Civil War days, was of Elijah Lovejoy's stamp.

FRED RUSSELL

935. Russell, Fred. *Bury Me in an Old Press Box: Good Times and Life of a Sportswriter.* New York: A. S. Barnes and Co., 1957. xvi + 235pp.

To the sports editor of the Nashville (Tenn.) *Banner,* the sports writer's life may not be the purest of pleasures — but it is not toil. This is a happy book, filled with Russell's accounts of experiences with scores of sports personalities he knew.

LABERT ST. CLAIR

936. St. Clair, Labert. *I've Met the Folks You Read About.* New York: Dodd, Mead and Co., 1940. 308pp.

The autobiography of an Indiana and Chicago journalist (*Inter-Ocean*) who was later retained by Barron G. Collier as a public relations man. There are recollections of associations with the great and near-great for more than a quarter-century.

ROBERT ST. JOHN

937. St. John, Robert. *This Was My World.* Garden City, N.Y.: Doubleday and Co., 1953. 380pp.

The autobiography of a midwestern reporter and later foreign correspondent, one of the group who came out of Chicago about 1920. In this book he covers in the main his youth: Chicago, Oak Park, Cicero.

938. ———. *Foreign Correspondent.* Garden City, N.Y.: Doubleday and Co., 1957. 283pp.

St. John's experiences in the Balkans early in World War II when the countries in that area crumbled before the German armies. He deals principally with Romania, telling the story of King Carol II and Magda Lupescu.

WILLIAM SALISBURY

939. Salisbury, William. *The Career of a Journalist.* New York: B. W. Dodge and Co., 1908. ix + 529pp.

A disappointed reporter writes of the ills, frustrations, and "mental serfdom" of newspaper work. Salisbury's disillusionment occurred chiefly in Kansas City, Omaha, and Chicago.

BRANDON SATTERLEE

940. Satterlee, Brandon. *The Dub of South Burlap: The Story of a Newspaper That Made a Holler in the Wilderness.* New York: Exposition Press, 1952. 243pp.

A Pacific Northwest writer's reminiscences of boyhood days in the 1890s, when his father went west from Neillsville, Wis., to run a weekly in South Burlap on the west shore of Puget Sound. The *Megaphone* did not last long, but father and son had an interesting time with it. Satterlee in later years was with the Seattle *Times*; "Dub" was a boyhood nickname.

A. A. SCHECHTER and EDWARD ANTHONY

941. Schechter, A. A., with Edward Anthony. *I Live on Air.* New York and Toronto: Frederick A. Stokes Co., 1941. viii + 456pp. + 64 full-page illustrations.

An adventurous, aggressive personal story of radio in the early 1930s. Schechter was director of news and special events for the National Broadcasting Co. and Anthony a magazine executive and writer of best-selling books. The story begins in the days of the press-radio war; emphasizes *rapprochement* between radio and press; then jumps around the world from scoop to scoop.

SAMMY SCHULMAN

942. Schulman, Sammy. *Where's Sammy?* New York: Random House, 1943. xi + 234pp. (Edited by Robert Considine.)

Sammy might have been anywhere, photographing Franklin Roosevelt, covering the election of a Pope, or riding "in a tank full of dead Russians." His is a rapid-fire autobiography, in the fire-chasing manner of the Hearst papers and the International News Service, for which Sammy worked, 1923–1943. The book includes 32 prints of Sammy's pictures.

EMILE C. SCHURMACHER

943. Schurmacher, Emile C. *Nothing's Sacred on Sunday.* New York: Thomas Y. Crowell Co., 1951. 243pp.

This could be titled "Ten Years of Stints for the *American Weekly*." Schurmacher reflects on the bewildering assignments of a reporter for a Hearst supplement — from the sex life of the penguin to a junket into Mexico for a scientific piece on the volcano Paricutin. Interspersed are descriptions of Morrill Goddard and Abe Merritt, the *Weekly* editors.

CARL SCHURZ

944. Schurz, Carl. *Intimate Letters of Carl Schurz, 1841–1869*. Madison: State Historical Society of Wisconsin, 1928. xx + 491pp. (Translated and edited by Joseph Schafer.)

Principally letters from Schurz to his wife and to his parents about his life before and during his residence in Wisconsin. Most of the letters were written in the 1850s, when Schurz lived in Watertown. They include material on his purchase of a half-interest in the St. Louis *Westliche-Post* in 1867.

945. ———. *The Reminiscences of Carl Schurz*. New York: The Mc-Clure Co., 1907–1908. 3 vols.

Published posthumously by Schurz's daughters and his son. Vol. I (1829–1852), vol. II (1852–1863), and vol. III (1863-1869) are all by Schurz, with vol. III continuing from 1869 to 1906 under the authorship of Frederic Bancroft and William A. Dunning. Schurz's newspaper career in Wisconsin and Missouri can be traced by careful reading; there are separate chapters on "Journalism" and "Editor of Harper's Weekly."

946. Easum, Chester V. *The Americanization of Carl Schurz*. Chicago: University of Chicago Press, 1929. xi + 374pp.

On Schurz's early years in Germany and in the United States to 1862. The volume is useful for that part of Schurz's journalistic career which preceded his life in St. Louis and New York: as a writer for newspapers in Germany and as a leader in the German-language press in Wisconsin in the 1850s (Watertown *Anzeiger* and *Deutsch Volks-Zeitung*).

947. Fuess, Claude M. *Carl Schurz, Reformer*. New York: Dodd, Mead and Co., 1932. xv + 421pp.

The standard political biography. See Chapter XIII, "Interlude," for Schurz's service with Horace Greeley in 1865 and later on the St. Louis *Westliche-Post*; Chapter XVI, "Greeley versus Grant," for Schurz's part in the campaign of 1872; and Chapter XXI, "A Mugwump Leader," for Schurz's brief editorship of the New York *Evening Post*.

HARVEY W. SCOTT

948. Oregon Historical Society. "Harvey W. Scott Memorial Number," in the *Quarterly* of the Society, vol. XIV, no. 2 (June 1913), pp. 87–213.

This entire issue was devoted to the life of the editor of the Portland *Oregonian*, 1865–1910. The historical society's study remains today the best single source on the career of this giant of Pacific Northwest journalism.

949. Pacific University. *Service in Memory of Harvey Whitefield Scott*. Forest Grove, Ore., 1910. 37pp.

Tributes and addresses, September 29, 1910, at the services for the deceased editor. Today of high regional value.

EDWARD W. SCRIPPS

950. Scripps, Edward W. *Damned Old Crank: A Self-Portrait of E. W.*

Scripps. New York: Harper and Brothers, 1951. xvii + 259pp. (Edited by Charles R. McCabe.)

Revealing accounts extracted from Scripps's unpublished writings to show his varied moods — from "rotund faith" to "hollow doubt." Worth reading. Scripps discusses his break with the Associated Press early in the century, describes Roy W. Howard, and analyzes the possibilities of "honest journalism." McCabe offers a brief analytical sketch of Scripps.

951. Cochran, Negley D. *E. W. Scripps.* New York: Harcourt, Brace and Co., 1933. vii + 315pp.

By a one-time editorial supervisor of Scripps newspapers who had access to E. W.'s files, correspondence, and other writings. Cochran presents Scripps in detail as an individual but does not tell the story of the Scripps newspapers. However, the book continues beyond the editor's death and includes a chapter on the purchase of the New York *World.*

952. Gardner, Gilson. *Lusty Scripps: The Life of E. W. Scripps, 1854–1926.* New York: Vanguard Press, 1932. xv + 274pp.

First of the Scripps biographies, by an associate of 20 years who was one of the trustees of Scripps's estate. In a way this book carries out Scripps's expressed wish that Gardner write the biography and be unconventional in portraying frailties as well as creditable characteristics. The appendix carries Scripps's will in full.

953. Ritter, William E. *Science Service as One Expression of E. W. Scripps's Philosophy of Life.* Washington, D.C.: Science Service, 1926. 31pp.

A report by the president of Science Service to the board of trustees. Ritter tells the story of the founding of and structure of the service.

954. Scripps, James E. *A Genealogical History of the Scripps Family and Its Various Alliances.* Detroit, 1903. iv + 87pp.

Printed for private circulation. Copies are available in the Detroit Public Library and in the Library of Congress.

GUY HAMILTON SCULL

955. Case, Henry J., comp. *Guy Hamilton Scull: Soldier, Writer, Explorer and War Correspondent.* New York: Duffield and Co., 1922. xviii + 267pp.

The biography of a correspondent whose name is missing in most narratives. From 1899 to 1910 Scull covered events in Africa, Manchuria, Russia, the Balkans, and Venezuela; he financed his own way to South Africa to report the Boer War for the New York *Globe* and *Commercial Advertiser.* This book was compiled from accounts contributed by Scull's associates, among them Lincoln Steffens and James H. Hare.

WILLIAM WINSTON SEATON

956. Seaton, Josephine. *William Winston Seaton of the National Intelligencer: A Biographical Sketch, with Passing Notices of His Associates and Friends.* Boston: James R. Osgood and Co., 1871. 385pp.

A family memoir, by Seaton's daughter, this book still remains a chief source of information on Seaton's life. Much of the content consists of extracts from material that Seaton wrote originally for his family. No index and no chapter divisions.

957. Smithsonian Institution. "Sketch of the Services of the Late Hon. W. W. Seaton in Connection with the Smithsonian Institution, and Some Notices of His Life and Personal Character," in *Annual Report of the Board of Regents of the Smithsonian Institution, 1866*, pp. 80–87. Washington, D.C.: Government Printing Office, 1872.

A brief memoir of the editor of the *National Intelligencer*. Seaton as mayor of Washington in 1846 had urged upon Congress the organization of the Smithsonian.

ELLERY SEDGWICK

958. Sedgwick, Ellery. *The Happy Profession*. Boston: Little, Brown and Co., 1946. x + 343pp.

The autobiography of a distinguished editor of the *Atlantic Monthly*, 1908–1938, who earlier had been with *Frank Leslie's Popular Monthly* and *McClure's*. Sedgwick tells of his purchase of the *Atlantic*, discusses contributors to the magazine and the *Atlantic*'s search for authors, and expresses himself on the degeneration of the English language.

GEORGE SELDES

959. Seldes, George. *Tell the Truth and Run*. New York: Greenberg, 1953. xxiv + 293pp.

Seldes's personal story is well worth reading. He covers his early newspaper experiences through World War I, his work abroad in the 1920s as correspondent for Robert R. McCormick on the Chicago *Tribune*, his experiences during the Spanish Civil War, and his unsuccessful venture into "completely free journalism" with *In Fact*.

LOUIS B. SELTZER

960. Seltzer, Louis B. *The Years Were Good*. Cleveland and New York: World Publishing Co., 1956. 318pp. (Introduction by Bruce Catton.)

A life of "Mr. Cleveland," editor of the Cleveland *Press* for 30 years: how an able, eager newspaperman, lacking material advantages early in life, forged to success in his home city and made his newspaper speak personally for everyone in a heterogeneous industrial metropolis. A great love of Cleveland and newspaper work is evident throughout.

ERIC SEVAREID

961. Sevareid, Eric. *Not So Wild a Dream*. New York: Alfred A. Knopf, 1946. 516pp.

The beautifully written autobiography of a young journalist who felt at the end of World War II that he already had lived through a lifetime. Sevareid had come out of North Dakota and the University of Minnesota to be a foreign correspondent on the eve of war, serving the Paris *Herald* and the Columbia Broadcasting Co. His book is marked by a decidedly philosophical note, unlike most personal narratives of journalists.

VINCENT SHEEAN

962. Sheean, Vincent. *Personal History*. Garden City, N.Y.: Doubleday, Doran and Co., 1935. 403pp.

A romantic and yet, on the surface, cynical autobiography of a widely known correspondent; a best seller in its time. Sheean traveled on assignment in the African Rif, the Near East, China in 1927, and Western Europe. His introspection and analysis set a new style in journalistic autobiography.

WILLIAM L. SHIRER

963. Shirer, William L. *Berlin Diary: The Journal of a Foreign Correspondent, 1934–1941*. New York: Alfred A. Knopf, 1941. vi + 695pp.

The best-selling narrative of a correspondent in Germany for the Columbia Broadcasting System, with entries from January 11, 1934, to December 13, 1940. Shirer's diary is a continuing observation of how Hitler carried Europe "down the road to Armageddon."

964. ———. *End of a Berlin Diary*. New York: Alfred A. Knopf, 1947. viii + 369pp.

The sequel to *Berlin Diary* runs from the date of the plot on Hitler's life (July 20, 1944) to December 9, 1945, with a postscript carrying it to the spring of 1947. The book is based chiefly upon Shirer's reading of documents captured from the Germans.

965. ———. *Midcentury Journal: The Western World through Its Years of Conflict*. New York: Farrar, Straus and Young, 1952. 310pp.

In an effort to picture Europe as Shirer had seen it from 1925 to 1950, he travels "back and forth not only in space but in time." Chapters treat of "Vienna — an Indestructible City"; "The Waning Star of France"; "Germany — the Master Race"; and "Will There Always Be an England?" He looks also into the question of European Union. The book is filled with personal introspection.

SIR CLIFFORD SIFTON

966. Dafoe, John W. *Clifford Sifton in Relation to His Times*. Toronto: The Macmillan Co. of Canada, Ltd., 1931. xxix + 552pp.

A tribute to a western Canadian political leader and newspaper owner by the editor who served him for many years. Dafoe deals almost wholly with Sifton's governmental career; however, he does spell out clearly Sifton's principles over 28 years for the *Manitoba Free Press* (later the Winnipeg *Free Press*). There is almost nothing on the Regina *Leader-Post* and Saskatoon *Star-Phoenix*, which Sir Clifford also owned.

SIME SILVERMAN

967. Stoddart, Dayton. *Lord Broadway: Variety's Sime*. New York: Wilfred Funk, 1941. x + 385pp.

Sime Silverman founded *Variety*, the theatrical weekly, in 1905. Stoddart's biography is heavily weighted with Sime's theatrical wars — the struggles of *Variety* against the Keith vaudeville circuit and the Shuberts. Included are facsimiles of *Variety* front pages.

UPTON SINCLAIR

968. Sinclair, Upton. *American Outpost: A Book of Reminiscences.* New York: Farrar and Rinehart, 1932. 280pp.

Sinclair's autobiography is told naively but honestly. The story of his work on *The Jungle* is relatively complete, that on *The Brass Check* is covered only incidentally. Over all, a somewhat unsatisfactory book.

GEORGE W. SMALLEY

969. Smalley, George W. *Anglo-American Memories.* New York and London: G. P. Putnam's Sons, 1911. ix + 441pp.

Excellent reminiscences of a half-century by one of the most intelligent of Civil War reporters. Smalley covered the war for the New York *Tribune*, later established the *Tribune*'s London bureau and covered the Franco-Prussian War, and from 1895–1905 was American correspondent for the London *Times*. There is worthwhile material on the draft riots of 1863 and the attack on the New York *Tribune*, changes in war correspondence, and the development of international journalism in the last 30 years of the 19th century.

KATHLEEN ANN SMALLZRIED

970. Smallzried, Kathleen Ann. *Press Pass: A Woman Reporter's Story.* New York: E. P. Dutton Co., 1940. 340pp.

A superficial autobiography of a small-city reporter (South Bend, Ind., *News-Times*). There is little here that rises above the level of opinions on obituary coverage, women's club lectures, and Notre Dame football games.

CARL SMITH

971. Smith, Carl. *Carl Smith in Washington: Twenty-Five News Years in the National Capital.* Portland, Ore.: Binfords and Mort, 1940. 133pp.

Smith represented the *Oregon Journal* (Portland) in Washington from 1915 to 1940. Although much of this book was written originally for the *Journal*, it has general as well as regional value.

H. ALLEN SMITH

972. Smith, H. Allen. *Low Man on a Totem Pole.* Garden City, N.Y.: Doubleday, Doran and Co., 1941. xvii + 295pp. (Introduction by Fred Allen.)

On the light side — and thin. There is considerable material from Smith's interviews and stories written for the New York *World-Telegram*.

973. ———. *Life in a Putty-Knife Factory.* Garden City, N.Y.: Doubleday, Doran and Co., 1944. xviii + 296pp.

In this companion piece (not a sequel) to *Low Man on a Totem Pole*, Smith attacks sports sections and writes of his "flight from city rooms." However, he includes material on "pride in journalism."

974. ———. *Lost in the Horse Latitudes*. Garden City, N.Y.: Doubleday, Doran and Co., 1944. 224pp.

Still more from Smith: 27 assorted essays, mostly from Hollywood, where Smith was writing for Paramount Pictures.

HAMPTON SIDNEY SMITH, JR.

975. Smith, Hampton Sidney, Jr. *Tramp Reporter*. Caldwell, Idaho: Caxton Printers, Ltd., 1937. 171pp.

Smith, who enjoyed the transient life, set up gradations among reporters as "floaters" and "drifters." Smith, a "floater," went from job to job; a "drifter," he says, merely "drifts."

I. NORMAN SMITH

976. Smith, I. Norman. *A Reporter Reports*. Toronto: Ryerson Press, 1954. x + 145pp.

Twenty-nine autobiographical narratives, 1938–1953, by the associate editor of the Ottawa *Journal*.

EDGAR SNOW

976a. Snow, Edgar. *Journey to the Beginning*. New York: Random House, 1958. 434pp.

An autobiographical narrative of 30 years of reporting in the Far East, from Snow's arrival in China in 1928 to the Cold War. He gives a penetrating analysis of the Communist problem. Snow began his career with the *China Weekly Review*, the Chicago *Tribune*, and the New York *Herald Tribune*, and in the 1940s became a world correspondent for the *Saturday Evening Post*.

EDGAR SNOWDEN

977. Quenzel, Carrol H. *Edgar Snowden, Sr.: Virginia Journalist and Civic Leader*. Charlottesville, Va.: Bibliographical Society of University of Virginia, 1954. 59pp.

A study of a pre-Civil War and Civil War editor of the Alexandria *Gazette*, 1831–1875. Contemporary sources, including the *Gazette*, were used.

E. J. STACKPOLE

978. Stackpole, E. J. *Behind the Scenes with a Newspaper Man: Fifty Years in the Life of an Editor*. Philadelphia: J. B. Lippincott Co., 1927. 325pp.

Reminiscences of politics and journalism in Pennsylvania. Stackpole was with the Harrisburg *Telegraph* for more than 40 years and was editor and president after 1901. He includes accounts of Pennsylvania newspapermen, with considerable detail on E. A. Van Valkenburg of the Philadelphia *North American*.

HENRY B. STANTON

979. Stanton, Henry B. *Random Recollections*. New York: Harper and Brothers, 1887. xv + 298pp.

By an 82-year-old journalist-politician who started his career before 1830. The volume centers chiefly on New York State, with extensive material on Thurlow Weed. Stanton was active in antislavery movements.

HAROLD STEARNS

980. Stearns, Harold E. *The Street I Know*. New York: Lee Furman, 1935. 411pp.

A sensitive account of hardship, success up to a point, and then failure. Stearns had served with the old New York *Evening Sun*, had been editor of the *Dial* in Chicago, and had been on the staff of the Paris *Daily Mail*.

EDMUND CLARENCE STEDMAN

981. Stedman, Laura, and George M. Gould. *Life and Letters of Edmund Clarence Stedman*. New York: Moffat, Yard and Co., 1910. 2 vols. 1292pp., total.

Stedman was a prominent critic and literary figure from 1860 to 1908. Part of vol. I is devoted to his journalistic career in Connecticut in the 1850s and later in New York; see also I:223–256 on "The War Correspondent." Most of the biography, however, is devoted to Stedman's business and literary career. An extensive bibliography and chronology, II:615–654, lists Stedman's works and all his Civil War press contributions.

LINCOLN STEFFENS

982. Steffens, Lincoln. *The Autobiography of Lincoln Steffens*. New York: Harcourt, Brace and Co., 1931. 2 vols. 884pp., total.

Among the most powerful and effective autobiographies ever written by a journalist. Its immediate impact was immense, its audience extending far beyond press circles; and it has continued to be widely read for more than a quarter-century. Steffens's story carries from a precocious childhood in post-Civil War California in the 1860s to the late 1920s. Muckraking, the Communist Revolution, the revolution in Mexico, Benito Mussolini, and post-World War I United States are treated at length.

983. ———. *The Letters of Lincoln Steffens*. New York: Harcourt, Brace and Co., 1938. 2 vols. 1072pp., total. (Edited by Ella Winter Steffens and Granville Hicks.)

Into these volumes are compressed scores of Steffens's personal comments — to family, friends, and political leaders — over a period of 47 years. Vol. I carries to 1920 and vol. II from 1920 to 1936. Exceptionally valuable is a bibliography of all Steffens's works, including magazine articles.

KENNETH STEWART

984. Stewart, Kenneth. *News Is What We Make It!* Boston: Houghton Mifflin Co., 1943. xii + 340pp.

BIOGRAPHY

A well-written report on the working press of America, to a great extent auto-biographical. Stewart had served in turn with the New York *Herald Tribune*, *Literary Digest*, and *PM*, had been a Nieman Fellow, and had taught journalism at Stanford. He is generous to newspapers and the employees who serve them, particularly copyreaders, rewrite men, and reporters.

WILLIAM JAMES STILLMAN

985. Stillman, William James. *The Autobiography of a Journalist*. Boston and New York: Houghton Mifflin Co., 1901. 2 vols. vi + 743pp., total.

The autobiography of a versatile man: art critic for the New York *Evening Post* under Bryant; founder of an art journal, the *Crayon*; U.S. consul in Rome during the Civil War and later in Crete; and for more than a decade late in his career world correspondent for the London *Times*.

WILLIAM O. STODDARD

986. Stoddard, William O. *Lincoln's Third Secretary: The Memoirs of William O. Stoddard*. New York: Exposition Press, 1955. 235pp. (Edited, with an introduction, by William O. Stoddard, Jr.)

Stoddard was a member of Abraham Lincoln's personal staff from 1861–1864. Before the Civil War Stoddard had been editor of the *Central Illinois Gazette* (West Urbana), and he is regarded as the first to have sounded an editorial call for Lincoln's nomination (May 4, 1859). The bulk of the book is devoted to Stoddard's association with Lincoln; his Illinois journalistic experience is treated only briefly and his long career as journalist and author after the war is neglected.

THOMAS L. STOKES

987. Stokes, Thomas L. *Chip Off My Shoulder*. Princeton, N.J.: Princeton University Press, 1940. 561pp.

The autobiography of a leading columnist for the United Press and Scripps-Howard newspapers. Stokes records his early life in Georgia and his move to the Washington scene in the early 1920s; thereafter the volume is mostly an analysis of political affairs, with portraits of Harding, Coolidge, Hoover, and Franklin D. Roosevelt.

MELVILLE E. STONE

988. Stone, Melville E. *Fifty Years a Journalist*. Garden City, N.Y., and Toronto: Doubleday, Page and Co., 1921. xiii + 379pp.

Among the better autobiographies in journalism, mostly because of the wealth of subject matter. Stone, one of the founders of the Chicago *Daily News* and the first general manager of the modern Associated Press, offers about 100 vignettes of highlights of his life. Although the many sketches that Stone gives may seem superficial when read separately, they nevertheless add up to a useful whole.

989. Associated Press. *"M. E. S." His Book: A Tribute and a Souvenir*

of the Twenty-Five Years 1893–1918 of the Service of Melville E. Stone as General Manager of the Associated Press. New York and London: Harper and Brothers, 1918. xi + 363pp.

A biographical sketch by John P. Gavit, managing editor of the New York *Evening Post*; tributes by Stone's associates; chapters on property rights in news; Stone's speeches and addresses on the AP, the American newspaper, and public opinion; by-laws of the AP; and a directory of AP officers, 1892–1918. This is excellent reference material apart from its promotional aspects.

990. ———. *"M. E. S." In Memoriam.* New York: The AP, 1929. 160pp.

Prepared after Stone's death by the Associated Press board of directors as a companion to *"M. E. S.," His Book.* Most helpful is the AP staff biography of Stone.

WILLARD STRAIGHT

991. Croly, Herbert. *Willard Straight.* New York: The Macmillan Co., 1925. xvi + 569pp.

A life of the founder of the *New Republic*, by the magazine's first editor and Straight's ardent friend. It is essentially concerned with Straight's career as a diplomat, businessman, and soldier, but there is some material on Straight as a journalist.

MARK SULLIVAN

992. Sullivan, Mark. *The Education of an American.* New York: Doubleday, Doran and Co., 1938. 317pp.

This is the deeply sincere autobiography of the magazine editor, columnist, and journalistic historian who was also the author of *Our Times*, a history of the first quarter of the 20th century. Sullivan's long association with *Collier's*, beginning in 1906, is dealt with at length.

JANE GREY SWISSHELM

993. Swisshelm, Jane Grey. *Crusader and Feminist: Letters of Jane Grey Swisshelm, 1858–1865.* St. Paul: Minnesota Historical Society, 1934. ix + 327pp. (Edited, with introduction and notes, by Arthur J. Larsen of the Society.)

Regional matter of high value. Mrs. Swisshelm was an aggressive, able frontier editor during the Civil War, writing for the St. Cloud (Minn.) *Visiter* and *Democrat* on the slavery issue, women's rights, pioneer journalism, frontier travel, Indian problems, and people in general. The first 32 pages carry a biography by Larsen. Some of the best letters are Mrs. Swisshelm's news reports on hospital service during the war.

994. ———. *Half a Century.* Chicago: Published by the Author, 1880. 363pp.

In this autobiography Mrs. Swisshelm sought to present her own inside history of the "Abolitionist War." She stresses her activities in hospitals during the Civil War; her newspaper work is subordinated.

BIOGRAPHY

ARTHUR TAPPAN

995. New York City Anti-Slavery Society. *Arthur and Lewis Tappan.* New York: West and Trow, 1883. 16pp.

Based upon an address by Clarence Winthrop Bowen on the occasion of the 50th anniversary of the Anti-Slavery Society, October 2, 1883.

996. Tappan, Lewis. *The Life of Arthur Tappan.* New York: Hurd and Houghton; Cambridge, Mass.: Riverside Press, 1870. 432pp.

By the brother of the antislavery leader and reformer who in 1827 founded the New York *Journal of Commerce*. He wrote primarily for Tappan's family and followers. Chapters of journalistic interest relate to the founding of the mercantile newspaper and the later sale of it to David Hale and Gerard Hallock; and to Arthur Tappan's support of the *Liberator, Emancipator, Colored American, National Era,* and *Anti-Slavery Reporter.* A useful appendix contains an analysis of the *Journal of Commerce.*

IDA MINERVA TARBELL

997. Tarbell, Ida Minerva. *All in the Day's Work.* New York: The Macmillan Co., 1939. 412pp.

The straightforward and unpretentious autobiography of the outstanding woman muckraker. There is considerable emphasis upon Miss Tarbell's years with *McClure's* and the *American Magazine.* Her interpretations of S. S. McClure, Lincoln Steffens, and Ray Stannard Baker are well worth reading.

ELLEN TARRY

998. Tarry, Ellen. *The Third Door: The Autobiography of an American Negro Woman.* New York: David McKay Co., 1955. ix + 304pp.

The life of a Montgomery (Ala.) girl who carved for herself a successful journalistic career in the 1930s and 1940s. The volume centers chiefly in New York City and Chicago.

BAYARD TAYLOR

999. Taylor, Bayard. *The Unpublished Letters of Bayard Taylor in the Huntington Library.* San Marino, Calif.: Huntington Library, 1937. xxvi + 231pp. (Edited, with an introduction, by John Richie Schultz.)

More than 125 of Taylor's letters covering the period 1844–1878. Many were to newspaper and magazine editors, among them Charles A. Dana, George W. Curtis, James T. Fields, Horace Greeley, Edmund C. Stedman, and James R. Osgood. Editor Schultz gives a brief sketch of Taylor.

1000. Beatty, Richmond Croom. *Bayard Taylor: Laureate of the Gilded Age.* Norman: University of Oklahoma Press, 1936. xv + 379pp.

Seeks to explain why an esteemed writer and journalist of the 19th century has been almost forgotten in the 20th. Beatty devotes considerable attention to Taylor's travel books and lectures, with good material on his trip to California in 1848 as correspondent for the New York *Tribune.*

1001. Hansen-Taylor, Marie, and Horace E. Scudder. *Life and Letters of Bayard Taylor.* Boston and New York: Houghton Mifflin Co., 1884. 2 vols. viii + 784pp., total.

The authors weave a story of Taylor's life from the letters he wrote over more than 30 years. Of particular interest is the material on Taylor's early career as editor of a country newspaper (Phoenixville, Pa., *Gazette*); on his literary life in New York; and on his service for Horace Greeley, including reporting from California in 1849.

1002. Smyth, Albert H. *Bayard Taylor.* Boston and New York: Houghton Mifflin Co., 1896. xii + 320pp. (American Men of Letters Series.)

Based heavily on the life of Taylor by Hansen-Taylor and Scudder. Smyth's volume is useful for the period 1848–1853 when Taylor was a newspaper reporter.

CHARLES H. TAYLOR

1003 Morgan, James. *Charles H. Taylor: Builder of the Boston Globe.* Boston: The Globe, 1923. 213pp.

A house biography, issued on the 50th anniversary of Taylor's editorship. Tritely written, with many testimonials and quotations from Taylor's speeches — even "Uncle Dudley" editorials.

JOHN ADAMS THAYER

1004. Thayer, John Adams. *Astir: A Publisher's Life Story.* Boston: Small, Maynard and Co., 1910. xv + 302pp.

The autobiography of one of the founders of *Everybody's* (1903), who also was associated with the *Ladies' Home Journal* and the *Delineator.* The most useful material is that concerned with the muckraking period and the discovery of Tom Lawson, author of a series for *Everybody's* on "Frenzied Finance."

EBENEZER THOMAS

1005. Thomas, Ebenezer Smith. *Reminiscences of the Last Sixty-Five Years, Commencing with the Battle of Lexington; Also, Sketches of His Own Life and Times.* Hartford, Conn.: Case, Tiffany and Burnham, printed privately for the author, 1840. 2 vols. 599pp., total.

One of the earliest autobiographies of a newspaper editor. Thomas, editor of the Charleston (S.C.) *City Gazette* and later the Cincinnati *Daily Evening Post,* gives a long backward view — to Samuel Adams, whom Thomas knew in 1792, and to his uncle, Isaiah Thomas.

ISAIAH THOMAS

1006. Marble, Annie Russell. *From 'Prentice to Patron: The Life Story of Isaiah Thomas.* New York and London: D. Appleton-Century Co., 1935. xii + 326pp.

Tells how a poor Colonial youth, without social influence or schooling, rose to become a Revolutionary patriot, editor of the *Massachusetts Spy,* founder of book stores and fine presses, benefactor of education, historian of printing, and founder of the American Antiquarian Society. There are extracts from Thomas's diaries and previously unpublished letters.

1007. Shipton, Clifford K. *Isaiah Thomas: Printer, Patriot and Philanthropist, 1749–1831.* Rochester, N.Y.: The Printing House of Leo Hart, 1948. xii + 94pp.

A scholarly monograph supplementing the Marble biography. Shipton wrote specifically for readers with an understanding of and appreciation for fine printing. Attractive plates depict Thomas's press, issues of the *Massachusetts Spy*, books, magazines, and theses which Thomas published, covers of Thomas-printed Bibles, and the Thomas paper mill.

EDWARD McCRAY THOMPSON

1008. Thompson, Edward McCray. *Leg Man.* New York: E. P. Dutton and Co., 1943. 187pp.

Experiences of a reporter for the St. Louis *Star-Times* and St. Louis *Globe-Democrat*. The volume does not rise much above commentary on multiple-alarm fires, executions, burglaries, and visiting celebrities.

SLASON THOMPSON

1009. Thompson, Slason. *Way Back When: Recollections of an Octogenarian.* Chicago: A. Kroch, privately published, 1931. 358pp.

The autobiography of a versatile editor who was also the biographer of Eugene Field, one of the first industrial public relations agents, and a devotee of drama and sports. His book is most helpful for the portions devoted to Chicago newspapers, 1880 to the early 1900s; the establishment of the Chicago *Herald*, in which Thompson joined; his editorship of the Chicago *Journal*; and his association with Herman Kohlsaat on the Chicago *Times-Herald*. Also included is information on General Managers Association, railway publicists.

EUNICE TIETJENS

1010. Tietjens, Eunice Hammond. *The World at My Shoulder.* New York: The Macmillan Co., 1938. 341pp.

The autobiography of a foreign correspondent, poet, and novelist. Mrs. Tietjens covered World War I for the Chicago *Daily News*, being one of the few accredited women correspondents of that day. She also served on the staffs of *Poetry* and the *Little Review*.

RICHARD L. TOBIN

1011. Tobin, Richard L. *Golden Opinions.* New York: E. P. Dutton and Co., 1948. 254pp.

Reminiscences over a quarter-century of a New York *Herald Tribune* radio columnist. Some of the pieces were published originally in the *Herald Tribune*. The book lacks depth.

L. FRANK TOOKER

1012. Tooker, L. Frank. *The Joys and Tribulations of an Editor.* New York and London: The Century Co., 1924. 369pp.

Tooker was a staff member of the *Century Magazine* for 40 years. Considerable background on the *Century* is woven into the autobiographical narrative, as well as personality portraits of Richard Watson Gilder and Robert Underwood Johnson, both editors of the *Century*.

CHARLES HANSON TOWNE

1013. Towne, Charles Hanson. *Adventures in Editing.* New York and London: D. Appleton and Co., 1926. viii + 239pp.

The rambling autobiography of a prolific writer and magazine editor, chiefly of the *Smart Set* and *Harper's Bazaar*. Towne also was a columnist for the New York *American*. There is good information on the competitive situation among leading circulation magazines.

W. B. TOWNSEND

1014. Townsend, W. B. *Observations from a Peak in Lumpkin: Or, the Writings of W. B. Townsend.* Atlanta, Ga.: Oglethorpe University, 1936. 342pp. (Edited by A. F. Dean.)

A collection of near-illiterate pieces which appeared in the Dahlonega (Ga.) *Nugget* over a 43-year period in the late 19th and early 20th centuries. Townsend put out this paper on a Washington hand-press in a town 20 miles from a railroad. Dean explains how an eccentric could gain a wide reputation regionally as a "second Benjamin Franklin."

IRWIN ST. JOHN TUCKER

1015. Tucker, Irwin St. John. *Out of the Hell-Box.* New York: Morehouse-Gorham Co., 1945. 179pp.

The autobiography of a man of "two sides" — priest in charge of St. Stephen's Church, Chicago, and, as "Friar Tuck," a copy editor for the Chicago *Herald-American*. The author was at one time managing editor of the *Christian Socialist* in Chicago.

AGNESS UNDERWOOD

1016. Underwood, Agness. *Newspaperwoman.* New York: Harper and Brothers, 1949. 297pp.

Agness Underwood more than held her own in the aggressive journalism of Los Angeles as city editor of the *Herald-Express*. Her unpretentious book is a report on "cops and crime," "newspaperwoman in court," "fires, floods, rapes and other minor disasters," plus Hollywood.

CARR VAN ANDA

1017. Fine, Barnett. *A Giant of the Press.* New York: Editor & Publisher, 1933. 108pp.

A life of Carr Van Anda, managing editor of New York *Times*, 1904–1932. See particularly the accounts of the *Times*'s handling of the sinking of the *Titanic* in 1912 and Van Anda's contribution to science in the handling of Einstein's theories. The book is based principally on secondary sources on the

Times, plus letters, personal interviews, and magazine and newspaper articles on Van Anda.

PIERRE VAN PAASSEN

1018. Van Paassen, Pierre. *Days of Our Years.* New York: Hillman Curl, 1939. 520pp.

Another best seller among journalists' autobiographies. Van Paassen, a European correspondent for the old New York *Evening World,* discusses his youth in Holland, his experiences in World War I, and his journalistic travels through most of Europe and North Africa. There is a strong religious note throughout.

PARKER VANAMEE

1019. Vanamee, Mary Conger. *Vanamee.* New York: Harcourt, Brace and Co., 1930. 307pp.

Parker Vanamee was a promising young New York *World* reporter for a short time in the 1900s; he resigned to enter the Episcopal clergy, and later died of wounds suffered in World War I. This book, by his widow, is a beautifully composed work.

CORNELIUS VANDERBILT, JR.

1020. Vanderbilt, Cornelius, Jr. *Farewell to Fifth Avenue.* New York: Simon and Schuster, 1935. 260pp.

Covers the first 35 years of Vanderbilt's life. The book is poorly written, with excessive attention to the failures of the social group into which he was born. There is some value in Vanderbilt's account of his effort to get the Los Angeles *Daily News* started in the 1920s.

1021. ———. *Personal Experiences of a Cub Reporter.* New York: George Sully and Co., 1922. 212pp.

Written when Vanderbilt was 23 and had had some experience on the New York *Herald.* His real career as publisher of unsuccessful tabloids, author and lecturer, and cinematographer came later.

HENRY VILLARD

1022. Villard, Henry. *Memoirs of Henry Villard: Journalist and Financier.* Boston and New York: Houghton Mifflin Co., 1904. 2 vols. 796pp., total.

Despite its subtitle, this autobiography of the owner of the *Nation* and the New York *Evening Post* contains relatively little journalistic material. Seven of eight sections deal wholly with Villard's experiences from his arrival in New York in 1853 through the Civil War; one section of 90 pages sums up the last 35 years of his life.

1023. Villard, Oswald Garrison. *Henry Villard: A True Fairy Tale.* New York: Henry Holt and Co., 1931. 12pp.

A beautiful piece, fact told as fiction, by a son moved by the memory and inspiration of his father.

THE LITERATURE OF JOURNALISM

OSWALD GARRISON VILLARD

1024. Villard, Oswald Garrison. *Fighting Years: Memoirs of a Liberal Editor.* New York: Harcourt, Brace and Co., 1939. 543pp.

An account of Villard's career as owner-editor of the New York *Evening Post* and the *Nation* and of his struggles in behalf of civil liberties. There are significant comments in connection with his activities in World War I, the accusations against him of pro-Germanism, and his unhappy friendship with Woodrow Wilson.

DANTON WALKER

1025. Walker, Danton. *Danton's Inferno: The Story of a Columnist and How He Grew.* New York: Hastings House, 1955. 312pp.

The recollections of a Broadway columnist of the New York *Daily News* — light in content but distinctive in style. Among Walker's train of celebrities are Joseph Medill Patterson and Mrs. Eleanor (Cissy) Patterson.

STANLEY WALKER

1026. Walker, Stanley. *Home to Texas.* New York: Harper and Brothers, 1956. v + 307pp.

Walker's autobiography, splendidly written, makes only limited reference to his quarter-century as a newspaperman in New York and is restricted almost wholly to the more adaptable life in Lampasas he chose later. He was at one time city editor of the New York *Herald Tribune.*

STANLEY WASHBURN

1027. Washburn, Stanley. *The Cable Game: The Adventures of an American Press-Boat in Turkish Waters during the Russian Revolution.* Boston: Sherman, French and Co., 1912. 222pp.

The life of a Chicago *Daily News* correspondent in the first decade of the 20th century. Washburn gives pictures of the Russo-Japanese War and of news races across India. To some extent this is a promotional piece on behalf of the *Daily News* and Victor F. Lawson.

HENRY WATTERSON

1028. Watterson, Henry. *The Compromises of Life: And Other Lectures and Addresses, Including Some Observations on Certain Downward Tendencies in Modern Society.* New York: Duffield and Co., 1906. 511pp.

1029. ———. *"Marse Henry": An Autobiography.* New York: George H. Doran Co., 1919. 2 vols. 629pp., total.

A discursive story by the editor of the Louisville *Courier-Journal* extending from Reconstruction to World War I. Watterson recalls people and events and philosophizes about changing times. Among those who crossed Watterson's path were Mark Twain, Murat Halstead, Samuel Bowles III, Horace White, Carl Schurz, Joseph Pulitzer, John W. Forney, and Charles A. Dana.

BIOGRAPHY

1030. Louisville Courier-Journal. *Marse Henry Edition.* Louisville, March 2, 1919. 32 tabloid pp., in color.

A testimonial to emeritus editor Watterson on the occasion of his completing 50 years with the newspaper. A collector's item, this edition is filled with fascinating cartoons of "Marse Henry."

1031. Marcosson, Isaac F. *"Marse Henry": A Biography of Henry Watterson.* New York: Dodd, Mead and Co., 1951. xviii + 269pp. (Foreword by Arthur Krock.)

Marcosson fails in this oversimplified biography to analyze thoroughly the complexities of Henry Watterson. Acknowledgments to sources refer almost wholly to previous secondary works on Watterson and his era.

1032. Wall, Joseph Frazier. *Henry Watterson: Reconstructed Rebel.* New York: Oxford University Press, 1956. xvi + 362pp. (Introduction by Alben W. Barkley.)

The latest addition to the Watterson literature. Wall draws on the Watterson papers in the Library of Congress and on other manuscript sources, as well as on the files of the *Courier-Journal.* The two most significant chapters come at either end of Watterson's career: the details of his taking over the *Journal* from George D. Prentice after the Civil War and his unhappy experiences on retiring from the newspaper after World War I.

NOAH WEBSTER

1033. Scudder, Horace E. *Noah Webster.* Boston: Houghton Mifflin Co., 1885. 302pp. (American Men of Letters Series.)

A life of the lexicographer and author who edited the *American Magazine* (1787–1788) and the *American Minerva* (1793–1798).

1034. Warfel, Harry R. *Noah Webster: Schoolmaster to America.* New York: The Macmillan Co., 1936. xiii + 460pp.

Devoted chiefly to Webster as teacher and lexicographer. However, adequate treatment is given to his career on the *American Magazine* and *American Minerva.*

JAMES A. WECHSLER

1035. Wechsler, James A. *The Age of Suspicion.* New York: Random House, 1953. 333pp.

The autobiography of the editor of the New York *Post.* The book carried political news value upon publication, since Wechsler had opposed Senator Joseph R. McCarthy in the anti-Communist imbroglios of the early 1950s. Wechsler gives background on his experiences in the Young Communist League and his withdrawal from the party, together with his later fight against it. The book may have increased value in another generation as a reflection of the temper of mid-20th century.

THURLOW WEED

1036. Weed, Thurlow. *Life of Thurlow Weed, Including His Autobiog-*

raphy and a Memoir. Boston: Houghton Mifflin Co., 1884. 2 vols. 1274pp. (Edited by Harriet A. Weed and Thurlow Weed Barnes.)

The first volume of this life of a politician and owner of the Albany *Evening Journal* is autobiographical, as edited by Weed's daughter; the second is a memoir, by his grandson. Weed wrote his life story in fragments over many years; the periods 1842–1848 and 1852–1860 are covered only sketchily. In the memoir, Barnes fits in missing links, particularly for 1850–1857. The volumes give excellent background for the period before and after the Civil War.

1037. Van Deusen, Glyndon G. *Thurlow Weed: Wizard of the Lobby.* Boston: Little, Brown and Co., 1947. xiv + 403pp.

A well-written life, based on numerous printed sources, including the Weed and William H. Seward papers. The content is essentially political, but there are many references to Weed's journalistic associations — particularly with Greeley and Raymond.

EDWARD WEEKS

1038. Weeks, Edward. *The Open Heart.* Boston and Toronto: Atlantic Monthly Press, Little, Brown and Co., 1955. xii + 235pp.

A series of 36 essays which add up to a warm autobiography by the editor of the *Atlantic Monthly.* There is an excellent chapter on how Adolph S. Ochs and Carr Van Anda built the modern New York *Times.*

LINTON WELLS

1039. Wells, Linton. *Blood on the Moon.* Boston and New York: Houghton Mifflin Co., 1937. viii + 418pp.

A highly romantic autobiography of a correspondent, globe-girdler, flier, and radio-broadcaster for some 25 years.

JOSEPH A. WHEELOCK

1040. Eide, Richard B. *North Star Editor: A Brief Sketch of Joseph A. Wheelock and His Policies as Editor of the St. Paul Pioneer-Press.* New York: King's Crown Press, Columbia University, 1944. viii + 77pp.

Traces Wheelock's career from his arrival in St. Paul in 1850 to his death in 1906, as editor first of the St. Paul *Press* and later the combined *Pioneer-Press.* Eide stresses Wheelock's conservative attitudes, his encouragement of civic development in St. Paul, and his attack upon exploitation of public lands.

DANIEL W. WHETSTONE

1041. Whetstone, Daniel W. *Frontier Editor.* New York: Hastings House, 1956. 287pp.

The autobiography of the editor of the Cut Bank (Mont.) *Pioneer Press* since 1909.

WILLIAM ALLEN WHITE

1042. White, William Allen. *The Autobiography of William Allen White.* New York: The Macmillan Co., 1946. 669pp.

BIOGRAPHY

One of the most valuable autobiographies of American newspapermen. This is the story of a Kansas editor who spoke forth strongly for more than 40 years, met with the great, but remained a reporter for his home-town Emporia. White carries the narrative only to the middle 1930s. His son, William L. White, rounds out the years up to his father's death in 1944. The book is well illustrated.

1043. ———. *Selected Letters of William Allen White.* New York: Henry Holt and Co., 1947. viii + 460pp. (Edited by Walter Johnson.)

These letters, from July 3, 1899, to November 23, 1943, only two months before White's death, are a treasure-trove for historians and general readers alike.

1044. Clough, Frank C. *William Allen White of Emporia.* New York and London: Whittlesey House, McGraw-Hill Book Co., 1941. xiv + 265pp.

"The Boss" of the Emporia *Gazette* as described by his managing editor. This unadorned biography shows throughout a regard for White as a truly great man.

1045. Hinshaw, David. *A Man from Kansas: The Story of William Allen White.* New York: G. P. Putnam's Sons, 1945. xi + 305pp.

Another appreciative biography, by one whose admiration for White went back to 1897. Hinshaw writes largely from memory, his common background with White, and a reading of Emporia *Gazette* editorials. He tries to interpret the nature of Kansas when Bill White was young; White's close association with Theodore Roosevelt in his middle years; and the editor's life as a national figure, 1916–1944.

1046. Johnson, Walter. *William Allen White's America.* New York: Henry Holt and Co., 1947. 621pp.

White's life in topical form. The book is based on unpublished letters of White's and on excerpts from the *Selected Letters* (1043). Newspaper sources were also used.

1047. Rich, Everett. *William Allen White: The Man from Emporia.* New York: Farrar and Rinehart, 1941. ix + 374pp.

A biography developed from a Ph.D. dissertation; first of the numerous recent books on White to be thoroughly documented.

BRAND WHITLOCK

1048. Whitlock, Brand. *Forty Years of It.* New York and London: D. Appleton and Co., 1914. xii + 374pp.

Autobiographical sketches written before Whitlock's service in World War I. The book deals chiefly with the author's opinions on morals, politics, religion, and literature; there are occasional glimpses of the press in the 1890s and 1900s.

1049. ———. *The Letters and Journal of Brand Whitlock.* New York and London: D. Appleton-Century Co., 1936. 2 vols. 1329pp., total. (Edited by Allan Nevins.)

Detailed material on the career of the Toledo journalist whose fame rests on his reform activities as mayor of Toledo and on his work as ambassador to Belgium in World War I. In a biographical introduction, Nevins sketches Whitlock's newspaper service, 1887–1890, on the Toledo *Blade* and in the 1890s in Chicago on the *Record-Herald*. Whitlock's diplomatic and literary careers are more extensively treated.

WALT WHITMAN

1050. Whitman, Walt. *Walt Whitman of the New York Aurora, Editor at Twenty-Two: A Collection of Recently Discovered Writings.* State College, Pa.: Bald Eagle Press, 1950. viii + 147pp. (Edited by Joseph Jay Rubin and Charles H. Brown.)

Collects nearly 200 articles and two poems written by Whitman for the New York *Aurora*, of which he was editor in the spring of 1842. For more than 100 years the material had been believed lost, until a file of the *Aurora* was found in the Paterson (N.J.) Library.

1051. Grebanier, Frances Vinciguerra [pseud. Frances Winwar]. *American Giant: Walt Whitman and His Times.* New York: Harper and Brothers, 1941. xiv + 341pp.

Portrays Whitman as the symbol of America: "generous, peace-loving, and mighty fighter for principle." There is a full discussion of Whitman as printer's devil, typesetter, editor of the Brooklyn *Eagle*, and follower of Paine and Jefferson.

1052. Holloway, Emory. *Whitman: An Interpretation in Narrative.* New York: Alfred A. Knopf, 1926. xv + 330pp.

A thorough account of Whitman's newspaper experiences.

1053. Rogers, Cameron. *The Magnificent Idler: The Story of Walt Whitman.* Garden City, N.Y.: Doubleday, Page and Co., 1926. 312pp.

An illustrated, popular appreciation of Whitman, by a young honor graduate of Harvard University.

1054. Willard, Charles B. *Whitman's American Fame: The Growth of His Reputation in America after 1892.* Providence, R.I.: Brown University, 1950. 269pp. (Brown University Studies, American Series, vol. XII.)

Summarizes what appear to the author to be major aspects in the solidification of Whitman's reputation after his death. There is a long chapter on the journalistic critics of Whitman, but the body of the book considers the views of him held by academicians, creative writers, Whitman enthusiasts, and general observers.

FREDERIC WILLIAM WILE

1055. Wile, Frederic William. *News Is Where You Find It.* Indianapolis: Bobbs-Merrill Co., 1939. 505pp.

Wile, who established a Chicago *Daily News* bureau in Berlin, is prolix but his autobiography contains valuable information about Germany from 1901 to 1914 and about the influence of Lord Northcliffe. Later Wile pioneered as a radio reporter.

BIOGRAPHY

FRANC B. WILKIE

1056. Wilkie, Franc B. *Personal Reminiscences of Thirty-Five Years of Journalism.* Chicago: F. J. Schulte and Co., 1891. 324pp.

Covers Wilkie's career from 1854, when he began with the Schenectady (N.Y.) *Evening Star*, through more than a score of years with the Chicago *Daily Times*. Well over half the book is virtually a biography of Wilbur F. Storey, eccentric editor of the *Times*, on whom little other material is readily available. Wilkie gives an objective, fair account of working for one of the most trying editors of the day.

TALCOTT WILLIAMS

1057. Dunbar, Elizabeth. *Talcott Williams: Gentleman of the Fourth Estate.* New York: Robert E. Simpson and Son, 1936. 400pp.

A tribute to the long-time Philadelphia newspaperman who, at age 63, became the first director of the Pulitzer School of Journalism at Columbia University. The writing is stodgy, but the book has real merit as an expression of high ideals for journalism.

WALTER WILLIAMS

1058. University of Missouri. *In Memoriam: Walter Williams, 1864–1935.* University of Missouri Bulletin, vol. 37, no. 5, journalism series no. 75, 1936. 79pp. (Edited by Roscoe Ellard.)

A pamphlet issued after the death of the emeritus dean of journalism at Missouri, who had also been president of the university. Williams founded the Missouri School of Journalism in 1908. Included are obituaries from the nation's press, editorials, commentaries of associates, and tributes from numerous Missouri editors.

WYTHE WILLIAMS

1059. Williams, Wythe. *Dusk of Empire: The Decline of Europe and the Rise of the United States, as Observed by a Foreign Correspondent in a Quarter Century of Service.* New York and London: Charles Scribner's Sons, 1937. xix + 325pp.

Williams served various American newspapers, including the New York *Times* and *World*, in the period after 1910. He gives excellent material on London and Paris before the wars; on the fall of Europe after World War I; and on Franklin D. Roosevelt. Among the better journalistic autobiographies.

NATHANIEL P. WILLIS

1060. Beers, Henry A. *Nathaniel Parker Willis.* Boston: Houghton Mifflin Co., 1885. viii + 365pp.

Willis founded the *American Monthly* in 1829 and was its editor for two years; he was also founder and editor of the *Home Journal*, 1846–1867.

SIR JOHN WILLISON

1061. Colquhoun, A. H. U. *Press, Politics and People: The Life and*

Letters of Sir John Willison, Journalist and Correspondent of the Times. Toronto: The Macmillan Co. of Canada, Ltd., 1935. 306pp.

Willison was a Canadian journalist of the late 19th and early 20th centuries (Toronto *Globe* and Toronto *News*) and from 1909 to 1927 Canadian correspondent of the London *Times*. The book is especially useful for its background on Sir Wilfrid Laurier and his connections with the press. Colquhoun had access to an immense bulk of Willison papers, 1885–1927.

WILLIAM H. WINANS

1062. Winans, William H. *Reminiscences and Experiences in the Life of an Editor.* Newark, N.J.: Privately published, 1875. 200pp.

Recollections of the middle 19th century by a small-city editor in upper New York State and in Newark, N.J. Winans began the first penny newspaper in Newark in 1848 — the Newark *Daily Mercury*.

WALTER WINCHELL

1063. McKelway, St. Clair. *Gossip, The Life and Times of Walter Winchell.* New York: Viking Press, 1940. 150pp.

A severe attack on the Broadway gossip columnist, spelling out Winchell's inaccuracies.

1064. Stuart, Lyle. *The Secret Life of Walter Winchell.* New York: Boar's Head Books, 1953. 253pp.

A diatribe against Winchell as an irresponsible gossip columnist. Perhaps an example of irresponsibility attacking irresponsibility.

1065. Weiner, Ed. *Let's Go to Press: A Biography of Walter Winchell, America's Most Controversial Newsman.* New York: G. P. Putnam's Sons, 1955. xviii + 270pp.

Weiner seeks to present a balanced biography of Winchell and produces probably the best work on this commentator yet done. The introduction quotes a wide range of praise and damnation directed at Winchell. The body of the book emphasizes Winchell's fights against naziism and communism more than his gossip writing. The over-all view is favorable toward him.

HENRY E. WING

1066. Tarbell, Ida Minerva. *A Reporter for Lincoln: The Story of Henry E. Wing, Soldier and Newspaperman.* New York: The Macmillan Co., 1927. 78pp.

A delightful short biography of a cub reporter for the New York *Tribune* in 1864, told as a piece of fiction but based on facts. Wing served Abraham Lincoln as well as the *Tribune* in carrying messages to and from Washington about Grant's Wilderness Campaign. After the war Wing bought a weekly, the Litchfield (Conn.) *Enquirer*, and was relatively unknown in journalistic circles.

WILLIAM E. WOODWARD

1067. Woodward, W. E. *The Gift of Life: An Autobiography.* New York: E. P. Dutton and Co., 1947. 436pp.

BIOGRAPHY

The autobiography of a popular historian (*A New American History, Tom Paine*, and *Meet General Grant*) who worked frequently on the fringes of journalism. There are interesting pictures of Hearst and of the operations of a book review syndicate.

SAMUEL J. WOOLF

1068. Woolf, Samuel Johnson. *Here Am I*. New York: Random House, 1941. x + 374pp.

Woolf was an artist and cartoonist whose sketches and interviews appeared for years in the New York *Times Sunday Magazine*. Included are 33 drawings of personalities from Mark Twain to Franklin Roosevelt.

ALEXANDER WOOLLCOTT

1069. Woollcott, Alexander. *Going to Pieces*. New York and London: G. P. Putnam's Sons, 1928. 256pp.

Light, personal observations by the New York dramatic critic. The best material includes accounts of a number of plays reviewed by Woollcott for the New York *World* — among them *An American Tragedy* and *East Lynne*. There are also some of Woollcott's city room memories.

1070. ———. *The Letters of Alexander Woollcott*. New York: Viking Press, 1944. xxiv + 409pp. (Edited by Beatrice Kaufman and Joseph Hennessey.)

Woollcott correspondence from childhood to his death in 1943. The bulk of the material covers his last five years. A biographical introduction offers a capsule survey of Woollcott's newspaper and literary career.

1071. Adams, Samuel Hopkins. *A. Woollcott: His Life and His World*. New York: Reynal and Hitchcock, 1945. 386pp.

Adams gives useful information on Woollcott's start on the New York *Times* and on his later career when he was known as "the seidlitz powder in Times Square."

EDWARD M. WOOLLEY

1072. Woolley, Edward Mott. *Free-Lancing for Forty Magazines*. Cambridge, Mass.: The Writer Publishing Co., 1927. viii + 320pp.

An autobiography on the theme "how to do it." Woolley, 60 at the time of writing, had had decades of experience in newspaper and magazine work.

THOMAS R. YBARRA

1073. Ybarra, Thomas R. *Young Man of Caracas*. New York: Garden City Publishing Co., 1941. 324pp. (Foreword by Elmer Davis.)

The early life of a New York *Times* reporter and author of works on Latin America.

1074. ———. *Young Man of the World*. New York: Ives and Washburn, 1942. xiii + 316pp.

A sequel to *Young Man of Caracas*, carrying Ybarra through college and his early experiences as a foreign correspondent. The author does not take himself too seriously.

THE LITERATURE OF JOURNALISM

ART YOUNG

1075. Young, Art. *Art Young: His Life and Times.* New York: Sheridan House, 1939. 467pp.

This autobiography lacks the fervor one would expect from a man of Young's background. A leading socialist, he started his career at the time of the Haymarket bombing in Chicago in 1886 and later was one of the founders of the *Masses.* As a cartoonist he served with Chicago, Denver, and New York newspapers. The book is illustrated with 100 of his drawings.

JAMES WEBB YOUNG

1076. Young, James Webb. *The Diary of an Ad Man: The War Years,* June 1, 1942–December 31, 1943. Chicago: Advertising Publications, 1944. 256pp.

Book publication of a series of weekly installments that had appeared in *Advertising Age.*

JOHN ORR YOUNG

1077. Young, John Orr. *Adventures in Advertising.* New York: Harper and Brothers, 1949. viii + 207pp.

The autobiography of the co-founder of the Young and Rubicam agency. Strongly anecdotal and inspirational in tone.

JOHN RUSSELL YOUNG

1078. Young, John Russell. *Men and Memories: Personal Reminiscences.* New York and London: F. Tennyson Neely, 1901. 2 vols. 617pp., total. (Edited by May D. Russell Young.)

Semi-autobiographical articles written for the New York *Herald,* the *North American Review,* the *Review of Reviews, Munsey's, Lippincott's,* and *McClure's.* Young started his career during the Civil War on Forney's Philadelphia *Press*; he later was managing editor of Greeley's *Tribune,* foreign correspondent for the younger Bennett, and eventually Librarian of Congress.

JOHN PETER ZENGER

1079. Almon, John. *The Trial of John Peter Zenger, of New York, Printer: Who Is Charged with Having Printed and Published a Libel against the Government; and Acquitted. With a Narrative of the Case.* London: John Almon, 1765. [San Francisco: Sutro Branch, California State Library, Occasional Papers, English Series No. 7, 1940. 59pp.]

A reissue of one of the many Colonial-period reprints of the Zenger trial. This modern edition, prepared by the Works Projects Administration, carries an added title page with the entry "The Trial of John Peter Zenger (1734)."

1080. Buranelli, Vincent, ed. *The Trial of Peter Zenger.* New York: New York University Press, 1957. viii + 152pp. (Foreword by H. V. Kaltenborn.)

A 20th-century reprint of the text of the Zenger trial, with the editor making a limited number of alterations in the original version to conform to present-day style and spelling. There are helpful preliminary sections giving biographical information on Zenger, Andrew Hamilton, William Cosby, and others involved in the case, plus an extensive discussion of "The Meaning of the Trial." Good bibliography.

1081. Heartman, Charles F. *John Peter Zenger and His Fight for the Freedom of the American Press: Together with a Genuine Specimen of the New-York Weekly Journal Printed by John Peter Zenger.* Highland Park, N.J.: Harry B. Weiss, 1934. 60pp.

A beautifully printed collector's item issued on the occasion of the 200th anniversary of Zenger's trial, with each copy having inserted in it a single original issue of the *Weekly Journal*. The work includes a general account of the period, going back to 1685; a review of "other actors" in the Zenger conflict (Cosby, De Lancey, Morris, etc.); and a report of the trial. There are full-page facsimiles of a brief of the case by John Chambers, Zenger's court-appointed attorney before Andrew Hamilton was brought in.

1082. Mott, Frank L., ed., "The Case and Tryal of John Peter Zenger," in *Oldtime Comments on Journalism*, vol. II. Columbia, Mo.: Press of the Crippled Turtle, 1954. v + 45pp.

An exact reprint of Zenger's original pamphlet on his trial, first issued in 1736. Earlier volumes reprinting the pamphlet were Howell's *State Trials*, London, 1816; Chandler's *American Criminal Trials*, London, 1841; and Rutherfurd's *John Peter Zenger*, New York, 1904. Mott inserted explanatory background notes.

1083. Osgood, Herbert L. "Controversies during the Administration of Cosby and Clarke, the Zenger Episode, 1730–1740," in *The American Colonies in the Eighteenth Century*, vol. II, part II, chap. V, pp. 443–482. New York: Columbia University Press, 1924.

An excellent account of the Zenger case as it fits into the history of New York rather than as a purely journalistic episode.

1084. Rutherfurd, Livingston. *John Peter Zenger: His Press, His Trial, and a Bibliography of Zenger Imprints.* New York: Dodd, Mead and Co., 1904. xiv + 275pp.

For years the only 20th-century book-length compilation of Zenger material. Its best features are the bibliography of the Zenger trial from the printer's own report in 1736 to Chandler's *American Criminal Trials* in 1841 and a list of the available issues of the *Weekly Journal*. Rutherfurd's own biography of Zenger and his description of political conditions in New York in 1733–1735 are somewhat dull. The book also contains a reprint of the text of the trial.

C. British Journalists

A'BECKETT FAMILY

1085. A'Beckett, Arthur William. *The A'Becketts of Punch: Memories of Father and Sons.* New York: E. P. Dutton and Co., 1903. 333pp.

THE LITERATURE OF JOURNALISM

SIR NORMAN ANGELL

1086. Angell, Sir Norman. *After All*. London: Hamish Hamilton, 1951. xiii + 370pp.

The autobiography of one of the oustanding British political-journalistic figures of the 20th century. Angell reviews his considerable experience as a youth in San Francisco and St. Louis and, for a decade before World War I, his association with Lord Northcliffe on the Paris *Daily Mail*; analyzes World War I and World War II crises; and considers the difficulties of the British press that led to the Royal Commission inquiry of 1946–1948.

THOMAS BARNES

1087. Hudson, Derek. *Thomas Barnes of the Times*. Cambridge, England: Cambridge University Press, 1944. xii + 196pp.

A scholarly biography of the editor of the London *Times*, 1817–1841, which places Barnes among England's political and literary leaders of his time. The volume includes a series of Barnes's essays and Parliamentary portraits of Coleridge, Byron, Wordsworth, and Goldsmith.

1088. The Times. *Thomas Barnes*. Cambridge, England: Cambridge University Press, 1935. 38pp. (Preface by W. Lewis.)

A sketch first printed on New Year's Day 1935 for the 150th anniversary edition of the London *Times*.

VERNON BARTLETT

1089. Bartlett, Vernon. *This Is My Life*. London: Chatto and Windus, 1937. 329pp. (Published in the United States under the title *Intermission in Europe: The Life of a Journalist and Broadcaster*. New York: Oxford University Press, 1938. 296pp.)

The autobiography of a reporter and radio commentator who served with Reuters and who from 1927 to 1933 was Great Britain's leading analyst on international affairs. It covers the period from the Versailles Conference to the Spanish Civil War. The writing is heavily charged with Bartlett's anger at the state of world affairs. Besides being shorter, the American edition has changes in the last chapter.

A. BEVERLEY BAXTER

1090. Baxter, A. Beverley. *Strange Street*. London: Hutchinson and Co., 1935. 286pp.

A brilliant young editor of Beaverbrook's London *Daily Express* in the 1920s and 1930s tells of Fleet Street. Woven into Baxter's own life story is an adulatory biography of Beaverbrook. A good book, both for its record of Baxter's enthusiasms and for the author's portraits of British life and politics.

COMYNS BEAUMONT

1091. Beaumont, Comyns. *A Rebel in Fleet Street*. London: Hutchinson and Co., n.d. (c. 1943). 158pp.

Recollections over 40 years (from the early 20th century to World War II)

BIOGRAPHY

of a reporter for various dailies and weeklies who was also a propagandist and publicist.

LORD BEAVERBROOK

1092. Beaverbrook, Lord [William Maxwell Aitken]. *Don't Trust to Luck.* London: Express Newspapers, Ltd., 1954. 108pp.

A revised and up-to-date version of *Success*, first published in 1921.

1093. Brittain, William J. *This Man Beaverbrook.* London: Hutchinson and Co., 1941. 63pp. (Leaders of Britain Series.)

A wartime propaganda biography introducing Beaverbrook "to the 45,000,000 people in Britain and the many millions in the Empire whose servant he is" (as minister of aircraft production). Brittain was a former employee on the *Daily Express*.

1094. Driberg, Tom. *Beaverbrook: A Study in Power and Frustration.* London: Weidenfeld and Nicholson, 1956. viii + 323pp.

A somewhat negative, yet honest analysis of Beaverbrook by a member of Parliament. Driberg treats principally of Beaverbrook's political career and his desire for authority. Operations of the *Daily Express* are discussed only as they relate to Beaverbrook's general career.

1095. Mackenzie, F. A. *Beaverbrook: An Authentic Biography.* London: Jarrolds, 1931. 296pp.

A member of the staff of the London *Times* and *Daily Mail* portrays Beaverbrook in romantic colors, as one who "is moulding a new force which bids fair to reshape the Empire." The author covers principally Beaverbrook's career from 1910 to 1930.

CEDRIC BELFRAGE

1096. Belfrage, Cedric. *Away from It All: An Escapologist's Notebook.* New York: Simon and Schuster, 1937. 411pp.

A very light book by a reporter, age 33, who seemingly took pride in being fired frequently. Belfrage was once a reviewer for the London *Daily Express*.

CHARLES F. MOBERLY BELL

1097. Bell, Enid Hester Chataway Moberly. *The Life and Letters of C. F. Moberly Bell, by His Daughter.* London: Richards Press, Ltd., 1927. 326pp. (Introduction by Sir Valentine Chirol.)

1098. Kitchin, F. Harcourt. *Moberly Bell and His Times: An Unofficial Narrative.* London: Philip Allan and Co., 1925. viii + 298pp. (Published in the United States as *The London Times under the Managership of Moberly Bell.* New York: G. P. Putnam's Sons.)

The life of the general manager of the London *Times* through most of that newspaper's tragic years from the death of Delane to its purchase by Northcliffe. Kitchin, a *Times* staff member, gives excellent accounts of the establishment of the Times Book Club, ventures into the reissuance of the *Encyclopedia Britannica*, and first publication of the newspaper's literary and financial supplements.

THE LITERATURE OF JOURNALISM

EDMUND BENTLEY

1099. Bentley, Edmund C. *Those Days*. London: Constable and Co., 1940. xv + 327pp.

A nostalgic account of the period from the 1880s to 1914. Bentley, for more than 30 years a staff member of the London *Daily News*, and after 1912 a leader-writer for the *Daily Telegraph*, portrays contemporary journalists and makes an interesting effort to define what a journalist is. He also tells the story of *Trent's Own Case* and *Trent's Last Case*, detective fiction for which Bentley was widely known.

EDWARD L. BLANCHARD

1100. Scott, Clement, and Cecil Howard. *The Life and Reminiscences of E. L. Blanchard, with Notes from the Diary of William Blanchard*. London: Hutchinson and Co., 1891. 2 vols. xv + 730pp., total.

Blanchard was a dramatic editor and critic for the *Sunday Times*, *Weekly Dispatch*, *Illustrated Times*, London *Figaro*, *Observer*, and *Daily Telegraph*. His biographers were associates of his. Unfortunately, the book is in an essentially unreadable diary form.

ROBERT BLATCHFORD

1101. Blatchford, Robert. *My Eighty Years*. London: Cassell and Co., Ltd., 1931. xix + 284pp.

The autobiography of a Labour journalist of integrity and courage. At one time associated with the London *Sunday Chronicle* and *Weekly Dispatch*, Blatchford helped to found the Socialist *Clarion* in 1891.

1102. Lyons, A. Neil. *Robert Blatchford: The Sketch of a Personality: An Estimate of Some Achievements*. London: The Clarion Press, 1910. 189pp.

A staff-produced biography of the editor of the *Clarion*, written by an intimate friend who, despite his own disagreement with many of the editor's opinions, regarded Blatchford as a "great man" and a prime mover in British socialism.

1103. Thompson, Laurence. *Robert Blatchford: Portrait of an Englishman*. London: Victor Gollancz, Ltd., 1951. 242pp.

A highly favorable biography of Blatchford, based principally on files of the *Clarion*, on Blatchford's writings and letters, and on records of the British Labour party.

HENRI GEORGES S. A. de BLOWITZ

1104. Blowitz, Henri Georges de. *Memoirs of M. de Blowitz*. New York: Doubleday, Page and Co., 1905. x + 321pp. (First published in England as *My Memoirs*. London: Edward Arnold, 1903. vi + 358pp.)

De Blowitz was one of England's most famous reporters in the late 19th century as Paris correspondent for the London *Times*. He recalls here his coverage of the Berlin Congress of 1878 and tells of interviews with Otto von Bismarck. There is excellent material on "Diplomacy and Journalism."

BIOGRAPHY

DAVID LOUIS BLUMENFELD (DAVID ELLBEY)

1105. Blumenfeld, David Louis [pseud. David Ellbey]. *Shooting the Bull.* London: Grayson and Grayson, 1933. 258pp.

Popularized reminiscences and correspondence of a reporter.

RALPH D. BLUMENFELD

1106. Blumenfeld, R. D. *The Press in My Time.* London: Rich and Cowan, Ltd., 1933. 253pp.

Blumenfeld, writing principally on the basis of personal experience, discusses the press and public opinion, Parliament, war, law and libel, pictorial journalism, the growth of Sunday journalism, the growth of British newspaper dynasties, the nature of Fleet Street, and prospects for the future.

1107. ———. *In the Days of Bicycles and Bustles.* New York: Brewer and Warren, 1930. viii + 248pp. (First published in England as *R.D.B.'s Diary.* London: William Heinemann, Ltd.)

Extracts over 27 years from the diary of a London correspondent of the New York *Herald* who later became editor of the London *Daily Express.* The comments, many gossipy items, span the period from Victoria's Golden Jubilee in 1887 to 1914.

1108. ———. *R. D. B.'s Procession.* New York: The Macmillan Co., 1935. viii + 285pp.

Fifty-five sketches of famous personalities whom Blumenfeld met in the years between Gladstone's prime ministries and that of David Lloyd George. Most of the accounts deal with Britishers, but four United States presidents are included.

J. B. BOOTH

1109. Booth, J. B. *A "Pink 'Un" Remembers.* London: T. Werner Laurie, Ltd., 1937. xx + 286pp. (Foreword by C. B. Cochran.)

Memories of a one-time *Sporting Times* reporter of the quarter-century from the accession of George V to the 1930s. Booth's volume includes accounts of music and the theater, British sports (particularly the derbies), the lecture circuit, and magazines of the period.

CHARLES BRADLAUGH

1110. Charles Bradlaugh Centenary Committee. *Champion of Liberty: Charles Bradlaugh.* London: C. A. Watts and Co., Ltd., 1933. xii + 346pp.

A memorial to a late-19th-century politician, journalist, and propagandist who was a leader in the free-thought movement. A biographical sketch of Bradlaugh is included, as are testimonials and sections on his free-thought doctrine. Bradlaugh's service to the press, carried on through the *National Reformer,* concerned chiefly the right of public meeting.

CHARLES WILLIAM (SHIRLEY) BROOKS

1111. Layard, G. S. *Shirley Brooks of Punch.* New York: Henry Holt and Co., 1907. 598pp. (First published in England as *A Great Punch Editor*. London: Sir Isaac Pitman and Sons, Ltd.)

Charles William (Shirley) Brooks was with *Punch* for more than 20 years and editor for the last four years of his life, 1870–1874. This biography is based principally on his letters and diaries and is well illustrated with *Punch* cartoons. The continuity is not too well handled.

IVOR BROWN

1112. Brown, Ivor. *The Way of My World*. London: Collins, 1954. 319pp.

Brown was editor of the London *Observer*, 1942–1948.

SIR DOUGLAS BROWNRIGG

1113. Brownrigg, Sir Douglas. *Indiscretions of the Naval Censor*. New York: George H. Doran Co., 1920. 315pp.

The autobiographical narrative of a retired Royal Navy rear admiral who from 1914 to 1919 was chief censor of radio-telegraphy. He gives a readable account of problems surrounding British publicity and propaganda, the Battle of Jutland, operations of the fleet, "doctoring of photographs," and relations with the Allied press.

JAMES SILK BUCKINGHAM

1114. Turner, Ralph E. *James Silk Buckingham, 1786–1855: A Social Biography*. New York: Whittlesey House, McGraw-Hill Book Co., 1934. 463pp.

Buckingham was a sailor, journalist, and reformer, a man of many talents who founded the Calcutta *Journal* in 1818 and sought in vain to establish a free press in India. Later he founded the *Athenaeum* and the *Parliamentary Review*. There is an extensive bibliography of contemporary original sources.

HARRY FINDLATER BUSSEY

1115. Bussey, Harry Findlater. *Sixty Years of Journalism*. Bristol: J. W. Arrowsmith; London: Simpkin, Marshall, Hamilton, Kent and Co., Ltd., 1906. 304pp.

Anecdotes and reminiscences of a provincial journalist (Liverpool and Brighton) who also served on London newspapers. Most useful is the contrast between journalism in 1844 and that of the early 1900s. There are numerous vignettes of political leaders.

J. F. BYRNE

1116. Byrne, J. F. *Silent Years: An Autobiography with Memoirs of James Joyce and Our Ireland*. New York: Farrar, Straus and Young, 1953. xi + 307pp.

The unorthodox story of an Irish journalist and literary figure.

GEORGE CADBURY

1117. Gardiner, A. G. *Life of George Cadbury*. London: Cassell and Co., Ltd., 1923. ix + 324pp.

BIOGRAPHY

The life of the liberal British chocolate and cocoa magnate who became owner of the London *Daily News* early in the 20th century. Although the book considers chiefly Cadbury's business, political, and religious activities, there is some helpful material on how he acquired the *Daily News* and on his support of David Lloyd George. Gardiner was editor of the *News* from 1901 to 1919.

NEVILLE CARDUS

1118. Cardus, Neville. *Autobiography*. London: Collins and the Book Society, 1947. 288pp.

1119. ———. *Second Innings*. London: Collins, 1950. 256pp.

Cardus combined, for the Manchester *Guardian*, music criticism and cricket reporting. During World War II he was music critic for the Melbourne *Herald*. His two autobiographies give excellent interpretations of "sport and the English."

RICHARD CARLILE

1120. Campbell, Mrs. Theophila Carlile. *The Battle of the Press, as Told in the Story of the Life of Richard Carlile*. London: A. and H. B. Bonner, 1899. vii + 319pp.

In this biography of a famous London bookseller and freethinker, his daughter gives an account of Carlile's trial for publication of Thomas Paine's *Age of Reason* and of his role in the Manchester riots of 1819. A list of Carlile's imprisonments in battles for liberty of the press is included.

THOMAS CATLING

1121. Catling, Thomas. *My Life's Pilgrimage*. London: John Murray, 1911. xviii + 384pp. (Introduction by Lord Burnham.)

Catling served for a half-century on *Lloyd's Weekly Newspaper*, for much of that period as editor. *Lloyd's* was a paper of the quality of the *Morning Post* and *Daily Telegraph*. Of most interest is Catling's discussion of "The Old Order Changeth," the rise of the "new journalism," 1890–1898.

WILLIAM CAXTON

1122. Aurner, Nellie Slayton. *Caxton: Mirrour of Fifteenth Century Letters: A Study of the Literature of the First English Press*. London: P. Allan and Co., Ltd., 1926. xvi + 304pp.

Caxton, of course, represents a period that preceded the development of the newspaper press, but his importance in the introduction of printing to England justifies his place in a bibliography on journalism.

1123. Knight, Charles. *William Caxton, the First English Printer: A Biography*. London: W. Clowes and Sons, 1877, new edition. ix + 158pp.

Originally published in 1844, then revised as part of one of Knight's works on *The Old Printer and the Modern Press* (London: J. Murray, 1854). The third issue in 1877 contains a list of books printed by Caxton. The issue of

1854 gave a view of the press of the mid-19th century, especially in its relation to popular literature.

1124. Plomer, Henry Robert. *William Caxton (1424–1491)*. London: L. Parsons, 1925; Boston: Small Maynard and Co., 1925. 195pp.

WINSTON SPENCER CHURCHILL

1125. Eade, Charles, ed. *Churchill, by His Contemporaries*. London: Hutchinson and Co., 1953. 528pp.

See "Churchill the War Correspondent," by G. Ward Price of the *Daily Mail* and *Sunday Dispatch*; "Churchill the Journalist," by Colin Coote, managing editor of the *Daily Telegraph*; "Churchill the Editor," by Beric Holt of the *Morning Post*; "Churchill and the Censorship," by Rear Admiral G. P. Thomson, chief press censor in World War II; "Churchill the Broadcaster," by Richard Dimbleby, BBC war correspondent; and "Churchill the Master of Words," by Ivor Brown, editor of the *Observer*. "Churchill and the Empire," by Sir Evelyn Wrench, and "Churchill the Biographer and Historian," by Malcolm Muggeridge, editor of *Punch*, are also valuable.

CLAUD COCKBURN

1126. Cockburn, Claud. *A Discord of Trumpets: An Autobiography*. New York: Simon and Schuster, 1956. 314pp. (Published in London under the title *In Time of Trouble: An Autobiography*. R. Hart-Davis, 1956. 264pp.)

Cockburn, a native of Peiping, was a correspondent in New York in 1929 for the London *Times*; later an active anti-Nazi in covering Europe; editor of a scandal news-letter in England; and a reporter for the London *Daily Worker* during the Spanish Civil War.

HENRY M. COLLINS

1127. Collins, Henry M. *From Pigeon Post to Wireless*. London: Hodder and Stoughton, 1925. xiii + 312pp. (Introduction by Sir Roderick Jones.)

In 1865 Paul Julius Reuter appointed Collins to organize Reuters activities in the East from Bombay to Yokohama. Almost the whole of the book concerns reminiscences of Reuters activity in obtaining a concession for news coverage in Persia, press relations with Russia in 1870s, managership of Reuters in Australasia, and the Boer War.

SIR EDWARD COOK

1128. Mills, J. Saxon. *Sir Edward Cook*. London: Constable and Co., Ltd., 1921. viii + 304pp.

A barrister's scholarly life of a distinguished liberal editor of the late 19th and early 20th century. Cook served on the early *Pall Mall Gazette* and later on the *Westminster Gazette* and London *Daily News*. He also had a distinguished literary career. There is considerable material on John Morley, J. A. Spender, and W. T. Stead, as well as on Cook's political associates.

BIOGRAPHY

CHARLES A. COOPER

1129. Cooper, Charles A. *An Editor's Retrospect: Fifty Years of Newspaper Work.* London: The Macmillan Co., Ltd. 1896. xv + 430pp.

The life of an editor of the Edinburgh *Scotsman.* There is a helpful history of the *Scotsman,* founded in 1817; also an account of Alexander Russel, an associate of Cooper's and his predecessor as editor. Cooper tells the story of carrying telegraphic news to regional newspapers in Britain after 1865.

W. L. COURTNEY

1130. Courtney, J. E. H. *The Making of an Editor: W. L. Courtney, 1850–1928.* London: The Macmillan Co., Ltd., 1930. viii + 233pp.

A worshipful memoir of the editor of the *Fortnightly Review,* 1895–1928, by his widow. She gives a view of Courtney's associations in Fleet Street, a short history of the *Fortnightly,* and accounts of four other editors: George H. Lewes, John Morley, T. H. S. Escott, and Frank Harris.

HARRY COZENS-HARDY

1131. Cozens-Hardy, Harry. *The Glorious Years: Random Recollections of Prominent Persons in Parliament, in Literature, on and off the Platform, on the Playing Fields, and in the Pulpit, the Prize Ring and the Press — Recaptured in London, Paris and New York between 1897 and 1952.* London: Robert Hale, Ltd., 1953. 255pp.

Cozens-Hardy for years was a staff member of the Colman press in Norwich and of the Cadbury newspapers (London *News-Chronicle*).

THOMAS WILLIAM H. CROSLAND

1132. Brown, W. Sorley. *The Life and Genius of T. W. H. Crosland.* London: Cecil Palmer, 1928. 490pp.

Crosland was a leading journalistic-literary figure of the late Victorian era and the first 20 years of the 20th century — contributor to Leeds *Mercury, Yorkshire Weekly Post, Outlook, Saturday Review,* and London *Evening Standard.* Brown gives considerable background on Crosland's violent assault upon Oscar Wilde and the latter's book *De Profundis.*

ICHABOD DAWKS

1133. Morison, Stanley. *Ichabod Dawks and His News-Letter, with an Account of the Dawks Family of Booksellers and Stationers, 1635–1731.* Cambridge, England: The University Press, 1931. 38pp.

A work of fine printing as well as a good biography. Selected facsimiles of Dawks's publications include the first issue of the *Philosophical Observator,* a weekly brought out by Dawks on January 22, 1695; others are from the *Protestant Mercury, Occurrences, Forein and Domestick,* published from 1696 to 1700, and *Dawks's News-Letter,* published from 1696 to 1716.

GEOFFREY DAWSON

1134. Wrench, Sir Evelyn. *Geoffrey Dawson and Our Times.* London: Hutchinson and Co., 1955. 487pp.

One of the outstanding biographies of a British journalist, by a friend of many years who was one of the owners of the *Spectator*. Dawson's career included two periods as editor of the London *Times* (1912–1919 and 1922–1941). There is solid information on Dawson's significant part in the abdication crisis of 1936.

DANIEL DEFOE

1135. Lee, William. *Daniel Defoe: His Life and Recently Discovered Writings*. London: John Camden Hotten, 1869. 3 vols.

A monumental work, including in vols. II and III a great amount of Defoe's journalistic output, 1716–1729. Vol. I is a biography of Defoe.

1136. Minto, William. *Daniel Defoe*. London: The Macmillan Co., Ltd., 1879. viii + 179pp. (English Men of Letters Series, edited by John Morley.)

A best-selling life of Defoe based chiefly on the more scholarly biography of Lee. There is extensive treatment of Defoe's journalistic career.

1136a. Moore, John Robert. *Daniel Defoe: Citizen of the Modern World*. Chicago: University of Chicago Press, 1958. xv + 409pp.

A well-written life of Defoe. Moore gives a sound analysis of Defoe as reporter and as pamphleteer and public servant.

1137. Payne, William Lytton. *Mr. Review: Daniel Defoe as Author of the Review*. New York: King's Crown Press, 1947. 147pp.

Payne makes a detailed examination of Defoe's career as editor of the *Review*, 1704–1713, and considers Defoe as an author, journalist, economist, and counselor and guide. There are extensive notes and bibliography.

1138. Sutherland, James. *Defoe*. London: Methuen and Co., Ltd., 1937. xiii + 300pp.

Objective and well balanced. Of particular interest are chapters on "Robert Harley's Man," in which the author goes into the beginnings of the *Review*; and on "Mist's Man," which considers Defoe and *Mist's Journal*. This book ranks near the top in any listing of material on Defoe.

1139. Watson, Francis. *Daniel Defoe*. London: Longmans, Green and Co., 1952. vii + 240pp. (Men and Books Series.)

Useful for quick reading but lacks the detail of other biographies of Defoe.

1140. Wright, Thomas. *The Life of Daniel Defoe*. London: Cassell and Co., Ltd., 1894. xxix + 432pp.

Too glowing a treatment and therefore not as valuable as other biographies of Defoe.

JOHN T. DELANE

1141. Cook, Sir Edward. *Delane of the Times*. London: Constable and Co., Ltd., 1916. 319pp. (In Makers of the Nineteenth Century Series, edited by Basil Williams.)

One of a scholarly series of biographies intended to portray the age from 1830 to the death of Queen Victoria. It is in part a life of Delane, in part a history of the London *Times*, and in part a chronicle of Europe during Delane's editorship, 1841–1877. Cook relied chiefly on the columns of the *Times*, on the correspondence of Delane's nephew, A. I. Dasent, and on Dasent's life of Delane.

1142. Dasent, Arthur Irwin. *John Thadeus Delane, Editor of the Times: His Life and Correspondence.* London: John Murray, 1908. 2 vols. 704pp., total.

Delane's nephew prepared this biography from Delane's correspondence and diaries accumulated over 40 years. An exceptionally rewarding book.

ROBERT DONALD

1143. Taylor, H. A. *Robert Donald: Being the Authorized Biography of Sir Robert Donald, B.G.E., LLD., Journalist, Editor and Friend of Statesmen.* London: Stanley Paul and Co., Ltd., n.d. (c. 1934). 288pp. (Foreword by J. Ramsey MacDonald.)

The life of a Scottish journalist who became an outstanding leader in Fleet Street in the World War I period. Taylor gives an account of Donald's work as editor of the *Daily Chronicle*; as president of the Institute of Journalists; as proprietor of the London *Globe*; and as one of the founders of the Empire Press Union in 1909. Appendixes carry Donald's addresses on journalistic principles before the Institute of Journalists, 1913–1928.

ANDREW DUNLOP

1144. Dunlop, Andrew. *Fifty Years of Irish Journalism.* Dublin: Hanna and Neale; London: Simpkin, Marshall and Co., 1911. xxi + 304pp.

Reminiscences of the half-century following 1857 by an Irish correspondent (chiefly for the London *Daily News*, 1867–1889). Written partly in 1889, partly just before publication, the book is disjointed. There is considerable detail on the *Irish Freeman's Journal* and *United Ireland*, and also on the Irish Home-Rule imbroglio.

BERNARD FALK

1145. Falk, Bernard. *Bouquets for Fleet Street: Memories and Musings over Fifty Years.* London: Hutchinson and Co., 1951. 427pp.

The autobiography of Falk and personality sketches by him of Fleet Street celebrities. Falk had long service on London *Evening News, Reynolds News,* and *Daily Mail.* This volume revises and adds to two previous autobiographies: *He Laughed in Fleet Street* (1935) and *Five Years Dead* (1937).

ARCHIBALD FORBES

1146. Forbes, Archibald. *Memories and Studies of War and Peace.* New York: Charles Scribner's Sons, 1895. 368pp.

The memoirs of a correspondent of the London *Morning Advertiser* and *Daily News* in the Franco-Prussian War. Two chapters are devoted wholly to war correspondence; the remainder of the book is political and descriptive.

SIR PHILIP FRANCIS (see also "JUNIUS")

1147. Francis, Sir Philip. *The Francis Letters*. London: Hutchinson and Co.; New York: E. P. Dutton and Co., 1901. 2 vols. 700pp., total. (Edited and compiled by Beata Francis and Eliza Keary.)

The letters of a British political writer believed by many to have been the author of the "Letters of Junius" in the London *Public Advertiser*. The book includes "A Note on the 'Junius' Controversy," by C. F. Keary, which gives the principal lines of evidence without attempting to settle the authorship controversy. The letters run from 1754 to 1818 but are most important in journalism for the years 1767–1771.

1148. *The Identity of "Junius," with a Distinguished Living Character Established*. London: Printed for Taylor and Hessey, 1816. viii + 366pp.

Fascinating material attributing the Junius letters to Sir Philip Francis. The author himself remained anonymous, but library records indicate that he might have been John Taylor, one of the publishers of the book. The book appeared two years before Francis's death and its attributions apparently were not controverted by him.

OLGA FRANKLIN

1149. Franklin, Olga Rose. *Born Twice*. London: P. Garnett, 1951. 180pp.

HARRY FURNISS

1150. Furniss, Harry. *The Confessions of a Caricaturist*. New York and London: Harper and Brothers, 1902. 2 vols. 582pp., total.

Furniss in his service with the *Illustrated London News*, *Punch*, and other periodicals covered Parliament and traveled over the world. His autobiography takes life not too seriously. There are several hundred excellent illustrations to go with the narrative.

1151. ———. *How to Draw in Pen and Ink*. London: Chapman and Hall, 1905. 115pp.

HAMILTON FYFE

1152. Fyfe, Hamilton. *My Seven Selves*. London: George Allen and Unwin, Ltd., 1935. 320pp.

Fyfe's service as reporter and editor ranged from the London *Times* to the *Daily Mail* and the Labour *Daily Herald*. In this first autobiography he gives a seven-step account of 49 of his years, from "foolish young fellow" at 14 to "poor and content" at 63. Enthusiastically written and highly informational.

1153. ———. *Sixty Years of Fleet Street*. London: W. H. Allen and Co., Ltd. 1949. 227pp.

Here Fyfe bridges the period from Victoria's Jubilee in 1887 to the close of World War II and the report of the Royal Commission on the Press. More than half the book looks back to the "Northcliffe-Pearson Revolution." There are helpful chapters on the press as a branch of commerce, on public distrust of the press, on Lord Beaverbrook, and on "The Future of Fleet Street."

BIOGRAPHY

LEONARD M. GANDER

1154. Gander, Leonard Marsland. *After These Many Quests*. London: MacDonald and Co., 1949. 367pp.

The life of a war correspondent, television and radio correspondent, and critic for the *Daily Telegraph*. Gander was also a radio correspondent for the New York *Times*.

J. L. GARVIN

1155. Garvin, Katharine. *J. L. Garvin: A Memoir*. London: William Heinemann, Ltd., 1948. ix + 215pp.

An intensely personal view of a father by his daughter rather than the story of the newspaper career of the editor of the London *Observer* for most of the first half of this century. Nevertheless, there is valuable material on Garvin's editorship of the fourteenth edition of the *Encyclopaedia Britannica*, 1926–1929, which he carried on simultaneously with his work on the *Observer*.

SIR PHILIP HAMILTON GIBBS

1156. Gibbs, Sir Philip Hamilton. *Adventures in Journalism*. London and New York: Harper and Brothers, 1923. 363pp.

Gibbs covers 20 years of his career as a young reporter for the *Daily Mail* and *Daily Chronicle*: the death of Edward VII; Dr. Frederick Cook's pretended discovery of the North Pole, one of Gibbs's important scoops; "explorations" in the underworlds of London; the more dignified activity of the literary critic; and finally foreign correspondence. The wartime career of Gibbs, author of *Now It Can Be Told*, is not treated.

1157. ———. *Crowded Company: In Which One Meets a Variety of Men and Women in High Places and Low, Famous and Unknown, among Whom Are Writers, Painters, Poets, Politicians, Pretty Ladies, and a Crowded Company of Ghosts from the Roll-Call of Remembrance*. London: A. Wingate; New York: Medill McBride Co., 1949. 286pp.

This is a story of the peaceful years before the world wars, of London and its "lure," and of the "pains of labor" in journalism and literature. Excellent reading.

LORD GLENESK

1158. Lucas, Reginald. *Lord Glenesk and the Morning Post*. London: Alston Rivers, Ltd., 1910. ix + 443pp.

The life of Sir Algernon Borthwick (Lord Glenesk), editor and owner of the *Morning Post*, 1876–1908. The first third of the book gives a history of the *Post* and of British journalism; the remainder is memoir. The book is weighted with quotations from correspondence, including that between Winston Churchill and the Borthwick family when Churchill corresponded for the *Morning Post* from South Africa.

CHARLES and PEGGY GRAVES

1159. Graves, Charles. *The Bad Old Days*. London: Faber and Faber, 1951. 227pp.

1160. Graves, Peggy [Leigh]. *Married to Charles*. London: William Heinemann, Ltd., 1950. 282pp.

Mrs. Graves writes under the pseudonym of Jane Gordon.

HARRY GREENWALL

1161. Greenwall, Harry J. *Round the World for News*. London: Hutchinson and Co., 1935. 286pp.

The breezy, colorful autobiography of a reporter for the *Daily Express* and *Continental Daily Mail* in the post-World War I period. Chapters are spotted geographically to give brief pictures of many countries around the globe.

1162. ———. *Scoops: Being Leaves from the Diary of a Special Correspondent*. London: S. Paul and Co., 1923. 287pp.

JOHN A. HAMMERTON

1163. Hammerton, J. A. *Books and Myself: Memoirs of an Editor*. London: MacDonald and Co., 1944. 343pp.

The autobiography of an editor and book publisher associated with many facets of British journalism for 55 years. The book includes an account of "ardent years with Northcliffe." Hammerton had been editor of the *Harmsworth Encyclopedia* and the *Harmsworth History of the World*.

CHARLES HAND

1164. Hand, Charles. *I Was After Money*. London: Partridge Publications, 1949. 223pp. (56 illustrations and 20 sketches by Adam E. Horne.)

LUKE HANSARD (HOUSE OF HANSARD)

1165. Trewin, J. C., and E. M. King. *Printer to the House: The Story of Hansard*. London: Methuen and Co., Ltd., 1952. xv + 272pp. (Foreword by Rt. Hon. W. S. Morrison, speaker of the House of Commons.)

The printing firm of Hansard carried on the journalistic assignment of publishing the House of Commons debates for years. Although a family biography, this work is centered principally on Luke Hansard (1752–1828), the founder. There is extensive treatment of the competitive relations between the Hansards and William Cobbett (*Cobbett's Parliamentary Debates*).

FRANK HARRIS

1166. Lunn, Hugh Kingsmill [pseud. Hugh Kingsmill]. *Frank Harris: A Biography*. New York: Farrar and Rinehart; London: Jonathan Cape, 1932. 252pp.

The life of a controversial editor and novelist in England and United States, 1883–1922. Harris was editor successively of the London *Evening News, Fortnightly Review, Saturday Review*, and *Vanity Fair*; and in the United States of *Pearson's* (1916–1922). The author takes a negative view of Harris.

BIOGRAPHY

1167. Root, E. Merrill. *Frank Harris*. New York: Odyssey Press, 1947. xi + 324pp.

A sympathetic biography and a psychological study. The volume is based on extensive materials originally collected by one of Harris's devoted supporters, Einar Lyngklip, and later deposited in the New York Public Library, where Root was the first to obtain access to them.

WILSON HARRIS

1168. Harris, [Henry] Wilson. *Life So Far*. London: Jonathan Cape, 1954. 321pp.

Harris's work covered most of the first half of the 20th century, first as a Liberal correspondent for the London *Daily News* and *News Chronicle*, and from 1932 to 1953 as editor of the *Spectator*. There is a useful interpretation of post-World War II journalism in England, including an analysis of the Report of the Royal Commission on the Press in 1949.

H. G. HIBBERT

1169. Hibbert, H. G. *Fifty Years of a Londoner's Life*. New York: Dodd, Mead and Co., 1916. xv + 304pp.

This is not so much the author's own life story as it is a report on the British theater in all its phases. Hibbert, who covered drama for the London newspapers, has fascinating material on stock companies, old theaters and music halls, ballet, stage society, the American chorus girl, and early movies.

SISLEY HUDDLESTON

1170. Huddleston, Sisley. *In My Time: An Observer's Record of War and Peace*. New York: E. P. Dutton and Co., 1938. ix + 411pp.

Truly excellent reminiscences of a cultured and temperate Englishman, covering the 25 years from World War I through the rise to power of Hitler. At various times Huddleston contributed to most of the distinguished newspapers of England and the United States: the London *Times*, *New Statesman*, *Christian Science Monitor*, and New York *Times*. He discusses Paris in World War I, including its press; censorship and spying; the failure of the press at Versailles; newspapers and their editors (chiefly the London *Times* and the *Christian Science Monitor*); and the rise of dictatorships.

SPENCER LEIGH HUGHES

1171. Hughes, Spencer Leigh. *Press, Platform, and Parliament*. London: Nisbet and Co., Ltd., 1918. xi + 320pp.

The autobiography of a parliamentary press reporter for a decade who later was elected to Parliament himself. Hughes was well known at the turn of the century under the pseudonym Sub Rosa. He served the *Morning Leader* and London *Star*.

EDWARD G. W. HULTON

1172. Hulton, Edward George W. *When I Was a Child*. London: Cresset Press, 1952. 234pp.

The autobiography of the chairman and managing director of Hulton Press, Ltd., publishers of the *Picture Post.*

LEIGH HUNT

1173. Hunt, Leigh. *The Autobiography of Leigh Hunt, with Reminiscences of Friends and Contemporaries.* New York: Harper and Brothers, 1850. 2 vols. (Later editions: London: Smith, Elder and Co., 1906, 1 vol., xvi + 413pp.; and London: Cresset Press, 1949, 1 vol., xxviii + 512pp., including introduction and notes by J. E. Morpurgo.)

Principally a literary autobiography. Of the 26 chapters 6 deal with Hunt's *Examiner,* his political troubles with the Prince Regent, and his imprisonment. The account carries to 1849, when Hunt revived the London *Journal.*

DOUGLAS HYDE

1174. Hyde, Douglas. *I Believed.* London: William Heinemann, Ltd.; New York: G. P. Putnam's Sons, 1950. vi + 312pp.

Hyde, who gave up communism for the Catholic Church, was on the staff of the London *Daily Worker* during World War II, later took to international free-lancing and contributed to the *Catholic Herald.*

LORD FRANCIS JEFFREY

1175. Cockburn, Lord. *Life of Lord Jeffrey, with a Selection from His Correspondence.* Edinburgh: Adam and Charles Black, 1852. 2 vols. 902pp., total.

Francis Jeffrey, British critic, was the first editor of the Edinburgh *Review* (1802). A history of the *Review* is included along with the biography, making this book extremely valuable journalistically. Vol. II contains Jeffrey's letters from 1793 to 1850 and a compilation of 200 of his articles from the *Review.*

HARRY JEFFS

1176. Jeffs, Harry. *Press, Preachers, and Politicians: Reminiscences, 1874–1932.* London: Independent Press, Ltd., 1933. 251pp.

SAMUEL JOHNSON

1177. Bloom, Edward A. *Samuel Johnson in Grub Street.* Providence, R.I.: Brown University Press, 1957. x + 309pp.

Bloom shows how extensive Johnson's offerings were to the English periodicals of the 18th century and how the Grub Street writers were responsible for the periodicity of publication which became an essential part of journalism. The book includes Johnson's views on liberty of the press, copyright, and authorship.

SIR RODERICK JONES

1178. Jones, Sir Roderick. *A Life in Reuters.* London: Hodder and Stoughton, 1951. 496pp.

Jones was the managing director of Reuters from 1915 to 1941. Early chapters relate Jones's experience with Reuters in South Africa, 1900–1915. He discusses the relations of the news agency with Northcliffe, the Associated Press of the United States, and the Press Association in Britain.

"JUNIUS" (see also SIR PHILIP FRANCIS)

1179. *Letters of Junius.* London: Faber and Gwyer, 1927. lviii + 410pp. (Edited, with an introduction, by C. W. Everett.)

An exact reprint of the Henry Sampson Woodfall edition of the *Letters of Junius* of 1772 comprising 69 letters from the files of the London *Public Advertiser.* The appendix to this edition includes private letters from Junius to Woodfall which were edited from manuscripts in the British Museum, and letters between Junius and John Wilkes. Everett lists in the appendix about 50 persons to whom the Junius authorship has been attributed; he suggests that the letters were written by the Earl of Shelburne. The extensive introduction goes into detail on the political-press struggle of 1760–1772.

1180. Symons, Jelinger Cookson. *William Burke the Author of "Junius": An Essay on His Era.* London: Smith, Elder and Co., 1859. iv + 144pp.

A British barrister attributes the Junius letters to the great parliamentarian Burke.

CHARLES SAMUEL KEENE

1181. Layard, George S. *The Life and Letters of Charles Samuel Keene.* London: Sampson Low, Marston and Co., Ltd., 1892. xxi + 463pp.

Keene was an artist and humorist for *Punch* for 40 years beginning in 1851. He also drew for the *Illustrated London News* and *Once a Week.* This detailed biography is a straightforward chronological account. There is no assessment of Keene's art.

HENRY LABOUCHERE

1182. Pearson, Hesketh. *Labby: The Life and Character of Henry Labouchere.* London: Hamish Hamilton, 1936. 318pp.

Labouchere was an extreme Radical member of Parliament in the 1880s and 1890s and editor of a sensational journal, *Truth,* which exposed crime and corruption.

1183. Thorold, Algar Labouchere. *The Life of Henry Labouchere.* London: Constable and Co., Ltd., 1913. xxi + 513pp.

A descendant of Labouchere's based this biography upon voluminous correspondence. Robert Bennett, editor of Labouchere's *Truth,* contributed a chapter on the founding of that journal in 1877, and there is considerable detail on the press during the Parnellite struggle over Home Rule for Ireland, on Labouchere and Charles Bradlaugh, and on Labouchere and socialism.

GEORGE LANSBURY

1184. Postgate, Raymond. *The Life of George Lansbury.* London and New York: Longmans, Green and Co., 1951. xiii + 332pp.

A Labour political leader and journalist, Lansbury was one of the early editors of the London *Daily Herald* (1913) and later of *Lansbury's Labour Weekly* (1925). In this well-written book, the author gives Lansbury a place among the great builders of the Labour party.

THOMAS LATIMER

1185. Lambert, Richard S. *The Cobbett of the West: A Study of Thomas Latimer and the Struggle between Pulpit and Press at Exeter*. London: Nicholson and Watson, Ltd., 1939. v + 254pp.

Latimer was a Radical 19th-century editor who conducted a significant battle against severe British libel statutes. As editor of the Exeter *Western Star* he maintained in 1847 the first successful plea of privilege in the right of the press to criticize the pulpit (*Queen v. Latimer*).

SIR ROGER L'ESTRANGE

1186. Kitchin, George. *Sir Roger L'Estrange: A Contribution to the History of the Press in the Seventeenth Century*. London: Kegan Paul, Trench, Truebner and Co., Ltd., 1913. xv + 440pp.

A scholarly, somewhat dull biography of the licensor of the press under Charles II and James II, 1663–1688. The book is based on contemporary sources and lists L'Estrange's political works; it also includes a London *Times* supplement on L'Estrange, September 10, 1912.

DAVID LOW

1187. Low, David. *Low's Autobiography*. New York: Simon and Schuster, 1957. 387pp.

The life of one of the most famous of 20th-century cartoonists, who worked principally for the London *Evening Standard* and *Daily Herald*. The volume includes more than 60 photographs and drawings. Considerable political history accompanies the personal record.

SIR SIDNEY LOW

1188. Chapman-Huston, Major Desmond. *The Lost Historian: A Memoir of Sir Sidney Low*. London: John Murray, 1936. xix + 388pp.

A splendid biography of an editor of the *St. James's Gazette* (1888–1897). Although remembered mainly as a brilliant journalist, Low was also a scholar and historian, the author of a book on the British constitution. This biography contains numerous references to British political and journalistic figures of the 19th and 20th centuries, a bibliography of Low's works, and a listing of his periodical articles, 1891–1931.

CHARLES LOWE

1189. Lowe, Charles. *The Tale of a Times Correspondent (Berlin 1878–1891)*. London: Hutchinson and Co., 1927. 315pp.

The autobiography of a Berlin correspondent for the London *Times*, with sections on Anglo-German relations, Otto von Bismarck, and "military memories." Lowe, dismissed by the *Times* in 1891 after a series of disagreements over his responsibilities in Berlin, tells his side of the story and offers some inside history of that great newspaper.

SIR HENRY LUCY

1190. Lucy, Sir Henry. *The Diary of a Journalist.* New York: E. P. Dutton and Co., 1920–1923. 3 vols.

A fascinating compilation of unedited extracts from the author's diary. Lucy was best known as a humorist for *Punch*, 1881–1916, to which he contributed satirical articles on contemporary politics under the pseudonym of Toby, M.P.

1191. ———. *Sixty Years in the Wilderness: Some Passages by the Way.* London: Smith, Elder and Co., 1909. x + 450pp.

A series of "Toby" reminiscences, originally published in *Cornhill Magazine*.

1192. ———. *Sixty Years in the Wilderness: More Passages by the Way.* London: Smith, Elder and Co., 1912. x + 398pp.

1193. ———. *Nearing Jordan: Being the Third and Last Volume of Sixty Years in the Wilderness.* London: Smith, Elder and Co., 1916. x + 453pp.

ARNOLD LUNN

1194. Lunn, Arnold. *Come What May: An Autobiography.* Boston: Little, Brown and Co., 1941. viii + 348pp.

Lunn, lecturer, author of books on skiing, traveler in America and Spain, deals with the fringes of journalism, but there is some relevant material in the chapter on "Wandering Journalist."

JUSTIN McCARTHY

1195. McCarthy, Justin. *An Irishman's Story.* New York and London: The Macmillan Co., 1904. 436pp.

An Irish Home-Rule parliamentarian, McCarthy was editor of a number of newspapers, the most important being the London *Morning Star*. He also served with the *Northern Daily Times* in Liverpool and contributed to the New York *Tribune* and *Harper's*. McCarthy gives full accounts of the Parnell Commission and the London *Times* forgeries.

JOHN HARRIES McCULLOCH

1196. McCulloch, John Harries. *North Range: A Record of Hard Living and Adventure on the Colourful Northern Rim of the British Empire.* London: W. and R. Chambers, 1954. 191pp.

JAMES MacDONNELL

1197. Nicoll, W. Robertson. *James MacDonnell: Journalist.* New York: Dodd, Mead and Co., 1897. xi + 416pp.

A sympathetic biography of a 19th-century Scottish journalist who rose from the Aberdeen *Free Press* and Edinburgh *Review* to become a leader-writer for the London *Daily Telegraph* and London *Times*. MacDonnell was highly successful because of his detailed knowledge of foreign politics and ecclesiastical history.

WILLIAM McKAY

1198. McKay, William. *Bohemian Days in Fleet Street*. London: John Long, Ltd., 1913. 312pp.

Nostalgic reminiscences of the Fleet Street of 1870–1890, with emphasis on romance and adventure. The book contains a provocative "forward look to 1960." It was issued anonymously as the work of "A Journalist."

CHRISTOPHER MARLOWE

1199. Bakeless, John. *Christopher Marlowe*. London: Jonathan Cape, 1938. 357pp.

1200. ———. *The Tragicall History of Christopher Marlowe*. Cambridge, Mass.: Harvard University Press, 1942. 2 vols. 807pp., total.

In each of his biographies of the Elizabethan dramatist, Bakeless gives an account of Marlowe's apparent use of late-16th-century "newsbooks" as a source of ideas for his plays. In *The Tragicall History* Bakeless discusses Marlowe's possible use of the newsbooks for *The Massacre at Paris*. Also, there is a general discussion of 16th-century journalistic methods. Bakeless has been a New York magazine editor and professor of journalism.

HARRIET MARTINEAU

1201. Nevill, John Cranstoun. *Harriet Martineau*. London: Frederick Muller, Ltd., 1943. 128pp.

This little book gives helpful background on the work of Miss Martineau as leader-writer for the London *Daily News* and on her writings in behalf of the abolitionist movement in the United States.

HENRY W. MASSINGHAM

1202. Massingham, H. W. *H. W. M.: A Selection from the Writings of H. W. Massingham*. London: Butler and Tanner, Ltd.; New York: Harcourt, Brace and Co., 1924. 368pp. (Preface by H. J. Massingham.)

Massingham, a Liberal editor of the London *Daily Chronicle* (1895–1899) and the British *Nation* (1907–1923), collects here a series of high-level articles written for various British newspapers on public men, war and peace, the press, men of letters, drama, religion, and personal impressions and experiences. See particularly "The Press and the People," "W. T. Stead," "The Religion of a Journalist" (on John Morley), and "Impressions of America."

NOEL MONKS

1203. Monks, Noel. *Eyewitness*. London: Frederick Muller, Ltd., 1956. 344pp.

BIOGRAPHY

An autobiographical narrative of an Australian who reported for London newspapers. A third is devoted to the 1930s and Monks's experiences in Abyssinia and Spain, the remainder to World War II, postwar crises, and Korea.

IRVING MONTAGU

1204. Montagu, Irving. *Things I Have Seen in War*. London: Chatto and Windus, 1899. x + 309pp.

Autobiographical pieces, each one complete in itself, of people, events, and scenes in the last quarter of the 19th century. Montagu, an artist for the *Illustrated London News*, could be called a precursor of Ernie Pyle. The scenes depicted are chiefly in Western Europe, the Near East, and Africa.

LORD MORLEY

1205. Morley, John, Viscount. *Recollections*. New York: The Macmillan Co., 1917. 2 vols. 770pp., total.

The autobiography of a distinguished political leader, man of letters, and journalist. Relatively slight attention is given to Morley's newspaper career with the *Pall Mall Gazette*, although he does discuss his choice of journalism as a career when he was a young man.

1206. Morgan, John H. *John, Viscount Morley*. Boston and New York: Houghton Mifflin Co., 1924. xiii + 215pp.

An appreciation of Morley, plus the author's personal reminiscences. Morgan discusses Morley's opposition to anonymity of leader-writers when he became editor of the *Fortnightly Review* in 1867.

1207. Staebler, Warren. *The Liberal Mind of John Morley*. Princeton, N.J.: Princeton University Press for the University of Cincinnati, 1943. vii + 216pp.

Staebler seeks to reveal Morley's mental processes. Nearly a fourth of the book is devoted to "The *Fortnightly Review* (1867–1882): Raising the Temperature of Thought through Journalism." Much less attention is paid to Morley's editorship of the *Pall Mall Gazette*.

HENRY MUDDIMAN

1208. Muddiman, J. G. *The King's Journalist, 1659–1689: Studies in the Reign of Charles II*. London: John Lane the Bodley Head, Ltd., 1923. ix + 294pp.

The life of Henry Muddiman, editor in 1665 of the Oxford *Gazette*, the first publication in England to be called a newspaper. There is valuable information on newsbooks, ballads of the times, and early newspapers, as well as accounts of Roger L'Estrange, the Popish plot of Titus Oates, and the English career of Benjamin Harris, printer of the first newspaper in the American colonies. The work is based upon manuscript materials and on Henry Muddiman's news letters, 1667–1689.

HENRY W. NEVINSON

1209. Nevinson, Henry W. *Changes and Chances*. New York: Harcourt, Brace and Co., 1923. xiii + 360pp.

Nevinson, a literary and political journalist, deals here wholly with the period 1875–1900, when he was a leader-writer for the *Daily Chronicle* and a Boer War correspondent. Nearly half the book concerns South Africa. There is an excellent analysis of H. W. Massingham of the *Daily Chronicle*.

1210. ———. *More Changes, More Chances.* New York: Harcourt, Brace and Co.; London: Nisbet and Co., Ltd., 1925. xvi + 427pp.

This continuation of *Changes and Chances* covers the period from the Boer War to the start of World War I, with accounts of the Russian Revolution of 1905, uprisings in the Balkans, and the gathering clouds in Europe before 1914. Nevinson served in this period on the *Daily News*, the *Nation*, the *Daily Chronicle*, and the Manchester *Guardian*.

1211. ———. *Last Changes, Last Chances.* New York: Harcourt, Brace and Co., 1929. xv + 359pp.

Nevinson's story from 1914 through the mid-1920s deals principally with World War I, the Washington Disarmament Conference, and Germany during the Ruhr occupation. The author added in this period work for the *New Leader*, a Labour paper. The three volumes as a unit make up one of the most detailed reportorial narratives one can find for the years 1875–1925.

SIR GEORGE NEWNES

1212. Friederichs, Hulda. *The Life of Sir George Newnes, Bart.* London, New York, and Toronto: Hodder and Stoughton, 1911. xi + 304pp.

George Newnes made a resounding success of popular journalism in England a decade before Northcliffe and before Hearst in America. His *Tit-Bits* came off the press in Manchester in 1881. Miss Friederichs's impressionistic biography, based upon personal acquaintance and supplemented by recollections of the Newnes family, is worth reading because of the perspective it gives on the early days of the "new journalism." There is good material on the inception of *Tit-Bits*, Newnes's contribution to stunt circulation, and his acquiring of the liberal *Westminster Gazette* in 1893.

LORD NORTHCLIFFE (ALFRED HARMSWORTH)

1213. Northcliffe, Lord. *My Journey round the World (16 July 1921–26 Feb. 1922).* London: John Lane; Philadelphia: J. B. Lippincott Co., 1923. xii + 326pp. (Edited by Cecil and St. John Harmsworth.)

Northcliffe's diary on a journey a year before his death is disconnected, abrupt, and inexact — yet vivid and forceful.

1214. Carson, W. E. *Northcliffe: Britain's Man of Power.* New York: Dodge Publishing Co., 1918. 456pp.

This heavily propagandistic volume by a former United States correspondent for Northcliffe newspapers is perhaps the weakest of the Northcliffe biographies.

1215. Clarke, Tom. *My Northcliffe Diary.* New York: Cosmopolitan Book Corp., 1931. xiii + 301pp.

Notations on Clarke's associations with Northcliffe from 1912 until the "Chief's" death in 1922. Clarke was an editor on the *Daily Mail*, although at the time of writing this book he had gone to the *Daily Chronicle*. He does not try to judge Northcliffe's power, but treats him as an interpreter of news and the public mind.

1216. ———. *Northcliffe in History: An Intimate Study of Press Power*. London and New York: Hutchinson and Co., 1951. 216pp.

Supplements Clarke's *My Northcliffe Diary*. He tries to rectify misunderstandings about Northcliffe that existed in the years immediately after the press lord's death.

1217. Fyfe, Hamilton. *Northcliffe: An Intimate Biography*. New York: The Macmillan Co., 1930. ix + 357pp.

Fyfe shows Northcliffe's strengths and weaknesses sympathetically. Like other biographers, he works around Northcliffe's conceptions that the press should be controlled by newspapermen, not by industrialists.

1218. Greenwall, Harry J. *Northcliffe: Napoleon of Fleet Street*. London: Allan Wingate, 1957. xii + 240pp.

A reporter (writer on politics, history, and travel) and novelist offers a biographical portrait of Northcliffe against the background of his period. Greenwall lets his fancy have free rein at the close by raising questions as to what might have happened to England (1922–1947) had Northcliffe lived to an advanced age.

1219. Pemberton, Max. *Lord Northcliffe: A Memoir*. London: Hodder and Stoughton, n.d. (c. 1922). 250pp.

An English novelist writes about Northcliffe as a friend. Material not included elsewhere: Northcliffe as motorist and golfer, in his daily habits, and on his reaction to stories relating to him.

1220. Ryan, A. P. *Lord Northcliffe*. London: Collins, 1953. 158pp. (Brief Lives Series.)

The only one of the 10 volumes in this series on a journalist. It is useful chiefly for a quick view of Northcliffe.

1221. Wilson, R. Macnair. *Lord Northcliffe: A Study*. London: Hazell, Watson and Viney, Ltd., 1927; Philadelphia: J. B. Lippincott Co., 1927. 304pp.

Unbounded praise of Northcliffe. Each of 51 short chapters is directed toward portraying some facet of Northcliffe's personality.

T. P. O'CONNOR

1222. Fyfe, Hamilton. *T. P. O'Connor*. London: George Allen and Unwin, Ltd., 1934. 351pp.

An excellent biography of an Irish politician-journalist who was an aide to Parnell and editor of Liberal-Radical newspapers (*Star*, *Sun*, and *T. P.'s Weekly*). There is good material on O'Connor's contribution to the "new journalism" and on the causes of the split in the Irish party in 1890.

ERIC PARKER

1223. Parker, Eric. *Memory Looks Forward: An Autobiography*. London: Seeley, Service and Co., Ltd., 1937. 368pp.

Parker served principally on newspapers devoted to the outdoors and to conservation. He started early in the 20th century with the *St. James's Gazette*, but for most of his career was on the staff of, and editor of, *Field*. The book is personal and gentle in tone.

CHARLES STEWART PARNELL

1224. Harrison, Henry. *Parnell, Joseph Chamberlain, and Mr. Garvin.* London: Robert Hale, Ltd., 1938. ix + 255pp.

A critical analysis of the ramifications of the Parnell-O'Shea divorce case of 1890 which split the Irish Home-Rule party and in which the press was deeply involved. Harrison's book is a vindication of Parnell.

1225. Robbins, Sir Alfred. *Parnell: The Last Five Years, Told from Within.* London: Thornton Butterworth, Ltd., 1926. 208pp.

Robbins was the London correspondent for the Birmingham *Post* during the British Royal Commission investigation into Irish crime involving the Home-Rule fight of the 1880s. This book is particularly valuable for the observation it affords of the London *Times*'s part in accusing Parnell of complicity in Irish murders. Virtually the whole book is concerned with the case. It discusses the relationships between the Irish *Freeman's Journal* and Parnell, quotes extensively from the Birmingham *Post*, and analyzes the work of journalist Henry Labouchere in connection with the case.

LESLIE ALLEN PAUL

1226. Paul, Leslie Allen. *Angry Young Man.* London: Faber and Faber, 1951. 302pp.

An introspective account by a free-lance journalist and novelist seeking the meaning of things in the world of the 1920s and 1930s.

SIR ARTHUR PEARSON

1227. Dark, Sidney. *The Life of Sir Arthur Pearson.* London: Hodder and Stoughton, 1918. vii + 228pp.

An employee's tribute to the founder of the London *Daily Express* (1900) and purchaser of the *Standard* (1904). Pearson in these years was a close competitor of Alfred Harmsworth for control of the mass-circulation field. Much of the content is devoted to Pearson's philanthropies.

STEPHEN WALTER POLLAK

1228. Pollak, Stephen Walter. *Strange Land behind Me.* London: Falcon, 1951. x + 337pp.

An account of the "strange land" of former comrades in Communist revolutionary service and an exposé of methods of the Communist underground in Europe.

ARTHUR PORRITT

1229. Porritt, Arthur. *More and More of Memories.* London: George Allen and Unwin, Ltd., 1947. 242pp.

The autobiography of a former editor of the *Christian World*.

BIOGRAPHY

G. WARD PRICE

1230. Price, G. Ward. *Extra-Special Correspondent*. London and Toronto: G. Harrap and Co., 1957. 346pp.

Reminiscences over nearly 50 years of a foreign and war correspondent for the *Daily Mail*. Among the better recent narratives, it gives a kaleidoscopic view of the complex world changes.

DOUGLAS REED

1231. Reed, Douglas. *Insanity Fair: A European Cavalcade*. New York: Random House, 1938. 420pp.

This autobiography includes a political analysis of Europe in the 1930s. Reed at one time had been secretary to Lord Northcliffe; later he represented the London *Times* in Europe. He devotes most of his story to Germany — the last days of the Weimar Republic and Hitler up to the march into Austria. There is some material on Balkan problems.

JOHN WILLIAM ROBERTSON-SCOTT

1232. Robertson-Scott, John William. *The Day before Yesterday: Memories of an Uneducated Man*. London: Methuen and Co., Ltd., 1951. x + 294pp.

HENRY CRABB ROBINSON

1233. Robinson, Henry Crabb. *Henry Crabb Robinson in Germany, 1800–1805*. London: Humphrey Milford, 1929. v + 194pp. (Edited by Edith J. Morley.)

Extracts from correspondence between Robinson and his brother Thomas. Robinson records political, social, and intellectual conditions during the Napoleonic wars. An appendix lists his contributions to the *Monthly Register* in 1802–1803.

1234. Baker, John Milton. *Henry Crabb Robinson of Bury, Jena, the Times, and Russell Square*. London: George Allen and Unwin, Ltd., 1937. 256pp.

This is particularly useful for Robinson's early journalistic and literary achievements. There is an excellent discussion of his reporting for the London *Times* in Germany in 1807. A good bibliography is included.

1235. Morley, Edith J. *The Life and Times of Henry Crabb Robinson*. London: J. M. Dent and Sons, Ltd., 1935. xii + 212pp.

The author places Robinson among those of lesser rank in 19th-century letters, philosophy, and politics, but she praises his excellent correspondence for the *Times*.

JONATHAN ROUTH

1236. Routh, Jonathan. *The Little Men in My Life*. London: Barrie, 1953. 138pp.

THE LITERATURE OF JOURNALISM

SIR WILLIAM HOWARD RUSSELL

1237. Atkins, J. B. *The Life of Sir William Howard Russell: The First Special Correspondent.* New York: E. P. Dutton and Co., 1911. 2 vols. 804pp., total.

This biography of the great *Times* war reporter is perhaps unsurpassed by any later writing on Russell. Besides recording Russell's career, Atkins carries through a running history of the Crimean War, Indian Mutiny, American Civil War, Austro-Prussian War, and Franco-Prussian War. The first eight chapters of vol. II deal wholly with the American Civil War.

1238. Furneaux, Rupert. *The First War Correspondent: William Howard Russell of the Times.* London: Cassell and Co., Ltd., 1945. 240pp.

Furneaux obtained material on the correspondent from one of Russell's descendants, previous works on him, and histories of the *Times*. Of interest in American journalism is "Russell Will Be Lynched," material devoted to the turmoil in public opinion arising from his penetrating accounts of the North in 1861.

GEORGE AUGUSTUS SALA

1239. Sala, George Augustus. *The Life and Adventures of George Augustus Sala, Written by Himself.* London: Cassell and Co., 1896. 746pp.

Sala, a famous correspondent of the London *Daily Telegraph*, ranges widely — on the theater and novels, journalists of the past, the Great Exhibition of 1851, the rise of the cheap press, and reporting in America during the Civil War, in France in 1870, in Russia in 1876, and throughout Europe in the 1880s.

CHARLES P. SCOTT

1240. Hammond, J. L. *C. P. Scott of the Manchester Guardian.* London: G. Bell and Sons, Ltd., 1934. xv + 365pp.

A solid biography of the great editor of the *Guardian* for more than a half-century, written by a friend and noted historian. In addition to biographical material on Scott, Hammond gives details on the *Guardian*'s views on Ireland, the Liberal-Conservative party struggles, British foreign policy, and World War I.

1241. Manchester Guardian. *C. P. Scott, 1846–1932: Memorial Number.* Special issue of Jan. 5, 1932. 12 tabloid pp.

A separate obituary section. It includes tributes from the British and American press at large and from leading British politicians. Well illustrated; worth reading in full.

1242. ———. *C. P. Scott, 1846–1932: The Making of the Manchester Guardian.* London: Frederick Muller, Ltd., 1946. 252pp.

Sketches by 16 contributors portraying phases of Scott's life and the history of the *Guardian* under his editorship. Special attention is paid to the newspaper's contribution to art, books, drama, music, special correspondence, and pictures. There are pieces by Scott himself on journalism, peace, liberalism,

BIOGRAPHY

labor, Ireland, and "men and movements." A closing chapter considers the *Guardian* after Scott's death.

FLORA SHAW

1243. Bell, Enid. *Flora Shaw*. London: Constable and Co., Ltd., 1947. 309pp.

The life of a *Times* correspondent in the late 19th and early 20th century who served special commissions to report on South Africa, the Klondike, and Australia, and later headed the newspaper's colonial department.

GEORGE SLOCOMBE

1244. Slocombe, George. *The Tumult and the Shouting: The Memoirs of George Slocombe*. New York: The Macmillan Co., 1936. 437pp.

Pictures of journalism and politicians by a newspaper and literary critic of the period 1912–1936. Slocombe was chief foreign correspondent of the *Daily Herald* in the 1920s and later was with the *Evening Standard*.

ERNEST SMITH

1245. Smith, Ernest. *Fields of Adventure: Some Recollections of Forty Years of Newspaper Life*. London: Hutchinson and Co., 1923; Boston: Small, Maynard and Co., 1924. ix + 319pp.

Smith started in provincial journalism with the *Isle of Wight Chronicle* and Portsmouth *Times*; later he was a Paris correspondent for the *Daily News*. He gives accounts of news coverage of Queen Victoria, the Vatican, the Dreyfus case (in which Smith played a big part as a journalist), South Africa, Germany, Greece, and the Holy Land after World War I.

ALEXANDER SOMERVILLE

1246. Somerville, Alexander. *The Autobiography of a Working Man*. Plymouth, England: Turnstile Press, 1951. xxiii + 282pp. (Reissue of original edition published in 1848; edited, with an introduction, by John Carswell.)

Somerville was a Cobdenite journalist in the Reform period of the 1830s and was a sponsor of corn law repeal. Beginning life as a cowherd and sawyer, he achieved recognition for his letters to the *Morning Chronicle* on the corn laws and became a correspondent of the Manchester *Examiner*. The autobiography deals only with the period to 1834.

VISCOUNT SOUTHWOOD

1247. Minney, Rubeigh James. *Viscount Southwood*. London: Odhams Press, Ltd., 1954. 384pp.

A house biography of Julius Salter Elias, Viscount Southwood of Fernhurst, publisher of the London *Daily Herald*. This is also a history of the unusual rise of a highly successful Labour–private capital press enterprise — Odhams. The development of other Odhams publications, including *John Bull* and the *People*, is discussed, as well as Southwood's activities in the Labour party.

THE LITERATURE OF JOURNALISM

JOHN ALFRED SPENDER

1248. Spender, J. A. *Life, Journalism and Politics*. London: Cassell and Co., Ltd., 1927. 2 vols. 471pp., total.

Spender was a scholar, politician, and journalist for 50 years, from the 1880s to the 1930s, editor of the *Westminster Gazette* from 1896 to 1922. This excellent autobiography weaves through the whole fabric of British history during the period, with chapters on the press interspersed with political history. There is a discussion of the history of the *Westminster Gazette*, the "art and craft of the journalist," and Lord Northcliffe.

1249. Harris, [Henry] Wilson. *J. A. Spender*. London: Cassell and Co., Ltd., 1946. viii + 246pp.

A sympathetic biography by a colleague. It leans heavily on Spender's own autobiography, supplementing the latter by carrying the story 15 years beyond 1927.

EARL OF STANHOPE (CHARLES MAHON)

1250. Kubler, George A. *The Era of Charles Mahon, Third Earl of Stanhope*. New York: Brooklyn Eagle Press, 1938. x + 120pp.

Charles Mahon was a mechanical genius, mathematician, scholar, politician, and member of a distinguished family related to the Pitts. This useful book brings together historical and biographical data that show the developments in the stereotyping process. Well illustrated.

HENRY MORTON STANLEY

1251. Stanley, Henry Morton. *The Autobiography of Henry Morton Stanley*. Boston and New York: Houghton Mifflin Co., 1909. xvii + 551pp. (Edited by Mrs. Dorothy Stanley.)

Partly Stanley's own story (limited to his early years) and partly an edited account of the remainder of his life as prepared by his widow from the journalist-explorer's journals and notes. The journalistic material begins with Stanley's coverage of the American Civil War, continues through Indian War campaigns, and goes on to the finding of David Livingstone. Mrs. Stanley portrays her husband as the victim of "ungenerous conduct" by a portion of press and public.

1252. ———. *How I Found Livingstone: Travels, Adventures, and Discoveries in Central Africa, Including an Account of Four Months' Residence with Dr. Livingstone*. New York: Scribner, Armstrong and Co., 1874. xliii + 736pp. (Centenary edition: Charles Scribner's Sons, 1913, with an introduction by Robert E. Speer, secretary of the Presbyterian Board of Foreign Missions.)

The bulk of this highly personal narrative concerns Stanley's troubles, thoughts, and impressions. The material runs chronologically from January 1871 to May 1872. There is an extensive appendix of official letters, some from Livingstone.

1253. Busoni, Rafaello. *Stanley's Africa*. New York: Viking Press, 1944. 288pp.

BIOGRAPHY

A popular biography. There is no material on Stanley's early life.

1254. Hird, Frank. *H. M. Stanley, the Authorized Life*. London: Stanley Paul and Co., Ltd., 1935. 320pp.

Based upon Stanley's letters, diaries, papers, and notebooks of his African expeditions over many years. The volume is devoted chiefly to his discoveries; his work as a newspaper correspondent is kept subordinate.

1255. Symons, A. J. A. *H. M. Stanley*. London: Camelot Press; New York: The Macmillan Co., 1933. 128pp.

Stanley's career in capsule form. The first half covers his newspaper career, with emphasis on the fact that his African assignments were sponsored by the London *Daily Telegraph* as well as the New York *Herald*.

1256. Wassermann, Jakob. *Bula Matari: Stanley, Conqueror of a Continent*. New York: Horace Liveright, 1933. xvi + 351pp. (Translated from the German by Eden and Cedar Paul. Published in England under the title *H. M. Stanley — Explorer*. London: Cassell and Co., Ltd.)

The life of Stanley in broad strokes, by a German essayist, novelist, and short-story writer.

RUSSELL STANNARD

1257. Stannard, Russell. *With the Dictators of Fleet Street: The Autobiography of an Ignorant Journalist*. London: Hutchinson and Co., 1934. 287pp.

Among British autobiographies, distinctive in its brashness. Stannard, who rose to become editor of the London *Sunday Express*, writes chiefly of the period 1914–1934. There are vignettes of Northcliffe, Beaverbrook, Rothermere, Camrose, and others; stories of the early days of "flying journalism"; and some material on sports writing and periodical journalism. Stannard admired all the newspaper barons.

WILLIAM T. STEAD

1258. Stead, Estelle. *My Father: Personal and Spiritual Reminiscences*. New York: George H. Doran Co., 1913. xii + 351pp.

W. T. Stead's daughter gives here numerous sketches of her father's activities, journalistic and religious. Writing a year after Stead lost his life on the *Titanic*, Miss Stead dwells heavily on his interest in spiritualism. She treats in lesser fashion his editorship of the *Northern Echo* in Darlington and the *Pall Mall Gazette*, and of his founding the *Review of Reviews*. A valuable account.

1259. Waugh, Benjamin. *William T. Stead: A Life for the People*. Chicago: Woman's Christian Temperance Publication Association, 1886. 36pp. (Foreword by Frances Willard.)

A propaganda piece defending Stead, then editor of the *Pall Mall Gazette*, for his crusade to wipe out prostitution in the Victorian London of the 1880s. The account centers on his articles on "The Maiden Tribute to Modern Babylon," which so shocked London that Stead was sent to jail. This gives a good view of what sensationalists did at the dawn of the "new journalism."

1260. Whyte, Frederic. *The Life of W. T. Stead.* London: Jonathan Cape; Boston: Houghton Mifflin Co., 1925. 2 vols. 713pp., total.

A balanced, thorough biography. Whyte covers separately Stead's editorship of various newspapers, with particular attention to the *Pall Mall Gazette* and *Review of Reviews.* There is also a valuable chapter on his first visit to America and on the effect of his sensational book, *If Christ Came to Chicago.*

HENRY WICKHAM STEED

1261. Steed, Henry Wickham. *Through Thirty Years, 1892–1922: A Personal Narrative.* Garden City, N.Y.: Doubleday, Page and Co., 1925. 2 vols. 830pp., total.

As good for general history as for journalism. Steed served the London *Times* as foreign correspondent in Rome and Vienna and later as foreign editor and editor for 27 of the 30 years covered. He left the *Times* shortly after Northcliffe's death to become editor of the *Review of Reviews.* Vol. I covers his career from student days in Germany to World War I; vol. II is almost wholly an analysis of the war and the peace conference of 1919. Steed gives a careful account of the sale of the *Times* to Northcliffe in 1908, analyzes Northcliffe's views on the war, discusses propaganda in 1917–1918, and concludes with extended comment on the power of the *Times* during his editorship (1919–1922). References to journalism as a career, journalistic ethics, changes in the press, and journalists and government are extensive.

GEORGE WARRINGTON STEEVENS

1262. Steevens, George W. *Things Seen: Impressions of Men, Cities and Books.* Indianapolis: Bowen-Merrill Co., 1900. xxvi + 326pp. (Selected and edited by G. S. Street, with a Memoir by W. E. Henley.)

Steevens, one of the most talented young reporters of his day, died of fever at Ladysmith in covering the Boer War for the *Daily Mail.* Henley's biography sketches Steevens's life sympathetically and somewhat emotionally. The selections from Steevens's writings are chiefly reprints from magazine articles; 5 are on Victoria's Jubilee in 1897 and 2 are penetrating analyses of the Dreyfus case.

JOHN ST. LOE STRACHEY

1263. Strachey, John St. Loe. *The Adventure of Living: A Subjective Autobiography.* New York and London: G. P. Putnam's Sons, 1922. xiv + 500pp.

The editor of the *Spectator* gives an account of the influences that affected his life. There is excellent material on the ethics of journalism and the place of journalism in modern life.

1264. Strachey, Amy. *St. Loe Strachey: His Life and His Paper.* London: Victor Gollancz, Ltd.; New York: Brewer and Warren, 1930. 387pp.

This biography by Strachey's wife covers his life from their marriage in 1887.

BIOGRAPHY

There is good material on the *Spectator*, on Strachey as a citizen and editor during World War I, and on relations between the *Spectator* and the United States during World War I.

ALLAN K. TAYLOR

1265. Taylor, Allan K. *From a Glasgow Slum to Fleet Street.* London: Alvin Redman, Ltd., 1949. xiii + 243pp.

A strange autobiography of a successful Scottish journalist who had less than two years' schooling and who in 1932 at age 42 was destitute. Then he made 1000 pounds with a piece in the *News of the World* on "Jock of Dartmoor," a story of life inside a prison. Taylor's early life bore some prison smudges which (aided by a good wife) he overcame.

ALEX THOMPSON

1266. Thompson, Alex ["Dangle"]. *Here I Lie: The Memorial of an Old Journalist.* London: George Routledge, 1937. xii + 324pp.

By an editor of a Liberal-Labour newspaper, the *Clarion*.

REGINALD THOMPSON

1267. Thompson, Reginald William. *The Pink House in Angel Street: The Story of a Family.* London: D. Dobson, 1954. 255pp.

J. C. TREWIN and H. J. WILLMOTT

1268. Trewin, J. C., and H. J. Willmott. *London-Bodwin, an Exchange of Letters.* London: Westaway Books, 1950. 198pp.

Twenty-two personal reminiscences (11 each) between Trewin, a metropolitan dramatic critic in Hampstead, and Willmott, news editor of a country newspaper in Bodmin, Cornwall. The period is spring and summer 1948. The material offers good insights into literary journalistic thought.

ERNEST ALFRED VIZETELLY

1269. Vizetelly, Ernest Alfred. *In Seven Lands: Germany — Austria — Hungary — Bohemia — Spain — Portugal — Italy.* New York: Duffield and Co., 1916. xiii + 393pp.

The joint experiences of Vizetelly and his father, Henry, whose companion Ernest was early in life while the father was correspondent for the *Illustrated London News* (1865–1872).

1270. ———. *My Days of Adventure: The Fall of France, 1870–71.* London: Chatto and Windus, 1914. xi + 337pp.

The experiences of Vizetelly based considerably upon memory although the author referred to old diaries and newspaper articles.

1271. ———. *My Adventures in the Commune.* London: Chatto and Windus, 1914. xv + 368pp.

A sequel to *My Days of Adventure.* Although this is more a political-military study of the effects of the Franco-Prussian War than a personalized narrative like the earlier book, it too is based heavily on personal recollections. A stronger anti-German bias creeps into this book.

THOMAS WAKLEY

1272. Sprigge, S. Squire. *The Life and Times of Thomas Wakley, Founder and First Editor of the Lancet, Member of Parliament for Finsbury, and Coroner for West Middlesex.* London and New York: Longmans, Green and Co., 1897. xix + 509pp.

The biography of a medical editor, politician, and reformer. Wakley founded the *Lancet* in 1823 to strike boldly at the ills of the medical profession.

EDGAR WALLACE

1273. Lane, Margaret. *Edgar Wallace: The Biography of a Phenomenon.* New York: Doubleday, Doran and Co., 1939. xii + 423pp.

The life of a journalistic oddity who as a spirited writer and editor for Harmsworth newspapers scored great scoops during the Boer War. Later, however, Wallace was discharged for inaccuracies that resulted in heavy libel damages. A fascinating account is given of this, and of Wallace's later ventures with the failing *Sunday News*, of successful novel and play writing, and of a whirl in Hollywood in the 1920s.

H. G. WELLS

1274. Brome, Vincent. *H. G. Wells, a Biography.* London and New York: Longmans, Green and Co., 1951. 255pp.

See chapter 6 for an account of Wells's sale of scientific romance to the *Pall Mall Gazette* in 1891–1892. There is also an account of Wells's association with the British Propaganda Ministry in World War I.

1275. Vallentin, Antonina. *H. G. Wells: Prophet of Our Day.* New York: The John Day Co., 1950. x + 338pp. (Translated from the French by Daphne Woodward.)

The author seeks to find the meaning of Wells's insistent message to mankind. The book is helpful for its over-all picture of the man and for such material as it gives of Wells's activities on the fringes of journalism.

WILLIAM WEST

1276. West, William. *Fifty Years' Recollections of an Old Bookseller.* London: The Author, 1837. vii + 200pp. (First issued in Cork, Ireland, 1830; reissued 1835.)

Anecdotes, character sketches of authors, artists, actors, and booksellers, and accounts of the periodical press of the half-century after 1780. This book is one of the earliest journalistic autobiographies.

JOHN WILKES

1277. Wilkes, John, and Charles Churchill. *The Correspondence of John*

BIOGRAPHY

Wilkes and Charles Churchill. London: Oxford University Press; New York: Columbia University Press, 1954. xxix + 114pp. (Edited, with an introduction, by Edward H. Weatherly.)

1278. Bleackley, Horace. *Life of John Wilkes.* London: John Lane the Bodley Head, 1917. xiii + 464pp.

A virtually full vindication of Wilkes, whose fame, the author argues, has been "influenced more adversely by political prejudice" than that of most public men.

1279. Postgate, R. W. *That Devil Wilkes.* New York: Vanguard Press, 1929. 267pp.

A scholarly life of Wilkes, telling the full story of his press troubles with the government, his civil outlawry and four-time expulsion from Parliament, his career as Lord Mayor of London, and his support of the American Colonial cause.

1280. Quennell, Peter. *The Profane Virtues: Four Studies of the Eighteenth Century.* New York: Viking Press, 1945. 220pp.

The most useful of these four vignettes is that on Wilkes. The other three are studies of James Boswell, Edward Gibbon, and Laurence Sterne.

1281. Treloar, William Purdie. *Wilkes and the City.* London: John Murray, 1917. xxvi + 299pp.

Concerns mostly Wilkes's relations with the Corporation of London during his career as Lord Mayor; however, some space is devoted to the *North Briton* episode.

1282. Watson, Rev. John Selby. *Biographies of John Wilkes and William Cobbett.* Edinburgh and London: William Blackwood and Sons, 1870. 407pp.

An interesting combination of biographies of these political-journalistic figures, but no clear indication as to why the two should have been drawn together. Neither biography would rate high in the literature on Wilkes or Cobbett. Toward Wilkes the author is antagonistic and toward Cobbett somewhat sympathetic.

HENRY SPENSER WILKINSON

1283. Wilkinson, Henry Spenser. *Thirty-Five Years, 1874–1909.* London: Constable and Co., Ltd., 1933. ix + 325pp.

The autobiography of a journalistic military expert, correspondent for the Manchester *Guardian* and London *Morning Post.* He reported events extending from Britain's Egyptian campaign in the 1880s to World War I; he later became a professor of military history at Oxford.

HAROLD WILLIAMS

1284. Tyrkova-Williams, Ariadna. *Cheerful Giver: The Life of Harold Williams.* London: Peter Davies, 1935. 337pp. (Preface by Sir Samuel Hoare.)

Williams was a leftist editor of World War I days; before that he had been a Methodist minister and an observer of pre-1917 Russia. He later joined the London *Times.*

VALENTINE WILLIAMS

1285. Williams, Valentine. *World of Action.* London: H. Hamilton, 1938. 479pp. Boston: Houghton Mifflin Co., 1938. vii + 429pp.

A well-written, worthwhile autobiography of a newspaperman, soldier, and novelist in the first third of the 20th century. There is a good description of Reuters late in the 19th century, when Williams's father was associated with that agency. Material on Northcliffe, World War I censorship, and military and political figures from the Kaiser to Franklin D. Roosevelt is useful.

A. E. WILSON

1286. Wilson, A. E. *Playgoer's Pilgrimage.* London: Stanley Paul and Co., Ltd., 1949. 276pp. (Foreword by Dame Sybil Thorndike.)

The life of a dramatic critic who worked for the London *Star.*

SIR JOHN EVELYN WRENCH

1287. Wrench, John Evelyn. *Uphill: The First Stage in a Strenuous Life.* London: Ivor Nicholson and Watson, Ltd., 1934. x + 316pp.

The first volume of a two-part autobiography by the owner of the *Spectator,* who devoted much of his career to seeking imperial and world union. *Uphill* carries from Wrench's childhood (1882) to 1912–1913, when he began his Empire crusade. The bulk of the book covers the years during which Wrench served Northcliffe as editor of the overseas edition of the *Daily Mail.* He left Northcliffe to found the magazine *Overseas.*

1288. ———. *Struggle, 1914–1920.* London: Ivor Nicholson and Watson, Ltd., 1935. 504pp.

In his second volume, Wrench deals wholly with World War I and his continued efforts for Empire unity. Heavy with detail, this book lacks the journalistic interest of *Uphill.*

EDMUND YATES

1289. Yates, Edmund. *Edmund Yates: His Recollections and Experiences.* London: Richard Bentley and Son, 1884. 2 vols. 701pp., total.

The life of a secondary novelist and literary journalist from the 1850s to the 1880s. Yates was editor of *Town Talk* and the *World,* a society journal, and in 1872–1873 European correspondent of the New York *Herald.* The book has useful material on a conflict between Yates and William Makepeace Thackeray involving a criticism of Thackeray in *Town Talk.*

D. Journalists of Other Countries

JEAN BEKESSY (HANS HABE)

1289a. Bekessy, Jean [pseud. Hans Habe]. *All My Sins: An Autobiography.* Sydney, Australia: Australasian Publishing Co., in association with George G. Harrap and Co., Ltd., London, 1957. 400pp. (Translated from the German by E. Osers.)

A deeply revealing account by a native Hungarian whose career of great success and equally great failure carried him through Hungary, Austria, Germany, and the United States from pre-Hitler days through the middle 1950s. Bekessy, both journalist and novelist, gives an excellent picture of sensational journalism in middle Europe in the 1920s; he claims to have been the first editor of the first denazified newspaper in Germany (*Neue Zeitung*) after the Allied victory in 1945.

FILIPPO BOJANO

1290. Bojano, Filippo. *In the Wake of the Goose-Step*. Chicago and New York: Ziff-Davis Publishing Co., 1945. 271pp. (Translated from the Italian by Gerald Griffin.)

An autobiography covering the period from 1929 to the defeat of Italy in 1943, by a reporter for Mussolini's *Popolo d'Italia*. Bojano served most of the period in Berlin; later he went to Moscow and Stockholm. A highly effective book, aided by a fine translation. There is a good account of il Duce's fall.

SALVATORE CORTESI

1291. Cortesi, Salvatore. *My Thirty Years of Friendships*. New York and London: Harper and Brothers, 1927. 296pp.

Reminiscences of a representative in Rome for the Associated Press. Cortesi is concerned largely with Italian affairs and persons; extensive detail on the papacy is included.

CAMILLE DESMOULINS

1292. Hartcup, John. *Love Is Revolution: The Story of Camille Desmoulins*. London and New York: Staples Press, 1950. 130pp.

The life of a journalist executed during the French Revolution. Desmoulins in 1789 harangued crowds at the Bastille, wrote *La France Libre*, and later published *La Tribune des Patriotes*.

KARL ESKELUND

1293. Eskelund, Karl. *My Chinese Wife*. Garden City, N.Y.: Doubleday, Doran and Co., 1945. 247pp.

This Danish newspaper correspondent reported world events for American press associations, the New York *Times*, and Danish and Chinese newspapers. His autobiography in part attempts to interpret the customs and culture of the Chinese through his story of his wife.

JOHN FAIRFAX

1294. Fairfax, J. F. *The Story of John Fairfax: Commemorating the Centenary of the Fairfax Proprietary of the Sydney Morning Herald, 1841–1941*. Sydney, Australia: John Fairfax and Sons, Ltd., 1941. xix + 169pp.

The life of the first of the Fairfaxes of the Sydney *Morning Herald, Art in Australia*, and the *Home*. Four generations of the family have been in control of the *Herald* or associated with it. J. F. Fairfax's account, which takes the paper's history to John Fairfax's death in 1877, is an excellent discussion of the Fairfax heritage, Sydney of a century ago, and the growth and progress of the newspaper.

A. FINN

1295. Finn, A. *Experiences of a Soviet Journalist*. New York: Research Program on the U.S.S.R. (East European Fund, Inc.), 1954. 27pp. (Mimeographed series No. 66.)

The author considers his life in the decade before World War II, his relationship with the Communist party and its activities, the social organization of the Soviet newspaper office, and censorship.

HOUSE OF FUGGER

1296. Klarwill, Victor von, ed. *The Fugger News-Letters: Being a Selection of Unpublished Letters from the Correspondents of the House of Fugger during the Years 1568–1605*. London: John Lane the Bodley Head, Ltd., 1924. xlv + 284pp. Second series, New York and London: G. P. Putnam's Sons, 1926. xlix + 348pp. (Series I translated from the German by Pauline de Chary, with a foreword by H. Gordon Selfridge and 30 illustrations; Series II translated by L. S. R. Byrne of Eton College, with 46 illustrations.)

These private reports from agents of the House of Fugger to their banking firm in Augsburg describe in early "journalistic narrative" the commercial and political happenings of the world as they viewed them. Von Klarwill's introduction in Series I summarizes the Fugger family background. The first series contains 240 letters, plus extensive historical notes and bibliography. The second series discusses Fugger coverage of English affairs under Elizabeth I and includes 748 letters and an appendix. The letters make fascinating reading — murders, driving out of devils, plagues, royal marriages, New World gold, political plots, and wars.

PAUL JOSEPH GOEBBELS

1297. Goebbels, Paul Joseph. *The Goebbels Diaries, 1942–1943*. Garden City, N.Y.: Doubleday and Co., 1948. ix + 566pp. (Edited and translated, with an introduction, by Louis P. Lochner.)

A record of Adolf Hitler's minister for public enlightenment and propaganda, January 21, 1942, to December 9, 1943, with numerous gaps. Lochner obtained the selections from Goebbels material found in Berlin after the Allied occupation in 1945. The introduction carries a useful biographical sketch of Goebbels. Lochner provides continuity.

1298. Riess, Curt. *Joseph Goebbels, a Biography*. London: Hollis and Carter, 1949. ix + 460pp. Garden City, N.Y.: Doubleday and Co., 1948. xvi + 367pp. (Preface by Louis P. Lochner.)

BIOGRAPHY

1299. Semmler, Rudolf. *Goebbels — the Man Next to Hitler*. London: Westhouse, 1947. 234pp. (Introduction by D. McLachlan.)

Based on a diary of Rudolf Semmler, a member of Goebbels's Propaganda Ministry, covering the period from December 1940 through the fall of Berlin. Two worthwhile accounts are Semmler's reactions to the plot against Hitler, July 20, 1944, and his report of Goebbels's joy at the news of Franklin D. Roosevelt's death, April 13, 1945.

GEORGE A. L. GREEN

1300. Green, George A. L. *An Editor Looks Back: South African and Other Memories, 1883–1946*. Cape Town and Johannesburg: Juta and Co., Ltd., 1947. 288pp. (Introduction by Field-Marshal the Right Hon. J. C. Smuts.)

The autobiography of the editor of the *Cape Argus*, in part a narrative, in part in diary form. Green, a native of England, went to South Africa in the days of Cecil Rhodes. He tells much about Rhodes and diamond development.

HEINRICH HAUSER

1301. Hauser, Heinrich. *The German Talks Back*. New York: Henry Holt and Co., 1945. xxiii + 215pp.

A German journalist who disliked America describes how Germans felt about World War II. His point of view is emotional and strong-minded, "in the spirit of Prussia." Hauser himself was a non-Nazi.

1302. ———. *Time Was: Death of a Junker*. New York: Reynal and Hitchcock, 1942. 308pp. (Translated by Barrows Mussey.)

A member of the Junker class, Hauser was a traveling correspondent for the *Frankfurter Zeitung* and *Hamburger Fremdenblatt* and for German illustrated magazines. He gives pictures of pre-Hitlerite Germany and changes wrought in it by the Nazis.

LAZAR HERRMANN (LEO LANIA)

1303. Herrmann, Lazar [pseud. Leo Lania]. *Today We Are Brothers: The Biography of a Generation*. Boston: Houghton Mifflin Co., 1942. 344pp. (Translated by Ralph Marlowe.)

The life of a Viennese journalist who fled from the Nazis and reached the United States early in World War II. Treated in some detail are the *Arbeiter-Zeitung*, for which Herrmann worked, and the *Neue Freie Press*, which went over to Hitler. The book is to some extent a sequel to *The Darkest Hour* (Boston: Houghton Mifflin, 1941) in which Herrmann describes his flight from Europe.

A. S. IYENGAR

1304. Iyengar, A. S. *All through the Gandhian Era*. Bombay: Hind Kitabs, Ltd., 1950. x + 327pp.

One of the few available memoirs of Asian journalists. It covers 35 years of experience as an Indian editor, with Reuters, the Associated Press (now the Press Trust of India), and the information office of the government of India. There is considerable political matter on Indian independence.

EGON E. KISCH

1305. Kisch, Egon. *Sensation Fair*. New York: Modern Age Books, 1941. 376pp. (Translated from the German by Guy Endore.)

A Czech journalist tells of his first 30 years. He covered crime news as a young reporter for the *Bohemia*, German newspaper in Prague, and the last days of the Austro-Hungarian Empire.

ARTHUR KOESTLER

1306. Koestler, Arthur. *Arrow in the Blue: An Autobiography*, vol. I; *The Invisible Writing*, vol. II. New York: The Macmillan Co., 1952 and 1954. 2 vols. viii + 352pp. and 431pp.

The life of an outstanding European journalist-author. These two volumes follow two earlier autobiographical works (*Dialogue with Death* and *Scum of the Earth*), both of which dealt with Spanish Civil War and World War II experiences. The later books treat more generally Koestler's whole life, vol. II dealing with his life as a Communist in the 1930s. A native of Hungary, Koestler began his career as a Middle East correspondent for the Ullstein Press.

HELENA KUO

1307. Kuo, Helena [Ching-Ch'iu]. *I've Come a Long Way*. New York and London: D. Appleton-Century Co., 1942. 369pp.

The delightful story of a Chinese newspaperwoman, born in Macao and educated in Canton and Shanghai. Forced to flee Hangkow in 1937 when the Japanese attacked, Miss Kuo tells of her struggles as a refugee, first in England and then in the United States. Her newspaper accounts include experiences with the *China Times*, *China Press*, and *North China Daily News*.

STEFAN LORANT

1308. Lorant, Stefan. *I Was Hitler's Prisoner*. New York: G. P. Putnam's Sons, 1935. 318pp. (Translated from the German by James Cleugh.)

The diary of the editor of the *Münchner Illustrierte Presse*, covering the period March 12–September 27, 1933, when he was held by the Nazis. This is an excellent historical account of early operations of the Third Reich.

ALEXANDER MacDONALD

1309. MacDonald, Alexander. *Bangkok Editor*. New York: The Macmillan Co., 1949. 229pp.

The autobiography of the editor of the Bangkok *Post*, English-language newspaper in Thailand founded by the author in 1946 after he left the United States Office of Strategic Services. A readable adventure about journalism in Asia.

BIOGRAPHY

SEIJI NOMA

1310. Noma, Seiji. *Noma of Japan: The Nine Magazines of Kodansha, Being the Autobiography of a Japanese Publisher.* New York: Vanguard Press, 1934. xi + 290pp. (Introduction by J. W. Robertson-Scott; translated by Shunkichi Akimoto.)

Owner of the Kodansha magazines, with circulation in the several millions, plus the Tokyo newspaper *Hochi Shimbun,* Noma sought to introduce himself "faithfully and candidly to the English-reading public." The result is a fascinating story of a young Japanese growing up in the end of the Japanese feudal age and his struggles for business success in modern Tokyo. There is a fairly close parallel between Noma and journalistic popularizers in England and the United States.

1311. Akimoto, Shunkichi. *Seiji Noma, Magazine King of Japan: A Sketch of His Life, Character, and Enterprises.* Tokyo: Dai Nippon Yubenkwai Kodansha, 1927. 36pp.

A sketch, originally issued in pamphlet form. Noma at the time controlled 70 per cent of the magazines of Japan, and Kodansha Enterprises had a gross circulation of about 10,000,000.

JOHN B. POWELL

1312. Powell, John B. *My Twenty-Five Years in China.* New York: The Macmillan Co., 1945. 436pp.

The autobiography of a University of Missouri School of Journalism graduate who went to China in 1917 and remained until repatriation after Japanese imprisonment during World War II. Powell was editor of the *China Weekly Review.* This is a helpful book for information on China's journalistic problems and for reports on Japan's practices during the "China incidents" of the 1930s. There is a long discussion of the Panay affair of 1937.

1313. *The Yun Gee Portrait of John B. Powell,* in University of Missouri Journalism Series, No. 94. Columbia, Mo.: University of Missouri, May 15, 1944. 8pp.

PIERRE JOSEPH PROUDHON

1314. Proudhon, Pierre Joseph. *Proudhon's Solution of the Social Problem.* New York: Vanguard Press, 1927. xvi + 225pp. (Editor's note by Henry Cohen.)

Besides Proudhon's own writings, this work includes Charles A. Dana's series of 1849 on "Proudhon and His Bank of the People," a short sketch by Dana of Proudhon's journalistic career in the mid-19th century, and an account by Cohen of Dana's change from his early support of Proudhon's radicalism.

PEPE ROMERO

1315. Romero, Pepe. *Mexican Jumping Bean.* New York: G. P. Putnam's Sons, 1953. 282pp.

A light, high-spirited autobiography of a Mexican journalist who calls himself "the Walter Winchell of Mexico." Romero has been a Mexican correspondent for the New York *Times*. He portrays Mexican life, Americans in Mexico, and Mexicans in Hollywood.

PETER SCHOEFFER

1316. Lehmann-Haupt, Hellmut. *Peter Schoeffer of Gernsheim and Mainz, with a List of His Surviving Books and Broadsides*. Rochester, N.Y.: Printing House of Leo Hart, 1950. xv + 146pp. (Printer's Valhalla Series.)

An account of one who was associated with Gutenberg and who "helped to remodel the international book market at the dawn of the modern age." Some material devoted to Schoeffer as "Publisher and Newsprinter" concerns his broadsides in the state-church struggles of the late 15th century.

FRANZ SCHOENBERNER

1317. Schoenberner, Franz. *Confessions of a European Intellectual*. New York: The Macmillan Co., 1946. x + 315pp.

Schoenberner was editor of a pre-Hitler weekly, *Simplicissimus*. This satirical paper, ever courageous and honest, was banned by the Nazis and Schoenberner was forced to flee Germany. Writing from exile in the United States, the author tells of the last days of *Simplicissimus* and recalls a publishing career running from 1913 to 1933.

MIKHAIL SOLOVIEV

1318. Soloviev, Mikhail. *My Nine Lives in the Red Army*. New York: David McKay Co., 1955. 308pp. (Introduction by Leslie C. Stevens; translation by Harry C. Stevens.)

An account of a Russian military correspondent and officer, from 1932 until his capture by the Nazis. Soloviev gives a view of the Soviet army from the inside, noting Russian army deficiencies, and takes up the Finnish War and the Nazi invasion of Russia. Heavily anecdotal.

ANNA LOUISE STRONG

1319. Strong, Anna Louise. *I Change Worlds: The Remaking of an American*. New York: Henry Holt and Co., 1935. x + 422pp.

Anna Strong, who left the United States in post-World War I days to live in Russia and to try to make the communistic ideal work, devoted her efforts to establishing the English-language Moscow *Daily News*. Some years after publication of her book, she herself was forced to flee Russia. Aided by hindsight, the reader may get more out of this book today than a quarter of a century ago; in any case the events since 1935 will influence the reader's reaction.

GENEVIEVE R. TABOUIS

1320. Tabouis, Genevieve R. *They Called Me Cassandra*. New York: Charles Scribner's Sons, 1942. xii + 436pp. (Introduction by Edgar Ansel Mowrer.)

BIOGRAPHY

Mme. Tabouis, one of the editors of *L'Oeuvre* in Paris, warned France of the Nazi peril throughout the 1930s. Her autobiography carries back to the early days of the century and memories of the Dreyfus affair, but it centers chiefly on the period growing out of days "when dictators were little" to a climax in "treason and war"; a prologue tells of the author's flight from France in 1940 to exile in the United States.

HOLLINGTON K. TONG

1321. Tong, Hollington K. *Dateline: China, the Beginning of China's Press Relations with the World.* New York: Rockport Press, 1950. xiii + 269pp.

Tong, vice-minister of information of the Republic of China in World War II, tells, after an autobiographical opening, the press story of China from the Japanese attack of 1937 to the end of the war. The book has been outdated by events since 1949.

HOUSE OF ULLSTEIN

1322. Ullstein, Hermann. *The Rise and Fall of the House of Ullstein.* New York: Simon and Schuster, 1943. 308pp.

The youngest of five Ullstein brothers, grandsons of the founder of a wholesale newsprint supply firm and sons of the builder of the *Berliner Zeitung*, tells his family history from its beginnings in the 1850s, through years of power and prestige, to the destruction of the distinguished Ullstein newspaper, magazine, and literary publishing firm during Hitler's seizure of the press and attack on the Jews.

THEODOR WOLFF

1323. Wolff, Theodor. *Through Two Decades.* London: William Heinemann, Ltd., 1936. xiv + 324pp. (Translated from the German by E. W. Dickes.)

A philosophical narrative by the exiled editor of the Berliner *Tageblatt*. The content bears only slightly on Wolff's newspaper and on himself as a man. Wolff was editor of the *Tageblatt* from 1906 to 1933.

H. G. W. WOODHEAD

1324. Woodhead, H. G. W. *Adventures in Far Eastern Journalism: A Record of Thirty-Three Years' Experience.* Tokyo: Hokuseido Press, 1935. ix + 266pp. (Issued in London under the title *A Journalist in China.*)

Reminiscences of a British editor in Shanghai, Peking, and Tientsin which go back to 1902. Woodhead, associated with the *Peking and Tientsin Times* and later editor of the *China Year Book*, covers a broad range, from the Chinese Revolution to the Manchukuoan Affair.

GREGOR A. ZIEMER

1325. Ziemer, Gregor A. *Education for Death: The Making of a Nazi.* New York and London: Oxford University Press, 1941. 209pp.

III

Narratives of Journalists at Work
and Anthologies of Journalistic Writing

A. General News and Features

1326. Austin, H. Russell. *The Milwaukee Story: The Making of an American City*. Milwaukee: The Journal Co., 1946. 219pp.

A general, popular history of Milwaukee, first run serially in the *Journal* on the occasion of the city's centennial and written by the newspaper's book editor. It includes brief accounts of 24 Milwaukee newspapers, with important dates.

1327. ————. *The Wisconsin Story: The Building of a Vanguard State*. Milwaukee: The Journal Co., 1948. viii + 382pp. (2nd edition, 1957.)

Similar to Austin's history of Milwaukee, this account was run in the *Journal* in commemoration of the Wisconsin statehood centennial. Some data are given on 28 historic Wisconsin newspapers, including 8 in Milwaukee. The articles by Austin are good examples of the service a newspaper can render in developing a sense of community and state history.

1328. Bolitho, William. *Camera Obscura*. New York: Simon and Schuster, 1930. 219pp. (Preface by Noel Coward.)

Collects essays written in the late 1920s for the New York *World*. High in quality, with a precise style, these cover a wide range of topics related to performances of both great and unknown persons. The author had been newsboy, author, laborer, and war correspondent.

1329. Boston Morning Post. *Selections from the Court Reports Originally Published in the Boston Morning Post from 1834 to 1837, Arranged and Revised by the Reporter of the Post*. Boston: Otis, Broaders and Co., 1837. 252pp.

Police and municipal court stories from the early days of the penny press. These are wholly human-interest items, written — before the day of the summary lead — in chronological narrative style.

1330. Bourne, George. *The Spirit of the Public Journals: Or, Beauties of the American Newspapers for 1805*. Baltimore: George Dobbin and Murphy, 1806. 300pp.

A fascinating collection of 121 pieces from 96 newspapers. This book offers welcome contrast to the vituperation characteristic of the press in this period by collecting material from newspapers of quality. Bourne specifically eliminated political discussion and caricature and included instead pieces on life and manners, education, poetry, advertisements — even an epitaph. Bourne, a clergyman, later wrote for the *Christian Intelligencer* in New York.

1331. Bowles, Samuel. *Our New West: Records of Travel between the Mississippi River and the Pacific Ocean.* Hartford, Conn.: Hartford Publishing Co., 1869. 524pp.

The founder and editor of the Springfield *Republican* was one of the first Americans to travel the route of the new Pacific Railroad. The book reveals how much newspapermen contributed to advertising the Far West.

1332. Brookhouser, Frank. *Our Philadelphia: A Candid and Colorful Portrait of a Great City.* Garden City, N.Y.: Doubleday and Co., 1957. xii + 224pp. (Drawings by Albert Gold.)

A newspaperman's account of his city. Much of the material appeared originally in the *Evening* and *Sunday Bulletin* and the *Inquirer*.

1333. Browning, Norma Lee. *City Girl in the Country and Other Stories.* Chicago: Henry Regnery Co., 1955. 291pp.

Articles, mostly from the late 1940s and early 1950s, by a feature writer for the Chicago *Tribune*. They include an exposé of quacks among Chicago doctors and of merchandisers like Dudley Le Blanc ("Hadacol").

1334. *Casual Columns: The Glasgow Herald Miscellany.* Glasgow, Scotland: George Outram and Co., Ltd., n.d. 317pp. (Introduction by James Holburn, editor of the Glasgow *Herald*.)

Articles, essays, and some fiction selected from the "Week-End Page" of the Saturday Glasgow *Herald*. Most of these appeared under the editorship of Sir William Robieson (1937–1955). The material demonstrates fullness and fairness in reporting.

1335. Chambers, [James] Julius. *The Mississippi River and Its Wonderful Valley: Twenty-Seven Hundred and Seventy-Five Miles from Source to Sea.* New York and London: G. P. Putnam's Sons, 1910. xvi + 308pp.

Chambers's own explorations around the source of the Mississippi in 1872, which he reported for the New York *Herald*, are sketched briefly. His work years later was granted scientific recognition by geographic and historical societies.

1336. Clemens, Samuel L. *Letters from the Sandwich Islands, Written for the Sacramento Union by Mark Twain.* Stanford, Calif.: Stanford University Press, 1938. xii + 224pp. (Introduction and conclusion by G. Ezra Dane; illustrations by Dorothy Grover.)

1337. ———. *Mark Twain of the Enterprise.* Berkeley and Los Angeles: University of California Press, 1957. 240pp. (Edited by Henry Nash Smith.)

Reprinted here are 30 revealing news stories, dispatches, and articles written by Samuel L. Clemens while he was on the staff of the *Territorial Enterprise* in Virginia City, Nev., during the Civil War.

1338. ———. *Mark Twain's Travels with Mr. Brown: Being Heretofore Uncollected Sketches Written by Mark Twain for the San Francisco Alta California in 1866 & 1867, Describing the Adventures of the Author and His Irrepressible Companion in Nicaragua, Hannibal, New York, and Other Spots on Their Way to Europe.* New York: Alfred A. Knopf, 1940. 296pp. (Introduction by Franklin Walker and G. Ezra Dane.)

"Mr. Brown" was an imaginary companion — vulgar, realistic, and philosophical. Explanatory notes are appended.

1339. ———. *The Washoe Giant in San Francisco: Being Heretofore Uncollected Sketches by Mark Twain Published in the Golden Era in the Sixties.* San Francisco: George Fields, 1938. 143pp. (Edited and with an introduction by Franklin Walker.)

Thirty-eight items of Mark Twain material from the *Golden Era* during Clemens's sojourn in Nevada and California, 1863–1866. The stories are carried in full, without change except for some typographical adaptation.

1340. Cobbett, W. W., and Sidney Dark, eds. *Fleet Street: An Anthology of Modern Journalism.* London: Eyre and Spottiswoode, 1932. xxiii + 426pp.

Nearly 100 pieces from British newspapers by writers distinguished and unknown. The articles, which appeared originally from the 1890s to the 1930s, include descriptive commentaries, personality sketches, literary pieces, leading articles, critiques on the theater, music, and art, sports stories, nature pieces, humor, and poetry.

1341. Cooke, [Alfred] Alistair. *Letters from America.* London: R. Hart-Davis, 1951. 260pp. (Published in the United States under the title *One Man's America.* New York: Alfred A. Knopf, 1952. 268pp.)

These 32 "radio essays" by the United States correspondent of the Manchester *Guardian* were originally delivered over the British Broadcasting Corp. Cooke makes observations on what America is like so that the British may understand her better.

1342. Denver Post. *Rocky Mountain Empire: Revealing Glimpses of the West in Transition from Old to New.* Garden City, N.Y.: Doubleday and Co., 1950. xiv + 272pp. (Edited by E. L. Howe; foreword by Palmer Hoyt.)

A reissue of material from the "Rocky Mountain Empire" magazine section of the Denver *Post.*

1343. Dunne, Finley Peter. *Mr. Dooley in Peace and in War.* Boston: Small, Maynard and Co., 1898–1899. xviii + 260pp.

A collection of pieces by this master of dialect and sage comment who was nationally quoted during the Spanish-American War period.

1344. ———. *Mr. Dooley's Opinions.* New York: R. H. Russell, 1901. vi + 212pp.

1345. ———. *Mr. Dooley's Philosophy*. New York: R. H. Russell, 1900. 263pp.

1346. Greeley, Horace. *An Overland Journey from New York to San Francisco in the Summer of 1859*. New York: C. M. Saxton, Barker and Co.; San Francisco: H. H. Bancroft and Co., 1860. 386pp.

Thirty-three letters, May 15 to October 20, 1859, sent by Greeley to the New York *Tribune* to describe his rugged trip to see the West for himself. Among the best pieces are "The American Desert," "The Poor Indian," and "Interviewing Brigham Young." Greeley closed with seven articles promoting California and a railroad to the Pacific. Like Horace Greeley, this book lives on.

1347. Greene, Laurence. *The Era of Wonderful Nonsense*. Indianapolis: Bobbs-Merrill Co., 1939. 290pp.

Some 25 entertaining and informative stories that made news between 1918 and 1933. This "casebook of the twenties" starts with a heroic picture of Sgt. Alvin York, continues with get-rich-quick schemes, the Ku Klux Klan, the Dayton monkey trial, and Aimee Semple McPherson, and ends with the Depression tragedy. Sources were the daily and periodical press. The book is in part a criticism of the press for feeding "editorial stimulation" to the public.

1348. *Headlining America: A Selection of Best News and Feature Stories*. Boston: Houghton Mifflin Co., 1937. 542pp. Revised edition, New York: Dryden Press, 1940. (Edited by Frank L. Mott.)

Earlier books in this series were issued under the titles *News Stories of 1933* and *News Stories of 1934* (Iowa City, Iowa: Clio Press, 340pp. and 305pp.). The series has been discontinued.

1349. Hearn, Lafcadio. *Children of the Levee: A Collection of Stories and Sketches of Lafcadio Hearn*. Lexington: University of Kentucky Press, 1957. 111pp. (Edited by O. W. Frost; introduction by John Ball; drawings by William K. Hubbell.)

Twelve narratives of Negro life on the levees of booming Cincinnati, 1874–1877, when Hearn was writing for the *Enquirer* and *Commercial*. These are among Hearn's earliest newspaper writings.

1350. Hecht, Ben. *1001 Afternoons in Chicago*. Chicago: Covici-McGee, 1922. 288pp. (Preface by Henry Justin Smith.)

Hechtian pieces that appeared during his heyday on the Chicago *Daily News* staff — comedies, dialogues, homilies, one-act tragedies, storiettes, word-etchings, and satires. Sixty-five articles are reproduced.

1351. *"In Regard to the News—"* New York: Time, Inc., 1956. 64pp.

Twenty-five pieces from the press section of *Time* during 1956. Interesting reading.

1352. Irwin, Will. *The City That Was: A Requiem of Old San Francisco*. New York: B. W. Huebsch, 1906. 47pp.

Irwin's highly descriptive report of San Francisco during the years before the 1906 earthquake. Originally published in the New York *Sun* on April 21, 1906, "three days after the Visitation came," this masterpiece of reporting interwoven with history has been reprinted in many publications, including the 100th anniversary edition of the *Sun*, September 2, 1933.

1353. Lawrence, Jack. *When the Ships Came In*. New York and Toronto: Farrar and Rinehart, 1940. 308pp. (Illustrated by John O'Hara Cosgrave II.)

Nostalgic stories and anecdotes gathered during ship-news reporting for the New York *Evening Mail*, 1910–1917. Included are reports on the *Titanic*, *Lusitania*, and *Deutschland*.

1354. Mackey, Joseph. *The Froth Estate*. New York: Prentice-Hall, 1946. xi + 236pp.

Mackey was for 10 years the New York *Sun*'s "nut editor," whose job it was to write of the "crackpot cavalcade — the loony *riff-polloi* that sometimes makes the front page."

1355. Mencken, H. L. *A Mencken Chrestomathy*. New York: Alfred A. Knopf, 1949. xvi + 626pp.

Mencken here revives the word *chrestomathy* in its true sense: "a collection of choice passages from an author or authors." His selections cover 30 different fields.

1356. Milwaukee Journal. *As the Journal Told It*. Milwaukee: The Journal Co., 1945–1947. 4 vols., pamphlets.

News features, background articles, staff columns, and book reviews written without by-lines by *Journal* staff members as run-of-the-day assignments. Most of the articles include staff photographs. Excellent writing.

1357. New York Times. *News of Presidential Inaugurations*. New York: The Times, 1933. 20 unpaged leaves.

Reprints of the *Times*'s coverage of inaugurations from Franklin Pierce in 1853 to Franklin Roosevelt in 1933.

1358. Owen, Russell. *The Antarctic Ocean*. New York: Whittlesey House, McGraw-Hill Book Co., 1941. xiii + 254pp.

A report of the explorations into South Polar regions by a correspondent for the New York *Times* who covered the Byrd Antarctic expeditions in 1928 and 1929.

1359. ———. *South of the Sun*. New York: John Day Co., 1934. 288pp. (Foreword by Roy Chapman Andrews.)

An earlier account of the Byrd expedition. The major part is in the form of a diary that Owen kept from February 24, 1929, to February 13, 1930. He tells how he covered the first South Pole flight for the New York *Times* (November 24 to December 2, 1929).

1360. Providence Journal. *In Perspective*. Providence, R.I.: Halladay, 1949. 124pp. (Preface by Sevellon Brown.)

Reprints of 48 pieces by 17 staff members of the Providence *Journal* and *Evening Bulletin*, chosen for book publication by a poll of readers. Each staff member appends a brief autobiography.

1361. Ralph, Julian. *Our Great West: A Study of the Present Conditions and Future Possibilities of the New Commonwealths and Capitals of the United States*. New York: Harper and Brothers, 1893. xii + 478pp.

These accounts, primarily of states admitted to the Union in 1889–1890 (the

Dakotas, Montana, Wyoming, Idaho, and Washington), appeared originally in *Harper's Magazine* and *Harper's Weekly*. They offer sound analysis by one of the most distinguished reporters of his day.

1362. Robinson, Solon. *Hot Corn: Life Scenes in New York, Illustrated.* New York: De Witt and Davenport, 1854. 408pp.

Robinson was a writer for Horace Greeley. His 10 reports here were aimed at promoting temperance and virtue in order "to lift up the lowly" and "to expose the hidden effects produced by Rum." Some of his scenes perhaps had no equal in human-interest reporting for that day, and they offer examples of Greeley and his good works in action. The title of the book refers figuratively to a waif who boiled sweet corn on a corner near the New York *Tribune* building.

1363. Scott, W. W., comp. *Breaks: Unintentional Humor by Tired Newspapermen and Others.* New York: Jonathan Cape and Harrison Smith, 1931. 84pp. (Illustrated by Nate Collier.)

Five hundred or so gems that should never have passed the copy desk — but did. Most of these, had they been caught, would have justified a replate.

1364. *Selections from the Tatler, the Spectator, and Their Successors.* New York: T. Nelson and Sons, 1928. 422pp. (Edited, with an introduction, by Walter Graham.)

1365. Sevareid, Eric. *In One Ear.* New York: Alfred A. Knopf, 1952. 258pp.

Sevareid's broadcasts given over the Columbia Broadcasting System are published as originally presented. He deals to a great extent with political issues and figures.

1366. ———. *Small Sounds in the Night: A Collection of Capsule Commentaries on the American Scene.* New York: Alfred A. Knopf, 1956. xiv + 305pp.

About 100 late-evening radio commentaries over the period from July 4, 1951, to September 9, 1955. Somewhat similar to *In One Ear.*

1367. *Star Reporters and 34 of Their Stories.* New York: Random House, 1948. xiii + 402pp. (Collected, with notes and an introduction, by Ward Greene.)

This anthology presents the news stories of famous reporters as first written for publication. The accounts range from Stanley's report on the finding of David Livingstone to the shooting of John Dillinger in 1934. Sports, crime, and war coverage are prominent. Greene provides background on time and place for each report.

1368. Thackeray, William Makepeace. *Contributions to the Morning Chronicle.* Urbana: University of Illinois Press, 1955. xix + 213pp. (Edited by Gordon N. Ray.)

Thackeray for a decade in the 1840s earned his living through contributions to newspapers and magazines. One of his longest connections was with the London *Morning Chronicle.*

1369. Thomas, Lowell. *History as You Heard It.* New York: Doubleday and Co., 1957. 486pp. (Foreword by William S. Paley.)

A collection of Thomas's Columbia Broadcasting System reports over a 25-year period, beginning September 29, 1930. The content is relatively thin.

1370. *A Treasury of Great Reporting: "Literature under Pressure" from the Sixteenth Century to Our Own Times.* New York: Simon and Schuster, 1949. xlv + 784pp. + 32pp. of news pictures. (Edited by Louis L. Snyder and Richard B. Morris; preface by Herbert Bayard Swope.)

Probably the best anthology of news stories so far published. Some 175 "masterpieces of journalism" from the time of the *Fugger News Letters* to the days following World War II are reprinted. The selections are somewhat heavy on war and spontaneous news breaks and somewhat shy on interpretative stories. The editors are professors of history with a strong interest in journalism.

1371. Webb, Charles Henry. *John Paul's Book: Moral and Instructive, Consisting of Travels, Tales, Poetry, and Like Fabrications.* Hartford, Conn., and Chicago: Columbian Book Co., 1874. 621pp.

A collection of Webb's contributions to the New York *Tribune*, written under the pseudonym John Paul. One of the best is "Horace Greeley's Funeral, and a Personal Reminiscence of the Man," a deeply reverent tribute.

1372. Wilkie, Franc B. *"Walks about Chicago" and Army and Miscellaneous Sketches.* Chicago: Church, Goodman, and Donnelley, 1869. 6 + 307pp.

Pieces that appeared originally in the Chicago *Times*, written by its returned Civil War correspondent. They include good descriptions of Chicago nearly a century ago, travel reports on a number of summer resorts, and army recollections.

1373. Woods, George Bryant. *Essays, Sketches, and Stories, Selected from the Writings of George Bryant Woods.* Boston: James R. Osgood and Co., 1873. xxii + 399pp.

Woods died in 1871 at the age of 27 after a brief journalistic career in which he contributed to at least 20 leading newspapers and periodicals, among them the New York *Tribune*, the *Atlantic*, and the *North American Review*. Most of the selections are on literary and dramatic topics, but Civil War correspondence is also included, notably an excellent news story on Lincoln's assassination. The book includes a biographical memoir.

B. Columns, Criticism, and Poetry

1374. Aldrich, Richard. *Musical Discourse from the New York Times.* New York and London: Oxford University Press, 1928. 304pp.

These miscellaneous essays include comments on program music, folk songs in America, "The Modernizing of Bach," Wagner, Brahms, Shakespeare and music, Jenny Lind and Barnum, and music lectures.

1375. Atkinson, [Justin] Brooks. *Once around the Sun.* New York: Harcourt, Brace and Co., 1951. 376pp.

A reporter and critic for the New York *Times* keeps a daily journal for a full year. He deals principally with the weather and the seasons, people, the meaning of holidays, and anniversaries of historic events. Interesting reading.

1376. Benchley, Robert. *My Ten Years in a Quandary and How They Grew.* New York: Harper and Brothers, 1936; Blue Ribbon Books, 1940. viii + 361pp.

A hundred-odd humorous pieces by the distinguished columnist who wrote for the *New Yorker*, the New York *Tribune*, the New York *World*, *Life*, and the Curtis Publishing Co. Illustrated with cartoons.

1377. Bentley, Eric. *The Dramatic Event — An American Chronicle.* New York: Horizon Press, 1954. 285pp.

A collection of play reviews and articles on the American theater, by a critic for the *New Republic*.

1378. Broun, Heywood. *Collected Edition of Heywood Broun.* New York: Harcourt, Brace and Co., 1941. xxx + 561pp. (Compiled by Heywood Hale Broun.)

These 184 selections of Broun's output from 1908 to his last column in the New York *Post* in 1939 are offered as those which Broun liked best, not as his best work. Most are from the New York *World* and *World-Telegram*.

1379. ———. *It Seems to Me.* New York: Harcourt, Brace and Co., 1935. xii + 335pp.

More than 100 excellent columns, August 5, 1927, to April 15, 1935, written for the New York *World*, *Telegram*, and *World-Telegram*. See particularly "The World Passes" (February 28, 1931); "A Certain City Editor" (on the death of Charles Chapin); and "A Union of Reporters" (on the American Newspaper Guild).

1380. ———. *Pieces of Hate and Other Enthusiasms.* New York: George H. Doran Co., 1922. 227pp.

Forty-two articles written early in Broun's career. It is difficult today to reconstruct the contemporary situations that led to their writing.

1381. ———. *Seeing Things at Night.* New York: Harcourt, Brace and Co., 1921. viii + 268pp.

Thirty-four newspaper and magazine articles on anything that struck Broun's fancy. Excellent are a history of left-handers through the ages, a comparison of Fleet Street and Park Row, a review of a biography of Margaret Fuller, and a piece on Heywood's son.

1382. ——— and George S. Chappell. *Nonsenseorship: Sundry Observations Concerning Prohibitions, Inhibitions, and Illegalities.* New York and London: G. P. Putnam's Sons, 1922. xiii + 181pp.

1383. Brown, John Mason. *Seeing Things.* New York: Whittlesey House, McGraw-Hill Book Co., 1946. viii + 341pp.

This and the two following entries are collections from Brown's department appearing under the title "Seeing Things" in the *Saturday Review*.

1384. ———. *Seeing More Things.* New York: Whittlesey House, McGraw-Hill Book Co., 1948. ix + 347pp.

1385. ———. *Still Seeing Things.* New York: McGraw-Hill Book Co., 1950. ix + 335pp.

1386. Buchwald, Art. *The Brave Coward*. New York: Harper and Brothers, 1957. 211pp. (Illustrated by Tomi Ungerer.)

Pieces by a columnist for the New York *Herald Tribune*, ostensibly reporting under a Paris dateline the activities of the International Set and also his own world adventures. High on hilarity.

1387. Burdette, Robert J. *The Rise and Fall of the Mustache and Other "Hawkeyetems."* Burlington, Iowa: Burlington Publishing Co., 1877. 328pp.

Burdette was a midwestern humorist who gained a wide reputation as columnist and editor of the Burlington *Hawkeye*.

1388. Cannon, James J. *Who Struck John?* New York: Dial Press, 1956. 267pp.

A compilation of the work of a columnist for the New York *Post*.

1389. Clapper, Raymond. *Watching the World*. New York: Whittlesey House, McGraw-Hill Book Co., 1944. ix + 372pp. (Introduction by Ernie Pyle.)

A representative selection from the work of one of the best columnists of his period: news dispatches, broadcasts, magazine articles, and special pieces, 1932–1944. Much of the material is on political subjects. Clapper lost his life in the Pacific in 1944. Mrs. Olive E. Clapper provides a biographical sketch.

1390. Crosby, John. *Out of the Blue: A Book about Radio and Television*. New York: Simon and Schuster, 1952. xi + 301pp.

Radio and television columns written for the New York *Herald Tribune*, which syndicated Crosby's material. This is more a collection of Crosby's personal comments than a review of the media.

1391. Davis, Franklyn P., and Athie S. Davis. *Anthology of Newspaper Verse*. Enid, Okla.: F. P. Davis Co., 1919–1940. 23 vols.

1392. Downes, Olin. *Olin Downes on Music*. New York: Simon and Schuster, 1957. xxxi + 473pp. (Edited by Irene Downes; preface by Howard Taubman.)

A selection of about 170 of Downes's music reviews, Sunday columns, and other pieces, 1906 to 1955. These provide an informal history of American music for the half-century. Downes's criticism appeared first in the Boston *Post* and for 31 years in the New York *Times*. A personality sketch and a brief biographical note are included.

1393. Fadiman, Clifton. *Party of One: The Selected Writings of Clifton Fadiman*. Cleveland and New York: World Publishing Co., 1955. 473pp.

Essays, reviews, and critical opinions. Fadiman now writes a column for *Holiday* under the title "Party of One."

1394. Ferril, Thomas Hornsby. *I Hate Thursday*. New York and London: Harper and Brothers, 1946. x + 233pp. (Illustrations by Anne Ferril Folsom.)

Columns by the poet-editor of the weekly Colorado *Rocky Mountain Herald*, from a series that ran from 1939 to 1946. The title reflects Ferril's irritation at having to prepare something for his newspaper once a week.

1395. Gray, James. *On Second Thought*. Minneapolis: University of Minnesota Press, 1946. 264pp.

> Comments from Gray's book reviews over 20 years in the St. Paul *Pioneer-Press* and *Dispatch*, with continuity added for the book. Gray discusses most of the distinguished literary figures of the 20th century, with emphasis on British and American authors.

1396. Haggin, Bernard H. *Music in the Nation*. New York: William Sloane Associates, 1949. ix + 376pp.

1397. Hammond, S. H., and L. W. Mansfield. *Country Margins and Rambles of a Journalist*. New York: J. C. Derby, 1855. x + 356pp.

> "Column writing" of an early day, from the Albany (N.Y.) *State Register*, chiefly in the form of letters between two writers on diverse subjects. Hammond was editor of the newspaper and Mansfield a prolific correspondent.

1398. Harris, Sydney J. *Strictly Personal*. Chicago: Henry Regnery Co., 1953. 244pp.

> Syndicated columns of a staff member of the Chicago *Daily News* whose materials have been distributed through United Features.

1399. McGill, Ralph. *The Fleas Come with the Dog*. New York and Nashville: Abingdon Press, 1954. 128pp.

> Forty selections from McGill's columns in the Atlanta *Constitution*, on the contemporary South, the nation as a whole, people big and little. The title is taken from a saying of McGill's North Georgia uncle: "You never get the dog without the fleas. Big dog, more fleas." Or, applied to the burgeoning United States: bigger country, more problems.

1400. McIntyre, O. O. *The Big Town: New York Day by Day*. New York: Dodd, Mead and Co., 1935. 204pp.

> Selected descriptions, random philosophical thoughts, and a diary of the New York columnist. The material demonstrates the stylistic qualities that made McIntyre so successful.

1401. Marquis, Don. *The Best of Don Marquis*. Garden City, N.Y.: Doubleday and Co., 1946. 670pp. (Introduction by Christopher Morley; illustrations by George Herriman.)

> An excellent selection from Marquis's work. Included are "The Lives and Times of Archy and Mehitabel," "The Old Soak," "The Old Soak's History of the World," "Short Stories," "Prefaces," "Hermione and Her Little Group of Serious Thinkers," "The Almost Perfect State," "Serious Poetry," and "Humorous Poetry." The illustrations are from "The Sun Dial," Marquis's humor column in the New York *Sun*.

1402. Nathan, George Jean. *The World of George Jean Nathan*. New York: Alfred A. Knopf, 1952. xxviii + 489pp. (Edited by Charles Angoff.)

> This anthology of a bellicose literary and dramatic critic covers a wide range of topics, among them language and censorship. A chronology of Nathan's journalistic career and a bibliography of his works are also included.

1403. New York Times. *A Century of Books: How More Than 100 Famous Books of the Past Century Were Judged by Contemporary Critics.* New York: The Times, 1951. 48pp.

The book section issued by the *Times* on its 100th anniversary. It reprints contemporary reviews of books that have achieved lasting fame, from Thackeray's *The History of Henry Esmond* (November 19, 1852) to Winston Churchill's *The Gathering Storm* (June 20, 1948).

1404. New York World. *The Second Conning Tower Book.* New York: Macy-Macius, 1927. 192pp.

Reprints the best of the verses published during 1926 in "The Conning Tower," edited by Franklin P. Adams for the New York *World.*

1405. Pyle, Ernest T. *Home Country.* New York: William Sloane Associates, 1947. vii + 472pp.

A collection of Pyle's newspaper columns, 1935–1940, written before he gained fame as a war correspondent.

1406. Sanborn, Kate. "Our Early Newspaper Wits," in *My Favorite Lectures of Long Ago, for Friends Who Remember*, pp. 217–266. Boston: Privately published, 1898.

An entertaining piece by a popular lecturer and teacher. She deals chiefly with Petroleum V. Nasby, Mark Twain, Artemus Ward, and others of the Civil War and post-Civil War periods.

1407. Taylor, Bert Leston. *The So-Called Human Race.* New York: Alfred A. Knopf, 1922. x + 330pp. (Foreword by Henry B. Fuller.)

Excerpts from Taylor's "Line o' Type or Two" column which ran in the Chicago *Tribune* for 20 years under the signature BLT.

1408. Thompson, Slason, comp. *The Humbler Poets: A Collection of Newspaper and Periodical Verse, 1870–1885.* Chicago: A. C. McClurg and Co., 1899. 459pp.

Reprints hundreds of poems by writers whose names and work, Thompson felt, would not be likely to appear in collections of standard poets. A few, however, became famous: Eugene Field and James Whitcomb Riley, for example.

1409. Thomson, Virgil. *Music, Right and Left.* New York: Henry Holt and Co., 1951. x + 214pp.

Reviews and Sunday articles published in the New York *Herald Tribune* between October 1947 and October 1950.

1410. ———. *The Musical Scene.* New York: Alfred A. Knopf, 1945. xiv + 301pp.

Essays on music and reviews of musical productions carried in the New York *Herald Tribune*, October 9, 1940, to July 23, 1944. They give a panoramic view of musical America in those years.

1411. Venturi, Lionello. *History of Art Criticism.* New York: E. P. Dutton and Co., 1936. xv + 345pp.

1412. Woollcott, Alexander. *The Woollcott Reader: Bypaths in the Realms of Gold.* New York: Viking Press, 1935. xi + 1010pp.

PERSONAL NARRATIVES AND ANTHOLOGIES
C. Editorials

1413. Bennett, Ira E. *Editorials from the Washington Post, 1917–1920.* Washington, D.C.: The Washington Post Co., 1921. xiv + 584pp.

Bennett was chief editorial writer for the *Post.* The book's value is limited by the lack of background notes; there is, for example, no explanation of why Bennett selected these particular editorials to express his views on World War I.

1414. Brisbane, Arthur. *The Book of "Today."* New York: International Magazine Co., 1923. 192pp.

A collection of Brisbane's platitudinous philosophical commentary that ran for years as editorial matter in the Hearst newspapers.

1415. ———, ed. *Editorials from the Hearst Newspapers.* New York: Albertson Publishing Co., 1906. viii + 402pp.

More than 100 editorials from various newspapers of the Hearst chain. Few have more than ephemeral value; further, there is no indication of the date of publication or of the particular paper from which each was taken.

1416. Chicago Tribune. *A Century of Tribune Editorials, 1847–1947.* Chicago: The Tribune Co., 1947. 156pp.

Issued as part of the *Tribune's* observance of its first 100 years.

1417. Cobb, Frank I. *Cobb of the World: A Leader in Liberalism.* New York: E. P. Dutton and Co., 1924. xxvii + 397pp. (Edited by John L. Heaton.)

The editorials and public addresses of the chief editorial writer of the New York *World,* 1904–1923. The volume includes a brief biography of Cobb by Lindsay Denison and personal tributes from Woodrow Wilson and Ralph Pulitzer. Exceptionally valuable are Cobb's editorials on the *World's* struggles with Theodore Roosevelt in the Panama Canal libel battle and on World War I, as well as four penetrating pieces on "The Profession of Journalism." This is a fine presentation of the intellectual force behind the *World* at its peak.

1418. Congdon, Charles Taber. *Tribune Essays.* New York: J. S. Redfield, 1869. xxiv + 406pp. (Introduction by Horace Greeley.)

Collects nearly 100 editorials that Congdon wrote for the New York *Tribune,* 1857–1863. They deal wholly with the slavery crisis and the Civil War. All are provocative, the more so because wit, scorn, and ridicule are directed against southerners and non-abolitionist northerners alike. Worth reading.

1419. De Voto, Bernard. *The Easy Chair.* Boston: Houghton Mifflin Co., 1955. xi + 356pp.

Selections from De Voto's articles for the "Easy Chair" department of *Harper's* after World War II. The volume was issued after the author's completion of 20 years' service as editor of the department and almost simultaneously with his death. The pieces include one on the meaning of journalism as a method of critical inquiry into current political and social problems. Highly readable, intelligent essays.

1420. Godkin, Edwin Lawrence. *Reflections and Comments.* New York: Charles Scribner's Sons, 1895. x + 328pp.

A collection of editorials by Godkin taken from the *Nation* during the 30 years, 1865–1895, when his influence was at its peak.

1421. Harris, [Henry] Wilson. *Ninety-Nine Gower Street*. London: Constable and Co., Ltd., 1943. viii + 192pp.

A selection of editorials from the authoritative London *Spectator* over the first 11 years of Harris's editorship, 1932–1943. The title derives from the *Spectator*'s publication address. Included are comments on the meaning of royalty (particularly in regard to the abdication crisis) and assessments of British and European political leaders, the Munich crisis, and the fall of France.

1422. Hearn, Lafcadio. *Editorials by Lafcadio Hearn*. Boston and New York: Houghton Mifflin Co., 1926. xx + 356pp. (Edited by Charles Woodward Hutson.)

Hearn's editorials first appeared in the New Orleans *Item* (June 24, 1878, to October 23, 1881) and the New Orleans *Times-Democrat* (July 23, 1882, to July 27, 1887). Many are literary pieces, although Hearn also wrote well on political, social, and economic subjects.

1423. Hearst, William Randolph. *Hearst Papers on the Issue of Temperance versus Prohibition*. N.p., 1933. 62pp.

Editorials from various Hearst morning, evening, and Sunday newspapers.

1424. Heaton, John L. *The Story of a Page*. New York and London: Harper and Brothers, 1913. x + 364pp.

Covers 30 years of opinions expressed on the editorial page of Pulitzer's New York *World*. The book includes also material on the background of the *World* before Pulitzer's purchase of it in 1883. Heaton served with the newspaper from 1899 to the time of the sale to Scripps-Howard.

1425. Lampman, Ben Hur. *How Could I Be Forgetting?* Portland, Ore.: The Oregonian Co., 1926. 196pp. (Foreword by Edgar B. Piper.)

Lampman's editorial essays and poems from the *Oregonian*. For many years his distinctive writing gave charm and substance to his newspaper's editorial page and earned him a reputation that extended far beyond the West Coast.

1426. Lerner, Max. *Actions and Passions: Notes on the Multiple Revolution of Our Time*. New York: Simon and Schuster, 1949. xv + 367pp.

A collection of pieces written originally for *PM*; similar to Lerner's earlier *Public Journal*. The 200 or so editorials, signed commentaries, and personal essays, covering the period from November 1944 to August 1948, have three major subjects: culture and ethics, economics and politics, and America and foreign affairs.

1427. ———. *Public Journal: Marginal Notes on Wartime America*. New York: Viking Press, 1945. xii + 434pp.

One hundred of Lerner's editorials from *PM*'s opinion section, 1943 and 1944.

1428. Lippmann, Walter. *Interpretations, 1931–1932*. New York: The Macmillan Co., 1932. xi + 361pp. (Selected and edited by Allan Nevins.)

Nevins chose what he regarded as 11 of the most substantial of Lippmann's articles for the New York *Herald Tribune* during the Depression years.

1429. ———. *Interpretations, 1933–1935.* New York: The Macmillan Co., 1936. x + 399pp. (Selected and edited by Allan Nevins.)

The second series of Lippmann pieces, principally on domestic problems during the first two years of the New Deal.

1430. London Times. *History through the Times: A Collection of Leading Articles on Important Events, 1800–1937.* London and Toronto: Cassell and Co., Ltd., 1937. xi + 619pp. (Selected by Sir James Marchant; introduction by Geoffrey Dawson, editor of the *Times*.)

An anthology of more than 100 *Times* leaders from the breaking of the Peace of Amiens to the abdication of Edward VIII. Since all are anonymous, the opinions expressed take on a kind of "corporate status." Each article carries a brief note on the contemporary event discussed.

1431. Nevins, Allan, ed. *American Press Opinion: Washington to Coolidge.* New York: D. C. Heath and Co., 1928. xxv + 598pp.

An extremely useful collection of nearly 400 magazine and newspaper editorials, 1786–1927. Many of these are historically famous; in addition, there are editorials by unknown writers for lesser known publications whose comments contributed to the history of the time. Preceding the editorials for each period is a synopsis of the journalism of the day.

1432. New York Sun. *Casual Essays of the Sun: Editorial Articles on Many Subjects, Clothed with the Philosophy of the Bright Side of Things.* New York: Robert Grier Cooke, 1905. xiv + 422pp.

These are mostly literary editorials covering 20 years toward the close of Dana's regime. The volume provides examples of the sort of good writing that made the *Sun* great. The "Santa Claus" editorial leads the group.

1433. New York World. *Give $1,000,000,000 to France: A Debt of Duty and Gratitude.* New York: The World, 1917. 20pp.

This and the next two entries are reprints of strong-voiced editorials from the *World* during the years of its great prestige.

1434. ———. *The Great Bond Conspiracy, Its Correct History.* New York: The World, 1904. 31pp.

1435. ———. *Woodrow Wilson: An Interpretation.* New York: The World, March 4, 1921. 16pp.

1436. Prentice, George D. *Prenticeana: Or, Wit and Humor in Paragraphs, by the Editor of the Louisville Journal.* New York: Derby and Jackson, 1860. 306pp.

These editorial "paragraphs" take on meaning historically when one recalls the important role Prentice played in helping to maintain a sense of reasonableness in slave-holding Kentucky.

1437. Roosevelt, Theodore. *Roosevelt in the Kansas City Star.* Boston: Houghton Mifflin Co., 1921. xlviii + 295pp.

The former President contributed editorials to the *Star* from September 1917 to his death in 1919. He was granted considerable editorial freedom.

1438. Scott, Harvey W. *History of the Oregon Country.* Cambridge, Mass.: Riverside Press, 1924. 6 vols. (Compiled by Leslie M. Scott.)

Commentaries by the editor of the Portland *Oregonian* over many years, as run on the newspaper's then nationally recognized editorial page. These make virtually a history of the Pacific Northwest.

1439. ———. *Religion, Theology and Morals.* Cambridge, Mass.: Riverside Press, 1917. 2 vols. xxiv + 351pp.; xvi + 403pp. (Compiled by Leslie M. Scott.)

Forty years of editorials and lectures by the *Oregonian* editor.

1440. ———. *Shakespeare: Writings of Harvey W. Scott.* Cambridge, Mass.: Riverside Press, 1928. viii + 160pp. (Compiled by Leslie M. Scott.)

Scott was known through the Pacific Northwest for his erudition. It was his editorials on literature, theology, and history that gave his newspaper leadership in a region of few outstanding journals.

1441. Stabley, Rhodes Rufus. *Newspaper Editorials on American Education.* Philadelphia: University of Pennsylvania Press, 1941. xii + 283pp.

A Ph.D. dissertation.

1442. Watterson, Henry. *The Editorials of Henry Watterson.* New York: George H. Doran Co., 1923. 430pp. (Compiled, and with an introduction, by Arthur Krock.)

An anthology of Watterson's comments over more than 50 years, beginning in 1868. The Watterson flavor is retained throughout, even to keeping peculiarities of spelling and punctuation.

1443. White, William Allen. *The Editor and His People.* New York: The Macmillan Co., 1924. xiii + 380pp. (Compiled by Helen Ogden Mahin.)

Editorials from the Emporia (Kan.) *Gazette*, 1895–1924. This volume is historically valuable as a representative commentary by one of the nation's most prominent small-city editors. The topics are personal and political, with some emphasis upon free speech.

1444. ———. *Forty Years on Main Street.* New York: Farrar and Rinehart, 1937. xv + 409pp. (Foreword by Frank C. Clough.)

A collection of White's editorials from the Emporia *Gazette*, 1895–1936. See especially "The Fourth Estate," in which White deals with the *Gazette* itself.

1445. Whitman, Walt. *I Sit and Look Out.* New York: Columbia University Press, 1932. 248pp. (Edited by Emory Holloway and Vernolian Schwarz.)

Editorials by Whitman in the Brooklyn *Daily Times*, May 1, 1857, to June 26, 1859. Holloway's introduction discusses Whitman's relations with the Brooklyn press, including also the *Eagle* and *Free-Soil Freeman*. The editorials cover Whitman's views on many topics, including the press. An excellent compilation.

D. Foreign Correspondence and War Correspondence

BEFORE WORLD WAR I

1446. Ames, Mary Clemmer. *Ten Years in Washington: Life and Scenes in the National Capital as a Woman Sees Them.* Hartford, Conn.:

A. D. Worthington and Co., 1873; Chicago: L. Lloyd and Co., 1874. xx + 587pp.

One of the earliest narratives of a woman reporter. Mrs. Ames was best known for her letters to the press during the Civil War, when she worked in army hospitals. She served the New York *Evening Post* and after the war contributed to the New York *Independent*.

1446a. Anderson, Frank Maloy. *The Mystery of "A Public Man": A Historical Detective Story*. Minneapolis: University of Minnesota Press, 1948. 256pp.

A careful study of the political-journalistic background of an anonymous diary relating to the start of the Civil War in 1860–1861 (see entry 1467 below). Anderson investigates the evidence pointing to Amos Kendall and others as authors of the "Public Man" diary; but he suggests that Samuel Ward, a lobbyist in the Civil War era, wrote it. The book carries the diary in full in an appendix and gives an excellent brief manuscript, press, and book bibliography.

1447. Barker, Jacob. *The Rebellion: Its Consequences, and the Congressional Committee Denominated the Reconstruction Committee, with Their Action*. New Orleans: Commercial Printing, 1866. 248pp.

Barker established the New Orleans *National Advocate* in 1862 and sought to operate on a middle ground between the Union conquerors of the city and the Confederate populace. He pleased neither, and his paper lasted only seven months. His book, in which he attempts to vindicate himself, is useful in showing the futility of reasonableness during the war.

1448. Barrett, Edwin Shepard. *What I Saw at Bull Run*. Boston: Beacon Press, 1886. 48pp.

Barrett had been a reporter for the Boston *Traveller*. This is an address he gave on the occasion of the 25th anniversary of Bull Run, July 21, 1886, to a reunion of Company G, Concord (Mass.) Artillery, 5th Regiment.

1449. Bickham, William Denison. *Rosecrans' Campaign with the Fourteenth Army Corps, or the Army of the Cumberland, a Narrative of Personal Observations . . . Official Reports of the Battle of Stone River*. Cincinnati: Moore, Wilstach, Keys and Co., 1863. viii + 476pp.

Bickham was a correspondent for the Cincinnati *Commercial*.

1450. Brooks, Noah. *Washington in Lincoln's Time*. New York: The Century Co., 1896. ix + 328pp. (Reissued, with a biographical introduction by Herbert Mitgang. New York and Toronto: Rinehart and Co., 1958. 309pp.)

Recollections of Civil War Washington by a correspondent of the Sacramento *Union*. Newspaper letters prepared nearly every day during the war form the basis of Brooks's narrative. There are good glimpses of Lincoln, Chase, and Grant.

1451. Browne, Junius Henri. *Four Years in Secessia: Adventures within and beyond the Union Lines*. Hartford, Conn.: O. D. Case and Co.; Chicago: George and C. W. Sherwood, 1865. vi + 450pp.

Browne was a special correspondent for the New York *Tribune* who was captured at Vicksburg in 1863 while trying to run southern batteries. This is an interesting patchwork of his experiences during imprisonments at Vicksburg, Jackson, Atlanta, and Richmond; his observations of the South in general; and his views on the anomalous position of the war correspondent.

1452. Burnett, Alf. *Incidents of the War, Humorous, Pathetic, and Descriptive.* Cincinnati: Rickey and Carroll, 1863. 310pp.

Entertaining sketches on the monotony of camp life, war and romance, battle scenes, and generals. Published long before personality reporting became common, this is a precursor of the "GI Joe" book. Burnett was a correspondent for the Cincinnati *Press, Times,* and *Commercial.*

1453. Churchill, Winston Spencer. *London to Ladysmith via Pretoria.* London, New York, and Bombay: Longmans, Green and Co., 1900. xiv + 498pp.

Young Winston Churchill's record of adventure during five months of the Boer War, October 26, 1899, to March 10, 1900, includes an account of British operations to relieve Ladysmith. Most of Churchill's correspondence appeared in the London *Morning Post.*

1454. Cisneros, Evangelina. *The Story of Evangelina Cisneros, Told by Herself; Her Rescue by Karl Decker.* New York: Continental Publishing Co., 1898. 257pp. (Illustrations by Frederic Remington.)

An example of yellow journalism's effectiveness at its peak. Miss Cisneros gives her own account of "infamies of Spanish prison life" and of her rescue by the New York *Journal,* and reporter Decker tells his story of the assignment from Hearst to free the Cuban heroine after diplomatic maneuvers had failed.

1455. Cochrane, Elizabeth [Nellie Bly]. *Nellie Bly's Book: Around the World in Seventy-Two Days.* New York: Pictorial Weeklies Co., 1890. 286pp.

1456. ———. *Six Months in Mexico.* New York: American Publishers Corp., 1888. 205pp.

Nellie Bly's report of her first extended newspaper assignment, before she gained international fame as an around-the-world reporter for the New York *World.* The Mexican stories were written in the first instance for a Pittsburgh newspaper.

1457. Coffin, Charles Carleton. *Four Years of Fighting: A Volume of Personal Observation with the Army and Navy from the First Battle of Bull Run to the Fall of Richmond.* Boston: Ticknor and Fields, 1866. xiv + 558pp.

One of the most talented and most creditable of Civil War correspondents, Coffin was a "special" for the Boston *Journal.* See particularly his account of Sherman's army and his assessment of the Rebel press.

1458. ———. *Freedom Triumphant: The Fourth Period in the War of the Rebellion — September 1864 to Its Close.* New York: Harper and Brothers, 1890. xv + 506pp.

1459. [Coffin, Charles Carleton.] *Stories of Our Soldiers: War Reminiscences by "Carleton" and by the Soldiers of New England.* Boston: Journal Newspaper Co., 1893. 263pp. (Illustrated by J. S. Barrows.)

Thirty years after the Civil War, the Boston *Journal* prepared this series of recollections. Coffin contributed accounts of his coverage of Ball's Bluff, Bull Run, Antietam, and Fredericksburg. There are also about 50 stories by soldiers, from general to private, and a brief biography of "Carleton," as Coffin was known to his readers.

1460. Conyngham, Capt. David P. *Sherman's March through the South: With Sketches and Incidents of the Campaign.* New York: Sheldon and Co., 1865. 431pp.

A correspondent for the New York *Herald* tells of getting information for James Gordon Bennett "with utmost despatch . . . with his horse, his revolver, his field-glass, his blanket, his note-book, and haversack." Conyngham regards Sherman's operations in 1864 as more significant than Grant's campaign in Virginia.

1461. Cook, Joel. *The Siege of Richmond: A Narrative of the Military Operations of Major General George B. McClellan during the Months of May and June 1862.* Philadelphia: G. W. Childs, 1862. viii + 358pp. (Introduction by B. J. Lossing.)

Cook was a reporter for the Philadelphia *Press.*

1462. Creelman, James. *On the Great Highway: The Wanderings and Adventures of a Special Correspondent.* Boston: Lothrop, Lee, Shepard Co., 1901. 418pp.

In its time a best-selling narrative of a Hearst foreign correspondent. Creelman gives accounts of his charge at El Caney, the Battle of Port Arthur in the Sino-Japanese War, an interview with Pope Leo XIII, and his impressions of William McKinley. He stanchly defends yellow journalism.

1463. Dana, Charles A. *Eastern Journeys: Some Notes of Travel in Russia, in the Caucasus and to Jerusalem.* New York: D. Appleton Co., 1898. iii + 146pp.

The editor of the New York *Sun* demonstrates his varied journalistic talents.

1464. Davis, Richard Harding. *The Notes of a War Correspondent.* New York: Harper and Brothers and Charles Scribner's Sons, 1910. 263pp.

Eleven adventures of the romantic war reporter. Four are on the Spanish-American War, including Davis's report of the Battle of San Juan Hill; three on the Boer War; and one each on war in Cuba before American intervention, the Greek-Turkish conflict, the Russo-Japanese War, and "A Correspondent's Kit" (paraphernalia needed in those swashbuckling days to be an army correspondent).

1465. ———. *Three Gringos in Venezuela and Central America.* New York: Harper and Brothers, 1903. xi + 282pp.

1466. ———. *A Year from a Reporter's Notebook.* New York: Harper and Brothers, 1903. ix + 304pp.

1467. *The Diary of a Public Man and a Page of Political Correspondence: Stanton to Buchanan.* New Brunswick, N.J.: Rutgers University Press,

1946. ix + 137pp. (Foreword by Carl Sandburg and prefatory notes by F. Lauriston Bullard.)

The author of this diary is still unknown. When it was originally published in the *North American Review*, August–November 1879, in an effort to get at the background of events leading to the southern bombardment of Fort Sumter, the diary caused a sensation. It covers the period December 28, 1860, to March 15, 1861. The introduction to this reprint gives useful background on the *North American Review* and on Allen Thorndike Rice, its owner in 1879, who made the decision to publish this volatile material. There are implications that journalist Amos Kendall might have been the "public man." (See also 1446a, above.)

1468. Dicey, Edward. *Six Months in the Federal States*. London and Cambridge: The Macmillan Co., 1863. 2 vols. in one, x + 310 + vi + 326pp.

Dicey, one of several British observers who reported the American Civil War for home newspapers, represented *Macmillan's Magazine* and the *Spectator*. In his extensive observations on the United States press, Dicey was particularly harsh toward the New York *Herald*. Vol. I is devoted to Washington, Congress, the Negro problem, American society, relations between England and the United States, and the quarrel engendered by the correspondence of William H. Russell for the London *Times*. Vol. II concerns various war theaters.

1469. Finerty, John F. *War-Path and Bivouac, or, The Conquest of the Sioux: A Narrative of Stirring Personal Experiences and Adventures in the Big Horn and Yellowstone Expedition of 1876 and in the Campaign on the British Border, in 1879*. Chicago: Donohue and Henneberry, 1890. xii + 460pp.

A correspondent of Wilbur Storey's Chicago *Times* gives an account of war on the Plains, including an on-the-scene report of the Custer Massacre of 1876 within a few days of the event.

1470. Fiske, Samuel Wheelock. *Mr. Dunn Browne's Experiences in the Army*. Boston: Nichols and Noyes; New York: O. S. Felt, 1866. xii + 390pp.

Fiske wrote during the Civil War for the Springfield *Republican* under the pseudonym Dunn Browne. He was assigned to the 14th Connecticut Infantry.

1471. Fogg, William Perry. *"Round the World": Letters from Japan, China, India, and Egypt*. Cleveland, Ohio: Privately printed, 1872. 237pp.

Thirty-three reports from a staff member of the Cleveland *Daily Leader* during a west-to-east trip in 1870 and 1871.

1472. Gilmore, James Roberts. *Personal Recollections of Abraham Lincoln and the Civil War*. Boston: L. C. Page and Co., 1898. 338pp.

Gilmore was a Civil War reporter for the New York *Tribune*.

1473. Gove, Capt. Jesse A. *The Utah Expedition, 1857–1858: Letters of Capt. Jesse A. Gove, 10th Inf., U.S.A., of Concord, N.H., to Mrs. Gove, and Special Correspondence of the New York Herald*. Concord,

N.H.: New Hampshire Historical Society, 1928. 442pp. (Society Collections No. 12, edited by Otis G. Hammond.)

Personal letters and news accounts of an officer who took part in the military campaign against the Mormons during Buchanan's administration. Gove wrote for the *Herald* over the signature Argus. The *Herald* reports provide an example of the intensity of the newspaper's coverage at the time.

1474. Hosmer, George Washington. *The Battle of Gettysburg.* New York: Press Publishing Co., 1913. 24pp.

Hosmer had been a reporter during the Civil War for the New York *Herald*. This recollection of Gettysburg was printed in the *Sunday World* on June 29, 1913, before the fiftieth anniversary of the battle.

1475. Kendall, George Wilkins. *Narrative of the Santa Fe Expedition.* Chicago: R. R. Donnelley and Sons Co., Lakeside Press, 1929. xxxiv + 585pp. (Historical introduction by Milo M. Quaife.)

A reissue of the first volume of a piece of travel and war reporting published in two volumes by Harper and Brothers in 1844. Kendall, founder of the New Orleans *Picayune*, tells of American-Mexican relations preceding the war of 1846–1848, and gives accounts of trips across the Texas prairies, hostile Indians, and capture by the Mexicans. After returning to New Orleans Kendall published in the *Picayune* sketches of this expedition, which was a forerunner of his later career as "the world's first great war correspondent" (1845–1848).

1476. Knox, Thomas W. *Camp-Fire and Cotton-Field: Southern Adventure in Time of War: Life with the Union Armies and Residence on a Louisiana Plantation.* New York: Blelock and Co., 1865. 524pp.

Experiences of a New York *Herald* correspondent. More than other war reporters of the period, Knox went into objective detail on economic matters. There is good material on the Memphis press and the "flight of the *Appeal*," the capture of Knox's colleagues at Vicksburg, and correspondents' problems in general.

1477. ———. *Overland through Asia: Pictures of Siberian, Chinese, and Tartar Life; Travels and Adventures in Kamchatka, Siberia, China, Mongolia, Chinese Tartary, and European Russia . . .* Hartford, Conn.: American Publishing Co.; San Francisco: H. H. Bancroft and Co., 1871. 608pp.

New York *Herald* reporter Knox had a threefold purpose in this Asian journey: pleasure, journalism, and promotion of a commercial company interested in telegraphic communication between the United States and Europe via the Bering Straits.

1478. Lawrence, George Alfred. *Border and Bastille.* New York: W. I. Pooley and Co., 1863; London: Tinsley Brothers, 1863. 291pp.

Lawrence, a pro-southern Englishman who was captured while trying to join the Confederate Army, had come to the United States under arrangement with the London *Morning Post* to contribute "any interesting matter . . . that fell my way." He made an excellent assessment of the nature of the conflict.

1479. MacGahan, J. A. *Campaigning on the Oxus, and the Fall of Khiva.* London: Sampson Low, Marston, Low, and Searle, 1874. x + 437pp.

A fascinating narrative by a distinguished reporter for the New York *Herald* and London *Daily News*. MacGahan covered the campaign of the Russians against the Khanate of Khiva in the deserts below the Aral Sea. The book is especially valuable for its information on Russian advances into Central Asia.

1480. Page, Charles A. *Letters of a War Correspondent.* Boston: L. C. Page and Co., 1899. xii + 397pp. (Edited, with biographical introduction and notes, by James R. Gilmore.)

Reprints reports written for the New York *Tribune* from June 1862 until May 1865. Page covers the activities of the Army of the Potomac under McClellan and Meade up to Gettysburg, Grant's campaign of 1864, and the final campaigns of the war. The report of Lincoln's funeral reveals a splendid news-writing style. Page was later Andrew Johnson's consul in Zurich.

1481. Parton, James. *General Butler in New Orleans: History of the Administration of the Department of the Gulf in the Year 1862.* New York: Mason Brothers, 1864. ix + 647pp.

A vindication of the Butler administration during the occupation of New Orleans. Parton gives a useful account of Butler's suppression of opposition newspapers and of the journalistic furor that followed Butler's famous "Woman Order" of May 1862. The general's relations with the New Orleans *Delta*, *True Delta*, *Bee*, and *Picayune* are treated, those with the *Delta* in some detail.

1482. Pike, James S. *First Blows of the Civil War: The Ten Years of Preliminary Conflict in the United States from 1850 to 1860.* New York: American News Co., c. 1879. xiv + 526pp.

Pike covered Washington for the New York *Tribune*. His account here is excellent journalistic exposition based upon public records and private correspondence with such men as Greeley, Dana, Owen Lovejoy, Donn Piatt, and George Ripley.

1483. Ralph, Julian. *War's Brighter Side: The Story of the Friend Newspaper Edited by the Correspondents with Lord Roberts's Forces.* New York: D. Appleton and Co., 1901. xvii + 471pp.

Ralph credits Roberts with being the first general to recognize the value of the press by establishing a newspaper as a source of information and entertainment for the army in the field. Included are 27 contributions from the first numbers of the *Friend*, March and April 1900. Among contributors to this Boer War journal were Rudyard Kipling, Arthur Conan Doyle, Bennet Burleigh, and General Roberts himself.

1484. Ray, George. *Echoes from a Regimental Paper.* Dover, England: St. George's Press, c. 1903. vii + 255pp.

Articles and poems contributed by Bt.-Maj. Ray to the *St. George's Gazette*, regimental newspaper of the 5th Fusiliers which was founded in 1883.

1485. Richardson, Albert D. *The Secret Service, the Field, the Dungeon and the Escape.* Hartford, Conn.: American Publishing Co., 1865. 512pp.

By another of the distinguished New York *Tribune* reporters. Early in the Civil War Richardson was sent beyond Confederate lines, and the first part of the book is a report on southern conditions. Later, with Junius Browne, he was captured at Vicksburg; thereafter Richardson records his suffering in Libby Prison. The book is less emotional than Browne's *Four Years in Secessia* (see 1451).

1486. Russell, Sir William H. *My Diary North and South.* London: Bradbury and Evans, 1863. 2 vols. 866pp., total. Reissued in one volume, New York: Harper and Brothers, 1955. xiii + 268pp. (Edited by Fletcher Pratt.)

An account of the activities of the correspondent of the London *Times* in covering the American Civil War, March 3, 1861, to December 28, 1861. Russell was coldly objective and outspoken in his opinions, many of which were resented in the North. Some of his reports at the time caused international news repercussions.

1487. *Russo-Japanese War: A Photographic Descriptive Review from the Reports, Records, and Cables of Collier's War Correspondents of the Great Conflict in the Far East.* New York: P. F. Collier and Son, 1905. 143pp.

Contributors include Richard Harding Davis, Frederick Palmer, James F. J. Archibald, Robert L. Dunn, and James H. Hare.

1488. Sala, George Augustus. *America Revisited: From the Bay of New York to the Gulf of Mexico, and from Lake Michigan to the Pacific.* London: Vizetelly and Co., 1882. 2 vols. 640pp., total.

Sixteen years after he reported the Civil War, British correspondent Sala took a second and more thorough look at the United States in 44 "letters" originally written for the London *Daily Telegraph.* The book includes nearly 400 engravings of the America of the 1880s.

1489. ———. *My Diary in America in the Midst of War.* London: Tinsley Brothers, 1865. 2 vols. 849pp., total.

Like many British reporters, Sala was sympathetic to the South, but principally this account is descriptive. The book does not measure up to the correspondence of Russell and Dicey.

1490. Taylor, Benjamin Franklin. *Mission Ridge and Lookout Mountain, with Pictures of Life in Camp and Field.* New York: D. Appleton Co., 1872; Chicago: S. C. Griggs and Co., 1872. vi + 272pp.

Taylor covered the western theater of the Civil War for the Chicago *Journal.*

1490a. Tibbles, Thomas Henry. *Buckskin and Blanket Days: Memoirs of a Friend of the Indians, Written in 1905.* Garden City, N.Y.: Doubleday and Co., 1957. 336pp. (Edited by Theodora Bates Cogswell.)

A distinctive analysis of Indian conflicts on the Great Plains, from the 1850s to 1890s, by a free-lance writer and newspaper editor. Tibbles was an assistant editor of the Omaha *Herald* and founder of a Populist newspaper in Lincoln, Neb. Mrs. Cogswell edited the work from a half-century-old manuscript.

1491. Townsend, George Alfred. *Rustics in Rebellion: A Yankee Reporter on the Road to Richmond, 1861–1865.* Chapel Hill: University of North Carolina Press, 1950. xx + 292pp. (Introduction by Lida Mayo.

First published as *Campaigns of a Non-Combatant.* New York: Blelock and Co., 1866. 368pp.)

These are the highly personal observations of one of the most literary of Civil War reporters, and they constitute some of the best descriptive material to come out of the war. The introduction gives an account of Townsend's full career, including his building of the Gapland Memorial to Civil War reporters on South Mountain, Maryland.

1492. Turner, Timothy G. *Bullets, Bottles, and Gardenias.* Dallas, Texas: South-West Press, 1935. 258pp.

Adventure and romance in Mexico during the revolutions from 1910 to 1916, with some account of Turner's early life in Illinois and Michigan. Turner makes war reporting seem more pleasant than the reality.

1493. Villard, Henry. *Lincoln on the Eve of '61: A Journalist's Story.* New York: Alfred A. Knopf, 1941. viii + 105pp. (Edited by Harold G. Villard and Oswald Garrison Villard.)

Reports from Henry Villard to the New York *Herald* in the interval between Lincoln's election and his inauguration when Villard was the only reporter of a major newspaper to be stationed in Springfield to give day-by-day accounts of doings of the President-elect. There is also an account of Villard's first meeting with Lincoln, at the Freeport debate with Douglas in 1858.

1494. Wilkie, Franc B. *Pen and Powder.* Boston: Ticknor and Co., 1888. 383pp.

Wilkie's Civil War experiences (1861–1863), chiefly as a reporter for the Dubuque (Iowa) *Herald* and later the New York *Times.* The volume is almost wholly concerned with the western theater, only briefly with Washington, D.C. See particularly chapter XXI for recollections of the postwar activities of Thomas Wallace Knox, A. D. Richardson, Junius H. Browne, Richard T. Colburn, J. B. McCullagh, and Whitelaw Reid.

WORLD WAR I AND THE PERIOD UP TO WORLD WAR II

1495. Adams, Benjamin Pettingill, ed. *You Americans.* New York and London: Funk and Wagnalls, 1939. xii + 348pp.

Fifteen foreign correspondents in the United States report their impressions of the country and of the political character of the American people.

1496. *Anywhere for a News Story: Being the Personal Narratives of Thirteen Adventurers in Search of News.* London: John Lane, 1934. 247pp. (Edited, and with an introduction, by H. W. Nevinson.)

Recollections of world events by British reporters as told in radio addresses sponsored by the British Broadcasting Corp. Heavily romantic slant.

1497. Associated Press. *The Unknown Soldier,* in Supplement Service Bulletin No. 64 of the AP. New York, December 1921. 24pp.

The complete Associated Press texts on "The Unknown Soldier" as sent from Washington on November 9, 10, and 11, 1921. Reporter Kirke L. Simpson's coverage of the Armistice Day dedication of Arlington National Cemetery brought him a Pulitzer Prize.

1498. Beals, Carleton. *Banana Gold.* Philadelphia and London: J. B. Lippincott Co., 1932. 367pp.

A free-lance writer's report on southern Honduras and Nicaragua during an insurrection involving American Marines. Beals includes interviews with insurrectionists.

1499. ———. *Glass Houses: Ten Years of Free-Lancing.* Philadelphia: J. B. Lippincott Co., 1938. 413pp.

Beals's account begins in Mexico and carries him through much of Latin America and to France, Spain, and Italy. There is a report of Mussolini's march on Rome.

1500. ———. *The Great Circle: Further Adventures in Free-Lancing.* Philadelphia and New York: J. B. Lippincott Co., 1940. 358pp.

A continuation of *Glass Houses*, recording journeys through Spain, Africa, Turkey, oil fields in South Russia (Baku), and Germany.

1501. Beaufort, J. M. de. *Behind the German Veil: A Record of a Journalistic War Pilgrimage.* New York: Dodd, Mead and Co., 1917. xix + 403pp.

Impressions, observations, interviews, and adventures of a Hollander, correspondent in Germany for the London *Daily Telegraph* before United States entry into World War I. The volume contains material on the German press in wartime and interviews with German political and military leaders.

1502. Berkes, Ross N. *Of the Multitude: A Journey around the World to Learn about People.* Los Angeles: Graphic Press, 1937. xiii + 212pp.

Observations made during a two-year assignment, with high praise for American foreign correspondents.

1503. Bernays, Robert. *Special Correspondent.* London: Victor Gollancz, Ltd.; New York: G. P. Putnam's Sons, 1934. 352pp.

Bernays, a devoted follower of the British Liberal party and a leader-writer for the London *Daily News*, describes early Nazi ruthlessness, Dollfuss of Austria, and Carol II of Rumania.

1504. Birchall, Frederick T. *The Storm Breaks: A Panorama of Europe and the Forces That Have Wrecked Its Peace.* New York: Viking Press, 1940. 366pp.

Birchall was a European correspondent for the New York *Times*.

1505. Blankenhorn, Heber. *Adventures in Propaganda: Letters from an Intelligence Officer in France.* Boston and New York: Houghton Mifflin Co., 1919. 166pp.

1506. Bolitho, William. *Italy under Mussolini.* New York: The Macmillan Co., 1926. 129pp.

Material from the New York *World* of December 1925, which the newspaper had specially commissioned Bolitho to write.

1507. Booker, Edna Lee. *News Is My Job: A Correspondent in War-Torn China.* New York: The Macmillan Co., 1940. xi + 375pp.

A correspondent for International News Service who was also a reporter for *China Press*, leading American daily in China, covers the Chinese Revolution and the rise of Chiang Kai-shek, 1922–1940.

1508. Byas, Hugh. *Government by Assassination.* New York: Alfred A. Knopf, 1942; London: G. Allen and Unwin, Ltd., 1943. 369pp.

Observations by the Tokyo correspondent of the New York *Times* on the rise of Japan before World War II. Byas served in Tokyo from 1914 to 1941 with the *Japan Advertiser*, London *Times*, and New York *Times*. The author includes some background on Japanese history.

1509. Chamberlin, William Henry. *The Russian Revolution, 1917–1921.* New York: The Macmillan Co., 1935. 2 vols. 511pp.; 556pp.

A heavily documented work by a European correspondent of the *Christian Science Monitor*.

1510. Chaplin, W. W. *Blood and Ink: An Italo-Ethiopian War Diary.* New York and Harrisburg, Pa.: Telegraph Press, 1936. 205pp. (Introduction by Floyd Gibbons.)

Day-by-day experiences of a correspondent for Universal Service in covering Mussolini's attack on Ethiopia, October 11, 1935 to January 25, 1936. Chaplin's sympathy is pro-Italian.

1511. Cobb, Irvin S. *Speaking of Prussians —* New York: George H. Doran Co., 1917. 80pp.

An emotional patriotic contribution to the World War I cause.

1512. Collings, Kenneth Brown. *Just for the Hell of It.* New York: Dodd, Mead and Co., 1938. vii + 373pp. Revised and republished under the title *These Things I Saw.* New York: Dodd, Mead and Co., 1939. vi + 346pp.

A readable narrative on the period from World War I to the late 1930s, with heavy emphasis upon aviation. It includes some war correspondence and experiences in France, Hong Kong, and Haiti.

1513. Cook, Sir Edward Tyas. *The Press in War-Time, with Some Account of the Official Press Bureau.* London: The Macmillan Co., Ltd., 1920. xv + 200pp.

1514. Cowles, Virginia. *Looking for Trouble.* New York and London: Harper and Brothers, 1941. xi + 447pp.

A report on the Spanish Civil War and early phases of World War II by an American woman reporting for the London *Daily Telegraph* and *Sunday Times*. There is good material on the siege of Madrid.

1515. Darrah, David. *Hail Caesar!* Boston: Hale, Cushman and Flint, 1936. x + 337pp.

A critical account of fascism in Italy. Darrah, a reporter for the Chicago *Tribune*, was expelled from Italy because he reported too factually the activities of the Mussolini government.

1516. Davis, Frances. *My Shadow in the Sun.* New York: Carrick and Evans, 1940. 318pp.

The author sold mail correspondence on the Spanish Civil War to a string of newspapers; later she became a staff writer for the London *Daily Mail* and the only woman to cover Franco's armies.

1517. Davis, Richard Harding. *With the Allies*. New York: Charles Scribner's Sons, 1915. xiii + 241pp.

1518. ———. *With the French in France and Salonika*. New York: Charles Scribner's Sons, 1916. xviii + 275pp.

Davis's World War I correspondence was this great reporter's last work. He died in 1916.

1519. Dosch-Fleurot, Arno. *Through War to Revolution: Being the Experiences of a Newspaper Correspondent in War and Revolution, 1914–1920*. London: John Lane the Bodley Head, Ltd., 1931. ix + 242pp.

A readable narrative by a correspondent for the New York *World*. The best part deals with the Russian Revolution and Kerensky, Lenin, and Trotsky.

1520. Dunn, Robert. *Five Fronts: On the Firing-Lines with English, French, Austrian, German, and Russian Troops*. New York: Dodd, Mead and Co., 1915. xiii + 308pp.

Dunn was a reporter for the New York *Evening Post*. His book is balanced, with an expressed effort being made to maintain a neutral spirit.

1521. Duranty, Walter. *Duranty Reports Russia*. New York: The Viking Press, 1934. xii + 401pp. (Selected and arranged by Gustavus Tuckerman, Jr.)

Includes a personal account of Duranty by Alexander Woollcott.

1522. ———. *I Write as I Please*. New York: Simon and Schuster, 1935. viii + 347pp.

A competent account of Duranty's 14 years in Russia, 1921–1935, as correspondent for the New York *Times*. The book is descriptive and conversational rather than analytical. Duranty judges Russia objectively by noting her accomplishments despite incredible difficulties.

1523. Farmer, Rhodes. *Shanghai Harvest: A Diary of Three Years in the China War*. London: Museum Press, Ltd., 1945. 294pp.

An analysis by a correspondent of the Melbourne *Herald* of China's struggle against Japan from the Marco Polo Bridge incident (July 7, 1937) through 1940. Farmer praises Chiang Kai-shek's policies.

1524. Farson, Negley. *Behind God's Back*. New York: Harcourt, Brace and Co., 1941. xii + 555pp.

A report on the equatorial regions of Africa and on South Africa just before World War II. The emphasis is on people "behind God's back" awaiting the brave new world.

1525. Fodor, Marcel W. *Plot and Counter-Plot in Central Europe: Conditions South of Hitler*. Boston: Houghton Mifflin Co., 1937. xvi + 317pp. (Introduction by John Gunther.)

A Hungarian-born Vienna correspondent of the Manchester *Guardian* analyzes the political and economic conditions of southeastern Europe, especially Austria, the Balkans, and Italy, in the mid-1930s. He includes an account of the Dollfuss murder. Some of the material appeared in the *Guardian, Foreign Affairs*, and *American Mercury*.

1526. ———. *The Revolution Is On*. Boston: Houghton Mifflin Co., 1940. xv + 239pp. (Introduction by Dorothy Thompson.)

Partly analysis, partly propaganda directed as a warning to the United States at the time of Germany's attacks in Europe.

1527. Gibbons, Floyd. *"And They Thought We Wouldn't Fight."* New York: George H. Doran Co., 1918. xx + 410pp.

1528. Gibbs, Sir Philip Hamilton. *Realities of War*. London: William Heinemann, Ltd., 1920. 455pp. (Published in the United States under the title *Now It Can Be Told*.)

Gibbs's plain-spoken narrative of World War I is among the most widely known volumes of war reporters ever written, one of the first of the type that became known as "I seen its." In a later edition in 1929 Gibbs softened some of his earlier views, particularly in regard to criticism of the British General Staff.

1529. ———. *More That Must Be Told*. London and New York: Harper and Brothers, 1921. 407pp.

A sequel to Gibbs's first book. Here he attacks "the Old Gang" among political leaders in Europe. He considers conditions in postwar Germany, the price of victory in France, problems of Austria, social changes in English life, the Irish problem, and the position of the United States.

1530. Gunther, John. *Inside Europe*. New York and London: Harper and Brothers, 1936. x + 470pp. Revised in 1938, 531pp.; completely revised in a war edition, 1940, 606pp.

First of the "Inside" series and probably the best, since it was Europe that Gunther knew most thoroughly as a foreign correspondent. The book provides an excellent background on the pre-World War II situation.

1531. ———. *Inside Latin America*. New York and London: Harper and Brothers, 1941. xi + 498pp.

1532. Hanighen, Frank C. *The Secret War*. New York: John Day Co., 1934. xi + 316pp. (Introduction by Quincy Howe.)

1533. ———, ed. *Nothing but Danger*. New York: Robert M. McBride and Co., 1939. 285pp.

Narratives by foreign correspondents who covered the Spanish Civil War. Contributors were Lawrence A. Fernsworth, London *Times*; Edmond Taylor, Chicago *Tribune*; Noel Monks, London *Daily Express*; Denis Weaver, London *News Chronicle*; Joseph Swire, Reuters; Jan Holman Yindrech, Madrid bureau of United Press; O. D. Gallagher, London *Daily Express*; and Keith Scott-Watson, London *Daily Herald*. Hanighen represented the New York *Post*.

1534. Hansen, Ferdinand. *The Unrepentant Northcliffe: A Reply to the London Times of October 19, 1920, by the Unrepentant Hun*. Hamburg, Germany: Overseas Publishing Co., 1920. 47pp.

The reply of a native German, reared in America, to a charge in the London *Times* that Germany was still unrepentant in defeat. Hansen is severe in his attack upon Lord Northcliffe.

1535. Howe, Quincy. *Blood Is Cheaper Than Water: The Prudent*

PERSONAL NARRATIVES AND ANTHOLOGIES

American's Guide to Peace and War. New York: Simon and Schuster, 1939. 223pp.

1536. ———. *England Expects Every American to Do His Duty*. New York: Simon and Schuster, 1937. xii + 238pp.

1537. Hubbard, Wyant. *Fiasco in Ethiopia: The Story of a So-Called War by a Reporter on the Ground*. New York: Harper and Brothers, 1936. ix + 391pp.

1538. Hunt, Frazier. *This Bewildered World, and Its Search for a New Rhythm*. New York: Frederick A. Stokes Co., 1934. viii + 371pp.

An effort to tell what was wrong with "the whole of the world in the 1930s." The book is interesting, but too ambitious.

1539. Irwin, Will. *A Reporter at Armageddon: Letters from the Front and Behind the Lines of the Great War*. New York and London: D. Appleton and Co., 1918. 355pp.

A series of personal experiences, March 24 to December 7, 1917, while Irwin was accompanying the Allied armies.

1540. Johnson, Thomas M. *Without Censor: New Light on Our Greatest World War Battles*. Indianapolis: Bobbs-Merrill Co., 1928. x + 411pp.

1541. Kaltenborn, H. V. *I Broadcast the Crisis*. New York: Random House, 1938. 359pp.

Broadcasts for the Columbia Broadcasting System, September 12 to October 2, 1938, on the Chamberlain-Hitler settlement at Munich. Most of these are by Kaltenborn, with news bulletins and a number of broadcasts by other commentators interposed. Kaltenborn extravagantly credited the Munich "turn for peace" in significant measure to radio. The appendix gives the text of the Munich settlement.

1542. ———. *Kaltenborn Edits the News*. New York: Modern Age Books, 1937. xiii + 183pp.

Summarizes Kaltenborn's analyses of the world situation in the 1930s as carried over the Columbia Broadcasting System. The author emphasizes radio's contribution to the dissemination of knowledge of world affairs.

1543. Kilgallen, Dorothy. *Girl around the World*. Philadelphia: David McKay Co., 1936. 219pp.

From October 1, 1936, to October 26, 1936, a 20th-century "Nellie Bly" raced with two male reporters around the globe by plane, blimp, motor, train, and bus. Dorothy came in second. She reported for the New York *Evening Journal*, International News Service, and King Features Syndicate. A fast-paced yarn intended to build circulation.

1544. Kirk, Betty. *Covering the Mexican Front: The Battle of Europe versus America*. Norman: University of Oklahoma Press, 1942. xix + 367pp. (Foreword by Josephus Daniels.)

A foreign correspondent for American newspapers made this careful study of Mexico in the 1930s and the early years of World War II. The book shows insight, fairness, and sound reporting.

1545. Knoblaugh, H. Edward. *Correspondent in Spain*. London and New York: Sheed and Ward, 1937. xii + 233pp.

A report on the first year of the Spanish Civil War by an Associated Press correspondent who was later forced to leave Spain as a result of conflicts with the Loyalist government. Several chapters deal with the Madrid propaganda machine.

1546. Lazareff, Pierre. *Deadline: The Behind-the-Scenes Story of the Last Decade in France*. New York: Random House, 1942. viii + 369pp. (Translated from the French by David Partridge.)

The editor of *Paris Soir* and, after the war, *France Soir*, records the collapse of the Third Republic, comments on corruption in the prewar French press, and analyzes the Havas monopoly. There is a full account of the rise and influence of *Paris Soir*.

1547. McCormick, Robert R. *With the Russian Army: Being the Experiences of a National Guardsman*. New York: The Macmillan Co., 1915. xiv + 306pp. (Includes maps, charts, and 24 full-page illustrations.)

As a major in the Illinois National Guard, the publisher of the Chicago *Tribune* surveyed the Russian front at the invitation of the Grand Duke Nicholas. This book reflects McCormick's intense interest in all things military, a lifelong characteristic.

1548. McKenzie, Vernon. *Through Turbulent Years*. New York: Robert M. McBride and Co., 1938. ix + 304pp.

An analysis of Europe in the 1930s, based upon personal observation and experience, by a former director of the University of Washington School of Journalism. There are comments on the European press in chapters called "Espionage Plague" and "Press, Propaganda and Friction."

1549. ———, ed. *Behind the Headlines: Journalistic Adventures of Today*. New York: Jonathan Cape and Harrison Smith, 1931. xxvi + 286pp.

News stories chosen to represent "reportorial go-and-get-it" achievements of newspapermen for whom their work retained glamour and romance in an age of "routine and rewrite."

1550. Matthews, Herbert L. *Two Wars and More to Come*. New York: Carrick and Evans, 1938. 318pp.

On the Ethiopian war and the Spanish Civil War, by a correspondent of the New York *Times*. Portions of the book had appeared originally in the *Times*.

1551. Millis, Walter. *Viewed without Alarm: Europe Today*. Boston: Houghton Mifflin Co., 1937. vi + 79pp.

1552. Mowrer, Edgar Ansel. *Germany Puts the Clock Back*. New York: William Morrow and Co., 1933. 325pp. (Introduction by Dorothy Thompson.)

A correspondent of the Chicago *Daily News* traces accurately the downfall of the Weimar Republic and analyzes the nature of Adolf Hitler. Because of this book Mowrer was forced to resign as president of the Berlin Association of Foreign Journalists and later to leave Germany itself. Pessimistic in tone.

1553. Northcliffe, Lord. *At the War.* New York: George H. Doran Co., 1916. viii + 355pp.

A compilation of Northcliffe's letters, telegrams, cablegrams, and other writings on World War I.

1554. ———. *Lord Northcliffe's War Book.* New York: George H. Doran Co., 1917. 283pp.

An expansion of *At the War.* It includes chapters on "America at War."

1555. Overseas Press Club. *Eye Witness.* New York: Alliance Book Corp., 1940. viii + 306pp. (Edited by Robert Spiers Benjamin.)

Each of 23 Overseas Press Club members writes of his most interesting and revealing reporting experience. Among the better known contributors were Linton Wells, George E. Sokolsky, and Eugene Lyons. Lyons's piece is on "What a Foreign Correspondent Is."

1556. ———. *The Inside Story.* New York: Prentice-Hall, 1940. x + 263pp. (Edited by Robert Spiers Benjamin.)

Behind-the-scenes stories of 20 foreign correspondents: Peggy Hull, William Parker, Eugene Lyons, Carol Weld, Arthur Settel, Morrill Cody, H. V. Kaltenborn, D. Thomas Curtin, S. Miles Bouton, Allan Finn, Joseph Israels II, George Sylvester Viereck, Mary Knight, Tom Morgan, Cornelius Vanderbilt, Jr., Hal Lehrman, Edward Hunter, Irene Kuhn, Burnet Hershey, and Wythe Williams. The period covered is World War I through the 1930s.

1557. Palmer, Frederick. *My Year of the Great War.* New York: Dodd, Mead and Co., 1915. vii + 464pp.

Covers 1914–1915, when Palmer was attached to British headquarters in France as a correspondent for *Collier's, Everybody's,* and American press associations. Pro-Allied.

1558. ———. *My Second Year of the War.* New York: Dodd, Mead and Co., 1917. 404pp.

Palmer continues his account to 1915–1916, stressing particularly the Somme and Canadian contributions to the Allied cause.

1559. Piper, Edgar B. *Somewhere near the War: Being an Authentic and More or Less Diverting Chronicle of the Pilgrimage of Twelve Journalists to the War Zone* . . . Portland, Ore.: The Morning Oregonian, 1919. viii + 141pp.

Twenty-six letters written by the editor of the *Oregonian* to his paper. The 12 journalists (including E. L. Ray of the St. Louis *Globe-Democrat* and Frank R. Kent of the Baltimore *Sun*) had been invited by the British Ministry of Information in 1918 to visit the western front. The reports actually were Allied propaganda.

1560. Powell, E. Alexander. *Vive la France!* New York: Charles Scribner's Sons, 1915. xiv + 254pp.

1561. Rue, Larry. *I Fly for News.* New York: Albert and Charles Boni, 1932. viii + 307pp.

High adventure — a correspondent for the Chicago *Tribune* writes as much about his airplane flights over perilous country as about newsgathering. The scene is laid principally in Afghanistan, the Mediterranean area, and the African Riff.

1562. Seldes, George. *Sawdust Caesar: The Untold Story of Mussolini and Fascism*. New York and London: Harper and Brothers, 1935. xv + 459pp.

1563. Sheean, Vincent. *Not Peace but a Sword*. New York: Doubleday, Doran and Co., 1939. viii + 367pp. (Published in London under the title *The Eleventh Hour*.)

Sheean pays the most attention to the Spanish Civil War, March 1938 to March 1939, which he regarded as a prelude to general war.

1564. Snow, Edgar. *Red Star over China*. New York: Random House, 1938. xiv + 474pp.

Snow was widely known as an interpreter of Far Eastern affairs. He was chief Far Eastern correspondent for the London *Daily Herald* in 1937; later he was on the staff of the *Saturday Evening Post*.

1565. Sokolsky, George E. *The Tinder Box of Asia*. Garden City, N.Y.: Doubleday, Doran and Co., 1932. x + 376pp.

1566. Thompson, Dorothy. *The New Russia*. New York: Henry Holt and Co., 1928. vii + 330pp.

A report on economic, cultural and social aspects of life under Communist doctrine in the early years of the Red regime.

1567. ———. *Refugees: Anarchy or Organization?* New York: Random House, 1938. xiv + 125pp. (Introduction by Hamilton Fish Armstrong.)

1568. Tolischus, Otto D. *They Wanted War*. New York: Reynal and Hitchcock, 1940. viii + 340pp.

A report on the building up of Adolf Hitler's war machine. Tolischus at the time was Berlin correspondent of the New York *Times* and much of his book is drawn from *Times* dispatches. See particularly "The Lap-Dog Press," on Nazi abrogation of freedom of speech and press.

1569. Vaughn, Miles W. *Covering the Far East*. New York: Covici-Friede, 1936. 408pp.

Vaughn was a correspondent in Japan and China for nine years in the 1920s and 1930s. His book analyzes Chiang Kai-shek's rise to power.

1570. Viereck, George Sylvester. *The Kaiser on Trial*. New York: Greystone Press, 1937. xx + 514pp.

1571. Waugh, Evelyn. *Waugh in Abyssinia*. London and New York: Longmans, Green and Co., 1936. 253pp.

Waugh sent back dispatches to the London press during the Italo-Ethiopian War. Here he provides a readable book with a pro-Italian bias.

1572. Whitaker, John T. *Americas to the South*. New York: The Macmillan Co., 1939. 300pp.

1573. ———. *And Fear Came*. New York: The Macmillan Co., 1936. 272pp.

A reporter's view of Europe in the late 1920s and early 1930s. There is considerable discussion of the failure of the League of Nations. The volume is directed toward thoughtful readers.

1574. ———. *We Cannot Escape History*. New York: The Macmillan Co., 1943. 374pp.

A correspondent for the New York *Herald Tribune* and Chicago *Daily News* summarizes world events in the period after 1934. His purpose was to analyze the nature of fascism and the reasons for its success in the 1930s. There is good material on Hitler's "blood purge" of 1934.

1575. White, William Allen. *The Martial Adventures of Henry and Me.* New York: The Macmillan Co., 1918. 338pp. (Illustrated by Tony Sarg.)

Editors White of the Emporia *Gazette* and Henry J. Allen of the Wichita *Beacon* observed the lighter side of World War I in Europe while gathering information on the American Red Cross. Well written.

1576. Whitlock, Brand. *Belgium: A Personal Narrative*. New York: D. Appleton and Co., 1919. 2 vols. xi + 661pp.; vi + 818pp.

1577. Wildes, Harry Emerson. *Japan in Crisis*. New York: The Macmillan Co., 1934. viii + 300pp.

A well-documented analysis of Japan under military dictatorship. Wildes treats the government's tampering with news.

1578. Williams, Wythe. *Passed by the Censor*. New York: E. P. Dutton and Co., 1916. 270pp. (Introduction by Myron T. Herrick.)

The experiences in France of the Paris correspondent of the New York *Times*, who was officially accredited to the French armies. Early chapters describe the hectic summer of 1914.

1579. Woodhead, Henry George W. *A Visit to Manchukuo*. Shanghai: The Mercury Press, 1932. 112pp.

A series of articles contributed to the Shanghai *Evening Post and Mercury*, October and November 1932.

1580. Woollcott, Alexander. *The Command Is Forward*. New York: The Century Co., 1919. xii + 304pp.

Chronicles of American battles as they appeared in *Stars and Stripes*, on which Woollcott served. Good reporting about humorous situations.

WORLD WAR II

1581. Abend, Hallett. *Japan Unmasked*. New York: Ives Washburn, 1941. 322pp.

Before the attack on Pearl Harbor a New York *Times* correspondent reports on areas threatened by Japan — the Malay Peninsula, Sumatra, Borneo, Celebes, Java, and the Philippines — and urges a reappraisal of American policy toward the Japanese.

1582. Alcott, Carroll. *My War with Japan*. New York: Henry Holt and Co., 1943. 368pp.

An extremely subjective analysis of Japan by a reporter, editor, and radio commentator with 15 years' experience in the Orient.

1583. Associated Press. *News Annual.* New York: Rinehart and Co., 1945 and 1946. (First volume compiled by Russell Landstrom; second by Dewitt Mackenzie.)

Each of these reports, which were discontinued after two volumes, gives a full picture of Associated Press coverage for one year in words and photographs compiled from dispatches of AP correspondents. They are excellent summaries of the last two years of war.

1584. ———. *Reporting to Remember: Unforgettable Stories and Pictures of World War II by Correspondents of the Associated Press.* New York: Associated Press, 1945. 71pp.

1585. Baillie, Hugh. *Two Battlefronts.* New York: United Press Associations, 1943. 139pp.

Dispatches by the president of United Press who personally covered the air offensive over Germany and the Sicilian campaign in the summer of 1943.

1586. Bartlett, Vernon. *Tomorrow Always Comes.* New York: Alfred A. Knopf, 1944. 159pp.

1587. Beattie, Edward W., Jr. *Diary of a Kriegie.* New York: Thomas Y. Crowell Co., 1945. vi + 312pp.

A United Press correspondent tells of life in German prison camps from September 12, 1944, until his liberation after Germany's surrender.

1588. ———. *"Freely to Pass."* New York: Thomas Y. Crowell Co., 1942. vi + 372pp.

The story of a passport, which grew from 32 to 92 pages in three years and four months of foreign and war correspondence. Beattie includes an account of the Nazi invasions of Poland and France and the bombing of London in 1940.

1589. Bernstein, Walter. *Keep Your Head Down.* New York: Viking Press, 1945. 213pp.

Eleven pieces by a reporter who covered Yugoslavia in 1944 and was the first foreign correspondent to interview Marshal Tito. Much of this had appeared first in the *New Yorker.* Good reading.

1590. Biddle, George. *Artist at War.* New York: Viking Press, 1944. 244pp. (Illustrated with 40 pen-and-ink drawings and 16 gravure portraits by the author.)

Biddle spent eight months in Tunisia, Sicily, and Italy in 1943. The emphasis is on the life of the common soldier.

1591. Booker, Edna Lee. *Flight from China.* New York: The Macmillan Co., 1945. x + 236pp. (In collaboration with John S. Potter.)

1592. Bourke-White, Margaret. *They Called It Purple-Heart Valley.* New York: Simon and Schuster, 1944. 182pp.

An account in text and photographs of war in Italy with the United States Fifth Army. Miss Bourke-White's stories of front-line soldiers parallel to some extent those of Ernie Pyle.

1593. Brines, Russell. *Until They Eat Stones.* Philadelphia and New York: J. B. Lippincott Co., 1944. 340pp.

Brines, an Associated Press reporter, was interned for 21 months after Pearl Harbor. His book covers the major wartime developments in occupied Asia and Japan during 1942 and 1943. The book is somewhat emotional in its treatment of Japan's plans to carry on a "diabolic war" for years.

1594. Brown, [Ernest] Francis. *The War in Maps: An Atlas of New York Times Maps*. New York: Oxford University Press, 1942. viii + 159pp. (Maps prepared by Emil Herlin.)

1595. Brown, John Mason. *To All Hands: An Amphibious Adventure*. New York and London: Whittlesey House, McGraw-Hill Book Co., 1943. xii + 236pp. (Foreword by Rear Admiral Alan G. Kirk, USN.)

Broadcasts by the author to soldiers and sailors on the flagship of the United States Atlantic Fleet's amphibious forces. The content centers particularly on the Sicilian campaign.

1596. Carpenter, Iris. *No Woman's World*. Boston: Houghton Mifflin Co., 1946. ix + 338pp.

An American reporter for the London *Daily Herald* reports chiefly on the last year of the war. She fought with the Maquis in Brittany and covered the last stages of the advance into Germany.

1597. Carroll, Gordon, ed. *History in the Writing*. New York: Duell, Sloan and Pearce, 1945. xii + 401pp.

A collection of war correspondence written by staff members of *Time, Life,* and *Fortune*. The volume summarizes through 82 selected pieces covering 1941–1944 some "X millions of words . . . enough to fill a half-dozen filing cabinets."

1598. Carroll, Wallace. *We're in This with Russia*. Boston: Houghton Mifflin Co., 1942. viii + 264pp.

1599. Casey, Robert J. *Battle Below: The War of the Submarines*. Indianapolis: Bobbs-Merrill Co., 1945. 380pp.

1600. ———. *I Can't Forget*. Indianapolis and New York: Bobbs-Merrill Co., 1941. 398pp.

Casey's observations early in the war in France, Luxembourg, Germany, Belgium, Spain, and England. Included is material on the "Sitzkrieg," the fall of France, and the Battle of Britain. Casey was a correspondent for the Chicago *Daily News*.

1601. ———. *This Is Where I Came In*. Indianapolis: Bobbs-Merrill Co., 1945. 307pp.

1602. ———. *Torpedo Junction: With the Pacific Fleet from Pearl Harbor to Midway*. Indianapolis: Bobbs-Merrill Co., 1942. 419pp.

Covers the first six months of United States activity in the war, including the Battle of the Coral Sea.

1603. Cassidy, Henry C. *Moscow Dateline, 1941–1943*. Boston: Houghton Mifflin Co., 1943. ix + 374pp.

An analysis of war on the Russian front in 1941 and 1942 by the then Associated Press bureau chief in Moscow. There is good material on the Battle of Moscow, the Battle of Stalingrad, and relations between Churchill and Stalin.

1604. Chaplin, W. W. *Seventy-Thousand Miles of War: Being One Man's Odyssey on Many Fronts*. New York and London: D. Appleton-Century Co., 1943. ix + 287pp.

1605. Childs, Marquis W. *This Is Your War*. Boston: Little, Brown and Co., 1942. 200pp.

1605a. Columbia Broadcasting System. *From D-Day through Victory in Europe: The Eye-Witness Story as Told by War Correspondents on the Air*. New York: Columbia Broadcasting System, 1945. 314pp.

1606. ———. *From Pearl Harbor into Tokyo: The Story as Told by War Correspondents on the Air*. New York: Columbia Broadcasting System, 1945. 313pp.

1607. Custer, Joe James. *Through the Perilous Night*. New York: The Macmillan Co., 1944. xii + 243pp.

A United Press correspondent's report of naval operations in the Pacific early in the war. Custer deals principally with the sinking by the Japanese of the *USS Astoria*. There is also interesting material about the *Bee*, the *Hornet*, and the *Enterprise* and about the naval battles of Guadalcanal and Savo Island.

1608. Daniell, Raymond. *Civilians Must Fight*. Garden City, N.Y.: Doubleday, Doran and Co., 1941. xiv + 322pp. (Foreword by W. Somerset Maugham.)

Recounts the experiences of the chief London correspondent of the New York *Times* during the Nazi bombings of 1940. Daniell gives considerable material on the British Ministry of Information, censorship, and the activities of correspondents.

1609. Dew, Gwen. *Prisoner of the Japs*. New York: Alfred A. Knopf, 1943. viii + 309pp.

1610. Ehrenburg, Ilya. *The Tempering of Russia*. New York: Alfred A. Knopf, 1944. viii + 356pp. (Translated from the Russian by Alexander Kaun.)

The report of a Soviet Union correspondent on Russia's war with Germany, July 3, 1941, to July 24, 1942. The material is based upon Ehrenburg's diaries and notes and his dispatches to the *Red Star*, *Pravda*, and *Izvestia*. It includes analyses of the German soldier, the Nazi mentality, and allies of the Soviet Union.

1611. Ford, Cory. *Short Cut to Tokyo: The Battle for the Aleutians*. New York: Charles Scribner's Sons, 1943. 141pp.

This material, which in part first appeared in *Collier's*, presents the argument that in June 1942 the history of the American continent may have swung on Japanese failure to take the Aleutians.

1612. Forman, Harrison. *Report from Red China*. New York: Henry Holt and Co., 1945. iv + 250pp.

1613. Fredborg, Arvid. *Behind the Steel Wall: A Swedish Journalist in Berlin, 1941–43*. New York: Viking Press; Stockholm: P. A. Norstedt and Sons, 1944. ix + 305pp.

A neutral journalist in Berlin reports on the year and a half following American entry into the war, when the United States had no official source of information from within Germany. He offers a picture of the foreign press in Berlin, the German ministry of propaganda, and censorship.

1614. Fyfe, Hamilton. *Britain's War-Time Revolution.* London: Victor Gollancz, Ltd., 1944. 248pp.

Fyfe's conception of the impact of World War II on British life, told in diary form, from September 3, 1939, to December 30, 1942.

1615. Geraud, André [Pertinax]. *The Gravediggers of France: Military Defeat, Armistice, Counter-Revolution.* Garden City, N.Y.: Doubleday, Doran and Co., 1944. xi + 612pp.

An account of Gamelin, Daladier, Reynaud, Petain, and Laval and the fall of France in 1940, by a distinguished French journalist of the 1930s. Under the pseudonym Pertinax, Geraud wrote for the *Echo de Paris* and his columns were widely circulated in the United States. The *Gravediggers* is an excellent piece of journalistic history.

1616. Gould, Randall. *China in the Sun.* Garden City, N.Y.: Doubleday and Co., 1946. xi + 403pp.

A useful book based upon years of correspondence in the Far East. It provides background material beginning with the Boxer Rebellion and takes up in detail the struggle between the Kuomingtang and communism, China in World War II, and China's future outlook.

1617. Gramling, Oliver. *Free Men Are Fighting: The Story of World War II.* New York and Toronto: Farrar and Rinehart, 1942. xvi + 488pp.

Reports by 65 Associated Press correspondents around the world, August 28, 1939, to July 4, 1942, published as a tribute to the AP. An appendix gives thumbnail sketches of the contributors. Special attention is paid to the Battle of Britain, Hitler's attack on Russia, and Pearl Harbor and Bataan.

1618. Gunther, John. *D-Day.* New York: Harper and Brothers, 1944. 276pp.

Gunther's coverage of the events leading up to the invasion of Europe and the plans for D-Day, June 6, 1944. Hastily prepared and somewhat superficial.

1619. ———. *Inside Asia.* New York: Harper and Brothers, 1939. x + 599pp. War edition, completely revised, 1942. xii + 637pp.

1620. Hailey, Foster Bowman. *Pacific Battle Line.* New York: The Macmillan Co., 1944. ix + 405pp.

1621. Hauser, Ernest O. *Shanghai: City for Sale.* New York: Harcourt, Brace and Co., 1940. 323pp.

1622. Hersey, John. *Hiroshima.* New York: Alfred A. Knopf, 1946. 117pp.

One of the literary classics of the war, an objective report as Hersey reconstructed it of what took place in Hiroshima the day the United States dropped the atomic bomb, August 6, 1945. The *New Yorker* devoted a full issue of its magazine to Hersey's account (August 31, 1946). The book is likely to remain permanently in the front rank of World War II narratives.

1623. ———. *Into the Valley: A Skirmish of the Marines.* New York:

Alfred A. Knopf, 1943. 138pp. (Illustrations by Major Donald L. Dickson.)

1624. ———. *Men on Bataan*. New York: Alfred A. Knopf, 1942. 313pp.

Excellent reporting on the surrender of the Philippines, including sketches of the men who fought there. Hersey drew heavily upon dispatches appearing in newspapers and in *Time* and *Life*.

1625. Hill, Helen, and Herbert Agar. *Beyond German Victory*. New York: Reynal and Hitchcock, 1940. viii + 117pp.

1626. Huie, William Bradford. *The Fight for Air Power*. New York: L. B. Fischer, 1942. 310pp.

1627. ———. *From Omaha to Okinawa: The Story of the Seabees*. New York: E. P. Dutton and Co., 1945. 257 + lxiv pp.

1628. Ingersoll, Ralph. *Action on All Fronts: A Personal Account of This War*. New York and London: Harper and Brothers, 1942. ix + 330pp.

The editor of *PM* reports on the Pacific, Chinese, Russian, Caucasian, Mediterranean, British, and Atlantic areas.

1629. ———. *The Battle Is the Payoff*. New York: Harcourt, Brace and Co., 1943. 217pp.

Battle-front reports on the war in North Africa in 1942, principally in Tunisia. Ingersoll also takes up the controversy occasioned by his own entry into the army.

1630. ———. *Top Secret*. New York: Harcourt, Brace and Co., 1946. viii + 373pp.

Ingersoll served with several commands engaged in planning the attack on Germany in 1944. This "uncensored inside account" of the campaign in Europe was written after Ingersoll's release from the service in 1945 and his return to *PM*.

1631. Johnston, Stanley. *Queen of the Flat-Tops*. New York: E. P. Dutton and Co., 1942. 280pp.

A "biography" of the *USS Lexington* by a reporter in the Pacific for the Chicago *Tribune*. Johnston includes sidelights on life aboard a carrier.

1632. Jordan, Max. *Beyond All Fronts: A Bystander's Notes on This Thirty Years' War*. Milwaukee: Bruce Publishing Co., 1944. xiv + 386pp.

Jordan, a one-time reporter for the *Berliner Tageblatt* and later a commentator for the National Broadcasting Co., emphasizes the interrelations between World Wars I and II. He takes a somewhat religious approach.

1633. Lardner, John. *Southwest Passage*. New York: J. B. Lippincott Co., 1943. 302pp.

A sports writer turned war correspondent tells of experiences in Australia early in the war. His volume is useful for background on Gen. Douglas MacArthur's arrival in Australia after the fall of the Philippines. Well written.

1634. Lauterbach, Richard E. *These Are the Russians*. New York and London: Harper and Brothers, 1945. 368pp.

A *Time* and *Life* correspondent's report on the Russian people during wartime. Written in a period of good will toward the Russians, the volume stresses that we must and can get along with the Soviet Union.

1635. Lear, John. *Forgotten Front.* New York: E. P. Dutton and Co., 1943. 256pp.

Lear, who served with the Associated Press and Wide World Photos, warns of Nazi enterprise and American neglect in South America.

1636. Liebling, A. J. *The Road Back to Paris.* Garden City, N.Y.: Doubleday, Doran and Co., 1944. 300pp.

Based on Liebling's reports to the *New Yorker.* The emphasis is on the human side of war.

1637. Lochner, Louis P. *What about Germany?* New York: Dodd, Mead and Co., 1942. xiv + 395pp.

By the former chief of the Associated Press in Berlin, written after Lochner's repatriation. Out of personal experience, Lochner provides considerable background on Hitler and on regimentation in the German press.

1638. Lucas, Jim. *Combat Correspondent.* New York: Reynal and Hitchcock, 1944. xi + 210pp.

The Marine Corps experiences, principally in the Pacific theater, of a Tulsa *Tribune* reporter from mid-1942 to the close of 1943.

1639. McMillan, Richard. *Mediterranean Assignment.* New York: Doubleday, Doran and Co., 1943. xii + 332pp.

A United Press reporter reviews desert warfare in Africa in 1942 and expresses high admiration for the triumphant British commander, Montgomery.

1640. Middleton, Drew. *Our Share of Night.* New York: Viking Press, 1946. 380pp.

A picture of the whole war in Europe, from the "phony war" of 1939 through the victorious drive across France and into Germany. The volume reflects Middleton's abhorrence of war, hatred of fascism, devotion to democracy, belief in internationalism, and pessimism about the future.

1641. Millis, Walter. *The Last Phase: The Allied Victory in Western Europe.* Boston: Houghton Mifflin Co., 1946. xi + 130pp.

A volume prepared for the Bureau of Overseas Publications, Office of War Information, for publication abroad as part of OWI's information services.

1642. ———. *This Is Pearl! The United States and Japan, 1941.* New York: W. Morrow and Co., 1947. xiii + 384pp.

1643. Mowrer, Edgar Ansel, and Marthe Rajchman. *Global War: An Atlas of World Strategy.* New York: W. Morrow and Co., 1942. 128pp. (Introduction by Frank Knox.)

1644. Mowrer, Lilian T. *Rip Tide of Aggression.* New York: W. Morrow and Co., 1942. viii + 247pp.

1645. New Yorker. *The New Yorker Book of War Pieces.* New York: Reynal and Hitchcock, 1947. 562pp.

Seventy-odd articles that appeared in the magazine from September 2, 1939, to August 6, 1945. They include John Hersey's report on Hiroshima.

1646. Oestreicher, J. C. *The World Is Their Beat*. New York: Duell, Sloan and Pearce, 1945. 254pp.

A correspondent for International News Service explains the manners and way of life of war correspondents.

1647. Patmore, Derek. *Balkan Correspondent*. New York and London: Harper and Brothers, 1941. xii + 319pp.

A correspondent for the London *News Chronicle* and *Exchange-Telegraph* covers the first 18 months of war. The bulk of the book concerns the German seizure of Rumania, the Bulgarian crisis, the Greco-Italian war, and Turkey.

1648. Poulos, Constantine, and Leland Stowe. *Challenge to Freedom: The Story of What Happened in Greece*. New York: Greek-American Council, 1945. 30pp.

1649. Pyle, Ernest. *Brave Men*. New York: Henry Holt and Co., 1944. 328pp.

Pyle's intensely personal story of Sicily, Italy, and England before D-Day and France from D-Day through Liberation. A thorough index lists the soldiers mentioned in the text.

1650. ———. *Here Is Your War*. New York: Henry Holt and Co., 1943. 304pp.

Human-interest accounts of the African campaign.

1651. ———. *Last Chapter*. New York: Henry Holt and Co., 1946. 143pp.

Covers the last weeks of Pyle's Pacific assignment, February–April, 1945, before he was killed on Ie. Like his other books, this one is about friendly GIs.

1652. Raleigh, John M. *Behind the Nazi Front*. New York: Dodd, Mead and Co., 1940. vii + 307pp.

1653. ———. *Pacific Blackout*. New York: Dodd, Mead and Co., 1943. ix + 244pp. (Foreword by Paul W. White.)

A Columbia Broadcasting System news commentator's account of Allied defense of the Netherlands East Indies and of war in Australia.

1654. Reynolds, Quentin. *Dress Rehearsal: The Story of Dieppe*. New York: Random House, 1943. xi + 278pp.

1655. ———. *Only the Stars Are Neutral*. New York: Random House, 1942. xi + 299pp.

Reynolds on the war in 1941 and early 1942, principally on London during Nazi bombings and Russia during the first stages of German invasion.

1656. ———. *The Wounded Don't Cry*. New York: E. P. Dutton Co., 1941. 253pp.

Largely concerns the Battle of Britain — descriptions of life during the blitzkrieg.

1657. Riess, Curt. *The Invasion of Germany*. New York: G. P. Putnam's Sons, 1943. 206pp.

Riess, an emigrant German, gives a picture of Germany under Nazism and outlines possible land and sea routes for Allied invasion. He overestimated Germany's strength.

1658. ———, ed. *They Were There: The Story of World War II and How It Came About, by America's Foremost Correspondents.* New York: G. P. Putnam's Sons, 1944. xliii + 670pp.

A chronicle of personal narrative by correspondents for newspapers, radio, and magazines covering the period 1924–1944. Riess's helpful foreword explains the nature of foreign correspondence. There are useful thumbnail biographies of the contributors.

1659. St. John, Robert. *From the Land of Silent People.* Garden City, N.Y.: Doubleday, Doran and Co., 1942. 352pp.

A correspondent for the Associated Press reports on the resistance of the Yugoslavs. He is critical of the waste of war and of reporters who try "to suck headlines out of death and suffering."

1660. Salisbury, Harrison E. *Russia on the Way.* New York: The Macmillan Co., 1946. 414pp.

An appraisal of social and economic progress in Russia, based in part on Salisbury's observations during his assignment as manager of the United Press Moscow bureau during the war. He points to the Far East as a possible postwar trouble spot.

1661. Sheean, Vincent. *Between the Thunder and the Sun.* New York: Random House, 1943. 422pp.

Strong on personalities — the French people before the occupation of Paris, the British during air raids, and the Chinese and peoples of the Pacific Islands before Pearl Harbor.

1662. Sherrod, Robert. *On to Westward: War in the Central Pacific.* New York: Duell, Sloan and Pearce, 1945. xv + 333pp.

Covers the war in the Pacific from June 1, 1944, to April 10, 1945: Saipan, Okinawa, and Iwo Jima. Many names and addresses of soldiers in action are included.

1663. Smith, Capt. Douglas M., and Cecil Carnes. *American Guerrilla Fighting behind the Enemy Lines.* Indianapolis: Bobbs-Merrill Co., 1943. 316pp.

1664. Snow, Edgar. *Battle for Asia.* New York: Random House, 1941. 433pp.

The story of China from 1937 through 1941, with an eye-witness account of the Battle of Shanghai, the rape of Nanking, and Japan's guerilla tactics.

1665. ———. *The Pattern of Soviet Power.* New York: Random House, 1945. xii + 219pp.

1666. ———. *People on Our Side.* New York: Random House, 1944. xi + 324pp.

Snow writes about the war in India, Iran, the Near East, Soviet Russia, and China, with considerable material on Chiang Kai-shek, Gandhi, Nehru, and Stalin. Snow foresaw postwar China's rise as a Communist power.

1667. Stowe, Leland. *No Other Road to Freedom*. New York: Alfred A. Knopf, 1941. 432pp.

Stowe's experiences from September 1939 through the spring of 1941 in covering Russia's invasion of Finland and events in Norway and the Balkans. Some of this material appeared originally in the Chicago *Daily News* and *Life*.

1668. ———. *They Shall Not Sleep*. New York: Alfred A. Knopf, 1944. 399pp.

Notes from Stowe's diary, July 1941 to December 1942. He seeks to shed light on potential postwar problems in China, Burma, and India. His theme is essentially that if tomorrow is not better than today "they [the dead] shall not sleep."

1669. ———. *While Time Remains*. New York: Alfred A. Knopf, 1946. xii + 379pp.

Severely criticizes United States policy concerning the atomic bomb, stresses the need for world government, and discusses the nature of fascism, communism, and democracy.

1670. Taylor, Edmond. *The Strategy of Terror: Europe's Inner Front*. Boston: Houghton Mifflin Co., 1940. 277pp.

1671. Thompson, Dorothy. *Listen, Hans*. Boston: Houghton Mifflin Co., 1942. x + 292pp.

More than half of this book consists of a series of short-wave broadcasts over the Columbia Broadcasting System, 1941–1942, in which Miss Thompson tried to re-establish contact with men and women of like mind in enemy territory. Hans was the disguised name of an old friend, a German patriot who was not a Nazi. The rest of the book is made up of articles on "The Invasion of the German Mind" by the Nazi regime.

1672. Time. *December 7: The First Thirty Hours*. New York: Time, Inc., 1941; Alfred A. Knopf, 1942. vi + 229pp.

Collects the reports of correspondents of *Time*, *Life*, and *Fortune* on December 7, 1941, during the first 30 hours after the Japanese attack on Pearl Harbor.

1673. Tolischus, Otto D., ed. *Through Japanese Eyes*. New York: Reynal and Hitchcock, 1945. 182pp.

Newspaper articles, broadcasts, speeches, magazine articles, and resolutions representing Japanese ideology, and personal accounts by Japanese and Allied soldiers of conditions in Japanese prison camps. The book attempts to foster an understanding of Japanese nationalism. Tolischus had been imprisoned by the Japanese after Pearl Harbor.

1674. ———. *Tokyo Record*. New York: Reynal and Hitchcock, 1943. 449pp.

This diary, January 24, 1941, through August 25, 1942, records Tolischus's 10 months as a correspondent in Japan and 6 subsequent months as a prisoner. He seeks to explain why the Japanese acted as they did.

1675. Treanor, Tom. *One Damn Thing after Another: The Adventures of an Innocent Man Trapped between Public Relations and the Axis*. Garden City, N.Y.: Doubleday, Doran and Co., 1944. ix + 294pp.

Treanor's best accounts are of desert warfare in North Africa, from which he was expelled, and of India, China, Sicily, and Italy (including Cassino and Anzio). He represented the Los Angeles *Times*.

1676. Tregaskis, Richard. *Guadalcanal Diary*. New York: Random House, 1943. 263pp.

Action-filled war reporting of gloomy days in the Southwest Pacific in the late summer of 1942, by a young correspondent for International News Service. The book is more colorful than informational.

1677. ———. *Invasion Diary*. New York: Random House, 1944. 241pp.

Tregaskis's diary for July 9, 1943, to January 13, 1944, covers the invasion of Italy. He tells chiefly of fighting men at the front, and also reports on hospital life.

1678. *The United States Marines on Iwo Jima, by Five Official Marine Combat Writers*. Washington, D.C.: The Infantry Journal, 1945. 312pp.

A report by Capt. Raymond Henri, 1st Lt. Jim G. Lucas, T. Sgt. W. Keyes Beech, T. Sgt. David Dempsey, and T. Sgt. Alvin M. Josephy, Jr.

1679. Weller, George. *Bases Overseas*. New York: Harcourt, Brace and Co., 1944. 424pp.

Based on the premise that future wars are inevitable, this book outlines what America should do *before* the next war, suggests a system of political and strategic bases in the Balkans, Africa, and the Far East, and discusses the politics of America in carrying out future needs. Weller was a correspondent for the Chicago *Daily News*.

1680. ———. *The Belgian Campaign in Ethiopia: A Trek of 2,500 Miles through Jungle, Swamps, and Desert Wastes*. New York: Belgian Information Center, 1941. 24pp.

1681. ———. *Singapore Is Silent*. New York: Harcourt, Brace and Co., 1943. 312pp.

Weller retreated down the Malay Peninsula during the Japanese advance in 1942 and was one of the last to be evacuated. There is good description of jungle fighting.

1682. Wheeler, Keith. *The Pacific Is My Beat*. New York: Books, Inc., distributed by E. P. Dutton and Co., 1943. 383pp.

A Chicago *Daily Times* correspondent's personal story of the first 14 months after Pearl Harbor. Wheeler traveled 50,000 miles through the Aleutians, Marshalls, Wake, and Hawaii. There is also an account of the Doolittle raid over Tokyo. Well illustrated.

1683. ———. *We Are the Wounded*. New York: E. P. Dutton and Co., 1945. 224pp.

A report on the dead and wounded among Marine and Navy personnel in the Battle of Iwo Jima. Wheeler himself was wounded on the second day of the battle and tells an intensely personal story.

1684. White, William L. *Report on the Russians*. New York: Harcourt, Brace and Co., 1945. 309pp.

1685. ———. *They Were Expendable.* New York: Harcourt, Brace and Co., 1942. 209pp.

The story of four men — "what was left of Motor Torpedo Boat Squadron Three" — against the tragic background of the Philippine campaign. Vivid writing.

1686. Williams, Wythe, and William Van Narvig. *Secret Sources: The Story behind Some Famous Scoops.* Chicago and New York: Ziff-Davis Publishing Co., 1943. 326pp. (Introduction by Lowell Thomas.)

Commentator Williams tells how he obtained accurate estimates of Nazi Germany's strength before the war and in the early years of the conflict. His source was Van Narvig, a onetime officer in the Imperial Russian Army who had become an American citizen. Williams guessed within three days the time of Hitler's attack upon Poland. The book includes a considerable portion of Van Narvig's correspondence to Williams.

1687. Wolfert, Ira. *American Guerrilla in the Philippines.* New York: Simon and Schuster, 1945. ix + 222pp.

Tells how a guerrilla army must operate, how it pays its forces, and what its tactics are, through the story of an American officer who remained in the Philippines after the Japanese seizure, coordinated guerrilla activities, and directed communications and public relations.

1688. ———. *Torpedo 8.* Boston: Houghton Mifflin Co., 1943. xi + 127pp.

A highly descriptive account of the men in Torpedo Squadron 8 during the Battle of Midway in 1942.

POST-WORLD WAR II PERIOD

1689. Attwood, William. *The Man Who Could Grow Hair: Or, Inside Andorra.* New York: Alfred A. Knopf, 1949; London: Wingate, 1950. xi + 240pp. (Drawings by Roger Duvoisin.)

Anecdotes of a United States foreign correspondent in Europe and Africa after World War II. Attwood, who served in Paris with the New York *Herald Tribune,* has some sharp words against the Communists.

1690. Beech, Keyes. *Tokyo and Points East.* Garden City, N.Y.: Doubleday and Co., 1954. 255pp.

This account by a correspondent of the Chicago *Daily News* is one of the better books to come out of the Korean War and the Indochina conflict of the early 1950s. There is good material on Communist Chinese "brainwashing" methods; there is also an autobiographical account of a year Beech spent at Harvard as a Nieman Fellow.

1691. Bourke-White, Margaret. *Halfway to Freedom.* New York: Simon and Schuster, 1949. 244pp.

A report on the birth of India and Pakistan, prepared originally on an assignment from *Life.* The volume includes an interview with Gandhi before his assassination.

1692. Brines, Russell. *MacArthur's Japan.* Philadelphia: J. B. Lippincott Co., 1948. 315pp.

PERSONAL NARRATIVES AND ANTHOLOGIES

1693. Cameron, James. *Mandarin Red.* New York: Rinehart and Co., 1955. vii + 334pp.

The report of a London *News Chronicle* reporter's visit to Communist China in 1954, including a fascinating chapter on his interview with the soldiers of the United Nations force who deserted to the Red Chinese in 1952. The account is more descriptive than analytical.

1694. ———. *Touch of the Sun.* London: H. F. and G. Witherby, Ltd., 1950. 311pp.

Cameron, reporting for the London *Daily Express* and *Picture Post*, covered the birth of independent India, atomic-bomb tests in the Pacific, and the first summer of the Korean War. His book is somewhat haphazard in organization.

1695. Childs, Marquis W. *The Ragged Edge: The Diary of a Crisis.* Garden City, N.Y.: Doubleday and Co., 1955. 251pp.

Childs's record of world events from the Big Four Ministers' meeting in Berlin through the Geneva Conference, February 15, 1954, to August 30, 1954. Childs puts the prolonged contest with communism in clear perspective and warns against the careless way in which Americans regard the situation.

1696. Cooke, Dwight. *There Is No Asia.* Garden City, N.Y.: Doubleday and Co., 1954. 320pp.

A news and public affairs analyst for the Columbia Broadcasting System reports on nations of Asia "vital to our political and economic survival": the Philippines, Japan, Korea, Formosa, Hong Kong, Indonesia, Malaya, Indochina, Thailand, Burma, India, and Pakistan.

1697. Dille, John. *Substitute for Victory.* Garden City, N.Y.: Doubleday and Co., 1954. 219pp.

An analysis of the Korean War by a correspondent for *Life.* Dille is optimistic about the long-range result of the Korean settlement.

1698. Ebener, Charlotte. *No Facilities for Women.* New York: Alfred A. Knopf, 1955. ix + 283pp.

Miss Ebener, an International News Service correspondent and free-lancer, covers a decade of postwar experiences in Russia and Red China, India, Indochina, Tibet, and the Holy Land, with occasional ventures into Europe. The book is far more solid than its flippant title indicates.

1699. Fernsworth, Lawrence. *Spain's Struggle for Freedom.* Boston: Beacon Press, 1957. vii + 376pp.

A correspondent who served the London *Times* in Spain for 10 years regards Spain's struggle as an "epic of unfaltering courage on the part of an unbeatable people." The book includes considerable history, with the Spanish Civil War put into perspective; there is also material on United States–Spanish relations.

1699a. Fischer, Louis. *Russia Revisited: A New Look at Russia and Her Satellites.* Garden City, N.Y.: Doubleday and Co., 1957. 288pp.

A foreign correspondent who had covered the Soviet Union from 1922 to 1938 returns 18 years later and reports his impressions of post-Stalin Russia. He analyzes the Soviet Union's contemporary problems in East Germany, Poland, and Hungary.

1700. Forman, Harrison. *Blunder in Asia.* New York: Didier, 1950. 190pp.

A report on the Red regime in China, from Manchuria to Shanghai, by a reporter of 20 years' service in the Far East. It includes interviews with both Communist and Nationalist leaders.

1701. Gayn, Mark. *Japan Diary.* New York: William Sloane Associates; Toronto: George J. McLeod, 1948. x + 517pp.

A reporter for the Chicago *Sun* seeks to interpret what happened in Japan and Korea under the American Occupation, December 5, 1945, to December 21, 1946, with a brief summary bringing the account down to May 3, 1948. Gayn is highly critical of the handling by the United States of the Korean situation and pessimistic about Japan's sincerity in professing peaceful intentions.

1702. Gunther, John. *Behind the Curtain.* New York: Harper and Brothers, 1949. 363pp.

1703. ———. *Inside Africa.* New York: Harper and Brothers, 1955. xxiii + 952pp.

A rapidly moving account of Gunther's travels to 105 African localities and of interviews with more than 1,500 persons. Gunther's "Inside" books are all highly readable but without depth of interpretation. They become quickly dated.

1704. ———. *Inside Russia Today.* New York: Harper and Brothers, 1958. 550pp.

A good description of the Russian people, with many details.

1705. ———. *The Riddle of MacArthur: Japan, Korea, and the Far East.* New York: Harper and Brothers, 1951. xiv + 240pp.

Gunther deals mostly with the MacArthur regime in Japan, which he regarded as "one of the worst-reported stories in history." The account carries through December 1950, six months after the North Korean invasion of South Korea. Parts of the book first appeared in *Look.*

1706. Hailey, Foster Bowman. *Half of One World.* New York: The Macmillan Co., 1950. x + 207pp.

An effort by a New York *Times* reporter to arouse interest among Americans in the problems of Asia. Hailey covered the Far East for the *Times* during World War II and in 1946–1947.

1707. Hartwell, Dickson, and Andrew A. Rooney, eds. *Off the Record: The Best Stories of Foreign Correspondents.* Garden City, N.Y.: Doubleday and Co., 1952. xxv + 324pp.

Nearly 100 correspondents contribute articles on censors, scoops, the Iron Curtain, and life among correspondents. Mostly light in treatment.

1708. Herrmann, Lazar [pseud. Leo Lania]. *The Nine Lives of Europe.* New York: Funk and Wagnalls Co., in association with United Nations World, 1950. x + 278pp.

Lania, a roving correspondent for *United Nations World* magazine, analyzes postwar spiritual and intellectual developments in Europe.

1709. Higgins, Marguerite. *Red Plush and Black Bread*. Garden City, N.Y.: Doubleday and Co., 1955. 256pp. (Illustrated with photographs by the author.)

> The report of a 13,500-mile trip through Russia and Siberia late in 1954. Miss Higgins, a reporter for the New York *Herald Tribune*, gives surface observations rather than analysis. She is fair-minded in her account.

1710. ———. *War in Korea: The Report of a Woman Combat Correspondent*. Garden City, N.Y.: Doubleday and Co., 1951. 223pp.

1711. *Indonesia Report: The Collected Dispatches of the American Correspondents Who Died in Bombay, India, July 12, 1949, on Their Return from a Tour of Indonesia*. Tucson, Ariz.: The Arizona Daily Star, 1949. About 50 bound leaves, illustrated. (Foreword by William R. Mathews, editor of the *Arizona Daily Star*.)

> Of 15 correspondents who made this trip to Indonesia, 13 were killed in a plane crash. Mathews and Dorothy Brandon of the New York *Herald Tribune* escaped death because they had returned to the United States independently. This memorial collection is representative of foreign correspondence at its best. Writers whose dispatches are included were Nathaniel A. Barrows, Chicago *Daily News*; James H. Branyan, Houston *Post*; Frederick W. Colvig, Denver *Post*; Charles E. Gratke, *Christian Science Monitor*; S. Burton Heath, Newspaper Enterprise Assn.; Bertram D. Hulen, New York *Times*; George Moorad, Portland *Oregonian*; William H. Newton, Scripps-Howard Newspaper Alliance; H. R. Knickerbocker, Radio Station WOR, New York; Thomas A. Falco, *Business Week*; Jack Werkley, *Time*; Vince Mahoney, San Francisco *Chronicle*; Elsie Dick, Mutual Broadcasting Co.

1712. Kato, Masuo. *The Lost War: A Japanese Reporter's Inside Story*. New York: Alfred A. Knopf, 1946. 264pp.

> The personal narrative of a former Domei correspondent who, after Japan's surrender, became managing editor of Kyodo, the new Japanese press association.

1713. Kelley, Frank, and Cornelius Ryan. *Star-Spangled Mikado*. New York: Robert M. McBride and Co., 1947. 282pp.

> A biased book by reporters for, respectively, the New York *Herald Tribune* and the London *Daily Telegraph*. Their treatment of Gen. Douglas MacArthur verges on the flippant; they criticize severely his censorship policies.

1714. Lauterbach, Richard E. *Danger from the East*. New York and London: Harper and Brothers, 1947. xi + 430pp.

> A postwar analysis of Japan, Korea, and China, based on material gathered during an assignment for *Life* and a year of study at Harvard as a Nieman Fellow. The work is well buttressed with documentary appendixes.

1715. Lazareff, Mrs. Helene, and Pierre Lazareff. *Soviet Union after Stalin*. London: Odhams Press, 1955; New York: Philosophical Library, 1956. 254pp. (Translated into English by David Hughes.)

> The Lazareffs of *France Soir* base their report on Russia on a survey made in 1954. Their comments are principally devoted to everyday life, art, automo-

biles, housing, the Soviet press, radio, television, literature, theater, and religion.

1716. Lucas, Jim. *Our Fighting Heart: The Story of the Republic of Korea Armed Forces*. Washington, D.C.: Korean Pacific Press, 1952. 17pp.

1717. Magidoff, Robert. *In Anger and in Pity: A Report on Russia*. Garden City, N.Y.: Doubleday, 1949. 278pp.

Magidoff, a Russian-born American journalist, was ordered to leave Russia after 12 years' service there as a foreign correspondent. His book, in part autobiographical, is dispassionate in its observations on life in Russia.

1718. ———. *The Kremlin vs. the People: The Story of the Cold Civil War in Stalin's Russia*. Garden City, N.Y.: Doubleday, 1953. 288pp.

1719. Matthews, Herbert. *The U.S. and Latin America*. New York: Foreign Policy Assn., 1953. 62pp. (Headline Series No. 100.)

1720. ——— and Nancie Matthews. *Assignment to Austerity: An American Family in Britain*. Indianapolis: Bobbs-Merrill Co., 1950. 338pp.

A narrative of four and a half years in England by a New York *Times* correspondent and his wife. Herbert contributes 11 pieces, principally on politics and economics; Nancie's 7 pieces are more personal.

1721. Middleton, Drew. *The Defense of Western Europe*. New York: Appleton-Century-Crofts, 1952. 313pp.

An assessment of the progress made by the United States and other powers of the North Atlantic Treaty Organization toward averting World War III, based on interviews with generals, politicians, and soldiers in the field. Middleton served the Associated Press and the New York *Times*.

1722. ———. *The Struggle for Germany*. Indianapolis: Bobbs-Merrill Co., 1949. 304pp.

1723. ———. *These Are the British*. New York: Alfred A. Knopf, 1957. viii + 290 + iii pp.

As London correspondent for the New York *Times*, Middleton analyzes the strengths and weaknesses of contemporary Britain. He includes a discussion of personalities and customs.

1724. Overseas Press Club of America. *Deadline Delayed*. New York: E. P. Dutton and Co., 1947. 311pp.

Twenty-two accounts by members of the Overseas Press Club of events that for various reasons (censorship, space, or failure to recognize significance) had not previously been reported. Each article contains a short biographical sketch of its author. Reporters whose selections appear include Bob Considine, Pierre J. Huss, Edgar Snow, Richard Tregaskis, Irene Kuhn, and Ruth Cowan.

1725. Overseas Writers. *The George Polk Case: Report of the Special Committee to Inquire into the Murder at Salonika, Greece, May 16, 1948, of Columbia Broadcasting System Correspondent George Polk*. Washington, D.C., n.d. 76pp.

Significant material going into all phases of the murder, presumably by conspirators, of an American reporter on assignment to cover the Greek Civil

War. The report includes a verbatim broadcast by Edward R. Murrow and others of CBS on April 27, 1949, summarizing the findings.

1726. Reed, Douglas. *Far and Wide*. London: Jonathan Cape, 1951. 398pp.

A one-time European correspondent for the London *Times* reports on travel in the United States and on post-World War II events generally.

1727. Reynolds, Quentin. *Leave It to the People*. New York: Random House, 1949. x + 341pp.

Reynolds records his travels through Germany, France, Italy, Greece, Norway, the Netherlands, and Israel; he talked to "average people" — farmers, clerks, chorus girls — and sometimes cabinet ministers and reports a strong faith in democracy. The book is somewhat superficial.

1728. Rowan, Carl T. *The Pitiful and the Proud*. New York: Random House, 1956. 432pp.

A Negro correspondent for the Minneapolis *Tribune* reports on a survey of southern and southeastern Asia, with particular reference to India. This is a competent piece of work on a difficult assignment — that of being objective and unmoved by "loyalties" of race, politics, or economics. There is an excellent discussion of the Indian press.

1729. St. John, Robert. *The Silent People Speak*. Garden City, N.Y.: Doubleday and Co., 1948. xvi + 397pp.

1730. ———. *Through Malan's Africa: Land of Hope and Fear*. Garden City, N.Y.: Doubleday and Co., 1954. 315pp.

An analysis of the South African situation, principally with regard to racial problems but taking up also other major issues, such as land distribution.

1731. Salisbury, Harrison E. *American in Russia*. New York: Harper and Brothers, 1955. x + 328pp.

As Moscow correspondent of the New York *Times*, 1949–1954, Salisbury traversed the whole of the Soviet Union. Writing after his return to New York and, therefore, free of censorship, he gives his personal impressions of political and social life in Russia. A portion of the book first appeared in the New York *Times*.

1732. Sheean, Vincent. *This House against This House*. New York: Random House, 1946. 420pp.

Sheean begins with Versailles, traces his own experiences in World War II, and carries through the San Francisco Conference of 1945. As in his other books, the philosophical slant is strong.

1733. Stowe, Leland. *Conquest by Terror: The Story of Satellite Europe*. New York: Random House, 1952. 300pp.

1734. Sulzberger, C. L. *The Big Thaw: A Personal Exploration of the "New" Russia and the Orbit Countries*. New York: Harper and Brothers, 1956. 275pp.

Based principally on reports to the New York *Times* concerning post-Stalin Soviet Russia. Because of travel restrictions on correspondents, Sulzberger can deal only in a limited way with Communist China, North Korea, North Vietnam, Mongolia, and Tibet.

1735. Taylor, Edmond. *Richer by Asia*. Boston: Houghton Mifflin Co., 1947. x + 432pp.

1736. Trumbull, Robert. *As I See India*. New York: William Sloane Associates, 1956. 256pp.

A report on observations of more than seven years by a New York *Times* correspondent. There is a good analysis of the creation of an independent India and Pakistan, Gandhi's last year of life, Nehru's problems, and the Communist issue. India's press is treated only incidentally.

1737. Visson, André. *As Others See Us*. Garden City, N.Y.: Doubleday and Co., 1948. 252pp.

Visson collects reports and descriptive observations of foreign journalists on the United States.

1738. White, Theodore H. *Fire in the Ashes: Europe in Mid-Century*. New York: William Sloane Associates, 1953. 405pp.

An analysis of Europe rising from the ruins of World War II, with particular emphasis on England, France, and West Germany. There is considerable material on the North Atlantic Treaty Organization.

1739. ——— and Annalee Jacoby. *Thunder Out of China*. New York: William Sloane Associates, 1946. xvi + 331pp.

Reporters for *Time* analyze the forces of change working "more critically and more explosively in China than anywhere else [in Asia]."

1740. White, William L. *Land of Milk and Honey*. New York: Harcourt Brace and Co., 1949. viii + 312pp.

The story of a Russian Air Force officer, Vasili Kotov, who left Russia after he had seen the Western world during World War II.

E. Political, Economic, and Social Reporting and Correspondence

1741. Allen, Robert S., ed. *Our Fair City*. New York: Vanguard Press, 1947. viii + 387pp.

Pieces on municipal affairs by reporters in 17 metropolitan areas. The writers are in general extremely critical of American municipal government. The cities covered are Boston, New York, Philadelphia, Miami, Birmingham (Ala.), Cleveland, Detroit, Chicago, Milwaukee, Memphis, St. Louis, Kansas City, Denver, Butte, Seattle, San Francisco, and Los Angeles.

1742. ———. *Our Sovereign State*. New York: Vanguard Press, 1949. xxxviii + 413pp.

Parallels *Our Fair City* on the state level. The volume characterizes American state government as "the tawdriest, most incompetent, and most stultifying unit of the nation's political structure." Included are Massachusetts, New York, Pennsylvania, Georgia, Ohio, Illinois, Wisconsin, Nebraska, Texas, Utah, and California.

1743. Allen, Robert S., and Drew Pearson. *Washington Merry-Go-Round*. New York: Horace Liveright, 1931. 366pp.

The "merry-go-round" books on inside Washington have been among the best sellers relating to the ways of politicians in the capital. As young men, the authors built reputations as dopester-columnists in part through these books.

1744. ———. *More Merry-Go-Round*. New York: Horace Liveright, 1932. 482pp.

1745. Allen, Robert S., and William V. Shannon. *The Truman Merry-Go-Round*. New York: Vanguard Press, 1950. 502pp.

1746. Andrews, Bert. *Washington Witch Hunt*. New York: Random House, 1948. 218pp.

A Washington correspondent analyzes the threats to civil liberties in early post-World War II years.

1746a. Ashmore, Harry S. *An Epitaph for Dixie*. New York: W. W. Norton and Co., 1958. 189pp.

The executive editor of the *Arkansas Gazette* (Little Rock) interprets the racial integration crisis in the South. A middle-ground southerner, Ashmore draws upon personal experience for his provocative and careful analysis.

1747. Beaverbrook, Lord. *Politicians and the Press*. London: Hutchinson and Co., 1925. 127pp.

1748. ———. *Politicians and the War, 1914–1916*. Vol. I, London: Thornton Butterworth, Ltd., 1928. Vol. II, London: Lane Publications, 1932. 254pp., total.

Beaverbrook treats extensively Britain's part in World War I, in particular justifying his own role. He refers at length to Lord Northcliffe's activities and to control of propaganda.

1749. Budenz, Louis F. *The Techniques of Communism*. Chicago: Henry Regnery Co., 1954. viii + 342pp.

A former managing editor of the *Daily Worker* tells how Americans can meet the threat of Soviet Communism. There is a chapter on the role of the Communist press.

1750. Childs, Marquis. *Eisenhower, Captive Hero: A Critical Study of the General and the President*. New York: Harcourt, Brace and Co., 1958. 310pp.

A columnist analyzes the wide discrepancy between Eisenhower's great reputation at the peak of his career and his apparent lack of accomplishment as President in achieving world peace. The book is based principally on Childs's own knowledge of events as a reporter, with some material being obtained from earlier "worshipful" literature on Eisenhower. Childs is fair-minded throughout.

1751. ———. *I Write from Washington*. New York and London: Harper and Brothers, 1942. ix + 331pp.

An excellent book on the capital scene written by Childs while he was a staff member of the St. Louis *Post-Dispatch*. The period covered is 1933 to United States entry into World War II. There is good material on the election campaigns of 1936 and 1940.

1752. Clapper, Olive Ewing. *Washington Tapestry*. New York and London: Whittlesey House, McGraw-Hill Book Co., 1946. 303pp.

The widow of columnist Raymond Clapper discusses Washington events from 1917 to the death of Franklin D. Roosevelt. Mrs. Clapper used her husband's diaries and notes and added material of her own. The information on Mrs. Eleanor Roosevelt is useful.

1753. Clark, Delbert. *Washington Dateline.* New York: Frederick A. Stokes Co., 1941. 322pp.

A report on how Washington was covered (at the beginning of World War II) by 500 correspondents of American and foreign newspapers. It is exceedingly useful today for its material on Franklin D. Roosevelt's press relations and the Office of Government Reports.

1754. Cochrane, Elizabeth [Nellie Bly]. *Ten Days in a Mad-House: Or, Nellie Bly's Experience on Blackwell's Island, Feigning Insanity in Order to Reveal Asylum Horrors.* New York: N. L. Munro, 1887. 120pp.

1755. Coffin, Tristram. *Missouri Compromise.* Boston: Little, Brown and Co., 1947. 315pp.

A readable account of the first two years of the Truman administration. Part of the material had been prepared as broadcasts for the Columbia Broadcasting System and as articles for *Coronet*, the *Nation*, and the *New Republic*.

1756. Davis, Elmer. *But We Were Born Free.* Indianapolis and New York: Bobbs-Merrill Co., 1954. 229pp.

A strong expression of the American's right to think as he pleases and to say what he thinks, by the chief news analyst of the American Broadcasting Co.

1757. ———. *Two Minutes to Midnight.* Indianapolis and New York: Bobbs-Merrill Co., 1955. ix + 207pp.

Davis warns of America's peril in the face of possible thermonuclear conflict.

1758. Deutsch, Albert. *The Shame of the States.* New York: Harcourt, Brace and Co., 1948. 188pp. (Introduction by Dr. Karl A. Menninger.)

Based on crusading articles originally prepared by Deutsch for *PM* and the New York *Star*. His findings helped to force a congressional investigation of conditions in mental hospitals.

1759. Donovan, Robert J. *Eisenhower: The Inside Story.* New York: Harper and Brothers, 1956. xviii + 423pp.

Donovan, a reporter for the New York *Herald Tribune*, had access to considerable unpublished information relating to the first Eisenhower administration. For the most part, his account is descriptive and objective. Part of the material was published in the *Herald Tribune* as "Eisenhower in the White House."

1760. Essary, J. Frederick. *Covering Washington: Government Reflected to the Public in the Press, 1822–1926.* Boston and New York: Houghton Mifflin Co., 1927. viii + 280pp.

A reporter for the Baltimore *Sun* aims to explain the relation between Washington reporters and government officials. His account is based largely on personal experience. There are good chapters on presidential travels, conflicts between press and Congress, and the development of the Gridiron Club.

1761. Godkin, Edwin Lawrence. *Problems of Modern Democracy: Political and Economic Essays.* New York: Charles Scribner's Sons, 1898. 332pp.

1762. ———. *Unforeseen Tendencies of Democracy.* New York: Houghton Mifflin Co., 1898. vii + 265pp.

1763. Greeley, Horace. *Essays Designed to Elucidate the Science of Political Economy while Serving to Explain and Defend the Policy of Protection to Home Industry as a System of National Co-operation for the Elevation of Labor.* Philadelphia: Porter and Coates, 1869. 384pp.

Horace Greeley found enough time amid his "exacting vocation" as an editor to write on economics with all the assurance gained by "experience and observation of nearly half a century." He wrote in a simple, lucid style in order to reach the "common people."

1764. ———. *Hints toward Reforms.* New York: Fowlers and Wells, 1854. 425pp.

A second edition of a work issued by Greeley in 1850 to compile his lectures and other writings. Among the more valuable essays are those on homestead exemption, slavery, and the nature and effect of alcoholic liquor and tobacco. Twenty-four of the 30 essays had first appeared in the New York *Tribune.*

1765. ———, with John F. Cleveland. *A Political Text-Book for 1860.* New York: New York Tribune Assn., Aug. 1, 1860. 253pp.

A magnificent drawing together of the issues of the Lincoln presidential campaign which reveals the thoroughness that Greeley exercised in his political activities.

1766. Gunther, John. *Inside U.S.A.* New York and London: Harper and Brothers, 1947. xvi + 979pp.

1767. Kent, Frank R. *The Great Game of Politics: An Effort to Present the Elementary Human Facts about Politics, Politicians, and Political Machines, Candidates and Their Ways for the Benefit of the Average Citizen.* Garden City, N.Y.: Doubleday, Page and Co., 1923. xiv + 322pp.

One of the most readable books on the practical philosophy and psychology of politics. Chapters on newspaper political coverage and newspaper political policy are included. Kent was a Baltimore *Sun* political reporter.

1768. Kiplinger, W. M. *Washington Is like That.* New York and London: Harper and Brothers, 1942. 522pp.

"Inside" reporting on the capital by the editor of the *Kiplinger News Letter.* Kiplinger ranges from Washington glamour and the White House to propaganda and censorship, the press corps, lobbyists, and tourists.

1769. Lawrence, David. *Diary of a Washington Correspondent.* New York: H. C. Kinsey and Co., 1942. 356pp.

Notes by the editor of *United States News and World Report,* May 1940 to May 1942.

1770. Lubell, Samuel. *Revolt of the Moderates*. New York: Harper and Brothers, 1956. ix + 308pp.

A political reporter noted as an interpreter of "grass-roots" sentiment studies the national trend toward conservatism during the Eisenhower presidency and provides good sketches of political leaders of the early 1950s.

1771. Lucy, Sir Henry. *Men and Manner in Parliament*. New York: E. P. Dutton and Co., 1919. 259pp. (First issued anonymously in 1874.)

A reissue of articles appearing in the *Gentleman's Magazine* many years earlier. Lucy for years wrote for *Punch* the humorous "Diary of Toby, M.P."

1772. Lynch, Denis Tilden. *Criminals and Politicians*. New York: The Macmillan Co., 1932. 256pp.

This series of articles was written originally for the New York *Herald Tribune*.

1773. MacDonagh, Michael. *The Book of Parliament*. London: Isbister and Co., Ltd., 1897. xii + 452pp.

A reporter's analysis of British parliamentary procedures.

1774. ———. *The Pageant of Parliament*. London: T. Fisher Unwin, Ltd., 1921. 2 vols. 493pp., total.

A description of Parliament's activities, including an analysis of "Parliament and the Press."

1775. ———. *The Reporters' Gallery*. London: Hodder and Stoughton, 1913. xii + 452pp.

A history of the struggle between Parliament and the press over the privilege of reporting debates in Commons and in Lords. The work is based upon a quarter-century of experience as a parliamentary reporter. There are good descriptions of Samuel Johnson, Samuel Taylor Coleridge, and Charles Dickens as parliamentary reporters, as well as an account of the rise of Hansard.

1776. Martineau, Harriet. *The Martyr Age of the United States*. Boston: Weeks, Jordan and Co., and Otis, Broaders and Co.; New York: John S. Taylor, 1839. 84pp.

A tract written after Miss Martineau's return to England from an American visit in which she expresses strong abolitionist views. There is considerable detail on the killing of Elijah P. Lovejoy, on James G. Birney, and on the congressional "Gag Bill" of 1836 to prohibit transmitting of abolitionist material through the mails. Miss Martineau's commentary first appeared in the *Westminster Review*.

1777. Mencken, H. L. *A Carnival of Buncombe*. Baltimore: Johns Hopkins Press, 1956. (Edited by Malcolm Moos.)

A collection of political pieces written for the Baltimore *Evening Sun* in the 1920s and 1930s and not before published in book form.

1778. Merz, Charles. *The Great American Band Wagon*. New York: The John Day Co., 1928. 263pp.

Merz, a staff member of the New York *Times*, offers good material on the political scene of the 1920s.

1779. Moley, Raymond. *After Seven Years.* New York and London: Harper and Brothers, 1939. xi + 445pp.

Moley's view of political events in the first two terms of Franklin D. Roosevelt. He gives an account of his break with the President and his later venture into journalism with the news magazine *Today* (now *Newsweek*).

1780. ————. *27 Masters of Politics in a Personal Perspective.* New York: Funk and Wagnalls Co., 1947. xii + 276pp.

Profiles based upon Moley's personal acquaintance with the subjects. The 27 include "political teachers," party nominees, party managers, advisers, and congressmen. One is Charles Michelson, newspaperman and publicity chairman for the Democratic party.

1781. Morris, Joe Alex. *What a Year!* New York: Harper and Brothers, 1956. xii + 338pp.

A history of 1929, with excellent material on bootlegging, show business, sports, the press, big business, and the Wall Street crash, as well as politics.

1782. Mowrer, Edgar Ansel. *Challenge and Decision: A Program for the Times of Crisis Ahead for World Peace under American Leadership.* New York: McGraw-Hill Book Co., 1950. ix + 291pp.

1783. ————. *The Nightmare of American Foreign Policy.* New York: Alfred A. Knopf, 1948. viii + 283pp.

1784. Mowrer, Paul Scott. *Our Foreign Affairs: A Study in National Interest and the New Diplomacy.* New York: E. P. Dutton and Co., 1924. xii + 348pp.

1785. Nicholas, H. G. *The British General Election of 1950.* London: The Macmillan Co., Ltd., 1951. x + 353pp.

Nearly a third of this research study is devoted to party manifestoes and broadcasts and to the press. There is also material on public opinion polls.

1786. Nock, Albert Jay. *A Journal of These Days, June 1932–December 1933.* New York: William Morrow and Co., 1934. x + 309pp.

Nock was formerly editor of the *Freeman* and a writer for the *New Republic* and the *Atlantic.*

1787. ————. *Journal of Forgotten Days, May 1934–October 1935.* Hinsdale, Ill.: Henry Regnery Co., 1948. 145pp.

A continuation of *A Journal of These Days.*

1788. Olmsted, Frederick Law. *The Cotton Kingdom: A Traveller's Observations on Cotton and Slavery in the American Slave States.* New York: Alfred A. Knopf, 1953. lxiii + 626 + xvi pp. (Edited, with an introduction and notes, by Arthur M. Schlesinger.)

During his short career as a reporter for the New York *Times* in the 1850s, Olmsted wrote penetrating analyses of the American South that have stood tests of accuracy for a century. In this anthology are collected reports from three of Olmsted's volumes on southern conditions. The full accounts are contained in *A Journey in the Seaboard Slave States* (New York: Dix and Edwards, 1856, 724pp.); *A Journey through Texas* (New York: Dix and Edwards,

1857, 516pp.); and *A Journey in the Back Country* (New York: Mason Brothers, 1860, 492pp.).

1789. Pearson, Drew, and Robert S. Allen. *The Nine Old Men.* Garden City. N.Y.: Doubleday, Doran and Co., 1936. 325pp.

An analysis, partly biographical, of the extremely conservative United States Supreme Court that invalidated much of the early New Deal legislation. The book was a best seller.

1790. Pearson, Drew, and Jack Anderson. *U.S.A.: Second Class Power?* New York: Simon and Schuster, 1958. xi + 334pp.

The authors impress upon America the need to face the fact that the United States must meet the challenge of Soviet advancement since the first successful satellite launching.

1791. Phillips, Cabell, ed. *Dateline: Washington — The Story of National Affairs Journalism in the Life and Times of the National Press Club.* New York: Doubleday and Co., 1949. vii + 307pp. (Introduction by Arthur Krock.)

Eighteen National Press Club members seek to tell the history of Washington reporting from 1800 to the present. A good book, even though not penetrating in its analysis; of most interest is a discussion of changes in writing style. Each chapter includes an identifying sketch of its author.

1792. Phillips, David Graham. *The Treason of the Senate.* New York: Monthly Review Press, by arrangement with Academic Reprints, Stanford University, 1953. 100pp.

A reissue of nine articles written by Phillips for *Cosmopolitan Magazine* in 1906, in which he exposed corrupt practices of members of the United States Senate. Phillips's series was among the most conspicuous muckraking of the period. Illustrated.

1793. Rosten, Leo C. *The Washington Correspondents.* New York: Harcourt, Brace and Co., 1937. xx + 435pp.

One of the earliest and most thorough empirical studies of the nature of the press corps in Washington, this book provides a mass of serviceable statistics on 127 correspondents for 186 different newspapers. Carefully considered are problems of press conferences, relationships with news sources, publicity, the meaning of news, and the relationship between the press and democracy. The bibliography is excellent. Even though dated, the book remains extremely valuable.

1794. Rowan, Carl T. *Go South to Sorrow.* New York: Random House, 1957. viii + 246pp.

Rowan, a Negro reporter for the Minneapolis *Tribune*, gives excellent background on the integration crises that made national headlines in the 1950s. He writes with anger and is pessimistic about the future of civil liberties in the South.

1795. ———. *South of Freedom.* New York: Alfred A. Knopf, 1952. viii + 270pp.

Rowan's moving story of his return to his native South after he had established himself professionally as a newspaperman. His account grew out of a series of articles written for the Minneapolis *Tribune*.

1796. Sidebotham, Herbert. *Political Profiles from British Public Life*. Boston and New York: Houghton Mifflin Co., 1921. viii + 256pp. (English edition carries the title *Pillars of the State*. London: Nisbet and Co.)

Useful for material on the parliamentary press gallery. There is also a series of articles on 18 leading Britons of the day. Sidebotham was a political commentator for the London *Times*.

1797. Smith, Merriman. *Meet Mr. Eisenhower*. New York: Harper and Brothers, 1955. x + 308pp.

An informal study of the general-become-President. The book includes material on Eisenhower and the press.

1798. ———. *A President Is Many Men*. New York and London: Harper and Brothers, 1948. x + 269pp.

Smith discusses the growth of responsibilities within the presidential office; this book is based upon his observations during the Roosevelt and Truman administrations.

1799. ———. *Thank You, Mr. President: A White House Notebook*. New York and London: Harper and Brothers, 1946. x + 304pp.

Smith, the United Press correspondent assigned to the White House, was the recognized spokesman for the press corps at presidential conferences. Here he tells about his experiences with Franklin D. Roosevelt and Harry S. Truman. There is a tendency toward flippancy in his describing White House coverage as a journalistic "rat race."

1800. Sprigle, Ray. *In the Land of Jim Crow*. New York: Simon and Schuster, 1949. viii + 215pp.

A Pulitzer-prize winning reporter for the Pittsburgh *Post-Gazette* who spent four weeks in the South impersonating a Negro recounts his experiences. The material first appeared as a series of news-feature articles.

1801. Steffens, Lincoln. *Lincoln Steffens Speaking*. New York: Harcourt, Brace and Co., 1936. xii + 315pp.

1802. ———. *The Shame of the Cities*. New York: McClure, Phillips and Co., 1907. v + 306pp.

Steffens's powerful accounts of corruption were written originally for *McClure's*. A half-century later these articles still sound a call "for civic pride." The cities discussed are St. Louis, Minneapolis, Pittsburgh, Philadelphia, Chicago, and New York.

1803. ———. *The Struggle for Self-Government: Being an Attempt to Trace American Political Corruption to Its Sources in Six States of the United States, with a Dedication to the Czar*. New York: McClure, Phillips and Co., 1906. xxiii + 294pp.

Steffens's account of the course of popular government in Missouri, Illinois, Wisconsin, Rhode Island, Ohio, and New Jersey.

1804. Sullivan, Mark, ed. *National Floodmarks: Week by Week Obser-*

vations on American Life as Seen by Collier's. New York: George
H. Doran Co., 1915. xvii + 391pp.

1805. Thompson, Dorothy. *Dorothy Thompson's Political Guide: A
Study of American Liberalism and Its Relationship to Modern Totali-
tarian States.* New York: Stackpole Sons, 1938. 120pp.

1806. ⸻. *Let the Record Speak.* Boston: Houghton Mifflin Co.,
1939. vii + 408pp.

1807. Townsend, George Alfred. *Washington, Outside and Inside: A Pic-
ture and a Narrative of the Origin, Growth, Excellences, Abuses,
Beauties, and Personages of Our Governing City.* Hartford, Conn.:
James Betts and Co., 1873. 751pp.

A distinguished Civil War reporter who became a Washington correspondent
for the Chicago *Tribune* gives a good view of a burgeoning city steeped in
Grant-era corruption. Thoroughly done is an account of the Credit Mobilier
scandal. There is also a good chapter on the press and its relations with government. Impressionistic, disorganized, and somewhat long-winded, but fascinating.

1808. *We Saw It Happen: The News behind the News That's Fit to
Print,* by 13 Correspondents of the New York *Times.* New York:
Simon and Schuster, 1939. viii + 379pp. (Edited by Shepard Stone
and Hanson W. Baldwin.)

"Descriptive history" written by newspaper observers to explain events of the
1930s. Arthur Krock writes on Roosevelt's Washington; G. E. R. Gedye on
Vienna; R. Raymond Daniell on the general United States scene; Frank Nu-
gent and Douglas Churchill on Hollywood; Elliott V. Bell on American
finance; Ferdinand Kuhn, Jr., on Great Britain; Russell Owen on the Antarctic;
John Kieran on sports; William R. Conklin on New York City politics; Hugh
Byas on Japan; Brooks Atkinson on drama; and Louis Stark on crime and
the Sacco-Vanzetti case. One of the best cooperative analyses of the period.

1809. Webb, Duncan. *Deadline for Crime.* London: Frederick Muller,
Ltd., 1955. 237pp.

A London reporter gives an account of major criminal investigations in which
he engaged in the early 1950s. The book is low in literary quality but strong
in detail on the British underworld.

1810. White, William Allen. *What It's All about: Being a Reporter's
Story of the Early Campaign of 1936.* New York: The Macmillan
Co., 1936. vii + 146pp.

1811. *The World at Home: Selections from the Writings of Anne O'Hare
McCormick.* New York: Alfred A. Knopf, 1956. xxi + 343 + viii pp.
(Edited by Marion Turner Sheehan; introduction by James B. Res-
ton.)

Thirty-three pieces, excellently written, on conditions in America from the
Florida real estate boom (1925) to the San Francisco Conference (1945). There
are penetrating interpretations of the South, Wall Street, and Franklin D.
Roosevelt. Mrs. McCormick wrote mainly on foreign affairs for the New York

Times, and this is the only readily available collection of her domestic reporting.

1812. *The World's Greatest 99 Days: Scissored and Pasted by Ben Duffy and Harford Powel.* New York: Harper and Brothers, 1933. 90pp.

A book based wholly on a reproduction of news headlines from the first months of the first Franklin D. Roosevelt administration — historically the famous "100 Days."

1813. Ybarra, Thomas R. *America Faces South.* New York: Dodd, Mead and Co., 1939. 321pp.

1814. Young, Eugene J. *Powerful America: Our Place in a Rearming World.* New York: Frederick A. Stokes Co., 1936. x + 386pp.

F. Photography and Cartooning

1815. Abbe, James E. *I Photograph Russia.* New York: Robert M. Mc-Bride Co., 1934. 324pp.

Abbe was a free-lance photographer who also represented the New York *Times* in the early Stalin period. This brash personal account is most interesting for the 80 pictures of Russia it contains, of which some were "forbidden."

1816. Auerbach-Levy, William, and Florence Von Wien. *Is That Me? A Book about Caricature.* New York: Watson-Guptill Publications, 1947. 155pp.

Includes nearly 200 reproductions of Auerbach-Levy's caricatures of modern figures, selected by him from examples of his work appearing in newspapers and magazines.

1817. Biddle, George. *George Biddle's War Drawings.* New York: Hyperion Press, distributed by Duell, Sloan and Pearce, 1944. 78pp.

1818. Block, Herbert. *The Herblock Book: Text and Cartoons.* Boston: Beacon Press, 1952. 244pp.

Block is staff cartoonist of the Washington *Post and Times-Herald.*

1819. ———. *Herblock's Here and Now.* New York: Simon and Schuster, 1955. 279pp.

Principally commentary on the first years of the Eisenhower administration, with text expanding upon the cartoons.

1819a. ———. *Herblock's Special for Today.* New York: Simon and Schuster, 1958. 255pp.

More than 400 Block cartoons, plus the artist's explanatory text, representing his work for the *Post and Times-Herald,* 1956–1958.

1820. Bourke-White, Margaret. *Shooting the Russian War.* New York: Simon and Schuster, 1942. xiv + 287pp.

A photographic account by a *Life* reporter of the Russian people's reaction to German invasion in 1941. It includes an account of how Miss Bourke-White became one of the few to photograph Joseph Stalin.

1821. Briggs, Clare. *The Selected Drawings of Clare Briggs: Memorial Edition.* New York: William H. Wise and Co., 1930. 7 vols.

Briggs's best cartoons, reproduced from the New York *Herald Tribune*. Among those most widely known are "When a Feller Needs a Friend," "There's at Least One in Every Office," and "That Guiltiest Feeling."

1822. Caldwell, Erskine, and Margaret Bourke-White. *Say, Is This the U.S.A.?* New York: Duell, Sloan and Pearce, 1941. 182pp.

A husband and wife collaborate in photographing and describing the United States as they saw it in a cross-country trip.

1823. Capa, Robert. *Slightly Out of Focus*. New York: Henry Holt and Co., 1947. 243pp.

A Hungarian-born photographer for *Collier's* and *Life* in World War II gives his impressions of North Africa in 1942, Sicily and Italy in 1943, invasion of France and liberation of Paris in 1944, and assault on Germany in 1945. The text, on the brash side, is inferior to the pictures.

1824. Craven, Thomas, ed. *Cartoon Cavalcade*. New York: Simon and Schuster, 1943. vii + 456pp. (Assisted by Florence and Sydney Weiss.)

A collection of some of the best American humorous cartoons from 1900 to the 1940s.

1825. Davenport, Homer. *Cartoons*. New York: De Witt Publishing Co. 1898. Unpaged. (Introduction by J. J. Ingalls.)

1826. Edom, Clifton C., ed. *Prize Pictures from the Annual Competition and Exhibition Sponsored by the School of Journalism* [University of Missouri]. Imprint varies, 1944–date.

These pictures first appeared (through 1947) as the *Annual 50-Print Exhibition of Spot News and Feature Pictures* (Columbia, Mo.: University of Missouri Journalism Series, Nos. 98, 104, 108, and 111). The pictures in 1948 were issued in cooperation with the Encyclopaedia Britannica Book of the Year as *The Great Pictures*. After 1949 the volumes carry the title *News Pictures of the Year* (Garden City, N.Y.: Garden City Publishing Co.; New York: Greenberg; and Chicago: L. Mariano).

1827. *Eyes on the World: A Photographic Record of History-in-the-Making*. New York: Simon and Schuster, 1935. 301pp. (Edited by M. Lincoln Schuster.)

Pictures and text attempting to "supplement history" for 1934 and the first part of 1935. The emphasis is heavy on the New Deal, personalities in the news, and United States folkways.

1828. *The Far West*. Boston: Houghton Mifflin Co., 1948. 402pp. (Introduction by Joseph Henry Jackson.)

The editors of *Look* picture the growing Far West in the years after World War II.

1829. Fitzpatrick, Daniel R. *As I Saw It: A Review of Our Times with 311 Cartoons and Notes*. New York: Simon and Schuster, 1953. xvi + 238pp. (Foreword by Joseph Pulitzer, Jr.)

The cartoons of a staff member of the St. Louis *Post-Dispatch* for more than 40 years. They are chiefly political criticism. A profile of Fitzpatrick by Thomas B. Sherman, music critic of the *Post-Dispatch*, is included.

PERSONAL NARRATIVES AND ANTHOLOGIES

1830. Fredericks, Pierce G., ed. *The People's Choice: The Issues of the Campaign as Seen by the Nation's Best Political Cartoonists.* New York: Dodd, Mead and Co., 1956. 100 unnumbered leaves.

A New York *Times* staff member selected these newspaper cartoons from the 1956 presidential election campaign. About 50 cartoonists from all over the country are represented. The selection is partial to neither political party.

1831. Herzberg, Max J., and Leon Mones, eds. *Humor of America.* New York: D. Appleton-Century Co., 1945. xi + 417pp.

1832. Hogben, Lancelot. *From Cave Printing to Comic Strip: A Kaleidoscope of Human Communication.* New York: Chanticleer Press, 1949. 287pp., including 20 in full color and 200 illustrations in black and white.

A survey in pictures and text of the art of communication over something more than 20,000 years. Newspaper strips are included in the contemporary material, as are news pictures of the "Babel of Tongues" in the United Nations.

1832a. Johnson, Gerald W. *The Lines Are Drawn: American Life since the First World War as Reflected in the Pulitzer Prize Cartoons.* Philadelphia: J. B. Lippincott Co., 1958. 224pp.

The most effective Pulitzer-cartoon anthology yet presented. Exceptionally helpful are Johnson's interpretations of the social and political conditions prevailing at the time the cartoons were drawn and his biographical sketches of the prize-winning artists.

1833. Kirby, Rollin. *Highlights: A Cartoon History of the Nineteen-Twenties.* New York: William Farquhar Payson, 1931. xv + 141pp. (Foreword by Walter Lippmann; edited by Henry B. Hoffmann.)

One of the best of the cartoon anthologies. The cartoons, which appeared in the New York *World* from April 11, 1920, to January 23, 1931, expressed that newspaper's editorial policy. Background is provided by reprints of news stories to which the cartoons refer.

1834. Kirkland, Wallace. *Recollections of a Life Photographer.* Boston: Houghton Mifflin Co., 1954. xiv + 272pp.

Kirkland's "adventures" for *Life*, illustrated with a variety of photographs from news and feature assignments. There is heavy emphasis upon oddity.

1835. Kouwenhoven, John A. *Adventures of America, 1857–1900: A Pictorial Record from Harper's Weekly.* New York and London: Harper and Brothers, 1938. Unpaged, 255 prints.

A valuable collection of news pictures of the pre-Civil War slavery conflict, the War and Reconstruction, the industrial era from 1877 to 1893, and the Spanish-American War. Text provides continuity.

1836. Laffan, William Mackay. *Engravings on Wood.* New York: Harper and Brothers, 1887. 15pp. + 25 mounted plates.

Laffan was an art expert and engraver who later became editor and owner of the New York *Sun* and a trustee of the Metropolitan Museum of Art. His illustrations were a feature of his newspaper work during his early career in post-Civil War San Francisco.

1837. Lardner, Ring W. *Regular Fellows I Have Met: With Illustrations by Regular Cartoonists.* Chicago: Privately printed, 1919. 2 leaves + 97 plates.

Scores of Ring Lardner's friends in sports and politics and business are honored in a Lardner limerick and a black-and-white cartoon. A collector's item.

1838. Look Magazine. *Look at the U.S.A.* Boston: Houghton Mifflin Co., 1955. 522pp.

Eight effective pictorial stories of America. Journalists of prominence among those who contributed regional introductions to the pictures are Gerald W. Johnson, Joseph Henry Jackson, and Frederick Lewis Allen.

1839. Los Angeles Press Photographers Assn. *50 Years of News Photography in Los Angeles.* Los Angeles: The Association, 1952. 72pp. (Foreword by Gov. Earl Warren.)

An anniversary promotion booklet. "Pictures of the year" are included, as is a historical account of Los Angeles photography.

1840. Low, David. *A Cartoon History of Our Times.* New York: Simon and Schuster, 1939. 171pp.

1841. ———. *Low on the War: A Cartoon Commentary of the Years 1939–1941.* New York: Simon and Schuster, 1941. 157pp.

Cartoons from the London *Evening Standard*, some subsequently reproduced in the New York *Times*. Brief textual matter gives necessary background for the drawings.

1842. ———. *Low's Cartoon History, 1945–1953.* New York: Simon and Schuster, 1953. 159pp.

Cartoons from the London *Evening Standard*, the London *Daily Herald*, and the Manchester *Guardian*, with explanatory text.

1843. ———. *Ye Madde Designer.* New York: Studio Publications, 1935. 128pp.

1844. Mauldin, William H. *Back Home.* New York: William Sloane Associates, 1947. 315pp.

1845. ———. *A Sort of a Saga.* New York: William Sloane Associates, 1949. 301pp.

A young World War II cartoonist tells here in text and drawings the story of his early life in Arizona and New Mexico. Good light reading.

1846. ———. *Up Front.* New York: Henry Holt and Co., 1945. 228pp.

Cartoons and narrative on World War II. Mauldin, a pictorial "find" of the war, was a 23-year-old artist who could picture vividly the life of "Willie" and "Joe" — unshaven, groggy GIs with soldiers' griefs, complaints, fears, opinions, and jokes.

1847. Murrell, William. *A History of American Graphic Humor.* Vol. I, New York: Whitney Museum of American Art, 1933. Vol. II, New York: The Macmillan Co., 1938. 516pp., total.

1848. Nevins, Allan, and Frank Weitenkampf. *A Century of Political Cartoons: Caricature in the United States from 1800 to 1900.* New

York: Charles Scribner's Sons, 1944. 190pp., including 100 cartoon reproductions.

Includes a brief historical introduction on the roles of the newspapers and magazines that carried the cartoons depicted. In the late century the work of Thomas Nast of *Harper's Weekly* and Joseph Keppler of *Punch* is heavily represented.

1849. New Yorker. *The New Yorker 1950–1955 Album.* New York: Harper and Brothers, 1955. Unpaged.

1850. ———. *Twenty-Fifth Anniversary Album, 1925–1950.* New York: Harper and Brothers, 1951. About 400pp.

1851. Parton, James. *Caricature and Other Comic Art in All Times and Many Lands.* New York: Harper and Brothers, 1877. 340pp.

Twenty-six well-written articles on comic art and satire, most of which Parton prepared for *Harper's Monthly Magazine* in 1875. There is good material on Benjamin Franklin's appreciation of comic art. Hundreds of cartoons are reproduced.

1852. Punch. *A Century of Punch Cartoons.* New York: Simon and Schuster; London: Bradbury, Agnew and Co., Ltd., 1955. 340pp. (Edited by R. E. Williams; foreword by Malcolm Muggeridge.)

Includes *Punch*'s parody on the *New Yorker,* April 7, 1954, more than 20 years after the *New Yorker* had originally parodied *Punch* as *Paunch.*

1853. Rayfield, Stanley. *How Life Gets the Story: Behind the Scenes in Photo Journalism.* Garden City, N.Y.: Doubleday and Co., 1955. 84pp. (Foreword by Edward K. Thompson.)

Life-size color and black-and-white prints of what the author and managing editor Thompson regarded as the most interesting of *Life*'s reporting and photographic activities. Rayfield is a *Life* promotion man.

1854. Sheridan, Martin. *Comics and Their Creators: Life Stories of American Cartoonists.* Boston: Hale, Cushman, and Flint, 1942. 304pp.

Sheridan discusses more than 80 comic strips and artists, with illustrations. He had worked with Russ Westover ("Tillie the Toiler").

1855. Shoemaker, Vaughn. *1940 A.D.: Cartoons by Vaughn Shoemaker.* Chicago: Chicago Daily News, 1941. 191pp.

A review of a single year through the cartoons of a *Daily News* staff member. The cartoons depict conditions in some war-ravished spot of the world. Shoemaker's series ran annually from 1938 through 1942.

1856. Spencer, Dick, III. *Pulitzer Prize Cartoons: The Men and Their Masterpieces.* Ames, Iowa: Iowa State College Press, 1953. 139pp.

Reproductions of the Pulitzer cartoons for the years 1922 to 1953, with biographical notes on each cartoonist and highlights of the news events behind each cartoon.

1857. Squier, Ephraim G. *Frank Leslie's Pictorial History of the American Civil War.* New York: F. Leslie Publishing House, 1861–1862. 2 vols. 452pp., total.

The Leslie publications, particularly *Frank Leslie's Illustrated Newspaper*, provided some of the best news pictures of the Civil War period.

1858. Waugh, Coulton. *The Comics.* New York: The Macmillan Co., 1947. xiii + 360pp.

A 50-year history of comic strips from the "Yellow Kid" of R. F. Outcault to the modern comic book. It includes more than 100 reprints of strips, as well as brief sketches of many cartoonists.

1859. Webster, H. T. *The Best of H. T. Webster: A Memorial Collection.* New York: Simon and Schuster, 1953. 255pp. (Preface by Robert E. Sherwood and biographical sketch by Philo Calhoun.)

Webster was an artist for the New York *Herald Tribune*; he created "Casper Milquetoast." These 250 or so drawings are from the period 1918 to 1953.

1860. ————. *Our Boyhood Thrills and Other Cartoons.* New York: George H. Doran Co., 1915. 215pp.

1861. ————. *The Timid Soul: A Pictorial Account of the Life and Times of Casper Milquetoast.* New York: Simon and Schuster, 1931. 127pp. + 731 cartoons.

1862. Weitenkampf, Frank. *American Graphic Art.* New York: Henry Holt and Co., 1912. x + 372pp. Revised edition, New York: The Macmillan Co., 1924. xxii + 328pp.

1863. Woolf, S. J. *Drawn from Life.* New York and London: Whittlesey House, McGraw-Hill Book Co., 1932. xiv + 387pp.

Forty-two charcoal and pencil drawings of the great and near-great whose pictures Woolf prepared for the New York *Times* or the New York *Herald Tribune*. Included with each is artist-writer Woolf's word-portrait of his subject.

1864. Young, Arthur Henry. *Hell up to Date.* Chicago: The Schulte Publishing Co., 1893. xi + 82pp. (First issued in 1892 under the title *Hades up to Date.*)

Young's illustrations of "the reckless journey" of R. Palasco Drant, a newspaper correspondent, through the "infernal regions."

G. Sports

1865. *Best Sports Stories of 1944, 1945*, etc. New York: E. P. Dutton and Co., 1944–date. (Edited by I. T. Marsh and Edward Ehre.)

An excellent annual collection of newspaper and magazine sports articles. In addition to the best stories each year, as selected by a group of judges, there are prize-winning sports photographs, a list of annual champions in each sport, and thumbnail biographies of the sports writers represented.

1866. Chicago Daily News. *My Greatest Day in Baseball, as Told to John P. Carmichael, Sports Editor of the Chicago Daily News, and Other Noted Sports Writers: Forty-Seven Dramatic Stories by Forty-Seven Stars.* New York: A. S. Barnes and Co., 1945. vi + 243pp.

1867. Danzig, Allison. *The History of American Football: Its Great*

Teams, Players, and Coaches. Englewood Cliffs, N.J.: Prentice-Hall, 1956. xii + 525pp.

Material gathered by Danzig during more than 25 years of reporting football for the New York *Times*; an outstanding piece of work. The volume includes pictures, records of outstanding teams, and a thorough index.

1868. *The Fireside Book of Baseball.* New York: Simon and Schuster, 1956. xxii + 394pp. (Edited by Charles Einstein; foreword by Ford C. Frick. Sequel issued as *The Second Fireside Book of Baseball.* New York: Simon and Schuster, 1958. xx + 395pp.)

Excellent anthologies of more than 200 baseball articles from the game's earliest years to 1958: spot news stories, biographies of stars, poetry, pieces on baseball history, and fiction. The contributors include most of the nationally known sports writers of the 20th century, plus some general writers. Editor Einstein was a baseball editor for International News Service. Illustrated.

1869. Graffis, Herbert B., ed. *Esquire's First Sports Reader.* New York: A. S. Barnes and Co., 1945. ix + 292pp.

1870. *The Greatest Sport Stories from the Chicago Tribune.* New York: A. S. Barnes and Co., 1953. xxiii + 448pp. (Edited by Arch Ward.)

An anthology covering 106 years of sports stories, with two thirds of the book covering the period 1920–1953. The emphasis is on spectator sports. Ward's introduction gives a brief history of *Tribune* sports coverage.

1871. *The Greatest Sport Stories from the New York Times: Sports Classics of a Century.* New York: A. S. Barnes and Co., 1951. xxi + 680pp. (Edited by Allison Danzig and Peter Brandwein.)

Issued on the occasion of the *Times*'s 100th anniversary. Most of the selections are from the period 1920–1951. The emphasis is on major spectator sports.

1872. Kieran, John. *The American Sporting Scene.* New York: The Macmillan Co., 1941. xii + 212pp. (Pictures by Joseph W. Golinkin.)

A collection of sports stories and art (80 photographs and drawings, half in color). The stories had appeared in various versions in the New York *Times*, while Golinkin's work had been shown in New York art galleries.

1873. ———. *The Story of the Olympic Games, 776 BC–1936 AD.* New York: Frederick A. Stokes Co., 1936. 319pp.

Includes a complete record of Olympic champions in all events, 1896–1936.

1874. Kofoed, Jack. *Thrills in Sports.* New York: Holborn House, 1932. viii + 120pp.

1875. Lardner, John. *It Beats Working.* Philadelphia: J. B. Lippincott Co., 1947. 253pp. (Foreword by Carl Van Doren; illustrations by Willard Mullin.)

A collection of well-written sketches on sports figures, from the author's columns in *Newsweek*, 1939–1945.

1876. Liebling, A. J. *The Sweet Science.* New York: The Viking Press, 1956. 306pp.

Urbane pieces on boxing, which appeared originally in the *New Yorker*. There is considerable detail on fights of the 1950s and on sights, sounds, and smells of arenas.

1877. Menke, Frank G. *The Encyclopedia of Sports: New and Revised Edition.* New York: A. S. Barnes and Co., 1953. ix + 1018 pp. (Earlier editions, 1939, 1944, and 1947. Cartoons by Willard Mullin; managing editor, Peter Brandwein.)

A magnificent compendium of sports commentary, history, and records on more than 70 major and minor sports — professional and amateur. Menke was for more than 20 years a sports reporter for King Features Syndicate and International News Service. Numerous newspapermen are contributors to the individual sections.

1878. Smith, Walter W. (Red). *Out of the Red: The Masters of Professional and Collegiate Mayhem as Seen through the Eyes of America's Most Entertaining Sports Writer.* New York: Alfred A. Knopf, 1950. 293pp. (Illustrated by Willard Mullin.)

More than 100 delightful selections from Smith's columns in the New York *Herald Tribune*, 1945 through 1949. Humor and satire predominate.

1879. *Sport's Golden Age: A Close-Up of the Fabulous Twenties.* New York: Harper and Brothers, 1948. xii + 296pp. (Edited by Allison Danzig and Peter Brandwein; foreword by John Kieran.)

1880. *Sports Extra: Classics of Sports Reporting.* New York: A. S. Barnes and Co., 1944. xv + 282pp. (Edited by Stanley Bernard Frank.)

1881. Sports Illustrated. *The Spectacle of Sport Selected from Sports Illustrated.* New York: Prentice-Hall, 1957. 317pp., including 202 pages in full color. (Compiled and edited by Norton Wood; foreword by Sidney L. James.)

A beautiful anthology of photographs and articles. Nationally known sports writers and general authors are among the contributors.

1882. Tunis, John R. *$port$: Heroics and Hysterics.* New York: John Day, 1928. 293pp.

An attack on commercialization of sports, particularly tennis, golf, and football. The picture is somewhat overdrawn, but provocative in its revelations of the sports "myth." Tunis was a free-lance writer and sports writer for the *New Yorker* and the New York *Evening Post*.

1883. *Wake Up the Echoes: From the Sports Pages of the New York Herald Tribune.* Garden City, N.Y.: Hanover House, 1956. 251pp. (Edited by Bob Cooke; preface by Bob Considine.)

Most of the great sports writers of the past 40 years appear to have written at one time for the *Herald Tribune*: Grantland Rice, Heywood Broun, John Kieran, Al Laney, W. O. McGeehan, Red Smith, and others. Here are about 100 of their best offerings.

1884. Woodward, Stanley. *Sports Page.* New York: Simon and Schuster, 1949. xvii + 229pp.

An outspoken, revealing analysis of sports editing and news coverage in all its phases, by the sports editor of the New York *Herald Tribune*.

Appraisals of the Press, Ethics of the Press, and Law of the Press

A. General Appraisals of the Press in the United States

1885. American Academy of Political and Social Science. "The Press in the Contemporary Scene," in the *Annals*, vol. 219, January 1942. viii + 175pp. (Edited by Ralph D. Casey and Malcolm M. Willey.)

Twenty-six articles on the press in modern life, the contemporary newspaper pattern, the relation of the press to fields of allied interest, and problems of press responsibility and reform. Although dated, the material still has significance. Contributors included editors, practicing newspapermen, and educators.

1886. American Newspaper Guild of the Twin Cities. *Newspaper Guild of the Twin Cities Memorial Lectures*. Minneapolis: University of Minnesota School of Journalism, 1947–date.

Annual lectures by distinguished journalists or students of the press who discuss contemporary press problems.

1887. American Society of Newspaper Editors. *Problems of Journalism: Proceedings of the Annual Meetings of the American Society of Newspaper Editors*. Washington, D.C.: The Society, 1923–date. (Current editor, Alice Fox Pitts.)

Addresses to the society by leading public figures are included, as are debates and convention reports. Each volume provides the year's membership list. Altogether, the series gives a good view of changing newspaper problems.

1888. Associated Press Managing Editors Association. *The APME Red Book*. New York: The Associated Press, 1948–date.

These volumes, similar to those of the ASNE, record the activities of managing editors of Associated Press newspapers. The *Red Book* is well illustrated with pictures of managing editors in formal and informal meetings, and includes detailed analyses of AP coverage in all its phases. It is highly useful for background on continuing news policies and for information on how service to member newspapers can be improved.

1889. Bellamy, Paul. *Attacks upon the Integrity of Journalism*. Washington, D.C.: American Society of Newspaper Editors, 1924. 16pp.

Pamphlet publication of an address by Bellamy, then managing editor of the Cleveland *Plain Dealer*, before the ASNE on April 25, 1924. He stanchly defends the press.

1890. Bent, Silas. *Ballyhoo: The Voice of the Press.* New York: Horace Liveright, 1927. xviii + 398pp.

One of the leading debunking books of a generation ago. Bent, who had had a varied newspaper career, deals with the problems and ills of metropolitan newspapers only, particularly as regards invasion of privacy, faults of the tabloids, and the "evil" influence of advertisers and chain newspapers.

1891. Bird, George L., and Frederick E. Merwin, eds. *The Press and Society.* New York: Prentice-Hall, 1951. xv + 655pp. (An earlier edition, 1942, was published under the title *The Newspaper and Society*.)

General readings, principally on the newspaper; the 1951 edition includes radio and other communication media. It is most useful as a textbook.

1892. Bleyer, Willard Grosvenor, ed. *The Profession of Journalism.* Boston: Atlantic Monthly Press, 1918. xxiii + 292pp.

These 19 articles selected from the *Atlantic Monthly* still make fruitful reading. Among men prominent in journalism who analyze the press are Rollo Ogden, H. L. Mencken, Melville E. Stone, Oswald Garrison Villard, and Professor Bleyer himself. There is some material on press ethics.

1893. Blumberg, Nathan B. *One Party Press?* Lincoln: University of Nebraska Press, 1954. 91pp.

An analysis of the way in which 35 metropolitan newspapers covered the presidential campaign of 1952. The author, although he did not use statistical sampling techniques, measured the space devoted to stories on Eisenhower and Stevenson and evaluated the political bias shown, if any.

1894. Boynton, Henry Walcott. *Journalism and Literature, and Other Essays.* Boston and New York: Houghton Mifflin Co., 1904. 226pp.

Chiefly essays previously published in the *Atlantic Monthly*. The author's approach is more thoughtful and temperate than most commentaries written in a day when sensational journalism was at its peak.

1895. Brucker, Herbert. *Freedom of Information.* New York: The Macmillan Co., 1949. 307pp.

The editor of the Hartford (Conn.) *Courant* offers an enlightened defense and analysis of the press. He goes into detail in discussing the nature of news and in emphasizing the economic independence of the American newspaper. This is among the best of the pro-press studies that have been written.

1896. Christian Writers' and Editors' Conference. *Christian Journalism for Today: A Resource Book for Writers and Editors.* Philadelphia: Judson Press, 1952. 252pp. (Collected and edited under the supervision of Benjamin P. Browne.)

Includes addresses delivered at the Christian Writers' conferences in Philadelphia and Green Lake, Wis., 1948–1951.

1897. Clark, Carroll DeWitt. *News: A Sociological Study.* Chicago: University of Chicago: 1931. 464pp.

A Ph.D. dissertation; includes a long historical account of the development of the concept of news.

1898. Clark, Wesley C., ed. *Journalism Tomorrow*. Syracuse, N.Y.: Syracuse University Press, 1958. 144pp.

An analytical evaluation of possible future developments in journalism. Faculty members of the Syracuse University School of Journalism are contributors of articles on specific fields. Dean Clark and Prof. Roland E. Wolseley write the general summary.

1899. Cole, Virginia Lee. *The Newspaper and Crime*, in University of Missouri Journalism Series, No. 44. Columbia, Mo.: University of Missouri, January 21, 1927. 84pp.

Provides a historical sketch of crime publicity, a statistical survey of crime news, and arguments for and against publicizing crime.

1900. Dale, Edgar. *How to Read a Newspaper*. Chicago and New York: Scott, Foresman and Co., 1941. x + 178pp.

1901. Dana, Charles A. *The Art of Newspaper Making*. New York: D. Appleton and Co., 1895. 114pp.

Three lectures by the old master of the New York *Sun* in his twilight years: "The Modern American Newspaper," "The Profession of Journalism," and "The Making of a Newspaper Man." The three offer an insight into the high ideals of the earlier Dana.

1902. Deutschmann, Paul J. *Attitudes toward the General Field of Newspaper Work*. East Lansing, Mich.: College of Communication Arts, Michigan State University, 1958. Mimeographed. 59pp. (Report No. 2 on "The Michigan Newspaperman.")

An analysis of the attitudes of 458 news and advertising employees of 41 nonmetropolitan newspapers.

1903. Dickinson, B. S. *The Newspaper and Labor: An Inquiry into the Nature and Influence of Labor News and Comment in the Daily Press*. Urbana: University of Illinois, 1930.

A Ph.D. dissertation.

1904. Drewry, John E. *Concerning the Fourth Estate*. Athens: University of Georgia Press, 1942. 2nd edition. xi + 167pp. (First edition, 1938.)

Essays on various problems of journalism.

1904a. ———, ed. *The What, Why, and How of Communications*. Athens: University of Georgia Press, 1958. viii + 214pp. (Vol. 11 in annual Bulletins of the Henry W. Grady School of Journalism.)

Begun in 1948, these appraisals are collected reports of comments on press, radio, television, periodicals, public relations, and advertising made during institutes and on special occasions at the Grady School of Journalism. See also *Journalism Enters a New Half-Century* (vol. 4, issued in 1951).

1905. Fenton, Frances. *The Influence of Newspaper Presentations upon the Growth of Crime and Other Anti-Social Activity.* Chicago: University of Chicago Press, 1911. iii + 96pp.

A Ph.D. dissertation.

1906. Ferguson, Le Roy C., and Ralph H. Smuckler. *Politics in the Press: An Analysis of Press Content in 1952 Senatorial Campaigns.* East Lansing, Mich.: Governmental Research Bureau, Michigan State College, 1954. 100pp.

1907. Given, John L. *Making a Newspaper.* New York: Henry Holt and Co., 1907. 325pp.

A critique on news and all phases of the newspaper that was highly regarded in its time; today the volume is valuable historically. Given was a news executive of the New York *Evening Sun.*

1908. Goddard, Morrill. *What Interests People — and Why; Modern Miracles; Underneath the Veneer of Civilized Man.* New York: The American Weekly, 1931. 60pp.

Collects three addresses by this Hearst news executive before annual conferences of the American Weekly Sales Organization in New York in 1928, 1929, and 1930.

1909. Harris, Frank. *Presentation of Crime in Newspapers: A Study of Method in Newspaper Research.* Minneapolis: The Sociological Press, 1932. xvi + 103pp.

An early quantitative study, today of historical interest in showing how far techniques for studying the press have advanced. Three Minneapolis daily newspapers were used.

1910. Hill, A. F. *Secrets of the Sanctum: An Inside View of an Editor's Life.* Philadelphia: Claxton, Remsen and Haffelfinger, 1875. 312pp.

A quaint description of what journalism was like in the 1870s, mostly in the context of the New York newspapers. The author's style is anecdotal and he wanders with little direction across the fields of reporting, editing, printing, personalities, libel, and the economics of the business. The commentary is oversimplified perhaps, but valuable in revealing how journalism has changed since Greeley's day.

1911. Holt, Hamilton. *Commercialism and Journalism.* Boston and New York: Houghton Mifflin Co., 1909. 105pp.

The managing editor of the *Independent* discusses the evils of sensational journalism, offers suggestions for meeting the pressure of advertisers, and suggests the endowing of newspapers to forestall all commercial pressures.

1912. Howe, Quincy. *The News and How to Understand It: In Spite of the Newspapers, in Spite of the Magazines, in Spite of the Radio.* New York: Simon and Schuster, 1940. x + 250pp.

A radio news commentator's advice to readers early in World War II. In a sense this is a textbook for mature readers who do not understand the intricacies of news gathering and news presentation.

1913. Hughes, Helen MacGill. *News and the Human Interest Story.* Chicago: University of Chicago Press, 1940. xxiii + 313pp. (University of Chicago Sociological Series; foreword by Robert E. Park.)

A sociological study of news, intended particularly to show the pervasiveness of human-interest elements. Some history of news development is included. The book is cited frequently by later researchers.

1914. Ickes, Harold L. *America's House of Lords: An Inquiry into the Freedom of the Press.* New York: Harcourt, Brace and Co., 1939. xvi + 214pp.

Franklin D. Roosevelt's strong-minded secretary of the interior gives his bill of particulars against the press. His book deserves a place beside those of Sinclair (1956 below), Seldes (1950), and Bent (1890) as one of the strongest and most articulate of attacks on the press.

1915. Irwin, Will. "The American Newspaper, a Study of Journalism in Its Relation to the Public," in *Collier's*, January 21, 1911, to July 22, 1911.

An excellent popular analysis of the press by one of its greatest reporters writing shortly after "yellow journalism" had passed its peak. His historical, descriptive, and critical analysis offers forceful observations that are still applicable.

1916. Kobre, Sidney. *Behind Shocking Crime Headlines: Searching Probe into Juvenile, Adult Crime, and Prisons.* Tallahassee: Florida State University, 1957. 274pp.

Kobre uses examples from news stories as his starting point in investigating the basic causes for criminal behavior.

1917. Krieghbaum, Hillier. *American Newspaper Reporting of Science News.* Manhattan: Kansas State College, 1941. 73pp. (Kansas State College Bulletin, Industrial Journalism Series No. 16.)

An analysis of science reporting from its begininngs in the days of Benjamin Franklin to the 1940s. The author includes a study of the Science Service and the National Association of Science Writers.

1918. ———, ed. *When Doctors Meet Reporters.* New York: New York University Press, 1957. 119pp.

A record of conferences, 1953–1956, that examined the state of medical news reporting and discussed ways of achieving a more friendly understanding between science writers and members of the medical profession. The conferences were sponsored by the Josiah Macy, Jr., Foundation.

1919. Lewinson, Minna, and Henry Beetle Hough. *A History of the Services Rendered to the Public by the American Press during the Year 1917.* New York: Columbia University Press, 1918. 31pp.

A Pulitzer prize-winning essay by two students of the Columbia University School of Journalism.

1920. Liebling, A. J. *The Wayward Pressman.* Garden City, N.Y.: Doubleday and Co., 1948. 284pp.

A collection of a number of the author's iconoclastic articles on the press written for the *New Yorker*, with additional autobiographical material. Liebling's satiric style must be kept in mind in judging the book.

1921. ———. *Mink and Red Herring: The Wayward Pressman's Casebook*. Garden City, N.Y.: Doubleday and Co., 1949. 251pp.

A continuation of Liebling's sharp barbs against the press. He centers on the 1948 presidential campaign.

1922. Lippmann, Walter. *Liberty and the News*. New York: Harcourt, Brace and Howe, 1920. vii + 104pp.

Based in part on two essays from the *Atlantic Monthly*, in which Lippmann drew a parallel between the crisis in Western democracy and a crisis in modern journalism.

1923. ——— and Charles Merz. "A Test of the News," *New Republic*, special supplement, vol. XXIII, part II, no. 296 (August 4, 1920). 42pp.

A provocative content study of news handling based on stories about the Russian Revolution appearing in the New York *Times* from March 1917 to March 1920. Frequent references to this study have been made in subsequent content analyses.

1924. Logan, Rayford W., ed. *The Attitude of the Southern White Press toward Negro Suffrage, 1932–1940*. Washington, D.C.: Foundation Publishers, 1940. xii + 115pp. (Foreword by Charles H. Wesley.)

An unsynthesized study of attitudes toward voting by Negroes as shown in the metropolitan press of 12 southern states, and an appeal for a campaign to educate southern leaders to accept Negro suffrage. Now outdated.

1925. London Times. "American Writing Today, Its Independence and Vigour," *Times Literary Supplement*, special number, September 17, 1954. 100pp.

An excellent British interpretation of American literature and communications in all phases, including a detailed treatment of the press and radio and television. *Times* reviews of distinguished American books dating back 40 years are reprinted.

1926. Lundberg, Ferdinand. *America's 60 Families*. New York: Vanguard Press, 1937. xxii + 544pp.

Among the families making up what Lundberg calls a modern industrial oligarchy are the McCormicks (Chicago *Tribune*), the Curtis-Boks (Curtis Publishing Co.), and the Pattersons (Chicago *Tribune* and New York *News*). Numerous other metropolitan press interests are also discussed.

1927. McCormick, Robert R. *The Freedom of the Press Still Furnishes That Check upon Government Which No Constitution Has Ever Been Able to Provide*. Chicago: The Tribune Co., 1934. 36pp.

A pamphlet by the publisher of the Chicago *Tribune*, directed in particular against early New Deal codes.

1928. ———. *What Is a Newspaper?* Chicago: The Tribune Co., 1924. 32pp.

A reprint of an address by McCormick giving his views on journalism.

1929. MacDougall, Curtis D. *Newsroom Problems and Policies*. New York: The Macmillan Co., 1941. x + 592pp.

An excellent analysis of the press, usable as a textbook at the graduate level. MacDougall considers at length the problem of whether the public should be given the news it wants or the news it needs, ethical problems involving suppression, and the necessity of meeting changing conditions.

1930. MacNeil, Neil. *Without Fear or Favor.* New York: Harcourt, Brace and Co., 1940. 414pp.

A good description of metropolitan journalism reflecting the perspective of the New York *Times,* of which MacNeil was an assistant managing editor. He discusses the responsibilities of news departments, the press associations, and law and ethics. There is also a forecast of possible press trends.

1931. Mahin, Helen Ogden. *The Development and Significance of the Newspaper Headline.* Ann Arbor, Mich.: George Wahr, 1924. x + 173pp.

The author regards the headline as the most significant feature of newspaper editing. Dozens of illustrative examples of headlines from 1762 to 1914 are given.

1932. "Mass Communications," *Atlantic Monthly,* special supplement, vol. 200, no. 6 (December 1957), pp. 80–160. (Introduction by Edward Weeks.)

A diverse set of articles on 13 phases of the communications industry. Well organized.

1933. Morley, Christopher. *Religio Journalistici.* Garden City, N.Y.: Doubleday, Page and Co., 1924. 62pp.

A humorous essay by a literary critic on the nature of newspaper work.

1934. Mott, Frank Luther. *The News in America.* Cambridge, Mass.: Harvard University Press, 1952. x + 236pp. (Library of Congress Series in American Civilization, edited by Ralph Henry Gabriel.)

A thoughtful essay for readers in any field who seek an understanding of the problems faced in gathering, distributing, and editing news in America and abroad. Mott also looks toward the future impact of the electronic communication media. The book is as good a general analysis of news as has yet been presented.

1935. ———, ed. *Journalism in Wartime.* Washington, D.C.: American Council on Public Affairs, 1943. 216pp.

Thirty-two valuable pieces by journalists on problems of the press in World War II. The subjects include censorship, radio and advertising, public-press relations, and postwar reconstruction plans.

1936. ——— and Ralph D. Casey, eds. *Interpretations of Journalism.* New York: F. S. Crofts and Co., 1937. x + 534pp.

A book of readings on general press problems; suitable as a textbook.

1937. Nieman Foundation. *Newsmen's Holiday: Nieman Essays — First Series.* Cambridge, Mass.: Harvard University Press, 1942. xv + 203pp. (Introduction by Louis M. Lyons, curator.)

First of the publications resulting from Nieman Foundation activities at Harvard. Newspapermen in an academic atmosphere write about how they hope to improve journalism.

THE LITERATURE OF JOURNALISM

1938. Nock, Albert Jay. *Free Speech and Plain Language*. New York: William Morrow and Co., 1937. 343pp.

A series of 17 outspoken essays written between the late 1920s and the mid-1930s for the *Atlantic* and *Harper's*. Nock was critical of the press.

1939. Novak, Benjamin J. *An Analysis of the Science Content of the New York Times*. Philadelphia: Temple University, 1942. viii + 60pp.

A doctor of education thesis.

1940. O'Laughlin, John Callan. *The Relation of Press Correspondents to the Navy before and during War*. Washington, D.C.: Government Printing Office, 1913. 16pp.

A lecture delivered at the Naval War College, urging generous release of factual information by the Navy. O'Laughlin, a Chicago *Tribune* staff member, had been associated with the *Army and Navy Journal*.

1941. *Oldtime Comments on Journalism*. Columbia, Mo.: Press of the Crippled Turtle, vol. 1, nos. 1–8, January 1953–April 1958. (Edited by Frank L. Mott.)

Historically valuable commentaries on news and newspapers gathered from almost forgotten sources and reprinted in limited editions. The following have been issued: "Ben Jonson's Satire on News" (1625), excerpts from *The Staple of Newes*, one of Jonson's later comedies, January 1953; "An Essay on Sensationalism in the Press," by Hercules, pseudonym of Fisher Ames writing in the *New-England Palladium* of Boston (1801), February 1953; "The Porcupine and the Pole-Cat," by Hugh Henry Brackenridge, from his *Modern Chivalry* part II (1804), satires on the Federalist and anti-Federalist press quarrels, April 1953; "Liang Chi-Chao's Comments on Journalism," words of a Chinese sage who died in the 20th century, July 1953; "Mark Twain's 'Journalism in Tennessee,'" which Clemens wrote for the Buffalo *Express* (1869), September 1955; "A Whip for the News-Writers," selections from the *Tatler*, the *Spectator*, and other 18th-century British newspapers, July 1956; "Benjamin Franklin on Newspapers," December 1956; and "Alex Sweet on Texas Journalism," comments from a humorous paper issued from 1880 to 1884 in Austin, April 1958. (See also Mott's reprint of the Zenger trial, published as vol. 2 of *Oldtime Comments*, 1082 above.)

1942. Philips, Melville, ed. *The Making of a Newspaper*. New York: G. P. Putnam's Sons, 1893. 322pp.

This collection of articles from *Lippincott's*, assembled by the literary editor of the old Philadelphia *Press*, gives a picture of what newspaper production was like in the early 1890s. The leading contributor was Julius Chambers, former managing editor of the younger Bennett's New York *Herald* and Pulitzer's New York *World*.

1943. Radder, Norman J. *Newspapers in Community Service*. New York: McGraw-Hill Book Co., 1926. x + 269pp.

Radder discusses the activities of newspapers and magazines in cooperating with municipalities toward development of their communities.

1944. Reid, Whitelaw. *Some Newspaper Tendencies: An Address Delivered before the Editorial Associations of New York and Ohio*. New York: Henry Holt and Co., 1879. 76pp.

1945. Rogers, James Edward. *The American Newspaper*. Chicago: University of Chicago Press, 1909. xiii + 213pp.

1946. Rowse, Arthur Edward. *Slanted News: A Case Study of the Nixon and Stevenson Fund Stories*. Boston: Beacon Press, 1957. 139pp. (Foreword by Erwin D. Canham.)

A study by a copyreader for the Boston *Traveler* of how 31 metropolitan newspapers representing 27 per cent of circulation in the nation handled news of the special fund raised in behalf of Richard M. Nixon in the campaign of 1952, and how any slant in presentation correlated with editorial policy. Facsimiles of representative pages are included.

1947. St. Louis Post-Dispatch. *Symposium on Freedom of the Press*. St. Louis: The Post-Dispatch, 1939. 76pp.

Opinions of 120 Americans on the meaning of the press are reprinted from the *Post-Dispatch* of December 13, 1938, to December 25, 1938.

1948. Seldes, George. *Facts and Fascism*. New York: In Fact, Inc., 1943. 286pp.

In this attack on fascist elements in America Seldes charges a conspiracy of silence on the part of the conservative press. He particularly singles out for attack Westbrook Pegler, the Chicago *Tribune*, the *Reader's Digest*, and Fulton Lewis, Jr.

1949. ———. *The Facts Are*. New York: In Fact, Inc., 1942. 128pp.

Seldes offers the "facts" as he sees them, sharply attacking "falsehood and propaganda" in the press and radio.

1950. ———. *Freedom of the Press*. Indianapolis: Bobbs-Merrill Co., 1935. 380pp.

With Upton Sinclair's *The Brass Check* (1956 below) and Silas Bent's *Ballyhoo* (1890 above), this is a major indictment of the press. Seldes marshals information to prove his thesis to his own satisfaction, if not always the reader's.

1951. ———. *One Thousand Americans*. New York: Boni and Gaer, 1947. viii + 312pp.

An indictment of "enemies of America," including "big magazines" — *Reader's Digest, Ladies' Home Journal, Woman's Home Companion, Good Housekeeping, American, Cosmopolitan, Life, Saturday Evening Post, Collier's, Look, Time, Liberty*, and *Newsweek*.

1952. ———. *The People Don't Know: The American Press and the Cold War*. New York: Gaer Associates, 1949. 342pp.

Seldes accuses the American press of misinforming the public about the world situation after World War II, particularly with regard to coverage of news in Hungary and Yugoslavia.

1953. ———. *You Can't Do That: A Survey of the Forces Attempting, in the Name of Patriotism, to Make a Desert of the Bill of Rights*. New York: Modern Age Books, 1938. xii + 307pp.

1954. ———. *You Can't Print That: The Truth behind the News — 1918–1928*. New York: Payson and Clarke, Ltd., 1929. 465pp.

1955. Siebert, Fred S., Theodore Peterson, and Wilbur Schramm. *Four Theories of the Press*. Urbana: University of Illinois Press, 1956. 153pp.

The authors hold that the press of any nation takes on the form and structure of the society within which it operates. Siebert writes on "The Authoritarian Theory" and "The Libertarian Theory," Peterson on "The Social Responsibility Theory," and Schramm on "The Soviet Communist Theory." There is a valuable selected bibliography.

1956. Sinclair, Upton. *The Brass Check: A Study of American Journalism*. Pasadena, Calif.: Published by the author, 1920. 445pp.

Probably the most famous indictment of the American press. Sinclair, widely known novelist and Socialist writer, bases his attack on his own experiences with the press and on the observations of others. He is particularly antagonistic toward policies of the Associated Press. The book today is of historical importance.

1957. Sweeney, John F. *A Study of the New York Times*. Cleveland, Ohio: The Sweeney and James Co., 1923. 23pp.

1958. Thorpe, Merle, ed. *The Coming Newspaper*. New York: Henry Holt and Co., 1915. vi + 323pp.

Contributors of speeches and essays in this collection include Roy W. Howard, Oswald Garrison Villard, and Hamilton Holt. Thorpe was one of the founders of the University of Washington School of Journalism.

1959. United States General Staff, War College Division. *The Proper Relationship between the Army and the Press in Time of War*. Washington, D.C.: Government Printing Office, 1916. 13pp.

1960. Villard, Oswald Garrison. *How Stands Our Press?* Chicago: Human Events Associates, 1947. 17pp. (Human Events Pamphlet No. 19.)

1961. ———. *The Press Today*. New York: The Nation, 1930. 96pp.

Expresses Villard's fears for the future of the press as a result of loss of liberal thought within it.

1962. ———. *Some Newspapers and Newspaper-Men*. New York: Alfred A. Knopf, 1923. 345pp.

Then editor of the *Nation*, Villard wrote these penetrating studies to illustrate tendencies toward extreme commercialization in the press. He discusses the leading newspapers and publishers in New York, Boston, Philadelphia, Baltimore, Washington, D.C., Chicago, and San Francisco, and adds accounts of five earlier editors: Henry Watterson, the Bennetts (father and son), Edwin L. Godkin, and William Lloyd Garrison.

1963. ———. *The Disappearing Daily: Chapters in American Newspaper Evolution*. New York: Alfred A. Knopf, 1944. vii + 285pp.

Principally a supplement to *Some Newspapers and Newspaper-Men*. Villard eliminates some earlier material and adds sketches on press associations, columnists, and publishers for the period 1923–1943. Together the two books reveal the visionary ideals of this distinguished editor and his disappointment in their failure to be realized.

1964. Walker, Stanley. *City Editor*. New York: Frederick A. Stokes Co., 1934. xi + 336pp. (Foreword by Alexander Woollcott.)

Among the best of the period's journalistic best sellers devoted to explaining intricacies and idiosyncrasies of the craft. Walker, a one-time city editor of the New York *Herald Tribune*, surveys the journalism of the early 1930s with both cynicism and idealism. In a sense this is a textbook on reporting, editing, libel, and ethics by one who himself debunks textbooks.

1965. Warner, Charles Dudley. *The American Newspaper: An Essay*. Boston: James R. Osgood and Co., 1881. 69pp.

A distinguished contributor to *Harper's* defends newspapers. The analysis remains today substantially accurate in its discussion of newspaper operations.

1966. Wertham, Frederic. *The Circle of Guilt*. New York: Rinehart and Co., 1956. 211pp.

An attack upon the pressures for prejudgment of murder cases exerted by newspapers, radio, and television.

1967. ———. *Seduction of the Innocent*. New York: Rinehart and Co., 1954. x + 400pp.

In this strongly worded attack upon comic books and television "horror" programs, Wertham exonerates newspaper comic strips since they benefit from the supervision of responsible editors. The author is a New York psychiatrist of 20 years' service.

1968. Whipple, Leon. *How to Understand Current Events: A Guide to an Appraisal of the News*. New York: Harper and Brothers, 1941. xi + 241pp.

Whipple seeks to explain how to judge newspaper content and how to evaluate radio programs and films. His volume is useful more for general reading than for analysis of specific problems.

1969. Willey, Malcolm M. *The Country Newspaper: A Study of Socialization and Newspaper Content*. Chapel Hill: University of North Carolina Press; London: Oxford University Press, 1926. xii + 153pp.

An early, excellent effort at newspaper content analysis that made use of research methods which in later years were considerably perfected. The study related chiefly to Connecticut weeklies. There is a good bibliography on the weekly press up to 1926.

1970. *William Allen White Memorial Lectures*. Lawrence, Kan.: William Allen White Foundation, 1950–date.

Annual addresses of distinguished newspapermen who discuss contemporary journalistic problems.

1971. Wilmer, Lambert A. *Our Press Gang: Or, a Complete Exposition of the Corruptions and Crimes of the American Newspapers*. Philadelphia: J. T. Lloyd; London: Sampson Low, Son and Co., 1859. 403pp.

One of the most violent criticisms of newspapers ever prepared, this book was written by a veteran of years of newspaper experience in Philadelphia, Baltimore, and Washington. Most of Wilmer's 14 indictments have since been set forth repeatedly; a few of them are still voiced today.

1972. Wingate, Charles F., ed. *Views and Interviews on Journalism.* New York: F. B. Patterson, 1875. 372pp.

Contemporary opinion on newspapers of the 1870s by widely known newspapermen of the time. Besides the standard practices of the day, they discuss possible future developments, among them prospects for college training of journalists and for illustrated journalism. See, particularly, the views on pictorial journalism by David G. Croly, editor of an early pictorial, the New York *Daily Graphic* (1873–1878).

1973. Wisehart, M. K. "Newspapers and Criminal Justice," in *Criminal Justice in Cleveland,* pp. 515–558. Cleveland: The Cleveland Foundation, 1922.

In his chapter on reporting and handling of crime news, Wisehart treats particularly of the practices of the Cleveland *Press, Plain Dealer,* and *News.* A fine contribution to understanding the newspaper in its environment.

B. General Appraisals of the British Press

1974. Angell, Norman. *The Press and the Organisation of Society.* London: Labour Publishing Co., Ltd., 1922. 123pp.

An analysis of press problems that might arise in the event of Labour control of the British government. While Angell favored conscious collective control of the press, he opposed any return to the governmental censorships of past generations.

1975. British Commonwealth of Nations. *Commonwealth Press Conference, 8th, in Australia and New Zealand* [1955]. London: Commonwealth Press Union, 1956. 80pp. (Compiled by Sir Henry Turner.)

Earlier reports of proceedings were issued under the title *Imperial Press Conference.* The conferences have been held at London, 1909; Canada, 1921 (see entry 1979 below); Australia, 1925; London, 1930; South Africa, 1935; London, 1946; and Canada, 1950.

1976. Churchill, Randolph Spencer. *What I Said about the Press.* London: Weidenfeld and Nicolson; New York: World Publishing Co., 1957. 112pp.

Three speeches on aspects of the British press and a report of Churchill's successful libel action against the *People* in October 1956.

1977. Cummings, A. J. *The Press and a Changing Civilisation.* London: John Lane the Bodley Head, 1936. xv + 139pp.

A popular account of the position of the press in society — American, German, and Russian press as well as British — with emphasis upon the need for competition among newspapers.

1978. Dibblee, G. Binney. *The Newspaper.* London: Williams and Norgate; New York: Henry Holt and Co., 1913. 256pp. (Home University Library of Modern Knowledge No. 58.)

A popular analysis treating continental European and American newspapers as well as London newspapers and the English provincial press.

1979. Donald, Robert. *The Imperial Press Conference in Canada.* London: Hodder and Stoughton, Ltd., c. 1921. xvi + 296pp. (Foreword by Viscount Burnham.)

A valuable contribution on the journalism of the British Empire. The book gives a full report of the Second Empire Press Conference in Ottawa in 1920 and useful biographical accounts of Canadian editors who were hosts.

1980. Matthews, T. S. *The Sugar Pill: An Essay on Newspapers*. London: Victor Gollancz, Ltd., 1957. 221pp.

A provocative analysis to the effect that the press is essentially a medium of entertainment — whatever its pretensions that it leads and informs. The book is exceptionally useful in its detailed appraisals of two journalistic extremes: the Manchester *Guardian* and the London *Daily Mirror*. The author is a former news executive of *Time* who now lives in England.

1981. Ockham, David. *Stentor: Or, the Press of Today and Tomorrow*. New York: E. P. Dutton and Co., 1928. 68pp.

A bitter assault upon the "dictatorial" nature of the British press. The author is principally critical of the newspaper combines formed in the 1920s.

1982. *Report on the British Press*. London: Political and Economic Planning, 1938. 333pp.

Although superseded by the parliamentary reports of the Royal Commission on the Press in the 1940s, this private research survey by PEP still is a helpful tool. Detailed attention is given to the national newspapers — their physical structure and financing, personnel, treatment of news, legal restrictions, readership, and relations with the public. Numerous appendixes carry tables on pulp and paper, circulation, and geographical distribution.

1983. Robbins, Sir Alfred. *The Press*. London: E. Benn, 1928. 80pp. (Benn's Six-Penny Library, No. 21.)

1984. Scott-James, R. A. *The Influence of the Press*. London: S. W. Partridge and Co., Ltd., 1913. 320pp.

A scholarly analysis, partly historical, to determine the influences inside and outside journalism that make the press in England and America what it is and prevent it from being what it might be.

1985. Soames, Jane. *The English Press: Newspapers and News*. London: Stanley Nott, 1936. 178pp. (Preface by Hilaire Belloc.)

Criticizes the increasing failure of the British press to perform its function of providing information. The author attacks particularly the withholding of essential news by newspaper owners.

1986. Steed, Henry Wickham. *The Press*. London: William Clowes and Sons, Ltd.; Penguin Books, Ltd., 1938. 250pp.

An excellent analysis by a former editor of the London *Times*, who discusses press freedom, press finances, evolution of newspapers, news-gathering, legal problems, and the rise of radio.

1987. Williams, Francis. *Dangerous Estate: The Anatomy of Newspapers*. London and New York: Longmans, Green and Co., 1957. 304pp.

A former editor of the *Daily Herald* provides a helpful, objective summary of the newspaper and its problems in meeting social needs. A considerable amount of historical material is compactly treated.

C. Ethical Studies of the Press

1988. Crawford, Nelson Antrim. *The Ethics of Journalism*. New York: Alfred A. Knopf, 1924. viii + 264pp.

1989. Flint, Leon Nelson. *The Conscience of the Newspaper*. New York: D. Appleton and Co., 1925. x + 470pp.

A casebook in principles and problems of journalism, long an established textbook and still of substantial value in its treatment of fairness, independence, accuracy, and service. Representative codes of ethics are included.

1990. Gibbons, William F. *Newspaper Ethics: A Discussion of Good Practice for Journalists*. Ann Arbor, Mich.: Edwards Brothers, 1926. 120 numbered leaves.

1991. Henning, Albert Frederick. *Ethics and Practices in Journalism*. New York: R. Long and R. R. Smith, 1932. viii + 204pp.

1992. Kingsbury, Susan M., Hornell Hart, and Associates. *Newspapers and the News: An Objective Measurement of Ethical and Unethical Behavior by Representative Newspapers*. New York: G. P. Putnam's Sons, 1937. xi + 238pp. (Bryn Mawr College Series in Social Economy No. 1.)

Discusses quantitatively bias, ethics, ethical codes, news interest, misleading medical advertisements, and social service activities. An extensive bibliography is included. This is a good example of early efforts to provide a methodology of journalism research.

1993. Lahey, Thomas A. *The Morals of Newspaper Making*. Notre Dame, Ind.: University of Notre Dame Press, 1924. 180pp.

Lahey reminds the journalist that he cannot make his own laws and that he must be responsible to the laws of God on questions of right and wrong in news. The book bears the imprimatur of the Catholic Church.

1994. Morris, Robert T. *Editorial Silence: The Third Era in Journalism*. Boston: The Stratford Co., 1927. iii + 256pp.

An eccentric criticism of the press. Morris asserts that the press prevents the people from obtaining necessary facts about meritorious industries by deliberately keeping silent about certain products — in this case nuts. The author tries, not too successfully, to use the press's own techniques of human interest in promoting nut-culture.

1995. Rathbone, H. B., ed. *Dynamic Journalism: Twelve Don R. Mellett Memorial Lectures*. New York: New York University, 1941. Paged individually by lecture.

Collects annual addresses, 1929–1940, delivered at schools of journalism in memory of a crusading editor of the Canton (Ohio) *Daily News* who was murdered in 1929 for exposing associations between criminals and public officials. All the lectures are historically valuable as statements of ideals by distinguished newspaper editors. Since 1941 the lectures have been published separately by the New York University Press.

1996. Reid, Richard. *The Morality of the Newspaper: A Series of Five*

Lectures Given at the University of Notre Dame. Notre Dame, Ind.: University of Notre Dame Press, 1938. 72pp.

1997. Schramm, Wilbur. *Responsibility in Mass Communication.* New York: Harper and Brothers, 1957. xxiii + 391pp. (Series 9 on Ethics and Economics of Society originated by a study committee of the National Council of Churches; foreword by Charles P. Taft; introduction by Reinhold Niebuhr.)

This is the most thorough study of ethics of the press in many years. Schramm redefines standards of press performance and seeks to delimit a new philosophy of public communication. Many case examples of ethical problems are offered and references to further reading are extensive.

1998. Sherover, Max. *Fakes in American Journalism.* Brooklyn, N.Y.: Free Press League, 1916. 89pp.

Brief case histories of newspaper fakes, and accounts of fakes in the early period of World War I. The author also attacks advertisers who exert pressures, the Associated Press, and William Randolph Hearst.

1999. Steed, Wickham. *Affirmations: God in the Modern World — Journalism.* London: E. Benn, Ltd., 1928. 32pp.

A statement of belief, with religious overtones, in the great opportunities of the press, by one of Great Britain's greatest journalists. The book is worth reading.

2000. Yost, Casper S. *The Principles of Journalism.* New York: D. Appleton and Co., 1924. ix + 170pp.

A commentary by the first president of the American Society of Newspaper Editors, long editor of the St. Louis *Globe-Democrat*, on truth in news handling, newspaper responsibility, and the concept of press freedom.

D. Freedom of the Press and Legal Analyses of the Press in the United States

2001. "Alien and Sedition Laws, Debates in the House of Delegates of Virginia," in *Senate Documents*, vol. 39, no. 873, 62nd Congress, 2nd Session. Washington, D.C.: Government Printing Office, 1912. 187pp.

A reissue of the verbatim record of debates on the Virginia Resolutions, December 1798, which opposed passage of the Alien and Sedition Acts.

2002. Angoff, Charles. *Handbook of Libel: A Practical Guide for Editors and Authors.* New York: Essential Books, Duell, Sloan and Pearce, 1946. ix + 410pp.

Angoff, a magazine editor for many years, discusses the underlying principles of libel, gives the significant libel laws of the various states, and summarizes the important legal decisions in libel cases.

2003. Arthur, William R., and Ralph L. Crosman. *The Law of Newspapers: A Text and Case Book for Use in Schools of Journalism and a Desk Book for Newspaper Workers.* New York and London: McGraw-Hill Book Co., 1940. xxxv + 615pp. (First published in 1928.)

Excellent in its day, this book now has been superseded by numerous later works, although its appendixes on court procedure are still helpful. It is stronger on the business side of journalism than some other texts.

2004. Ashley, Paul P. *Say It Safely: Legal Limits in Journalism and Broadcasting.* Seattle: University of Washington Press, 1956. x + 117pp. (An earlier edition was published under the title *Essentials of Libel: A Handbook for Journalists,* 1948.)

A manual designed to help publishers and broadcasters avoid the perils of libel, invasion of privacy, and contempt of court. Useful for quick reference.

2005. Associated Press. *Charter and By-Laws of the Associated Press.* New York: Associated Press, 1928. 22nd edition. 69pp.

2006. ———. *The Law of the Associated Press.* New York: Associated Press, 1914. 732pp.

Discusses litigation involving the AP, notably the *Inter-Ocean Publishing Co. v. Associated Press* case, for which the complete record is given. Other contents deal with membership regulations, protection of news, and copyright.

2007. ———. *Member Editorials on the Monopoly Complaint Filed by the Government against the Associated Press on August 28, 1942.* New York: Associated Press, 1942. 2 vols. About 600pp.

This case, in which the AP lost its fight to keep the Chicago *Sun* from membership, was decided in the U.S. Supreme Court in 1945 under the title *U.S. v. Associated Press.* An addendum in vol. II carries facsimiles of comments from a special supplement to *Editor & Publisher,* November 21, 1942.

2008. Barth, Alan. *The Loyalty of Free Men.* New York: Viking Press, 1951. xxxi + 253pp. (Foreword by Zechariah Chafee.)

An editorial writer of the Washington *Post* stanchly defends civil liberties and analyzes the attacks on nonconformity at the height of the Communist investigations in the early 1950s. He notes the tendencies of the press to give currency to accusations through sensational display of news.

2009. Beman, Lamar T., comp. *Selected Articles on Censorship of Speech and the Press.* New York: H. W. Wilson Co., 1930. 507pp.

This anthology includes historical and contemporary arguments on both sides of the subject. There is a useful bibliography.

2010. Berns, Walter. *Freedom, Virtue and the First Amendment.* Baton Rouge: Louisiana State University Press, 1957. xiii + 264pp.

The author reviews what he regards as widespread dissatisfaction with U.S. Supreme Court decisions in First Amendment cases in the 1950s. He analyzes censorship and obscenity and "freedom and loyalty." The table of cases is extensive.

2011. Blanshard, Paul. *The Right to Read: The Battle against Censorship.* Boston: Beacon Press, 1955. 339pp.

An analysis for the general reader, based in part on censorship reports of *Publishers' Weekly,* the American Book Publishers Council, the American Civil Liberties Union, the Committee on Intellectual Freedom of the American Library Association, and the National Education Association.

2012. Bowker, Richard Rogers. *Copyright: Its History and Its Law*. Boston: Houghton Mifflin Co., 1912. xxiii + 709pp.

A summary of the principles and practices of copyright, with special reference to the American Code of 1909 and the British Copyright Act of 1911.

2013. Brown, Rome G. *Some Points on the Law of the Press*, in University of Missouri Journalism Series, No. 24. Columbia, Mo.: University of Missouri, May 1922. 39pp.

2014. Chafee, Zechariah, Jr. *The Blessings of Liberty*. Philadelphia and New York: J. B. Lippincott Co., 1956. 350pp.

Eleven selections from Chafee's writings and addresses that stress civil liberties; much is personal recollection. Included are a discussion of Chafee's own work with the United Nations in advocating worldwide freedom of speech and press and a report on the McCarthy hearings of the early 1950s.

2015. ———. *Free Speech in the United States*. Cambridge, Mass.: Harvard University Press, 1941. xiv + 634pp. (First published as *Freedom of Speech*. New York: Harcourt, Brace and Howe, 1920. 431pp.)

The most authoritative study of the concept of free speech. Chafee traces the philosophical background and analyzes thoroughly the specific cases that have shaped interpretation of the First Amendment. There is heavy emphasis on the law of sedition and, in the 1941 edition, on the condition of free speech and free press on the eve of World War II.

2016. ———. *Government and Mass Communications: A Report from the Commission on Freedom of the Press*. Chicago: University of Chicago Press, 1947. 2 vols. xvii + 829pp., total.

Chafee deals with libel and compulsory correction of errors, obscenity, post office and customs services, treason and sedition, censorship, and contempt of court. He also considers the role of government as itself a possible disseminator of ideas. The book is the most specific to come out of the commission studies.

2017. ———. *Thirty-Five Years with Freedom of Speech*. New York: Roger N. Baldwin Civil Liberties Foundation, 1952. 40pp.

A lecture at Columbia University, March 12, 1952.

2018. Chenery, William L. *Freedom of the Press*. New York: Harcourt, Brace and Co., 1955. 256pp.

A former editor of *Collier's* writes feelingly on the value of press freedom. Drawing upon his own wealth of experience and knowledge, Chenery weaves past event and past meaning into present crisis and present need.

2019. Chunn, Calvin Ellsworth, ed. *Oklahoma Publication Laws*. Tulsa, Okla.: University of Tulsa, 1948. 83pp. Revised edition published under the title *The Publication Laws of Oklahoma*. St. Louis, Mo.: Educational Publishers, 1950. 146pp.

2020. Colorado Press Association. *Publication Laws of the State of Colorado*. Boulder: Colorado Press Assn., 1932. 277pp. (Preface by Edwin A. Bemis.)

Includes a review of important court decisions in addition to the compilation of laws.

2021. Commission on Freedom of the Press. *A Free and Responsible Press*. Chicago: University of Chicago Press, 1947. xii + 140pp. (Foreword by Robert M. Hutchins.)

Summarizes the findings of the commission set up by Time, Inc., and the Encyclopaedia Britannica and makes recommendations for more responsible operation of the mass media.

2022. Cooper, Kent. *The Right to Know: An Exposition of the Evils of News Suppression and Propaganda*. New York: Farrar, Straus, and Cudahy, 1956. 335pp.

The retired general manager of the Associated Press presents here a fervent appeal for press freedom. He draws a broad historical picture of government suppression through the centuries and advocates that peoples of the world urge their governments to withdraw from news-gathering activities. Cooper goes into detail on the case of the AP's Edward Kennedy, who defied a censorship order delaying release of news concerning the end of World War II.

2023. Cross, Harold L. *The People's Right to Know: Legal Access to Public Records and Proceedings*. New York: Columbia University Press, 1953. xxiv + 405pp.

A reference book and textbook prepared for the Freedom of Information Committee of the American Society of Newspaper Editors. Cross carefully analyzes the rights of the press in gathering information about government, outlines statutes of the states relating to public records, and discusses newspapers as parties to litigation involving records. The case list is extensive.

2024. Cushman, Robert E. *Civil Liberties in the United States*. Ithaca, N.Y.: Cornell University Press, 1956. xiii + 248pp.

A factual survey of the state of 11 forms of civil liberty, among them speech and press. The author engages in little commentary or interpretation, leaving conclusions to the reader.

2025. ———. *Keep Our Press Free*. New York: Public Affairs Committee, 1946. 32pp. (Pamphlet No. 123 in Public Affairs Series.)

The content is elementary.

2026. Davis, Jerome. *Character Assassination*. New York: Philosophical Library, 1950. xix + 259pp. (Introduction by Robert M. Hutchins.)

A defense of civil liberties by a former Yale professor and leader in the American Federation of Teachers. The book is useful for its details on a libel action which Davis carried on against the *Saturday Evening Post*, 1939–1943, after he had been called a leader in Communist activities.

2027. Davis, Norris G. *The Press and the Law in Texas*. Austin: University of Texas Press, 1956. x + 244pp.

Traces in detail how Texas press laws operate, with examples drawn from actual news-reporting situations. Davis does not take up federal regulations of the press.

2028. Dawson, Samuel Arthur. *Freedom of the Press: A Study of the Legal Doctrine of Qualified Privilege*. New York: Columbia University Press, 1924. 120pp.

An analysis of the right of newspapers to publish information about legislatures, courts, and governmental officials. Now out of date.

2029. Dennett, Mrs. Mary Ware. *Who's Obscene?* New York: Vanguard Press, 1930. xxxiii + 281pp.

Mrs. Dennett was arrested in April 1929 for distributing through the mails a pamphlet on *The Sex Side of Life.* She discusses in detail her successful defense and quotes extensively from newspaper editorials supporting her cause. She also considers the general problem of censorship by the post office.

2030. Digges, I. W. *The Modern Law of Advertising and Marketing.* New York: Funk and Wagnalls Co., 1948. xxiv + 310pp. (Issued in association with Printers' Ink Publishing Co.)

Considers state laws on advertising, trademarks, fair trade regulations, property rights in ideas and copyright, right of privacy, and libel and slander.

2031. *A Dissertation upon the Constitutional Freedom of the Press.* Boston: Joseph Nancrede, printed by David Carlisle, 1801. 54pp.

The writer (identified only as "An Impartial Citizen") argues in a manner surprisingly reasonable for the period both sides of the Alien and Sedition Acts controversy.

2032. Douglas, William O. *An Almanac of Liberty.* Garden City, N.Y.: Doubleday and Co., 1954. xx + 409pp.

Many of these brief legal-philosophical essays, in calendar form, deal with free speech, free press, contempt, censorship, and copyright.

2033. Duniway, Clyde Augustus. *The Development of Freedom of the Press in Massachusetts.* New York: Longmans, Green and Co., 1906. xv + 202pp.

A scholarly study of the early constitutional struggles over freedom of the press in the colony and state of Massachusetts. British precedents are emphasized. Appendixes give transcripts of the censure of James Franklin (*New-England Courant*) in 1722. The study carries to 1827.

2034. Eaton, Clement. *Freedom of Thought in the Old South.* Durham, N.C.: Duke University Press, 1940. xix + 343pp.

In this cultural study of the South, 1790–1860, Eaton gives detailed accounts of the proscribing of newspapers over the slavery issue and reports of trials of numerous editors who flouted state controls. All the material is carefully documented.

2035. Ernst, Morris L. *The Best Is Yet.* New York and London: Harper and Brothers, 1945. xiii + 291pp.

This American lawyer and author was for many years a leader in defense of civil liberties and both a critic and a defender of the press. Part of his autobiography contains excellent information on the American Civil Liberties Union, Heywood Broun's struggles to get the American Newspaper Guild established, censorship, and the right to privacy.

2036. ———. *The First Freedom.* New York: The Macmillan Co., 1946. xiv + 316pp.

A provocative analysis of "concentrated economic power" in the structure of the press. Ernst attacks newspaper and film monopolies, the trend toward one-newspaper cities, the rise in absentee ownership of newspapers, and interlocking radio-newspaper control. He also offers remedies.

2037. ———. *So Far So Good.* New York: Harper and Brothers, 1948. 271pp.

A sequel to *The Best Is Yet,* with considerably more discussion on press invasions of privacy and recommendations for a wider flow of news under the Bill of Rights.

2038. ——— and Alexander Lindey. *The Censor Marches On: Recent Milestones in the Administration of the Obscenity Law in the United States.* New York: Doubleday, Doran and Co., 1940. xi + 346pp.

An account of efforts to "save society from sex," with emphasis on obscenity prosecutions from 1925 to 1940.

2039. ———. *Hold Your Tongue: Adventures in Libel and Slander.* New York: William Morrow and Co., 1932. xi + 357pp. London: Methuen and Co., Ltd., 1936. xv + 312pp. (Introduction in Methuen edition by A. P. Herbert, M.P.)

For the lay reader, a book treating libel and slander as "live, merry topics." The cases are chiefly those which have involved prominent personalities — among them, Theodore Roosevelt, James Abbott McNeill Whistler and John Ruskin, James Fenimore Cooper, and Oscar Wilde. The criminal libel prosecution involving the New York *World* as a result of its Panama Canal Zone investigations in the early 1900s is also discussed in detail.

2040. Ernst, Morris L., and William Seagle. *To the Pure: A Study of Obscenity and the Censor.* New York: Viking Press, 1928. xiv + 336pp.

Little material on newspapers is included.

2041. *The Federalist, or the New Constitution, by Alexander Hamilton, John Jay, and James Madison.* New York: E. P. Dutton and Co.; London: J. M. Dent and Sons, Ltd., 1911. xx + 456pp. (No. 519 in Everyman's Library; introduction by W. J. Ashley.)

One of numerous editions of *The Federalist,* 85 essays written to urge adoption of the Constitution in 1787–1788. Hamilton, Jay, and Madison in the first instance wrote the articles for publication in New York newspapers. The Everyman's edition contains a brief summary and a short bibliography.

2042. *The Federalist: The Enduring Federalist.* Garden City, N.Y.: Doubleday and Co., 1948. xvi + 391pp. (Edited and analyzed by Charles A. Beard.)

Beard's useful abridgment of the complete *Federalist* for modern readers. Illustrated with 24 halftones.

2043. Ferguson, George V. *Press and Party in Canada: Issues of Freedom.* Toronto: Ryerson Press, 1955. vii + 46pp. (Foreword by W. A. Mackintosh, Queen's University, Kingston.)

Lectures by the editor of the Montreal *Star* providing an excellent brief summary of the meaning of press freedom. Ferguson opposes state intervention and urges press owners to pursue responsible policies.

2044. Field, Marshall, III. *Freedom Is More Than a Word*. Chicago: University of Chicago Press, 1945. xvii + 190pp.

Field's explanation of the way he sought through *PM* and the Chicago *Sun* to promote his faith in democracy, and his version of the *Associated Press v. U.S.* case, by which the *Sun* eventually gained an AP franchise.

2045. Fraenkel, Osmond K. *Our Civil Liberties*. New York: Viking Press, 1944. x + 277pp.

2046. ———. *The Supreme Court and Civil Liberties: How Far Has the Court Protected the Bill of Rights?* New York: American Civil Liberties Union, 1949. 3rd revision. 80pp.

2047. "Freedom of the Press," in the *American Annual Cyclopaedia and Register of Important Events*. New York: D. Appleton and Co., 1861–1902. (The title after 1874 was *Appleton's Annual Encyclopaedia*.)

The articles covering the Civil War period (vol. I, pp. 328–330; II, 480–481; III, 423–425; IV, 389–394) are most valuable; they contain considerable information on suppression of newspapers during that conflict.

2048. Gerald, J. Edward. *The Press and the Constitution, 1931–1947*. Minneapolis: University of Minnesota Press, 1948. viii + 173pp.

Discusses the development of the concept of freedom of the press through constitutional law from the invalidation of the Minnesota gag law (*Near v. Minnesota*) to the revision of the Wagner Labor Relations Act. Problems that are analyzed concern the contempt power, picketing as a form of free speech, fair labor standards and taxation of the press, and censorship and licensing. There is a selected bibliography.

2049. Haight, Anne Lyon. *Banned Books: Informal Notes on Some Books Banned for Various Reasons at Various Times and in Various Places*. New York: R. R. Bowker Co., 1955. 2nd edition, revised and enlarged. xvii + 172pp. (First edition, 1935.)

Considers book censorship from the expurgation of *The Odyssey* to the 1950s, discusses freedom of the press as it relates to book firms and libraries, and notes court decisions concerning censorship and the postal power.

2050. Hale, William G. *The Law of the Press*. St. Paul: West Publishing Co., 1948. 3rd edition. xiii + 691pp. (Published under the same title in 1923 and revised in 1933; the second edition was under the joint authorship of Hale and Ivan Benson.)

A case book on press law, principally as it concerns the newspaper. In addition to the cases, carried in full or in part, there is a useful general discussion of courts and court procedure, libel, privacy, contempt, constitutional guarantees, copyright, business law of the press, and miscellaneous statutes.

2051. Harper, Fowler, and Fleming James, Jr. "Defamation," in *The Law of Torts*, vol. 1, pp. 349–473. Boston and Toronto: Little, Brown and Co., 1956.

An excellent concentrated coverage of the substantive aspects of defamation, by two Yale professors of law.

2052. Hays, Arthur Garfield. *Let Freedom Ring.* New York: Horace Liveright, 1928. 341pp.

An appeal in behalf of civil liberties by a famed legal defender of them. Hays discusses cases with which he was associated between 1922 and 1927, including *Massachusetts and U.S. v. H. L. Mencken*, in which Hays was counsel for the editor of the *American Mercury* when Mencken was charged with violating obscenity laws.

2053. Hocking, William Ernest. *Freedom of the Press: A Framework of Principle.* Chicago: University of Chicago Press, 1947. xi + 243pp.

One of the members of the Commission on Freedom of the Press discusses cogently the philosophical problems of press freedom in the 20th century.

2054. Hughes, Frank. *Prejudice and the Press: A Restatement of the Principle of Freedom of the Press with Specific Reference to the Hutchins-Luce Commission.* New York: Devin-Adair Co., 1950. xi + 642pp.

A Chicago *Tribune* staff member aggressively criticizes the 1947 report of the Commission on Freedom of the Press. Hughes's book is marred by his personal attacks on commission members, but he does provide substantive material clearing up some matters covered carelessly or neglected by the commission.

2055. Ickes, Harold L., comp. *Freedom of the Press Today: A Clinical Examination by 28 Specialists.* New York: Vanguard Press, 1941. 308pp.

Ickes invited leaders in journalism and other fields to contribute their views on how well American newspapers had fulfilled their responsibilities under the First Amendment. The tone is distinctly liberal.

2056. Inglis, Ruth A. *Freedom of the Movies: A Report on Self-Regulation.* Chicago: University of Chicago Press, 1947. x + 244pp.

This Freedom of the Press Commission report on the film phase of its mass communication studies recommends particularly that the constitutional guarantee of free press be broadened to include films. There is an extensive discussion of newsreels.

2057. Jenkins, Arthur D. *Illinois Newspaper Law.* St. Louis, Mo., and Mascoutah, Ill.: Oxford Publishing House, 1942. 291 + 26pp.

A textbook on notice and publication laws, annotated.

2058. Johnson, Gerald W. *Peril and Promise: An Inquiry into Freedom of the Press.* New York: Harper and Brothers, 1958. vii + 110pp.

An eloquent expression of the need for greater press responsibility, by a distinguished Baltimore newspaperman. The material is highly literary and philosophical.

2059. Jones, Robert William. *The Law of Journalism.* Washington, D.C.: Washington Law Book Co.; Brooklyn, N.Y.: Metropolitan Law Book Co., 1940. xii + 395pp.

A textbook on freedom of the press, libel, contempt of court, property rights in news, and regulation of advertising. It is less adequate in general than other works on the same subjects.

2060. Kinsley, Philip. *Liberty and the Press*. Chicago: The Chicago Tribune, 1944. xi + 99pp.

The *Tribune* argument in support of the newspaper's continual fight "to preserve a free press for the American people," published while the *Tribune* was contesting the government's action to bring about changes in the membership by-laws of the Associated Press.

2061. Konvitz, Milton R. *Bill of Rights Reader*. Ithaca, N.Y.: Cornell University Press, 1954. xix + 591pp.

A solid case book of leading constitutional decisions involving civil rights, mostly from the 1930s, 1940s, and early 1950s. The press cases take up the question of freedom *not* to speak and *not* to listen. In some respects Konvitz brings Chafee's *Free Speech in the United States* (2015 above) up to date.

2062. ———. *Fundamental Liberties of a Free People: Religion, Speech, Press, Assembly*. Ithaca, N.Y.: Cornell University Press, 1957. xiii + 420pp.

A critical study, with extensive details on scores of major cases. There is good treatment of the concepts of freedom *not* to speak and *not* to listen, of test oaths and loyalty oaths, and of the clear-and-present-danger doctrine. An appendix analyzes the background leading to the adoption of the Bill of Rights in 1791.

2063. Koop, Theodore F. *Weapon of Silence*. Chicago: University of Chicago Press, 1946. xi + 304pp.

A deputy director of the United States Office of Censorship in World War II discusses the office's operations, including those affecting the press and radio.

2064. Lassiter, William C. *Law and Press: The Legal Aspects of News Reporting, Editing and Publishing in North Carolina*. Raleigh, N.C.: Edwards and Broughton Co., 1956. xvi + 262pp. (Earlier edition, 1954.)

A detailed treatise on all phases of press law in North Carolina. The author is an attorney and legal representative of press associations.

2065. Lehmann, Frederick W. *The Law and the Newspaper*, in University of Missouri Journalism Series, No. 15. Columbia, Mo.: University of Missouri, December 1917. 26pp.

2066. Lindey, Alexander. *Plagiarism and Originality*. New York: Harper and Brothers, 1952. xv + 366pp.

A helpful and readable commentary on the legal problems of writing in various fields: books and magazines, plays, motion pictures, and music.

2067. McKeon, Richard, Robert K. Merton, and Walter Gellhorn. *The Freedom to Read: Perspective and Program*. New York: National Book Committee, published by R. R. Bowker Co., 1957. xvii + 110pp.

A study of censorship problems, including material on the validity of state and local censorship laws, on federal censorship through postal and customs administration, and on possible community defense against censorship.

2068. Meiklejohn, Alexander. *Free Speech and Its Relation to Self-Government*. New York: Harper and Brothers, 1948. xiv + 107pp.

2069. Merrill, Samuel. *Newspaper Libel: A Handbook for the Press.* Boston: Ticknor and Co., 1888. 304pp.

An early text on defamation intended for use in newspaper offices. The author, an attorney, was on the staff of the Boston *Globe.* The cases cited are still interesting, although no longer timely.

2070. Miller, John C. *Crisis in Freedom: The Alien and Sedition Acts.* Boston: Little, Brown and Co., 1951. 253pp.

One of the more useful books on this critical period, with excellent detailed accounts of the trials conducted under the Sedition Act against James T. Callender, Thomas Cooper, William Duane, and Matthew Lyon. There is a good bibliography.

2071. Mock, James R. *Censorship 1917.* Princeton, N.J.: Princeton University Press; London: Oxford University Press, 1941. ix + 250pp.

An account of all phases of World War I censorship, including newspaper cases. There is considerable material on George Creel, director of the Committee on Public Information.

2072. National Association of Radio and Television Broadcasters. *Broadcasting and the Bill of Rights.* Washington, D.C.: The Association, 1947. 322pp.

A compilation of statements made at a hearing in May 1947 on a bill to amend the Communications Act of 1934. Appendixes give the text of the proposed bill and radio program standards of the National Association of Radio and Television Broadcasters.

2073. National Civil Liberties Bureau. *War-Time Prosecutions and Mob Violence Involving the Rights of Free Speech, Free Press, and Peaceful Assemblage.* New York: Civil Liberties Bureau, 1919. 56pp.

An annotated pamphlet listing 655 prosecutions under World War I statutes, including 56 espionage cases involving statements made in public print or distribution of literature.

2074. New York State, Supreme Court Common Law Reports. *Reports of Cases Adjudged and Determined in the Supreme Court of Judicature . . . of the State of New York.* Newark, N.J.: Lawyers' Co-operative Publishing Co., 1883.

The appendix of Book I (pp. 717–741) contains a full report of the famous New York case of *People v. Croswell* (1804), which helped to establish truth as a defense in criminal libel prosecutions.

2075. Nicholson, Margaret. *A Manual of Copyright Practice for Writers, Publishers, and Agents.* New York: Oxford University Press, 1956. 2nd edition. x + 273pp. (First edition, 1945. x + 255pp.)

A useful work for anyone who seeks specific information on copyright. Newspaper and magazine problems are carefully considered.

2076. Outland, Ethel R. *The "Effingham" Libels on Cooper: A Documentary History of the Libel Suits of James Fenimore Cooper Centering around the Three-Mile Point Controversy and the Novel "Home as Found"—1837–1845*. Madison, Wis.: University of Wisconsin, 1929. 272pp.

The author discusses the history and significance of Cooper's controversies with the press. Those whom he sued included Thurlow Weed, Horace Greeley, James Watson Webb, William L. Stone, and Park Benjamin.

2077. Patterson, Giles J. *Free Speech and a Free Press*. Boston: Little, Brown and Co., 1939. ix + 261pp.

2078. Pfeffer, Leo. *The Liberties of an American: The Supreme Court Speaks*. New York: Beacon Press, 1956. xi + 309pp.

Prepared for the general reader, this book takes up eight aspects of American liberty, among which are the right of speech and the right to remain silent. Numerous cases are cited.

2079. Pollard, James E. *Laws of the 48 States Bearing on: I. Definition of "Newspaper"; II. "Open Meetings of Public Bodies"; III. Definition of Public Records*. Columbus, Ohio: Ohio State University Press, 1957. 26pp. (In Journalism Series No. 18.)

Based chiefly on information obtained in 1956 from the offices of the attorneys general of the 48 states. It brings up to date Pollard's *The Newspaper as Defined by Law*.

2080. ———. *The Newspaper as Defined by Law*. Columbus, Ohio: Ohio State University Press, 1940. viii + 82pp.

2080a. ———. *Ohio Newspapers and the Law: A Handbook and Digest of Ohio Laws and Other Material Related to Editing and Writing for Newspapers and Other Media*. Columbus: Ohio State University Press, 1956. 18pp. (In Journalism Series No. 17.)

2081. ——— and Edward M. Martin, eds. *Newspaper Laws of Ohio*. Columbus, Ohio: Ohio State University Press, 1937. xiii + 174pp. Revised edition, *Ohio Newspaper and Publication Laws*. 1954. 210pp. (In Journalism Series No. 16.)

2082. Pritchett, C. Herman. *Civil Liberties and the Vinson Court*. Chicago: University of Chicago Press, 1954. xi + 297pp.

A sequel to an earlier work by the same author on *The Roosevelt Court*, this covers the period of Fred M. Vinson's chief justiceship, 1946–1953. There are three chapters on free speech.

2083. *Report of the New York State Joint Legislative Committee Studying Publication and Dissemination of Objectionable and Obscene Materials*. Albany, N.Y.: Williams Press, 1956. 172pp. (Issued as State of New York Legislative Document No. 32.)

This committee, which operated from 1949 to 1955, made a study of offensive publications, motion and still pictures, radio and television programs; and it considered possible remedial legislation that would not restrain or abridge liberty of the press. Illustrated.

2084. Rich, W. E. *The History of the U.S. Post Office to the Year 1829*. Cambridge, Mass.: Harvard University Press, 1924. vii + 190pp.

2085. Roberts, Martin A. "Records in the Copyright Office of the Library of Congress Deposited by the United States District Court, 1790–1870," in *Papers of the Bibliographical Society of America,* vol. 31, part 2, pp. 81–101. Chicago: University of Chicago Press, 1937.

Summarizes briefly early copyright legislation.

2086. Rutland, Robert Allen. *The Birth of the Bill of Rights, 1776–1791.* Chapel Hill: University of North Carolina Press, 1955. vi + 243pp. (Published under the sponsorship of the Institute of Early American History and Culture.)

A careful study of the background and adoption of the Bill of Rights.

2087. *Safeguarding Civil Liberty Today: The Edward L. Bernays Lectures of 1944.* New York: Peter Smith, 1949. x + 158pp.

The lectures are "Political Freedom," by Carl L. Becker; "Freedom, Image and Reality," by Max Lerner; "Freedom of Speech and the Press," by James Lawrence Fly; "Civil Liberty and Public Opinion," by Robert E. Cushman; "Civil Rights and the Federal Law," by Francis Biddle; and "Freedom to Learn," by Edmund Ezra Day.

2088. Salmon, Lucy Maynard. *The Newspaper and Authority.* New York: Oxford University Press, 1923. xxviii + 505pp.

A companion volume to Miss Salmon's *The Newspaper and the Historian* (see 25 above). She discusses the problem of how far restrictions — censorship, taxes, etc. — placed on newspapers by external authority have limited their usefulness for the historian in his attempt to reconstruct the past. The approach is scholarly.

2089. Savage, W. Sherman. *The Controversy over the Distribution of Abolition Literature.* [Washington, D.C.]: Association for the Study of Negro Life and History, 1938. xv + 141pp.

Traces the conflict over the distribution of abolition literature through the mails, 1830–1860, and the attempts in this period (particularly in the South) to control the press.

2090. Schroeder, Theodore. *Free Speech for Radicals.* New York: The Free Speech League, 1916. viii + 206pp.

2091. ———. *A New Concept of Liberty.* Berkeley Heights, N.J.: Oriole Press, privately published, 1940. lxxx + 153pp.

Eight selections from the writings of this controversial defender of civil liberties, 1900–1938, with a biography of Schroeder by Joseph Ishill. See especially "An Indictment of Puritan Censorship" and "Our Vanishing Liberty of the Press."

2092. ———. *"Obscene" Literature and Constitutional Law: A Forensic Defense of Freedom of the Press.* New York: Privately published, 1911. 439pp.

The author attacks obscenity laws of the time as a pernicious curtailment on liberty of the press and makes a strong attack against Anthony Comstock.

2093. ———, comp. *Free Press Anthology.* New York: Free Speech League and Truth Seeker Publishing Co., 1909. viii + 267pp.

Although old, poorly indexed, and only sketchily footnoted, this book collects a mass of useful and interesting material relating to free speech and press from the time of Milton to 1909. See especially the complete reprint of "An Explanation concerning Obscenities," by Pierre Bayle, French philosopher of the 17th century.

2094. Schuyler, Livingston Rowe. *The Liberty of the Press in the American Colonies before the Revolutionary War, with Particular Reference to Conditions in the Royal Colony of New York.* New York: Thomas Whittaker, 1905. 86pp.

Much of the author's treatment of the New York Colonial press (including the Zenger case) is based upon the proceedings of the General Assembly of the colony and upon O'Callaghan's *Documents Relative to the Colonial History of New York.* Originally this was a doctoral thesis.

2095. Shaw, Ralph R. *Literary Property in the United States.* Washington, D.C.: Scarecrow Press, 1950. v + 277pp.

A book for general readers in which the author seeks to determine just what literary property is.

2096. Siebert, Fredrick Seaton. *The Rights and Privileges of the Press.* New York and London: D. Appleton-Century Co., 1934. xvii + 429pp.

A standard general work, suitable as a college text although now dated. Siebert approaches the subject from the angle of what the press can do under the law rather than what it cannot do because of restrictive legislation. As a result, libel is relatively subordinated.

2097. Smith, Bradford. *A Dangerous Freedom.* Philadelphia and New York: J. B. Lippincott Co., 1952 and 1954. 308pp.

A study of a neglected phase of the first amendment — freedom of assembly as distinct from religion, speech, and press.

2098. Smith, James Morton. *Freedom's Fetters: The Alien and Sedition Laws and American Civil Liberties.* Ithaca, N.Y.: Cornell University Press, 1956. xv + 464pp. (Published in cooperation with the Institute of Early American History and Culture.)

The first of a projected two-volume study. Smith goes into careful detail on cases involving Benjamin Franklin Bache (Philadelphia *Aurora*); John Daly Burk (New York *Time-Piece*); Matthew Lyon (*Vermont Gazette*); the Boston *Independent Chronicle*; William Duane (the *Aurora*); James T. Callender (Richmond *Examiner*); Anthony Haswell (*Vermont Gazette*); and Charles Holt (New London, Conn., *Bee*). The text of the Alien and Sedition Acts is carried.

2099. Spring, Samuel. *Risks and Rights in Publishing, Television, Radio, Motion Pictures, Advertising, and the Theater.* New York: W. W. Norton and Co., 1956. 2nd edition, revised. xviii + 365pp. (First issued in 1952. xviii + 385pp. Foreword by Harold M. Stephens, chief judge, United States Court of Appeals, Washington, D.C.)

A "lawbook for laymen," touching upon most phases of communications. Spring treats chiefly of privacy, defamation, copyright, and unfair competition. An appendix includes the complete text of the U.S. Copyright Act. Numerous press cases are cited.

2100. Steigleman, Walter A. *The Newspaperman and the Law*. Dubuque, Iowa: William C. Brown Co., 1950. x + 427pp.

The author treats the law and the press as social agencies that interact and deals less with specific legal cases than do writers of most texts of this type. He also considers the history of press law.

2101. Sullivan, Harold W. *Contempts by Publication: The Law of Trial by Newspaper*. New Haven, Conn.: Yale University Press, 1941. 3rd edition. xiv + 230pp.

An anti-press interpretation. The author supports the conservative point of view that the courts should be strict in enforcing judicial controls over newspaper comment on trials. Both the American and British laws of contempt are considered.

2102. Swindler, William F. *Problems of Law in Journalism*. New York: The Macmillan Co., 1955. xxii + 551pp.

A modified case book, with procedural details omitted and background added by the author. The book is stronger on the business side of newspapers than most other books on law of the press.

2103. Syracuse University School of Journalism. *A Digest of New York Laws Relating to Publications*. Syracuse, N.Y.: The School of Journalism, 1943. 186pp.

2104. Thayer, Frank. *Legal Control of the Press*. Brooklyn, N.Y.: Foundation Press, 1956. 3rd edition. xv + 749pp. (Earlier editions, 1950 and 1944.)

Strongest of the general works on press law in its treatment of the historical background in the struggle for freedom of the press and in its attention to trial procedure in libel cases. There are extensive appendixes on terminology, bibliography, second-class mailing privileges, and cases.

2105. United States Congress, House of Representatives Committee on Government Operations. *Availability of Information from Federal Departments and Agencies*. Hearings, 84th Congress, 1st Session–85th Congress, 2nd Session, November 7, 1955–February 7, 1958. Washington, D.C.: Government Printing Office, 1956–1958. 15 parts, 3564pp., numbered consecutively.

Important legislative hearings on freedom of information from federal executive offices. They were held before a subcommittee under the chairmanship of Rep. John E. Moss (D, Calif.). Contents: Pt. 1, Panel discussion with editors, *et al.*; pt. 2, Civil Service Commission, Post Office, Treasury, and Agriculture; pt. 3, Panel discussion with legal experts; pt. 4, Panel discussion on scientific and technical information; pt. 5, Department of Defense, first section; pt. 6, Department of Commerce; pt. 7, Department of Defense, second section; pt. 8, Department of Defense, third section; pt. 9, Department of Defense, fourth section; pt. 10, Department of Defense, fifth section (Army, Navy, Air Force information chiefs); pt. 11, Amendment of "Housekeeping Statute"; pt. 12, Panel discussion with government lawyers; pt. 13, Department of Defense, sixth section; pt. 14, Second hearing on amendment of "Housekeeping Statute," later passed as Revised Statutes 161 (5 U.S.C. 22), proposed by H.R. 2767, H.R. 2768, H.R. 2769, H.R. 3497, and H.R. 2810; pt. 15, Restrictions on flow of scientific and technological information.

2106. ———. *Availability of Information from Federal Departments and Agencies (Department of Defense)*. House Report No. 1884, 85th Congress, 2nd Session. Washington, D.C.: Government Printing Office, June 16, 1958. ix + 295pp. (Union Calendar No. 745.)

Twenty-seventh report of the full Committee on Government Operations transmitted to the House of Representatives and based on the study made by the Moss subcommittee (2105 above). This report was presented by William L. Dawson (D, Ill.), chairman. It contains recommendations for alleviation of censorship controls, and 15 exhibits (chiefly correspondence, news stories, and editorials on information difficulties).

2107. ———. *Freedom of Information Legislation during the 85th Congress*. Washington, D.C.: Government Printing Office, October 30, 1958. Committee print. 24pp.

A useful, brief summary of the extensive activities of the Moss Committee (2105 above).

2108. United States Copyright Office. *Decisions of the United States Courts Involving Copyright*, Bulletins 17–. Washington, D.C.: Library of Congress Copyright Office, 1915–date.

These volumes contain substantially all significant cases on copyright, and many involving related subjects in the field of literary property, decided since 1909. There have been 30 bulletins to date, carrying the decisions through 1956. A cumulative index, compiled and edited by Wilma S. Davis, was issued in 1956; it covers Bulletins 17 through 29.

2109. United States Department of State, Office of Public Affairs. *Freedom of Information in American Policy and Practice*. Washington, D.C.: Foreign Policies Studies Branch, Division of Historical Policy Research, 1948. vi + 65pp. (Prepared by William Gerber and Letitia A. Lewis.)

2110. United States Office of Censorship. *Code of Wartime Practices for the American Press*. Washington, D.C.: Government Printing Office, 1942–1945.

These pamphlets set forth the principles of the voluntary censorship code under which the press operated during World War II. Four major editions were circulated: June 15, 1942, 6pp.; February 1, 1943, 16pp.; December 1, 1943, 14pp.; and May 15, 1945, 4pp.

2111. ———. *Code of Wartime Practices for American Broadcasters*. Washington, D.C.: Government Printing Office, 1942–1943.

Edition of June 15, 1942, 8pp.; February 1, 1943, 9pp.; December 1, 1943, 8pp.

2112. ———. *A Report on the Office of Censorship*. Washington, D.C.: Government Printing Office, 1945. 54pp.

A historical report on the administration of the office during World War II.

2113. United States Post Office Department. *Postage Rates, 1789–1930: Abstract of Laws Passed between 1789 and 1930 Fixing Rates of Postage and According Free Mail Privileges*. Washington, D.C.: Government Printing Office, 1930. 55pp.

2114. ———. *Postal Laws and Regulations of the United States of America*. Washington, D.C.: Government Printing Office, annually.

2115. Weinberger, Harry. *Free Speech and Free Press*. New York: The Author, n.d. 8pp.

A stanch proponent of press freedom and member of the New York bar argues that the first casualties of war are free speech and free press. This piece was first published in the *Fra*, a monthly issued from 1908 to 1917.

2116. ———. *The Liberty of the Press*. Berkeley Heights, N.J.: Oriole Press, 1934. 39pp.

Two addresses delivered on the occasion of the 200th anniversary of John Peter Zenger's establishment of the New York *Weekly-Journal*. The memorial speeches are as much in recognition of Andrew Hamilton, Zenger's attorney, as of Zenger.

2117. Whipple, Leon. *The Story of Civil Liberty in the United States*. New York: Vanguard Press, 1927. x + 366pp.

A competent account for general readers covering the history of American civil liberties from 1776 to 1917. There is a detailed discussion of the abolitionist controversy, 1830–1860; the Civil War; civil liberty and labor; and freedom of social thought.

2118. Wiggins, James Russell. *Freedom or Secrecy*. New York: Oxford University Press, 1956. xi + 242pp.

Wiggins, executive editor of the Washington *Post and Times-Herald*, was chairman of the Freedom of Information Committee of the American Society of Newspaper Editors and the Associated Press Managing Editors Association. He analyzes provocatively the people's right of free access to information about Congress and legislatures, the judiciary, government executive departments, and the military.

2119. Wittenberg, Philip. *Dangerous Words: A Guide to the Law of Libel*. New York: Columbia University Press, 1947. ix + 335pp.

Among general books on libel this is the most readable for the nonprofessional and the student. Wittenberg includes an extensive list of terms judged libelous since 1800. He is a libel and copyright attorney.

2120. ———. *The Law of Literary Property*. Cleveland and New York: World Publishing Co., 1957. 284pp.

In attempting to discuss in layman's language the contradictory and technical elements of the law on literary property, Wittenberg perhaps oversimplifies. The book relates chiefly to copyright.

2121. ———. *The Protection and Marketing of Literary Property*. New York: Julian Messner, 1937. 395pp.

A handbook for the general reader on copyright, infringement, piracy, libel, contracts, and radio use of literary property. Some material on newspaper copyright is included.

2122. Wortman, Tunis. *A Treatise, Concerning Political Enquiry, and the Liberty of the Press*. New York: George Forman, for the author, 1800. 296pp.

A philosophical and legal analysis of the meaning of free expression, in which Wortman strikes at the dangers arising from the criminal prosecutions under the Alien and Sedition Acts. The date of publication, just before the election of Jefferson, gives the book special significance.

2123. Yankwich, Leon R. *"It's Libel or Contempt If You Print It."* Los Angeles: Parker and Co., 1950. xvi + 612pp. (The first edition was published under the title *Essays in the Law of Libel*, 1929.)

A practical book on libel, contempt, freedom of the press, and kindred topics for students and newspaper workers. The disposition of the cases presented is given in the judge's own words. Yankwich was a United States district judge in California.

E. Freedom of the Press and Legal Analyses of the Press in Great Britain

2124. Aspinall, A. *Politics and the Press, 1780–1850*. London: Hone and Van Thal, Ltd., 1949. xv + 511pp.

An analysis of the emancipation of the British press from control by and subservience to political interests, based upon manuscript sources and contemporary periodicals and newspapers. The passage of Lord Campbell's Act in 1843 is detailed.

2125. Belloc, Hilaire. *The Free Press*. London: George Allen and Unwin, Ltd., 1918. vii + 102pp.

2126. Blackstone, Sir William. *Blackstone's Commentaries on the Law*. Washington, D.C.: Washington Law Book Co., 1941. 1041pp. (Edited by Bernard C. Gavit.)

These *Commentaries*, first issued in 1765–1769, have become the foundation for legal interpretation of the meaning of freedom of the press.

2127. Bury, J. B. *A History of Freedom of Thought*. London: Williams and Norgate; New York: Henry Holt and Co., 1913. 256pp. (Holt edition issued as No. 69 in Home University Library.)

Bury discusses the philosophical development of freedom of thought from ancient Greece and Rome through the 19th century. He offers a good conceptual base for the idea of a free press.

2128. Clyde, William M. *The Struggle for the Freedom of the Press from Caxton to Cromwell*. London: Oxford University Press, H. Milford, 1934. 360pp.

Except for an opening chapter covering printing as a royal prerogative from 1476 to 1637, this book deals primarily with the press from 1640 to 1658. Clyde considers Milton's views, ordinances relating to news-books, the history of the Stationers' Company, and development of the freedom of the press concept. Included are the texts of Star Chamber decrees regulating printing.

2129. Collet, Collet Dobson. *History of the Taxes on Knowledge; Their Origin and Repeal*. London: T. F. Unwin, 1899. 2 vols. 433pp., total. (Introduction by George Jacob Holyoake.)

A history of newspaper stamp taxes.

2130. Dean, Joseph. *Hatred, Ridicule or Contempt: A Book of Libel Cases*. London: Constable and Co., Ltd., 1953. 271pp.

A summary of the law and facts relating to 40 British libel litigations from 1824 to 1946. The cases involved some noted personalities (Winston Churchill and Lord Gladstone) and some significant decisions, including that in *E. Hulton v. Jones* (peril of anonymous libel). Well written and useful.

2131. Defoe, Daniel. *The Best of Defoe's Review: An Anthology*. New York: Columbia University Press, 1951. xxi + 289pp. (Edited by William L. Payne.)

Eight articles among these selections, dated 1705–1713, are on "The Press: License and Liberty." Others cover Defoe's views on such matters as economics and politics.

2132. ———. *An Essay on the Regulation of the Press*. Oxford: Published by Blackwell for the Luttrell Society, 1948. xvi + 29pp.

2133. General Council of the Press. *The Press and the People: The First Annual Report of the General Council of the Press*. London: The Council, 1954. 48pp.

The purpose of this council, set up after the report of the British Royal Commission on the Press, is to make periodic analyses in order to suggest improvements in press performance.

2134. Gillett, Charles R. *Burned Books: Neglected Chapters in British History and Literature*. New York: Columbia University Press, 1932. 2 vols. 702pp., total.

A list of "burned books" is included in vol. II, pp. 667–682.

2135. Hanson, Laurence. *Government and the Press, 1695–1763*. London: Oxford University Press, H. Milford, 1936. ix + 149pp.

Hanson traces the relationship between government and press, primarily newspapers, from the expiration of the Licensing Act to the publication of John Wilkes's *North Briton No. 45*. There is extensive detail on the nature of the British law and its administration as applied to the press. The bibliography lists manuscript sources and contemporary printed sources.

2136. Hyde, Harford Montgomery, ed. *Privacy and the Press: The Daily Mirror Press Photographer Libel Action*. London: Thornton Butterworth, Ltd., 1947. v + 250pp.

The case of *Thomas Lea v. Justice of the Peace, Ltd., and R. J. Acford, Publishers, Ltd.*, tried in 1947, involved the taking of a photograph at a wedding against the wishes of the bridegroom.

2137. Inglis, Brian. *The Freedom of the Press in Ireland, 1784–1841*. London: Faber and Faber, Ltd., 1954. 256pp.

Analyzes the British Empire restrictions that delayed the growth of Irish newspapers into a "Fourth Estate." There is an extensive bibliography.

2138. Martin, Kingsley. *The Press the Public Wants.* London: Hogarth Press; Toronto: Oxford University Press, 1947. 143pp.

The editor of the *New Statesman and Nation* discusses a central problem of the 20th-century press: how to avoid the evils of corporate ownership and "monopolistic tendency" without loss of freedom through government control. Martin's analysis in behalf of the public demand for press responsibility complements the Royal Commission on the Press reports.

2139. Mill, John Stuart. *On Liberty.* London: J. W. Parker and Son, 1859. 207pp. Boston: Ticknor and Fields, 1863. 223pp. (In modern paperback edition, No. 61 of The Library of Liberal Arts, edited and with an introduction by Currin V. Shields. New York: Liberal Arts Press, 1956. xxviii + 141pp.)

Mill's essay is one of the fundamental expressions of libertarian thought and opinion. Insofar as speech and press are concerned, Mill raises many questions on the limits of collective and individual action.

2140. Milton, John. *Areopagitica: A Speech by Mr. John Milton for the Liberty of Unlicenc'd Printing, to the Parliament of England.* London: 1644; London: N. Douglas, 1927, replica from the British Museum. 40pp.

Numerous reprints of this historic discourse are available. See also *Harvard Classics*, vol. 3, pp. 193–244.

2141. O'Sullivan, Richard. *A Guide to the Defamation Act, 1952.* London: Sweet and Maxwell, Ltd.; Stevens and Sons, Ltd., 1952. 50pp. (Current Law Guide No. 10.)

Provides background on the extensive changes made in the British law of libel in 1952 and lists leading libel cases. The author is one of Her Majesty's counsel.

2142. P.E.N. International. *Freedom of Expression: A Symposium.* London and New York: Hutchinson International Authors, 1944. 184pp. (Edited by Herman Ould.)

Thirty-one articles from a conference called by the London Centre of International P.E.N. to commemorate the tercentenary of Milton's *Areopagitica*. See particularly "An American's Tribute," by Herbert Agar (Louisville *Courier-Journal*); "An Editor's View," by Kingsley Martin (*New Statesman and Nation*); and "The *Areopagitica* after 300 Years," by Harold J. Laski.

2143. Ransom, Harry. *The First Copyright Statute: An Essay on an Act for the Encouragement of Learning, 1710.* Austin: University of Texas Press, 1956. 145pp.

Appended to the essay is a short calendar of leading cases before 1710. The essay is the first in a series in the history of British and American copyright, to include British cases from 1710 to 1950 and American from the Colonial period to the present.

2144. Routledge, James. *Chapters in the History of Popular Progress,*

Chiefly in Relation to the Freedom of the Press and Trial by Jury, 1660–1820, with an Application to Later Years. London: Macmillan and Co., 1876. vii + 631pp.

In effect a British constitutional history of the press, plus an account of the growth of the London metropolitan press. The detailed treatment of the contributions to press freedom of the bookseller and parodist William Hone is excellent.

2145. Royal Commission on the Press. *Minutes of Evidence Taken before the Royal Commission on the Press, 19 June 1947–10 June 1948.* London: His Majesty's Stationery Office, 1948. Paged individually in 38 separate reports.

More than 1000 pages record the 38 days of testimony in the commission hearings.

2146. ———. *Report Presented to Parliament by Command of His Majesty, June 1949.* London: His Majesty's Stationery Office, 1949. x + 363pp.

The official report of the Royal Commission which sat in 1947–1948 to study the manner in which free expression of opinion operated through the British press. The commission had been set up by Parliament at the behest of the Labour Government and the National Union of Journalists.

2147. St. John-Stevas, Norman. *Obscenity and the Law.* London: Secker and Warburg; New York: The Macmillan Co., 1956. xxii + 289pp.

A barrister combines law and literature in this scholarly study of obscenity law from ecclesiastical courts and Star Chamber to the contemporary period. He advocates liberalization and reform of the law of obscenity.

2148. *A Selection of Essays Prepared for the Royal Commission on National Development in the Arts, Letters, and Sciences.* Ottawa: Edmond Cloutier, 1951. vii + 430pp.

Issued as a Royal Commission study, this work includes articles on the press of Canada by Wilfred Eggleston, director of the Department of Journalism, Carleton College, Ottawa.

2149. Siebert, Fredrick Seaton. *Freedom of the Press in England, 1476–1776: The Rise and Decline of Government Controls.* Urbana: University of Illinois Press, 1952. xiv + 411pp.

An excellent study of the English origins of American principles relating to press freedom, particularly with regard to theoretical concepts, licensing of corantos and early newspapers, and the first efforts to report proceedings of Parliament. The work is extensively footnoted.

2150. *The Trials of Oscar Wilde.* London: William Hodge and Co., Ltd., 1948. 384pp. (Edited, with an introduction by H. Montgomery Hyde; Notable British Trials, vol. 70.)

Wilde was involved in three sensational trials in 1894 and 1895 that represented a series of major news developments. This book provides complete background on the state of British libel law at the time, trial evidence in the Wilde cases, the Criminal Law Amendment Act of 1888, and treatment of the trials in the press of the day.

APPRAISALS, ETHICS, AND LAW OF THE PRESS

2151. Wickwar, William H. *The Struggle for the Freedom of the Press, 1819–1832*. London: George Allen and Unwin, Ltd., 1928. 325pp.

Wickwar treats thoroughly the post-Waterloo changes in government and press that marked the development of a more democratic base in journalism. He considers changes in the law of criminal libel, struggles over the press in Parliament, and the careers of pamphleteers and booksellers who fought for press freedom. Among these were Richard Carlile, Francis Place, and William Hone.

2152. Williams, Francis. *Press, Parliament and People*. London and Toronto: William Heinemann, Ltd., 1946. 254pp.

An excellent study of problems of press freedom during and immediately after World War II. Williams was editor of the *Daily Herald* and served in the Ministry of Information.

2153. Williamson, Geoffrey. *Morality Fair: Vagaries of Social Conduct as Reflected in the Press*. London: Watts and Co., 1955. xii + 260pp. 31 illustrations.

Surveys the quirks and changes over 100 years in ideas of morality as reflected in newspapers, magazines, and the printed word generally and calls for reform in the British laws relating to morality.

V

Techniques of Journalism, Including Textbooks

2154. Alden, Henry Mills. *Magazine Writing and the New Literature.* New York and London: Harper and Brothers, 1908. xi + 320pp.

Alden had been editor of *Harper's Magazine* for nearly 40 years. He strives to show the relation between periodical and general literature; more than half the book concerns creative values, with comment on the rewards of authorship.

2155. Allen, Charles L. *Country Journalism.* New York: T. Nelson and Sons, 1928. 504pp.

2156. Allen, John Edward. *The Modern Newspaper: Its Typography and Methods of News Presentation.* New York and London: Harper and Brothers, 1940. ix + 234pp.

An extension of an earlier book by Allen, *Newspaper Makeup* (1936), and based on a series of articles that had appeared in the *Linotype News*, of which Allen was editor.

2157. ———. *Newspaper Designing.* New York: Harper and Brothers, 1947. x + 478pp.

A more extensive analysis of the mechanics of newspaper makeup than Allen's earlier book.

2158. Alsop, Joseph, and Stewart Alsop. *The Reporter's Trade.* New York: Reynal and Co., 1958. v + 377pp.

These capable brothers worked as a Washington columnist team through post-World War II years. Here they record their techniques of political reporting, with an emphasis on "leg work" to get directly at the news. They buttress their personal narrative and analysis of public affairs with the reprinting of chosen columns written between 1945 and 1957.

2159. Arnold, Edmund C. *Functional Newspaper Design.* New York: Harper and Brothers, 1956. 340pp.

Ways to make the daily newspaper more attractive and readable are suggested. The author, associated with *Publishers' Auxiliary*, provides about 200 illustrations.

2160. Bailey, Robeson. *Techniques in Article-Writing.* New York: D. Appleton-Century Co., 1947. xi + 272pp.

Bailey analyzes nonfiction articles, with the help of 11 authors, and gives advice to aspiring writers.

2161. Bakeless, John. *Magazine Making*. New York: The Viking Press, 1931. xi + 323pp.

2162. Barnard, M. C. [pseud., Ben Arid]. *Putting "It" in the Column: With Comments on the Philosophy and Art of Human Interest*. Los Angeles: De Vorss and Co., 1939. 218pp.

Barnard discusses newspaper columns — metropolitan and small city. The book is presented as a guide on how to write a column, but considerable background information is included along with instruction in technique, thereby making it broader than a textbook.

2163. Barnhart, Thomas F. *Weekly Newspaper Makeup and Typography*. Minneapolis: University of Minnesota Press, 1949. ix + 267pp.

2164. ———. *Weekly Newspaper Writing and Editing*. New York: Dryden Press, 1949. xii + 302pp.

2165. Bastian, George C., Leland D. Case, and Floyd K. Baskette. *Editing the Day's News*. New York: The Macmillan Co., 1956. 4th edition. xii + 373pp.

The third revision of a pioneer copy-editing textbook, first issued in 1922 by Bastian. The revision, now chiefly the work of Baskette, emphasizes small-city newspaper practices. There is material on the teletypesetter.

2166. Bernstein, Theodore M. *Watch Your Language*. Great Neck, N.Y.: Channel Press, 1958. 287pp.

Analyzes word uses that are undesirable in writing for newspapers, from outright errors to worn and wasteful grammatical constructions. Many of the examples are from the New York *Times*, of which the author is assistant managing editor.

2167. Berryman, Clifford K. *Development of the Cartoon*, in University of Missouri Journalism Series, No. 41. Columbia, Mo.: University of Missouri, June 7, 1926. 19pp.

By a Washington *Evening Star* cartoonist.

2168. Bierce, Ambrose. *Write It Right: A Little Blacklist of Literary Faults*. New York and Washington, D.C.: Neale Publishing Co., 1910. 73pp.

The precise, strong-minded Bierce here provided a tiny book on the art of writing. After nearly half a century it could still be used as a newspaper style book.

2169. Bing, Phil C. *The Country Weekly*. New York: D. Appleton and Co., 1917. x + 347pp.

An early manual for rural journalists.

2170. Bird, George L. *Article Writing and Marketing*. New York: Rinehart and Co., 1956. Revised edition. xii + 506pp. (Earlier edition, 1948.)

For students in college classes and for writers seeking to teach themselves professional techniques. There are useful appendixes and illustrations.

2171. Bleyer, Willard G. *How to Write Special Feature Articles*. Boston: Houghton Mifflin Co., 1920. viii + 373pp.

One of the early texts, the first to attempt systematically to teach the techniques of writing for sale to newspapers and popular magazines. Almost half the book consists of articles appearing in contemporary magazines — examples of those that "sold" during the World War I period.

2172. ———. *Newspaper Writing and Editing*. Boston: Houghton Mifflin Co., 1932. 482pp. (Earlier editions, 1923, 412pp.; 1913, 365pp.)

This is becoming a classic among early textbooks in journalism. The closing chapter outlines on a high ethical plane the function of a newspaper.

2173. Bond, F. Fraser. *Introduction to Journalism*. New York: The Macmillan Co., 1954. 358pp.

An introductory textbook in broad strokes. It covers all media, with greatest attention to the editorial phase of newspapers.

2174. Borland, Hal. *How to Write and Sell Non-Fiction*. New York: The Ronald Press Co., 1956. 217pp.

By a highly successful free-lance writer.

2175. Brazelton, Ethel Maude. *Writing and Editing for Women*. New York and London: Funk and Wagnalls Co., 1927. xvii + 258pp.

Surveys the opportunities for women in newspaper, magazine, and other writing work. There is useful material for women reporters.

2176. Brennecke, Ernest, Jr., and Donald L. Clark, eds. *Magazine Article Writing*. New York: The Macmillan Co., 1942. xi + 486pp. (Earlier edition, 1931.)

2177. Brown, Charles H. *Informing the People: A Basic Text in Reporting and Writing the News*. New York: Henry Holt and Co., 1957. x + 341pp.

Seeks to apply at the beginning reporting level the findings of social scientists about readability and interest. The book is chiefly devoted to newspaper work, but it also takes up such special fields as writing for radio and television and preparing interpretative articles and features.

2178. ———. *News Editing and Display*. New York: Harper and Brothers, 1952. 457pp. (Foreword by Fayette Copeland.)

Brown emphasizes techniques on a small-city newspaper and goes into print-shop practices. Headline writing is covered somewhat cursorily. There is strong emphasis on ethical principles.

2179. Brucker, Herbert. *The Changing American Newspaper*. New York: Columbia University Press, 1937. x + 111pp.

An effective book that broke fresh ground in such techniques as news summaries and departmentalization, flush-left headlines, and "modernistic make-up." Many of Brucker's suggestions have since become commonplace practices.

2180. Burch, George Edward. *Of Publishing Scientific Papers*. New York: Grune and Stratton, 1954. 40pp.

Burch deals with medical journalism.

2181. Bush, Chilton R. *The Art of News Communication.* New York: Appleton-Century-Crofts, 1954. ix + 246pp.

A beginning textbook for classes in news writing which aims to encourage the use of research findings on readability in the presentation of news. The volume is limited to writing style and structure; there is almost nothing on news gathering. Adult in approach.

2182. ———. *Editorial Thinking and Writing: A Textbook with Exercises.* New York: D. Appleton and Co., 1932. xi + 453pp.

Although more than a quarter-century old, this work is still useful because of the emphasis the author puts on the thinking processes that must be developed in dealing with social problems. The editorial as a literary form and the editor's relations with his readers are treated as secondary.

2183. ———. *Newspaper Reporting of Public Affairs.* New York: Appleton-Century-Crofts, 1951. 3rd edition. 346pp. (Earlier editions: D. Appleton-Century Co., 1940, 455pp.; D. Appleton and Co., 1929, 406pp.)

Earliest of the books on reporting public affairs. Bush emphasizes court and police coverage; there is some material on municipal and county affairs, politics, business and finance, and labor. The volume is strong on specialized terminology and court procedures.

2184. Butler, Kenneth B. *Practical Handbook on Headline Design and Publication Layout.* Mendota, Ill.: Butler Typo-Design Research Center, 1954. 95pp.

2185. Callihan, E. L. *Grammar for Journalists.* New York: Ronald Press Co., 1957. xiii + 397pp.

A straightforward text on grammar slanted to the needs of students planning careers in journalism. Numerous examples are taken from newspaper stories. The book, although excellent, may be too detailed to be a ready reference aid.

2186. Campbell, Laurence R., and Roland E. Wolseley. *Newsmen at Work: Reporting and Writing News.* Boston: Houghton Mifflin Co., 1949. x + 560pp.

2187. Charnley, Mitchell V., and Blair Converse. *Magazine Writing and Editing.* New York: Cordon Co., 1938. xv + 352pp.

Describes the processes in considering magazine articles for purchase, editing of manuscripts, and carrying articles through to publication. *Better Homes and Gardens* is used as a representative magazine office.

2188. Clayton, Charles C. *Newspaper Reporting Today.* New York: Odyssey Press, 1947. x + 422pp. (Foreword by Frank L. Mott.)

A newspaperman's "practical" book on reporting. Clayton covers the role of the reporter, the rewards of reporting, the mechanics of news writing, and specialized reporting. The author was with the St. Louis *Globe-Democrat.*

2189. Corbin, Charles R. *Why News Is News.* New York: Ronald Press Co., 1928. v + 191pp.

An early textbook on news judgment, by a former managing editor of the Toledo *Blade*. Fairly elementary approach: news is weather, combat, fire, religion, children and animals, prominent persons, and success. Many reprints of stories are used.

2190. Costa, Joseph, ed. *Complete Book of Press Photography*. New York: National Press Photographers Assn., 1950. 206pp.

More than 30 articles, illustrated by several hundred pictures, discuss all aspects of news photography. The volume includes a good bibliography, a glossary of terms, information for free-lancers, and biographies of the cameramen who contributed articles.

2191. Crawford, Robert P. *The Magazine Article*. New York: McGraw-Hill Book Co., 1931. xii + 340pp.

2192. Danilov, Victor J. *Public Affairs Reporting*. New York: The Macmillan Co., 1955. xiv + 487pp.

A recent textbook on this subject, covering basically the same ground as Bush (2183) and MacDougall (2238). It includes a section on agricultural news coverage not found in other public affairs texts. There is an extensive glossary of specialized terminology.

2193. Davis, Hallam Walker. *The Column*. New York and London: Alfred A. Knopf, 1926. ix + 166pp. (Borzoi Handbooks on Journalism, edited by N. A. Crawford.)

A handbook on columns, with various contributors giving their views on technique.

2194. Deckoff, Harold B. *The Free-Lance Photographer's Hand-Book*. New York: Falk Publishing Co., 1956. 249pp.

2195. Desmond, Robert W. *Newspaper Reference Methods*. Minneapolis: University of Minnesota Press, 1933. xv + 229pp.

Dated, but has a useful history of newspaper libraries and reference procedures. It outlines methods of organization and classification of such libraries, the value of news indexes, and the types of books valuable in the newspaper library.

2196. Drewry, John E. *Book Reviewing*. Boston: The Writer, Inc., 1945. ix + 231pp.

Drewry emphasizes to some extent newspaper reviewing and gives background on "how the experts do it." He stresses also appreciation of book reviewing as an art.

2197. Eastman, Max. *Journalism versus Art*. New York: Alfred A. Knopf, 1916. 146pp.

Reprints four essays critical of methods in magazine art and writing: "What Is the Matter with Magazine Art?" from the *Masses*; "Magazine Writing," from *Vanity Fair*; "Lazy Verse," from the *New Republic*; and "Why English Does Not Simplify Her Spelling," from the *North American Review*. Eastman was then editor of the *Masses*.

2198. Edson, C. L. *The Gentle Art of Columning: A Treatise on Comic Journalism*. New York: Brentano's, 1920. 177pp.

The passing of several decades since publication has failed to dull this little book on punning, jingling, news-slanting, contributing, and humorous editorializing. There are four introductory essays — by Don Marquis, Christopher Morley, Franklin P. Adams, and George Horace Lorimer.

2199. Ezickson, A. J. *Get That Picture! The Story of the News Cameraman.* New York: National Library Press, 1938. 200pp.

A popular treatment of news photography, by a staff member of Wide World Photos. The emphasis is heavy on the "big-story" approach.

2200. Farrar, Larston. *How to Make $18,000 a Year Free-Lance Writing.* New York: Hawthorne Books, 1957. 276pp.

A practical book that covers the subject down to the free-lancer's way of life.

2201. Fishbein, Morris. *Medical Writing: The Technic and the Art.* New York: Blakiston Division, McGraw-Hill Book Co., 1957. 3rd edition. x + 262pp. (Earlier editions: Chicago: American Medical Assn., 1938, 212pp.; and 1925, by George H. Simmons and Morris Fishbein, under the title *The Art and Practice of Medical Writing.*)

The various editions represent the evolution in theory and practice of medical journalism during Fishbein's 35 years in the editorial department of the American Medical Association. The body of the third edition is devoted to style, bibliographical material, preparation of manuscripts, illustrations, proof-reading, and indexing.

2202. Flesch, Rudolf. *The Art of Plain Talk.* New York and London: Harper and Brothers, 1946. xiii + 210pp. (Foreword by Lyman Bryson, Columbia Broadcasting System.)

Flesch's immensely successful and provocative book offers sound and practical rules for producing readable writing. With this and his later studies, Flesch laid the groundwork for style changes among newspaper writers. Here Flesch outlined his original "yardstick" formulas for measuring readability.

2203. ———. *The Art of Readable Writing.* New York and London: Harper and Brothers, 1949. xiv + 237pp. (Foreword by Alan Gould, executive editor, Associated Press.)

A refinement of *The Art of Plain Talk.* Many of Flesch's techniques were adopted by the Associated Press.

2204. Flint, Leon Nelson. *The Editorial.* New York: D. Appleton and Co., 1928. Revised edition. xiii + 319pp. (Earlier edition, 1920.)

Among the early texts on editorial writing. It includes a history of editorial writing and emphasizes ethical considerations and responsibility.

2205. Floherty, John J. *Shooting the News: Careers of the Camera Man.* Philadelphia and New York: J. B. Lippincott Co., 1949. viii + 150pp.

A popular history of news photography, including an account of picture coverage for the films.

2206. Fox, Rodney. *Agricultural and Technical Journalism.* New York: Prentice-Hall, 1952. vii + 229pp.

Provides a wealth of information on how to handle technical subject matter, without excessive use of jargon, for newspapers, radio, and magazines.

2207. Friedman, Harry A. *Newspaper Indexing*. Milwaukee: Marquette University Press, 1942. viii + 261pp.

2208. Gard, Wayne. *Book Reviewing*. New York: Alfred A. Knopf, 1927. 159pp. (Borzoi Handbooks on Journalism.)

A condensed, well-considered treatment.

2209. Garst, Robert E., and Theodore M. Bernstein. *Headlines and Deadlines*. New York: Columbia University Press, 1940. Revised edition. 217pp. (First issued in 1933.)

An excellent volume for specialized desk work, although too limited for a general survey. The authors stick to newspaper staff organization, standards of copy-editing, grammar, and headlines. There is a good list of headline words.

2210. Gavit, John P. *The Reporter's Manual: A Handbook for Newspaper Men*. Albany, N.Y.: Privately printed, 1903. 81pp.

A small-city newspaper style book (Albany *Evening Journal*), including tips for better news coverage, from a day when detailed style books were uncommon.

2211. Gunning, Robert. *The Technique of Clear Writing*. New York: McGraw-Hill Book Co., 1952. x + 289pp.

By a one-time newspaperman who became a readability counselor for the United Press, newspapers, and *Newsweek*. His book is somewhat similar to those by Flesch (2202, 2203). ✓

2212. Harral, Stewart. *The Feature Writer's Handbook: With a Treasury of 2,000 Tested Ideas for Newspapers, Magazines, Radio, and Television*. Norman: University of Oklahoma Press, 1958. xiii + 342pp.

A reference book providing advice to writers, devices by which ideas can be made more effective, suggestions on titles and ways of asking questions, and other hints from experts.

2213. ———. *Keys to Successful Interviewing*. Norman: University of Oklahoma Press, 1954. 223pp.

An ambitious work directed toward all writers who use interviews in their work — reporters and those in fields quite divorced from journalism. The book attempts too much in too little space.

2214. Harrington, Harry Franklin, and Elmo Scott Watson. *Modern Feature Writing*. New York and London: Harper and Brothers, 1935. xi + 541pp.

A revision and expansion of an earlier book called *Chats on Feature Writing*. It is directed toward the needs of young writers.

2215. Harris, Emerson Pitt, and Mrs. Florence Harris Hooke. *The Community Newspaper, Its Promise and Development*. New York: D. Appleton and Co., 1923. xiv + 378pp.

2216. Heath, Harry, and Lou Gelfand. *How to Cover, Write and Edit Sports*. Ames, Iowa: Iowa State College Press, 1957. Revised edition. 536pp. + 75 illustrations. (Earlier edition, 1951.)

A comprehensive textbook. It deals separately with all major sports and discusses the history of sports writing, problems of photography and publicity, and the roles of radio and television. There is a good bibliography of general sports books. The collaborators were a journalism professor and a St. Paul, Minn., sports writer, respectively.

2217. Hemstreet, Charles. *Reporting for the Newspapers.* New York: A. Wessels Co., 1901. 140pp.

This early textbook develops the concept that experience is the best teacher. The author outlines news in a simple manner, tells how it is collected and written, and explains how reporters work. The most extensive treatment is given to the technique of handling court evidence.

2218. Herzberg, Joseph G. *Late City Edition.* New York: Henry Holt and Co., 1947. 282pp.

Herzberg, city editor of the New York *Herald Tribune*, and members of that newspaper's staff collaborated on this book for students and general readers. Although much of it is devoted to local reporting, there is interesting and useful material on how the present-day news room operates.

2219. Hicks, Wilson. *Words and Pictures: An Introduction to Photo-journalism.* New York: Harper and Brothers, 1952. 171pp.

2220. Hinkle, Olin, and John Henry. *How to Write Columns.* Ames, Iowa: Iowa State College Press, 1952. 288pp. (Illustrated by Harry E. Walsh.)

2221. Howard, Clive, ed. *A Guide to Successful Magazine Writing.* New York: Charles Scribner's Sons, 1954. 521pp. (Sponsored by the Society of Magazine Writers.)

Thirty articles from 19 leading magazines showing how ideas for articles originated, how facts were gathered, how the material was prepared, and how the marketing was handled.

2222. Hyde, Grant Milnor. *Newspaper Editing.* New York: D. Appleton and Co., 1925. 2nd edition. 364pp. (First edition, 1915.)

2223. ———. *Newspaper Handbook.* New York and London: D. Appleton-Century Co., 1941. 3rd edition. xix + 337pp. (Earlier editions, 1926 and 1921, published under the title *Handbook for Newspaper Workers.*)

A reference handbook for beginners in journalism, dealing principally with English usage.

2224. ———. *Newspaper Reporting.* New York: Prentice-Hall, 1952. vi + 599pp.

Based upon years of reporting and teaching experience and on a series of earlier books by this pioneer among writers of texts on reporting. Hyde considers the writing of news stories, problems of newspapers, and problems of gathering news and gaining reportorial background.

2225. ———. *Newspaper Reporting and Correspondence: A Manual for Reporters, Correspondents, and Students of Newspaper Writing.* New York: D. Appleton and Co., 1912. xi + 347pp.

2226. Johnson, Gerald W. *What Is News? A Tentative Outline.* New

York: Alfred A. Knopf, 1926. 98pp. (Borzoi Handbooks on Journalism.)

Many of Johnson's general concepts of news still hold good: news is what is in the newspapers, and newspapers are what newspapermen make them. He considers selectivity in news, policy and compulsions, ethics, and public interest and significance.

2227. Jones, John Paul. *The Modern Reporter's Handbook*. New York: Rinehart and Co., 1949. xvi + 430pp.

Organized as a reference book (the author calls it a "cook book"), with numerous problems and examples.

2228. Jones, Llewellyn. *How to Criticize Books*. New York: W. W. Norton and Co., 1928. 190pp.

For professional and nonprofessional critics. Jones goes into both the mechanics of criticism and its philosophy.

2229. Kalish, Stanley E., and Clifton C. Edom. *Picture Editing*. New York: Rinehart and Co., 1951. xvi + 207pp.

Primarily for those concerned with the techniques of picture editing and with judging the news value of photos. A brief history of the news picture and numerous prints of famous news pictures are included.

2230. Kemsley Newspapers. *The Kemsley Manual of Journalism*. London: Cassell and Co., Ltd., 1954. xiii + 424 + xlvi pp. (First issued in 1950; foreword by Viscount Kemsley.)

An important British book on newspaper techniques as engaged in by one major chain. Of particular value is a discussion of the in-training program of the Kemsley Press.

2231. Kinkaid, James C. *Press Photography*. Boston: American Photographic Publishing Co., 1936. vi + 281pp.

2232. Kobre, Sidney, and Juanita Parks. *Psychology and the News*. Tallahassee, Fla.: Florida State University Bureau of Media Research and Services, 1955. Mimeographed. 174pp.

Stresses the importance to students of a knowledge of psychology in understanding and writing about news of the day.

2233. Krieghbaum, Hillier. *Facts in Perspective: The Editorial Page and News Interpretation*. New York: Prentice-Hall, 1956. 518pp.

Aims to give a broad picture of editorial writing and the problems involved in getting at "essential truth." There are chapters on news magazines, weekly news summaries, and interpretative writing. Perhaps the best of recent books on editorial writing.

2234. Leech, Harper, and John C. Carroll. *What's the News?* Chicago: P. Covici, 1926. xviii + 183pp.

2235. Lieder, Paul Robert, and Robert Withington, eds. *The Art of Literary Criticism*. New York: D. Appleton-Century Co., 1941. xii + 689pp.

2236. Lundy, Miriam, ed. *Writing up the News: Behind the Scenes of the Great Newspapers; Top-Ranking Editors and Reporters Tell*

Their Own Inside Stories. New York: Dodd, Mead and Co., 1939. x + 254pp.

2237. MacDougall, Curtis D. *Covering the Courts.* New York: Prentice-Hall, 1946. xvi + 713pp.

An intensive analysis of courts and court reporting, with far more background on legal history and procedure than most texts give. The book is excellent in its discussion of trends in law.

2238. ————. *Interpretative Reporting.* New York: The Macmillan Co., 1957. 3rd edition. vii + 592pp. (Earlier editions, 1948 and 1938.)

Among the best of the textbooks on general reporting. Included are discussions of the nature of newspaper work, principles of news writing, and handling of important assignments.

2239. Macy, John. *The Critical Game.* New York: Boni and Liveright, 1922. 335pp.

Sketches on the nature of literary criticism and on literary figures and journalists. Most of the accounts originally were published in leading reviews.

2240. Mansfield, F. J. *The Complete Journalist: A Study of the Principles and Practice of Newspaper Making.* London: Sir Isaac Pitman and Sons, Ltd., 1935. xviii + 389pp.

A high-level British textbook. Mansfield describes how newspapers in Britain are produced and gives a quick 300-year survey of journalism history. Numerous plates illustrating pages of outstanding newspapers are included.

2241. ————. *Sub-Editing.* London: Sir Isaac Pitman and Sons, Ltd., 1932. xv + 248pp.

This text on British desk practice pays much more attention than American textbooks to the historical development of news-editing processes. Some attention is given to editing techniques learned from American journalism. Mansfield was associated with the London *Times.*

2242. *A Manual of Style.* Chicago: University of Chicago Press, 1952. 11th edition. x + 521pp.

With the United States Government Printing Office manual (2291) and some of the style books of metropolitan newspapers, this is one of the best available guides for authors, reporters, printers, and publishers.

2243. *The Masthead.* Washington, D.C.: National Conference of Editorial Writers, 1947–date. Issued quarterly.

This association publication is aimed "to stimulate the conscience and the quality of the American editorial page." Regularly included are articles on editorial writers, on how to write editorials, on controversial subjects of the day, and on the history of editorials. It is more useful in many ways than textbooks and anthologies.

2244. Mavity, Nancy Barr. *The Modern Newspaper.* New York: Henry Holt and Co., 1930. xiii + 320pp.

A textbook on all phases of newspaper work. Mrs. Mavity was on the staff of the Oakland (Calif.) *Tribune.*

2245. Mich, Daniel D., and Edwin Eberman. *The Technique of the Pic-*

ture Story. New York and London: McGraw-Hill Book Co., 1945. 239pp.

A practical guide to the preparation of "visual articles," by the executive editor and the art director of *Look*.

2246. Milwaukee Journal. *Production of R.O.P. Color in the Milwaukee Journal*. Milwaukee: The Journal Co., 1950. viii + 177pp.

A promotional piece devoted chiefly to one newspaper's long use of color. The emphasis is on advertising, but the book has general value in its good discussion of techniques. A glossary of terms and a select bibliography are included. Illustrated in color.

2246a. ———. *Three-Color Process Reproduction in Newspapers*. Milwaukee: The Journal Co., 1951. 28pp.

A supplement to *Production of R.O.P. Color*.

2247. Neal, Robert M. *Editing the Small-City Daily*. New York: Prentice-Hall, 1946. Revised edition. xiv + 498pp (First published in 1939; forewords by Eugene W. Sharpe and John M. Imrie.)

An enthusiastically written text on copy-editing, in which an "old desk hand" gives instruction to a cub employee.

2248. ———. *News Gathering and News Writing*. New York: Prentice-Hall, 1949. 2nd edition. 580pp. (First published in 1940.)

2248a. New York Times. *How to Read and Understand Financial and Business News: Prepared by the Financial and Business News Staff of the New York Times*. New York: The Times, 1957. 7th edition. 122pp. (First issued in 1937; title varies.)

2249. ———. *News: The Story of How It is Gathered and Printed*. New York: New York Times Co., 1945. Revised edition. 39pp. (Earlier edition, 1934.)

2250. ———. *The Newspaper: Its Making and Its Meaning*. New York: Charles Scribner's Sons, 1945. vi + 207pp.

Useful in providing discussion of the policies of one great newspaper, of the processes involved in news publication, and of the newspaper's place in the community.

2251. ———. *Style Book*. New York: New York Times Co., 1956. 102pp. (Earlier editions, 1950, 1928, and 1914.)

Among the most detailed and comprehensive of the metropolitan newspaper style books.

2252. *News and the Newspaper*, in University of Missouri Journalism Series, No. 28. Columbia, Mo.: University of Missouri, September 1923. 124pp.

An extensive analysis of news in all its phases compiled from addresses delivered at the University of Missouri.

2253. *Newsmen Speak: Journalists on Their Craft*. Berkeley and Los Angeles: University of California Press, 1954. ix + 197pp. (Edited by Edmond D. Coblentz.)

An anthology of newspaper "know-how," by three dozen technicians from the senior Bennett to the junior Hearst, with a piece by Lord Northcliffe giving the British view. The content includes press association techniques, syndication, photography, typography, and production.

2254. Olson, Kenneth E. *Typography and Mechanics of the Newspaper.* New York: D. Appleton and Co., 1930. 441pp.

Among the better textbooks on newspaper printing and makeup, although now long out of date. A clear and brief history of printing is included.

2255. Opdyke, John Baker. *Get It Right! A Cyclopedia of Correct English Usage.* New York: Funk and Wagnalls Co., 1941. Revised edition. xvii + 673pp. (Earlier editions, 1939 and 1935.)

An excellent compendium on the fine points of grammar and style, with useful information on library service, indexing, and preparation of direct-mail and newspaper copy. It serves well on a news desk for quick answers to tricky questions.

2256. Patterson, Helen M. *Writing and Selling Feature Articles.* Englewood Cliffs, N.J.: Prentice-Hall, 1956. 3rd edition. 527pp. (Earlier editions, 1949 and 1939. Introduction by Grant Milnor Hyde.)

Includes a suggested library for free-lance writers and a list of references and guides for journalists wishing to market articles.

2257. Peterson, Theodore. *Writing Non-Fiction for Magazines.* St. Louis: Educational Publishers, 1949. 93pp.

2258. Porter, Philip W., and Norval Neil Luxon. *The Reporter and the News.* New York: D. Appleton-Century Co., 1935. xiii + 560pp.

2259. Price, Jack. *News Photography.* New York: Industries Publishing Co., 1932. 165pp.

2260. ———. *News Pictures.* New York: Round Table Press, 1937. xii + 192pp.

2261. Radder, Norman, and John E. Stempel. *Newspaper Editing, Make-up and Headlines.* New York and London: McGraw-Hill Book Co., 1942. 2nd edition. xvi + 398pp. (The first edition, 1924, was published under the title *Newspaper Makeup and Headlines.*)

A copy-editing textbook with good discussion on methods of condensing, good taste, headline essentials, and ethics.

2262. Reddick, De Witt C. *Modern Feature Writing.* New York: Harper and Brothers, 1949. x + 457pp.

A textbook on feature-writing techniques.

2263. Rigby, Charles. *The Staff Journalist.* London: Sir Isaac Pitman and Sons, Ltd., 1950. 186pp.

Similar to Mansfield's books on British newspaper practices (2240, 2241). It has the advantage of more recent publication than Mansfield's.

2264. Robbins, Alan Pitt. *Newspapers Today.* London: Oxford University Press, 1956. 142pp.

2265. Ross, Charles G. *The Writing of News.* New York: Henry Holt and Co., 1911. xii + 236pp.

Ross, 40 years later President Truman's press secretary, wrote this early textbook while he was a young assistant professor of journalism at the University of Missouri. Other texts of the period were perhaps more substantial.

2266. Rothstein, Arthur. *Photojournalism: Pictures for Magazines and Newspapers.* New York: American Photographic Book Publishing Co., 1956. 197pp.

A survey of the entire field, with major emphasis upon creativity in pictures. Some 200 excellent news and feature pictures are reproduced, but the text attempts too much in too little space. The author is technical director of *Look.*

2267. Saturday Review. *Writing for Love or Money: Thirty-Five Essays Reprinted from the Saturday Review of Literature.* New York: Longmans, Green and Co., 1949. ix + 278pp.

Articles on the lives, problems, and opportunities of writers. Among journalists included are Elmer Davis and Henry Seidel Canby.

2268. Scribner, B. W. *Preservation of Newspaper Records.* Washington, D.C.: National Bureau of Standards, July 19, 1934. 10pp. (Miscellaneous Publications No. 145.)

2269. Sherriff, Andrew, and others. *News: Its Scope and Limitations.* in University of Missouri Journalism Series, No. 57. Columbia, Mo.: University of Missouri, December 7, 1929. 42pp.

Sherriff deals with coverage of the courts by the press. Six other contributors discuss general reporting, why news is printed, gathering world news, independence in politics, women's reporting, and covering South America.

2270. Shuman, Edwin L. *Practical Journalism: A Complete Manual of the Best Newspaper Methods.* New York: D. Appleton and Co., 1903. xix + 265pp.

Among the earliest textbooks on metropolitan journalism, by an editor of Chicago newspapers, later managing editor of *Current History.* Today it is highly interesting reading for the perspective it gives on changes in techniques and in journalism instruction.

2271. ———. *Steps into Journalism: Helps and Hints for Young Writers.* Evanston, Ill.: Correspondence School of Journalism, 1894. x + 229pp.

A still earlier reporting text, this one an outgrowth of Shuman's Chautauquan course in journalism. It is inferior to his *Practical Journalism* and of historical value only.

2272. Sipley, Louis Walton. *A Half Century of Color.* New York: The Macmillan Co., 1951. xv + 216pp.

Based upon collections of the American Museum of Photography.

2273. Skillin, Marjorie E., Robert M. Gay, and others. *Words into Type.* New York: Appleton-Century-Crofts, 1948. xx + 585pp.

A guide for writers, editors, proofreaders, and printers. The book deals with the physical form of manuscripts, techniques for preparing copy, the mechanics of typography, illustrations, and grammar and usage.

2274. Smith, C. R. F., and Kathryn M. Rheuark. *Management of Newspaper Correspondents*. Baton Rouge, La.: Louisiana State University Press, 1944. xiv + 158pp. (Journalism Monograph Series, No. 3.)

A reference book for newspaper editors who manage country correspondents, with emphasis upon means of selecting personnel.

2275. Smith, Henry Justin. *It's the Way It's Written*. Chicago: The Daily News, 1923. 52pp. (Chicago Daily News Reprints, No. 7.)

A valuable article by the managing editor of the *Daily News* in which he stresses the merit of sound literary practices in daily newspaper writing.

2276. Smith, S. Stephenson. *The Command of Words*. New York: Thomas Y. Crowell Co., 1935. vi + 290pp.

A helpful text that journalists can use to help build vocabulary, although its approach is general. There are good chapters on fine shades of meaning among synonyms, on slang and jargon, and on special and technical vocabularies, plus exercises with keys.

2277. ———. *The Craft of the Critic*. New York: Thomas Y. Crowell Co., 1931. ix + 416pp.

2278. ———. *How to Double Your Vocabulary*. New York: Thomas Y. Crowell Co., 1947. 360pp.

Similar to *The Command of Words* (2276 above). Included here is good material on how words change meaning and on the history of words.

2279. Solomon, Leo M. *There's Money in Pictures*. New York: Funk and Wagnalls, 1952. x + 198pp. (Published for *Newsweek* in Newsweek Book Series.)

2280. Sorrells, John H. *The Working Press: Memos from the Editor about the Front and Other Pages*. New York: Ronald Press Co., 1930. ix + 116pp.

2281. Spencer, Dick, III. *Editorial Cartooning*. Ames, Iowa: Iowa State College Press, 1949. xii + 110pp.

An excellent guide to the editorial cartoon, with reproductions of several dozen famous cartoons going back to Franklin's "Join or Die" of pre-Revolutionary days. There is helpful material on cartoon prizes and the influence of cartoons in elections.

2282. Spencer, Matthew Lyle. *Editorial Writing: Ethics, Policy, Practice*. Boston and New York: Houghton Mifflin Co., 1924. viii + 364pp.

One of the early textbooks on this subject. It includes a bibliography and collections of editorials.

2283. Stabler, Norman C. *How to Read the Financial News*. New York: Harper and Brothers, 1951. 54pp.

The eighth edition of a reference book for courses in reporting and editing as they touch upon financial and business news. The series began in 1922. The New York *Herald Tribune* is used as a base.

2284. Stewart, Donald Ogden, ed. *Fighting Words*. New York: Harcourt, Brace and Co., 1940. 167pp.

This volume is concerned with problems of writing technique and of gathering and disseminating information. There is interesting shoptalk of magazine journalists, poets, novelists, playwrights, critics, scenario writers, and radio writers.

2285. Straumann, Heinrich. *Newspaper Headlines: A Study in Linguistic Method.* London: George Allen and Unwin, Ltd., 1935. 263pp.

One of only a few studies that carefully dissect newspaper headline methods, purposes, and effects on a historical, semantic, and psychological basis. Although based on British practice, the book has general application.

2286. Strauss, Leo. *Persecution and the Art of Writing.* Glencoe, Ill.: The Free Press, 1952. 204pp.

Discusses the peculiar techniques of writing developed by adversaries of regimes under which free discussion is suppressed.

2287. Sutton, Albert A. *Design and Makeup of the Newspaper.* New York: Prentice-Hall, 1948. xiv + 483pp.

Basically a textbook, but useful in general for its excellent condensation of factual information on printing. It is somewhat weak on the contemporary development of the teletypesetter.

2288. Svirsky, Leon, ed. *Your Newspaper: Blueprint for a Better Press.* New York: The Macmillan Co., 1947. xii + 202pp.

Nine Nieman Fellows of 1945–1946 put forth their ideas on what constitutes good journalistic news practice. See particularly their "Design for a Daily," a theoretical view of how the future newspaper can be produced in better fashion and also be financially stable. The work is thoughtful and challenging.

2289. Taylor, Howard B., and Jacob Scher. *Copy Reading and News Editing.* New York: Prentice-Hall, 1951. xi + 386pp.

This volume gives heavier emphasis to metropolitan procedures than do other works on news editing. There is an excellent treatment of press association copy and of developing news stories. The authors have been staff members of the Chicago *Tribune* and the Chicago *Sun-Times.*

2290. Tunis, John R. *This Writing Game: Selections from Twenty Years of Free-Lancing.* New York: A. S. Barnes and Co., 1941. xv + 357pp. (Introduction by Frederick Lewis Allen.)

About 40 articles, with sports perhaps somewhat overrepresented. Tunis explains in each case how he happened to write the article.

2291. United States Government Printing Office. *Style Manual.* Washington, D.C.: Government Printing Office, annually. About 500pp.

2292. United States War Department. *A Guide for Army Newspaper Editors.* Washington, D.C.: Government Printing Office, 1947. 90pp.

2293. Vitray, Laura, John Mills, Jr., and Roscoe B. Ellard. *Pictorial Journalism.* New York: McGraw-Hill Book Co., 1939. xvi + 437pp.

Dated, but still a valuable textbook. Based to a great extent on the experience of the first two authors on the Washington *Post.*

2294. Waddell, Robert. *Grammar and Style.* New York: Dryden Press, 1951. v + 380pp.

A descriptive textbook on grammar, useful for newspaper workers who want grammar "interpreted."

2295. Waldrop, A. Gayle. *Editor and Editorial Writer.* New York: Rinehart and Co., 1955. Revised edition. xiv + 511pp. (Earlier edition, 1948.)

Discusses the mission of the editorial page, techniques of writing editorials, how to understand the reader, how editorial writers work, and "allies" and "rivals" of the editorial (letters, columnists, cartoonists, and pollsters).

2296. Ward, William B. *Reporting Agriculture through Newspapers, Magazines, Radio, Television.* Ithaca, N.Y.: Comstock Publishing Associates, 1952. xi + 362pp.

2297. Warren, Carl N. *Modern News Reporting.* New York: Harper and Brothers, 1951. Revised edition. xix + 498pp. (Earlier editions, 1934, 449pp.; and, as *News Reporting,* 1929, 236pp.)

Among the most widely used of beginning reporting texts. The material is sound, although handled in a simplified manner; it is especially strong in vocational guidance, "shoptalk," reporting exercises, and diagrams. Warren has been a metropolitan newspaperman, radio editor, and journalism teacher.

2297a. Weil, B. H., ed. *Technical Editing.* New York: Reinhold Publishing Corp.; London: Chapman and Hall, Ltd., 1958. xiii + 278pp.

A compilation of 19 papers on specific phases of specialized journalism, including the use of graphic aids. Weil is chief editor of the technical information division of the Esso Research and Engineering Co. Included is material on editing business magazines, handling news releases, and editing organization-sponsored newsletters.

2298. Westley, Bruce. *News Editing.* Boston: Houghton Mifflin Co., 1953. viii + 431pp.

Treats the copy-desk practices of both large and small newspapers. Westley stresses the psychological aspects of news and the changes in news interpretation and definition that have been effected through recent motivational research.

2299. Williams, Walter, and Frank L. Martin. *The Practice of Journalism: A Treatise on Newspaper Making.* Columbia, Mo.: Stephens Publishing Co., 1911. 330pp.

2300. Wimer, Arthur Cecil. *Writing for the Business Press: A Complete Reference Book on Writing for the Business Papers, with Contributions by One Hundred Editors and Publishers.* Dubuque, Iowa: William C. Brown Co., 1950. xi + 351pp.

2301. Wolseley, Roland E. *Interpreting the Church through Press and Radio.* Philadelphia: Muhlenberg Press, 1951. xv + 352pp.

A handbook for ministers, church secretaries, and others responsible for parish publications and for church radio programs. Wolseley analyzes press association and syndicate channels, and radio and television, as well as secular newspaper outlets. Highly useful for specific problems.

2302. ———— and Laurence R. Campbell. *Exploring Journalism: With Emphasis on Its Social and Professional Aspects.* Englewood Cliffs, N.J.: Prentice-Hall, 1957. 3rd edition. xi + 636pp. (Earlier editions, 1943 and 1949.)

A widely used textbook surveying all fields at the college elementary level.

VI

Journalism Education and Vocational Guidance

2303. American Council on Education for Journalism. *Choosing a Career in Journalism.* Bloomington, Ind.: The Council, n.d. 32pp.

A brochure directed toward prospective students in United States schools of journalism. Outlined are the scope of the field, working conditions and pay, personal qualifications needed, descriptions of available jobs, and the nature of schools of journalism. Illustrated.

2303a. Angel, Juvenal L. *Careers in Journalism.* New York: World Trade Academy Press, 1957. 26pp. (Monograph No. 46.)

An oversimplified survey of occupational outlets and qualifications for prospective journalists.

2304. Austin, Alvin E. *Recruiting New Talent for News Staffs.* New York: Wall Street Journal, 1958. 12pp.

A booklet summarizing a more extensive study by Austin into the supply of and demand for fresh talent in reporting and editing on United States newspapers. The full report may be consulted in the libraries of the *Wall Street Journal* and the University of North Dakota. Austin is head of the University of North Dakota School of Journalism.

2305. Baker, Richard Terrill. *A History of the Graduate School of Journalism.* New York: Columbia University Press, 1954. 144pp.

Provides excellent background on Joseph Pulitzer's views during negotiations that led to establishment of the Columbia School of Journalism; on Pulitzer prizes; on the establishment of the American Press Institute; and on "The Columbia Journalist," a composite of the 2500 students who had gone through the school.

2306. Black, Marvin M. *The Pendulum Swings Back.* Nashville, Tenn.: Cokesbury Press, 1938. 229pp.

This is a philosophical book that aims to present a broad rather than a particularistic view of various fields of education. One of 10 chapters is devoted to "Journalistic Education and the Synoptic Viewpoint." Black was a teacher and journalist.

2307. Campbell, Laurence R., ed. *Careers in Journalism.* Chicago: Quill and Scroll Foundation, Northwestern University, 1949. Revised edition. ix + 105pp. (First edition, 1946. x + 80pp.)

2308. Desmond, Robert W. *Professional Training of Journalists*. Paris: United Nations Educational, Scientific, and Cultural Organization, 1949. 95pp. (In Press, Film and Radio in World Today Series.)

An examination of the worldwide problems in the training of journalists, particularly those working for the daily press. The history of journalism instruction is considered and sample curriculums are offered.

2309. Ellard, Roscoe. *General Lee and Journalism*. Lexington, Va.: Washington and Lee University, 1926. 24pp. (Bulletin XXV, No. 11.)

A brief sketch of the efforts made by Robert E. Lee as president of Washington College in 1869 to set up scholarships for "young men intending to make practical printing and journalism their business in life."

2310. *Kappa Tau Alpha Yearbook*. Columbia, Mo.: Kappa Tau Alpha, 1946–date. About 30pp.

The annual report of meetings of this national society dedicated to promoting scholarship in journalism. Each year's pamphlet includes the annual Kappa Tau Alpha lecture given at the convention of the Association for Education in Journalism.

2311. Lee, James Melvin. *Opportunities in the Newspaper Business*. New York and London: Harper and Brothers, 1919. 99pp. (Opportunity Books Series.)

2312. Lent, Henry B. *I Work on a Newspaper*. New York: The Macmillan Co., 1948. 152pp. (Photos by James B. Walsh.)

Light guidance material with a romantic tinge.

2313. Lord, Chester S. *The Young Man and Journalism*. New York: The Macmillan Co., 1922. ix + 221pp.

Lord, for 33 years managing editor of the New York *Sun* under Charles A. Dana and Edward P. Mitchell, tells of the rewards of journalism for young people thinking of entering the field. Although dated, this still has value.

2314. Nash, Vernon. "Educating for Journalism." Unpublished Ph.D. thesis, Columbia University, 1938. x + 178pp.

2315. ———. *What Is Taught in Schools of Journalism: An Analysis of the Curricula of the Members of the American Association of Schools and Departments of Journalism*, in University of Missouri Journalism Series, No. 54. Columbia, Mo.: University of Missouri, December 1, 1928. 77pp.

2316. National Society for the Study of Education. *Mass Media and Education*. Chicago: Distributed by University of Chicago Press, 1954. x + 290pp. (Edited by Nelson B. Henry.)

Concerned with the contributions of mass media to the learning experiences of school children. Contributors include professors of journalism.

2317. Nieman Foundation. *The Nieman Fellows Report: An Account of an Educational Experiment in Its Tenth Year.* Cambridge, Mass.: Harvard University Press, 1948. 135pp. (Edited by Louis M. Lyons.)

This report summarizes the Foundation's background, purposes, dinners and seminars, and projects undertaken by newspapermen during their fellowship years with supplementary information on their subsequent careers and their published works.

2318. Odell, De Forest. *The History of Journalism Education in the United States.* New York: Teachers College, Columbia University, 1935. vii + 116pp. (Columbia Contributions to Education, No. 653.)

This book recites the views of pioneers in journalism education up to 1902 (much of this being in the form of undigested quotation) and lists principles and curriculums. Inadequate, with many inaccuracies, especially in names.

2319. Oldcastle, John. *Journals and Journalism: With a Guide for Literary Beginners.* London: Field and Tuer, 1880. 151pp.

An early reporting and vocational guidance work aimed at encouraging beginners in literary pursuits to take up journalism. Included is a good period directory of English newspapers and magazines.

2320. Olin, Charles H. *Journalism: Explains the Workings of a Modern Newspaper Office, and Gives Full Directions for Those Who Desire to Enter the Field of Journalism.* Philadelphia: Penn Publishing Co., 1906. 192pp.

2321. Pitkin, Walter B., and Robert F. Harrel. *Vocational Studies in Journalism.* New York: Columbia University Press, 1931. vii + 158pp.

An analysis, now dated, of qualities contributing to success in journalism. It is devoted principally to news and editorial judgments.

2322. *Prize-Winning Essays: American Newspaper Publishers Association Journalism Contest.* New York: The Association, 1943–date.

Essays by winners of awards made annually by the ANPA to students in United States schools and departments of journalism, published in pamphlet form.

2323. Ralph, Julian. *The Making of a Journalist.* New York: Harper and Brothers, 1903. 200pp.

An inspiring, exceedingly well written "text" for prospective practitioners from one of the greatest reporters of the quarter century 1875–1900 (New York *Sun* and Hearst's New York *Journal*). The book is partly autobiographical.

2324. Redmond, Pauline, and Wilfrid Redmond. *Business Paper Writing, a Career: New Opportunity in a Misunderstood Field of Journalism.* New York and Chicago: Pitman Publishing Corp., 1939. xi + 194pp.

2325. Reid, Whitelaw. "Journalism," in *Careers for the Coming Men,* pp. 201–213. New York: Tribune Association, 1902; Saalfield Publishing Co., 1904.

Journalism is one of 23 fields covered in this volume of occupational guidance sponsored by the New York *Tribune* as a community service. See also the chapters on "Advertising" by M. M. Gillam, pp. 179–189; "Publishing" by

F. N. Doubleday, pp. 219–227; and "Authorship" by Cyrus Townsend Brady, pp. 237–245.

2326. Rogers, Charles Elkins. *Journalistic Vocations.* New York and London: D. Appleton-Century Co., 1937. 2nd edition. xi + 354pp. (First published in 1931.)

A guide to editorial work, advertising, circulation, free-lance writing, publicity, and related fields.

2327. Seitz, Don C. *Training for the Newspaper Trade.* Philadelphia and London: J. B. Lippincott Co., 1916. 162pp.

2328. Shuler, Marjorie, Ruth Adams Knight, and Muriel Fuller. *Lady Editor: Careers for Women in Journalism.* New York: E. P. Dutton and Co., 1941. 288pp.

Occupational guidance for women desiring work on newspapers, on magazines, and in book publishing.

2329. Sontheimer, Morton. *Newspaperman: A Book about the Business.* New York and London: Whittlesey House, McGraw-Hill Book Co., 1941. xii + 336pp.

Personal recollections by a Scripps-Howard news editor who, in effect, provides an informal textbook for those who want to become newspapermen.

2330. Sorrells, John H. *A Letter to a Young Man Considering Entering the Newspaper Business.* Cincinnati: E. W. Scripps Co., 1948. 14pp.

A Scripps-Howard executive editor tells a prospective journalist of the qualities journalism needs.

2331. Steffler, C. W. *Columbia Journalism Graduates: A Study of Their Employment and Earnings.* New York: Columbia University Press, 1926. 96pp. (Foreword by Roscoe C. E. Brown.)

An analysis of responses to a questionnaire on the activities of graduates of the Columbia School of Journalism. Long since outdated, but of historical interest.

2332. Sutton, Albert A. *Education for Journalism in the United States from Its Beginning to 1940.* Evanston, Ill.: Northwestern University, 1945. x + 148pp. (Studies in the Humanities No. 14.)

A competent history and account of contemporary journalism education. Sutton discusses programs, enrollments, graduates, teaching staffs, placement problems, and library and laboratory facilities. There is a good bibliography.

2333. United Nations Educational, Scientific, and Cultural Organization. *Education for Journalism, 1953.* Paris: Clearing House, Department of Mass Communication, 1954. 44pp. (Reports and Papers No. 8.)

An outline of the status of journalistic educational programs in all countries in whch UNESCO was able to obtain information. On-the-job training methods are included.

2334. ———. *The Training of Journalists: A World-Wide Survey on the Training of Personnel for the Mass Media.* The Hague, Holland, 1958. 222pp. (In Press, Film and Radio in the World Today Series.)

This expansion of earlier publications considers journalism education with regard to the role of UNESCO, the roles of professional organizations and schools of journalism, trends in curriculums, and mass media research. Among 21 articles on journalism training in various countries there is one of the few as yet available on training in the Soviet Union.

2335. Warren, Low. *Journalism*. London: Cecil Palmer, 1922. xx + 352pp. (Foreword by Alan Pitt Robbins.)

An introductory British book for prospective journalists, partly vocational guidance and partly textbook. In comparison with American books of the same period, it is somewhat more mature in its treatment of every phase of the press. Warren was a member of the National Union of Journalists and Robbins was news editor of the London *Times*.

2335a. Wilcox, Walter. *Critique of Twenty Journalism Education Units by ACEJ Accrediting Teams*. Iowa City, Iowa: American Council on Education for Journalism, 1957. Mimeographed. ii + 39pp.

A summary of critical comments in reports made by ACEJ representatives who visited 20 schools and departments of journalism during the 1956–1957 accrediting year. Wilcox is executive secretary of the ACEJ accrediting committee.

2336. Will, Allen Sinclair. *Education for Newspaper Life: An Account of the Co-operation of a University and the Press*. Newark, N.J.: The Essex Press, 1931. 314pp.

A useful report on the origin, development, and stabilization of instruction in journalism in New Jersey. Professor Will established the Rutgers University journalism curriculum in 1926.

2337. Williams, Sara Lockwood. *Twenty Years of Education for Journalism: A History of the School of Journalism of the University of Missouri*. Columbia, Mo.: E. W. Stephens Publishing Co., 1929. ix + 474pp.

2338. Williams, Talcott. *The Newspaper Man*. New York: Charles Scribner's Sons, 1922. 209pp. (Scribner's Vocational Series.)

A guidance book by the first director of the Pulitzer School of Journalism at Columbia University. The author was both a working newspaperman and an early journalism educator.

2339. Wolseley, Roland E. *Careers in Religious Journalism*. New York: Association Press, 1955. 116pp.

VII

Magazines

A. History of Magazines in the United States

2340. Allen, Frederick L. *The Function of a Magazine in America*, in University of Missouri Journalism Series, No. 101. Columbia, Mo.: University of Missouri, August 1945. Pp. 3–12.

2341. Bainbridge, John. *Little Wonder: Or, The Reader's Digest and How It Grew*. New York: Reynal and Hitchcock, 1946. 177pp.

A satire, complete to digest format, on the magazine of DeWitt Wallace and his wife. Most of the account had appeared originally as articles in the *New Yorker*. Bainbridge uses a stiletto-like technique, but through the book runs a vein of good humor.

2342. Cooke, George Willis. *An Historical and Biographical Introduction to the Dial*. Cleveland, Ohio: The Rowfant Club, 1902. 2 vols. 436pp., total.

Vol. I tells the history of Transcendentalism and the origin of the *Dial*, Transcendentalist magazine of the 1840s; vol. II discusses noted contributors, including Charles A. Dana and Theodore Parker. The author was a clergyman.

2343. Drewry, John E. *Some Magazines and Magazine Makers*. Boston: The Stratford Co., 1924. 237pp.

Characterizes the principal magazines of various periods by fields covered, appeals, and contributors.

2344. Facsimile Text Society. *The American Magazine, or a Monthly View of the Political State of the British Colonies*. New York: The Society, 1937. 120pp. (Publication No. 39.)

Reproduced from the original edition, 1740–1741, of the first known magazine to be published in the American Colonies. In a note, Lyon N. Richardson discusses the personal controversy between Andrew Bradford, publisher of this short-lived magazine, and Benjamin Franklin, publisher of the competing *General Magazine*.

2345. ———. *The General Magazine and Historical Chronicle*. New York: Columbia University Press, 1938. 426pp. (Publication No. 41.)

2346. Flanders, Bertram Holland. *Early Georgia Magazines: Literary*

Periodicals to 1865. Athens: University of Georgia Press, 1944. xiv + 289pp.

A study based upon the contents of these magazines.

2347. Garwood, Irving. *American Periodicals from 1850 to 1860.* Macomb, Ill.: Privately printed, Commercial Art Press, 1931. 83pp.

Garwood lists periodicals of the decade, with place of publication, editors, and proprietors; he connects them with their political, economic, and social interests; and he estimates their influences upon literary movements.

2348. Gohdes, Clarence L. F. *The Periodicals of American Transcendentalism.* Durham, N.C.: Duke University Press, 1931. vii + 264pp.

An analysis of 11 periodicals conducted or controlled by the Transcendentalists: the *Western Messenger*, Boston *Quarterly Review*, the *Dial* (Boston), the *Present*, the *Harbinger*, the *Spirit of the Age, Aesthetic Papers, Massachusetts Quarterly Review*, the *Dial* (Cincinnati), the *Radical*, and the *Index*. Included is material on journalists associated with Transcendentalism: Charles A. Dana, Albert Brisbane, and George Ripley.

2349. Grimes, Alan Pendleton. *The Political Liberalism of the New York Nation, 1865–1932.* Chapel Hill: University of North Carolina Press, 1953. ix + 133pp. (James Sprunt Studies in History and Political Science No. 34.)

2350. Gundell, Glenn, ed. *Writing — From Idea to Printed Page.* New York: Doubleday and Co., 1949. ix + 374pp. (Foreword by Frank L. Mott.)

Six case histories of articles, short stories, and an illustration project, all of which had appeared in the *Saturday Evening Post*. The volume is designed to take the reader behind the scenes in the editorial offices of the magazine and into the lives of its writers.

2351. Harper, J. Henry. *The House of Harper: A Century of Publishing in Franklin Square.* New York and London: Harper and Brothers, 1912. 689pp.

This combination biography-history of the Harper brothers (James, John, Joseph Wesley, and Fletcher) and their business contains considerable information about the policies of the editors of *Harper's*.

2352. Hersey, Harold Brainerd. *Pulpwood Editor: The Fabulous World of the Thriller Magazines Revealed by a Veteran Editor and Publisher.* New York: Frederick A. Stokes Co., 1937. viii + 301pp.

Hersey, for more than 25 years associated as editor or owner with over 75 magazines (from *True Story* and *Physical Culture* to *Zoom*), tells how the pulps are made and edited. The book is heavily autobiographical.

2353. Hoffman, Frederick J., Charles Allen, and Carolyn F. Ulrich. *The Little Magazine, a History and a Bibliography.* Princeton, N.J.: Princeton University Press, 1946. ix + 440pp.

A critical account of the magazines which in literary-journalistic history were "sponsors of innovation" and "the gathering place of irreconcilables." The material on Margaret Anderson's *Little Review* is extensive. Nearly half the book is bibliographical.

2354. *Literature for Ladies, 1830–1930.* Manhattan: Kansas State Agricultural College Press, 1930. 54pp.

Three brief accounts of women's magazines, the most useful being that on *Godey's Lady's Book*, by Elizabeth H. Davis. Others are on "Modern Women's Magazines," by Lilian Hughes Neiswanger; and "The Woman Reader of 1930," by Mrs. Leslie Wallace.

2355. Luxon, Norval Neil. *Niles' Weekly Register: News Magazine of the Nineteenth Century.* Baton Rouge: Louisiana State University Press, 1947. viii + 337pp.

In part this is a biography of Hezekiah Niles, who created a publication that printed significant news of the period 1811–1849 and preserved for posterity speeches, documents, and correspondence of public officials. The *Register* remains today an important historical source.

2356. Merritt, Abraham. *The Story behind the Story.* New York: Privately published, 1942. 188pp.

The editor of the *American Weekly* explains for the advertising sales organization of this Hearst supplement how and why each of a series of 18 articles was published.

2357. Mims, Edwin. "Southern Magazines," in *The South in the Building of the Nation*, vol. 7, pp. 437–469. Richmond, Va.: Southern Historical Publication Society, 1909.

This history of southern magazine journalism begins with the establishment of the *Southern Review* in 1828 and includes material on the *Southern Literary Messenger*, the *Southern Quarterly Review*, and *De Bow's Review*.

2358. Mott, Frank Luther. *Golden Multitudes: The Story of Best Sellers in the United States.* New York: The Macmillan Co., 1947. xii + 357pp.

A comprehensive study of popular reading which with Mott's histories of magazines and newspapers (2359 and 18) rounds out his work across three fields. This book, covering the years 1662–1945, provides material on the influence of magazines and newspapers upon the development of best-selling books.

2359. ———. *A History of American Magazines.* Vol. I, 1741–1850, New York: D. Appleton and Co., 1930. xviii + 848pp. Vol. II, 1850–1865, Cambridge, Mass.: Harvard University Press, 1938. xvi + 608pp. Vol. III, 1865–1885, Cambridge, Mass.: Harvard University Press, 1938. xiii + 649pp. Vol. IV, 1885–1905, Cambridge, Mass.: Harvard University Press, 1957. xvii + 858pp.

A general history of American magazines, unequaled in thoroughness and skill in presentation. It was awarded the Pulitzer prize in history. The content includes, besides accounts of every periodical of importance in the periods covered, analyses of magazine problems, the relation of magazines to science and the arts, the business of publishing, readership, geographical factors, and the effect on magazines of politics and wars. The volumes also offer literary criticism and are generously illustrated with facsimiles and examples of contemporary magazine art.

2360. Noel, Mary. *Villains Galore: The Heyday of the Popular Story Weekly*. New York: The Macmillan Co., 1954. xi + 320pp.

An account of popular literature in the mid-19th century as found in such publications as Bonner's *New York Ledger* and Street and Smith's *New York Weekly*. The author includes an analysis of advertising, circulation, illustrations, publicity tricks, and copyright infringement practices.

2361. Peterson, Theodore. *Magazines in the Twentieth Century*. Urbana: University of Illinois Press, 1956. x + 456pp.

A thorough coverage of commercial magazines for the lay public in the period from the late 19th century through 1955; trade, technical, scientific, and professional journals are omitted. The study is based in part upon corporate records. Well illustrated.

2362. Reynolds, Quentin. *The Fiction Factory: Or, From Pulp Row to Quality Street*. New York: Random House, 1955. 283pp.

A history of 100 years of Street and Smith, from their *New York Weekly* of 1855 to the mass magazine-book-comic-paperback-yearbook operation of 1955. It is illustrated extensively with color prints from Street and Smith publications and facsimiles of old magazines. Interesting biographies of the founders, Francis Smith and Francis Street, are included.

2363. Richardson, Lyon N. *A History of Early American Magazines, 1741–1789*. New York: Thomas Nelson and Sons, 1931. xi + 414pp.

A study of 37 colonial magazines which covers the same ground as Mott (2359) but less effectively. Richardson's work is extremely detailed but he lacks Mott's ability to draw general conclusions.

2364. Shackleton, Robert. *The Story of Harper's Magazine*. New York: Harper and Brothers, 1917. 32pp.

A good source for quick review. The volume includes a short account of the development of "The Easy Chair" column.

2365. Smyth, Albert H. *The Philadelphia Magazines and Their Contributors, 1741–1850*. Philadelphia: Robert M. Lindsay, 1892. 264pp.

Sketches of numerous Philadelphia magazines in the century between Franklin's *General Magazine* and *Graham's*. Most useful, perhaps, is the analysis of Joseph Dennie's *Port Folio*.

2366. Stern, Madeleine B. *Imprints on History: Book Publishers and American Frontiers*. Bloomington, Ind.: Indiana University Press, 1956. 492pp.

An analysis of America's "mental frontiers" as represented by printer, bookseller, and publisher. There is considerable material on magazines and newspapers, particularly with regard to Transcendentalist publishers and to James Redpath, George W. Childs, and the Frank Leslies. The book has extensive notes on primary source materials.

2367. Stewart, Paul R. *The Prairie Schooner Story*. Lincoln, Neb.: University of Nebraska Press, 1955. x + 203pp.

A history of the first 25 years of a Nebraska "little magazine," 1927–1951.

2368. Tassin, Algernon. *The Magazine in America*. New York: Dodd, Mead and Co., 1916. 374pp.

An informal history of magazines, long since superseded by Mott (2359). Tassin merely assembles published opinions about the leading magazines (principally the *Atlantic*, *Putnam's*, *Harper's*, and *Scribner's*), 1741–1900.

2369. Time, Inc. *What Makes Time Tick*. New York: Time, Inc., 1956. Unpaged brochure. (First issued in 1953.)

An illustrated promotional folio aiming to answer all possible questions about the operation of the Luce publications: *Time*, *Time International*, *Life*, *Life International*, *Fortune*, *Sports Illustrated*, *Architectural Forum*, and *House and Home*.

2370. True Story Magazine. *The American Economic Evolution*. New York: Macfadden Publications, 1930. 92pp.

A fantastic piece of magazine promotion, set in flamboyant type.

2371. Van Every, Edward. *Sins of New York, as "Exposed" by the Police Gazette*. New York: Frederick A. Stokes Co., 1930. xvi + 299pp. + more than 100 prints. (Introduction by Franklin P. Adams.)

An exhaustive survey — with 153 pages in pale pink — of the *Leading Illustrated Sporting Journal of the World*, as the *Police Gazette* (later the *National Police Gazette*) called itself. This is also an informal history of American tastes, violences, and recreations as reported in the magazine in the half-century after 1845. The account of Richard K. Fox's revolutionizing of journalistic standards with the *National Police Gazette* after 1876 is excellent.

2372. ———. *Sins of America, as "Exposed" by the Police Gazette*. New York: Frederick A. Stokes Co., 1931. xx + 297pp. (Introduction by Thomas Beer.)

A sequel to the *Sins of New York*. There are two extensive chapters on newspaper coverage of the Tilton-Beecher trial and the Charley Ross kidnaping case of the 1870s.

2373. Wolseley, Roland E. *The Magazine World: An Introduction to Magazine Journalism*. New York: Prentice-Hall, 1951. xii + 427pp.

A basic text on the magazine for those planning to enter the field. It includes a brief history of magazines and a good treatment of their business operations.

2374. Wood, James Playsted. *Magazines in the United States*. New York: Ronald Press, 1956. 2nd edition. xiii + 390pp. (First edition, 1949. x + 312pp.)

Wood discusses the influence over the years of general magazines on American tastes, manners, habits, interests, beliefs, and political and social reform. The major emphasis is on the "slicks," although the digests, magazine supplements to newspapers, and important specialized magazines are also considered.

2375. ———. *Of Lasting Interest: The Story of the Reader's Digest*. New York: Doubleday and Co., 1958. 264pp.

B. History of British Magazines

2376. Bevington, Merle Mowbray. *The Saturday Review, 1855–1868: Representative Educated Opinion in Victorian England*. New York:

Columbia University Press, 1941. x + 415pp. (Columbia University Studies in English and Comparative Literature, No. 154.)

The *Saturday Review* was important in mid-Victorian times, both as an index of leading political opinion and as an influence upon literary taste. This study covers the period of the *Review*'s first editor, John Douglas Cook.

2377. Bond, Richmond P., ed. *Studies in the Early English Periodical.* Chapel Hill: University of North Carolina Press, 1957. 206pp.

Discusses the growth of the periodical press, 1700–1760, and the forces responsible for its development. Six contributors prepared articles on Richard Steele and the *Tatler* (1709–1711), the *British Apollo* (1708–1709), the *Free-Thinker* (1718–1721), the *Prompter* (1734-1735), the *Female Spectator* (1744–1746), and the *World* (1753–1756).

2378. Carlson, C. Lennart. *The First Magazine: A History of the Gentleman's Magazine, with an Account of Dr. Johnson's Editorial Activity and of the Notice Given America in the Magazine.* Providence, R.I.: Brown University, 1938. ix + 281pp.

The *Gentleman's Magazine*, founded by Edward Cave in 1731, was one of the most important influences for liberation of the press and broadening of intellectual interests in the 18th century. This scholarly history includes a bibliography on manuscript and printed sources of the period.

2379. Cook, Sir Edward. *Literary Recreations.* London: The Macmillan Co., Ltd., 1919. x + 329pp.

Nine papers by a distinguished journalist of the old *Pall Mall Gazette*. One, "Fifty Years of a Literary Magazine," is on the *Cornhill*. A second, "Literature and Modern Journalism," is helpful for its defense of journalists against the critical attitudes of literary figures.

2380. Graham, Walter. *The Beginnings of English Literary Periodicals: A Study of Periodical Literature, 1655–1715.* New York and London: Oxford University Press, 1926. iv + 92pp.

2381. ———. *English Literary Periodicals.* New York: Thomas Nelson and Sons, 1930. 424pp.

2382. Liveing, Edward. *Adventure in Publishing: The House of Ward Lock.* London and Melbourne: Ward Lock and Co., Ltd., 1954. 108pp. (Preface by Dornford Yates.)

A concise centennial history of a firm that has been the English publisher of leading American magazines and associated with a number of well-known British magazines. The account includes a chapter on the Fleet Street of the 1850s.

2383. Marchand, Leslie A. *The Athenaeum: A Mirror of Victorian Culture.* Chapel Hill: University of North Carolina Press, 1941. xiv + 411pp.

An analysis of the *Athenaeum*'s fight for independent literary criticism and of how it reflected 19th-century tastes. There is biographical material on Sir Charles Dilke, editor from 1830 to 1846.

2384. Marr, George S. *The Periodical Essayist of the Eighteenth Cen-*

MAGAZINES

tury. London: J. Clark and Co.; New York: D. Appleton and Co., 1924. 263pp.

Chronological and alphabetical lists of periodicals and illustrated extracts from the rarer periodicals are included.

2385. Mineka, Francis E. *The Dissidence of Dissent: The Monthly Repository, 1806–1838*. Chapel Hill: University of North Carolina Press, 1944. xiv + 458pp.

An account of this liberal religious, political, social, and literary magazine under the editorships of Robert Aspland, William Johnson Fox, Richard Hengist Horne, and Leigh Hunt, with special emphasis on Fox (1828–1836). The *Repository* published the early work of John Stuart Mill.

2386. Morgan, Charles. *The House of Macmillan, 1843–1943*. New York: The Macmillan Co., 1944. 248pp.

See especially the material on *Macmillan's Magazine* and the account of John Morley's influence on publishing. (The volume also relates the story of publishers against the London *Times* in the newspaper's losing battle from 1906 to 1908 to circulate quality books to subscribers at low newspaper-subscription rates.)

2387. Nesbitt, George L. *Benthamite Reviewing: The First Twelve Years of the Westminster Review, 1824–1836*. New York: Columbia University Press, 1934. vi + 208pp.

A scholarly account of an early magazine that in its first years was the official organ of the Radical followers of the Utopian Jeremy Bentham.

2388. Oliphant, Margaret. *Annals of a Publishing House: William Blackwood and His Sons, Their Magazine and Friends*. New York: Charles Scribner's Sons, 1897. 3 vols. (Vol. 3 has the title *John Blackwood and His Daughter, Mrs. Gerald Porter*.)

By a staff member of *Blackwood's Magazine* for 40 years.

2389. Sampson, Anthony. *Drum: A Venture into the New Africa*. London: Collins, 1956. 256pp.

An account of a South African magazine of which the author was editor for three years. The views are those of a white editor of a publication for blacks; there is good material on the problem of apartheid.

2390. Spielmann, M. H. *The History of Punch*. New York: Cassell Publishing Co., 1895. xvi + 592pp.

A detailed history of the first 50 years of *Punch*, with biographical material on Mark Lemon, the first editor, and Shirley Brooks, Lemon's successor. There are numerous illustrations and reproductions of *Punch* cartoons.

2391. Thomas, Sir William Beach. *The Story of the Spectator, 1828–1928*. London: Methuen and Co., Ltd., 1928. ix + 250pp.

A history of the serious-minded periodical whose contributors in 100 years included many of England's outstanding political and literary figures. The book is also in a sense a biography of four *Spectator* editors: Robert Stephen Rintoul, Richard Holt Hutton, Meredith Townsend, and John St. Loe Strachey.

2392. Thrall, Miriam M. H. *Rebellious Fraser's: Nol Yorke's Magazine in the Days of Maginn, Thackeray, and Carlyle.* New York: Columbia University Press, 1934. xii + 332pp.

An account of the early years (1830s) of a magazine that exposed frailties and foibles of its generation with wit, erudition, and common sense. William Maginn, with Hugh Fraser, was one of the founders. The book is well documented.

2393. Wiles, R. M. *Serial Publication in England before 1750.* Cambridge, England: Cambridge University Press, 1957. xv + 391pp.

A scholarly work tracing the growth of installment publication of material on all conceivable subjects, with the development of newspapers, magazines, books, and trade catalogues interwoven in the study. An extensive appendix gives serial titles from 1678 to 1749, a list of printers and booksellers, and a select bibliography.

2394. *Wipers Times.* London: Eveleigh Nash and Grayson, Ltd., 1930. About 300pp. (Edited by Lieut. Col. F. J. Roberts and Maj. J. H. Pearson; foreword by Field Marshal Lord Plumer.)

This is a complete facsimile reproduction of the *Wipers Times*, a World War I trench magazine issued from Ypres, Belgium, 1915–1918. The material offers some of the most interesting original news and entertaining writing to be found on the war.

C. Collections of Magazine Material

2395. A'Beckett, Gilbert Abbott. *The Comic Blackstone of Punch.* Detroit: Collector Publishing Co., 1897. 3 parts, 198pp.

Light satires on the law and its operations that appeared originally in *Punch* about 1840.

2396. American Mercury. *The American Mercury Reader: A Selection of Distinguished Articles, Stories, and Poems Published in the American Mercury during the Past 20 Years, 1924–1944.* New York: The American Mercury, 1943. 208pp.

2397. ———. *Readings from the American Mercury.* New York: Alfred A. Knopf, 1926. x + 328pp. (Edited by Grant C. Knight.)

2397a. *The Armchair Esquire.* New York: G. P. Putnam's Sons, 1958. 354 + 24pp. (Edited by Arnold Gingrich and L. Rust Hills; introduction by Granville Hicks.)

An excellent anthology of 29 articles covering *Esquire's* first 25 years, 1933–1958, together with a brief account of the magazine's history by editor Gingrich. A helpful appendix gives a check list of literary contributions in the period, alphabetized by author.

2398. Atlantic Monthly. *Atlantic Harvest: Memoirs of the Atlantic.* Boston: Little, Brown and Co., 1947. xxxviii + 682pp.

2399. ———. *Jubilee: One Hundred Years of the Atlantic.* Boston and Toronto: Little, Brown and Co., 1957. xxi + 746pp. (Selected and edited by Edward Weeks and Emily Flint.)

A splendid anniversary anthology compiling nearly 150 *Atlantic* articles, stories, and poems.

2400. *Best Articles of the Year.* New York: Hermitage House, 1953–date. About 350pp. (Selected and edited by Rudolf Flesch.)

An annual collection of the editor's choice of the 25 most memorable articles from 75 magazines. A good anthology.

2401. Ladies' Home Journal. *Ladies' Home Journal Treasury.* New York: Simon and Schuster, 1956. 580pp. (Edited by John Mason Brown.)

A collection of stories, articles, and illustrations appearing in the *Journal* over many years.

2402. Nation. *The Best of the Nation: A Selection of the Best Articles of Lasting Value to Appear in the Nation during the Recent Past.* New York: The Nation Associates, 1952. 96pp.

2403. ———. *Critical and Social Essays Reprinted from the New York Nation.* New York: Leypoldt and Holt, 1867. iv + 230pp.

2404. ———. *Fifty Years of American Idealism: The New York Nation, 1865–1915.* Boston and New York: Houghton Mifflin Co., 1915. ix + 468pp. (Edited by Gustav Pollak.)

An anniversary anthology prepared by an author and editor who contributed to the *Nation* from 1874 to 1919. A history of the *Nation's* first half-century and accounts of its contributors are included in addition to editorials and essays from the magazine's earlier years. (Wendell Phillips Garrison's obituary of E. L. Godkin is among these.)

2405. New Republic. *40th Anniversary Issue.* New York: The New Republic, November 22, 1954. 127pp.

A collection of representative articles, poems, and stories from earlier years, as well as contemporary pieces on the America of 1954. Bruce Bliven, editor for more than 10 years, writes on *New Republic* history. Also included is material on the magazine's founder, Herbert Croly.

2406. *Prize Articles, 1954, 1955,* etc. New York: Ballantine Books, 1954–date. About 200pp. (Edited by Llewellyn Miller.)

Reprints the articles winning the annual Benjamin Franklin awards for the best work in American magazines of general circulation. These are a kind of magazine equivalent of the Pulitzer prizes in newspaper journalism.

2407. Punch. *The Best Humor from Punch.* New York: World Publishing Co., 1953. 350pp.

2408. Reader's Digest. *Getting the Most out of Life: An Anthology from the Reader's Digest.* Pleasantville, N.Y.: Reader's Digest Assn., 1946. 250pp.

2409. ———. *The Reader's Digest Reader.* New York: Doubleday, Doran and Co., 1940. xii + 495pp.

2410. ———. *Twentieth Anniversary Anthology.* Pleasantville, N.Y.: Reader's Digest Assn., 1941. 125pp.

2411. Reporter. *The Reporter Reader.* Garden City, N.Y.: Doubleday and Co., 1956. 314pp.

Selections from the fortnightly news-interpretative magazine edited by Max Ascoli. The articles cover the *Reporter*'s early years, beginning in 1949.

2412. Saturday Evening Post. *One Issue: Just One 52nd of a Year.* Philadelphia: Curtis Publishing Co., 1919. 382pp.

Published for agents of the *Post* to promote sales of the magazine, this puts in book form 15 stories, articles, and editorials from one copy of the magazine.

2413. ———. *Saturday Evening Post Treasury.* New York: Simon and Schuster, 1954. xvi + 544pp. (Selected by Roger Butterfield and the editors of the *Saturday Evening Post.*)

A magnificent anthology — stories, poems, articles, and reproductions of cover pages and advertisements. Butterfield provides a sketch of *Post* history under Cyrus H. K. Curtis and George Horace Lorimer. He and other editors write introductions giving background on the articles and fiction selected.

2414. Saturday Review. *Designed for Reading: An Anthology Drawn from the Saturday Review of Literature, 1924–1934.* New York: The Macmillan Co., 1934. xviii + 614pp.

2415. ———. *Twenty-Fifth Anniversary Edition.* New York: The Saturday Review, August 6, 1949.

2416. Smart Set. *The Smart Set Anthology.* New York: Reynal and Hitchcock, 1934. xlviii + 884pp. (Edited by Groff Conklin and Burton Rascoe.)

2417. South Atlantic Quarterly. *Fifty Years of the South Atlantic Quarterly, 1902–1952: An Anthology.* Durham, N.C.: Duke University Press, 1952. vi + 397pp. (Edited by William B. Hamilton.)

2418. *Ten Years of Holiday.* New York: Simon and Schuster, 1956. xi + 596pp. (Introduction by Clifton Fadiman.)

Forty travel and descriptive pieces, of high quality, chosen from those published in the magazine in its first decade.

2419. Time, Inc. *Time Book of Science.* New York: Random House, 1955. xii + 356pp. (Prepared by Jonathan Norton Leonard, science editor.)

These science articles from *Time* cover a 10-year period, 1945–1955. There is heavy emphasis on articles relating to atomic-energy developments.

VIII

Periodicals of the Press

The titles in this section represent a selected list of the more important periodicals of the press and allied media. The reader who wishes an extensive treatment should refer to the trade publication entries of Ayer's *Directory of Newspapers and Periodicals* (no. 3085 below) and *Ulrich's Periodicals Directory* (no. 3117 below) under appropriate headings: Advertising and Marketing, Books, Book Trade and Authors, Journalism, Newsdealers, Printing and Typography, and Radio and Television.

2420. *Advertising Age: The National Newspaper of Marketing.* Chicago: Advertising Publications, 200 E. Illinois Street, 1930–date. Weekly. (S. R. Bernstein, editorial director.)

Carries news and statistics on advertising.

2421. *Advertising Requirements: Workbook of Advertising and Sales Promotion.* Chicago: Advertising Publications, 200 E. Illinois Street, 1953–date. Monthly. (S. R. Bernstein, editorial director.)

Regular departments include material on radio and television and printing. This magazine is of exceptionally high quality.

2422. *American Editor.* Hartford, Conn.: New England Society of Newspaper Editors, Box 1619, 1957–date. Quarterly. (William H. Heath, editor.)

An intelligently edited magazine that examines the performance of the American press in a concentrated effort to improve its quality. The circulation is general and nationwide.

2423. *American Press: An Independent Magazine for Hometown Newspapers.* Stanton, N.J.: American Press, 1882–date. Monthly. (Don Robinson, editor and publisher.)

A controlled-circulation periodical directed to small newspapers, mostly weeklies and semiweeklies.

2424. *American Pressman.* Pressmen's Home, Tenn.: International Printing Pressman's Union, 1890–date. Monthly. (Thomas E. Dunwody, editor.)

A periodical of a labor organization that has wide influence in general journalism.

2425. American Society of Newspaper Editors. *Bulletin.* Wilmington, Del.: The Society, Box 1053, 1941–date. Monthly, August through June. (Fredric G. Pitts, editor.)

A news and opinion magazine with special reference to policies of newspaper editorial executives. There is a cumulative index through 1955.

2426. Associated Press. *The AP World.* New York: Associated Press, 50 Rockefeller Plaza, 1946–date. Quarterly. (Oliver Gramling, assistant general manager.)

The house magazine for Associated Press staff members throughout the world; it is useful for personnel information. Extensively illustrated.

2427. *Author and Journalist.* Topeka, Kan.: Author and Journalist Publishing Co., 1313 National Bank of Topeka Building, 1916–date. Monthly. (Nelson Antrim Crawford, editor and publisher.)

A useful free-lance writer's periodical. The magazine includes contributions from readers, reviews of books for writers, and general market lists.

2428. *Broadcasting: The Business Weekly of Television and Radio.* Washington, D.C.: Broadcasting Publications, 1735 De Sales Street, N.W., 1931–date. Weekly. (Sol Taishoff, editor and publisher.)

This news magazine was established as *Broadcasting: The News Magazine of the Fifth Estate.* It took over *Broadcast Advertising* in 1932, *Broadcast Reporter* in 1933, and *Telecast* in 1953.

2429. *Canadian Markets.* Toronto, Ont.: Canadian Daily Newspaper Assn., 55 University Avenue, 1941–date. Monthly. (Paul Reading, editor.)

Publishes general newspaper-trade news, with editorial and business departments.

2430. *Canadian Weekly Editor.* Vancouver, B.C.: L. C. Way, 207 W. Hastings Street, 1946–date. Monthly. (Dean Miller, editor.)

2431. *Circulation Management.* Plainfield, N.J.: Galloway Publishing Co., 120 W. Seventh Street, 1935–date. Monthly. (Howard P. Galloway, editor and publisher.)

Covers circulation in all fields of publishing.

2432. *Editor & Publisher: The Fourth Estate.* New York: Editor & Publisher Co., 1475 Broadway, 1884–date. Weekly. (Robert U. Brown, publisher and editor.)

The most important general news organ of the daily newspaper industry in the United States. It covers the editorial, business, and mechanical fields and provides useful information on personnel changes, current views of editors, new books on journalism, and developments in journalism education.

2433. *Gazette: International Journal of the Science of the Press.* Leiden and Amsterdam, Holland, 1955–date. Quarterly. (Published by H. E. Stenfert Kroese.)

A periodical devoted to the study of international world opinion, newspapers, propaganda, advertising, radio and television, and film. Bibliographical information on the international press is included. The contents are published in English, German, and French.

2434. *Graphic Arts Monthly and the Printing Industry*. Chicago: Graphic Arts Publishing Co., 608 S. Dearborn Street, 1929–date. Monthly. (D. B. Eisenberg, editor.)

2435. *Guild Reporter*. Washington, D.C.: American Newspaper Guild, 1126 Sixteenth Street, N.W., 1933–date. Semimonthly. (Charles E. Crissey, editor.)

The official publication of the Guild. Labor interests take precedence over general news of the field.

2436. *Impressions*. Jamaica, N.Y.: Fairchild Graphic Equipment, 1950–date. Quarterly. (James B. Moore, editor.)

Useful for photojournalists. The magazine carries no advertising.

2437. *Inland Printer*. Chicago: MacLean-Hunter Publishing Corp., 79 W. Monroe Street, 1883–date. Monthly. (Wayne V. Harsha, editor.)

A periodical of exceptionally high quality, both in its coverage of developments in the printing and allied industries and in its typographical display.

2438. International Council of Industrial Editors. *Reporting for People in Industrial Communications*. Denver, Colo.: The Council, 810 S. Vallejo Street, 1948–date. Monthly.

Directed toward improving industrial communications through company periodicals. The magazine circulates among employees in industry, customers, and the public.

2439. International Press Institute. *IPI Report: Monthly Bulletin of the International Press Institute*. Zurich, Switzerland: The Institute, 1952–date.

This is one of the most helpful periodicals on current information relating to the foreign press. The publication is privately supported and its contents are not under the control of any foreign government.

2440. *Iowa Publisher and Bulletin of the Iowa Press Association*. Iowa City, Iowa: School of Journalism, State University of Iowa, 1929–date. Monthly. (John M. Harrison, editor.)

2441. *Japanese Press*. Tokyo: Japan Newspaper Publishers' and Editors' Association, 1949–date. Annually. About 100pp.

Publishers' handbooks, giving capsule summaries of current activities, newsprint and business data, and a "who's who" among press personnel. The first issue in 1949 was historical in nature and carried the title *The Japanese Press, Past and Present*.

2442. *Journalism Quarterly*. Minneapolis and Iowa City: Association for Education in Journalism, 1924–date. (Currently edited by Raymond B. Nixon; founded under the title *Journalism Bulletin*.)

This is one of the few periodicals devoted wholly to expanding knowledge of techniques in journalism and allied fields, particularly radio and television. It contains full book reviews and in each issue a selected bibliography of articles on mass communications that have appeared in American magazines and foreign journals. There are also annual summaries of communications research in progress and enrollment in schools of journalism. A cumulative index to articles and reviews is carried in vol. 25, no. 4 (December 1948).

2443. *Journalist.* London: National Union of Journalists, 22 Great Windmill Street, 1908–date. Monthly.

The official organ of the British working newspapermen's labor union.

2444. *Kansas Publisher.* Topeka: Kansas Press Association, 701 Jackson Street, 1923–date. Monthly. (Forrest G. Inks, editor.)

2445. *Listener.* London: British Broadcasting Corporation Publications, 35 Marylebone High Street, 1929–date. Weekly. (Distributed in the United States by Eastern News Co., New York.)

Contains chiefly scripts and broadcast talks and commentaries on world affairs.

2446. *Matrix: A Magazine for Women Who Write.* Austin, Texas: Theta Sigma Phi, 408 W. 38½ Street, 1915–date. Bimonthly. (Frances Dewberry, editor.)

A publication sponsored by the national society for women in journalism.

2447. *Missouri Press News.* Columbia, Mo.: Missouri Press Association, School of Journalism, University of Missouri, 1933–date. Monthly. (William A. Bray, editor.)

2448. National Association of Science Writers. *News Letter.* Port Washington, N.Y.: The Association, 1953–date. Quarterly.

2448a. *National Press Photographer.* New York: National Press Photographers Assn., 235 E. 45th Street, 1946–date. Monthly. (Joseph Costa, executive editor.)

The official publication of the association, directed toward advancement of news photography. Extensively illustrated.

2449. *National Publisher.* Chicago: National Editorial Association, 608 S. Dearborn Street, 1920–date. Monthly. (Clinton W. Loomis, editor.)

Devoted principally to the needs of small daily newspapers and weeklies.

2450. *Newsdealer: The Trade Magazine of Periodical Distribution.* New York: W. H. Cobb, 141 E. 44th Street, 1946–date. Weekly. (Roger M. Damio, editor.)

An illustrated publication dealing in magazine market information. It carries bibliographical material.

2451. *Newspaper News.* Sydney, Australia: David Yaffa, Newspaper News, Ltd., 1928–date. Monthly.

A general newspaper trade publication giving contemporary information on the Australian press. See particularly the 25th anniversary issue (1953, 96pp.) for historical background on Australian journalism, including facsimiles of front pages covering more than 50 years.

2452. Nieman Alumni Council. *The Nieman Reports.* Cambridge, Mass.: Nieman Foundation, Holyoke House, 1947–date. Quarterly. (Louis M. Lyons, editor.)

General commentaries on current press problems by Nieman Fellows and contributors from the working press and from education. The approach is generally highly idealistic and liberal. This quarterly contains outstanding book reviews on works of importance to journalism and it frequently republishes significant public addresses on journalism.

2453. *Ohio Newspaper*. Columbus: School of Journalism, Ohio State University, 1919–date. Monthly, October to June.

2454. *Oklahoma Publisher*. Oklahoma City: Oklahoma Press Association, Biltmore Hotel, 1930–date. Monthly. (Ben Blackstock, editor.)

2455. *Oregon Publisher*. Eugene: Oregon Newspaper Publishers Association, School of Journalism, University of Oregon, 1932–date. Monthly. (Carl C. Webb, editor.)

News and personnel information on the Oregon press and general articles. Much of the material is helpful for recent history of Oregon journalism.

2456. *Pen Woman*. Washington, D.C.: National League of American Pen Women, 1300 Seventeenth Street, N.W., 1933–date. Monthly, October to June.

2457. *PNPA Press Bulletin*. Harrisburg, Pa.: Pennsylvania Newspaper Publishers Association, Telegraph Building, 1929–date. Monthly.

Contains general information on the Pennsylvania press, illustrations, and book reviews.

2458. *Printers' Ink: The Weekly Magazine of Advertising and Marketing*. New York: Printers' Ink Publishing Co., 635 Madison Avenue, 1888–date. Weekly. (Robert T. Lund, publisher; Woodrow Wirsig, editor.)

2459. *Printing Equipment Engineer*. Cleveland, Ohio: Willsea Publishing Co., 1276 W. Third Street, 1911–date. Monthly. (Mac D. Sinclair, editor.)

Devoted to printing techniques.

2460. *Public Opinion Quarterly*. Princeton, N.J.: Princeton University Press, 1937–date. (Frederick F. Stephan, editor.)

Next to the *Journalism Quarterly* (2442) this is the most helpful scholarly journal for communication analysis. It is broader in perspective than the *Journalism Quarterly* and more inclined to treat purely political and psychological phases of communication. Summaries of the more important current polls and book reviews are included.

2460a. *Public Relations Journal*. New York: Public Relations Society of America, 375 Park Avenue, 1945–date. Monthly. (Verne Burnett, editor.)

The official journal of the society, this magazine carries articles, opinion, and book reviews in the field of public relations practice. Well illustrated.

2461. *Publication Management*. Plainfield, N.J.: Galloway Publishing Co., 120 W. Seventh Street, 1935–date. Monthly. (Howard P. Galloway, editor and publisher.)

2462. *Publishers' Auxiliary.* Chicago: Western Newspaper Union, 210 S. Desplaines Street, 1866–date. Weekly. (Byron V. Cook, editor.)

Among the oldest continuously published trade journals of the newspaper industry. It is the only one that attempts to meet the needs of printers, publishers, and editors, especially of small newspapers.

2463. *Quill: A Magazine for Journalists.* Chicago: Sigma Delta Chi, 35 E. Wacker Drive, 1912–date. Monthly. (Charles Clayton, editor.)

The periodical of the national professional fraternity in journalism. It contains articles on problems of newspapers and magazines by working journalists and teachers of journalism, and reports on fraternity news, annual service awards, and convention meetings; it also carries book reviews. Well illustrated.

2464. *Sooner State Press.* Norman, Okla.: School of Journalism, University of Oklahoma, 1908–date. Weekly.

2465. *Sponsor.* New York: Sponsor Publications, 40 E. 49th Street, 1946–date. Weekly. (Norman R. Glenn, editor.)

For buyers of broadcast advertising.

2466. *Standard Rate and Data Service.* Evanston, Ill.: Standard Rate and Data Service, 1740 Ridge Avenue, 1919–date. Monthly.

An exceptionally useful periodical for current information on newspaper rates and other business developments. The service is issued in 10 publications, each with separate circulation and subscription list: *Newspaper Section; Business Publication Section; Consumer Magazine and Farm Publication Rates and Data; Spot Radio Rates and Data; Spot Television Rates and Data; Films for Television; Network Rates and Data; Transportation Section; Canadian Media Section;* and *ABC Weekly Newspaper Advertising* (semiannually).

2467. *Stet: The House Magazine for House Magazine Editors.* Hamilton, Ohio: Champion Paper and Fiber Co., 1940–date. Monthly.

2468. *Technical Writing Review.* Boston: Society of Technical Writers, 28 Newbury Street, 1954–date. Quarterly.

2469. *Tide: The Advertising Magazine for Executives.* New York: Executive Publications, 386 Fourth Avenue, 1926–date. Semimonthly. (Morgan Browne, editor.)

2470. *Typographical Journal.* Indianapolis, Ind.: International Typographical Union, 2820 N. Meridian Street, 1889–date. Monthly. (Don Hurd, editor.)

2471. *United States Camera Magazine.* New York: U.S. Camera Publishing Corp., 9 East 40th Street, 1938–date. Monthly. (Also published annually under the title *United States Camera*, 1935–date. T. J. Maloney, editor.)

The title of the annual varies, those of 1950–1952 being called *United States Camera Annual.* See particularly the annuals of 1947–1948, subtitled *Great News Pictures,* and 1944–1945, *U.S.A. at War.*

2472. *Utah Publisher and Printer.* Salt Lake City, Utah: Utah State Press Association, 34 W. Broadway, 1952–date. Monthly.

2473. *Washington Newspaper.* Seattle, Wash.: Washington Newspaper

Publishers Association, School of Journalism, University of Washington, 1915–date. Monthly. (C. B. Lafromboise, editor.)

2474. *Western Advertising.* San Francisco: Ramsey Oppenheim Publications, 580 Market Street, 1919–date. Weekly as a newspaper under the title *Western Advertising News*; monthly as a magazine; special annual issue. (Frank J. Bruguiere, editor.)

2475. *World's Press News and Advertisers' Review: The National Weekly for Press and Advertising.* London: World Press News and Publishing Co., 9 Old Bailey, 1929–date. (K. R. Viney, editor.)

Serves newspapers, advertisers, magazines, printers, the British trade press, publicity and public relations groups, television and radio.

2476. *Writer.* Boston: The Writer, Inc., 8 Arlington Street, 1887–date. Monthly. (A. S. Burack, editor.)

A periodical for free-lance writers. See also the *Writer's Handbook*, an annual guide published since 1936.

2477. *Writer's Digest.* Cincinnati, Ohio: F. and W. Publishing Corp., 22 E. Twelfth Street, 1920–date. Monthly. (Richard K. Abbott, editor.)

A periodical for free-lance writers. The company also publishes annually *The Writer's Market* (16th edition, 1958, edited by Ruth A. Jones and Aron M. Mathieu) and the *Writer's Year Book* (edited by Mathieu). The three publications give information on about 2500 general and specialized markets and instruction on manuscript preparation and copyright; they list sales agents and make suggestions on selling book-length manuscripts. Well indexed.

IX

Management of the Press

A. General Studies and Texts

2478. American Newspaper Guild. *For All Newspaper Workers: Economic Independence and Security.* New York: The Guild, 1946. Mimeographed. ii + 48pp.

Sets forth the economic goals of the Guild as presented to the National Collective Bargaining Conference, St. Louis, Mo., September 7–8, 1946. Included are extensive tables and charts on newspaper editorial salaries and newspaper general revenues.

2479. Baker, C. *Technical Publications: Their Purpose, Preparation, and Production.* London: William Clowes and Sons, Ltd.; New York: John Wiley and Sons, 1955. xiii + 302pp.

Interesting chiefly because its material is on British technical journalism, with emphasis on scientific journals.

2480. Barnhart, Thomas F. *Weekly Newspaper Management.* New York: Appleton-Century-Crofts, 1952. 539pp. (First edition, 1936.)

One of the most serviceable textbooks on the weekly newspaper.

2481. Bentley, Garth. *Editing the Company Publication.* New York: Harper and Brothers, 1953. 242pp.

A revised and enlarged edition of *How to Edit an Employee Publication* (New York and London: Harper and Brothers, 1944).

2482. Byxbee, O. F. *Establishing a Newspaper: A Handbook for the Prospective Publisher, Including Suggestions for the Financial Advancement of Existing Daily and Weekly Journals.* Chicago: The Inland Printer, 1901. 113pp.

2483. Chicago Tribune. *The W. G. N.: A Handbook of Newspaper Administration — Editorial, Advertising, Production, Circulation — Minutely Depicting in Word and Picture "How It's Done."* Chicago: The Tribune Co., 1922. 302pp.

2484. Elfenbein, Julien. *Business Journalism, Its Function and Future.* London and New York: Harper and Brothers, 1945. xx + 341pp.

Discusses the duties of business-paper publishers, editors, and advertising and circulation managers and clearly shows the place of the business press in the journalistic structure.

2485. ———, ed. *Business Paper Publishing Practice.* New York: Harper and Brothers, 1952. 422pp.

Book publication of a series of lectures on the management of business publishing enterprises and on editorial and public responsibility.

2486. Hungerford, Herbert. *How Publishers Win: A Case Record Commentary on Personal Experiences and Interviews with Prominent Publishers Showing How Books and Periodicals Are Made and Marketed.* Washington, D.C.: Ransdell, 1931. 324pp.

A former editor of the *American News Trade Journal* tells what publishers are like and why some publications fail, discusses circulation methods, and gives some history of publishing.

2487. Moore, W. Clement, and Herman Roe, comps. *The First National Survey of the Weekly Newspaper Publishing Business of the United States.* St. Paul: National Editorial Assn., 1929. 47pp. (Second survey, 1930, 64pp.; third survey, 1932, 32pp.; then discontinued.)

2488. Murasken, Estelle. *Newswriters' Unions in English-Speaking Countries.* New York: U.S. Works Progress Administration, 1937. Mimeographed. 55 + 65 + 24pp.

Three accounts of news-editorial union organization: the Australian Journalists' Association, the British National Union of Journalists, and the Canadian International Typographical Union (newswriters' unit).

2489. National Industrial Conference Board. *Employe Magazines in the United States.* New York: The Board, 1925. x + 89pp.

2490. Pollard, James E. *Principles of Newspaper Management.* New York and London: McGraw-Hill Book Co., 1937. x + 462pp.

One of the better textbooks on newspaper management. More than half the book considers circulation and advertising; the rest is devoted to newspaper financing, accounting, business-legal problems, industrial relations, and office management.

2491. Porte, R. T. *The New Publisher: A Tale of Twelve Cities.* Salt Lake City, Utah: Porte Publishing Co., 1924. 239pp.

An account of management of small-city newspapers by a publisher educated in a school of journalism. The twelve cities are representative of the country at large but are not specifically identified.

2492. Radder, Norman J. *The Small-City Daily and the Country Weekly.* Bloomington: Department of Journalism, Indiana University, 1927. 58pp.

An early textbook on editorial problems, circulation, advertising, promotion, accounting, administration, and handling of mechanical equipment.

2493. Rogers, Jason. *Fundamentals of Newspaper Building: A Brief Consideration of the General Business Principles in Starting a Daily Newspaper or Turning a Moribund Property into a Successful One.* New York: Jason Rogers, 1919 and 1922. 156pp.

An early-day textbook, by the publisher of the New York *Globe*. Rogers's suggestions remain sound.

2494. ———. *Newspaper Building: Application of Efficiency to Editing, to Mechanical Production, to Circulation and Advertising*. New York and London: Harper and Brothers, 1918. xi + 312pp.

Records the publishing methods used successfully by Melville E. Stone, Victor Lawson, William Rockhill Nelson, Joseph Pulitzer, William L. McLean of the Philadelphia *Bulletin*, Adolph S. Ochs, Hugh Graham (Lord Atholstan) of the Montreal *Star*, and Rogers himself with the New York *Globe*.

2495. Rucker, Frank W., and Herbert Lee Williams. *Newspaper Organization and Management*. Ames: Iowa State College Press, 1955. xvii + 547pp.

A textbook for newspaper practitioners seeking to improve mechanical methods. Rucker takes up newspaper organization and equipment, advertising and circulation production and service, financial and legal questions, public relations, and within-the-plant relations. There is a useful bibliography.

2496. Safley, James Clifford. *The Country Newspaper and Its Operation*. New York: D. Appleton and Co., 1930. x + 390pp.

2497. Thayer, Frank. *Newspaper Business Management*. New York: Prentice-Hall, 1954. x + 438pp.

Perhaps the best of the management textbooks. Thayer does an excellent job in correlating the editorial and business problems of the newspaper.

2498. Williams, Walter. *Organization of Journalists in Great Britain*, in University of Missouri Journalism Series, No. 58. Columbia, Mo.: University of Missouri, December 14, 1929. 39pp.

2499. Wisconsin, University of, School of Journalism. *The Outlook for Newspaper Management*. Madison: Office of Editorial Services, University Extension Division, 1955. 31pp.

Papers presented in celebration of 50 years of journalism education at the University of Wisconsin.

2500. Wood, Donald J. *Newspaper Personnel Relations*. Oakland, Calif.: Newspaper Research Bureau, 1952. 70 leaves.

2501. Wyckoff, Edith Hay. *Editing and Producing the Small Publication*. New York: D. Van Nostrand Co., 1956. 289pp.

The editor and publisher of the *Locust Valley Leader* (Long Island) provides details on printing methods and equipment; news and feature gathering; advertising and circulation.

B. Advertising

2502. American Newspaper Publishers Association, Bureau of Advertising. *The Newspaper as an Advertising Medium: A Handbook of the Newspaper in North America, Its Beginnings, Its Development, Its Services to the Public, and Its Usefulness to Buyers of Advertising*. New York: The Bureau, 1940. 170pp.

2503. American Newspaper Publishers Association and Advertising Research Foundation. *The Continuing Study of Newspaper Reading.* New York: The Association and the Foundation, 1939–1952. 142 numbers.

These extensive studies of newspaper reading habits covered newspapers in all sections of the United States, mostly the larger metropolitan areas. These were among the early reading studies; the methodology later became more precise.

2504. Association of National Advertisers. *The Measured Effectiveness of Employee Publications.* New York: The Association, 1953. 109pp.

A study of depth of readership and readability of seven leading employee publications.

2505. Ballinger, Raymond A. *Layout.* New York: Reinhold, 1956. 244pp. ✓

Theoretical and practical material on designing pages, principally for advertising. Examples from magazine and newspaper advertisements are given.

2506. Bedell, Clyde. *Let's Talk Retailing.* New York: Retail Division, Bureau of Advertising, American Newspaper Publishers Assn., 1946. xiii + 129pp.

A text for newspaper retail-advertising staffs and retail-store advertising personnel.

2507. Birren, Faber. *Selling Color to People.* New York: University Books, 1956. 219pp.

Discusses commercial uses of color in advertising, television, and marketing.

2508. Borden, Neil H. *The Economic Effects of Advertising.* Chicago: R. D. Irwin, 1942. xl + 988pp.

A study of the role advertising plays in the national economy, by a Harvard professor of advertising.

2509. ———, Malcolm D. Taylor, and Howard T. Hovde. *National Advertising in Newspapers.* Cambridge, Mass.: Harvard University Press, 1946. xiv + 486pp.

2510. Cheskin, Louis. *How to Predict What People Will Buy.* New York: Liveright Publishing Corp., 1957. 241pp. (Introduction by Van Allen Bradley.)

A handbook on the use of techniques in marketing, advertising, and selling, by the director of the Color Research Institute.

2511. Clark, Thomas Blake. *The Advertising Smoke Screen.* New York and London: Harper and Brothers, 1944. ix + 228pp.

An exposé of dishonest advertising.

2512. Davis, Donald W. *Basic Text in Advertising.* Pleasantville, N.Y.: Printers' Ink Books, 1955. xxii + 665pp. (Foreword by C. B. Larrabee, chairman of the board, *Printers' Ink.*)

An extensive history of advertising, an analysis of the psychological and creative forces affecting it, and data on production, media, coverage, and rates.

2513. De Voe, Merrill. *Effective Advertising Copy.* New York: The Macmillan Co., 1956. xxix + 717pp.

Sets forth the technical principles for preparing advertising copy that have evolved through research.

2514. Dunn, S. Watson. *Advertising Copy and Communication*. New York: McGraw-Hill Book Co., 1956. ix + 545pp.

The communicative aspects of advertising are kept secondary to a conventional discussion. There is useful information on the variety of tasks performed by copywriters.

2515. Fortune Magazine. *The Amazing Advertising Business*. New York: Simon and Schuster, 1957. xi + 178pp.

Eleven articles on advertising that appeared originally in *Fortune*. The business of advertising, products, techniques, and economic problems are discussed. A useful inclusion is an interchange among writer Bernard De Voto and two businessmen, retailer Richard Weil and advertising executive Albert Lynd.

2516. Freeman, William M. *The Big Name*. New York: Printers' Ink Books, 1957. 230pp. (Foreword by Jules Alberti, president of Endorsements, Inc.)

A study of the testimonial ad, with emphasis on the need for greater honesty in its presentation.

2517. French, George. *20th Century Advertising*. New York: D. Van Nostrand Co., 1926. xii + 588pp.

2518. Gill, Leslie E. *Advertising and Psychology*. London: Hutchinson House, 1954. vii + 192pp. (Hutchinson's University Library.)

Although press advertising is only slightly treated, this is interesting for its emphasis on the effect large-scale advertising has on social life. A good bibliography of British publications on advertising is included.

2519. Gundersen, Gilbert N. *The Story of Classified Ads and Their Relation to Human Progress*. New York: New York Telegram and Evening Mail, 1924. 59pp.

A useful historical summary. The account goes back to 1795 and includes reproductions of selected ads.

2520. Harding, Thomas Swann. *The Popular Practice of Fraud*. London and New York: Longmans, Green and Co., 1935. vii + 376pp.

An examination of nostrums and devices for which extreme claims have been made in commercial advertising. Written in a racy style.

2521. Hepner, Harry Walker. *Modern Advertising: Practices and Principles*. New York: McGraw-Hill Book Co., 1956. 740pp. (An earlier edition was published under the title *Effective Advertising*.)

A textbook that successfully integrates advertising with other marketing processes. Attention is given to motivation research studies.

2522. Hotchkiss, George Burton. *An Outline of Advertising*. New York: The Macmillan Co., 1950. 3rd edition. xxvi + 605pp. (Earlier editions, 1933 and 1940.)

The third edition of a general-survey textbook that is heavy in statistics, recent case material, and illustrations. Excellent as a handbook.

2523. Hower, Ralph M. *The History of an Advertising Agency: N. W. Ayer & Son at Work, 1869–1939.* Cambridge, Mass.: Harvard University Press, 1939. xxxv + 652pp. (Vol. 5 in Harvard Studies in Business History.)

A thoroughly documented study. There is a good account of the development of Ayer's *American Newspaper Annual.*

2524. Hymes, David. *Production in Advertising and the Graphic Arts.* New York: Henry Holt and Co., 1958. Revised edition. 376pp. (First issued under the title *Production in Advertising.* New York: Colton Press, 1950. 392pp.)

An excellent handbook explaining advertising processes and procedures. Supplementary line drawings, samples of paper stocks, and type specimens are helpful.

2525. Kenner, H. J. *The Fight for Truth in Advertising.* New York: Round Table Press, 1936. xxi + 298pp.

An account of what business has done and is doing to establish and maintain accuracy and fairness in advertising.

2526. Kleppner, Otto. *Advertising Procedure.* New York: Prentice-Hall, 1950. 4th edition. xviii + 775pp. (First published in 1925; revised in 1933 and 1941.)

A general text and reference book on advertising in all its phases. Newspapers, magazines, radio, and television, although subordinated in the book as a whole, are still treated in detail. This is probably the most extensively used advertising textbook.

2527. Lambert, Isaac. *The Public Accepts: Stories behind Famous Trade-Marks, Names, and Slogans.* Albuquerque, N.M.: University of New Mexico Press, 1941. 253pp. (Introduction by William Allen White.)

2528. Lund, John V. *Newspaper Advertising.* New York: Prentice-Hall, 1947. xiii + 459pp.

Emphasizes local advertising in newspapers, principally non-metropolitan newspapers. The material, based on the author's 12 years as a publisher of a small newspaper, is presented clearly. There is an extensive bibliography.

2529. Lyon, Marguerite. *And So to Bedlam: A Worm's Eye View of the Advertising Business.* Indianapolis and New York: Bobbs-Merrill Co., 1943. 302pp. (Illustrated by Lois Fisher.)

A rollicking book in which information is subordinated to entertainment.

2530. McClure, Leslie Willard. *Newspaper Advertising and Promotion.* New York: The Macmillan Co., 1950. xiv + 479pp.

Stresses developments since World War II — new types of markets, consumer research projects, and the growing use of visual aids. It is useful as reference and textbook. The emphasis is on larger newspapers.

2531. McCormick, Robert R. *A Preliminary Study of the Freedom of the Press as It Affects the Rights of Advertisers.* Chicago: The Tribune Co., 1935. 18pp.

McCormick argues that the First Amendment protects the advertiser's right of expression as much as the editor's.

2532. Martineau, Pierre. *Motivation in Advertising: Motives That Make People Buy*. New York: McGraw-Hill Book Co., 1957. 224pp.

The director of research and marketing for the Chicago *Tribune* analyzes advertising from the perspectives of psychology, sociology, and symbolic communication.

2533. Mayer, Martin. *Madison Avenue, U.S.A.* New York: Harper and Brothers, 1958. xiii + 332pp.

A fair-minded, objective analysis of American advertising in all its phases. The principal emphasis is on agency operation. The section on the media deals chiefly with newspapers, radio, television, and the big consumer magazines.

2534. Meynell, Francis. *The Typography of Newspaper Advertisements*. London: E. Benn, 1929. 240pp.

Meynell provides examples of English, American, French, Dutch, and German typefaces; a table for calculating the number of words of any type which can be fitted into any given space; and a gallery of contemporary advertisements.

2535. Mills, G. H. Saxon. *There Is a Tide*. London: William Heinemann, Ltd., 1954. viii + 197pp.

The life and work of Sir William Crawford, to whom advertising owed much, and a historical account of modern British advertising, principally since 1914. This book is concerned mostly with creative-aesthetic achievements in advertising and with raising professional standards.

2536. Munsey, Frank A. *Advertising in Some of Its Phases*. New York, 1898. 42pp.

An address by Munsey before the Sphinx Club on October 12, 1898.

2537. Presbrey, Frank. *The History and Development of Advertising*. Garden City, N.Y.: Doubleday, Doran and Co., 1929. ix + 642pp.

Long the standard history of advertising. Presbrey, the experienced head of an advertising agency, includes considerable general journalistic history.

2538. Price, [Charles] Matlack. *Advertising and Editorial Layout*. New York: McGraw-Hill Book Co., 1949. xi + 359pp.

Discusses the theory and practice of advertising design and layout in newspapers and magazines.

2539. *Principles and Practices of Classified Advertising*. Culver City, Calif.: Association of Newspaper Classified Advertising Managers, 1952. 470pp. (Edited by M. J. A. McDonald; a revision of *Encyclopedia of Classified Advertising*, 1947.)

Sixteen authors discuss classified advertising in historical and practical terms. The volume may be used as a textbook or "self-help" manual.

2540. Rorty, James. *Our Master's Voice: Advertising*. New York: John Day, 1934. x + 394pp.

Heavy in ridicule, sarcasm, and irony, this book maintains that the "master" of the American press is "business for profit."

2541. Sandage, C. H., and Vernon Fryburger. *Advertising Theory and*

Practice. Homewood, Ill.: Richard D. Irwin, 1958. 5th edition. 690pp. (First issued in 1936.)

This expanded text incorporates into its earlier general material new develop-ments in marketing and research and new studies of media audiences.

2542. Swan, Carroll J. *Tested Advertising Copy.* Pleasantville, N.Y.: Printers' Ink Books, 1955. 208pp.

An editor of *Printers' Ink* presents the factual results of readership and sales studies in advertising.

2543. Thomson, William A. *Making Millions Read and Buy: The Influ-ence and Use of the Newspaper in Advertising.* New York: W. Drey, 1934. xiv + 248pp.

2544. Turner, E. S. *The Shocking History of Advertising.* London: M. Joseph, 1952. 303pp. New York: E. P. Dutton and Co., 1953. 351pp.

Despite its title, this is not a direct attack on advertising but an informative account with suggestions for improvements. The author is most critical of testimonial advertising. There are excellent reproductions of advertisements of many periods.

2545. Wales, Hugh G., Dwight L. Gentry, and Max Wales. *Advertising Copy, Layout and Typography.* New York: Ronald Press Co., 1958. 491pp.

This book on techniques seeks to bring together all the communicative de-vices of advertising. There is a strong emphasis on creativity.

2546. Watkins, Julian Lewis. *The 100 Greatest Advertisements — Who Wrote Them and What They Did.* New York: Moore Publishing Co., 1949. 201pp.

2547. Whittier, Charles L. *Creative Advertising.* New York: Henry Holt and Co., 1955. xviii + 585pp.

2548. Wood, James Playsted. *The Story of Advertising.* New York: Ronald Press Co., 1958. viii + 512pp.

A general history of advertising going back to the earliest English newspapers. The approach is critical, yet balanced and fair. Extended treatment is given to Phineas T. Barnum, John Wanamaker, and Cyrus H. K. Curtis. There is a good bibliography of secondary works on advertising.

2549. Woolf, James Davis. *Getting a Job in Advertising.* New York: Ronald Press Co., 1946. xi + 103pp.

Woolf describes the different types of work in advertising and the personal qualities required for success in each.

2550. Young, James Webb. *A Technique for Producing Ideas.* Chicago: Advertising Publications, 1944. 61pp.

An exposition on the intellectual process involved in meeting advertising problems — actually a book on practical psychology.

C. Circulation and Distribution

2551. Allen, Charles L. *Free Circulation: A Study of Newspapers Having*

Free or Controlled Circulation. University: Louisiana State University Press, 1940. viii + 78pp. (Journalism Monographs No. 1.)

Some 81 free-circulation newspapers published in Chicago and Chicago suburbs, 1936–1937, were studied.

2552. American News Company. *Covering a Continent: A Story of Newsstand Distribution and Sales.* New York: American News Co., 1930. 61pp.

2553. ———. *Serving the Reading Public: America's Leading Distributor of Books, Magazines, and Newspapers Celebrates 80 Years of Growth.* New York: American News Co., 1944. 66pp.

An illustrated promotional pamphlet recording the history of this distribution agency for newspapers, magazines, and books. Interesting reading but lacking in substance.

2554. Boyenton, William H. *Audit Bureau of Circulations.* Chicago: The Bureau, 1952. x + 126pp. (Earlier editions, 1948 and 1949.)

In this history of the bureau Boyenton analyzes audit reports, publishers' circulation statements, and membership. There is extensive tabular matter.

2555. Burroughs, Harry E. *Boys in Men's Shoes: A World of Working Children.* New York: The Macmillan Co., 1944. xx + 370pp.

This account of the Burroughs Newsboys Foundation of Boston is directed more toward the issue of child protection than toward problems of newspaper circulation.

2556. Davenport, John Scott. *Newspaper Circulation, Backbone of the Industry.* Dubuque, Iowa: William C. Brown Co., 1949. xii + 132pp.

Much of the material in this book is from a master of arts thesis, University of Illinois, 1947.

2557. *Gordon & Gotch — London: The Story of the G. & G. Century, 1853–1953.* London: Gordon & Gotch, Ltd., 1953. viii + 152pp. (Foreword by Leslie W. Berrill, chairman of G. & G.)

The history of a British Empire newspaper distribution firm, advertising agency, and subscription and book agency, with considerable biographical material on the founders (Alexander Gordon and John Speechly Gotch). Well illustrated, partly in color.

2558. McDaniel, Henry Bonner. *The American Newspaperboy: A Comparative Study of His Work and School Activities.* Los Angeles, Calif.: Wetzel Publishing Co., 1941. 139pp.

A quantitative study of newspaperboys, by a vocational counselor for the San Diego city schools. McDaniel makes suggestions for the correction of practices that hamper the carriers.

2559. Rucker, Frank W. *Newspaper Circulation . . . What . . . Where and How.* Ames: Iowa State College Press, 1958. xvi + 390pp. (Foreword by H. Phelps Gates of the *Christian Science Monitor.*)

An excellent textbook and handbook on distribution of newspapers, carrier-boy accounting, circulation and readership, legal issues, and liaison with other newspaper departments. The book is extensively illustrated and has a good bibliography.

2560. Scott, William Rufus. *Scientific Circulation Management for Newspapers*. New York: Ronald Press Co., 1915. xvi + 310pp.

2561. Texas Circulation Managers Association. *Newspaper Circulation: Principles and Development of Modern Newspaper Circulation Methods*. Austin, Texas: Steck Co., 1948. 231pp.

Written especially as a study of the American newspaperboy and a guide for his training.

2562. Watson, Elmo Scott. *History of Newspaper Syndicates in the United States, 1865–1935*. Chicago: Western Newspaper Union, 1936. 98pp.

Issued originally as a supplement to the *Publishers' Auxiliary*, November 16, 1935, on the 70th anniversary of the establishment of the first independent newspaper syndicate.

2563. Wood, Donald J. *Newspaper Circulation Management: A Profession*. Oakland, Calif.: Newspaper Research Bureau, 1952. viii + 104pp.

2564. Wyman, Phillips. *Magazine Circulation: An Outline of Methods and Meanings*. New York: The McCall Co., 1936. 193pp.

By the circulation director of *McCall's*.

D. Production and Labor Relations in the Printing Industry

2565. Barnett, George E. "The Introduction of the Linotype," in *Chapters on Machinery and Labor*, pp. 3–29. Cambridge, Mass.: Harvard University Press, 1926.

One of a series of essays analyzing problems raised by the displacement of skilled labor by machinery. Barnett discusses the reaction of the International Typographical Union to the linotype machine after 1887. The article was first published in the *Yale Review*, November 1904.

2566. ———. "The Printers: A Study of American Trade Unionism," *Quarterly of the American Economic Association*, vol. X (October 1909), pp. 443–819.

2567. Current, Richard N. *The Typewriter and the Men Who Made It*. Urbana: University of Illinois Press, 1954. 149pp.

The story of Christopher Latham Sholes, Wisconsin newspaper publisher who invented the typewriter, and of James Densmore, who promoted it, includes a complete account of the early period of the machine that radically changed the newspaper city room after the 1870s. There are excellent pictures and diagrams.

2568. Deutschmann, Paul J. *The Manpower Problem*. East Lansing: College of Communication Arts, Michigan State University, 1957. Mimeographed. (Report No. 1 on "The Michigan Newspaperman.")

2569. Drake, Leonard A. *Trends in the New York Printing Industry*. New York: Columbia University Press, 1940. xiii + 135pp.

This monograph reporting on New York City printers — unionism, wages, competition, etc. — includes information on newspapers.

2570. Ellis, L. Ethan. *The Print Paper Pendulum: Group Pressures and the Price of Newsprint.* New Brunswick, N.J.: Rutgers University Press, 1948. ix + 215pp.

A study examining the relations between newsprint manufacturers and newspaper publishers, 1878–1938. Well written and carefully compiled from government, publisher, and newsprint manufacturing sources.

2571. Guthrie, John A. *The Economics of Pulp and Paper.* Pullman: State College of Washington, 1950. xi + 194pp.

2572. ———. *The Newsprint Paper Industry: An Economic Analysis.* Cambridge, Mass.: Harvard University Press, 1941. xxiii + 274pp. (Harvard Economic Studies, vol. LXVIII.)

2573. Hollander, Jacob H., and George E. Barnett, eds. *Studies in American Trade Unionism.* New York: Henry Holt and Co., 1905. v + 380pp.

Two of these twelve studies provide good background on newspaper-printer relations: "The Government of the Typographical Union" and "Collective Bargaining in the Typographical Union."

2574. Hunter, Dard. *Papermaking in Pioneer America.* Philadelphia: University of Pennsylvania Press, 1952. xiv + 178pp.

2575. ———. *Papermaking: The History and Technique of an Ancient Craft.* New York: Alfred A. Knopf, 1943. xviii + 398pp.

2576. ———. *Papermaking through Eighteen Centuries.* New York: W. E. Rudge, 1930. xvii + 358pp.

2577. Kellogg, Royal S. *Newsprint Paper in North America.* New York: Newsprint Service Bureau, 1948. 94pp.

2578. ———. *Pulpwood and Wood Pulp in North America.* New York: McGraw-Hill Book Co., 1923. xii + 273pp.

2579. Kjaer, Swen. *Productivity of Labor in Newspaper Printing.* Washington, D.C.: Government Printing Office, March 1929. 253pp. (Issued as Bulletin No. 475, U.S. Bureau of Labor Statistics Productivity of Labor Series.)

A comprehensive economic report by a member of the Bureau of Labor Statistics staff. He includes comparative figures on production and costs, 1896–1926, a history of newspaper mechanical production after 1800, and a discussion of employment trends.

2580. Lipset, Seymour Martin, Martin A. Trow, and James S. Coleman. *Union Democracy: The Internal Politics of the International Typographical Union.* Glencoe, Ill.: The Free Press, 1956. xxviii + 455pp. (Foreword by Clark Kerr.)

The text, heavy with statistical findings, reads slowly, but the book is an invaluable, definitive study of the ITU. It was developed through a combination of historical and survey-research methods.

2581. Loft, Jacob. *The Printing Trades.* New York and Toronto: Farrar and Rinehart, 1944. xiii + 301pp.

2582. Lynch, James M. *Epochal History of the International Typographical Union.* Indianapolis: The Union, 1925. 108pp.

The official history of the union, compiled by a former ITU president. Introductory chapters record the origin of printing and discuss early printing organizations.

2583. McMurtrie, Douglas C. *The Pacific Typographical Society and the California Gold Rush of 1849: A Forgotten Chapter in the History of Typographical Unionism in America.* Chicago: Ludlow Typograph Co., 1928. 20pp.

A volume of fine printing recalling a controversy over wages between the the first newspaper labor organization in California and the publishers of the *Alta California.*

2584. Margolin, Edward, and William P. McLendon. *Transportation Factors in the Marketing of Newsprint.* Washington, D.C.: United States Department of Commerce, Office of the Undersecretary of Transportation, 1952. ix + 126pp.

2585. New York State Department of Labor. *New York Typographical Union No. 6: Study of a Modern Trade Union and Its Predecessors.* Albany, N.Y.: The Department, 1912. xix + 717pp. (Prepared by George A. Stevens, senior statistician, under the direction of John Williams, labor commissioner; in the department's report for 1911, vol. 2.)

A thorough analysis covering some 135 years and placing the story of the typographical union in the general pattern of industrial reform and newspaper history. Horace Greeley's work with the typographers is discussed in detail.

2586. Porter, Arthur R., Jr. *Job Property Rights: A Study of the Job Controls of the International Typographical Union.* New York: King's Crown Press, 1954. vi + 110pp.

A study of the concept among employees in composing rooms of the printing industry that a job is a property right.

2587. Seybold, John W. *The Philadelphia Printing Industry: A Case Study.* Philadelphia: University of Pennsylvania Press, for the Labor Relations Council of the Wharton School of Finance and Commerce, 1949. v + 109pp.

2588. Stewart, Ethelbert. *A Documentary History of the Early Organization of Printers.* Indianapolis: International Typographical Union, 1907. 194pp.

2589. Sutermeister, Edwin. *The Story of Papermaking.* Boston: S. D. Warren Co., 1954. xi + 209pp.

A readable account of paper, its history, and its manufacture. Well illustrated.

2590. Tracy, George A. *History of the Typographical Union.* Indianapolis: International Typographical Union, 1913. 1165pp.

An authorized history, by a one-time vice-president of the ITU. Plodding and discursive, this book discusses printers' organizations from 1786 and provides extensive reports of ITU conventions from 1850 to 1912.

2590a. United States Congress, House Committee on Interstate and Foreign Commerce. *Newsprint Study: Hearing before the Committee on Interstate and Foreign Commerce, House of Representatives, 85th Congress, 1st Session, on the Newsprint Situation* (February 18, June 3, and June 17, 1957). Washington, D.C.: Government Printing Office, 1958. iii + 121pp.

2591. United States Congress, Senate Committee on Interstate and Foreign Commerce. *Newsprint Inquiry*. Washington, D.C.: Government Printing Office, 1957. iv + 261pp.

Hearings before the Senate committee, 85th Congress, 1st Session, pursuant to Senate Resolution 26 providing for an investigation of problems affecting interstate and foreign commerce, February 26 to 28, 1957.

2592. United States Congress, Senate Committee on Small Business. *Newsprint for Tomorrow: Report and Conclusions of the Select Committee on Small Business*. Washington, D.C.: Government Printing Office, 1952. vi + 239pp.

2593. United States Federal Trade Commission. *Newsprint Paper Industry: Letter from the Chairman of the Federal Trade Commission Transmitting, in Response to Senate Resolution No. 337 (70th Congress), a Report on Certain Phases of the Newsprint Paper Industry*. Washington, D.C.: Government Printing Office, 1930. ix + 116pp.

2594. ———. *Report of the Federal Trade Commission on the Newsprint Paper Industry in the United States*. Washington, D.C.: Government Printing Office, 1917. 162pp.

2595. United States National Labor Relations Board. *Collective Bargaining in the Newspaper Industry*. Washington, D.C.: Government Printing Office, 1939. x + 194pp. (Issued in October 1938 as Bulletin No. 3, Division of Economic Research, NLRB.)

A study of newswriters' organizations and representative unions in the mechanical trades, and an analysis of the effects upon interstate commerce of industrial conflict within the industry.

2596. Weeks, Lyman Horace. *History of Paper Manufacturing in the United States, 1690–1916*. New York: Lockwood Trade Journal Co., 1916. xv + 352pp.

A nontechnical, comprehensive historical account of paper-making, with good material on the colonial activities of William Bradford and William Parks and on the modern-day supplying of paper to major newspapers.

2597. Wiegman, Carl. *Trees to News: A Chronicle of the Ontario Paper Company's Origin and Development*. Toronto, Ont.: McClelland Stewart, Ltd., 1953. xii + 364pp.

A history of the Chicago *Tribune*'s business activities in Canada (1900–1952) in developing forest resources, newsprint mills, and hydroelectric plants. The author is a *Tribune* staff member.

X

Public Opinion, Propaganda, and Public Relations

A. General Studies in Public Opinion

2598. Albig, William. *Modern Public Opinion*. New York: McGraw-Hill Book Co., 1956. xii + 518pp. (First issued as *Public Opinion*. New York: McGraw-Hill Book Co., 1939. xiii + 468pp.)

A complete revision of the author's earlier textbook. The volume is good on history, somewhat weak on press and radio.

2599. Altick, Richard D. *The English Common Reader: A Social History of the Mass Reading Public, 1800–1900*. London: Cambridge University Press; Chicago: University of Chicago Press, 1957. viii + 430pp.

A careful study, in which the author includes an account of the effect of British periodicals and newspapers upon mass reading and opinion. An extensive bibliography and tables of periodical and newspaper circulation are provided.

2600. Bailey, Thomas A. *The Man in the Street: The Impact of American Public Opinion on Foreign Policy*. New York: The Macmillan Co., 1948. v + 334pp.

Somewhat popular in approach. Bailey discusses in detail propaganda and pressure groups and the newspaper and radio.

2601. Barnouw, Erik. *Mass Communication: Television, Radio, Film, Press — the Media and Their Practice in the United States of America*. New York and Toronto: Rinehart and Co., 1956. 280pp.

The newspaper is subordinated in this volume, in which the author tries to cover the history and psychology of communications, the major media, and the sponsors of communications.

2602. Berelson, Bernard, and Morris Janowitz, eds. *Reader in Public Opinion and Communication*. Glencoe, Ill.: The Free Press, 1953. Enlarged edition. xi + 611pp. (First edition, 1950. xi + 505pp.)

Articles by journalists and social scientists on such subjects as theories of and formation of public opinion; content of magazines, radio, and books; American audiences and effects of communication media upon them; and public opinion objectives.

2603. Bernays, Edward L. *Crystallizing Public Opinion.* New York: Boni and Liveright, 1923. viii + 218pp.

One of the better early studies. For a full description of all Bernays's work, see *Public Relations, Edward L. Bernays and the American Scene* (2940).

2604. Bogardus, Emory S. *The Making of Public Opinion.* New York: Association Press, 1951. 265pp.

2605. Boyd, Malcolm. *Crisis in Communication: A Christian Examination of the Mass Media.* Garden City, N.Y.: Doubleday and Co., 1957. 128pp.

Boyd, once in advertising, radio, and television, and now a clergyman, examines mass media as channels of Christian communication in an effort to show how people can use the media for the highest ends.

2606. Buchanan, William, and Hadley Cantril. *How Nations See Each Other: A Study in Public Opinion.* Urbana: University of Illinois Press, 1953. ix + 220pp.

2607. Cauter, T., and J. S. Downham. *The Communication of Ideas.* London: Chatto and Windus, for the Reader's Digest Assn., Ltd., 1954. xviii + 324pp. (Foreword by Sir Arthur Bowley, University of London.)

A study of opinion formation in a British urban community, with particular reference to the city of Derby. See particularly Part I, Chapters 9–11: "Radio and Television," "Newspapers and Magazines," and "Books and Libraries" (pp. 138–202).

2608. *Communications Research.* New York: Harper and Brothers, 1948. (Earlier published under the title *Radio Research.* New York: Duell, Sloan and Pearce, 1941; Essential Books, 1942–1943. Edited by Paul F. Lazarsfeld and F. N. Stanton, Bureau of Applied Social Research, Columbia University.)

The latest of these books gives the results of methodological studies in all fields of communications.

2609. Doob, Leonard W. *Public Opinion and Propaganda.* New York: Henry Holt and Co., 1948. viii + 600pp. (First issued as *Propaganda: Its Psychology and Technique,* 1935. 424pp.)

Doob's book gives adequate treatment to the sampling of public opinion, polling evaluation, and the communication media. There is a helpful bibliography.

2610. Heckman, Dayton F., Franklin H. Knower, and Paul H. Wagner. *The Man behind the Message: Personal Characteristics of Professional Communicators.* Columbus: Ohio State University Press, 1956. iv + 132pp.

An effort to determine systematically whether professional communicators (lawyers, teachers, clergymen, newspapermen, and broadcasters) possess characteristics which differentiate them from other professional men.

2611. Hovland, Carl I., Irving L. Janis, and Harold H. Kelley. *Communication and Persuasion: Psychological Studies of Opinion Change.* New Haven: Yale University Press, 1953. xii + 315pp.

2612. *Information Please!* Des Moines, Iowa: Wallaces' Farmer and Iowa Homestead, 1956. 202pp. (Prepared by T. A. Bancroft, director, Statistical Laboratory, Iowa State College.)

A report on farmers' sources of information, third in a series begun in 1947 and continued in 1951. The study includes an analysis of the survey method and material on what farm men and women read, listen to on the radio, and watch on television. Prestige ratings of the various media are given.

2613. Inkeles, Alex. *Public Opinion in Soviet Russia: A Study in Mass Persuasion.* Cambridge, Mass.: Harvard University Press, 1950. xviii + 377pp.

A social science analyst in the Department of State describes and analyzes the functioning of the mass communication media in the Soviet Union, with detailed treatment of the functions and personnel of the press, censorship controls, and manner of operation.

2614. Innis, Harold A. *The Bias of Communication.* Toronto: University of Toronto Press, 1951. ix + 226pp.

An extension of Innis's broad arguments in *Empire and Communications.* Significant essays directly concerned with journalism are "The English Publishing Trade in the Eighteenth Century" and "Technology and Public Opinion in the United States." The second places heavy emphasis on journalistic mechanics and the pulp-paper industry.

2615. ———. *Empire and Communications.* Oxford, England: Clarendon Press, 1950. 230pp.

A historical-philosophical-economic study of how communication has occupied a crucial position in government organization and, in turn, in the development of empires. There is good treatment of the enormous expansion of the printing industry and its contribution in bringing together dispersed communities.

2616. ———. *The Press, a Neglected Factor in the Economic History of the Twentieth Century.* London and New York: Oxford University Press, 1949. 48pp. (Also carried in Innis's *Changing Concepts of Time*, pp. 77–125. Toronto: University of Toronto Press, 1952.)

Concentrates on the industrialization of the press after the process of obtaining newsprint from wood pulp had been perfected.

2617. Institute for Religious and Social Studies, Jewish Theological Seminary of America. *The Communication of Ideas, a Series of Addresses.* New York: Distributed by Harper and Brothers, 1948. ix + 296pp. (Edited by Lyman Bryson.)

Sixteen addresses on general problems of communication, delivered during 1946–1947 by leading social scientists and religious leaders. See particularly "Mass Communication, Popular Taste, and Organized Social Action," by Paul F. Lazarsfeld; "Radio," by C. A. Siepmann; and "Science and Writing," by J. M. Clarke.

2618. Institute of Citizenship, Emory University. *Public Opinion and the Press.* Atlanta, Ga.: Emory University, 1933. 177pp. (Edited by Cullen Bryant Gosnell and Raymond B. Nixon.)

2619. Irion, Frederick C. *Public Opinion and Propaganda.* New York: Thomas Y. Crowell Co., 1950. xvi + 782pp.

2620. Jacobson, David J. *The Affairs of Dame Rumor.* New York and Toronto: Rinehart and Co., 1948. 492pp.

A disorganized book on the public's tendency to believe rumors. There is considerable discussion of newspapers as carriers of rumor.

2621. Katz, Elihu, and Paul F. Lazarsfeld. *Personal Influence: The Part Played by People in the Flow of Mass Communications.* Glencoe, Ill.: The Free Press, 1955. xx + 400pp. (Foreword by Elmo Roper.)

An excellent work showing the role of opinion leaders and groups, as distinct from the mass media, in influencing opinion change. The book is based in part upon a study undertaken in Decatur, Ill., and known since in opinion research as the Decatur Study.

2622. Klineberg, Otto. *Tensions Affecting International Understanding: A Survey of Research.* New York: Social Science Research Council, 1950. xi + 227pp.

2623. Laprade, William Thomas. *Public Opinion and Politics in Eighteenth Century England to the Fall of Walpole.* New York: The Macmillan Co., 1936. vii + 463pp.

2624. Lippmann, Walter. *The Phantom Public.* New York: Harcourt, Brace and Co., 1925. xii + 281pp.

2625. ———. *Public Opinion.* New York: Harcourt, Brace and Co., 1922. x + 427pp.

Still a leading analysis of public opinion as a force and particularly valuable for journalists because of its authorship by a newspaperman.

2626. Lowell, Abbott Lawrence. *Public Opinion and Popular Government.* New York: Longmans, Green and Co., 1926. New edition. 415pp. (First edition, 1913.)

2627. ———. *Public Opinion in War and Peace.* Cambridge, Mass.: Harvard University Press, 1923. xi + 302pp.

2628. Lydgate, William A. *What America Thinks.* New York: Thomas Y. Crowell Co., 1944. 167pp.

An editor of the American Institute of Public Opinion argues that the American people show more common sense in regard to public issues than their leaders in Washington.

2629. MacDougall, Curtis D. *Hoaxes.* New York: The Macmillan Co., 1940. viii + 336pp.

A helpful analysis of how falsehoods spread and acquire influence. There are numerous examples of hoaxes put forth by journalists and public relations men.

2630. ———. *Understanding Public Opinion: A Guide for Newspaper-*

men and Newspaper Readers. New York: The Macmillan Co., 1952. xii + 698pp.

Drawing upon diverse disciplines, MacDougall provides materials that help one to understand public opinion; he also discusses related problems of journalistic ethics.

2631. Markel, Lester, ed. *Public Opinion and Foreign Policy.* New York: Harper and Brothers, 1949. xii + 227pp.

A study of the growing power of propaganda in international relations and of changes in techniques in influencing public opinion through mass communication media. Numerous newspaper foreign correspondents contributed reports.

2632. Mills, C. Wright. *White Collar; The American Middle Class.* New York: Oxford University Press, 1951. xx + 378pp.

See particularly "The Mass Media," a somewhat gloomy report of the equalizing power of "culture machines."

2633. Odegard, Peter. *The American Public Mind.* New York: Columbia University Press, 1930. ix + 308pp.

A political scientist's interpretation of why we behave like Americans. Especially relevant for journalists are the chapters on "The Fourth Estate," "Pressure and Propaganda," and "Censorship and Democracy."

2634. Ogle, Marbury Bladen, Jr. *Public Opinion and Political Dynamics.* Boston: Houghton Mifflin Co., 1950. iv + 361pp.

More than half of this book is devoted to terminology, language, myths, and social behavior. The rest deals with propaganda, opinion measurement, press, radio, and motion pictures.

2635. Ortiz, Santiago. *American Press Opinion with Reference to Politics and Government in Puerto Rico, 1932–1939.* Washington, D.C.: Georgetown University, 1946. (Foreword by Emilio M. Colon.)

This analysis was limited to prestige newspapers in New York, Washington, and St. Louis, and to high-quality magazines.

2636. Packard, Vance. *The Hidden Persuaders.* New York: David McKay Co., 1957. viii + 275pp.

A former newspaperman writes a popular book about what makes us buy, believe, and even vote the way we do. Packard criticizes motivational research as an invasion of the privacy of men's minds.

2637. Park, Robert E. *Society: Collective Behavior, News and Opinion, Sociology, and Modern Society.* Glencoe, Ill.: The Free Press, 1955. 358pp. (Preface by Everett Cherrington Hughes.)

Park's pioneering work in newspaper research first appeared chiefly between 1923 and 1941; this volume reprints his important articles on news and opinion, including "The Natural History of the Newspaper."

2638. Pool, Ithiel de Sola. *Symbols of Democracy.* Stanford, Calif.: Stanford University Press, 1952. xi + 80pp. (Hoover Institute Studies, Series C.: Symbols, No. 4.)

2639. ———. *Symbols of Internationalism.* Stanford, Calif.: Stanford

University Press, 1952. 73pp. (Hoover Institute Studies, Series C: Symbols, No. 3.)

2640. Postman, Leo, and Gordon W. Allport. *The Psychology of Rumor.* New York: Henry Holt and Co., 1947. xiv + 247pp.

2641. Powell, Norman. *Anatomy of Public Opinion.* New York: Prentice-Hall, 1951. 619pp.

A more extensive treatment than in most public opinion textbooks is given to the press, motion pictures, radio, and television. The bibliography is extensive.

2642. *The Press and Its Readers.* London: Art and Technics, Ltd., 1949. 128pp.

A British report prepared by Mass Observation for the Advertising Service Guild. It gives statistics on what Britons think of their press, principally the London mass-circulation newspapers.

2643. Quastler, Henry, ed. *Information Theory in Psychology: Problems and Methods — Proceedings of a Conference on the Estimation of Information Flow, Monticello, Illinois, July 5–9, 1954, and Related Papers.* Glencoe, Ill.: The Free Press, 1955. x + 436pp.

2644. Rosenberg, Bernard, and David Manning White, eds. *Mass Culture: The Popular Arts in America.* Glencoe, Ill.: The Free Press (The Falcon's Wing Press), 1957. x + 561pp.

Readings on the impact upon society of the mass media. Rosenberg, a sociologist, takes a somewhat pessimistic view; White, with a literary and journalistic background, is more optimistic. The book offers a strong intellectual appeal.

2645. Schramm, Wilbur, ed. *Communications in Modern Society.* Urbana: University of Illinois Press, 1948. 252pp.

This reader appraises research in mass communications at the University of Illinois.

2646. ———. *Mass Communications: A Book of Readings Selected and Edited for the Institute of Communications Research in the University of Illinois.* Urbana: University of Illinois Press, 1949. 552pp.

A manual for students, teachers, and researchers, supplementing *Communications in Modern Society.* The emphasis is on the press, radio, and film.

2647. ———. *The Process and Effects of Mass Communication.* Urbana: University of Illinois Press, 1954. 586pp.

2648. Smith, Charles William, Jr. *Public Opinion in a Democracy.* New York: Prentice-Hall, 1939. ix + 598pp.

Out of date, and at best one of the less useful textbooks.

2649. Society for the Psychological Study of Social Issues. *Public Opinion and Propaganda.* New York: Dryden Press, 1954. xx + 779pp. (Edited by Daniel Katz, Dorwin Cartright, Samuel Eldersveld, and Alfred McClung Lee.)

These readings include contributions from more than 90 scholars in social science and journalism. Useful pieces on the mass media are included.

2650. Truman, David B. *The Governmental Process: Political Interests and Public Opinion*. New York: Alfred A. Knopf, 1951. xii + 544pp.

2651. *The Use of the Mass Media of Communication for Community Relations Purposes*. New York: National Community Relations Advisory Council, 1956. 88pp. (Prepared by Walter A. Lurie and Samuel Spiegler.)

A report for the National Community Relations Advisory Council of a meeting of its special committee on reassessment.

2652. Waples, Douglas. *People and Print: Social Aspects of Reading in the Depression*. Chicago: University of Chicago Press, 1938. xvi + 228pp. (Studies in Library Science.)

2653. Willey, Malcolm M., and Stuart A. Rice. *Communication Agencies and Social Life*. New York: McGraw-Hill Book Co., 1933. xv + 229pp.

Discusses the development and utilization of the media of communication and their relationships. With its numerous statistical tables, this remains a valuable source book.

2654. Wisehart, M. K. "The Pittsburgh Newspapers and the Steel Strike," in *Public Opinion and the Steel Strike*, pp. 87–162. New York: Harcourt, Brace and Co., 1921.

A study of the coloring and suppression of news, advertiser influence, handling of news of violence, and attitudes of the clergy as reported in seven English-language dailies during the period September–November 1919. The report was one of seven relating to the steel strike and was compiled by a Commission of Inquiry of the Interchurch World Movement, with technical assistance from the New York Bureau of Industrial Research.

2655. Woodward, Julian Lawrence. *Foreign News in American Morning Newspapers: A Study in Public Opinion*. New York: Columbia University Press, 1930. 122pp.

An early quantitative study of the press, now outdated by advances in methodology. Forty metropolitan newspapers were surveyed.

B. Public Opinion Measurement and Media Analysis

2656. *The Audiences of Nine Magazines: A National Study*. New York: Cowles Magazines, 1955. 86pp.

Provides statistics on the readers of *Collier's, Life, Look, Saturday Evening Post, Better Homes and Gardens, Good Housekeeping, Ladies' Home Journal, McCall's*, and *Woman's Home Companion* — employment status and occupation, household possessions, exclusive readership, etc. The study was conducted by Alfred Politz Research, Inc.

2657. Berelson, Bernard. *Content Analysis in Communication Research*. Glencoe, Ill.: The Free Press, 1952. 220pp.

A scholarly examination of how new social science techniques can be applied to communication media. The bibliography contains most of the content analyses published through 1950.

2658. ———, Hazel Gaudet, and Paul F. Lazarsfeld. *The People's Choice: How the Voter Makes up His Mind in a Presidential Campaign.* New York: Duell, Sloan and Pearce, 1944. vi + 178pp.

Popularly known as the Erie County Study. Through use of a panel-interviewing technique, the authors studied the Roosevelt-Willkie campaign of 1940 in Erie County, Ohio. Voters answered questions on the role of press, radio, and magazines in the campaign, as well as on their attitudes toward formal propaganda. The method has been considerably refined in subsequent years.

2659. Berelson, Bernard, Paul F. Lazarsfeld, and William N. McPhee. *Voting: A Study of Opinion Formation in a Presidential Campaign.* Chicago: University of Chicago Press, 1954. xix + 395pp.

Popularly known as the Elmira Study. A case analysis of voting habits and processes by which voters made up their minds in Elmira, N.Y., in the Dewey-Truman campaign of 1948. The panel technique of interviewing was used.

2660. Bogart, Leo. *The Age of Television.* New York: Frederick Ungar Publishing Co., 1956. 347pp.

A review of scores of television studies. One of the best single references available.

2660a. Brinton, James E., Chilton R. Bush, and Thomas M. Newell. *The Newspaper and Its Public: A Standardized Test to Measure the Public's Attitude toward a Newspaper.* Stanford, Calif.: Institute for Communication Research, Department of Communication and Journalism, Stanford University, 1957. ix + 126pp.

A measurement device for the use of individual newspapers, based upon studies extending over 10 years.

2661. Cantril, Hadley, ed. *Public Opinion, 1935–1946.* Princeton, N.J.: Princeton University Press, 1951. lix + 1191pp. (Assisted by Mildred Strunk.)

Provides the results of hundreds of public opinion polls for the years covered. No effort is made to discuss methodology.

2662. Cantril, Hadley, and Research Associates in Office of Public Opinion Research. *Gauging Public Opinion.* Princeton, N.J.: Princeton University Press; London: Oxford University Press, 1944. xiv + 318pp.

Still a valuable book on polling methodology, although somewhat outdated by later refinements in technique.

2663. Chall, Jeanne S. *Readability: An Appraisal of Research and Application.* Columbus: Ohio State University Press, 1958. xiv + 202pp.

Treats exhaustively 24 readability formulas developed since 1923.

2664. Ernst, Morris L., and David Loth. *The People Know Best: The Ballots vs. the Polls.* Washington, D.C.: Public Affairs Press, 1949. 169pp.

A sharp attack on polling and pollsters on the basis of their errors in the

Dewey-Truman campaign of 1948. The authors make no suggestions for improvements in the polls.

2665. Faville, David E. *How Sunset Magazine Subscribers Evaluate the Magazines They Read: A Study of Magazine Preferences.* Stanford, Calif.: Stanford University Graduate School of Business, 1940. 107pp.

One of many analyses conducted in recent decades to study readership trends. The report on *Sunset* covers the seven westernmost states.

2666. Gallup, George A. *A Guide to Public Opinion Polls.* Princeton, N.J.: Princeton University Press, 1948. 2nd edition. xxiv + 117pp. (First issued in 1944.)

A helpful manual, in layman's language, to explain the methods employed in public opinion research. It is highly useful for background information on election predictions, including the *Literary Digest* failure of 1936.

2667. ———— and Saul Forbes Rae. *The Pulse of Democracy.* New York: Simon and Schuster, 1940. vii + 335pp.

An early popular discussion of polling techniques.

2668. Handel, Leo A. *Hollywood Looks at Its Audience: A Report of Film Audience Research.* Urbana: University of Illinois Press, 1950. xvii + 240pp.

2669. Hansen, Morris H., William N. Hurwitz, and William G. Madow. *Sample Survey Methods and Theory.* New York: John Wiley, 1954. 2 vols. xxii + 638pp.; xiii + 332pp.

2670. Hobart, Donald M., ed. *Marketing Research Practice.* New York: Ronald Press Co., 1950. ix + 471pp.

2671. Hyman, Herbert, and others. *Interviewing in Social Research.* Chicago: University of Chicago Press, 1954. xvi + 415pp.

2672. ————. *Survey Design and Analysis: Principles, Cases and Procedures.* Glencoe, Ill.: The Free Press, 1955. xxviii + 425pp. (Foreword by Paul F. Lazarsfeld.)

Helpful for those who make surveys and for instructors in survey methodology. Much of the content bears on problems of the media researcher.

2673. Iowa Conference on Attitude and Opinion Research. *The Polls and Public Opinion.* New York: Henry Holt and Co., 1949. x + 355pp. (Edited by Norman C. Meier and Harold W. Saunders.)

One of the numerous studies discussing the failure of the polls in predicting the results of the 1948 presidential election.

2674. Klapper, Joseph T. *The Effects of Mass Media.* New York: Columbia University, Bureau of Applied Social Research, 1949. 192pp. (Foreword by Paul F. Lazarsfeld.)

A report on the impact of the mass media upon public taste; the comparative effects of the various media; and the functions and effects of escapist communication.

2675. Klare, George R., and Byron Buck. *Know Your Reader: The*

Scientific Approach to Readability. New York: Hermitage House, 1954. 192pp.

2676. Lasswell, Harold D., Daniel Lerner, and Ithiel de Sola Pool. *The Comparative Study of Symbols: An Introduction.* Stanford, Calif.: Stanford University Press, 1952. v + 87pp. (Hoover Institute Studies, Series C: Symbols, No. 1.)

Gives the reader an insight into the design of content analysis and the technical problems involved in this method of analyzing the contents and performance of the press.

2677. Lazarsfeld, Paul F., and Morris Rosenberg. *The Language of Social Research.* Glencoe, Ill.: The Free Press, 1955. xiii + 590pp.

A reader in social research methodology. Studies relating to public opinion and the press are included.

2678. Mosteller, Frederick. *The Pre-Election Polls of 1948.* New York: New York Social Science Research Council, 1949. xx + 396pp.

2679. *Motivation Research Looks at Detroit Newspaper Readers.* Detroit: Detroit Free Press, 1955. 108pp. (Prepared by the Promotion-Research Department of the *Free Press,* in cooperation with Social Research, Inc., Chicago; text by Dorian Hyshka.)

An exhaustive study of reader attitudes toward the Detroit newspapers. The general significance of newspaper motivation research is discussed.

2680. Nafziger, Ralph O., and Thomas A. Barnhart. *Red Wing and Its Daily Newspaper.* Minneapolis: University of Minnesota Press, 1946. 54pp. (The Community Basis for Postwar Planning Series, No. 9.)

This study considered the effects of war upon a small-city newspaper and the influence of a newspaper upon its community in wartime. Nafziger surveyed news content and readership, Barnhart management problems. Extensive graphs and tabulations on news and advertising readership are included. The authors were members of the University of Minnesota School of Journalism faculty.

2681. Nafziger, Ralph O., and David Manning White, eds. *Introduction to Mass Communications Research.* Baton Rouge: Louisiana State University Press, 1958. ix + 244pp. (Sponsored by Council on Communication Research, Association for Education in Journalism.)

Succeeds *An Introduction to Journalism Research* (2682) and brings up to date developments in communication research techniques. Writing from a behavioral point of view, seven contributors discuss the challenge of communication research, research planning, experimental method, field methods, statistical methods, measurement, and scientific method.

2682. Nafziger, Ralph O., and Marcus M. Wilkerson, eds. *An Introduction to Journalism Research.* Baton Rouge: Louisiana State University Press, 1949. v + 143pp.

The first effort to describe research techniques that can be made useful to journalism; the methodology has since been considerably perfected. This work considers research method in connection with legal problems of communication, content analysis, interviewing, and history.

2683. National Opinion Research Center. *Interviewing for NORC*. Denver: National Opinion Research Center, 1945. ix + 154pp.

2684. Parten, Mildred. *Surveys, Polls, and Samples: Practical Procedures*. New York: Harper and Brothers, 1950. xii + 624pp.

A detailed manual on polling techniques. Newspaper polling is only cursorily treated, however. There is an extensive bibliography.

2685. Payne, Stanley L. *The Art of Asking Questions*. Princeton, N.J.: Princeton University Press, 1951. xiv + 249pp. (Foreword by Hadley Cantril.)

Exceptionally useful on the methodology of polling and market research. The author takes a practical approach and writes in a popular style. The study was issued under the editorial sponsorship of the *Public Opinion Quarterly*.

2686. Robinson, Claude E. *Straw Votes: A Study of Political Prediction*. New York: Columbia University Press, 1932. xxi + 203pp.

An early study; long since outdated.

2687. Rogers, Lindsay. *The Pollsters*. New York: Alfred A. Knopf, 1949. xi + 239pp.

A severe critic of polling presents his bill of particulars against opinion measurement. He uses as his base of attack the failure of the polls in the presidential election of 1948.

2688. Smith, George Horsley. *Motivation Research in Advertising and Marketing*. New York: McGraw-Hill Book Co., 1954. 242pp.

2689. Social Research, Inc. (Chicago). *The Sunday Comics: A Socio-Psychological Study of Their Functions and Character, Prepared for Metropolitan Sunday Newspapers, Inc.* New York: Metropolitan Sunday Newspapers, 1955. 66pp.

2690. Stephan, Frederick F., and Philip J. McCarthy. *Sampling Opinions*. New York: John Wiley and Sons, 1958. 451pp.

An examination and evaluation of sampling: accuracy, cost, feasibility, and acceptability. The authors show tolerance for non-probability sampling, such as quota selection and purposive selection.

2691. *The Story behind the Gallup Poll*. Princeton, N.J.: American Institute of Public Opinion, 1957. 31pp.

2692. *A Study of the Accumulative Audience of Life*. New York: Time, Inc., 1950. 134pp. (Conducted by Alfred Politz Research, Inc.)

An endeavor to give an insight into the dimensions of audiences: how *Life*'s audience accumulates and what its characteristics are. The report includes an analysis of how Politz Research established its sample.

2693. *The Sunday Comics: A Socio-Psychological Study with Attendant Advertising Implications*. New York: Puck, the Comic Weekly, 1956. 236pp. (Prepared by Science Research Associates.)

A study by *Puck* seeking to explore the real meaning of the Sunday comics by going beyond the indices of readership and Sunday newspaper circulation.

2694. Time, Inc. *Where Stands Freedom? A Report on the Findings of* an *International Survey of Public Opinion Conducted by Elmo Roper for Time*. New York: February–March 1948. 45pp.

2694a. *A Twelve Months' Study of Better Homes & Gardens Readers*. Des Moines, Iowa: Meredith Publishing Co., 1956. 148pp. (Conducted by Alfred Politz Research, Inc.)

A readership survey covering these categories: reader characteristics, possessions, purchase patterns, extent of reading, actions taken as a result of reading, and editorial and advertising content to which readers respond in answer to questions.

2695. White, David Manning, and Seymour Levine. *Elementary Statistics for Journalists*. New York: The Macmillan Co., 1954. 83pp.

Discusses how to apply to journalistic problems basic statistical tools — standard error, correlation, sampling, tests of significance.

C. Propaganda

2696. Alsop, Stewart, and Thomas Braden. *Sub Rosa: The O.S.S. and American Espionage*. New York: Reynal and Hitchcock, 1946. 237pp.

Two journalists report on the espionage and sabotage activities of the Office of Strategic Services in World War II; there is good material on how the O.S.S. aided the Resistance movements.

2697. Barghoorn, Frederick C. *The Soviet Image of the United States: A Study in Distortion*. New York: Harcourt, Brace and Co., 1950. xviii + 297pp. (Institute of International Studies, Yale University.)

Barghoorn, press attaché to the American embassy in Moscow, 1942–1947, discusses Soviet propaganda against the United States as one of the main instruments of the Kremlin's foreign policy.

2698. Barrett, Edward W. *Truth Is Our Weapon*. New York: Funk and Wagnalls, 1953. xviii + 355pp.

A report on problems in operating the United States overseas propaganda service, by a former director of overseas operations for the Office of War Information who is now dean of the Columbia University School of Journalism.

2699. Bernays, Edward L. *Propaganda*. New York: Liveright Publishing Corp., 1936. 159pp.

2700. ———. *Speak up for Democracy: What You Can Do — a Practical Plan of Action for Every American Citizen*. New York: Viking Press, 1940. xiv + 127pp.

2701. Bruntz, George G. *Allied Propaganda and the Collapse of the German Empire in 1918*. Stanford, Calif.: Stanford University Press, 1938. xiii + 246pp. (Hoover War Library Publication No. 13.)

Discusses the propaganda organization of the World War I allies and goes into internal conditions in Germany. There is an excellent bibliography of documents.

2702. Carroll, Wallace. *Persuade or Perish*. Boston: Houghton Mifflin Co., 1948. 392pp.

An analysis of World War II political warfare, based in part on the author's work as United States director of psychological warfare operations in the European theater.

2703. Childs, Harwood L. *Propaganda and Dictatorship: A Collection of Papers.* Princeton, N.J.: Princeton University Press, 1936. vi + 153pp.

A discussion of propaganda in Germany, in Italy, and in Soviet Russia. There is some comment on the press in these countries and on foreign news distribution.

2704. Creel, George. *How We Advertised America: The First Telling of the Amazing Story of the Committee on Public Information That Carried the Gospel of Americanism to Every Corner of the Globe.* New York: Harper and Brothers, 1920. 466pp.

Creel's own report of the activities of the World War I Committee on Public Information, which he headed from 1917 to 1919. A more objective analysis can be found in other studies.

2705. Davidson, Philip. *Propaganda and the American Revolution, 1763–1783.* Chapel Hill: University of North Carolina Press, 1941. xvi + 460pp.

Contains excellent material on the propaganda activities of the colonial newspapers.

2706. Fay, Sidney Bradshaw. "The Influence of the Pre-War Press in Europe," in Massachusetts Historical Society *Proceedings,* vol. 64 (1931), pp. 113–142.

Analyzes press activity in "fomenting national hatred and war" (before 1914). The study is limited to England, Germany, France, and Russia.

2707. Ford, Lt. Col. Corey, and Maj. Alastair MacBain. *Cloak and Dagger: The Secret Story of the OSS.* New York: Random House, 1946. vii + 216pp.

This account of the Office of Strategic Services is written in a more popular style than that of Alsop and Braden (2696).

2708. *Germany Speaks, by 21 Leading Members of Party and State.* London: Thornton Butterworth, Ltd., 1938. 406pp. (Preface by Joachim von Ribbentrop, Reich Minister of Foreign Affairs.)

Self-justification by the Nazis, including the Third Reich's theory of propaganda and the press. See especially, "The Essence of 'Propaganda' in Germany," by Dr. G. Kurt Johannsen, managing director of *Hanse Press,* and "The Press in World Politics," by Dr. Hans Dietrich, Reich chief of press. Historically interesting.

2709. Gordon, Matthew. *News Is a Weapon.* New York: Alfred A. Knopf, 1942. viii + 268pp. (Introduction by Elmer Davis.)

A popularly written guide to help Americans guard against Axis propaganda; the material is based upon analysis of enemy news reports.

2710. Hale, Oron James. *Germany and the Diplomatic Revolution: A Study in Diplomacy and the Press, 1904–1906.* Philadelphia: University of Pennsylvania Press; London: Oxford University Press, 1931. ix + 233pp.

2711. ———. *Publicity and Diplomacy, with Special Reference to England and Germany, 1890–1914.* New York and London: D. Appleton-Century Co., 1940. xi + 481pp. (University of Virginia Institute for Research in the Social Sciences.)

A thoroughly documented study on the effect of popular literacy, suffrage, and the mass-circulation press upon international affairs in the quarter-century before World War I. There is good detail on the intervention of the English and German press in foreign affairs.

2712. Hargrave, John. *Propaganda, the Mightiest Weapon of All: Words Win Wars.* London: W. Gardner, Darton and Co., Ltd., 1940. ix + 218pp.

An expostulation against alleged lethargy on the part of the British Ministry of Information.

2713. Holtman, Robert B. *Napoleonic Propaganda.* Baton Rouge: Louisiana State University Press, 1950. xv + 272pp.

An account of Napoleon's use of propaganda (1799–1815) as a tool of politics and statesmanship. The study is based upon materials available in the United States.

2714. Irwin, Will. *Propaganda and the News: Or, What Makes You Think So?* New York and London: Whittlesey House, McGraw-Hill Book Co., 1936. vii + 325pp.

Easy reading, but too popular in treatment to be of substantial value.

2715. Kent, Sherman. *Strategic Intelligence: For American World Policy.* Princeton, N.J.: Princeton University Press, 1949. xiii + 226pp.

Provides background on the operation of the Central Intelligence Agency, including the role of the press in the activities of the CIA.

2716. Lasker, Bruno, and Agnes Roman. *Propaganda from China and Japan: A Case Study in Propaganda Analysis.* New York: American Council, Institute of Pacific Relations, 1938. xiv + 120pp.

2717. Lasswell, Harold D. *Propaganda Technique in the World War.* New York: Alfred A. Knopf, 1927. 229pp.

A thorough and readable study of World War I propaganda by a Chicago political science professor. This pioneering work became the base for many subsequent developments and refinements in content analysis.

2718. ——— and Dorothy Blumenstock. *World Revolutionary Propaganda.* New York and London: Alfred A. Knopf, 1939. xii + 392 + xii pp.

A study of revolutionary propaganda in an industrial center (Chicago) during economic depression. It is especially useful for its section on the channels of propaganda, including Communist newspapers and periodicals. There are extensive illustrations and tables.

2719. Lavine, Harold, and James Wechsler. *War Propaganda and the United States.* New Haven: Yale University Press, 1940. x + 363pp.

2720. Lee, Alfred McClung. *How to Understand Propaganda*. New York: Rinehart and Co., 1952. xii + 281pp.

An excellent introduction to propaganda for the layman not versed in the technicalities of the subject.

2721. —— and Elizabeth Briant Lee, eds. *The Fine Art of Propaganda: A Study of Father Coughlin's Speeches*. New York: Harcourt, Brace and Co., 1939. xi + 140pp.

2722. Lerner, Daniel, ed. *Propaganda in War and Crisis: Materials for American Policy*. New York: George W. Stewart, 1951. xvi + 500pp.

2723. Lumley, Frederick E. *The Propaganda Menace*. New York: D. Appleton-Century Co., 1933. 454pp.

Too prejudiced to be effective; Lumley works on the assumption that all propaganda is evil, regardless of source.

2724. McKenzie, Vernon. *Here Lies Goebbels!* London: Michael Joseph, Ltd., 1940. 319pp.

An analysis of the evils of Nazi propaganda, based on observations in Europe over seven years. There is good material on Goebbels's manipulations of the press.

2725. Macmahon, Arthur W. *Memorandum on the Postwar International Information Program of the United States*. Washington, D.C.: Government Printing Office, 1945. xx + 135pp. (U.S. Department of State Publication No. 2438.)

The report of a Department of State consultant on the possibility of international agreements regarding the use of information services.

2726. Martin, L. John. *International Propaganda: Its Legal and Diplomatic Control*. Minneapolis: University of Minnesota Press, 1958. viii + 284pp.

An extensive study of the laws, treaties, and diplomatic maneuvers to limit undesirable propaganda. Martin records the history of international propaganda and outlines the propaganda activities of the United States, Great Britain, and the Soviet Union.

2727. Mock, James R., and Cedric Larson. *Words That Won the War: The Story of the Committee on Public Information, 1917–1919*. Princeton, N.J.: Princeton University Press, 1939. xvi + 372pp.

An excellent history of the work of George Creel's wartime committee, based on materials in the National Archives. Creel is assessed generously. There are photographs, facsimiles and cartoons, and extensive bibliographic notes.

2728. Noble, George Bernard. *Policies and Opinions at Paris, 1919: Wilsonian Diplomacy, the Versailles Peace, and French Public Opinion*. New York: The Macmillan Co., 1935. x + 465pp.

2729. Norman, Albert. *Our German Policy: Propaganda and Culture*. New York: Vantage Press, 1951. 85pp.

2730. "Office of War Information," in *Public Opinion Quarterly*, vol. 7, No. 1 (Spring 1943). 188pp. (Foreword by Harwood L. Childs.)

Historically valuable articles on public opinion and informational problems of World War II. Elmer Davis, director of OWI, Lester G. Hawkins and George S. Pettee, OWI staff members, and Paul Scott Mowrer, then editor of the Chicago *Daily News*, were contributors.

2731. Peterson, H. C. *Propaganda for War: The Campaign against American Neutrality, 1914–1917*. Norman: University of Oklahoma Press, 1939. viii + 357pp.

2732. Read, James Morgan. *Atrocity Propaganda, 1914–1919*. New Haven: Yale University Press; London: Oxford University Press, 1941. ix + 319pp.

2733. Riegel, O. W. *Mobilizing for Chaos: The Story of the New Propaganda*. New Haven: Yale University Press, 1934. 231pp.

An impartial analysis of the effect of post-World War I nationalism on communication agencies. The author compares the American concept of news "objectivity" and methods of communication systems operated elsewhere under government control.

2734. Riess, Curt. *Underground Europe*. New York: The Dial Press, 1942. xiii + 325pp.

Reports of activities by residents of Nazi-occupied countries in resisting German occupation in World War II. There are helpful accounts of underground news sheets and of activities of the British Broadcasting Corp.

2735. Riley, Norman. *999 and All That*. London: Victor Gollancz, Ltd., 1940. 223pp.

The story of press frustration during the first few months under the British Ministry of Information in World War II as told by a newspaperman. The book outlines a postwar plan for better handling of news.

2736. Rogers, Cornwell B. *The Spirit of Revolution in 1789: A Study of Public Opinion as Revealed in Political Songs and Other Popular Literature at the Beginning of the French Revolution*. Princeton, N.J.: Princeton University Press, 1949. ix + 363pp.

2737. Sayers, Michael, and Albert E. Kahn. *The Great Conspiracy: The Secret War against Soviet Russia*. Boston: Little, Brown and Co., 1946. ix + 433pp.

2738. ———. *Sabotage! The Secret War against America*. New York: Harper and Brothers, 1942. 266pp.

Emphasizes German sabotage and "Fifth Column" tactics in the United States before World War II. Sayers was a writer-investigator and Kahn editor of the *Hour*, a publication exposing Axis activities in the United States.

2739. Sington, Derrick, and Arthur Weidenfeld. *The Goebbels Experiment*. New Haven: Yale University Press, 1943. 261pp.

Includes an account of the Nazi propaganda machine and an analysis of the Ministry of Public Enlightenment. This is a dispassionate piece of good reporting; source references, however, are limited.

2740. Squires, J. Duane. *British Propaganda at Home and in the United*

States from 1914 to 1917. Cambridge, Mass.: Harvard University Press, 1935. x + 113pp.

2741. Stephens, Oren. *Facts to a Candid World: America's Overseas Information Program.* Stanford, Calif.: Stanford University Press, 1955. 164pp.

Seeks to present "basic guidelines" in the international propaganda battle. There is more on the philosophy and substance of United States propaganda than on techniques.

2742. Stouffer, Samuel A. *Communism, Conformity, and Civil Liberties: A Cross-Section of the Nation Speaks Its Mind.* Garden City, N.Y.: Doubleday and Co., 1955. 278pp.

Summarizes the results of interviews conducted under the auspices of the Fund for the Republic to determine the reactions of Americans to the dangers of Communism.

2743. *Target: The World.* New York: The Macmillan Co., 1956. 362pp. (Edited by Evron M. Kirkpatrick.)

A factual report, based upon governmental data, on Communist activities around the world for the year 1955. Numerous tables contain lists of organs of Communist persuasion.

2744. Thomson, Charles A. H. *Overseas Information Service of the United States Government.* Washington, D.C.: The Brookings Institution, 1948. xii + 397pp.

Principally a descriptive account of personal experiences with information services in the early post-World War II period. Included are helpful sections on information control in occupied Germany, Austria, and Japan. There is insufficient detail on Thomson's relations with the mass media.

2745. United States Committee on Public Information. *Complete Report of the Chairman of the Committee on Public Information, 1917, 1918, 1919.* Washington, D.C.: Government Printing Office, 1920. 290pp.

George Creel's official report of his work in World War I.

2746. Viereck, George Sylvester. *Spreading Germs of Hate.* New York: Horace Liveright, 1930. xiii + 327pp. (Foreword by Col. E. M. House.)

Viereck, a German-born journalist who was associated with German propaganda agencies in World War I, tells his "inside story" of propaganda to save Americans from "future pitfalls."

2747. Warburg, James P. *Unwritten Treaty.* New York: Harcourt, Brace and Co., 1946. 186pp.

The deputy director of propaganda policy for the Office of War Information analyzes propaganda and psychological warfare and advocates international interchange of information at the treaty level.

2748. Wilkerson, Marcus M. *Public Opinion and the Spanish-American War: A Study in War Propaganda.* Baton Rouge: Louisiana State University Press, 1932. 141pp.

One of the most useful, scholarly studies of the period. Wilkerson drew extensively from files of the New York *World* and the New York *Journal*. The bibliography of governmental documents and general works is helpful.

2749. Wisan, Joseph E. *The Cuban Crisis as Reflected in the New York Press (1895–1898).* New York: Columbia University Press; London: P. S. King and Son, Ltd., 1934. 477pp.

A detailed, heavily documented study of all phases of yellow journalism in the years before the conflict with Spain. Included is an extensive bibliography.

2750. *Worldwide Communist Propaganda Activities.* New York: The Macmillan Co., 1955. viii + 222pp. (Edited by F. Bowen Evans.)

These materials on the nature, volume, and cost of the total Communist propaganda effort during 1954 were obtained principally from eye-witness reports of United States government representatives and correspondents stationed around the world. An extensive and valuable chapter covers Communist use of the international media of information.

D. Publicity and Public Relations

2751. Bernays, Edward L. *Public Relations.* Norman: University of Oklahoma Press, 1952. x + 374pp.

A summary of Bernays's ideas about public relations after more than 40 years' experience; much of the material is historical.

2752. ———, ed. *The Engineering of Consent.* Norman: University of Oklahoma Press, 1955. viii + 246pp.

Eight articles examining public relations from a philosophical point of view rather than as a technique. Contributors in addition to Bernays include Howard T. Cutler and Benjamin Fine.

2753. Canfield, Bertrand R. *Public Relations: Principles, Cases, and Problems.* Chicago: Richard D. Irwin, 1956. Revised edition. 691pp. (First issued in 1952.)

A textbook usable in a survey course in public relations; includes many case descriptions.

2754. Center, Allen H., ed. *Public Relations Ideas in Action.* New York: McGraw-Hill Book Co., 1957. 327pp.

A how-to-do-it compilation of about 50 successful public relations projects.

2755. Cutlip, Scott M., and Allen H. Center. *Effective Public Relations.* Englewood Cliffs, N.J.: Prentice-Hall, 1958. 2nd edition. xiii + 450pp. (First issued in 1952.)

A comprehensive coverage of both fundamentals and practice. The authors draw upon their own experience as newspapermen and as public relations workers in government, education, and industry.

2756. *Dartnell Public Relations Handbook.* Chicago: The Dartnell Corp., 1957. About 1000pp. (Edited by J. C. Aspley and L. F. Van Houten.)

Aims to bring into one volume the information needed to establish a public relations program. Only a small part of the book is directly concerned with journalistic media.

2757. Dyar, Ralph E. *Newspaper Promotion and Research.* New York and London: Harper and Brothers, 1942. ix + 270pp.

2758. Fine, Benjamin. *Educational Publicity.* New York: Harper and Brothers, 1951. Revised edition. xi + 561pp. (First edition, 1943.)

A standard textbook in educational publicity. Fine is a former education editor of the New York *Times.*

2759. Goldman, Eric F. *Two-Way Street: The Emergence of the Public Relations Counsel.* Boston: Bellman Publishing Co., 1948. 23 + vii pp.

A helpful brochure sketching the main outlines of the development of public relations, giving brief biographies of Ivy Lee and Edward L. Bernays, and providing notes to additional sources of information.

2760. Griswold, Glenn, and Denny Griswold, eds. *Your Public Relations: The Standard Public Relations Handbook.* New York: Funk and Wagnalls Co., 1948. xix + 634pp.

A practical working manual for management executives, public relations directors and counsel, teachers, and students.

2761. Harral, Stewart. *Profitable Public Relations for Newspapers.* Ann Arbor, Mich.: J. W. Edwards, 1957. 184pp.

Comprehensive, but principally applicable to small-city newspapers. Useful as a textbook.

2762. Kelley, Stanley, Jr. *Professional Public Relations and Political Power.* Baltimore: Johns Hopkins Press, 1956. 247pp.

Revealing case studies of political campaigns in which public relations men have played important parts in selling candidates or ideologies. Included is a thorough report on Clem Whitaker and Leone Baxter, public relations counselors.

2763. Lee, Ivy. *Publicity: Some of the Things It Is and Is Not.* New York: Industries Publishing Co., 1925. 64pp.

Reprints of two addresses by this first of the public relations counsels. Lee oversimplified the problems involved.

2764. Levy, Harold P. *Public Relations for Social Agencies: A Guide for Health, Welfare, and Other Community Organizations.* New York: Harper and Brothers, 1956. x + 208pp.

Case studies in public relations, including material on informing the public through press, radio-television, and films.

2765. Lindsay, Robert. *This High Name: Public Relations and the U.S. Marine Corps.* Madison: University of Wisconsin Press, 1956. xi + 101pp.

A history of the Marine Corps' pioneering activity in military public relations, from 1775 to the end of the Korean War. The volume also sketches the development of the combat correspondent system.

2766. McCamy, James L. *Government Publicity: Its Practice in Federal Administration.* Chicago: University of Chicago Press, 1939. xv + 275pp.

2767. MacDonald, James C. *Press Relations for Local Officials.* Ann

Arbor, Mich.: University of Michigan Institute of Public Administration, Bureau of Government, 1956. 50pp. (Michigan Pamphlets No. 25.)

A report giving the conscientious public official an opportunity to understand the journalist.

2768. Newcomb, Robert, and Margaret Sammons. *Speak Up, Management!* New York: Funk and Wagnalls, 1951. 308pp.

Tells how to communicate with employees and public through modern industrial magazines.

2769. Norton, William Bernard. *Church and Newspaper.* New York: The Macmillan Co., 1930. xi + 271pp.

Written by a pastor who was former religious editor of the Chicago *Tribune* to help ministers and church laymen understand better the daily newspaper and obtain more and better church publicity.

2770. *Public Relations Handbook.* New York: Prentice-Hall, 1950. xxvi + 902pp. (Edited by Philip Lesly.)

A comprehensive reference work, one of the best in the field.

2771. Samstag, Nicholas. *Persuasion for Profit.* Norman: University of Oklahoma Press, 1957. xvi + 208pp. (Illustrated by Irwin Glusker.)

Analyzes promotion, market research, and writing and editing for purposes of persuasion. Samstag also discusses the status and conscience of the promotion man.

2772. Steinberg, Charles S. *The Mass Communicators: Public Relations, Public Opinion, and Mass Media.* New York: Harper and Brothers, 1958. x + 470pp.

A general account, suitable as a textbook on public relations. There is a section on ethical considerations. The author is director of press information for CBS radio.

2773. Stephenson, Howard, and Wesley Fiske Pratzner. *Publicity for Prestige and Profit.* New York: McGraw-Hill Book Co., 1953. xi + 304pp. (Foreword by Harold C. Case.)

An informal treatment of the position and function of publicity in the American economy, with considerable material on the cultivation of news sources among communication media, on news and feature releases, and on corporate journalism.

2774. Washburn, Charles. *Press Agentry.* New York: National Library Press, 1937. 153pp.

A simple, uncritical handbook based on the show-business type of press-agentry. It is most useful for its material on Edward L. Bernays and opinions on press agents collected from metropolitan newspaper editors.

2775. Wright, J. Handly, and Byron H. Christian. *Public Relations in Management.* New York: McGraw-Hill Book Co., 1949. ix + 229pp.

There is ample discussion of the social responsibilities and ethics of public relations practitioners.

XI

Radio and Television

2776. Abbot, Waldo, and Richard L. Rider. *Handbook of Broadcasting.* New York: McGraw-Hill Book Co., 1957. 4th edition. 531pp. + 98 illustrations. (Earlier editions, 1937, 1941, and 1950.)

Covers all fields of radio and television except technique. There are good chapters on news programs, sports programs, vocations, and the law as it affects broadcasting. A glossary of terms is included.

2777. Archer, Gleason Leonard. *Big Business and Radio.* New York: American Historical Co., 1939. vi + 503pp.

Supplements Archer's *History of Radio to 1926* for the period 1922–1936. Included is background material on the National Broadcasting Co., the Mutual Broadcasting System, and the Columbia Broadcasting System.

2778. ———. *History of Radio to 1926.* New York: American Historical Co., 1938. 421pp.

Fundamental for background on the early development of radio. There is little, however, on press use of radio communications.

2779. Association of Radio News Analysts. *History, Constitution, and Membership, 1942–1954.* New York, 1954. 73pp.

2780. *At Year's End, 1956.* New York: Columbia Broadcasting System, December 30, 1956. Pamphlet in three parts, about 150 leaves.

Provides the full text of a public affairs broadcast summarizing the major events of 1956. This is an excellent example of electronic journalism at its best.

2781. Bickel, Karl A. *New Empires: The Newspaper and the Radio.* Philadelphia: J. B. Lippincott Co., 1930. 112pp.

An early discussion of the impact of radio upon the press, by the then president of United Press Associations. The book contains a helpful appendix on newspapers affiliated with radio stations in 1930.

2782. Bickford, Leland. *News While It Is News: The Real Story of the Radio News.* Boston: G. C. Manthorne and Co., 1935. 137pp.

Paints the accomplishments of news broadcasting in glowing colors and points out errors and shortcomings of the newspaper press.

2783. Borkin, Joseph, and Frank C. Waldrop. *Television: A Struggle for Power.* New York: William Morrow and Co., 1938. xii + 299pp.

2784. Bretz, Rudy. *Techniques of Television Production.* New York: McGraw-Hill Book Co., 1953. v + 474pp.

2785. Brown, Donald E., and John Paul Jones. *Radio and Television News.* New York: Rinehart and Co., 1954. v + 472pp.

A classroom exercise book, with practical assignments.

2785a. Canada, Royal Commission on Broadcasting. *Report.* Ottawa: Queen's Printer, 1957. 2 volumes in one. About 500pp.

2786. Cantril, Hadley. *The Invasion from Mars: A Study in the Psychology of Panic, with the Complete Script of the Orson Welles Broadcast.* Princeton, N.J.: Princeton University Press, 1940. xv + 224pp.

An analysis of the panic that swept the United States the night of October 30, 1938, when Welles's *Mercury Theatre* broadcast "The War of the Worlds." Included is a summary of the treatment of the event as carried in the newspapers.

2787. Charnley, Mitchell V. *News by Radio.* New York: The Macmillan Co., 1948. v + 403pp.

One of the better radio-news textbooks. Charnley makes extensive comparisons between newspaper and radio practices.

2788. Chase, Francis, Jr. *Sound and Fury: An Informal History of Broadcasting.* New York and London: Harper and Brothers, 1942. vii + 303pp.

The story of radio in terms of people and anecdotes instead of statistics. Among the more important personalities discussed are Fulton Lewis, Jr., H. V. Kaltenborn, and Orson Welles.

2789. Chester, Giraud, and Garnet R. Garrison. *Radio and Television: An Introduction.* New York: Appleton-Century-Crofts, 1956. 2nd edition. xv + 652pp. (First edition, 1950.)

For introductory courses in broadcasting. There is a good bibliography.

2790. Crews, Albert. *Radio Production Directing.* Boston: Houghton Mifflin Co., 1944. v + 550pp.

2791. Dryer, Sherman H. *Radio in Wartime.* New York: Greenberg, 1942. xiv + 384pp.

A criticism of the failure of wartime radio to be fully effective.

2792. Elliott, William Y., ed. *Television's Impact on American Culture.* East Lansing: Michigan State University, 1956. xvi + 382pp.

A balanced discussion of the potential role of educational television and the potential educational role of commercial television. There is a detailed discussion of the Educational Television and Radio Center.

2793. Franklin, O. Thomas. *Broadcasting the News: A Practical Handbook for the Radio Newsman.* New York: Pageant Press, 1955. vii + 145pp.

A radio news editor from the Pacific Coast provides a handbook on newscast techniques. Useful for beginners.

2794. Gorham, Maurice A. C. *Television: Medium of the Future.* London: P. Marshall, 1949. xiv + 142pp.

2795. ———. *Training for Radio.* Paris: United Nations Educational, Scientific, and Cultural Organization, 1949. 105pp. (In Press, Film and Radio in World Today Series.)

Stresses improvement in radio's professional standards. The author has been editor of *Radio Times* and of the television service for the British Broadcasting Corporation.

2796. Grandin, Thomas. *The Political Use of the Radio.* Geneva, Switzerland: Geneva Research Centre, 1939. 116pp. (Geneva Studies, vol. X, no. 3.)

Discusses broadcasting for national and European consumption, intercontinental broadcasting, effects of political programs on the public, and efforts to control the political use of radio.

2797. Head, Sydney W. *Broadcasting in America: A Survey of Television and Radio.* Boston: Houghton Mifflin Co., 1956. xv + 502pp.

Discusses technology, history, economics, and social control of American radio and television. The appendix compares radio, television, and motion picture codes.

2798. Hills, Lee, and Timothy J. Sullivan. *Facsimile.* New York and London: McGraw-Hill Book Co., 1949. xiii + 319pp. (Foreword by John V. L. Hogan, president of Radio Inventions, Inc.)

Gives a history of facsimile and outlines how facsimile newspapers can be produced by electronics. There is also material on freedom of the press on the air. Hills was at the time of writing managing editor of the Miami (Fla.) *Herald* and Sullivan was its facsimile editor.

2799. Holt, Robert T. *Radio Free Europe.* Minneapolis: University of Minnesota Press, 1958. xii + 249pp.

An account of the privately supported agency that aims to relieve the plight of captive peoples under Soviet domination. The book covers the period 1949–1957. There is a full chapter on the handling of information about the uprisings in Poland and Hungary in 1956.

2800. Jones, Charles Reed. *Facsimile.* New York: Murray Hill Books, 1949. xiii + 422pp.

A technical work on the nature of facsimiles.

2801. Kingson, Walter K., Rome Cowgill, and Ralph Levy. *Broadcasting Television and Radio: How-to Techniques of Writing, Directing and Acting, Plus a Behind-the-Scenes Survey of the Radio and Television Industry.* New York: Prentice-Hall, 1955. x + 274pp.

2802. Lazarsfeld, Paul F. *Radio and the Printed Page: An Introduction to the Study of Radio and Its Role in the Communication of Ideas.* New York: Duell, Sloane and Pearce, 1940. xxii + 354pp.

2803. Mercier, Claude. *Low Cost Radio Reception.* Paris: United Nations Educational, Scientific, and Cultural Organization, 1950. 118pp. (In Press, Film and Radio in World Today Series.)

2804. Nicol, John, Albert A. Shea, and G. J. P. Simmins. *Canada's Farm Radio Forum*. Paris: United Nations Educational, Scientific, and Cultural Organization, 1954. 235pp. (In Press, Film and Radio in World Today Series.)

A report on 12 years of service to rural Canada by a radio discussion-group project.

2805. Paulu, Burton. *British Broadcasting: Radio and Television in the United Kingdom*. Minneapolis: University of Minnesota Press, 1956. xii + 457pp.

This thorough description and appraisal includes a history of the British Broadcasting Corporation and an analysis of the structure and staffs of the radio and television organizations, plus material on programs and news.

2806. Payne, George Henry. *The Fourth Estate and Radio*. Boston: The Microphone Press, 1936. 112pp.

2807. *The People Look at Radio*. Chapel Hill: University of North Carolina Press, 1946. ix + 158pp. (Survey conducted by National Opinion Research Center, University of Denver; research directed by Paul F. Lazarsfeld, Bureau of Applied Social Research, Columbia University.)

This survey asked about attitudes on radio advertising, types of programs, and broadcasters.

2808. Phillips, David C., John M. Grogan, and Earl H. Ryan. *Introduction to Radio and Television*. New York: Ronald Press Co., 1954. ix + 423pp.

Two professors of speech and a television production manager (Grogan) cover chiefly current procedures and problems of radio and television. There is some material on writing for radio and television and on newswriting and newscasting.

2809. *Radio Listening in America: The People Look at Radio Again*. New York: Prentice-Hall, 1948. v + 178pp. (Analyzed by Paul F. Lazarsfeld and Patricia L. Kendall.)

The National Association of Broadcasters sponsored this follow-up to the survey reported in *The People Look at Radio* (2807).

2810. Seehafer, E. F., and J. W. Laemmar. *Successful Radio and Television Advertising*. New York: McGraw-Hill Book Co., 1951. vii + 574pp.

2811. Seldes, Gilbert. *The Great Audience*. New York: The Viking Press, 1951. viii + 299pp.

In this revision of an earlier book (*The Seven Lively Arts*. New York: Harper and Brothers, 1924) Seldes considers at length mass entertainment — movies, radio, and television — and the influence of mass media on freedom of expression.

2812. ———. *The Public Arts*. New York: Simon and Schuster, 1956. viii + 303pp.

A popular analysis of movies, radio, and television. There is good detail on the problem of commentary on the air, with particular reference to Edward R. Murrow.

2813. ———. *Writing for Television*. New York: Doubleday and Co., 1952. 254pp.

A survey of principles and practices in television writing, from commercials to full-length plays.

2814. Settel, Irving, Norman Glenn, and Associates. *Television Advertising and Production Handbook*. New York: Thomas Y. Crowell Co., 1953. viii + 480pp.

2815. Siepmann, Charles A. *Radio, Television, and Society*. New York: Oxford University Press, 1950. vii + 410pp.

Analyzes the "cultural revolution" effected by radio and television and their influence on tastes, opinions, and values. Siepmann surveys the history of these media, discusses their legal structure (including comments on freedom of speech in theory and practice), and provides material on British, Canadian, and other foreign systems. The bibliography is extensive.

2816. ———. *Radio's Second Chance*. Boston: Little, Brown and Co., 1946. xiv + 282pp.

A critical analysis of radio based upon the author's first-hand experience with the Federal Communications Commission and the British Broadcasting Corporation. Freedom of speech on the air is treated extensively.

2817. Simon, Ernest D. S., Lord, of Wythenshawe. *The BBC from Within*. London: Victor Gollancz, Ltd., 1953. 360pp.

A detailed work on the organization of the British Broadcasting Corporation by its chairman from 1947 to 1952. There is an appendix on Swiss radio.

2818. Smythe, Dallas W. *New Haven Television*. Urbana, Ill.: National Association of Educational Broadcasters, Monitoring Study No. 5, May 15–21, 1952. iii + 119pp.

2819. ———. *New York Television*. Urbana, Ill.: National Association of Educational Broadcasters, Monitoring Studies Nos. 4, 6, and 7, 1951–1954. 3 vols. (Study No. 7 was directed by the Purdue Opinion Panel, headed by H. H. Remmers.)

2819a. ———, and Angus Campbell. *Los Angeles Television, May 23–29, 1951*. Urbana, Ill.: National Association of Educational Broadcasters, Monitoring Study No. 2, 1951. v + 94pp.

2820. Straight, Michael. *Trial by Television*. Boston: The Beacon Press, 1954. 282pp. (Illustrations by Robert Osborn.)

The editor of the *New Republic* makes a critical analysis of the United States Army — Joseph R. McCarthy hearings as televised in the spring of 1954.

2821. *The Television Code*. Washington, D.C.: National Association of Radio and Television Broadcasters, 1956. 3rd edition. 8pp. (Earlier editions, 1952 and 1954.)

An outline of ethical standards.

2822. *Television News Reporting*. New York: McGraw-Hill Book Co.,

1958. 182pp. (Prepared by the staff of Columbia Broadcasting System; introduction by John F. Day.)

An inclusive textbook covering television newsroom operation, filming news, scripting and editing, and handling equipment. A brief history of television news and specific story examples are included.

2822a. Thomson, Charles A. H. *Television and Presidential Politics: The Experience in 1952 and the Problems Ahead.* Washington, D.C.: Brookings Institution, 1956. viii + 173pp.

Includes helpful material on television equipment for convention coverage, news presentation, arguments for and against open convention proceedings, and editorial preferences of networks.

2823. Tomlinson, John D. *The International Control of Radio-Communications.* Ann Arbor, Mich.: J. W. Edwards, 1945. 314pp.

A well-documented history of the rise of international radio legislation after 1903. Tomlinson does not take up the World War II period.

2824. *Top TV Shows of the Year: Complete Scripts of the Best Television Programs.* New York: Hastings House, 1955–date. About 275pp.

Scripts in all the major categories of television shows are included, among these being the best of Lawrence E. Spivak's *Meet the Press* program (NBC). A dictionary of television terms is also provided.

2825. United Nations Educational, Scientific, and Cultural Organization. *Television and Education in the United States.* Paris: UNESCO, 1952. 131pp. (Prepared by Charles A. Siepmann; in Press, Film and Radio in World Today Series.)

First of a series of UNESCO reports intended to cover world television.

2826. Warner, Harry P. *Radio and Television Law: A Standard Reference Book on the Legal and Regulatory Structure of the Radio Industry.* Albany, N.Y.: M. Bender and Co., 1948. xii + 1095pp.

2827. ———. *Radio and Television Rights.* Albany, N.Y.: M. Bender and Co., 1953. xi + 1254pp.

2828. Warren, Carl N. *Radio News Writing and Editing.* New York: Harper and Brothers, 1947. xix + 439pp.

A college textbook.

2829. West, Robert. *The Rape of Radio.* New York: Rodin Publishing Co., 1941. 546pp.

An oversimplified, disjointed book that concentrates on the entertainment phases of radio.

2830. White, Llewellyn. *The American Radio: A Report on the Broadcasting Industry in the United States from the Commission on Freedom of the Press.* Chicago: University of Chicago Press, 1947. xxi + 255pp.

One of the commission's major reports, by the assistant director. This indispensable study includes material on radio history, legal organization and problems of self-regulation, radio news analysis, and studies of listenership, and proposals for improvement of radio quality.

2831. White, Paul W. *News on the Air*. New York: Harcourt, Brace and Co., 1947. x + 398pp.

A textbook that includes an annotated bibliography.

2832. Williams, Albert N. *Listening: A Collection of Critical Articles on Radio*. Denver: University of Denver Press, 1948. 152pp.

2833. Williams, J. Grenfell. *Radio in Fundamental Education in Undeveloped Areas*. Paris: United Nations Educational, Scientific, and Cultural Organization, 1950. 152pp. (In Press, Film and Radio in World Today Series.)

The author was head of the colonial service for the British Broadcasting Corporation.

2834. Wylie, Max. *Clear Channels: Television and the American People*. New York: Funk and Wagnalls Co., 1955. viii + 408pp.

A defense of television and a call for wider use of the medium by education. Extensive appendixes relate to the Army-McCarthy hearings of 1954, radio and television codes of ethics, and news releases on juvenile problems.

XII

Foreign Press and International Communication Facilities

2835. Banner, Franklin C. *A Study of the Australian Press.* State College: Pennsylvania State College, 1950. 30pp.

A cursory history and analysis based upon a trip to Australia.

2836. Bardens, Dennis. *A Press in Chains.* London: Batchworth Press, 1953. 40pp. (Background Books on World Affairs.)

The author, editor of current affairs documentary programs for the British Broadcasting Corporation, discusses the press of the Soviet Union and its satellites.

2837. Barns, Margarita. *The Indian Press: A History of the Growth of Public Opinion in India.* London: George Allen and Unwin, Ltd., 1940. xv + 491pp.

Press history is placed in the context of the history of British occupation in India. The volume is thorough in dealing with the foundations of Indian journalism and with the vernacular press. Library files of Indian newspapers in Calcutta, Bombay, and London are indicated.

2838. Bauchard, Philippe. *The Child Audience: A Report on Press, Film and Radio for Children.* Paris: UNESCO, 1952. 198pp. (In Press, Film and Radio in World Today Series.)

Investigates at the international level the measures adopted to protect children from undesirable influences through press, film, and radio.

2839. Britton, Roswell S. *The Chinese Periodical Press, 1800–1912.* Shanghai: Kelly and Walsh, Ltd., 1933. vi + 151pp. + 24 plates.

In addition to a historical sketch, this volume carries a bibliography of the indigenous press, the new native press, the foreign and missionary press, and printing.

2840. *Central News Agency of China.* Taipei, April 1, 1954. 20pp.

A history of the Nationalist news agency, 1927 to 1954. The text is printed in both Chinese and English; maps and photographs are included.

2841. Cooper, Kent. *Barriers Down: The Story of the News Agency Epoch.* New York: Farrar and Rinehart, 1942. x + 324pp.

Although Cooper, a retired general manager of the Associated Press, is over-concerned with justifying AP policy, his book is a significant contribution to the history of international communication. Most valuable is the detailed account of AP's success, from 1914 to 1934, in breaking the international news cartel and striking out as a worldwide agency.

2842. Coughlin, William J. *Conquered Press: The MacArthur Era in Japanese Journalism.* Palo Alto, Calif.: Pacific Books, 1952. 165pp.

A history of the contemporary Japanese press and an account of the activities of American correspondents during the Occupation, 1945–1951. The author, who is highly critical of MacArthur's press policies, had access to original letters and documents as well as monographs and special studies.

2843. *Current Digest of the Soviet Press.* Washington, D.C.: Joint Committee on Slavic Studies, 1949–date. (Vol. 1 begins Feb. 1, 1949.)

Issued weekly by a committee appointed by the American Council of Learned Societies and the Social Science Research Council. Selected contents of the Soviet press are translated into English as objectively as possible. A weekly index to *Pravda* and *Izvestia* is included.

2844. Dávila, Carlos G. *The Journalism of Chile*, in University of Missouri Journalism Series, No. 53. Columbia, Mo.: University of Missouri, December 7, 1928. 14pp.

By the ambassador from Chile to the United States.

2845. De Palma, Samuel. *Freedom of the Press: An International Issue.* Washington, D.C.: Office of Public Affairs, Department of State, 1950. 24pp. (Department of State Bulletin of November 14, 1949.)

2846. Desmond, Robert W. *The Press and World Affairs.* New York and London: D. Appleton-Century Co., 1937. xxvi + 421pp. (Introduction by Harold J. Laski.)

Although somewhat outdated by events of the 1940s and 1950s, this volume still is of great value for the historical background it provides on the development of international news coverage, news networks, and transmission facilities. There is an extensive bibliography.

2847. Economist (London). *Paper for Printing and Writing: Tentative Forecasts of Demand in 1955, 1960, 1965.* Paris: UNESCO, Clearing House, Department of Mass Communication, 1954. 108pp. (Reports and Papers No. 12.)

2848. ———. *Paper for Printing (Today and Tomorrow).* Paris: UNESCO, 1952. 139pp. (In Press, Film and Radio in World Today Series.)

Provides material on the availability of wood pulp, the location of paper industries, newsprint and newsprint problems, and international legislation on newsprint.

2849. ———. *The Problem of Newsprint and Other Printing Paper.* Paris: UNESCO, 1949. 111pp. (In Press, Film and Radio in World Today Series.)

Covers 19 countries and emphasizes particularly rising demands for newsprint.

2850. Fliess, Peter J. *Freedom of the Press in the German Republic,*

1918–1933. Baton Rouge: Louisiana State University Press, 1955. 147pp. (Louisiana State Social Science Series No. 4.)

Includes a good account of how the press laws of the Weimar Republic protected only expression of opinion and not publication of news as fact.

2851. Great Britain Foreign Office. *The Press Laws of Foreign Countries, with an Appendix Containing the Press Laws of India*. London: H.M. Stationery Office, 1926. 328pp. (Edited by Montague Shearman, assistant legal adviser in the Foreign Office, and O. T. Rayner of the Foreign Office.)

2852. Hanazono, Kanesada. *The Development of Japanese Journalism*. Tokyo: Tokyo Nichi-Nichi; Osaka: Osaka Mainichi, 1924; revised 1934. 100pp.

A member of the editorial staff of *Nichi-Nichi* analyzes the modern-day development of the Japanese press for foreign readers. Numerous facsimiles of early newspapers are included.

2853. Heberle, Rudolf. *From Democracy to Nazism: A Regional Case Study of Political Parties in Germany*. Baton Rouge: Louisiana State University Press, 1945. ix + 130pp.

Includes material on the role of the German press in preparing a people for a new political order.

2854. *Indian Press Digests*. Berkeley: University of California Bureau of International Relations of Department of Political Science, 1952–date, published irregularly. (Edited by Mrs. Margaret Fisher.)

This series includes an examination of Indian periodicals; a description of the publications from which the items are drawn is given. The *Indian Press Digest Monographs* series was begun in February 1956.

2855. International Federation of Free Journalists of Central and Eastern Europe and Baltic and Balkan Countries. *Press behind the Iron Curtain*. London: The Federation, 1952. 62pp.

On the post-World War II press in the Baltic States, the Balkans, Czechoslovakia, Hungary, Poland, and the Ukraine.

2856. International Labour Office. *Conditions of Work and Life of Journalists*. Geneva, Switzerland: League of Nations; London: P. S. King and Son, Ltd., 1928. 219pp. (Series L, Studies and Reports on Professional Workers, No. 2.)

An economic study of the profession, with historical background on press-labor disputes.

2857. International Press Institute. *As Others See Us*. Zurich, Switzerland: The Institute, 1954. 5 vols., each subtitled *Studies in Press Relations*.

Each volume gives correspondents' views of news coverage in the countries to which they were assigned — the United States, Great Britain, Germany, France, Italy, and India.

2858. ———. *The Flow of the News*. Zurich, Switzerland: The Institute, 1953. xi + 266pp.

A significant content analysis of news movement among leading countries — the United States, the nations of Western Europe, and India. Valuable appendixes list the nearly 200 United States and foreign newspapers studied with tables of news categories and readership.

2859. ———. *Improvement of Information*. Zurich, Switzerland: The Institute, 1952. 32pp.

First of the IPI surveys directed toward broadening the flow of news among peoples and publicizing international restrictions on news movement.

2860. ———. *The News from Russia*. Zurich, Switzerland: The Institute, 1952. 52pp.

The second of the IPI surveys gives background on the Russian press, reports by correspondents in Moscow, and suggestions for improvement.

2861. ———. *The News from the Middle East*. Zurich, Switzerland: The Institute, 1954. 115pp.

The nations studied are Egypt, Iraq, Jordan, Libya, Lebanon, Syria, Saudi Arabia, Yemen, the Sudan, Iran, Arabia (general), and Israel. There are valuable tables outlining restrictions on news coverage and giving cable and telephone rates.

2862. ———. *News in Asia*. Zurich, Switzerland: The Institute, 1956. 113pp.

A report incorporating preliminary research data and the proceedings of the International Press Institute's Asian Conference in Tokyo, March 1956.

2863. ———. *The Proceedings*. Zurich, Switzerland: The Institute, 1952–date. About 100pp.

Summaries of the general assemblies of this privately supported international press organization that works for improved worldwide news communications.

2864. Jacobi, Claus. "The New German Press," in *Foreign Affairs*, vol. 32, no. 2 (January 1954), pp. 323–330.

A useful survey of the German press after World War II by the correspondent in Bonn of the German news-magazine *Der Spiegel*.

2865. Japan Times. *Short History of the Japan Times*. Tokyo: The Times, 1941. viii + 156pp.

2866. Joesten, Joachim. *German Periodicals in 1947*. New York: Privately printed by the author, 1947. 19 leaves. (New Germany Reports No. 2.)

2867. ———. *The German Press in 1947*. New York: Privately printed by the author, 1947. 20 leaves. (New Germany Reports No. 1.)

2868. Kawabe, Kisaburo. *The Press and Politics in Japan: A Study of the Relation between the Newspaper and the Political Development of Modern Japan*. Chicago: University of Chicago Press, 1921. 190pp.

The period covered is 1868–1920. There is an excellent bibliography.

2869. Kayser, Jacques. *One Week's News: Comparative Study of 17 Major Dailies for a Seven-Day Period*. Paris: UNESCO, 1953. 102pp.

A content study of leading world newspapers for the week of March 4–10, 1951. Kayser explains structural differences among the 17 newspapers, differences in treatment of news and features, and differences in ownership and political predilection. The 17 are *Borba* (Yugoslavia); *Times of India*; *La Nación* (Argentina); *Al Misri* (Egypt); *Hürriyet* (Turkey); *Rand Daily Mail* (South Africa); *Daily Express* (England); *La Prensa* (Mexico); *Il Nuovo Corriere della Serra* (Italy); *Pravda* (USSR); New York *Daily News* (U.S.A.); *Le Parisien libéré* (France); *Rudé Právo* (Czechoslovakia); *O Estado de São Paulo* (Brazil); *Ta Kung Pao* (China); *Dagens Nyheter* (Sweden); and *Daily Telegraph* (Australia).

2870. Kruglak, Theodore Edward. *The Foreign Correspondents: A Study of the Men and Women Reporting for the American Information Media in Western Europe*. Geneva, Switzerland: Librairie E. Droz, 1955. 163pp. (Etudes d'Histoire Economique Politique et Sociale XV.)

An excellent detailed report on the nature of the European press corps, based on interviews and questionnaires. It includes correspondents' views on international problems and newsgathering difficulties and the author's assessment of their performance. There are numerous statistical appendixes.

2871. Lepidus, Henry. *The History of Mexican Journalism*, in University of Missouri Journalism Series, No. 49. Columbia, Mo.: University of Missouri, January 21, 1928. 87pp.

2872. Liebling, A. J., ed. *The Republic of Silence*. New York: Harcourt, Brace and Co., 1947. viii + 522pp.

This account of the French Resistance movement includes articles from the French underground press, 1940–1944.

2873. Lin, Yu'tang. *A History of the Press and Public Opinion in China*. Chicago: University of Chicago Press, 1936. 179pp.

Although dated, one of the most serviceable works on this subject.

2874. McFadden, Tom J. *Daily Journalism in the Arab States*. Columbus: Ohio State University Press, 1953. xi + 103pp. (Journalism Series, No. 15.)

Includes a brief history of Arab journalism. The author was director of the Office of War Information news operations in Lebanon and Syria during World War II.

2875. Mance, Brig. Gen. Sir Osborne. *International Telecommunications*. London: Oxford University Press, 1943. xi + 90pp. (Assisted by J. E. Wheeler.)

Mance gives material on the technical development of telegraphy and telephony, on press services, on police services, and on cable and wireless concessions. The volume was issued under the auspices of the Royal Institute of International Affairs.

2876. Martin, Frank L. *The Journalism of Japan*, in University of Missouri Journalism Series, No. 16. Columbia, Mo.: University of Missouri, April 1918. 38pp.

2877. Merrill, John C. *A Handbook of the Foreign Press*. Natchitoches, La.: Privately printed by the author, 1958. Bound typescript. 136pp.

Reviews major world newspapers, country by country, and provides an international glossary of press terminology. The book is useful as a text but is not nearly so complete as the UNESCO publications.

2878. Millard, Oscar E. *Underground News: The Complete Story of the Secret Newspaper That Made War History.* New York: Robert M. McBride and Co., 1938. 287pp. (Published in England under the title *Uncensored.* London: Hale, 1937.)

A fascinating history of *La Libre Belgique*, clandestine publication issued in Brussels during World War I. There is good biographical material on Eugene Van Doran, founder of the paper, and on Victor Jourdain, another Belgian journalistic hero.

2879. Miller, Edmund Morris. *Pressmen and Governors: Australian Editors and Writers in Early Tasmania.* Sydney and London: Angus and Robertson, 1952. ix + 308pp.

Includes biographical and bibliographical notes.

2880. Murdock, Harold R. *Newsprint in Japan.* Tokyo: General Headquarters, Supreme Command Allied Powers, Natural Resources Section, 1949. 31pp.

2881. *Office of the German Press in the U.S. Occupied Area, 1945–1948, Special Report.* Frankfurt: Office of Military Government for Germany (U.S.). 1948. 39pp.

Material on the German press prepared by the Information Services Division of OMGUS.

2882. Patterson, Don D. *The Journalism of China,* in University of Missouri Journalism Series, No. 26. Columbia, Mo.: University of Missouri, December 1922. 89pp.

The author was business editor of the Shanghai *Weekly Review* for three years.

2883. Pers, Anders Yngve. *Newspapers in Sweden.* Stockholm: The Swedish Institute, 1954. 66pp. (Translated by Gunnar Beckman.)

A good account of the Swedish press. Pers lists major newspapers in 1954, with circulations and political affiliations; traces newspaper history and ownership; and takes up press organizations, press codes, and standards.

2884. Pilgert, Henry P. *Press, Radio and Film in West Germany, 1945–1953.* Bad Godesberg-Mehlem: Office of U.S. High Commissioner for Germany, 1953. viii + 123pp.

A compact treatment, with emphasis upon the restoration of a democratic spirit in the German press. Heavily documented.

2885. Pool, Ithiel de Sola. *The "Prestige Papers": A Survey of Their Editorials.* Stanford, Calif.: Stanford University Press, 1952. vii + 146pp. (Hoover Institute Studies, Series C: Symbols, No. 2.)

A content analysis of editorials from newspapers regarded in their time as organs of elite opinion in the world. Included are the *Times of London* (1890–1949); *Novoe Vremia* of Czarist Russia (1892–1917); *Izvestia* of the Soviet Union (1918–1949); the New York *Times* (1900–1949); *Le Temps* of France (1900–1942) and *Le Monde* of France (1945–1949); *Norddeutsche Allgemeine*

Zeitung of Imperial Germany (1910–1920); *Frankfurter Zeitung* of the Weimar Republic (1920–1932); and the *Volkischer Beobachter* of the Third Reich (1933–1945). The book offers a valuable historical picture of press influence on world politics and national policy.

2886. La Prensa. *Defense of Freedom.* New York: John Day Co., 1952. 315pp. (Edited by the staff of *La Prensa.*)

Dedicated to maintaining the ideals of *La Prensa,* forced out of existence for several years by dictator Juan Perón in 1951. The volume includes biographical sketches of owners José C. Paz, Ezequiel Pedro Paz, and Alberto Gainza Paz, and editorials on press freedom.

2887. *Press Congress of the World.* Columbia, Mo.: E. W. Stephens Publishing Co., 1922, 1928, 1934. 3 vols. (Edited by Walter Williams.)

The proceedings of three international press congresses held in Honolulu (1921), Switzerland (1926), and Mexico (1931) are included in these manuals, as well as material relating to censorship, ethical standards, and journalistic education and organization. They are useful historically as background on early efforts at international press cooperation.

2888. *The Press in Africa.* Washington, D.C.: Ruth Sloan Associates, 1956. iii + 96pp. (Edited by Helen Kitchen; introduction by Abiodum Aloba, editor of the *Sunday Times,* Lagos, Nigeria.)

Summaries and statistics on the press of 23 countries, with considerable emphasis on the native press. Egypt is omitted.

2889. Rothenberg, Ignaz. *The Newspaper: A Study in the Workings of the Daily Press and Its Laws.* New York and London: Staples Press, 1948. xvi + 352pp.

A heavily documented study of international press law. The book is particularly valuable for its material on newspaper corruption, on libel and rights of reply to libel, and on coverage of governmental proceedings. The greatest emphasis is on Great Britain, France, and Germany.

2890. Saturday Review. *America and the Mind of Europe: Mid-Century.* New York: Library Publishers, 1952. 125pp. (Introduction by Lewis Galantiere.)

Three of these nine articles on cultural relations between the United States and Europe concern communications: Stephen Spender on "Britain — Culture in Official Channels"; Arthur Koestler on "The War of Ideas"; and Leo Lania on "Germany — Journalism and Publishing." The pieces appeared originally as a special issue of the *Saturday Review.*

2891. Schneider, Maarten. *The Netherlands Press Today.* Leiden: E. J. Brill, 1951. 48pp.

A capsule history of the press in the Netherlands, a survey of current conditions, organizations and institutions of journalists, and the relation of press to people. Included is a bibliography of works on the press in Dutch.

2892. Schreiner, George Abel. *Cables and Wireless and Their Role in the Foreign Relations of the United States.* Boston: The Stratford Co., 1924. 269pp. (Introduction by Edward F. McSweeney.)

An analysis of international policy in 1924 regarding the laying out and operating of cable lines, by a war correspondent of World War I.

2893. Sharp, Eugene W. *The Censorship and Press Laws of Sixty Countries*, in University of Missouri Journalism Series, No. 77. Columbia, Mo.: University of Missouri, November 1, 1936. 49pp.

2894. ———. *International News Communications: The Submarine Cable and Wireless as News Carriers*, in University of Missouri Journalism Series, No. 45. Columbia, Mo.: University of Missouri, January 14, 1927. 43pp.

2895. Suzuki, Bunshiro. *Japanese Journalism*. Tokyo: Japanese Council, Institute of Pacific Relations, 1929. 20pp.

2896. Suzuki, Hidesaburo. *Early Japanese Newspapers*. Kyoto: Occasional Papers of Kansai Asiatic Society, 1954. 13pp.

An informal survey of the types of newspapers published in Japan during the decades just before and after the Imperial Revolution of 1867. A bibliography of original prints, 1837–1881, is included.

2897. Sydney Morning Herald. *A Century of Journalism: The Sydney Morning Herald and Its Record of Australian Life, 1831–1931*. Sydney and London: John Fairfax and Sons, Ltd., 1931. xii + 805pp.

A centennial history and, in effect, a general history of Australia, with the introduction carrying back to 1770. The account is heavily based on *Herald* files. There are 12 color plates.

2898. Terrou, Fernand, and Lucien Solal. *Legislation for Press, Film and Radio*. Paris: UNESCO, 1951. 420pp. (In Press, Film and Radio in World Today Series.)

A comparative study of regulations. Included is a section on limitations of freedom of expression.

2899. Thorsen, Svend. *Newspapers in Denmark*. Copenhagen: Det Danske Selskab, 1953. 171pp. (Danish Information Handbooks; translated by Sigurd Mammen.)

A history and analysis emphasizing the 20th-century press, with a good account of Nazi treatment of the press under occupation in World War II. The book lacks source notes and bibliography.

2900. *The Times Book of India*. London: Times Publishing Co., Ltd., 1930. xix + 288pp.

Reprint in book form of a special "India Number" of the London *Times*, February 18, 1930. The *Times* has issued several books of this type; among them are studies of Russia (1916), Canada (1920), Argentina (1927), and Egypt (1937).

2901. Tompkins, Stuart Ramsay. *The Russian Mind*. Norman: University of Oklahoma Press, 1953. 291pp.

Chapters on the press are included in this study of the period between Peter I and Nicholas I.

2902. United Nations Educational, Scientific, and Cultural Organization. *The Daily Press: A Survey of the World Situation in 1952*. Paris:

UNESCO Clearing House, Department of Mass Communication, December 1953. 46pp. (Reports and Papers No. 7.)

A helpful guide giving quantitative data on the press of the world: number of dailies, circulation, nature of distribution, subscription prices, and languages in which printed.

2903. ———. *News Agencies, Their Structure and Operation*. Paris, 1953. 208pp.

An inventory of the worldwide technical facilities of news agencies, as well as a survey of the agencies' history and problems. Loose-leaf maps and charts illustrate international agency operations.

2904. ———. *Newsprint Trends, 1928–1951*. Paris: UNESCO Clearing House, Department of Mass Communication, 1954. 64pp. (Reports and Papers on Mass Communication No. 10.)

A study of the effect of the world shortage of paper for printing and writing on educational, cultural, and economic development. Extensive tables give statistical data.

2905. ———. *Newsreels across the World*. Paris, 1952. 100pp. (Prepared by Peter Bächlin and Maurice Muller-Strauss.)

Surveys the techniques of news films, the machinery of exchange between nations, and the impact of television. Well illustrated.

2906. ———. *Paper for Printing (Other Than Newsprint) and Writing: 1929–1951 Trends*. Paris: UNESCO Clearing House, Department of Mass Communication, 1954. 44pp. (Reports and Papers No. 11.)

2907. ———. *Press, Film, Radio: Reports on the Facilities of Mass Communication*. Paris, 1947–1952. 5 vols.

A factual survey of structure, work, and equipment of news agencies, press, cinema, and radio in 157 countries and territories. Vol. 5 summarizes the project and its purposes.

2908. ———. *The Problems of Transmitting Press Messages*. Lausanne, Switzerland, and Paris, 1956. 95pp.

A joint study by UNESCO and the International Telecommunication Union focused on proposals to secure cheaper, faster, and more extensive telecommunication facilities for news. There are extensive tables on comparative rates.

2909. ———. *Trade Barriers to Knowledge: A Manual of Regulations Affecting Educational, Scientific and Cultural Materials*. Paris, 1956. 2nd edition. 364pp. (First issued in 1951. 167pp.)

2910. ———. *Universal Copyright Convention*. Paris and Geneva, 1952. 2nd edition. 24pp. (Drawn up by the Intergovernmental Conference on Copyright, meeting in Geneva.)

A convention for universal protection of literary, artistic, and scientific works, adopted in 1952. It is printed in French, English, and Spanish.

2911. ———. *Visual Aids in Fundamental Education: Some Personal Experiences*. Paris, 1952. 168pp. (In Press, Film and Radio in World Today Series.)

First-hand accounts by specialized workers in Africa, Asia, Australasia, Italy, Venezuela, Jamaica, and the United States. The volume gives useful comparative information on how communication reaches areas inadequately served by the major media.

2912. ———. *World Communications: Press, Radio, Film, Television.* Paris, 1956. 3rd edition. 262pp. (First issued in 1950.)

Describes the facilities throughout the world for conveying information and ideas by the four media. There are exceptionally helpful pictographs and an extensive bibliography.

2913. Valenzuela, Jesus Z. *History of Journalism in the Philippine Islands.* Manila: The Author, 1933. xix + 217pp. (Introduction by Willard G. Bleyer.)

A general account by a one-time correspondent for the New York *World*, later a teacher in the University of the Philippines.

2914. Villard, Oswald Garrison. *The German Phoenix: The Story of the Republic.* New York: Harrison Smith and Robert Haas, 1933. 358pp.

The closing chapters of this analysis of pre-Hitlerite Germany give a picture of the effect of World War I upon the press and of the failure of the press to exercise responsibility in the early 1930s.

2915. Wang, Y. P. *The Rise of the Native Press in China.* New York: Columbia University Press, 1924. 50pp.

A history of the Chinese vernacular press, including the legal and business phases. The author had been assistant manager of *Shun Pao*, oldest vernacular daily in China.

2916. Weber, Karl. *The Swiss Press: An Outline.* Berne, Switzerland: Herbert Lang, 1948. 40pp.

2917. White, Llewellyn, and Robert D. Leigh. *Peoples Speaking to Peoples: A Report on International Mass Communication from the Commission on Freedom of the Press.* Chicago: University of Chicago Press, 1946. ix + 122pp.

One of the best of the commission's reports. This is a broad synthesis of international communication problems, with suggestions for improving accuracy in news transmission, removing political and physical controls on news flow, and encouraging the United States to enter the cultural and informational fields.

2918. Wildes, Harry Emerson. *Social Currents in Japan, with Special Reference to the Press.* Chicago: University of Chicago Press, 1927. ix + 391pp.

Though many years out of date, this book still offers extensive background on the Japanese press. There is good material on the *Japan Advertiser*, the American newspaper, and a helpful bibliography.

2919. Williams, Francis. *Transmitting World News: A Study of Telecommunications and the Press.* Paris: UNESCO, 1953. 96pp.

A history of the news agencies and a survey of technical facilities, including facsimile and telephoto and multiple address systems. The author was editor of the London *Daily Herald* in World War II.

2920. Williams, Walter. *A New Journalism in a New Far East*, in University of Missouri Journalism Series, No. 52. Columbia, Mo.: University of Missouri, December 1, 1928. 19pp.

2921. ———. *The World's Journalism*, in University of Missouri Journalism Series, No. 9. Columbia, Mo.: University of Missouri, February 1915. 44pp.

2922. Wolseley, Roland E., ed. *Journalism in Modern India*. Bombay and Calcutta: Asia Publishing House, 1953. xxiii + 308pp.

Articles covering English-language newspapers, the vernacular press, news agencies, techniques of journalism, and education for journalism. Brief biographies of the 14 Indian journalists who contributed to the book and a bibliography are included.

2923. Wordley, Derek. *The Third Front: Europe's Underground Press*. London: Hammond, Hammond and Co., Ltd., 1944. 63pp.

A wartime patriotic booklet. Names of the more prominent secret newspapers are given.

2924. Young, Eugene J. *Looking behind the Censorships*. Philadelphia: J. B. Lippincott Co., 1938. 368pp.

An exposé of the art of international news manipulation, with particular reference to world news developments of the 1930s. The author was cable editor of the New York *Times*.

XIII

Bibliographies and Directories

A. General Bibliographies

2925. Barnhart, Thomas F. *The Weekly Newspaper: A Bibliography, 1925–1941*. Minneapolis, Minn.: Burgess Publishing Co., 1941. Mimeographed. 107pp.

Books and articles on weekly newspapers are listed topically under history, editors, news processes, photography, management, advertising, circulation, mechanics, and law.

2926. Brigham, Clarence S. *History and Bibliography of American Newspapers (1690–1820)*. Worcester, Mass.: American Antiquarian Society, 1947. 2 vols. xvii + 1508pp., total.

The most thorough single bibliographical work on American journalism, by the director of the Antiquarian Society. Brigham includes sketches of founders and salient facts in newspaper histories; libraries in which newspapers are available; holdings of some foreign libraries; and an index to 2820 printers, publishers, and editors. For newspapers after 1820 see Winifred Gregory's list (3026).

2927. Cannon, Carl L., comp. *Journalism: A Bibliography*. New York: New York Public Library, 1924. vi + 360pp.

This work has been the most thorough available for journalistic output of the 19th and early 20th centuries. Entries are categorized over 37 journalistic fields; they include numerous magazine articles and county histories, and some foreign works. Relatively little of the material is annotated.

2928. Ely, Margaret. *Some Great American Newspaper Editors*. New York: H. W. Wilson Co., 1916. 33pp.

Supplements Julia Stockett's *Masters of American Journalism* (2943) for Samuel Bowles III, George W. Childs, Henry W. Grady, Nathan Hale, Whitelaw Reid, Carl Schurz, and Thurlow Weed.

2929. Ford, Edwin H. *A Bibliography of Literary Journalism in America*. Minneapolis, Minn.: Burgess Publishing Co., 1937. Mimeographed. 68pp.

A listing of books and magazine articles within "the twilight zone that divides literature from journalism." Some English writers are included. The work of humorists, novelists, short-story writers, poets, essayists, and critics is listed.

2930. ———. *History of Journalism in the United States: A Bibliography of Books and Annotated Articles*. Minneapolis, Minn.: Burgess Publishing Co., 1938. Mimeographed. 42pp.

Includes most of the established general books on journalism up to the date of publication; these entries are not annotated. More valuable is the list of selected magazine articles, which are annotated briefly. All in all, less serviceable than Ford's literary bibliography.

2931. Ginsburg, Claire. *A Newspaperman's Library*, in University of Missouri Journalism Series, No. 22. Columbia, Mo.: University of Missouri, 1921. 123pp.

2932. Graham, Robert X., comp. *A Bibliography in the History and Backgrounds of Journalism*. Pittsburgh: University of Pittsburgh, February and November 1940, two editions. 20pp.

A list of about 300 books on history, analysis of the press, biography, and adventures of journalists. Well chosen, but too limited to be of general value.

2933. *Harvard Guide to American History*. Cambridge, Mass.: Harvard University Belknap Press, 1954. xxiv + 689pp. (Edited by Oscar Handlin, Arthur M. Schlesinger, Samuel Eliot Morison, Frederick Merk, Arthur M. Schlesinger, Jr., and Paul Herman Buck.)

This most recent of thorough single-volume general bibliographies in American history has many journalistic entries under various subject headings, principally "Journalism, Letters and the Arts" and "Newspapers."

2934. Kane, Charles E. *The Journalist's Library: Books for Reference and Reading*, in University of Missouri Journalism Series, No. 13. Columbia, Mo.: University of Missouri, January 1916. 89pp.

2935. Lunn, A. J. E. "Bibliography of the History of the Canadian Press," in *Canadian Historical Review*, vol. XXII (1941), pp. 416–433. Toronto: University of Toronto Press.

Includes general works on the Canadian press and works categorized by provinces. Most of the entries are from periodicals. Highly useful.

2936. Marks, Besse B. *Recent Books for Journalists*, in University of Missouri Journalism Series, No. 37. Columbia, Mo.: University of Missouri, December 10, 1925. 35pp.

2937. Mott, Frank Luther. *One Hundred Books on American Journalism*, in University of Missouri Journalism Series, No. 131. Columbia, Mo.: University of Missouri, 1953. 18pp. (Earlier editions: Series No. 115, 1949; and Series No. 95, 1944.)

As choice a selection of what constitute the best 100 books on and about journalism as one could find, although Professor Mott modestly presents the books as his choices only. He includes some fiction titles.

2938. Peet, Hubert W. *A Bibliography of Journalism: A Guide to the Books about the Press and Pressmen*. London: Sells, Ltd., 1915. 44pp. (Also in 1915 edition of *Sell's World's Press*, pp. 34ff.)

A helpful British list of works on journalism preceding Cannon's bibliography (2927) by nine years, but not so detailed or authoritative. Peet lists about 400 titles, with some annotation, in journalistic history, biography, techniques, law, and periodicals. The listing unfortunately is chronological by date of publication and therefore difficult to use.

2939. Porter, Bernard H., comp. *H. L. Mencken: A Bibliography.* Pasadena, Calif.: Geddes Press, 1957. 24pp.

An annotated compilation of Mencken's writings, 1903–1956, and books and pamphlets about Mencken. It includes about 200 titles.

2940. *Public Relations, Edward L. Bernays and the American Scene: Annotated Bibliography of and Reference Guide to Writings by and about Edward L. Bernays from 1917 to 1951.* Boston: F. W. Faxon Co., 1951. 86pp.

An exceptionally detailed, descriptive bibliography of Bernays's own writing in books and periodicals and of material about him in other publications. A summary of Bernays's published addresses is included. The material was published as a supplement to the *Bulletin of Bibliography and Dramatic Index,* vol. 20, no. 3 (September–December 1950).

2941. Quinby, Henry Cole. *Richard Harding Davis, a Bibliography: Being a Record of His Literary Life, of His Achievements as a Correspondent in Six Wars, and His Efforts in Behalf of the Allies in the Great War.* New York: E. P. Dutton and Co., 1924. xxi + 294pp.

Most useful is an alphabetized list of all Davis's work which appeared in newspapers and magazines. Included also are Davis's plays, moving pictures of his works, his books for the blind, translations of his books in foreign languages, and biographical and critical works about him.

2942. Scott, Leslie M., ed. *Catalogue of Public Addresses and Lectures of Harvey W. Scott, Forty Years Editor-in-Chief, Morning Oregonian.* Portland, Ore., 1915. 14 unnumbered pp.

A chronological bibliography of 61 major addresses Scott made from 1872 to 1910, compiled by his son.

2943. Stockett, Julia Carson. *Masters of American Journalism.* New York: H. W. Wilson Co., 1916. 40pp.

Bibliographies of James Gordon Bennett, Charles A. Dana, Edwin L. Godkin, Horace Greeley, Joseph Pulitzer, and Henry J. Raymond. The listing of references to these editors in encyclopedias, periodicals, general reference books, books and book reviews, and collected biographies is complete for the period up to 1916.

2944. Tobin, James E. *Eighteenth Century English Literature and Its Cultural Background: A Bibliography.* New York: Fordham University Press, 1942. vii + 190pp.

Some distinctive journalism entries are included, pp. 46–50.

2945. United States Department of State, Division of Library and Reference Services. *American Correspondents and Journalists in Moscow, 1917–1952: A Bibliography of Their Books on the U.S.S.R.* Washington, D.C.: Government Printing Office, 1953. ii + 52pp. (Bibliography No. 73.)

Lists 695 books by 190 authors. Annotations include information on the correspondents' chief assignments.

2946. Wolseley, Roland E. *The Journalist's Bookshelf*. Chicago: Quill and Scroll Foundation, 1955. 6th edition. 212pp. (First issued in 1939.)

The most serviceable of the contemporary general bibliographies of books on journalism, with the 1955 edition carrying about 1300 titles and an introductory essay. Wolseley defines journalism narrowly and hence does not include many titles from allied fields. His entries are highly useful for fiction and works on high school journalism.

B. Bibliographies on Special Fields of Journalism

ADVERTISING

2947. Advertising Federation of America. *Books for the Advertising and Marketing Man: A Classified Bibliography on Advertising, Marketing, Selling, and Related Subjects*. New York: Bureau of Research and Education of the Federation, 1957. 37pp. (Supplement issued in 1958. 16pp.)

Lists more than 1500 titles, unannotated, in 60 categories related to advertising; there is also an index to publishers and authors. The years covered are 1937–1956.

2948. Jones, Donald H., comp. *100 Books on Advertising*, in University of Missouri Journalism Series, No. 128. 6th edition. Columbia, Mo.: University of Missouri, 1952. 25pp.

Intended to complement Mott's *100 Books on American Journalism* (2937), this selected list covers the whole advertising field. Still useful are the listings in two earlier editions, Journalism Series No. 107 and No. 100, issued in 1946 and 1945, respectively, and both edited by E. K. Johnston.

FOREIGN PRESS AND INTERNATIONAL COMMUNICATIONS

2949. Dahl, Folke. *Dutch Corantos, 1618–1650*. The Hague, Netherlands: Koninklijke Bibliotheek, 1946. 87pp.

2950. Fellows, Otis. *The Periodical Press in Liberated Paris: A Survey and a Checklist*. Syracuse, N.Y.: Syracuse University Press, 1946. 29pp.

Lists about 75 weekly periodicals which played an important role in the first 18 months after the liberation of France. There is also a listing of the Paris daily press as of 1946. Brief annotations are given.

2951. Gropp, Arthur E., comp. *Union List of Latin American Newspapers in Libraries in the United States*. Washington, D.C.: Department of Cultural Affairs, Pan American Union, 1953. x + 235pp. (Bibliographic Series No. 39.)

Expands on Gregory's *Union List of American Newspapers* (3026) to include the 20 countries of the Americas outside the United States and Canada. Holdings in 56 libraries are listed, totaling more than 5000 titles. An index of titles on microfilm is included. The arrangement is geographical by country and city. Main entries give the newspaper title, frequency, and dates of publication if known.

2951a. Khurshid, Abdus Salam. *Newsletters in the Orient, with Special Reference to the Indo-Pakistan Sub-Continent.* Assen: Van Gorcum, 1956. 123pp.

2952. Löwenthal, Rudolf. *Western Literature on Chinese Journalism.* Tientsin: Nankai Institute of Economics, 1937. x + 60pp.

Some 680 titles on Chinese journalism which have appeared in Western languages are listed; of these 609 are in English.

2953. Nafziger, Ralph O. *Foreign News Sources and the Foreign Press: A Bibliography.* Minneapolis: Burgess Publishing Co., 1937. 57 leaves.

Entry 2954 is a book-length expansion of this publication.

2954. ———. *International News and the Press: Communications, Organization of News Gathering, International Affairs and the Foreign Press — an Annotated Bibliography.* New York: H. W. Wilson Co., 1940. xxix + 193pp.

Still the only general bibliography on the international press; with Cannon (2927) and Smith, Lasswell, and Casey (2984, 2986) a leading journalistic bibliography. The organization is topical. References to the press of foreign countries are listed alphabetically by continent and country. An introductory essay gives a brief analysis of the development of foreign-news coverage.

2955. Pan American Union. *Catalogue of the Newspapers and Magazines in the Columbus Memorial Library of the Pan American Union.* Washington, D.C.: The Union, 1931. Mimeographed. 112pp. (Bibliographic Series No. 6.)

2956. Perry, Ruth Robinson. *Clandestine Publications Issued in Belgium during the German Occupation, 1914–1918.* Rochester, N.Y.: University of Rochester Press, for Association of College and Reference Libraries, 1953. iii + 67 leaves.

Includes a check list of clandestine serials in the Hoover Library of War, Revolution, and Peace.

2957. United Nations Educational, Scientific, and Cultural Organization. *Current Mass Communication Research — I.* Paris: UNESCO Clearing House, Department of Mass Communication, December 1956. 60pp. (Reports and Papers No. 21.)

A register of mass-communication research projects in progress and planned and a bibliography of books and articles on mass communication published since January 1, 1955. This is the first of a proposed series to keep research workers informed about methodological studies of information media. Nearly 400 projects from 24 countries are listed.

2958. ———. *A Selected Inventory of Periodical Publications.* Paris, 1951. 129pp. (UNESCO, Department of Social Sciences, Publication No. 798.)

2959. ———. *Tentative International Bibliography of Works Dealing with Press Problems (1900–1952)*. Paris: UNESCO Clearing House, Department of Mass Communication, 1954. 96pp.

Limited to books; no annotations. Forty nations are covered, including all major countries except those under USSR influence. Titles are given in the native language and in French and English. Of 1500 entries, those from the United States, United Kingdom, France, and Germany comprise a fourth. Manuals and directories are excluded.

2959a. United Nations General Assembly. *Report of the Expert Committee on United Nations Public Information*. New York: The United Nations, 13th Session, Agenda Item 55, August 28, 1958. 105pp. + 8 appendixes (46pp.).

This report includes a review of UN activity in public information relating to press, radio, and television services; films and graphics; publications; and public liaison activities.

2960. United States Library of Congress, European Affairs Division. *The European Press Today*. Washington, D.C., 1949. 152pp.

A six-page supplement carries the subtitle *The Press in Turkey*.

2961. ———. *Freedom of Information: A Selective Report on Recent Writings*. Washington, D.C., 1947. 153pp. *Revised Supplement*, 1952. v + 40pp. (Compiled by H. J. Krould; revised by Helen F. Conover.)

2962. United States Library of Congress, Reference Department. *African Newspapers Currently Received in Selected American Libraries*. Washington, D.C., 1956. iv + 16pp.

2963. ———. *Periodicals of Africa Currently Received in Selected American Libraries*. Washington, D.C., 1956. ix + 34pp.

LEGAL BIBLIOGRAPHIES

2964. Schroeder, Theodore. *Free Speech Bibliography: Including Every Discovered Attitude toward the Problem, Covering Every Method of Transmitting Ideas and of Abridging Their Promulgation upon Every Subject Matter*. New York: H. W. Wilson Co.; London: Grafton and Co., 1922. 247pp.

Comprehensive and thorough, listing works from 1506 up to the date of publication. Many of the entries are annotated. One of the most useful sections is that listing suppressed publications.

2965. Summers, Robert E., comp. *Federal Information Controls in Peacetime*. New York: H. W. Wilson Co., 1949. 301pp.

2966. ———. *Wartime Censorship of Press and Radio*. New York: H. W. Wilson Co., 1942. 297pp.

2967. Swindler, William F. *A Bibliography of Law on Journalism*. New York: Columbia University Press, 1947. x + 191pp.

One of the few available annotated bibliographies on journalistic law. Included are 1154 entries for books, monographs, periodical articles, and other publications, principally works of the past 100 years. There is a helpful introductory essay.

2968. United States Library of Congress, Division of Bibliography. *The Bill of Rights: A List of References.* Washington, D.C., 1940. Mimeographed. 21pp. (Compiled by Grace Hadley Fuller.)

About 200 references, including Library of Congress call numbers.

2969. ———. *List of References on Freedom of the Press and Speech and Censorship in Time of War, with Special Reference to the European War.* Washington, D.C., 1916. 9pp.

2970. United States National Archives. *Preliminary Inventory of the Records of the Office of Censorship, Record Group 216.* Washington, D.C.: Government Printing Office, 1953. 16pp. (Compiled by Henry T. Ulasek.)

PRINTING

2971. Bigmore, Edward Clements, comp., with C. W. H. Wyman. *A Bibliography of Printing, with Notes and Illustrations.* New York: P. C. Duschnes, 1945. 2nd edition. 2 vols. xii + 449pp.; vii + 412 + 115pp. (First published in the *Printing Times and Lithographer,* vol. 2, no. 11, 1876–1887.)

2972. Lehmann-Haupt, Hellmut. *One Hundred Books about Bookmaking: A Guide to the Study and Appreciation of Printing.* New York: Columbia University Press, 1949. Unpaged.

A descriptive bibliography that is serviceable for titles of volumes devoted to the history of printing.

2973. McMurtrie, Douglas C. *Printing History, Typography, and Techniques of Printing: A List of Books and Pamphlets.* Chicago: Albert H. Allen, 1935. 28pp.

A useful bibliography of more than 200 McMurtrie publications.

2974. Mills, George J. *Guide to Films, Periodicals and Books in Printing, Paper, Publishing, Printed Advertising, and Their Closely Related Industries.* Pittsburgh: Privately published for the author by Carnegie Institute of Technology, 1956. 64pp.

2975. ———. *Sources of Information in the American Graphic Arts.* Pittsburgh: Carnegie Press, 1951. vii + 70pp.

2976. New York Public Library. *Printing from the 16th to the 20th Century.* New York: The Library, 1940. 24pp. (Introduction by Charles F. McCombs.)

A catalog prepared for an exhibition commemorating the 500th anniversary of printing from movable types; there are bibliographical footnotes.

PUBLIC OPINION, PROPAGANDA, AND
PUBLIC RELATIONS

2976a. *Abstracts from the Experimental Literature on the Effects of*

Mass Communication. Stanford, Calif.: Institute for Communication Research, Stanford University, 1957. About 225 unpaged leaves.

Prepared by graduate students in communications at Stanford, under the direction of Wilbur Schramm. Entries, listed alphabetically by author, include annotations on research methods used, findings obtained, and implications involved in the various studies.

2977. Beuick, Marshall. *Bibliography of Public Relations.* New York: M. Beuick, privately printed, 1947. 40 numbered leaves.

2978. *A Bibliography of Theory and Research Techniques in the Field of Human Motivation.* New York: Advertising Research Foundation, 1956. v + 117pp.

A helpful guide, particularly for motivational material on marketing and advertising. Several hundred books, articles, and pamphlets are listed, with extensive annotations.

2979. Childs, Harwood L., ed. *A Reference Guide to the Study of Public Opinion.* Princeton, N.J.: Princeton University Press, 1934. 105pp.

2980. Cutlip, Scott M., comp. *A Public Relations Bibliography, and Reference and Film Guides.* Madison, Wis.: University of Wisconsin Press, 1957. xviii + 313pp. (Sponsored by Public Relations Society of America.)

An excellent comprehensive annotated bibliography of approximately 3600 entries on public relations, public opinion, and communications literature dating from 1900.

2981. Dale, Edgar, and Norma Vernon. *Propaganda Analysis: An Annotated Bibliography.* Columbus: Ohio State University Press, 1940. 29pp.

2982. *The Edward L. Bernays Collection on Public Relations.* New York: New York Public Library, 1947. 17pp.

An annotated bibliography of 150 titles representing key publications in a public opinion and public relations collection of 4500 titles.

2983. Jamieson, John. *Books for the Army: The Army Library Service in the Second World War.* New York: Columbia University Press, 1950. xiv + 335pp.

Includes reference materials on such journalistic interests as publicity on books for soldiers, "lightweight magazines," and censorship.

2984. Lasswell, Harold D., Ralph D. Casey, and Bruce Lannes Smith. *Propaganda and Promotional Activities: An Annotated Bibliography.* Minneapolis: University of Minnesota Press, 1935. xvii + 450pp.

See Smith, Lasswell, and Casey (2986 below).

2985. Nielander, William A. *A Selected and Annotated Bibliography of Public Relations.* Austin: Bureau of Business Research, University of Texas, 1956. 42pp. (First published in 1948 under the title *A Selected and Annotated Bibliography of Literature on Public Relations.*)

2986. Smith, Bruce Lannes, Harold D. Lasswell, and Ralph D. Casey. *Propaganda, Communication, and Public Opinion: A Comprehensive*

Reference Guide. Princeton, N.J.: Princeton University Press, 1946. vii + 435pp.

This volume and *Propaganda and Promotional Activities: An Annotated Bibliography* (2984 above) offer the most complete bibliography available for material on this field. Together they list about 7500 titles, including periodical articles. The earlier volume covers the period through 1934; the second, 1934–1946. The second volume includes four essays surveying the field of communications — on communication channels, communication specialists, communication content, and communication effects; the first has an essay by Lasswell on the study and practice of propaganda. The books are invaluable.

2987. Smith, Bruce Lannes, and Chitra M. Smith. *International Communications and Public Opinion: A Guide to the Literature*. Princeton, N.J.: Princeton University Press, 1956. xi + 325pp. (Prepared for the Rand Corporation through the Bureau of Social Science Research.)

Announced as a continuation of *Propaganda, Communication, and Public Opinion*, but concentrates on materials dealing with international communication. A preliminary essay takes up "Trends in Research on International Communications and Public Opinion, 1954–1955." There is useful material on the Voice of America and on Soviet channels of information.

2988. Smith, Chitra M., Berton Winograd, and Alice R. Jwaideh. *International Communication and Political Warfare: An Annotated Bibliography*. Santa Monica, Calif.: The Rand Corp., 1952. Mimeographed. 508pp.

Covers the period from mid-1943 to mid-1951, with 39 separate bibliographies on specialized fields, plus a note on the research value of periodical literature in the field. Of 1659 entries, nearly 200 concern press, radio, and motion pictures.

2989. Summers, Robert E., ed. *America's Weapons of Psychological Warfare*. New York: H. W. Wilson Co., 1951. 206pp.

2990. United States Department of State, Division of Library and Reference Services. *Overseas Information Programs of the United States Government: A Bibliography of Selected Materials, with Annotations*. Washington, D.C.: Government Printing Office, 1951. 34pp.

2991. Young, Kimball, and Raymond D. Lawrence. *Bibliography on Censorship and Propaganda*. Eugene: University of Oregon Press, 1928. 133pp.

RADIO AND TELEVISION

2992. Beuick, Marshall. *Bibliography of Radio Broadcasting*. New York: M. Beuick, privately printed, 1947. 60pp.

2993. British Broadcasting Corporation. *British Broadcasting: A Bibliography*. London: Broadcasting House, BBC, 1954. 36pp.

Includes books published in England on sound and television broadcasting; articles in monthly and quarterly journals; debates on the BBC in both houses of Parliament; and official publications relating to the BBC. About 700 titles are listed.

2994. Paulu, Burton, comp. *A Radio and Television Bibliography*. Urbana, Ill.: National Association of Educational Broadcasters, 1952. vii + 129pp.

2995. *Radio and Television Bibliography*. Washington, D.C.: Government Printing Office, 1956. 46pp. (Bulletin No. 2, United States Department of Health, Education, and Welfare; prepared by Gertrude G. Broderick.)

The emphasis is on books devoted to historical, philosophical, and sociological aspects of the media, together with textbooks on careers in radio and television. Except for standard texts, publications more than 10 years old are omitted.

2996. "Radio Journalism: An Annotated Bibliography," in *Journalism Quarterly*, vol. 23 (June 1946), pp. 193–201.

2997. Rose, Oscar, ed. *Radio Broadcasting and Television: An Annotated Bibliography*. New York: H. W. Wilson Co., 1947. 120pp.

C. Check Lists of Newspapers and Magazines

UNITED STATES

2998. Alabama Department of Archives and History. *Checklist of Newspaper and Periodical Files in the Department of Archives and History of the State of Alabama*. Montgomery: Brown Printing Co., 1904. 65pp.

2999. American Antiquarian Society. "Alabama, Mississippi, and Tennessee Newspaper Files in the Library of the American Antiquarian Society," in *Proceedings*, vol. 17 (1906), pp. 274–279.

3000. Ander, Oscar Fritiof, comp. *Swedish-American Political Newspapers: A Guide to the Collections in the Royal Society, Stockholm, and the Augustana College Library*. Stockholm and Uppsala: Almqvist and Wiksells; Rock Island, Ill.: Augustana Library Publications, 1936. 28pp.

3001. Ayer, Mary Farwell, comp. *Check-List of Boston Newspapers, 1704–1780, with Bibliographical Notes by Albert Matthews*. Boston: Colonial Society of Massachusetts, 1907. 527pp. (Vol. 9 of the *Publications* of the Society.)

3002. Bardolph, Richard. *Agricultural Literature and the Early Illinois Farmer*. Urbana: University of Illinois Press, 1948. 200pp.

3003. Barton, Albert O. *The Beginnings of the Norwegian Press in America*. Madison: State Historical Society of Wisconsin, 1916. (Also in the Society's *Proceedings*, no. 174, pp. 186–212.)

3004. Blair, Emma H. *Annotated Catalogue of Newspaper Files in the Library of the State Historical Society of Wisconsin*. Madison: The Society, 1898. 375pp. *Supplementary Catalogue of Newspaper Files*. Madison, 1918. 91pp.

3005. Brayer, Herbert Oliver. "Preliminary Guide to Indexed Newspapers in the United States, 1850–1900," in *Mississippi Valley Historical Review*, vol. 33 (September 1946), pp. 237–258.

3006. Brigham, Clarence S. "Wallpaper Newspapers of the Civil War," in *Bibliographical Essays: A Tribute to Wilberforce Eames*, pp. 203–210. Cambridge, Mass.: Harvard University Press, 1924.

A check list of 13 wallpaper newspapers in Louisiana, Mississippi, and Alabama.

3007. Brown, Warren. *Check List of Negro Newspapers in the United States, 1827–1946*. Jefferson City, Mo.: Lincoln University School of Journalism, 1946. 37pp. (Lincoln University Journalism Series No. 2.)

Lists more than 450 Negro newspapers and indicates editors, dates of founding and expiration, and depositories of known copies.

3008. Cappon, Lester J. *Virginia Newspapers, 1821–1935: A Bibliography with Historical Introduction and Notes.* New York and London: D. Appleton-Century Co., for the Virginia Institute in the Social Sciences, 1936. xiii + 299pp.

Lists 1763 newspapers alphabetically by city of publication. The entries give key data on each paper and the location of files. There is also a title index, a chronological guide, and a limited general bibliography.

3009. Chicago, University of. *Newspapers in the Libraries of Chicago: A Joint Check List.* Chicago: University of Chicago Libraries Documents Section, 1936. iv + 257 numbers.

Lists by state and city of publication the detailed newspaper holdings of the University of Chicago, Newberry Library, Chicago Public Library, Chicago Historical Society Library, John Crerar Library, Northwestern University Library, and McCormick Historical Association Library. The work includes a title index.

3010. Chicago Historical Society Library. *A Check List of the Kellogg Collection of "Patent Inside" Newspapers of 1876.* Chicago: WPA Historical Records Survey Project, 1939. Mimeographed. ix + 99 numbers.

A catalog of the exhibit prepared originally for the Centennial Exposition in Philadelphia, 1876.

3011. Common Council for American Unity. *Foreign Language Publications in the United States.* New York: The Council, 1926, 1930. 2 vols.

Vol. I lists publications by language, vol. II by state of publication.

3012. Crandall, Marjorie Lyle. *Confederate Imprints: A Check List Based Principally on the Collection of the Boston Athenaeum.* Boston: The Athenaeum, printed by the Athoensen Press of Portland, Me., 1955. 2 vols. xxxv + 910pp., total.

Vol. I contains the official imprints of the Confederate States of America and of each of the 11 seceded states, plus Kentucky; vol. II contains unofficial imprints, among them names and available dates of 181 Confederate newspapers and periodicals owned by the Athenaeum. The work is especially useful for its material on these important Confederate newspapers: Charleston *Daily Courier* and Charleston *Mercury*, Augusta (Ga.) *Chronicle and Sentinel*, Memphis *Daily Appeal*, and Richmond *Daily Enquirer* and Richmond *Examiner*.

3013. Dawson, Muir. *History and Bibliography of Southern California Newspapers, 1851–1876*. Los Angeles: Dawson's Book Shop, 1950. 86pp.

Reprinted and revised from articles in the *Quarterly of the Historical Society of Southern California*, March and June 1950. Dawson lists 76 newspapers in 18 southern California cities, with a sketch of each and notes on early editors, and locates files in southern California and in some large general libraries.

3014. Delmatier, Royce. *American Newspaper Files in Eight California Libraries, 1900–1954: A Listing of Metropolitan Newspapers Having a Circulation of Over 50,000*. Berkeley: Regional Resources Co-ordinating Committee of the California Library Assn., 1954. 47 leaves.

3015. Dill, William Adelbert. *The First Century of American Newspapers*. Lawrence: University of Kansas, Bulletin of Department of Journalism, 1925. 23pp.

A check list of periodicals published from 1690 to 1790.

3016. Drewry, John E. *Contemporary American Magazines: A Selected Bibliography and Reprints of Articles Dealing with Various Periodicals*. Athens: University of Georgia Press, 1940. 3rd edition. 80 numbered leaves. (Earlier editions, 1938 and 1939.)

3017. Duke University. *A Checklist of United States Newspapers (and Weeklies before 1900) in the General Library*. Durham, N.C.: Duke University, 1932–1937. 6 parts. (Compiled by Mary Wescott and Allene Ramage.)

3018. Ellison, Rhoda Coleman. *A Checklist of Alabama Imprints, 1807–1870*. University: University of Alabama Press, 1946. 151pp.

3019. ———. *History and Bibliography of Alabama Newspapers in the Nineteenth Century*. University: University of Alabama Press, 1954. xii + 209pp.

About 1000 entries, arranged alphabetically by cities. Included are dates of founding, sketches of owners, and indications of holdings in libraries.

3019a. Fessler, Aaron L., comp., assisted by Saro J. Riccardi. *Current Newspapers, United States and Foreign: A Union List of Newspapers Available in the Libraries of the New York Metropolitan Area*. New York: New York Public Library, 1957. Provisional edition. 66pp.

3020. Ford, Worthington C. "Broadsides, Ballads &c, Printed in Massachusetts, 1639–1800," in Massachusetts Historical Society *Collections*, vol. 75. Boston, 1922. vi + 483pp.

A check list of 3423 entries beginning with the Massachusetts Bay Colony "Freeman's Oath" of 1639 and including an extensive listing of publications of Isaiah Thomas, Samuel Adams, and other Boston patriots. Profusely illustrated. Ford gives a helpful commentary on the broadside as a precursor of the newspaper.

3021. Foreman, Carolyn Thomas. *Oklahoma Imprints, 1835–1907: A History of Printing in Oklahoma before Statehood.* Norman: University of Oklahoma Press, 1936. xxiv + 499pp.

A valuable record of all early newspapers in Indian Territory and Oklahoma Territory. There is a brief account of the establishment of the first Oklahoma press and the founding of the *Cherokee Phoenix* and an extended treatment of the press of the Five Civilized Tribes, the early mission press, and magazines, books, pamphlets, and newspapers. A bibliography of secondary sources and an excellent index are included.

3022. Fox, Louis H. "New York City Newspapers, 1820–1850: A Bibliography," in *Papers of the Bibliographical Society of America*, vol. 21. Chicago: University of Chicago Press, 1928. 131pp.

Includes all newspapers in New York City for the period. It is most useful for those devoted to special subjects and causes. Annotations are detailed. Appendix graphs show the length of publication of each newspaper.

3023. Fraenkel, Josef, comp. *The Jewish Press of the World.* London: World Jewish Congress, 1956. 4th edition. 78pp. (First issued in 1953.)

3024. Gavit, Joseph. *A List of American Newspaper Reprints.* New York: New York Public Library, 1931. 16pp.

Notes on the complete separate reproductions of early or historic newspaper issues.

3025. Giffen, Helen S. *California Mining Town Newspapers, 1850–1880: A Bibliography.* San Fernando Valley, Calif.: Westernlore Press, 1954. 102pp.

An alphabetical list of scores of these early papers, together with sketches of editors and a listing of publication dates. Some facsimiles are included. The author succeeds in recapturing the spirit of early California in her accompanying essay.

3026. Gregory, Winifred, ed. *American Newspapers, 1821–1936: A Union List of Files Available in the United States and Canada.* New York: H. W. Wilson Co., 1936. 791pp.

Indispensable in any scholarly study of American newspapers. Miss Gregory picks up where Brigham left off (see 2926). The volume alphabetizes newspapers by states or provinces and by city, and lists files in libraries and, as far as possible, files preserved in courthouses, newspaper offices, and private collections. Also included is a bibliography of union lists of newspapers compiled by the New York Public Library.

3027. Griswold, Ada Tyng. *Annotated Catalogue of Newspaper Files in the Library of the State Historical Society of Wisconsin.* Madison, Wis.: The Society, 1911. 591pp.

3028. Hamilton, Milton W. "Anti-Masonic Newspapers, 1826–1834," in *Papers of the Bibliographical Society of America*, vol. 32, pp. 71–97. Chicago: University of Chicago Press, 1938.

The author gives founder, date of founding, and a brief annotation for each anti-Masonic sheet.

3029. Harwell, Richard Barksdale. *More Confederate Imprints.* Richmond, Va.: Virginia State Library, 1957. 2 vols. in one. xxxvi + 345pp.

A supplement to *Confederate Imprints* by Marjorie Lyle Crandall (3012).

3030. Henry, Edward A. "The Durrett Collection, Now in the Library of the University of Chicago," in *Papers of the Bibliographical Society of America*, vol. 8, pp. 57–94. Chicago: University of Chicago Press, 1914.

A check list of newspapers from 19 states, Mexico, and England in the collection of Col. Reuben T. Durrett, who was in the 1850s editor-in-chief of the Louisville (Ky.) *Courier*. Durrett specialized in works printed in Kentucky and his collection includes a complete file of *Niles' Register* and an extensive file of the Maysville (Ky.) *Eagle* and the Louisville *Public Advertiser*.

3031. Hewett, Daniel. "Daniel Hewett's List of Newspapers and Periodicals in the United States in 1828," in *Proceedings* of the American Antiquarian Society, vol. 44, new series, part I, pp. 365–396. Worcester, Mass., 1934.

Listed are 681 newspapers and 119 magazines, with name of publisher, period of publication, place of publication, and subscription price. This is invaluable in identifying printers of the early press. Hewett prepared the list in 1828 for his *Traveller and Monthly Gazeteer*.

3032. Historical Records Survey, Arkansas. *Union List of Arkansas Newspapers, 1819–1942.* Little Rock: Historical Records Survey Division of Community Service Programs, Works Projects Administration, 1942. 240pp.

Locates 536 newspapers in 18 Arkansas libraries and lists them alphabetically by cities. Chronological and title indexes are included.

3033. Historical Records Survey, Mississippi. *Mississippi Newspapers, 1805–1940: A Preliminary Checklist of Mississippi Newspaper Files Available in the Mississippi Department of Archives and History.* Jackson: Historical Records Survey, 1942. 102 leaves.

The 661 entries are alphabetized by city, with a chronological index and a title index.

3034. Historical Records Survey, Texas. *Texas Newspapers, 1813–1939: A Union List of Newspaper Files Available in Offices of Publishers, Libraries, and a Number of Private Collections.* Houston: San Jacinto Museum of History Assn., 1941. xiii + 293 leaves.

Alphabetized by city, with a chronological index and a title index.

3035. Historical Records Survey, Vermont. *Index to the Burlington Free Press in the Billings Library, University of Vermont.* Montpelier: Historical Records Survey, 1940–1942. 10 vols.

3036. Illinois State Historical Library. *Newspapers Published in Illinois prior to 1860: A Bibliography.* Springfield, Ill.: Phillips Bros., State Printers, 1899. 94pp. (Prepared by Edmund J. James.)

Lists all Illinois newspapers for the period that could be located in public and private libraries. The entries are given alphabetically by city, each with a note on the founding of the paper, its early editors, and changes in name and ownership. An appendix gives a chronological list of Illinois and Missouri newspapers, 1808–1897, in the St. Louis Mercantile Library.

3037. Indiana State Library. *A List of Indiana Newspapers Available in the Indiana State Library, the Indianapolis Public Library, the Library of Indiana University, and the Library of Congress.* Indianapolis: State Library Bulletin, vol. XI, no. 4 (December 1916). 31pp.

An alphabetical listing, by city and newspaper, including available dates.

3038. Kansas State Historical Society. *A List of Kansas Newspapers and Periodicals, Corrected to Aug. 1, 1911.* Topeka: State Printing Office, n.d. 47pp. (Issued by George W. Martin.)

3039. Lincoln University. *Bibliography of the Negro Press.* Jefferson City, Mo.: Lincoln University, 1946. 11pp.

3040. Lutrell, Estelle. *Newspapers and Periodicals of Arizona, 1859–1911.* Tucson: University of Arizona, 1949. 123pp. (Issued as University of Arizona Bulletin, vol. XX, no. 3.)

The first attempt to record Arizona's territorial newspapers and periodicals. Entries are alphabetized by city; there is also a chronological listing of periodicals. A biographical section contains 100 accounts of newspapermen of early Arizona.

3041. McMurtrie, Douglas C. *Early Printing in Tennessee, with a Bibliography of the Issues of the Tennessee Press, 1793–1830.* Chicago: Chicago Club of Printing House Craftsmen, 1933. 141pp.

In addition to the bibliography, McMurtrie provides an essay on the first Tennessee newspapers, with brief sketches of George Roulstone, first printer in the state (Knoxville *Gazette*, 1791), and Roulstone's successors. Some facsimiles of early governmental proclamations are included. The volume was issued in a limited edition as a work of fine printing.

3042. ———. *Oregon Imprints, 1847–1870.* Eugene: University of Oregon Press, 1950. xxi + 206pp.

3043. ———, comp. *A Check List of Eighteenth Century Albany Imprints.* Albany, N.Y.: University of the State of New York, 1939. 83pp. (Bibliographic Bulletin No. 80.)

Entries are listed by date beginning with 1772; most are annotated. The volume is most useful for printing history. There is considerable material on Thomas Paine.

3044. ——— and Albert H. Allen, comps. *A Check List of Kentucky Imprints.* Louisville: Historical Records Survey, Kentucky, 1939. 2 vols. xxvii + 205pp.; xiii + 235pp.

The first volume covers the period 1787–1810 and the second 1811–1820.

3045. Micro-Photo, Inc. *Newspapers on Micro-Film.* Cleveland, Ohio: Micro-Photo, 1956. 4th edition. 24pp.

Lists more than 1,000 newspapers for which microfilmed papers are available.

3046. Miller, Daniel. *Early German-American Newspapers*. Lancaster: Pennsylvania German Society, 1911. 107pp.

3047. Millington, Yale O. "A List of Newspapers Published in the District of Columbia, 1820–1850," in *Papers of the Bibliographical Society of America*, vol. 19, pp. 43–65. Chicago: University of Chicago Press, 1925.

Supplements Brigham (2926) for the District of Columbia. There are nearly 100 entries, entered alphabetically, with dates of publication and names and political leanings of editors.

3048. Mostar, Roman, and J. Ronald Todd, comps. *A Check List of Pacific Northwest Newspapers Held by the University of Washington Library*. Seattle: University of Washington, 1950. 16pp.

Includes Alaska, British Columbia, Idaho, Montana, Oregon, Washington, and Yukon Territory.

3049. *New Serial Titles: A Union List of Serials Commencing Publication after December 31, 1949*. Washington, D.C.: Library of Congress, 1958. iv + 938pp. (2nd series, 1957 cumulation, prepared under sponsorship of the Joint Committee on the *Union List of Serials*.)

A continuing supplement to the union lists prepared through 1949 by the H. W. Wilson Co. (3061). The *New Serial Titles* are published monthly and cumulated annually, with further cumulations over five-year periods. The first series of five-year cumulations was concluded December 31, 1954. Entries have been supplied by the Library of Congress and cooperating libraries.

3050. New York Public Library. *Check List of Newspapers and Official Gazettes in the New York Public Library*. New York: The Library, 1915. ix + 579pp. (Compiled by Daniel C. Haskell.)

3051. Oehlerts, Donald E., comp. *Guide to Wisconsin Newspapers, 1833–1957*. Madison: State Historical Society of Wisconsin, 1958. xiv + 338pp.

Lists all newspapers published in the state (Green Bay *Intelligencer* in 1833 to the present) and includes references to Wisconsin libraries which contain files. Editors and dates of editorship are given, as well as a name index of editors. The listings are alphabetical by counties and cities within counties.

3052. Paine, Nathaniel, comp. "Early American Broadsides," in *Proceedings* of the American Antiquarian Society, vol. 11, pp. 455–516. Worcester, Mass., 1898.

3053. Pease, Marguerite [Jenison]. *A Check List of Newspapers in the Illinois Historical Survey*. Urbana: Illinois Historical Survey, 1953. 66 leaves.

3054. Pride, Armistead. *Negro Newspapers on Microfilm: A Selected List*. Washington, D.C.: Library of Congress Photo-duplication Service, 1953. 8pp.

3055. Rowell, George P., and Co., comp. *Centennial Newspaper Exhibition*. New York: George P. Rowell, 1876. 298pp.

A complete list of newspapers in 1876. Includes population and characteristics of cities in which they were published; historical data on selected "great newspapers"; and statistical tables of periodicals, state by state. Most of the historical material refers to newspapers in New York State.

3056. Schwegmann, George A., Jr. *Newspapers on Microfilm: A Union Check List*. Philadelphia: Association of Research Libraries, 1948. 176pp.

Lists all newspapers on microfilm which were reported to the National Union Catalog by libraries and other producers of microfilm. The entries are alphabetized by states and cities within the states.

3057. Scott, Franklin William. *Newspapers and Periodicals of Illinois, 1814–1879, Revised and Enlarged Edition*. Springfield, Ill.: Illinois State Historical Library, 1910. civ + 610pp.

Expands on the Illinois State Historical Library compilation (3036). An extensive introduction gives the general background on Illinois journalism. Papers are listed alphabetically by counties; there is a historical annotation for each and an indication of ownership to 1909. Indexes show libraries in which the papers are held.

3058. Shearer, Augustus H., George Parker Winship, and William Beer. [French Newspapers in the United States from 1790 to 1800], in *Papers of the Bibliographical Society of America*, vol. 14, pp. 45–147. Chicago: University of Chicago Press, 1920.

Eight bibliographies in narrative form on 15 early French newspapers in the United States. The more important of these were *Courier de Boston, Courier de L'Univers* (Boston), *Le Courier de L'Amerique* (Philadelphia), and *Moniteur de La Louisiane* (New Orleans). The articles are a useful reference on a press rarely discussed in the history of the period.

3059. Streeter, Thomas W. *Bibliography of Texas, 1795–1845*. Cambridge, Mass.: Harvard University Press, 1955. 2 vols. lxxi + 616pp., total.

A monumental critical bibliography of Texas imprints, with 670 minutely annotated entries. Included are a sketch of printing in Texas to 1845; an alphabetized list of Texas newspapers through 1845, with historical accounts; an index of printers, presses, editors, and publishers; and a list of public documents and journals of conventions. Vol. I covers 1817–1838; vol. II, 1839–1845. Perhaps the most thorough of all the single-state bibliographies.

3060. Tinker, E. L. *Bibliography of the French Newspapers and Periodicals of Louisiana*. Worcester, Mass.: American Antiquarian Society, 1933. 126pp.

3061. *Union List of Serials in Libraries of the United States and Canada*. New York: H. W. Wilson Co., 1943. 2nd edition. 3065pp. (Edited by Winifred Gregory.) *Supplement 1941–1943*. New York: H. W. Wilson Co., 1945. 1123pp. (Edited by Gabrielle E. Malikoff.) *Supplement 1944–1949*. New York: H. W. Wilson Co., 1953. 1365pp. (Edited by Marga Franck.)

Descriptions of some 115,000 to 120,000 periodicals and other serials are given, as well as the holdings of more than 600 libraries. These volumes were continued after 1949 under the title *New Serial Titles* (3049), compiled by the Library of Congress.

3062. United States Bureau of the Census. *Negro Newspapers and Periodicals in the United States.* Washington, D.C., 1938. 18pp.

3063. United States Department of Labor Library. *American Trade Union Journals and Labor Papers Currently Received by the Library.* Washington, D.C.: The Library, 1938–date. Annually. About 50pp.

Lists newspapers of national and international federations of labor and of affiliated unions, state labor organizations, and local and miscellaneous papers. Includes a trade-union index.

3064. United States Library of Congress. *A Check List of American Eighteenth Century Newspapers in the Library of Congress.* Washington, D.C.: Government Printing Office, 1912. 186pp. (Compiled by John Van Ness Ingram.) Reissued, 1936. 401pp. (Compiled by Henry S. Parsons.)

3065. United States Library of Congress, Periodicals Division. *A Check List of American Newspapers in the Library of Congress.* Washington, D.C.: Government Printing Office, 1901. 292pp.

3066. ———. *A Check List of Foreign Newspapers in the Library of Congress.* Washington, D.C.: Government Printing Office, 1929. 209pp. (New compilation under the direction of Henry S. Parsons; earlier compilation, 1904.)

3067. United States Library of Congress, Serials Division. *Postwar Foreign Newspapers, a Union List.* Washington, D.C.: Government Printing Office, 1953. vi + 231pp.

3068. United States Library of Congress, Union Catalog Division. *Newspapers on Microfilm.* Washington, D.C.: Government Printing Office, 1953. 2nd edition. ix + 126pp. (First edition, 1948, by George A. Schwegmann, Jr., published by Association of Research Libraries. See 3056 above.)

3069. Weeks, Lyman, and Edwin M. Bacon, comps. *An Historical Digest of the Provincial Press.* Boston: Society for Americana, 1911. xiii + 564pp.

3070. Yale University Library. *A List of Newspapers in the Yale University Library*, in Yale Historical Publications, Miscellany II. New Haven: Yale University Press, 1916. 216pp.

CANADA

3071. Canadian Library Association. *Newspaper Microfilming Project Catalogue (Microfilms de Journaux).* Ottawa, 1954. 22pp. (Introduction by Robert Blackburn, University of Toronto Library.)

BIBLIOGRAPHIES AND DIRECTORIES

This is issue No. 4 in a series that lists cumulatively Canadian newspapers on microfilm and provides historical notes on the newspapers.

3072. Tremaine, Marie. *A Bibliography of Canadian Imprints, 1751–1800.* Toronto: University of Toronto Press, 1952. xxvii + 705pp.

A scholarly study listing chronologically by imprint more than 1200 entries — books, pamphlets, laws, leaflets, broadsides, handbills, some pictorial publications, and newspapers and magazines. There are extensive annotations. The newspaper section contains brief histories of Canada's first 23 newspapers and first 2 magazines.

GREAT BRITAIN

3073. Bond, Richmond Pugh, and Katherine Kirtley Weed. *Studies of British Newspapers and Periodicals from Their Beginning to 1800.* Chapel Hill: University of North Carolina Press, 1946. vi + 233pp.

3074. Crane, R. S., and F. B. Kaye. *A Census of British Newspapers and Periodicals, 1620–1800.* Chapel Hill: University of North Carolina Press; London: Cambridge University Press, 1927. 205pp.

A detailed list of holdings of British newspapers, magazines, reviews, essay sheets, and annuals (Scotch, Irish, and Welsh as well as English) in American libraries and of those not in American libraries. There is also a chronological index and a geographical index.

3075. Cranfield, Geoffrey Alan. *A Handlist of English Provincial Newspapers and Periodicals, 1700–1760.* Cambridge, England: Bowes and Bowes, 1952. viii + 31pp.

3076. Dahl, Folke. *A Bibliography of English Corantos and Periodical Newsbooks, 1620–1642.* London: Bibliographical Society, 1952. 282pp.

3077. Milford, R. T., and D. M. Sutherland. *A Catalogue of English Newspapers and Periodicals in the Bodleian Library, 1622–1800.* Oxford: Oxford University, Bodleian Library, 1936. (Appears as vol. IV, part II, pp. 163–364, of *Proceedings* of Oxford Bibliographical Society, 1935.)

3078. Muddiman, J. G. *Handlist of English and Welsh Newspapers, Magazines and Reviews: A Chronological Bibliography of the British Press from 1620–1920.* London: Academic and Bibliographical Publications, Ltd., 1954. 8 vols.

D. Almanacs, Directories, Manuals, and Yearbooks

UNITED STATES

3079. *A.A.A.A. Roster.* New York: American Association of Advertising Agencies, 1956. 105pp.

An alphabetical and geographical list of the member agencies and a guide to the organization of the A.A.A.A.

3080. *American Labor Press: An Annotated Directory.* Washington, D.C.: American Council on Public Affairs, 1940. vii + 120pp. (Compiled by Wisconsin Works Projects Administration, Official Project No. 9422.)

3081. *American Labor Press Directory.* New York: Labor Research Department of the Rand School of Social Science, 1925. 82pp.

Primarily concerned with the United States and Canada, but important international labor newspapers are listed in a special section.

3082. American Press Association. *Complete Directory of Country Newspaper Rates, with Which Is Included a Listing of Advertising Agencies and National Advertisers.* New York, 1923–1939. Discontinued.

3083. ———. *Independent Daily and Weekly Newspapers of the United States That Use Plate Matter: A Complete and Accurate List Compiled by the American Press Association for the Convenience of National and State Publicity Committees.* Washington, D.C., 1916. 24pp.

3084. Association for Education in Journalism. *Directory of Journalism Films.* Ames: Iowa State College Press, 1954. Mimeographed. 95pp. (Edited by Harry Heath.) *Supplement* issued in 1956. 56pp. (Edited by Royal H. Ray.)

Gives locations and dates of films relating to advertising and the business side of the press, graphic arts, magazines and newspapers, public relations, public opinion, propaganda, and radio and television. The annotations provide the names of film sponsors and information on charges.

3085. Ayer, N. W., and Son. *Directory of Newspapers and Periodicals: A Guide to Publications Printed in the United States and Its Possessions, the Dominion of Canada, Bermuda, Cuba, and the Republics of Panama and the Philippines.* New York: N. W. Ayer, 1880–date. About 1500 pages, plus individual state maps.

The most complete annual guide to periodical publications; includes circulations, periodicity of publication, ownership, descriptions of communities of publication, and economic features of trading areas. It is indispensable for information on local publishing situations.

3086. Batten, George. *Batten's Agricultural Directory of the United States and Canada.* New York: George Batten Co., 1948. 212pp.

3087. *Broadcasting-Telecasting Yearbook-Marketbook.* New York: Broadcasting Publications, 1931–date, now issued semiannually. (Sol Taishoff, editor.)

Founded in 1931 as *Broadcasting: The News Magazine of the 5th Estate.* Provides information on radio-television advertising, agencies, audiences, awards, equipment, the Federal Communications Commission, networks, newspaper control of stations, regional networks, individual stations, and transcriptions; lists station personnel by states and includes the names of news directors of radio and television stations.

3088. *Brooklyn Daily Eagle Almanac: A Book of Information of the World and Special to New York City and Long Island.* Brooklyn: The Daily Eagle, 1886–1926. Discontinued.

During its 40 years of publication, one of the leading almanacs published by metropolitan newspapers.

3089. Burke, W. J., and Will D. Howe. *American Authors and Books, 1640–1940*. New York: Gramercy Publishing Co., 1943. ix + 858pp.

A manual of facts on writing, editing, illustrating, reviewing, publishing, selling, and preserving American books. More than 400 newspapers are described, and especially valuable is the alphabetical listing (with short biographies) of famous newspaper staff members.

3090. Caspar, Carl. *Caspar's Directory of the American Book, News and Stationery Trade, Wholesale and Retail — Hints and Suggestions, Trade Bibliographies, Trade Journals, Etc.* Milwaukee, Wis.: C. N. Caspar, 1889. 1434pp.

3091. Catholic Press Association. *Catholic Press Directory*. New York, published annually since 1923.

The official listing of Catholic newspapers and magazines in the United States and Canada. Information is provided by the publications themselves.

3092. *Chicago Daily News Almanac and Yearbook*. Chicago: The Daily News, 1880–1937. Discontinued.

An excellent reference book that appeared for 57 years under various titles, including *Chicago Daily News Almanac and Political Register* and *Chicago Daily News Almanac and Book of Facts*.

3093. Coggeshall, William Turner. *The Newspaper Record*. Philadelphia: Lay and Brother, 1856. xiv + 205pp.

One of the earliest complete newspaper directories to be issued. Lists all newspapers, United States and Canada, and gives a historical sketch of the origin and progress of printing and some history of newspapers in Europe and America. Today it is mostly of curiosity value, although its discussion of mechanical processes then coming into newspaper use is still helpful.

3094. Dodd Firm. *Advertisers' Newspaper Manual Containing a list of American Newspapers*. Boston: Dodd's Advertising and Checking Agency, 1895. 378pp.

3095. *Editor & Publisher International Yearbook*. New York: Editor & Publisher Co., published annually. About 450pp.

A directory published by the trade journal of the newspaper industry. Lists all daily newspapers in the United States and Canada alphabetically by state or province and city; gives circulations, news services subscribed to, departmental executives (both news and business), and departmental editors. The foreign press section is strong on Great Britain and Latin America. Listed also are schools of journalism in the United States and Canada, with the names of deans and directors, the number of students, and the number of graduates. There is a limited title list of books on journalism and in allied fields (unannotated).

3096. *Editor & Publisher Market Guide*. New York: Editor & Publisher Co., 1924–date. About 500pp.

A detailed annual survey of more than 1500 newspaper markets in the United States, Canada, and the Philippine Islands. Economic information about the individual trading areas is helpful for advertisers. State maps are included.

3097. Educational Press Association of America. *America's Education Press, 25th Yearbook*. Washington, D.C.: The Association, 1955. 63pp.

A classified list of educational publications in the United States, an index to educational periodicals and editors, and a list of association members. The *Yearbook* was first issued in 1895. The association also issues an "Education Press News Letter."

3098. *Edwin Alden and Bro.'s American Newspaper Catalogue, Including Lists of All Newspapers and Magazines Published in the United States and the Canadas — Their Politics, Class or Denomination, Size, and Estimated Circulation. Also Special Lists of Religious, Agricultural, and Various Class Publications, and of All Newspapers Published in Foreign Languages*. Cincinnati and New York: E. Alden and Bro.'s Advertising Agency, 1883. 838pp.

3099. Ettinger, Karl E., ed. *Public Relations Directory and Yearbook*. New York: Longacre Press, 1945. vii + 855pp.

3100. *Facts on File: Weekly World News Digest with Cumulative Index*. New York: Facts on File, 1941–date. (Edward Van Westerborg, president; H. V. Kaltenborn, news analysis; William L. Shirer, world affairs.)

Records without comment or bias news of each week in world, national, and foreign affairs; finance and economics; arts and sciences; education and religion; sports, obituaries, and miscellaneous. Indexes are issued biweekly, monthly, quarterly, and annually. Yearbooks have been available since 1942.

3101. Farrell, Tom, publisher. *The Working Press of the Nation*. New York: Public Relations Press, Farrell Publications Corp., 1945–date. About 375pp. (Title varies; begun in 1945 as *The Working Press of New York City*.)

An annual guide to newspapers, news services, news magazines, feature syndicates, photo services, radio, and television. Lists every newspaper in the United States and gives the executive personnel, in many cases members of reportorial staffs also. There is an introduction on "How to Meet the Press."

3101a. Gebbie Press. *House Magazine Directory*. New York: The Gebbie Press, 1958. 457pp.

A listing of some 4,000 house publications that gives useful information to specialists in industrial editing and to free-lance writers. Included are locations of magazines, names of editors, frequency of publication, size, circulation, and name of printing firms publishing the magazines. An earlier edition in 1952 carried the title *The Nation's Leading House Magazines* (181pp.).

3102. Guild, C. H., and Co. *Advertising in New England: A Complete Handbook for 1896–1897 — Description of All Newspapers and Periodicals Published in New England*. Boston: C. H. Guild and Co., 1896. 324pp.

BIBLIOGRAPHIES AND DIRECTORIES

3103. Herbert, Benjamin Briggs. *The First Decennium of the National Editorial Association of the United States.* Chicago: The Association, by B. B. Herbert, 1896. xxxii + 682pp.

Reports of 10 of the society's conventions, accounts of convention cities, and reviews of excursions. Includes 128 pages of illustrations. Discontinued after one volume.

3104. *Information Please Almanac.* New York: Issued through the Macmillan Co., 1947–date. About 900pp. (Planned and supervised by Dan Golenpaul Associates.)

With the *World Almanac* (3119), the leading present-day reference manual of facts. The content is essentially the same in both, although the *Information Please Almanac* is somewhat more popular in its treatment of events and typographically somewhat easier to read.

3105. *Kellogg's Lists: 1925 Family Weekly Newspapers of the Better Class.* Chicago and New York: A. N. Kellogg Newspaper Co., 1903. 48 unnumbered pp., in color, and maps.

An advertisers' directory of leading weeklies in areas served by Kellogg: Chicago, St. Louis, Cleveland, Kansas City, Cincinnati, Memphis, Little Rock, and Wichita. Kellogg began as an advertising agency in 1865, and this manual offers good material on advertising development.

3106. Kennedy, Joseph Camp Griffith. *Catalogue of the Newspapers and Periodicals Published in the United States, Showing the Town and County in Which the Same Are Published, How Often Issued, Their Character and Circulation; Compiled from the United States Census Statistics for 1850.* New York: J. Livingston, 1852. 56pp.

Among the earliest newspaper catalogues published, preceding Rowell's *American Newspaper Directory* (3115) by 17 years. Kennedy, once editor of the Crawford (Penn.) *Messenger*, was superintendent of the 7th and 8th United States Censuses.

3107. Kenny, Daniel J. *The American Newspaper Directory and Record of the Press: Containing an Accurate List of All the Newspapers, Magazines, Reviews, Periodicals, etc., in the United States and British Provinces of North America. Also, a Concise General View of the Origin, Rise, and Progress of Newspapers.* New York: Watson and Co., 1861. 123 + xxix pp.

This statistical-historical-advertising book provides a good reflection on the period, but the accuracy is open to question. In a "Record of the Press," Kenny offers a 45-page history of journalism from Gutenberg to the Civil War.

3108. *Literary Market Place: The Business Directory of American Book Publishing.* New York: R. R. Bowker Co., 1940–date.

An annual register of personnel in publishing and allied fields and a guide to publishing services. It provides information on book agencies, columnists and commentators, magazines and newspapers significant in book coverage, literary prizes and awards, and radio and television outlets, as well as book publishers.

3109. *Lord and Thomas' Pocket Directory of the American Press.* Chicago: Lord and Thomas Advertising Agency, 1890–1928. Discontinued.

A list of newspapers, magazines, and periodicals in the United States and possessions, Canada, and Cuba, with circulation figures. The title varied from time to time. It is less valuable than other guides listed here.

3110. *Mike and Screen Press Directory.* New York: Radio-Newsreel-Television Working Press Association, 1955–date. Annually.

3111. *Pettengill's Newspaper Directory and Advertisers' Handbook.* New York: S. M. Pettengill Co., 1878–1899. Discontinued.

A complete list of newspapers and other periodicals published in the United States and British America, as well as prominent European and Australasian newspapers. Includes material on newspaper advertising as an outlet, hints to advertisers, and comments on the value of newspapers as historical records.

3112. *Radio Annual — Television Yearbook.* New York: Radio Daily Corp. 1938–date. (Edited by Jack Alicoate.)

Radio and television stations in the United States and Canada are listed by state or province and city. There is also material on advertising agencies, radio-television program producers, network billings, newspaper associations, and legal matters; personality sketches; and a summary of the year's events.

3113. *Remington Brothers Newspaper Manual: A Complete Catalogue of the Newspapers of the United States, Canada, Porto Rico and Cuba.* New York: Remington Brothers Newspaper Advertising, 1884–1898. Discontinued. About 600pp.

Similar to the Rowell directory (3115). Newspaper trade ads, taking up half of each volume, are themselves of historical value.

3114. Rhodes, James Ford. "Newspapers as Historical Sources," in *Historical Essays*, pp. 81–89. New York: The Macmillan Co., 1909.

A valuable assessment of the worth of newspapers as research tools in the study of history. The article appeared also in the *Atlantic Monthly*, May 1909.

3115. *Rowell's American Newspaper Directory.* New York: George P. Rowell and Co., 1869–1908. Discontinued.

Until absorbed by N. W. Ayer (see 3085), this was the most useful compendium of newspaper information in the United States. It listed all newspapers and periodicals in the country and its territories, Canada, and British North America. Rowell also classified publications by specialty and by circulation. The 1869 issue has highly valuable material on Rowell's concept of his directory; it gives also the earliest and perhaps most thorough record of the southern press in the immediate post-Civil War period.

3116. Standard Rate and Data Service, Inc. *Consumer Markets.* Evanston, Ill.: The Service, 1920–date. About 700pp.

A helpful annual guide for business information of importance to the press: data on counties and cities, farms, households, income, metropolitan areas, newspaper rates and circulations, population, radio use in homes, retail sales.

3117. *Ulrich's Periodicals Directory: A Classified Guide to a Selected List of Current Periodicals, Foreign and Domestic.* New York: R. R.

Bowker Co., 8th edition. 1956. x + 730pp. (Edited by Eileen C. Graves, succeeding Carolyn F. Ulrich.)

More than 16,000 periodicals are grouped by subject classification. Each entry includes title, date of origin, frequency of publication, price, publisher, and place of publication. Invaluable.

3118. Weekly Newspaper Representatives, Inc. *National Directory of Weekly Newspapers*. New York: Weekly Newspaper Representatives, 1927–date.

Information about the weekly press: advertising rates, circulation, publishers of newspapers, and community data. Semi- and tri-weekly newspapers are included.

3119. *World Almanac*. New York: New York World, 1886–1931; World-Telegram, 1931–1950; and World-Telegram and Sun, 1950–date. About 900pp. (Edited in 1958 by Harry Hansen.)

Founded by the *World* in 1868 but discontinued, this almanac was revived by Joseph Pulitzer in 1886 and acquired by Scripps-Howard upon purchase of the *World* in 1931. Perhaps the most useful of all journalistic almanacs for quick reference, it contains a large amount of newspaper information in summaries of major news events, historical flashbacks in news, and winners of journalistic prizes and awards.

GREAT BRITAIN

3120. Cambridge University Library. *List of Current English Periodicals 1950, with a Subject Index*. Cambridge, England, 1950, vi + 179pp.

First issued in November 1906 as *Select List of Current English Periodicals*.

3121. *The Fleet Street Annual*. London: Fleet Publications, 1951–date. (Edited by Harold Herd.)

Editorial notes on the preceding year in journalism: reports of activities of British press organizations; changes among newspapers; comments on outstanding news events; obituaries of deceased press celebrities; and lists of journalistic societies. There is also a literary market section for prospective writers. Exceptionally compact.

3122. *N. F. Yearbook*. London: National Federation of Retail Newsagents, Booksellers and Stationers, 1950–date. About 200pp.

3123. *Newspaper Press Directory and Advertisers' Guide*. London: Benn Brothers, Ltd., Bouverie House, 1846–date. About 700pp.

A comprehensive manual on the British Commonwealth press: newspapers and periodical press both general and specialized (house magazines, directories, annuals, and yearbooks); mechanical and art service; press and advertising and kindred societies; summaries of Commonwealth, Colonial, and foreign press; and lists of distributors of foreign publications. It is akin to Ayer's directory in the United States (3085). A descriptive foreword reviews conditions of the press in the previous year.

3124. *Newspaper World*. London: Benn Brothers, Ltd., Bouverie House, 1898–date. Weekly. (Richard Wooley, editor.)

See particularly the fiftieth anniversary issue (*The Press, 1898–1948*, 160pp.) for good summaries of the vast developments in the 20th-century British metropolitan press.

3125. *Official Handbook of the Periodical Proprietors Association, Ltd.* London: The Association, 1950. 284pp.

3126. *A Perfect Diurnall of Some Passages in Parliament (1643–1649): An Annotated Bibliography and Summary.* San Francisco: California State Library, Sutro Branch, 1939. 68pp.

3127. *Sell's World's Press: The Handbook of the Fourth Estate.* London: Henry Sell, 1884–1921. 36 vol., discontinued. (Title varies; also published as *Sell's Directory of the World's Press.*)

This annual contained biographical material on important journalists.

3128. *Willing's Press Guide.* London: Willing's Press Service, Ltd., 1875–date.

An annual handbook on the press of the United Kingdom, British Commonwealth, and colonial and foreign publications. It lists alphabetically newspapers and periodicals, with dates of issue, subscription price, and ownership. Also included is information on newsreels, typesetters, electrotypers, engravers, news agencies, chain ownerships, and titular changes and amalgamations.

OTHER FOREIGN

3129. Cambridge University Library. *List of Current Foreign Periodicals, Including Those Published in Countries of the British Commonwealth Overseas.* Cambridge, England, 1950. vi + 283pp.

3130. Crow, Carl, Inc. *Newspaper Directory of China, Including Hong Kong.* Shanghai, 1931. 2 vols.

3131. Nash, Vernon, comp. *Trindex.* Peiping: Yinte Press of the Harvard-Yenching Institute, 1936. 654pp.

Provides a system of numerical conversion based upon three Chinese dictionaries whereby Westerners can use materials in written Chinese. A serviceable reference in foreign journalism.

E. Indexes

3132. American Historical Review. "Guide to the *American Historical Review*, 1895–1945," in *Annual Report* of the American Historical Assn., 1944, pp. 69–285. Washington, D.C.: Government Printing Office, 1945.

Dozens of articles published through the years in the *American Historical Review* offer a wealth of information on journalistic history, and this guide to the journal's contents should not be neglected. Annotated.

3132a. *Biography Index: A Cumulative Index to Biographical Material in Books and Magazines.* New York: H. W. Wilson Co., January 1946–date. Monthly, and cumulated triennially. (Edited by Bea Joseph.)

Lists current books on biography in English, wherever published, and biographical material from 1500 periodicals. The index includes biographies, autobiographies, diaries, letters, memoirs, obituaries, and pictorial works. Journalistic subject headings are editors, journalists, newspapermen, and printers.

3133. *Book Review Digest.* New York: H. W. Wilson Co., 1905–date. (Currently edited by Mertrice M. James and Dorothy Brown.)

Issued monthly and cumulated annually, these volumes digest and index book reviews appearing in some 75 American and English periodicals. The contents are alphabetized by author and by subject and title. In most cases excerpts from selected reviews are included. Among the 4000 or so books listed each year are volumes by journalists and about newspapers, journalism, and allied fields.

3134. Cappon, Lester J., and Stella F. Duff. *Virginia Gazette Index, 1736–1780.* Williamsburg, Va.: Institute of Early American History and Culture, 1950. 2 vols. 1314pp., total.

3135. *International Index to Periodicals: A Quarterly Guide to Periodical Literature in the Social Sciences and Humanities.* White Plains, N.Y., and New York City: H. W. Wilson Co., 1907–date.

Indexes by author and subject the contents of about 170 periodicals. In 1955, scientific, psychological, and foreign-language periodicals were dropped. The title varies, from 1907 to 1920 being *Readers' Guide to Periodical Literature Supplement.*

3136. Mississippi Valley Historical Review. *Indexes: Topical Guide to the Mississippi Valley Historical Review.* Lincoln, Neb.: The Review, 1932.

Covers vols. I–XIX, 1914–1932. As with the *American Historical Review,* numerous entries relate to journalism, the press, printing, newspapers, and public opinion.

3137. ———. *Cumulative Index.* Cedar Rapids, Iowa: Torch Press, 1932 and 1940.

The issue of 1932, compiled by Louise Rau, indexes vols. I–XV, 1914–1929; that of 1940, compiled by Bertha E. Josephson, covers vols. XVI–XXV, 1929–1939.

3138. New York Times. *Index.* New York: The New York Times Co., 1913–date.

The most complete index of an American daily newspaper.

3139. New York Tribune Association. *New York Daily Tribune Index.* New York: The Tribune, 1876–1907. Discontinued.

The 31 volumes cover 1875–1906.

3140. *Poole's Index to Periodical Literature,* by William Frederick Poole, with the Assistance as Associate Editor of William I. Fletcher. New York: Peter Smith, 1938. Revised edition. 6 vols. in 7.

Indexes the subjects treated in important American and English periodicals of the 19th century. There are many references to book reviews. First issued in 1848, it appeared in later editions in 1853, 1882, and 1893. Five supplements were prepared with the cooperation of the American Library Association to cover the period up to 1906.

3141. *Readers' Guide to Periodical Literature.* Minneapolis, Minn.: H. W. Wilson Co., 1900–1913; White Plains, N.Y., and New York City: H. W. Wilson Co., 1913–date.

An author and subject index to a selected list of general periodicals. Wilson has also issued the *Nineteenth Century Readers' Guide to Periodical Literature, 1890–1899, with Supplementary Indexing, 1900–1922* (2 vols., 1516pp. and 1558pp.).

3142. Shaw, Thomas Shuler, comp. *Index to Profile Sketches in the New Yorker Magazine.* Boston: F. W. Faxon Co., 1946. 100pp. (Useful Reference Series No. 72.)

Indexes profiles appearing in the *New Yorker* from vol. 1, no. 1 (February 21, 1925) to vol. 16, no. 1 (February 17, 1940), when the *Readers' Guide to Periodical Literature* began indexing the magazine.

3143. Shine, Hill, and Helen Chadwick Shine. *The Quarterly Review under Gifford, 1809–1824.* Chapel Hill: University of North Carolina Press, 1949. xx + 108pp.

Some 733 contributions to this noted British periodical are identified by author, with notes.

3144. *Subject Index to Periodicals.* London: Library Association, 1953. xii + 336pp. (Edited by T. Rowland Powell.)

3145. The Times (London). *The Official Index to the Times.* London: J. P. Bland, at the Times Office, 1914–date. Issued quarterly. (Begun as the *Monthly Index to the Times,* January 1906–June 1914.)

These and *Palmer's Index* (3146) give a complete guide to this leading international newspaper for a period of nearly a century.

3146. ———. *Palmer's Index to the Times Newspaper.* London: S. Palmer, 1867–1905. 39 volumes.

3147. Weatherford, Willis Duke. *Analytical Index of De Bow's Review.* Santa Barbara, Calif.: Privately issued, 1952. vi + 200pp.

This painstaking guide to the contents of De Bow's economic journal (from 1846 through the last issue in 1880) makes it possible to find information on almost all phases of De Bow's coverage of the ante-bellum and Civil War South.

Index

NOTE ON INDEX

THE VALUE *of any bibliography hinges to a great extent upon its index, and I have tried to make the index analytical and detailed. Every effort has been made to draw out the journalistic content from the many books and to enter an appropriate subject reference in the index.*

Straight alphabetization by author's name and by subject heading has been followed. There are only a few title entries in the index; a general title index has been omitted because a reader who knows an author's name or the subject he is seeking information on can find a book through the table of contents or the author-subject listings. In cases in which the reader knows only the title, he will note that this frequently gives a hint about the subject.

References to journalism, newspapers, and the press are so numerous that general indexing under these subjects would not be feasible. The reader, therefore, should look under specific subheadings, such as Agriculture and journalism, Freedom of the press, Military affairs and the press, Politics and the press, Religion and journalism, Reporters and reporting, names of newspapers, and names of cities and states. For the United States, Canada, and Great Britain, newspapers are indexed under the city of publication. Newspapers of other countries are listed within the entry for each country.

The index carries also a long listing of textbooks in all major journalistic categories; these are brought together for convenience under the heading Textbooks rather than under each subject category.

Index

All references are to entry numbers, *not* pages

INDEX

INDEX

Beecher, Rev. Edward, 770
Beecher, Rev. Henry Ward, 334–335, 368, 497, 2372
Beer, Thomas, 493, 2372
Beer, William, 3058
Beers, Henry A., 1060
Bekessy, Jean, 1289a
Belfrage, Cedric, 1096
Belgium, 1049, 1251–1256, 1680, 2956: *La Libre Belgique*, 2878
Bell, C. F. Moberly, 1097–1098. *See also* London *Times*
Bell, Elliott V., 1808
Bell, Enid Hester, 1097, 1243
Bell, John Browne, 188
Bellamy, Edward, 310
Bellamy, Paul, 1889
Belleville (Kan.) *Telescope*, 821
Belloc, Hilaire, 1985, 2125
Belo, Col. Alfred H., 91
Beman, Lamar T., 2009
Benchley, Nathaniel, 369
Benchley, Robert, 369, 1376
Benét, Stephen Vincent, 103
Benjamin, Park, 370, 2076
Benjamin, Robert Spiers, 1555–1556
Benjamin, S. G. W., 293
Benjamin Franklin Magazine Awards, 2406
Bennett, Ira E., 1413
Bennett, James Gordon, Sr., 12, 50, 292, 298, 305, 320, 371–374, 497, 739, 1460, 1962–1963, 2253, 2943. *See also* New York *Herald*
Bennett, James Gordon, Jr., 141, 360, 375, 447, 460, 489, 1078, 1251–1253, 1255, 1962–1963. *See also* New York *Herald*
Bennett, James O'Donnell, 807
Benson, Ivan, 466–467, 2050
Bent, Silas, 294, 1890
Bentham, Jeremy, 2387
Bentley, Edmund, 1099
Bentley, Eric, 1377
Bentley, Garth, 2481
Berelson, Bernard, 2602, 2567–2659
Berger, Meyer, 104, 376
Berkes, Ross N., 1502
Berkshire (England) *Chronicle*, 58
Bernays, Edward L., 2087, 2603, 2699–2700, 2751–2752, 2759, 2774, 2940, 2982
Bernays, Robert, 1503
Berns, Walter, 2010
Bernstein, Theodore M., 2166, 2209
Bernstein, Walter, 1589
Berrey, R. Power, 188

Berry brothers, *see* Camrose and Kemsley, Viscounts
Berryman, Clifford K., 2167
Berryman, John, 494
Berthel, Mary Wheelhouse, 626
Berthold, S. M., 862
Bertier de Sauvigny, Guillaume de, 28
Bessie, Simon Michael, 105
Best, Mary Agnes, 863
Best Articles of the Year, 2400
Best Sports Stories, 1865
Better Homes & Gardens, 2187, 2656, 2694a
Beuick, Marshall, 2977, 2992
Bevington, Merle Mowbray, 2376
Bibliographical Society of America, 2085, 3028, 3030, 3047, 3058
Bibliographies, 2442, 2925–3078: advertising, 2518, 2528, 2548, 2947–2948, 2974, 2978; African press, 2962–2963; Asiatic press, 2896, 2918, 2922, 2952; British press, 2938, 2944, 2993, 3073–3078; Canadian press, 2935, 3071-3072; check lists, 2998–3078; circulation, 2559; community-weekly field, 1969, 2925; early newspapers, 285, 2926; European press, 2891; fiction, 2946; films, 2980; foreign-language press, 3000, 3003, 3011, 3046, 3058, 3060, 3066–3067; freedom of the press, 2048, 2961, 2964, 2968–2969; frontier press, 3013, 3021, 3025; high school journalism, 2946; history of journalism, 7, 18, 2925–2946; individual journalists, 520a, 630, 651, 667, 677, 688, 691, 759, 775, 824, 846, 903, 981, 983, 1080, 1084, 1114, 1137, 1188, 1234, 1296, 2928, 2939–2943, 2945; international communications, 2433, 2949–2963, 2986–2988; journalism education, 2332; *Journalist's Bookshelf*, 2946; labor press, 3063; law of the press, 2964–2970; literary journalism, 2929, 2944; magazines, 753, 2353, 2393, 2930, 3016; management, 2495; market research, 2978; Negro press, 3007, 3039, 3054, 3062; newspapers as historical sources, 3114; newspapers on microfilm, 3045, 3054, 3056, 3068, 3071; *One Hundred Books on Journalism*, 2937; Overseas Information Service, 2990; printing, 273, 289, 2971–2976; propaganda, 2981, 2984–2986, 2991; psychological warfare, 2988–2989; public opinion, 2599, 2685, 2979, 2986–2987; public relations, 2940, 2977, 2980, 2982–2983; radio and television, 2815, 2992–2997; religious press, 3023; sports, 2216; USSR press, 2945

439

INDEX

844, 1026, 1028–1032; in West, 400, 415, 474, 542, 695–702, 852–854, 915, 1016, 1020; of press associations and syndicates, 529, 743, 802, 950–954, 988–990, 1178

Photographers, cartoonists, artists, 323, 409–410, 485, 514, 614, 674, 733, 791, 793, 839, 875, 942, 1068, 1075, 1085, 1111, 1150, 1181, 1187, 1204

Political journalists, 395, 420–423, 461–463, 479–482, 497, 533–537, 567, 599–608, 725, 739, 761, 770–773, 782–783, 843, 846, 882–883, 919, 928–929, 944–947, 956–957, 979, 1036–1037, 1048–1049, 1086, 1125, 1133, 1147–1148, 1171, 1173, 1177, 1179–1180, 1182–1184, 1188, 1195, 1201, 1208, 1224–1225, 1277–1282

Printers, 284, 290, 302, 315, 819, 836, 1006–1007, 1122–1124, 1165, 1250

Promoters and propagandists, 339–340, 361–362, 496, 557, 907, 936

Radio commentators, 297, 662, 735–736, 754, 941, 961, 1089, 1154

Regional journalists, 355, 405–406, 530, 597, 618–619, 626, 632, 659, 667, 750, 766, 787, 821, 911, 934, 948–949, 977–978, 986, 993–994, 1005, 1040, 1062, 1115–1116, 1129, 1185, 1196, 1232, 1240–1242, 1268

Reporters, 982–983: for Hearst, 389, 531, 559, 574, 872–873; in Hollywood, 632a, 835, 974; in London, 1091, 1096, 1105, 1126, 1131, 1144, 1149, 1159–1162, 1164, 1174, 1194, 1198, 1226, 1236, 1265, 1267, 1273; in Middle West, 442–443, 704, 757, 828, 939, 959, 1008; in New York City, 376, 459, 615, 625, 703, 744, 855, 878, 891, 916–917, 924, 972–973, 980, 984, 1019, 1021; in South, 717, 921; in West, 574, 730, 825, 975; women, 324, 357–359, 483, 488, 657, 689, 711, 738, 741, 746, 776, 820, 970, 998

Specialized journalists, 318, 334–336, 345, 351, 368, 390–393, 429, 458, 584, 664, 686, 705, 797, 818, 829, 874, 967, 995–996, 1015, 1101–1104, 1110, 1223, 1229, 1246, 1266, 1272, 1284

Sports writers, 365, 435, 594–595, 748, 792, 801, 912, 930–931, 935, 1109

Washington correspondents, 363, 516, 592, 620, 877, 885, 914, 971

Biography Index, 3132a

Birchall, Frederick T., 1504

Bird, George L., 1891, 2170

Bird, Harry Lewis, 388

Birdwell, Russell, 389

Birmingham (Alabama), 1741

Birmingham (England) *Post*, 1225

Birney, James Gillespie, 390–393, 603, 1776

Birney, William, 391

Birren, Faber, 2507

Bishop, Jim, 706

Bismarck, Otto von, 1104

Black, Alexander, 394

Black, H. C., 98

Black, Marvin M., 2306

Black, Van Lear, 98

Blackburn family (Canada), 148

Blackmon, Robert E., 415

Blackstone, Sir William, 2126

Blackwood, William, 2388

Blair, Emma H., 3004

Blair family, 108a, 395, 413, 739, 788

Blanchard, Edward L., 1100

Blankenhorn, Heber, 1505

Blanshard, Paul, 2011

Blatchford, Robert, 1101–1103

Bleackley, Horace, 1278

Bleyer, Willard G., 2, 1892, 2171–2172, 2913

Bliven, Bruce, 2405

Block, Herbert (Herblock), 1818–1819a

Block, Paul, 94, 327

Bloom, Edward A., 1177

Blowitz, Henri Georges de, 1104

Blumberg, Nathan B., 1893

Blumenfeld, David Louis, 1105

Blumenfeld, Ralph D., 1106–1108

Blumenstock, Dorothy, 2718

Blunden, Edmund, 189

Bly, Nellie, *see* Cochrane, Elizabeth

Blythe, Samuel G., 396

Boardman, Samuel L., 550

Boer War, 955, 1158, 1209, 1273, 1453, 1464, 1483. *See also* Africa; Foreign and war correspondence (before World War I)

Boettiger, John, 757

Bogardus, Emory S., 2604

Bogart, Leo, 2660

Bojano, Filippo, 1290

Bok, Edward William, 292, 397–398, 498

Bolitho, William, 1328, 1506

Bolles, Joshua A., 399

Bolles, Joshua K., 399

Bond, F. Fraser, 822, 2173

Bond, Richmond Pugh, 2377, 3073

Bonelli, William G., 106

Bonfils, Fred G., 147, 400. *See also* Denver *Post*

Bonfils, Helen, 326

INDEX

INDEX

Cust, Harry, 210
Custer, Gen. George Armstrong, 1469
Custer, Joe James, 1607
Cut Bank (Mont.) *Pioneer-Press*, 1041
Cutler, Howard T., 2752
Cutlip, Scott M., 2755, 2980
Czechoslovakia, 1269, 2855: *Bohemia*, 1305; *Rudé Právo*, 2869

Dabney, Thomas Ewing, 118
Dafoe, John Wesley, 162, 500–501, 569, 966
Dahl, Folke, 2949, 3076
Dahlonega (Ga.) *Nugget*, 1014
Dakin, Edwin Franden, 548
Dale, Edgar, 1900, 2981
Dallam, Frank M., Jr., 489
Dallas *Morning News*, 91, 523
Dana, Charles A., 1432, 2943: and Civil War, 53, 291, 1482; and Transcendentalism, 2342, 2348; biographies of, 502–507; colleagues and contemporaries of, 413, 631, 650, 827, 918, 999, 1029; early radicalism of, 1314; foreign correspondence of, 1463; on newspaper techniques, 1901; *Story of the Sun*, 163. *See also* New York *Sun*
Dana, Marshall N., 119
Dane, G. Ezra, 1336, 1338
Daniel, John M., 239
Daniell, Raymond, 1608, 1808
Daniels, Jonathan, 513
Daniels, Josephus, 508–513, 1544
Danilov, Victor J., 2192
Danzig, Allison, 1867, 1871, 1879
Dark, Sidney, 1227, 1340
Darling, Jay N., 326
Darlington (England) *Northern Echo*, 1258
Darrah, David, 1515
Dartnell Public Relations Handbook, 2756
Dasent, Arthur Irwin, 1142
Davenport, Homer, 514, 1825
Davenport, John Scott, 2556
Davenport, Russell, 515
Davenport (Iowa) *Democrat*, 142
Davenport (Iowa) *Gazette*, 934
Davenport (Iowa) *Times*, 142
Davidson, Philip, 2705
Dávila, Carlos G., 2844
Davis, Athie S., 1391
Davis, Charles Belmont, 517–518
Davis, Donald W., 2512
Davis, Elizabeth H., 2354
Davis, Elmer, 120, 1073, 1756–1757, 2267, 2709, 2730
Davis, Frances, 1516

Davis, Franklyn P., 1391
Davis, Hallam W., 2193
Davis, Henry R., 170
Davis, Jerome, 2026
Davis, Norris G., 2027
Davis, Oscar King, 516
Davis, Rebecca Harding, 518
Davis, Richard Harding, 31, 291, 296, 356, 517–518, 1464–1466, 1487, 1517–1518, 2941
Davis, Robert H., 519–520, 887
Dawks, Ichabod, 90, 1133
Dawks's News-Letter, 1133
Dawson, Geoffrey, 68, 1134, 1430. *See also* London *Times*
Dawson, Muir, 3013
Dawson, Samuel A., 2028
Day, Benjamin, 159. *See also* New York *Sun*
Dayton (Ohio) *Daily News*, 491, 766
Dealey, George B., 91, 523
Dean, A. F., 1014
Dean, Joseph, 2130
De Armond, Anna Janney, 407
De Bow, James D. B., 520a–521, 3147
De Bow's Review, 520a–521, 567, 2357, 3147
De Castro, Adolphe, 377
Decker, Karl, 1454
Deckhoff, Harold B., 2194
Defoe, Daniel, 59, 61, 90, 197, 1135–1140, 2131–2132
De Forest, Henry, 306
De Kalb (Miss.) *Democrat*, 899
Delane, John Thadeus, 63, 1098, 1141–1142. *See also* London *Times*
Delineator, 539, 1004
Delmatier, Royce, 3014
Demaree, Albert Lowther, 224
Deming, William Chapin, 524–525
De Morse, Charles, 522
Dempsey, David K., 1678
Denmark, 1293, 2879
Denmore, James, 2567
Dennett, Mrs. Mary Ware, 2029
Dennie, Joseph, 128, 317, 526–527, 2365
Dennis, Charles H., 560, 749
Denver, 496, 1741
Denver *Post*, 147, 400, 574, 1342, 1711
De Palma, Samuel, 2845
De Quille, Dan, 226, 471
Des Moines, 318
[Des Moines] *Iowa State Register*, 530
Des Moines *Register and Tribune*, 490
Desmond, R. G. C., 196
Desmond, Robert W., 2195, 2308, 2846

INDEX

INDEX

Ford, Worthington C., 38, 434, 543, 3020
Foreign Affairs, 610
Foreign and war correspondence, 17, 749,
1125, 2954: anthologies, 1370, 1707, 1724;
before World War I, 27, 31, 33, 53, 55,
493–494, 517–518, 981, 1446–1494; European press corps, 2870, 2945; flow of the
news, 2857–2858; in World War I, 401–
402, 517–518, 572, 612–613, 679, 1495–
1580; in World War II, 350, 617, 1581–
1688; nature of the correspondents' corps,
1646, 1658; period from World War I to
World War II, 1495–1580; since World
War II, 1689–1740, 2842, 2870; views on
U.S. of foreign correspondents, 1341,
1737. *See also* Biographies (foreign and
war correspondents); Reporters and re-
porting
Foreign-language press, 40, 140, 216, 242–
243, 252, 259, 275, 686, 705, 944–947,
3000, 3003, 3011, 3046, 3058
Foreman, Carolyn Thomas, 3021
Forkert, Otto Maurice, 265
Forman, Harrison, 1612, 1700
Forman, Samuel E., 586
Forney, John W., 570–571, 751, 1029, 1078
Forrest, Wilbur, 572
Fortescue, Granville, 573
Fortune, 515, 1597, 2369, 2515
Forum, 859–860
Fowler, Gene, 389, 400, 574
Fox, Louis H., 3022
Fox, Richard K., 2371–2372
Fox, Rodney, 2206
Fox, William Johnson, 2385
Fox-Bourne, H. R., 63
Fra, 2115
Fraenkel, Josef, 3023
Fraenkel, Osmond K., 2045–2046
France, 1512, 1560, 1738, 2857, 2889: cor-
ruption in press, 1546; *Daily Mail* (Paris
edition), 980, 1086; defeat by Hitler,
1320, 1421, 1600, 1615, 1661; defeat in
Franco-Prussian War, 1269–1271; Drey-
fus case, 1245, 1262, 1320; *Echo de Paris*,
1615; *La France Libre*, 1292; *France Soir*,
1546; in Napoleonic period, 28, 2713;
liberation in World War II, 2950; *Le
Monde*, 2885; *L'Oeuvre*, 1320; opinion during World War I, 1505, 1517–1518, 2728;
Paris *Herald*, 141, 447, 730, 961; Paris
Tribune, 746; *Le Parisien libéré*, 2869;
radical journalists, 502, 1314; Resistance
press in World War II, 2696, 2872, 2923;
Revolution (*1789–1793*), 1292, 2736;

since World War II, 965; *Le Temps*,
2885; *La Tribune des Patriotes*, 1292;
Underground movement, 1596
Francis, Sir Philip, 61, 1147–1148. *See also*
Junius
Franco-Prussian War, 969, 1146, 1237–1239,
1269–1271
Frank, Gerald, 632a
Frank, Stanley, 1880
Frank Leslie's Illustrated Newspaper, see
Leslie Publications
Franklin, Benjamin, 22, 46, 2344–2345: as
humorist, 1851; as printer and typogra-
pher, 275; biographies of, 3, 317, 352,
575–583; in American Revolution, 54;
letters to the press, 577; on newspapers,
1941
Franklin, James, 294, 580, 582–583, 2033
Franklin, Jay, 441
Franklin, Olga, 1149
Franklin, O. Thomas, 2793
Fraser, Hugh, 2392
Fraser's Magazine, 305, 2392
Fredborg, Arvid, 1613
Frederick Douglass' Paper, 533–537
Fredericks, Pierce G., 1830
Free-lancing, *see* Magazines (free-lancing)
Free-Soil Freeman, 1445
Free Thinker, 2377
Freedman, David, 907
Freedom of assembly, 2062, 2073, 2097
Freedom of religion, 2062
Freedom of speech, *see* Freedom of the
press
Freedom of the press, 1914, 1927, 1938,
1947, 1950, 1953, 1955, 2001–2153, 2964:
Alien and Sedition Laws, 23, 434, 688,
784–785, 1941, 2001, 2031, 2070, 2098,
2122; anthologies, 2009, 2055, 2061, 2093;
antislavery controversy, 427, 461–463, 770–
772, 2089; case books, 2010, 2023, 2102;
censorship suppression, 1402, 2009, 2011,
2047, 2049, 2067, 2071, 2134, 2924, 2966,
2969–2970; Chicago *Tribune's* views, 790,
2054, 2531; civil liberties and, 1024, 1035,
1746, 2008, 2014, 2024, 2035–2037, 2045–
2046, 2052, 2073, 2082, 2087, 2098, 2117,
2742; constitutional analyses, 2015–2016,
2032, 2036, 2041–2042, 2048, 2061–2062,
2968; contempt of court and, 2101, 2123;
Daniel Defoe on, 1137–1138; for anarch-
ists and radicals, 2090; history, 669–670,
2015, 2017–2018, 2033, 2086, 2088, 2094,
2104, 2124, 2127–2129, 2135, 2144, 2149,
2151; in Canada, 2043; in Germany, 1568;

in Great Britain, 51, 64, 69, 71, 73, 80, 189, 209, 1110, 1120, 1147–1148, 1173, 1177, 1179–1180, 1277–1282, 2124–2153, 2378; in India, 1114; international problems, 2841, 2845–2846, 2850–2851, 2889, 2917; local problems, 703, 896–897; Moss Committee hearings, 2105–2107; philosophical concepts, 564, 2053, 2058, 2087, 2139–2140, 2286; postal controls, 668, 2029, 2034, 2049, 2067, 2084, 2089, 2104, 2113–2114; privilege, 1185, 1775, 2028; public meetings and right to know, 1110, 1819a, 2022–2023, 2079, 2096, 2109, 2118; seizure of *La Prensa*, 2886; Supreme Court cases, 2007, 2010, 2015–2016, 2046, 2078, 2082; taxes on knowledge, 2129; unfair legislation, 125; Zenger trial, 35, 1079–1085. *See also* Copyright; Libel; Obscenity; Privacy and the press

Freeman, Andrew A., 557
Freeman, Joseph, 584
Freeman, Legh R., 126
Freeman, William M., 2516
Freeman's Journal (Freneau's), 587
French, George, 2517
Freneau, Philip, 22, 54, 294, 585–588
Fresno (Calif.) *Morning Republican*, 316
Friederichs, Hulda, 1212
Friedman, Harry A., 2207
Friend, 1483
Frontier Index, 126
Frontier journalism, *see* West and Far West
Frothingham, Octavius B., 918
Fry, William Henry, 589
Fryburger, Vernon, 2541
Fuess, Claude, 947
Fugger, House of, 1296, 1370
Fuhrmann, Otto W., 266
Fuller, Margaret, 22, 310, 590–591, 648, 1381
Fuller, Muriel, 2328
Furman, Bess, 592
Furneaux, Rupert, 1238
Furniss, Harry, 1150–1151
Fyfe, Hamilton, 1152–1153, 1217, 1222, 1614

Gaine, Hugh, 306, 593
Gales, Joseph, 108a, 124, 311, 788
Gales, Seaton, 124
Gales, Weston, 124
Galesburg (Ill.) *Hemlandet*, 686
Gallagher, O. D., 1533
Gallico, Paul, 594–595

Galloway, Joseph, 128a
Gallup, George A., 325, 2666–2667, 2691. *See also* Public opinion (measurement)
Galveston (Tex.) *News*, 91
Gander, Leonard M., 1154
Gandhi, Mohandas K., 1666, 1691. *See also* India
Gannett, Frank, 327, 596
Gannett, Guy P., 597
Gard, Wayne, 2208
Gardiner, A. G., 1117
Gardner, Gilson, 952
Garrison, Francis Jackson, 601
Garrison, Garnet B., 2789
Garrison, Wendell Phillips, 598, 601, 2404
Garrison, William Lloyd, 22, 310, 533, 535–536, 599–608, 782, 1962–1963
Garst, Robert E., 2209
Garvin, J. L., 68, 210, 314, 1155, 1224
Garvin, Katharine, 1155
Garwood, Irving, 2347
Gaudet, Hazel, 2658
Gauvreau, Emile, 609, 794
Gavit, John P., 989, 2210
Gavit, Joseph, 3024
Gay, Edwin F., 610
Gay, Robert M., 2273
Gay, Sydney, 53
Gaylord, Edward K., 680
Gayn, Mark J., 611, 1701
Gazette, 2433
Gebbie Press, 3101a
Gedye, G. E. R., 1808
Gelfand, Lou, 2216
Gellhorn, Walter, 2067
General Magazine, 2345, 2365
Genesee Farmer, 318
Genius of Universal Emancipation, 391, 782–783. *See also* Abolitionism
Gentleman's Magazine, 1771, 2378
Gentry, Dwight L., 2545
Gentry, Helen, 267
Georgia, 29, 96, 223, 228, 366, 987, 1014, 1742, 2346. *See also* Atlanta newspapers
Georgia, University of, 1904a
Georgia Press Association, 228
Gerald, J. Edward, 64, 2048
Geraud, André, 1615
Germany, 946, 1104, 1245, 1269–1271, 1500, 1570, 1625, 2729, 2744, 2746, 2857, 2889–2890: *Arbeiter-Zeitung*, 1303; attitude in defeat, 1534; *Berliner Tageblatt*, 1323, 1632; *Berliner Zeitung*, 1322; coverage of, in Napoleonic period, 1233–1235; defeat in World War I, 2701; exiled journalists,

Graves, Charles, 1159–1160
Graves, Peggy, 1160
Gray, James, 1395
Grayson, David, *see* Baker, Ray Stannard
Great Britain, 965, 1430, 1536, 1614, 1723, 1738, 1808, 2711, 2740, 2851, 2857, 2889–2890: abdication crisis (Edward VIII), 204, 1134, 1421, 1430; age of Queen Anne, 62, 1941; austerity in, 1720; Commonwealth Press Union, 1975; Criminal Law Amendment Act, 2150; Defamation Act of *1952*, 2141; Empire Press Union, 1143; General Council of the Press, 2133; Imperial World Union, 1287–1288; Institute of Journalists, 1143; journalistic history, 2, 56–90, 188–213, 299, 1986–1987; Ministry of Information and Propaganda, 1608, 2152, 2712, 2726, 2735; "new journalism," 1121, 1212–1222, 1227, 1258–1260; Parliament and press, 80, 82, 86, 194, 209, 1094, 1106, 1114, 1117, 1131, 1141–1142, 1165, 1171, 1176–1177, 1179–1180, 1182–1183, 1186, 1190–1193, 1261, 1503, 1747–1748, 1771, 1773–1775, 1796, 2140, 2145–2146, 2151–2152, 2623, 3126; Parnell Commission, 1144, 1225; Periodical Proprietors Association, 3125; policy toward press in American colonies, 51; the Press Association, 87; press trusts, 1106, 1981–1982; provincial press, 85, 196, 208, 213, 299, 1115, 1978; Reform Bill, 63, 1246; Royal Commission on the Press, 69, 299, 1086, 1153, 1168, 2133, 2138, 2145–2146; trade press, 2475, 2479. *See also* British Broadcasting Corporation; National Union of Journalists; Reuters
Greatest Sport Stories, 1870–1871
Grebanier, Mrs. Frances Vinciguerra, 1051
Greece, 1245, 1648, 1725
Greeley, Horace, 22, 50, 463, 843, 869, 1036–1037, 1362, 1371, 1418; and Abraham Lincoln, 633, 640, 653; and Typographical Union No. *6*, 651, 2585; as pioneer in socialism, 650; bibliography of, 2943; biographies of, 298, 320, 633–656; colleagues of, 413, 487, 503, 589–591, 660–661, 909, 918, 947, 999–1002, 1078, 1482; economic views of, 1763–1764; election of *1860*, 1765; election of *1872*, 395, 635–636, 643, 648; *Overland Journey*, 1346. *See also* New York *Tribune*
Greeley-Smith, Nixola, 324
Green, Beriah, 393
Green, Duff, 108a, 739
Green, George A. L., 1300

Green, Samuel, 42
Greene, Laurence, 10, 1347
Greene, Ward, 1367
Greenhood, David, 267
Greenslet, Ferris, 342
Greenville (Miss.) *Delta Democrat Times*, 440
Greenwall, Harry J., 1161–1162, 1218
Greenwood, Frederick, 61, 211
Gregory, Elizabeth Hiatt, 657
Gregory, Winifred, 3026
Gridiron Club of Washington, 122, 544, 885 1760
Griffin, Frederick, 658
Griffin, Solomon B., 659
Griffis, William Elliot, 484
Griffith, Louis Turner, 228
Grimes, Alan Pendleton, 2349
Grimke, Archibald H., 602
Griswold, Ada Tyng, 3027
Griswold, Denny, 2760
Griswold, Glenn, 2760
Griswold, Rufus Wilmot, 660–661, 880–881
Grogan, John M., 2808
Gropp, Arthur E., 2951
Gross, Ben, 662
Grozier, Edwin A., 920
Grub Street (London), 305, 1177
Guest, Edgar A., 325
Guild, C. H., & Company, 3102
Guild Reporter, 2435. *See also* American Newspaper Guild
Gulfport (Miss.) *Dixie Guide*, 899
Gundell, Glenn, 2350
Gunderson, Gilbert N., 2519
Gunning, Robert, 2211
Gunther, John, 1525, 1530–1531, 1618–1619, 1702–1705, 1766
Gutenberg, Johann, 263, 265, 273–274, 276, 1316. *See also* Printers and printing (history)
Guthrie, John A., 2571–2572
Gwynne, H. A., 201

Habe, Hans, 1289a
Hadden, Briton, 663. *See also* Time, Inc.
Haggin, Bernard H., 1396
Haight, Anne Lyon, 2049
Hailey, Foster Bowman, 1620, 1706
Hale, David, 664, 668, 996
Hale, Nathan, 2928
Hale, Oron James, 2710–2711
Hale, Sarah Josepha, 332, 665–666
Hale, William G., 2050
Hale, William Harlan, 638

INDEX

INDEX

Hovde, Howard T., 2509
Hovland, Carl I., 2611
Howard, Cecil, 1100
Howard, Clive, 2221
Howard, Henry W. B., 108
Howard, Leon, 774
Howard, Roy W., 150, 181, 325, 327, 826, 893, 950, 1958. *See also* Scripps, Edward W.; Scripps-Howard Newspapers
Howe, Edgar Watson, 325, 718
Howe, Gene, 326
Howe, Joseph, 719–720
Howe, Mark Antony De Wolfe, 307
Howe, Quincy, 1532, 1535–1536, 1912
Howe, Will D., 3089
Howells, William Dean, 307, 356, 721–723
Hower, Ralph M., 2523
Howe's Monthly, 718
Howey, Walter, 308
Hoyt, Palmer, 821, 1342
Hubbard, Frank McKinney, 724
Hubbard, Wyant, 1537
Huddleston, Sisley, 360, 1170
Hudson, Derek, 70, 1087
Hudson, Frederic, 12, 53
Hudson, William Cadwalader, 725
Hughes, Frank, 2054
Hughes, Helen MacGill, 1913
Hughes, Spencer Leigh, 1171
Huie, William Bradford, 1626–1627
Hulton, Sir Edward, 68, 85
Hulton, Edward George W., 1172
Hulton Press, Ltd., 1172
Hume, Hugh, 489
Humor and humorists, *see* Biography (literary journalists); Literature and journalism (humor)
Hungary, 1269, 1289a, 1306, 1699a, 1952, 2799, 2855
Hungerford, Herbert, 2486
Hunt, Frazier, 309, 726, 1538
Hunt, Frederick Knight, 71
Hunt, Leigh, 61, 189, 1173, 2385
Hunter, Dard, 2574–2576
Hurwitz, William N., 2669
Huss, Pierre J., 1724
Hutchins, Robert M., 2021, 2054
Hutchinson, Bruce, 501
Hutton, Bud, 133
Hutton, Richard Holt, 2391
Hyde, Douglas, 1174
Hyde, Grant Milnor, 2222–2225
Hyde, Harford Montgomery, 2136
Hyman, Herbert, 2671–2672
Hymes, David G., 2524

Ickes, Harold L., 1914, 2055
Iconoclast, 411
Idaho, 1361, 3048
If Christ Came to Chicago, 1260
Illinois, 116, 667, 902, 986, 1333, 1493, 1742, 1803, 3002: Decatur Study, 2621; publication laws, 2057. *See also* Chicago
Illinois State Historical Library, 3036
Illinois State Historical Society, 3053, 3057
Impressions, 2436
In Fact, 959, 1948–1949
Independent (Beecher's), 368, 643
Independent (20th century), 1911
Index, 2348
Indexes, 3131–3147
India, 2857–2858: analysis, description, and interpretation, 806, 976a, 1027, 1666, 1668, 1675, 1728, 2900; Calcutta *Journal*, 1114; Government Information Office, 1304; independence of, 1691, 1694, 1736; Indian Mutiny, 1237; *Indian Press Digests*, 2854; newsletters, 2951a; press in, 1728, 2837, 2922; press law, 2851; press techniques, 2922; Press Trust of India, 1304; *Times of India*, 2869; vernacular press, 2837
Indian affairs (U.S. West) and the press, 474, 1251, 1469, 1475, 1490a
Indiana, 221, 898, 970
Indiana State Library, 3037
Indianapolis News, 724
Indochina, 1690, 1734
Indonesia, 1581, 1653
Indonesia Report, 1711
Information Please, 2612
Information Please Almanac, 3104
Ingersoll, L. D., 641
Ingersoll, Ralph, 727, 1628–1630
Inglis, Brian, 2137
Inglis, Ruth A., 2056
Inkeles, Alex, 2613
Inland Printer, 2437
Innis, Harold A., 2614–2616
"Inside" Series (Gunther), 1530–1531, 1619, 1703–1704, 1766
Institute for International Social Research, 747
Institute for Religious and Social Studies, 2617
Inter-Mountains Freeman, 126
International communications, 2433, 2439, 2835–2924, 2959a, 3129–3131: barriers to, 2841, 2908–2909, 2917; comparative press law, 2889, 2893, 2898, 2909–2910; comparative studies, 2869, 2911; concepts of,

INDEX

INDEX

834, 1027, 2494. *See also* Chicago *Daily News*

"Lay Preacher" essays, 526–527

Layard, G. S., 1111, 1181

Lazareff, Helene, 1715

Lazareff, Pierre, 1546, 1715

Lazarsfeld, Paul F., 2608, 2617, 2621, 2658–2659, 2672, 2674, 2677, 2802, 2807, 2809

Leach, Frank A., 750

Lear, John, 1635

Leary, Lewis, 587

Lee, Alfred McClung, 14, 2649, 2720–2721

Lee, Elizabeth Briant, 2721

Lee, Ivy Ledbetter, 2759, 2763

Lee, James Melvin, 15, 777, 2311

Lee, Gen. Robert E., 2309

Lee, William, 1135

Lee Newspapers, 142

Leech, Harper, 2234

Leech, Margaret, 486

Leeds (England) *Mercury*, 1132

Leeds (England) *Yorkshire Post*, 199, 1132

Leggett, William, 151

Lehmann, Frederick W., 2065

Lehmann-Haupt, Hellmut, 1316, 2972

Leigh, Robert D., 2917

Leland, Charles Godfrey, 751–752

Lemon, Mark, 2390

Lent, Henry B., 2312

Leonard, Jonathan Norton, 2419

Lepidus, Henry, 2871

Lerner, Daniel, 2676, 2722

Lerner, Max, 1426–1427, 2087

Leslie, Mrs. Frank, 753, 823

Leslie Publications, 674, 753, 958, 1857, 2366

Lesly, Philip, 2770

L'Estrange, Sir Roger, 61, 80, 90, 1186, 1208

Levine, Seymour, 2695

Levy, Harold P., 2764

Levy, Ralph, 2801

Lewes, George H., 1130

Lewinson, Minna, 1919

Lewis, Fulton, Jr., 297, 754, 1948, 2788

Lewis, John, 418

Lewis, Sinclair, 755–756

Lewis, William Draper, 670

Lewis, Sir Willmott, 325

Liang, Chi-Chao, 1941

Libel: casebooks, 2002–2004, 2050–2051, 2059, 2069, 2099, 2102, 2104, 2119, 2123, 2130; correction of errors, 2016, 2889; famous personalities involved in, 2026, 2039, 2074, 2076; in Great Britain, 63,

1106, 1273, 1976, 2124, 2130, 2141; Oscar Wilde prosecution, 2150; Panama Canal case, 895. *See also* Freedom of the press; Privacy and the press

Liberator (Eastman), 546

Liberator (Garrison), 599–608, 996. *See also* Abolitionism

Liberty, 531, 1951

Library Journal, 404

Liebling, A. J., 792, 1636, 1876, 1920–1921, 2872

Lieder, Paul Robert, 2235

Life (19th century), 349, 356, 369, 614

Life (20th century), 323, 675, 1597, 1624, 1691, 1697, 1714, 1823, 1834, 1853, 1951, 2369, 2656, 2692. *See also* Time, Inc.

Lin Yu'tang, 819, 2873

Lincoln, Abraham, 409–410, 690, 839, 986, 1066, 1450, 1472, 1493, 1765: assassination of, 620, 1373, 1480; Greeley's influence on, 640, 653; press relations, 39, 50. *See also* Civil War

Lincoln (Neb.) *Star*, 142

[Lincoln] *Nebraska State Journal*, 766

Lincoln University, 3039

Lindbergh, Charles A., 389, 875

Lindey, Alexander, 2038–2039, 2066

Lindley, Ernest K., 301

Lindsay, Robert, 2765

Lingle, Alfred (Jake), 757

Linn, James Weber, 737

Linn, William Alexander, 644

Linotype, *see* Management and production

Lippmann, Walter, 297, 301, 758–759, 1428–1429, 1833, 1922–1923, 2624–2625

Lipset, Seymour Martin, 2580

Listener, 2445

Litchfield (Conn.) *Enquirer*, 1066

Literary Digest, 984, 2666

Literary Market Place, 3108

Literature and journalism, 424–426, 565, 667, 734, 1894, 2154, 2929: anthologies, 184, 187, 1330, 1349, 1355, 1364, 1368, 1373, 1376, 1391, 1401, 1404, 1406, 1408, 1412, 1425, 1436, 1439–1440, 1445, 1580, 1824, 2395, 2407; criticism and reviews, 738, 1118–1119, 1925, 2066, 2239, 2379; history, 3, 4, 22, 220a; humor, 341, 349, 464–473, 724, 801, 1181, 1338, 1343–1345, 1363, 1387, 1452, 1831–1832, 1847–1848, 1851, 1854, 1858, 1862; in American Revolution, 43; in Canada, 6; in Colonies, 32; in Great Britain (18th century), 197–198, 2380; in Great Britain (19th

463

INDEX

465

INDEX

INDEX

INDEX

INDEX

INDEX

Shoemaker, Vaughn, 1855
Sholes, Christopher Latham, 2567
Short History of Printing, 282
Shuler, Marjorie, 2328
Shuman, Edwin L., 2270–2271
Sidebotham, Herbert, 1796
Siebert, Frederik S., 1955, 2096, 2149
Siepmann, C. A., 2617, 2815–2816, 2825
Sifton, Sir Clifford, 500–501, 760, 966
Sigma Delta Chi, 127, 2463
Silverman, Sime, 967
Simmins, G. J. P., 2804
Simon, Ernest D. S., Lord of Wythenshawe, 2817
Simonis, H., 85
Simpson, George E., 250
Simpson, Kirke L., 1497
Sinclair, Upton, 300, 968, 1956
Sington, Derrick, 2739
Sino-Japanese War, 1462
Sipley, Louis Walton, 2272
Skillin, Marjorie E., 2273
Skinner, John Stewart, 224, 318
Skipper, Ottis C., 520a
Skowhegan (Me.) *Independent Reporter*, 134
Slocombe, George, 1244
Smalley, George W., 33, 296, 314, 969
Smallzreid, Kathleen Ann, 970
Smart Set, 814–817, 1013, 2416
Smith, Amelie de Fonfride, 251
Smith, Bradford, 2097
Smith, Bruce Lannes, 2984, 2986–2987
Smith, C. R. F., 2274
Smith, Carl, 971
Smith, Charles William, Jr., 2648
Smith, Chitra M., 2987–2988
Smith, Capt. Douglas M., 1663
Smith, Ernest, 1245
Smith, Francis, 2360, 2362
Smith, George Horsley, 2688
Smith, George Murray, 211
Smith, H. Allen, 972–974
Smith, Hampton Sidney, Jr., 975
Smith, Harrison, 755
Smith, Henry Justin, 328, 1350, 2275
Smith, Henry Ladd, 7
Smith, I. Norman, 681, 976
Smith, J. Eugene, 183
Smith, James Morton, 2098
Smith, Merriman, 1797–1799
Smith, Rixey, 619
Smith, S. Stephenson, 2276–2278
Smith, Walter W. (Red), 1878, 1883
Smith, William, 52

Smith, William Ernest, 395
Smithsonian Institution, 957
Smuckler, Ralph H., 1906
Smyth, Albert H., 1002, 2365
Smythe, Dallas W., 2818–2819a
Snoqualmie (Wash.) *Valley Record*, 871
Snow, Edgar, 976a, 1564, 1664–1666, 1724
Snowden, Edgar, 977
Snyder, Louis L., 1370
Soames, Jane, 1985
Social Research, Inc., 2679, 2689
Society for the Psychological Study of Social Issues, 2649
Society of Magazine Writers, 2221
Sokolsky, George E., 297, 1555, 1565
Solal, Lucien, 2898
Solomon, Leo M., 2279
Soloviev, Mikhail, 1318
Soltes, Mordecai, 252
Somerville, Alexander, 1246
Sontheimer, Morton, 2329
Sooner State Press, 2464
Sorrells, John H., 181, 2280, 2330
Sotheran, Charles, 650
South (U.S.), 355: antebellum period, 36, 520a–521, 567, 855, 911, 977, 1436, 1788, 3147; attitude of press on Negro suffrage, 1924; economic analyses, 1476, 1788; in contemporary America, 1399; New South, 222, 627–631; newspapers in, 136, 222–223, 228, 235–236, 239, 258, 260; race problem, 1746a, 1794–1795, 1800; suppression of press, 2034, 2089. *See also* Civil War
South Atlantic Quarterly, 2417
South Bend (Ind.) *News-Times*, 970
South Carolina, 177, 223, 235, 260. *See also* Charleston newspapers
South Carolina Gazette, 115
South Dakota, 1361
Southern California Associated Newspapers, 116
Southern Literary Messenger, 567
Southern Newspaper Publishers Association, 136
Southern Quarterly Review, 2357
Southern Review (Charleston), 2357
Southwood, Julius S. Elias, Viscount, 1247. *See also* London *Daily Herald*
Spain, 806, 1269, 1499–1500, 1699
Spanish-American War, 296, 493–494, 861, 867, 1343–1345, 1454, 1462, 1464, 1466, 1835, 2748–2749
Spanish Civil War, 959, 1089, 1126, 1203, 1306, 1514, 1516, 1533, 1545, 1550, 1563

INDEX

INDEX

Woollcott, Alexander, 184, 1069–1071, 1412, 1521, 1580, 1964
Woolley, Edward M., 1072
Worcester, Rev. Samuel A., 216a
Wordley, Derek, 2923
World (18th century), 2377
World Almanac, see New York *World*
World at Home, 1811
World War I, 510–511, 729, 859, 867, 959, 1024, 1049, 1086, 1210–1211, 1264, 1283, 1288, 1353, 1413, 1433, 1435, 1520, 1528–1529, 2701, 2717, 2727: atrocities, 2732; Brand Whitlock in Belgium, 1576; camp newspapers, 184, 2394; censorship, 1113, 1285, 2071; clandestine press, 2878, 2956; espionage prosecutions, 2073; false armistice, 826; press influence on, 1919; problems of neutrality, 2731; Red Cross, 1575; sedition, 2015–2016; Unknown Soldier, 1497; Versailles conference, 1089, 1170, 1261, 1732, 2728. *See also* Foreign and war correspondence; Propaganda
World War II, 963–965, 1306, 1952, 2970: air power, 1585, 1626; Aleutians, 1611; atomic bomb, 1669; Battle of Britain, 1588, 1600, 1608, 1617, 1655–1656, 1661; Battle of Germany, 1640–1641; broadcasts, 1605a–1606; camp newspapers, 133, 187; cartoons, 1817; censorship, 1608, 1613, 1935, 2063, 2110–2112, 2152; D-Day, 1618, 1630, 1649; Dieppe, 1654; espionage and sabotage, 2696, 2707; fall of Berlin, 1299; fall of Italy, 1290; fall of Singapore, 1681; Finland invasion, 1667; Goebbels diaries, 1297; guerrilla fighting, 1663; humor and pathos, 898, 1590, 1592, 1636, 1649–1651; Pacific sector, 1602, 1607, 1620, 1631, 1651, 1653, 1662, 1676, 1678, 1682–1683; Pearl Harbor, 1617, 1642, 1661, 1672; Philippines, 1617, 1624, 1633, 1685, 1687; photography, 1823; prisoners of war, 350, 1587, 1593, 1609, 1673–1674; radio in, 1605a; Seabees, 1627; secret news sources, 1686; Sicilian campaign, 1585, 1595; strategy, 1679; terrorism, 1670; underground press, 2734, 2923; V-E Day, 2022. *See also* Foreign and war correspondence; Propaganda
World's Greatest 99 Days, 1812
World's Press News and Advertisers' Review, 2475
World's Work, 804

Worldwide Communist Propaganda Activities, 2750
Wortman, Tunis, 2122
Wrench, Sir Evelyn, 1125, 1134, 1287–1288
Wright, Frederic Victor, 213
Wright, J. Handly, 2775
Wright, Richardson, 332
Wright, Thomas, 1140
Writer, 2476
Writer's Digest, 2477
Wroth, Lawrence C., 285, 289–290
Wyckoff, Edith Hay, 2501
Wylie, Max, 2834
Wyman, Phillips, 2564
Wyoming, 126, 524–525, 848, 1361

Yaffa, David, 2451
Yale University Library, 3070
Yank, 187
Yankwich, Leon R., 2123
Yates, Edmund, 1289
Ybarra, Thomas R., 1073–1074, 1813
Yellow journalism, *see* Appraisals of the press; Hearst, William Randolph; Pulitzer, Joseph; Tabloids
Yindrich, Jan Holman, 1533
Yorke, Nol, 2392
Yorkshire Post, see Leeds (England) *Yorkshire Post*
Yost, Casper S., 2000
Young, Alexander, 128
Young, Art, 1075, 1864
Young, Brigham, 95, 1346
Young, Charles de, 261
Young, Edward J., 874
Young, Eugene J., 1814, 2924
Young, James Webb, 1076, 2550
Young, John Orr, 1077
Young, John Philip, 261
Young, John Russell, 1078
Young, Kimball, 2991
Young, M. H. de, 261, 377
Young and Rubicam, 1077
Yukon, 99, 3048
Yust, Walter, 326

Zabriskie, Francis N., 656
Zenger, John Peter, 23, 35, 52, 290, 306, 308, 669–670, 1079–1084, 2094, 2116
Ziemer, Gregor A., 1325
Zoom, 2352
Zuver, Dudley, 597